MW01629174

ALBERTUS SEBA

Cabinet of Natural Curiosities

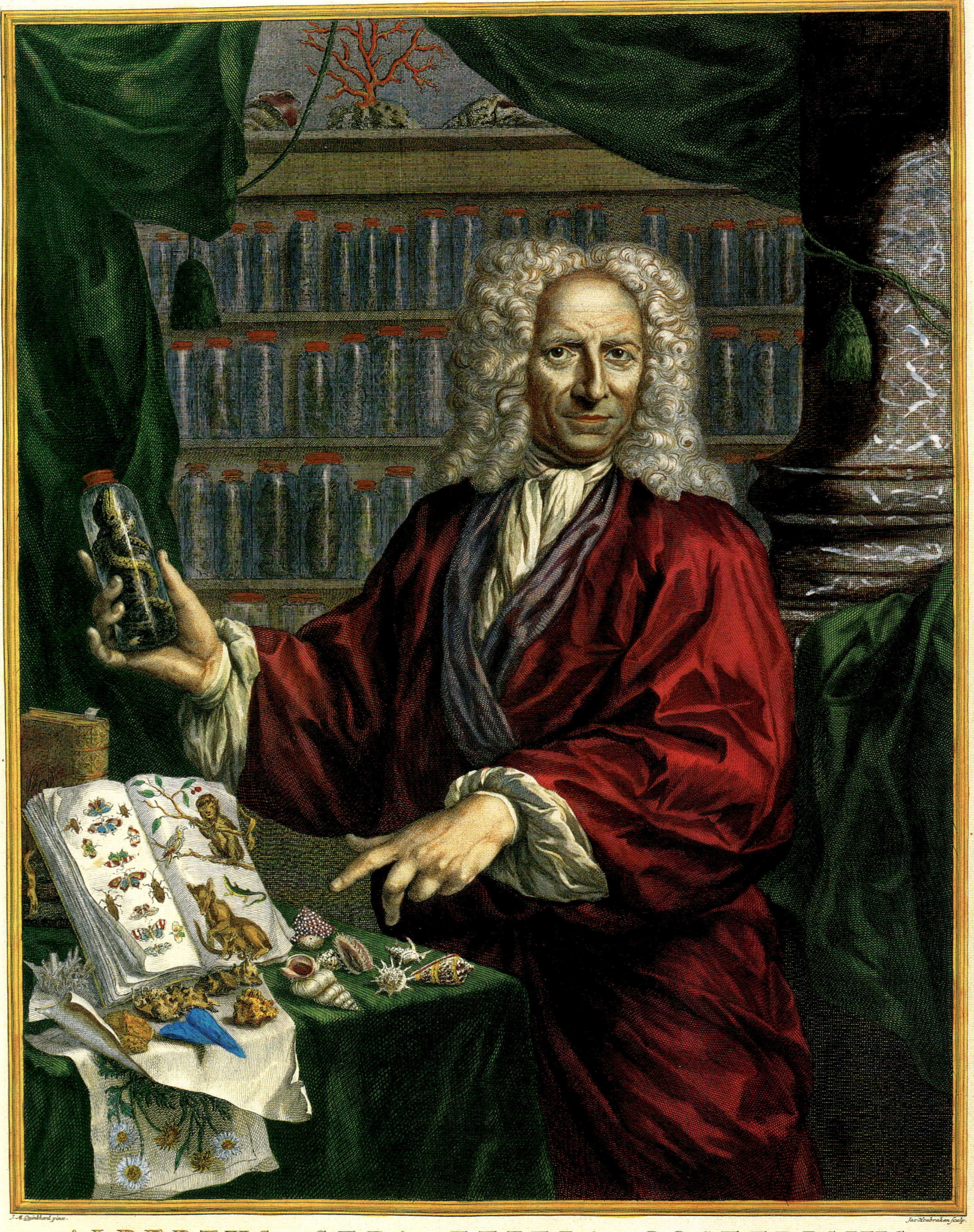

J. M. Quinkhard pinx. Jac. Houbraken sculp.

ALBERTVS SEBA, ETZELA OOSTFRISIVS

Pharmacopoeus Amſtelaedamenſis

ACAD: CAESAR: LEOPOLDINO CAROLINAE NAT: CVRIOS: COLLEGA XENOCRATES DICTVS;

SOCIET: REG: ANGLICANAE, et ACAD: SCIENTIAR: BONONIENSIS INSTITVTVS SODALIS.

AETATIS LXVI. ANNO CIƆIƆCCXXXI.

ALBERTUS SEBA

Cabinet of Natural Curiosities

Locupletissimi rerum naturalium thesauri
1734–1765

A selection of the most important plates from the copy
in the Koninklijke Bibliotheek, The Hague

BARNES & NOBLE
NEW YORK

Contents

37

THESAURUS
Tomus 1

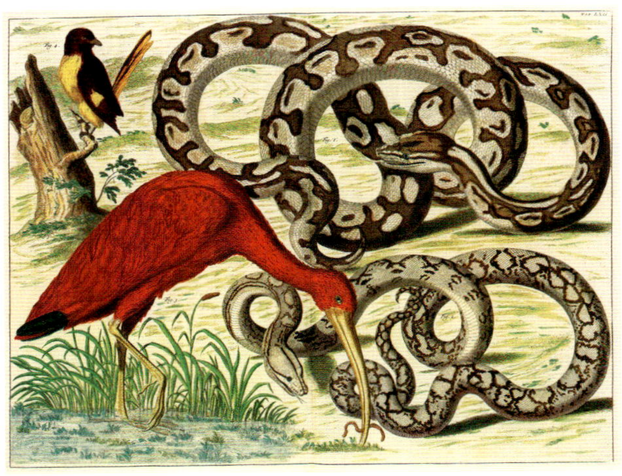

Amstelaedami, Apud Janssonio-Waesbergios.
& J. Wetstenium, & Gul. Smith.
MDCCXXXIV (1734)

139

THESAURUS
Tomus 2

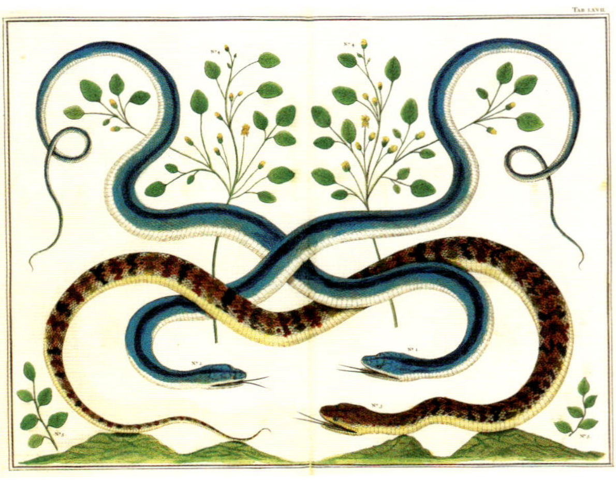

Amstelaedami, Apud J. Wetstenium,
& Gul. Smith, & Janssonio-Waesbergios.
MDCCXXXV (1735)

6

Albertus Seba's Collection of Natural Specimens
and its Pictorial Inventory

IRMGARD MÜSCH

27

The Zoology and Botany
in Albertus Seba's *Thesaurus*

RAINER WILLMANN
JES RUST

219

THESAURUS

Tomus 3

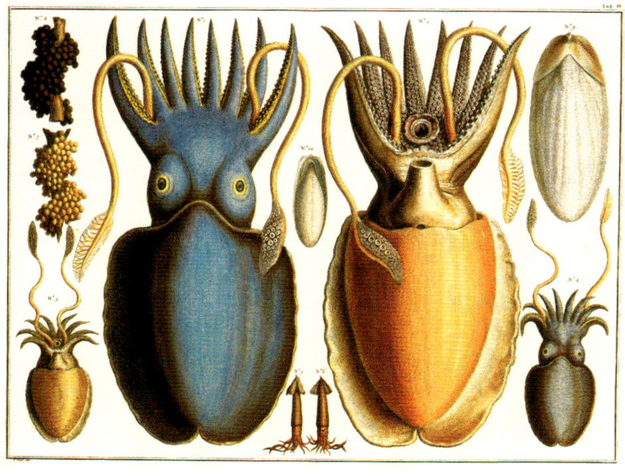

Amstelaedami, Apud Janssonio-Waesbergios.
MDCCLVIII (1758)

335

THESAURUS

Tomus 4

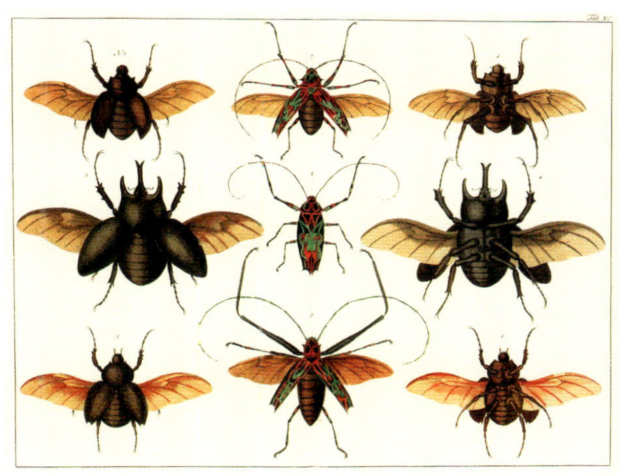

Amstelaedami, Apud H. C. Arksteum et
H. Merkum, et Petrum Schouten.
MDCCLXV (1765)

414

APPENDIX

The Scientists and the Authors
Acknowledgements
Photographic Credits

And there are no other
collections in all of Europe
wherein so many rare pieces
are to be found

ALBERTUS SEBA

ALBERTUS SEBA'S *collection of natural specimens and its* PICTORIAL INVENTORY

Albertus Seba (1665–1736) in Amsterdam was proud indeed of his collection of natural specimens, the work of many decades. Having emphasized its uniqueness in a letter to a potential buyer, composed in c. 1725, he expanded further on its scope, writing that it included *all sorts of exquisite pieces from the East and West Indies,* among these no less than *700 jars containing the rarest exotic animals* and *many particularly rare snakes.* Also *brought together thus are every exceptional sort of beautiful and rare conch, the finest and most complete butterflies from the 4 corners of the Earth.* Completing this list are samples *of all the plants, some familiar pieces, but unfamiliar ones too.* Seba commissioned artists to make meticulous drawings of these diverse objects from his collection. He went on to publish these drawings, supplemented by commentary, in a four-volumed set entitled *Loccupletissimi Rerum Thesauri Accurata Descriptio* (abbreviated in the following as *Thesaurus*). The large and magnificent work, incorporating an impressive total of 446 copperplates, was published between 1734 and 1765, hence also posthumously. This pictorial record of Seba's unique collection is now available in reprint. For a better appreciation of this major publishing enterprise, it is necessary to take a closer look at the life and historical context of the man behind it.

An APOTHECARY *and* COLLECTOR *in* AMSTERDAM

By becoming an apothecary, Albertus Seba, who was born in 1665 in the East Frisian town of Etzel, chose a profession with close ties to natural history. Doctors and apothecaries were pioneers of the empirical sciences, which had been growing significantly in importance since the Renaissance. Unlike today, medications were not synthetically made but mixed together from natural constituents. A whole range of traditional recipes were available to those versed in the art of creating remedies from animal, vegetable and mineral ingredients. But many did not stop there. They continued the search for new methods, collecting natural specimens from distant lands, studying them, and testing their potential uses. Their passion for collecting and researching often extended beyond immediate pharmaceutical applications. In many instances apothecaries started major natural history collections and contributed personally to the growing knowledge of nature.

Seba's collection of natural specimens also went far beyond what was required for the normal exercise of his profession (ill. p. 2). His portrait, programmatically placed at the front of the *Thesaurus,* depicts him amidst his collection. The wall behind him is completely lined with shelves of glass jars in which he stored his large collection of preserved snakes. Seba is holding one of these jars, probably filled with alcohol, in his right hand as well. He is pointing with his left hand at shells, loose sheets of drawings and an open book before him. This still-life arrangement illustrates the evolutionary course of the publication – from collected specimen to drawing to printed work. Indeed, the animals depicted on the right-hand page of the book can be found in two of the plates in the actual *Thesaurus* (I, 33 and 38). The portrait of Seba himself, executed by the copper engraver Jakob Houbraken (1698–1780) after a painting by Jan Maurits Quinkhard (1688–1772), shows Seba in the pose of a scholar of his day. The characteristic workroom, the periwig appropriate to his rank, the dignified drapery complete with pillar, signal that, even without a university education, it was possible to regard oneself as a member of the republic of letters in the 18th century.

In his day, Seba's profession, pharmaceutical science, was not a subject of academic study but of vocational training. Manuals already existed on the topic, of course, but they only contained excerpts of the empirical knowledge that continued to be transmitted mainly orally and in professional day-to-day practice. Apprenticeships and years as journeymen, entailing frequent changes of workplace, were thus essential for a good command of the profession. Seba started his training in 1684 in Neustadt-Gödens, not far from his home town, completing it in Groningen, Amsterdam, Nuremberg and Strasbourg. Each different location enabled him not only to deepen his pharmaceutical knowledge but also to acquaint himself with and study some natural

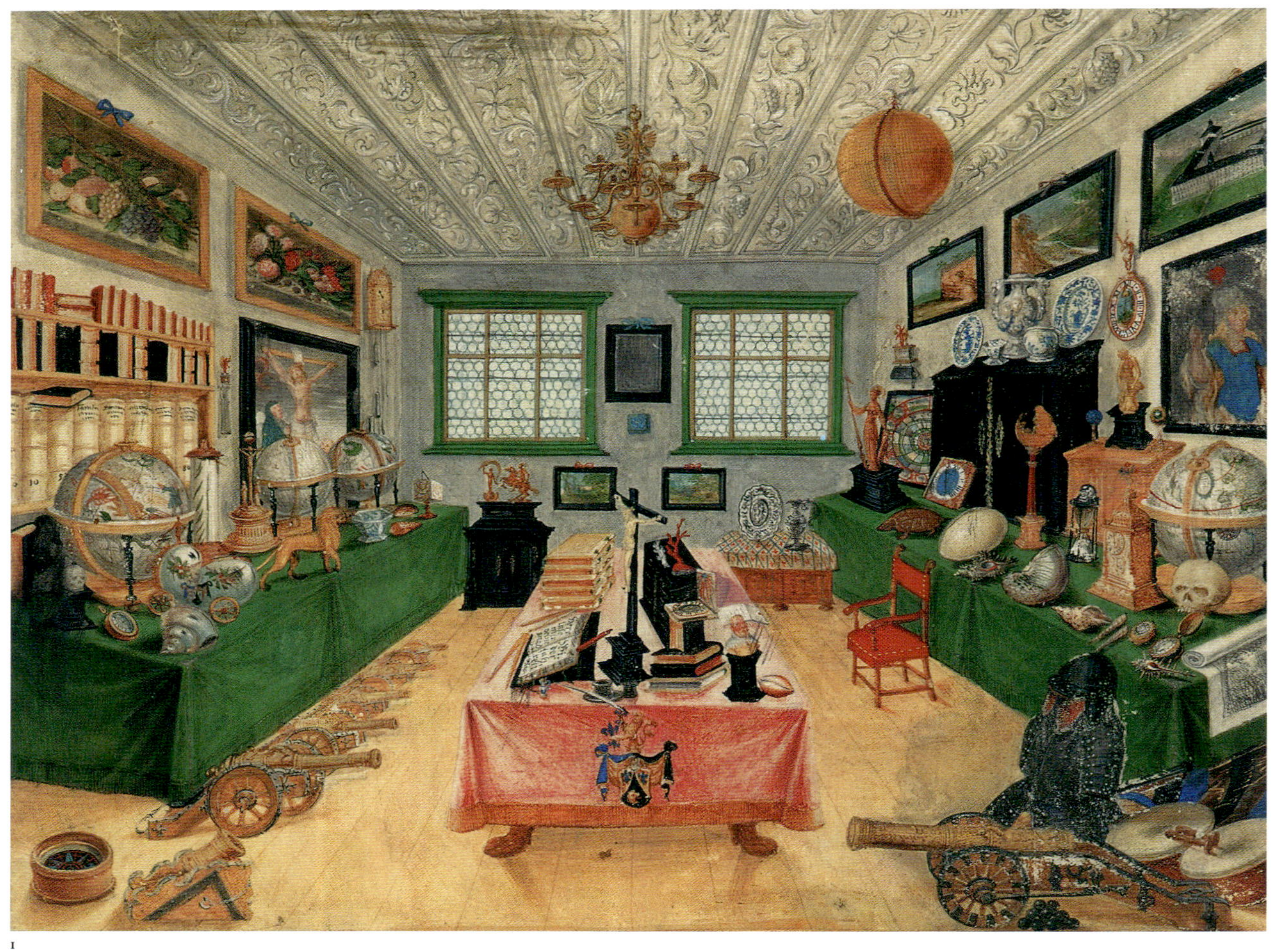

1

Fig. 1
Joseph Arnold:
The curiosity cabinet of the Dimpfel family of wholesale iron-mongers and miners from Regensburg, 1668?

Opaque pigment with heightening in gold on parchment
Ulm, Ulmer Museum

history collections. His employer in Nuremberg, for example, the apothecary Johann Leonhard Stöberlein (1636–1696), maintained an extensive collection of art and natural specimens. Each of the many such collections, large and small, were one little mosaic piece in the incomplete picture that naturalists around 1700 were able to form of the rich diversity of nature. Each collection, bearing the peculiar stamp of its owner's interests and astuteness, could make its own contribution to the advancing knowledge about nature, and hence each was a valuable instrument of research.

After his time of travel as a journeyman, Seba returned to Amsterdam, becoming a citizen there in 1697. In the same year, he passed his apothecary examinations, for which he was required to prepare various medicaments. Marrying Anna Loopes, the daughter of one of his colleagues, Seba bought a house and settled down as an independent apothecary in Amsterdam.

With his "Die Deutsche Apotheke" (German Apothecary's Shop), as he called his business, Seba rapidly earned an excellent reputation for himself. Even the Russian tsar Peter the Great trusted his pharmaceutical expertise, purchasing medicines from him for many years. Financially, too, he was successful – something which would enable him to establish his comprehensive collection of natural specimens. Not relying solely on casual customers who happened to pass by his apothecary, Seba actively sought them out. He traded in drugs from overseas, advertising his prices in an Amsterdam newspaper. He supplied departing ships with cases of medicines and treated their crews. It is related how, whenever a ship arrived in port, Seba would hasten down to the harbour without delay and administer his medicines to the exhausted sailors. Any natural specimens that they had brought with them he would then be able to purchase at a good price or accept in exchange for his medications.

In Amsterdam, Seba was ideally situated for starting such a collection of natural curios. The city on the Amstel river was still the flourishing centre of international maritime trade that it had first become in the 17th century. The Low Countries had, after 1580, liberated themselves in a series of stages from domination by Catholic Spain and had united as a Protestant republic. The succeeding century was a Golden Age, an extraordinary blossoming of the arts, sciences and commerce. The influx of Protestant refugees from the Spanish-occupied southern regions (now Belgium) enriched intellectual and economic life, and capital and know-how poured into the city. Amsterdam replaced Antwerp – still firmly in the grip of the Spanish – as the most important port, and trade with the colonies was expanded. Enjoying special political privileges, the Dutch East India Company imported spices, textiles, gems and other colonial goods on a grand scale, reselling them all over Europe at an enormous profit.

The sciences benefited directly from this flourishing trade. The Hortus Botanicus of Amsterdam, established in 1638 as a garden for medicinal herbs, was substantially enlarged with exotic plants brought home by representatives of the East India Company. These rare plants in Europe transformed the botanical garden, which still exists today, into an important focal point for naturalists. The research that the Swede Carl Linnaeus (1707–1778) conducted there led to his ground-breaking book *Systema Naturae* (1735), which continues to form the methodological basis of the classification of plants and animals. Numerous private collections of natural specimens likewise profited from the foreign trade and developed into important natural history collections offering indispensable visual material for domestic and foreign naturalists.

Dutch researchers were respected members of the republic of letters, that international network in which information was exchanged and open questions debated without regard for social class or national boundary. Seba, too, fostered relations with important researchers throughout Europe, such as Sir Hans Sloane (1660–1753), the influential president of the scientific Royal Society in London, Johann Jakob Scheuchzer (1672–1733), the Zurich-based naturalist and physician, Johann Jacob Baier (1677–1735), president of the Leopoldina Academy of Science, and Count Luigi Ferdinando de Marsigli (1658–1730) in Bologna. These were just a few of Europe's many collectors of natural specimens. The long letters between these scholars shed light on details about their collections. They sent each other unusual pieces, discussed observations of natural phenomena and established contacts amongst themselves. They founded academies and societies which, partly assisted by public funds, collated their research and published their findings in periodicals. Seba's achievements, helped along by his good contacts, were rewarded with membership of the Royal Society, the Bologna Academy and the Leopoldina.

The so-called republic of letters rose not only above issues of nationality or class; it tended to leave religious quarrels behind it, as well. During the turbulent first half of the 17th century, bloody wars raged between Catholics and Protestants, yet the sciences offered a generally neutral sphere in which a new, more or less objective understanding of the world could be developed beyond theological controversy. It was a sphere in which natural history collections could play an important part.

From CABINETS OF CURIOSITIES *to* COLLECTIONS OF NATURAL SPECIMENS

Under the influence of humanist scholarship, around 1500 there began to appear – initially at the courts of Italian princes – collections of a special type, known as *Kunstkammern* or cabinets of curiosities.

Very different things found their way into these collections: antique objects such as figurines and coins, artistically crafted artefacts, scientific instruments, books, pictures, items from faraway lands, and for the first time on a larger scale, natural specimens. One particularly large cabinet – built upon older precursors – was established by Francesco I de' Medici, Grand Duke of Tuscany, around 1570 in Florence. Early examples north of the Alps are the collections of Duke Albrecht V of Bavaria in Munich (from 1563) and the Tyrolean archduke Ferdinand at Ambras castle (from 1573). The cabinet of curiosities that Emperor Rudolph II established around 1600 in Prague, which filled many rooms, gained legendary fame. In emulation of their princes, members of the middle classes also began compiling private collections in the second half of the 16th century. Famous examples include the collections by Abraham Ortelius (1527–1598), a geographer and cartographer in Antwerp, and Herman Boerhaave (1668–1738), professor of medicine at Leiden, who, incidentally, wrote a glowing preface to Seba's *Thesaurus*.

A small gouache by the Ulm artist Joseph Arnold (?–1671), executed in 1668(?), portrays the *Kunstkammer* owned by the 17th-century Regensburg ironmonger Dimpfel (fig. 1). We see a room amply stocked with an assortment of very different objects. Paintings, weaponry, celestial and terrestrial globes, clocks, books, shells, small sculptures, and much more stand in decorative arrangements on the floor, on tables, shelves, and little cabinets. Although Arnold's depiction seems somewhat idealized, it is documented that splendid displays aimed at pleasing aesthetic tastes were quite commonplace. In order to be able to display a collection artistically while protecting it from dirt and damage, in the 16th and 17th century a new piece of furniture was specially developed: the collector's cabinet. In the description of his collection which he published in 1706, the Dutch cloth merchant Vincent Levin (1658–1727) illustrated individual areas of his collection just as they had been arranged in their cabinets (fig. 2). The selected plate shows an artistic display of corals and other sea creatures in an open cabinet. It is easy to imagine the effect on the visitors when Levin threw open the cabinet doors and drew out the drawers to reveal the secretly hidden treasures. A drawer that was once a part of a seashell cabinet dating from about 1725 also gives us a sense of the charm of such beautifully arranged collections (fig. 5). Equally impressive is the illustration of a collector's room which precedes a description by the Danish naturalist Ole Worm (1588–1654) of his cabinet (fig. 3). Worm's collection includes domestic utensils and natural specimens, so-called exotica, from overseas: musical instruments, a canoe, preserved animals, shells and much more besides.

The multifarious and disparate objects united in early encyclopaedic collections appeared to later generations as confused cabinets of curiosities. For all its variety, however, Worm's collection is far from a random hotchpotch. Besides its clear focus on natural specimens, its pieces are sorted and clearly arranged on shelves and inside drawers, all neatly identified. The labels reveal that Worm ordered his objects according to different criteria, for example, by material: thus there are labels for metal and *Ligna* (wood).

Advice on arranging and ordering such collections was provided by theoretical guides, the first of which was written by Samuel van Quiccheberg (1529–1567) in 1565. In his *Inscriptiones vel tituli theatri amplissimi*, this Flemish doctor and administrator of the ducal art collection in Munich outlines an ideal cabinet of curiosities. In his system of five departments, the first was devoted to noble lineage, i.e. genealogy. The second department was dedicated to handicrafts from Antiquity to his own day, the third department to natural specimens, and the fourth to technical and cultural objects. Quiccheberg's fifth department was a picture gallery comprising paintings, drawings and engravings. In addition to these departments he also saw as necessary not only a library and workshops, but also an apothecary's shop. It is precisely these last which make it clear that the *Kunstkammer* was intended not merely as a collection, but as a place of learning.

In a world becoming ever more complex with each new geographic and scientific discovery, the ideal cabinet of curiosities constituted an attempt to produce an overall picture of this world, the cosmos. Within its limited space, the cabinet of curiosities presented a microcosm, reproducing the general picture, the macrocosm, on a reduced scale. The early cabinets of curiosities thereby spotlighted areas on the fringes of the known world. These included medical "curiosities" such as so-called freaks of nature, as well as handicrafts and natural specimens from foreign lands, and many other rarities which in Europe provoked astonishment and raised questions. The aim was to bring together – at least in representative form – the most complete collection pos-

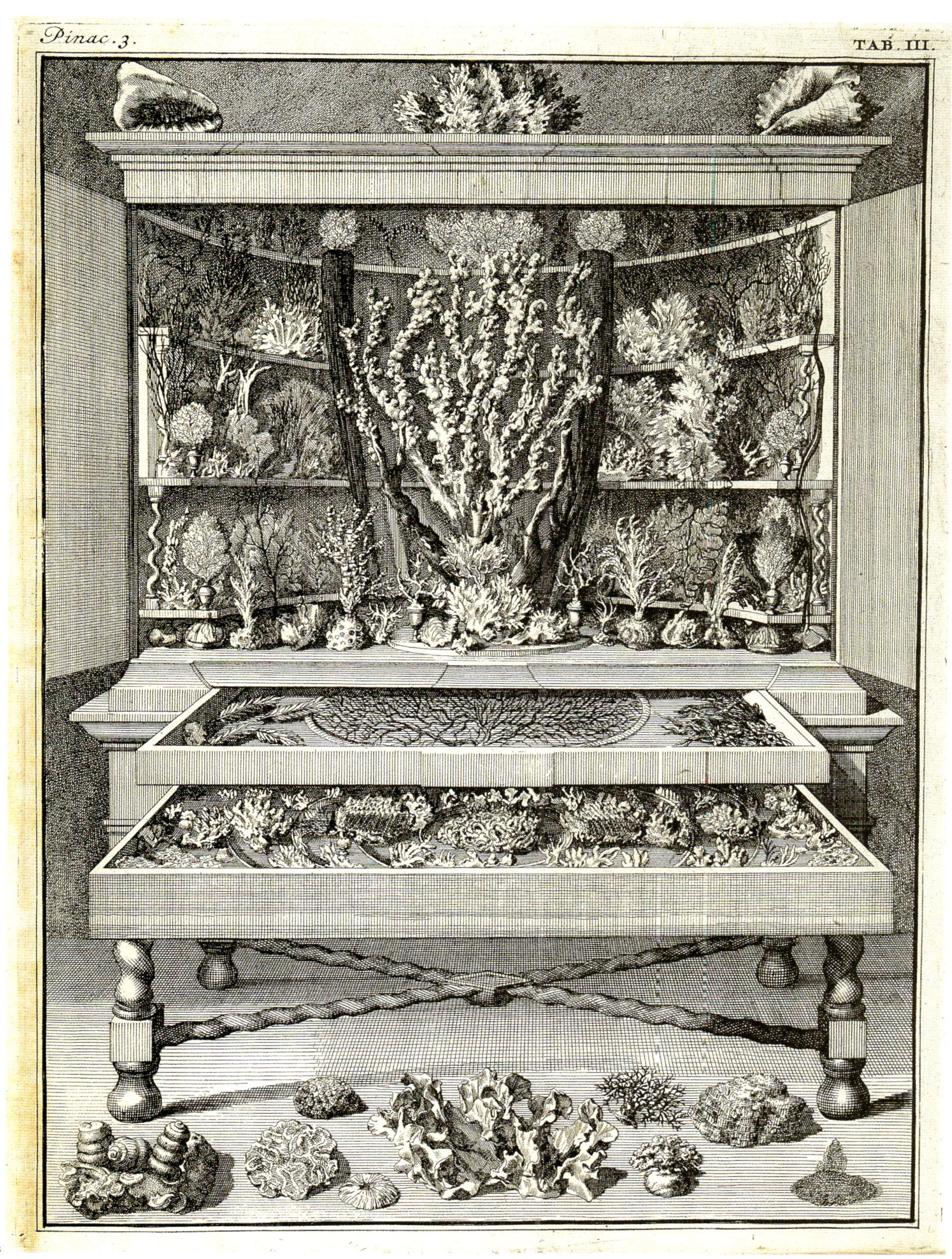

2

Fig. 2
Vincent Levin: *Het Wondertooneel der Natuure*, 1706
Plate III

Göttingen, Niedersächsische Staats- und Universitätsbibliothek

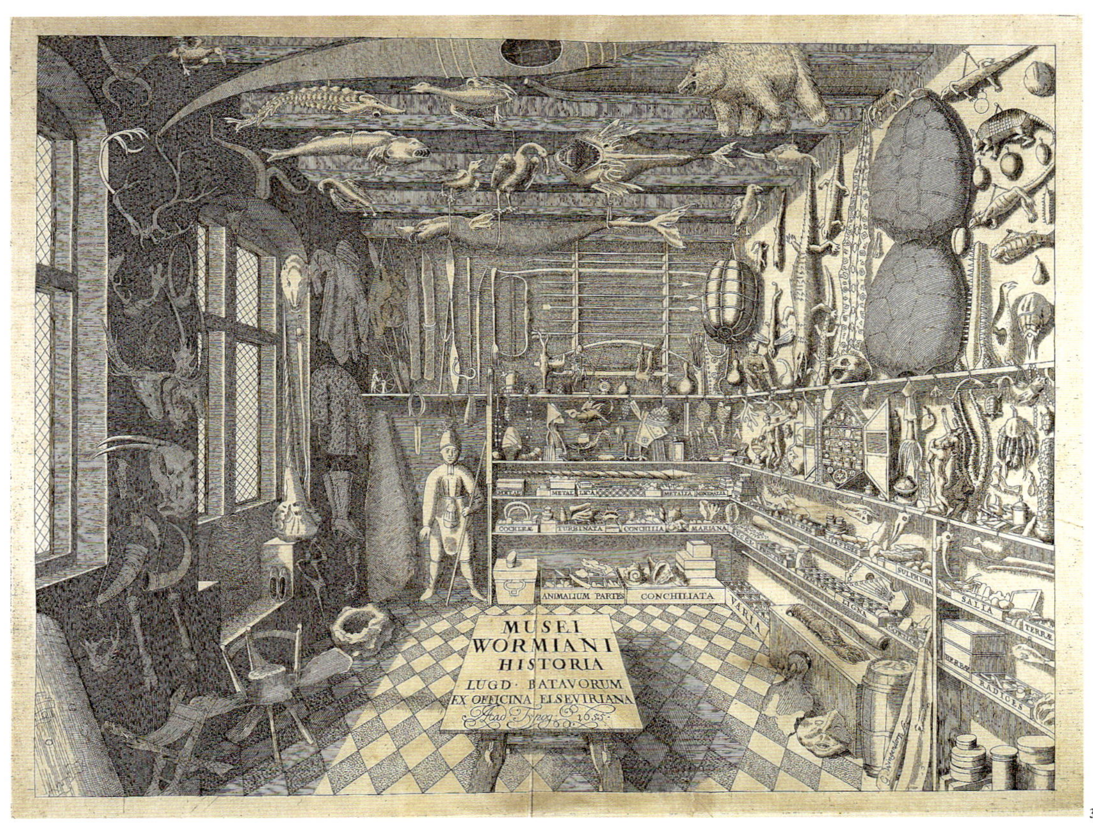

3

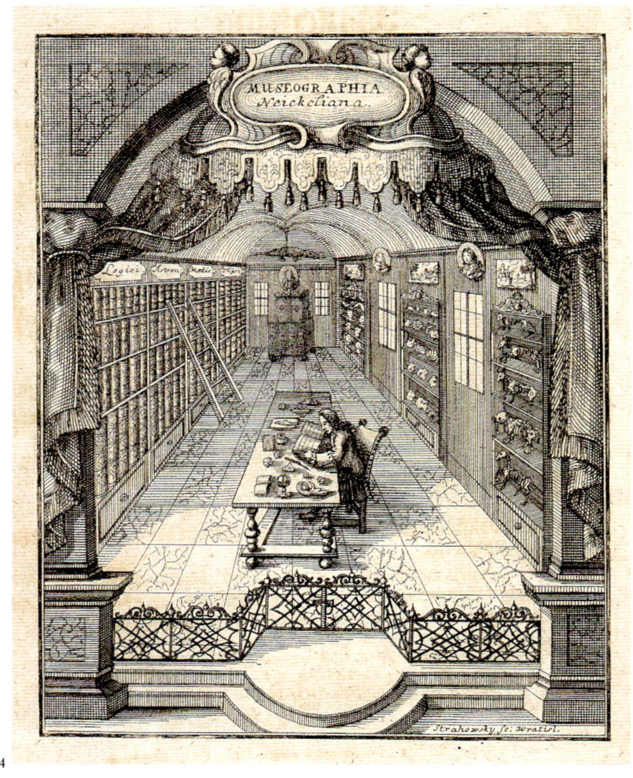

4

Fig. 3
Ole Worm: *Musei Wormiani Historia*, 1655
Frontispiece

Göttingen, Niedersächsische Staats- und Universitätsbibliothek

Fig. 4
Caspar Friedrich Neickel: *Museographia*, 1727
Frontispiece

Göttingen, Niedersächsische Staats- und Universitätsbibliothek

sible of all things knowable and worth knowing, to record them and thus to make them easier to grasp. The arrangement of the various objects in a room – some laid out on tabletops – gave the viewer the opportunity to relate the individual objects to one another visually and to draw connections between them. A given natural specimen, a piece of coral for instance, which was represented in the collections of Levin, Dimpfel and Seba (ill. p. 2; figs. 1-2), thereby acquired quite different meanings. Initially it was regarded as a remedy for illnesses such as anaemia, but was subsequently also imputed magical powers, such as protection against lightning bolts or the evil eye. Its brilliant colour made it an aesthetic ornament, intricately set in gold by fine metalsmiths. But coral excited scientific interest as well, because it was not easily assigned either to the kingdom of animals or plants, while the fact that it hardened to stone once out of the water meant it might even belong to the mineral kingdom. Thus objects like coral could suggest a variety of links to different fields. What today seems the very heterogeneous organization of cabinets of curiosities was grounded in this network of meanings, and arose out of correlations with religion and alchemy as well as out of the classification of objects by their specific material properties.

The cosmological view of the world that governed the encyclopaedic pretensions of early collections began to lose importance after 1600. In the 17th and 18th century, cabinets of curiosities were replaced by more specialized collections. The new aim was less to reflect, in representative samples, the whole cosmos than to cover comprehensively a chosen area of speciality. Natural history collections became tools of empirical research. Through description, comparison and ordering of their pieces, collectors strove to reach a scientific understanding of nature. An illustration from 1727 (fig. 4) shows a collector working with his objects in such an ideal "research laboratory". Caspar Friedrich Neickel placed it at the front of his *Museographia*, published by the Breslau physician Johann Kanold (1679–1729). This manual on early museum science combined a guide to collecting with descriptions of existing collections, including Seba's own.

There were motivations enough for collecting – whether to act as an intellectual stimulus, to satisfy an investigative spirit, or to display wealth and erudition. And of course, collections raised the social prestige of their owners. Large collections, or ones containing rare pieces, attracted foreign visitors, and even royalty. And it was not unheard of for complete collections to be resold at a handsome profit.

Collecting was naturally subject to fashion. Shells, for example, were a popular item and from the Renaissance onwards were collected and studied in ever-growing numbers. As an employee of the Dutch East India Company on the island of Amboina (in modern Indonesia), Georg E. Rumphius (1627–1702) was well placed to build up an exquisite collection that became the subject of *D'Amboinsche Rariteitkamer*, an influential volume of 1705 with which Seba was also familiar (fig. 6). Around 1700 the Netherlands were seized by a veritable conch mania; market prices soared to almost absurd levels for these fascinatingly pretty natural specimens. Alongside the countless little shell collections which formed as a consequence, there were a few larger ones – with Seba's collection being among the most comprehensive.

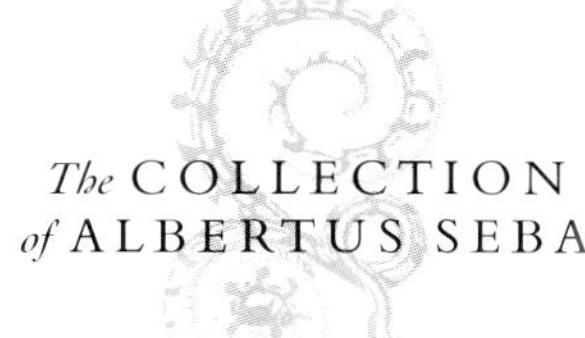

The COLLECTION *of* ALBERTUS SEBA

In assembling his collection, Seba was thus following a trend of his time. As an apothecary, however, he was already *per se* a collector and researcher of natural specimens. Contemporary reports testify to his being a well-versed member of this species. His tactic of buying the souvenirs from sailors just returned from the distant seas, sometimes even before they had disembarked from their vessels, has already been mentioned. He may well have made arrangements with the odd seafarer to bring back specific natural samples that rarely reached Europe and were scarcely known at home. Many remarks in the *Thesaurus* indicate that Seba exchanged correspondence with contacts in Sri Lanka, Greenland, Virginia, Batavia (now Jakarta, Indonesia) and elsewhere, from whom he obtained specimens. With other collectors he swapped duplicates from his collection, or sold them – with his usual business acumen – at a profit.

Seba succeeded in assembling a wealth of natural specimens whose fame spread beyond the bounds of Amsterdam. The full extent of his collection has come down to posterity as a consequence of an exceptionally fortunate transaction that Seba made in 1717. He had heard about the impending visit of the Russian tsar, Peter

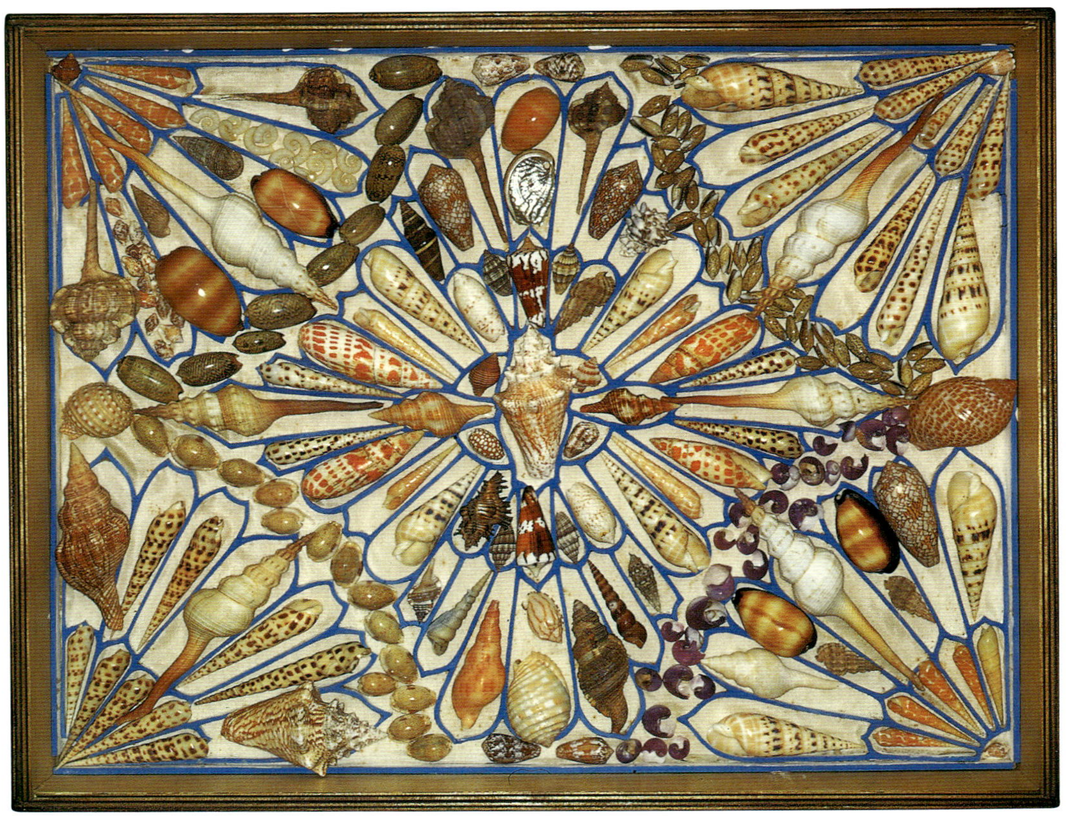

5

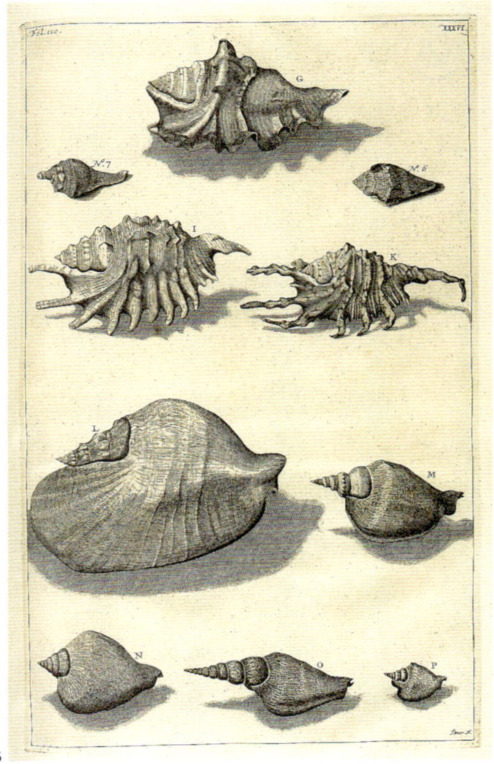

6

Fig. 5
Drawer from a cabinet of seashells, 1725

Amsterdam, Zoölogisch Museum, Universiteit van Amsterdam

Fig. 6
Georg E. Rumphius: *D'Amboinsche Rariteitkamer*, 1705
Plate XXXVI

Göttingen, Niedersächsische Staats- und Universitätsbibliothek

the Great, who wanted to see the Netherlands and at the same time shop for acquisitions for his own cabinet of wonders. The adroit Seba sent him a written itemization of his collection in advance and thus prepared the way for its sale. This sale actually took place after Peter had paid a visit to his home. The full scope of Seba's first collection is revealed in an inventory drawn up by an administrator from St. Petersburg upon arrival of the newly purchased pieces. Among other things, it comprised no less than 72 drawers full of shells, 32 drawers displaying 1,000 European insects, and 400 jars of animal specimens preserved in alcohol.

After selling his first collection, Seba immediately set about establishing a second one that eventually became even larger. As the *Thesaurus* shows, the main emphases of this collection were marine animals, insects and reptiles. With this approach Seba was in good company. As already mentioned, naturalists around 1700 were generally tending to concentrate their collecting activities on a few specific aspects of the natural kingdom. Instead of amassing the broadest possible assortment of rarities, they strove to put together a detailed overview of selected fields. What made a collection scientifically valuable was less the worth of some of its single pieces than its completeness in covering a particular branch of the natural world, including native flora and fauna.

Leafing through the *Thesaurus,* one is struck by a certain ambivalence in the selection. The Amsterdam apothecary succeeded in assembling a collection of the greatest scientific importance in the areas of reptiles, insects and marine animals, and made a major contribution towards the identification of the various species. And yet his collection retains a clear link with the older cabinets of wonders and curiosities. It continues to make room for the peculiar, the rare and the strange. It is more out of curiosity than in the name of science, for instance, that a deformed baby from Curaçao, preserved in alcohol, is separately depicted. The *Thesaurus* also includes an illustration of a malformed goat with one head and two bodies (I, 46). What found its way into Seba's book was not necessarily the typical representative of a given species but the occasional anomaly, which was certain to excite much greater interest. Unlike earlier cabinets of curiosities, however, Seba's collection of natural specimens made no room for ancient coins, exotic weapons or the like. Untouched nature was the main interest of this professional apothecary. Only the nautilus shell is elaborately adorned by the work of a human hand (III, 84).

One general problem facing natural history collections was storage and conservation. While objects such as hard, calcareous seashells were not subject to major decay, other natural specimens required complex conservation measures. Procedures were borrowed from other disciplines, such as medicine, and developed further. At the end of the 17th century another Amsterdam apothecary, Frederik Ruysch (1638–1731), who was also a doctor, naturalist and friend of Seba's, adapted existing techniques for preserving human corpses. His conservation by means of coloured wax and oils was so effective that the bodies looked as if they were still alive. Although he kept his formula secret, it is possible that Seba had at least some understanding of the processes involved. Seba, for example, employed a method by which he could isolate the skeleton of a leaf. He submitted the leaf to an accelerated rotting process to expose its internal structure. In 1730 he published an article on this technique. Specimens prepared in this way are displayed on the first few pages of the *Thesaurus.*

Seba's large collection of preserved natural specimens, which he exhibited in a specially designated room of his house, was famous far afield. Naturalists from many countries came to view it. After Seba's death in 1736 the collection passed to his heirs. In order to assure continued publication of the still incomplete *Thesaurus,* they eventually found it necessary to sell the collection. The auction took place in 1752. Thanks to a printed auction catalogue containing handwritten notes, we know the considerable sums which were paid for some of the pieces. Some items have survived the centuries and form a part of the holdings of European natural history museums, including the Zoological Institute in St. Petersburg, the Natural History Museum in Stockholm, the Zoological Museum in Amsterdam and the British Museum in London.

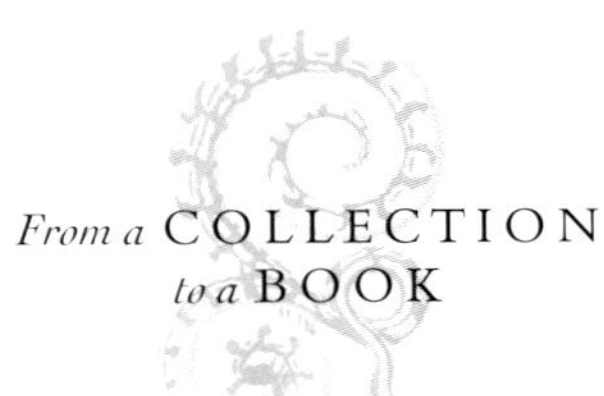

From a COLLECTION *to a* BOOK

Natural history collections and books about the natural world are inextricably linked to each other. While naturalists from the late Renaissance onwards increasingly emphasized the primacy of immediate, empirical studies of nature over knowledge from books, this did not, by any means, completely preclude reading. As with *Kunstkammern*, books formed a part of every natural history collection and also served as commentaries on them. They provided access to the subject matter and enabled identification and ordering. Books and their illustrations also served to supplement collections of natural specimens, closing any gaps and making up for any deficiences with pictures. As Seba's *Thesaurus* exemplifies, some collections were themselves made into books.

Works devoted to plant identification, to individual collections, and to natural history in general reveal the close tie between books and collections. Indeed, books themselves could constitute collections of natural specimens, as in the case of herbaria, which became increasingly popular from the 16th century onwards. Herbaria are blank volumes of highly absorbent, soft paper on which pressed and dried plants were glued. An example still extant today was compiled by Boëtius, court physician to Emperor Rudolph II in Prague (fig. 8). The two dried plants illustrated are members of the geranium family, as the handwritten label at the top of the page indicates. A small drawing in the lower margin, showing a stork, refers to the botanical name given to the plants in German – *Storchschnabelgewächse* (cranesbill). After 1700, compiling herbaria with personally collected plant samples was considered a useful pastime and even an important element of education. One went out to "botanize", exploring and recording one's natural surroundings. Everyone could participate in scientific inquiry, acquire a personal first-hand grasp of the current state of knowledge and possibly even contribute to it.

Assembling an extensive collection of natural specimens required considerable financial outlay, however. Since, moreover, many objects were not so easily obtained or were difficult to preserve, collections of drawings could act as a substitute or supplement. Like the plants in a herbarium, these pictures were glued in the desired order onto the blank pages of folio volumes. The results were veritable "museums on paper", such as the *Museo Cartaceo* by the Italian naturalist and classical scholar Cassiano dal Pozzo (1589–1627), which comprises over 7,000 drawings.

When a collector or naturalist commissioned an artist to draw specimens of interest to him, and in a second stage even to transfer them onto a plate for the press, the plant or animal in question underwent considerable abstraction and distillation on its way to becoming a scientific illustration (fig. 7). Just as a specimen was regarded as representative of its species, so its appearance was systematized. Individual traits not typical of its kind were minimized and the scientifically significant ones were accentuated. This process becomes clear upon comparison of a jar containing a snake preserved in alcohol, such as seen in Seba's portrait (ill. p. 2), with one of the numerous snake depictions in the *Thesaurus*. A convoluted, compressed, often faded and partly decomposed creature suspended in a murky fluid is transformed into a very clear and distinct illustration. The elements important for human identification of the animal are rendered better and considerably more clearly in the picture than in the actual specimen itself. This pictorial abstraction may also be understood as one way of taming the multifariousness of nature.

From the 16th century onwards, books on the natural world contained detailed and realistic depictions permitting identification of the specimens in question. First came large botanical works, since the identification of plants played a crucial role in pharmaceutics. The epoch-making *Historia Stirpium* by the botanist Leonhart Fuchs (1501–1566) is illustrated with a handsome 511 woodcuts. The important contribution which the artists made to this work is also acknowledged pictorially: they can be seen drawing and transferring a drawing onto the wooden block (fig. 7).

The example set by botany was soon followed by medicine, with its plate volumes on anatomy, and zoology, with richly illustrated books on animals. The 17th century subsequently saw the appearance of ever more specialized books, such as the *Metamorphosis Naturalis* by the Dutch painter and naturalist Jan Goedaert (?– c. 1668), a three-volume work on insects which was published in various languages in the 1660s. Goedaert was the first to present the developmental stages of these creatures systematically in a single picture; thus we see a larva, a caterpillar and a butterfly together on one sheet (fig. 9). The book on *Ornithologiae libri tres* by the Englishman Francis Willughby (1635–1672), which first appeared in 1676, presents 78 plates of native and "exotic" birds, arranged by specific category, such as birds of prey or water fowl (fig. 10).

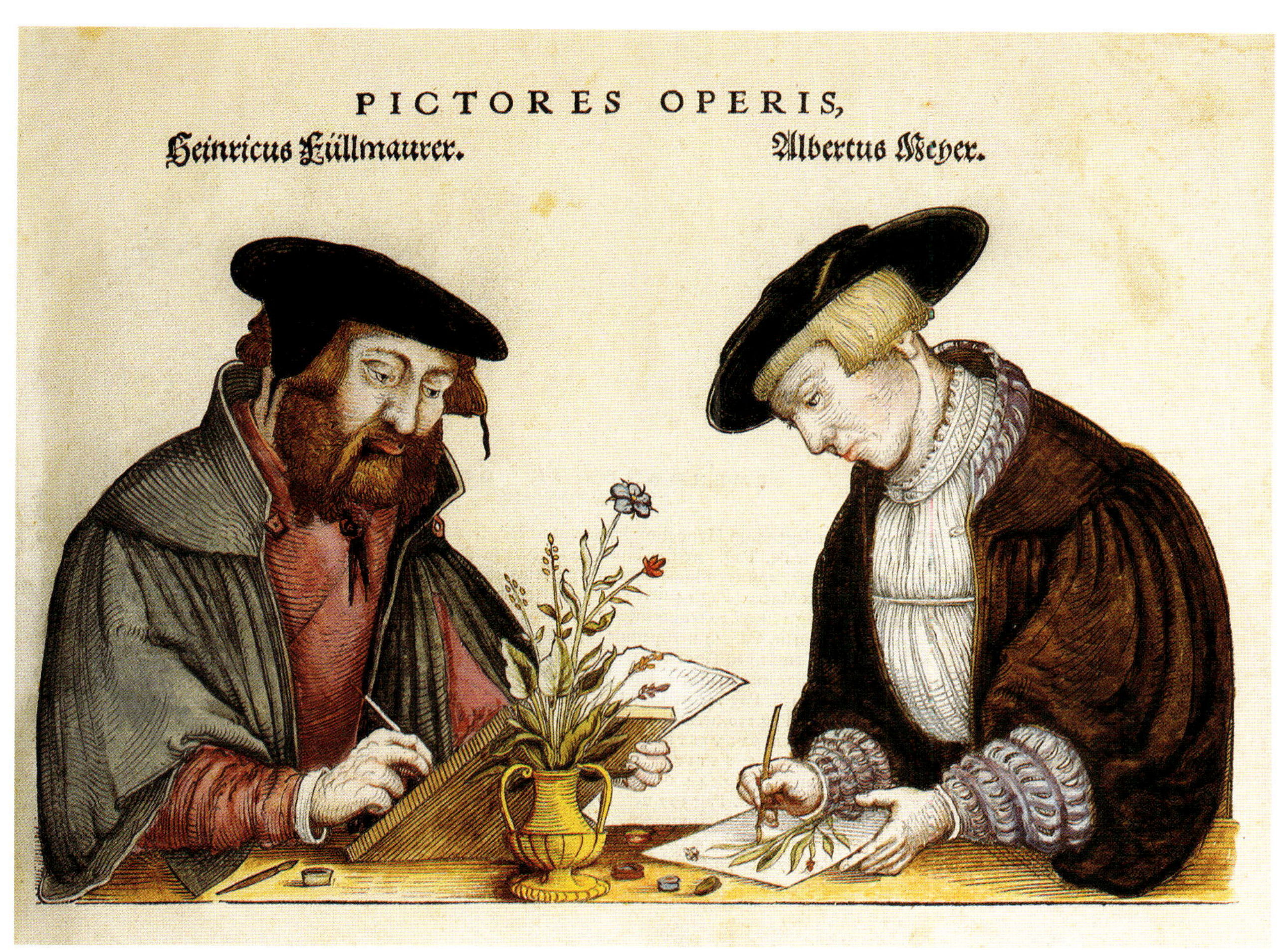

9

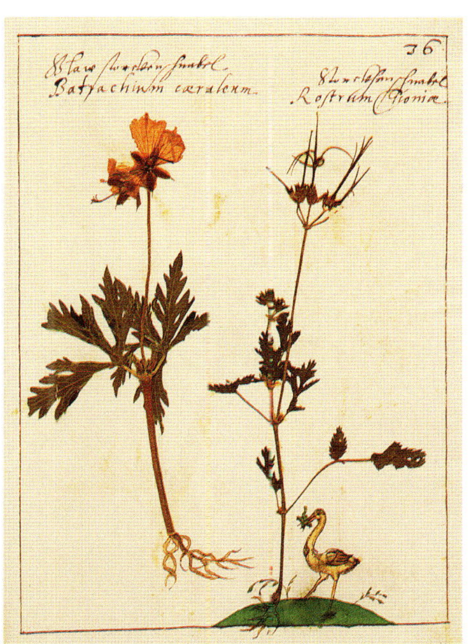

8

Fig. 7
Leonhart Fuchs: *Historia Stirpium*, 1542
Ulm, Stadtbibliothek

Fig. 8
Boëtius, Herbarium

Braunschweig, Technische Universität Carolo-Wilhelmina zu Braunschweig, Universitätsbibliothek

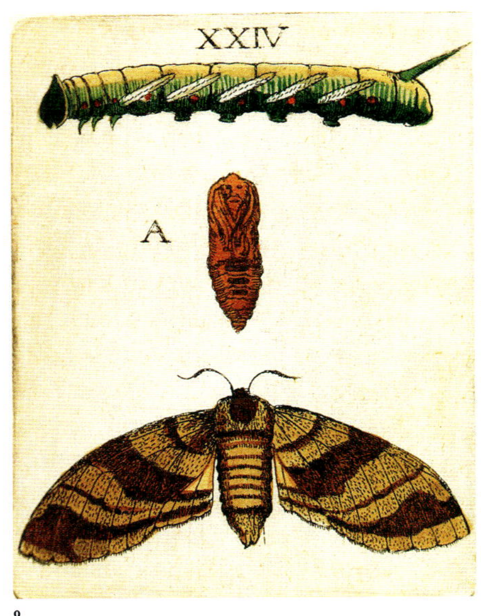

9

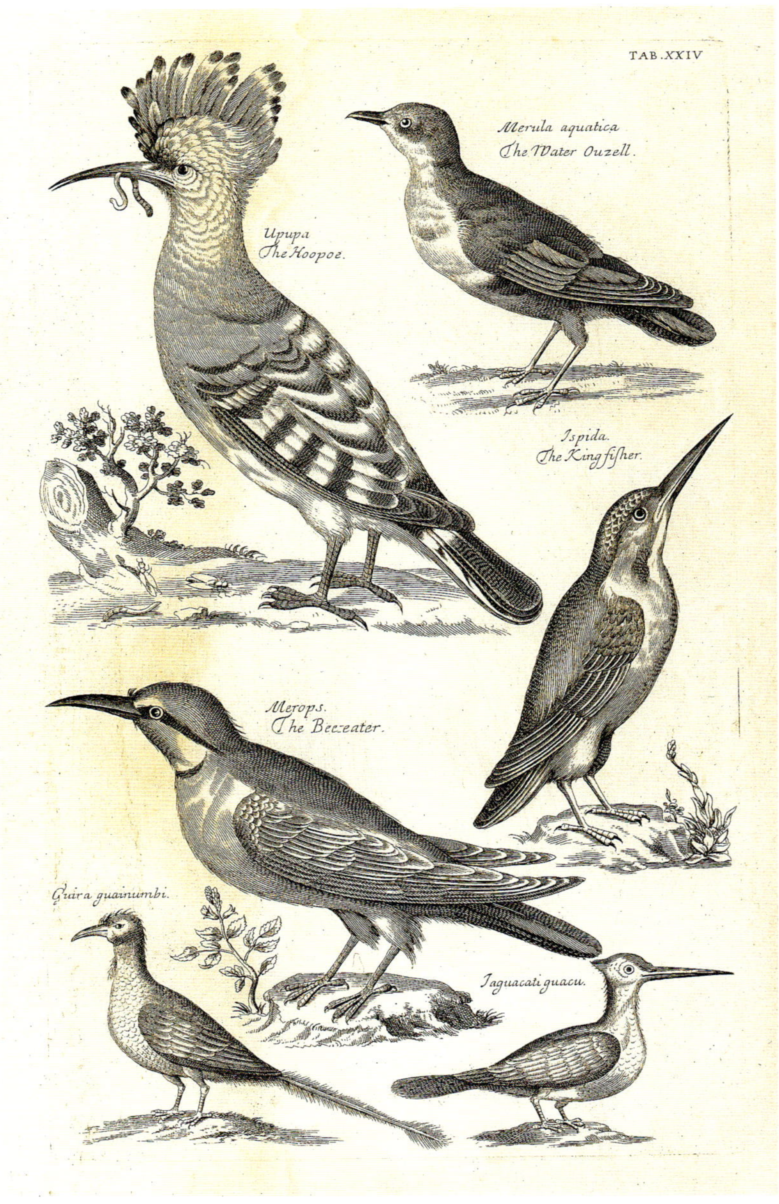

10

Fig. 9
Jan Goedaert: *Metamorphosis Naturalis*, 1662
Plate XXIV

Göttingen, Niedersächsische Staats- und Universitätsbibliothek

Fig. 10
Francis Willughby: *Ornithologiae libri tres*, 1676
Plate XXVI

Göttingen, Niedersächsische Staats- und Universitätsbibliothek

Scholars like Willughby were usually not acquainted at first hand with the animals and plants from distant parts of the world. Rather, they consulted illustrated travel accounts in which such unfamiliar fauna and flora were described and depicted. To obtain more accurate information, they provided ship's captains or other voyagers with detailed questionnaires to help them record what they saw. Towards the end of the 17th century, more naturalists began to travel abroad themselves. They documented what they saw in pictures or had artists accompany them on their travels to carry out this task. After their return, the sketches and descriptions made on site were subsequently turned into travel books which were simultaneously regular natural histories of the regions visited. Hans Sloane, a naturalist who corresponded with Seba, published his travel account in 1707 and 1725 as a *Natural History of Jamaica*. It is very likely that Seba knew these two volumes, containing plates of a variety of reptiles and insects.

A particularly exceptional work was compiled by Maria Sybilla Merian (1647–1717), an artist from Frankfurt-on-Main who set out for Surinam at her own expense and on her own initiative on a voyage that lasted between 1699 and 1701. She was particularly interested in insects, but also studied other animals and plants in this South American country. In 1705 she published the work *Metamorphosis Insectorum Surinamensium*, which consisted of 60 large illustration plates and detailed descriptions (fig. 11). Her artistic still-life compositions are strikingly beautiful and influenced the design of the first volume of the *Thesaurus*.

Works of natural history from this era were illustrated in many very different ways. This is explained by their various purposes. Many books followed the tradition of earlier botanical works, whose illustrations were designed for unambiguous plant identification in herbal medicine. The specimens are depicted individually on a neutral background, so that they do not overlap and their characteristic traits are visible as clearly as possible (figs. 8, 9, 10). A different emphasis, on the other hand, is offered by a book from 1681, the *Anatome Animalium* by the Amsterdam physician Gerard Blasius (fig. 12). Here the author attempts to reach a deeper understanding of nature by examining the internal organs and bone structure of animals. Each of his plates is devoted to a single species. Its skeleton and the results of anatomical analysis are presented next to a view of the animal in a natural setting. Maria Sybilla Merian placed particular importance on conveying an impression of the habitat in which the plants and animals lived and interacted. Her carefully designed scenes presented the individual elements distinctly and identifiably in an aesthetically pleasing manner (fig. 11). The Swiss naturalist Johann Jakob Scheuchzer (1672–1733) had another purpose in mind with his *Kupfer-Bibel*, which was also called the *Physica Sacra* (fig. 14). He discussed the animals, plants and natural phenomena mentioned in the Bible in the light of the latest scientific findings. This work, published between 1731 and 1735, was intended to help elucidate the Bible and to demonstrate its authenticity from the point of view of natural history. Depictions of biblical events are combined with illustrations from natural science. For example, the scene of Eve succumbing to the serpent's temptations and persuading Adam to taste the forbidden apple as well is accompanied by depictions of various kinds of snakes. While such representations of the natural world are clearly embedded within a specific worldview, Carl Linnaeus (1707–1778) sought to free his *Systema Naturae* from any such extraneous ballast (fig. 13). This book, which first appeared in 1735, developed the system of classification of plants and animals which still holds today. Linnaeus chose the reproductive organs as the main distinguishing factor between the genera and species of living organisms. The illustrations in his book are correspondingly reduced to simple diagrams of the relevant plant parts. It is easy to see how much Seba's *Thesaurus* diverges from this example of cutting-edge contemporary science.

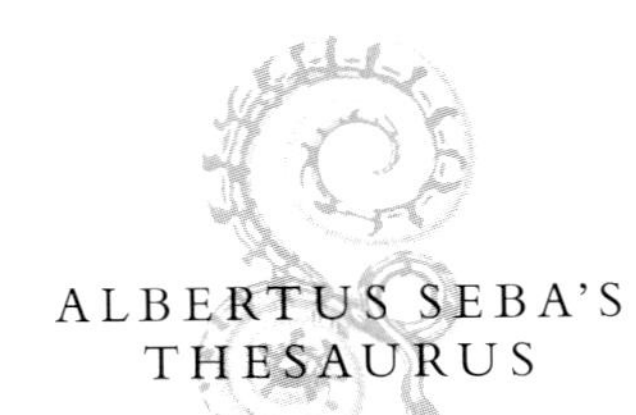

ALBERTUS SEBA'S THESAURUS

On 30 October 1731 a contract was signed in Amsterdam between three parties: Seba and the agents of two publishing houses agreed to produce a major work of 400 plates depicting Seba's collection. Ultimately, the *Thesaurus* incorporated a magnificent 446 plates, 175 of them double-page. The four volumes appeared over a span of 30 years, for after the appearance of the first two volumes in 1734 and 1735, Seba's death delayed the last two to 1758 and 1765. The commentary on the plates was published in a Latin-French and a Latin-Dutch edition, so as to reach a broad international readership of natural historians, collectors and book lovers. Seba wrote the text for the first two volumes largely himself, but also had other naturalists assist him. Frederik Ruysch, for example, helped him identify the snakes. Seba also entrusted the task of writing the commentary about fish in the third volume to an expert on the subject, the Swede Peter Artedi (1705–1735). When Albertus Seba died, his notes for the fourth volume were ready, but had to be revised a little and updated.

Volume I of the *Thesaurus* opens with a few pages devoted to illustrations of the plant skeletons that Seba had prepared and conserved using his own special technique. These are followed by depictions of plants and animals from South America and Asia. Alongside lizards, birds, frogs, spiders and other creatures, Seba includes a few fantastical creatures, such as dragons. Volume II is dedicated primarily to snakes, but a few plants and other animals are also depicted on the plates for decorative purposes and in order to illustrate the reptiles' environment. Volume III is devoted to marine life. The imposing variety of sea creatures includes scallops, starfish, squid, sea urchins and fish. Volume IV presents, in nearly 100 plates, a large collection of insects followed by a few pages of minerals and fossils from Seba's cabinet.

These natural-history plates are preceded not only by the author's portrait (ill. p. 2) but also by an allegorical frontispiece typical of books of the Baroque era (fig. 15). Figures embodying abstract concepts are here combined into a composition which yields a complex message and which represents a programmatic statement of the aims of the book. The original drawing was executed by the Dutch painter and draughtsman Louis Fabritius Dubourg (1693–1775) and then transferred onto a copperplate for printing by Pieter Tanjé (1706–1761), an engraver in Amsterdam. The Latin motto at the lower edge of the picture provides important clues for decoding its message. The female figure seated in the centre is thus to be understood as *Industria*, the personification of Industry and Diligence, who is motivated by her love of the sciences. She is busily carrying out her task, symbolized by the beehive beside her, under the protection of the enlightened personification of Truth, *Veritas*. Time, represented by the allegorical figure of *Chronos* with his scythe idle, is giving her the opportunity to pursue her work, namely, collecting. She is receiving from a winged messenger, who personifies Commerce, natural specimens from the different parts of the world. These last are personified in turn by allegorical figures standing behind Commerce. A Native American represents the New World, followed by a dark-skinned inhabitant of the African continent, and an oriental from Asia. Europe is not represented, indicating that natural specimens from overseas – brought back on the large sailing ships visible in the background – are the focus of attention. Since Australia was still unknown to Europeans, its symbolical representative is missing. Many putti are scampering about at *Industria*'s feet, engaged in gathering specimens, examining and discussing them. As can be seen, pictures and books are also part of this study of nature. Two spirits are descending from the heavens to acknowledge *Industria*'s tireless collecting for the benefit of knowledge about the natural world. The one in front is carrying a circlet wrought in the shape of a snake biting its tail. This symbol of eternity, together with the laurel wreath in the hands of the second spirit, stands for lasting fame. The personification of diligent collecting thus outshines the idle reaper *Chronos* and is rewarded with symbols of enduring honour. The frontispiece of course reflects how Seba saw himself: its allegorical composition celebrates his own industriousness as an indefatigable collector and as the author of a comprehensive catalogue of his collection.

Publication of a work like the *Thesaurus* called for considerable sums of money. Hugely expensive to produce were above all the many illustration plates, whose engraving was a laborious and drawn-out task. The names of no less than 13 artists are recorded as being employed on the transferral of the drawings, frontispiece, and portrait to the copperplates. Besides Houbraken and Tanjé, who have already been mentioned, these included copper engravers from Amsterdam such as Frans de Bakker (active from 1736–1765), Adolf van der Laan (active from 1717–1740), and Jan Punt (1711–1779). But first Seba had to find a publisher willing to take on the financial risk associated with such an elaborate enterprise. It was customary in the Netherlands for several

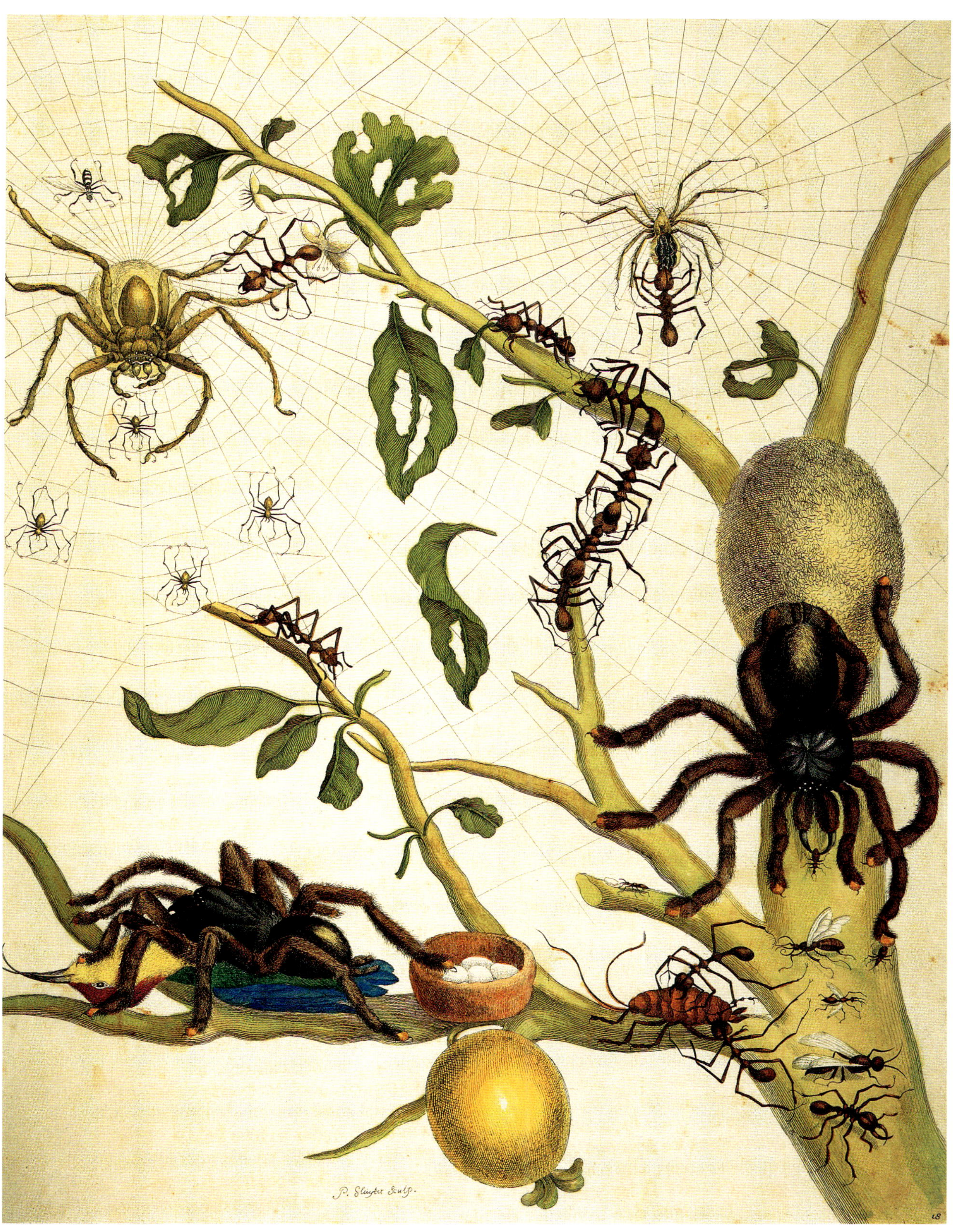
11

Fig. 11
Maria Sybilla Merian: *Metamorphosis Insectorum Surinamensium*, 1705
Plate XVIII

Göttingen, Niedersächsische Staats- und Universitätsbibliothek

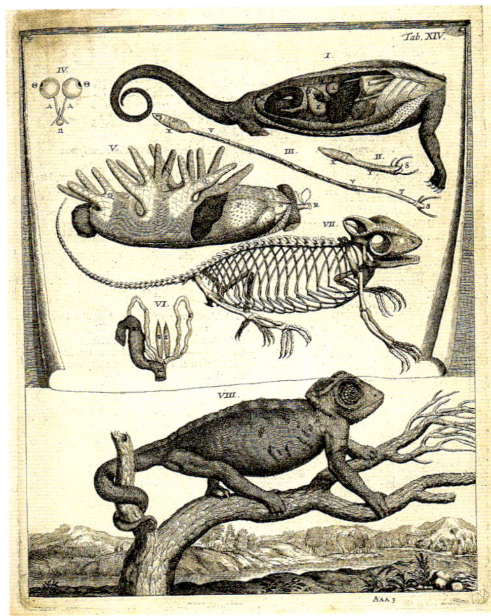

12

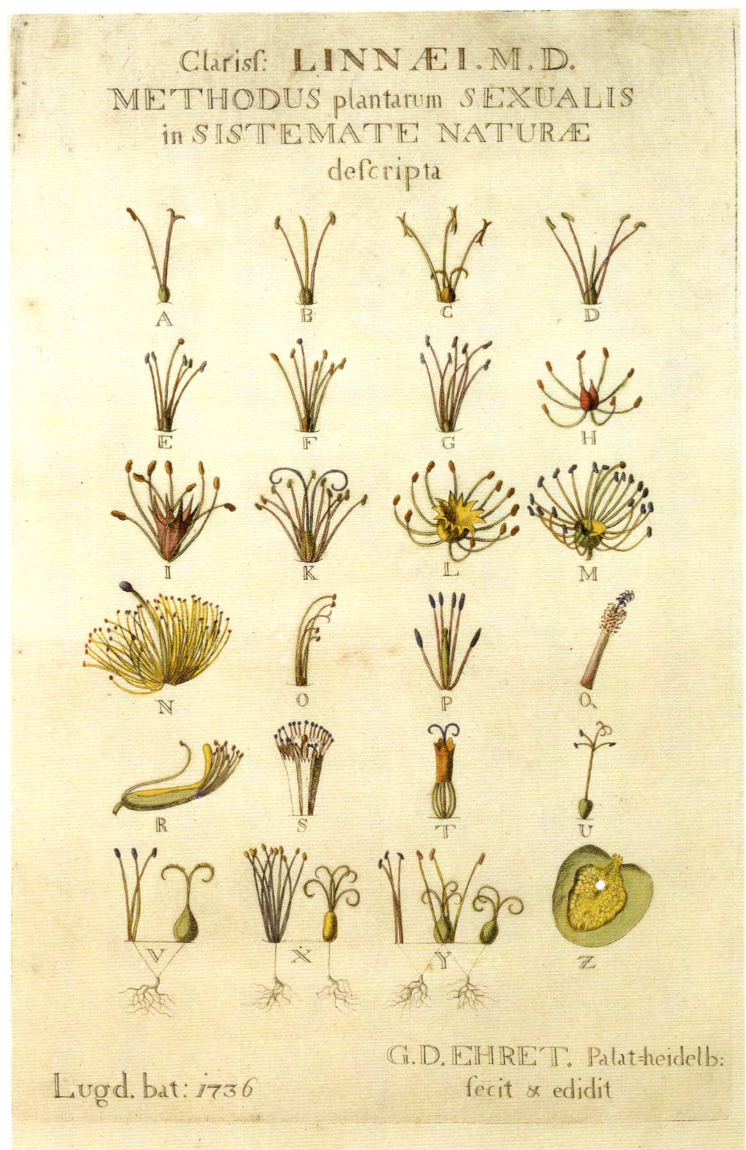

13

Fig. 12
Gerard Blasius: *Anatome Animalium,* 1681
Plate XIV

Göttingen, Niedersächsische Staats- und Universitätsbibliothek

Fig. 13
Carolus Linnaeus: *Systema Naturae,* 1735
Vienna, Österreichische Nationalbibliothek

publishers to join forces in the case of such costly book projects. The contract drawn up between the two publishers of the *Thesaurus* reveals that the author was still obliged to put up one third of the money himself. Initial production costs were funded by means of a subscription: future customers placed their names on a list, paid at least a partial amount in advance and were granted in return a discount of 30 per cent.

The expensive work was initially published in black-and-white, in other words, without the vibrant colouring of the copy upon which this reprint is based. It is not known whether the publishers also offered a hand-painted edition, which would naturally have raised the price and profit margin considerably. Buyers probably had the work painted at their own extra expense by specialist colourists. One such was J. Fortuÿn, whose biographical dates are not known. Because he signed his work, several coloured copies of the *Thesaurus* can be traced back to him, including the present volumes, reprinted here from the copies in the Royal Library in The Hague. Since Fortuÿn followed his signature with the word "Hague", he must have lived and worked in The Hague as well. One of Fortuÿn's bills preserved in the archive in The Hague is dated 1767, which suggests that he carried out his colouring work only after all the volumes had been published.

The gorgeous colours add substantially to the attractiveness of the plates, but their purpose was not just aesthetic enhancement. They had a scientific use as well. Some specimens, such as those of butterflies, snakes and shellfish, are only distinguishable by their colouring, and the differences in patterning of many fauna can barely be discerned in black-and-white. The colourist's skill and knowledge of the subject played an important part in enabling the illustrations to convey their message. Fortuÿn occasionally deviated from reality, however, and added colours for purely aesthetic effect. This happened in his interpretation of the pearly nautilus. The satin-white shell of this creature was highly valued and was often finely decorated with engraved motifs. Fortuÿn coloured one such ornamented nautilus in the *Thesaurus* in multiple hues, although the original shell would undoubtedly have been engraved simply in black (III, 84).

In his introduction Seba asserted that all the illustrations in his *Thesaurus* were based on specimens taken from his collection. The fabulous seven-headed creature in Volume I casts some doubt on this statement (I, 102). It is also known that, while writing the fourth volume, Seba drew upon a manuscript containing insect illustrations that he had purchased, and also incorporated into the *Thesaurus* drawings of animals from South Africa that a colleague had lent him. The Leipzig apothecary Johann Heinrich Linck (1674–1734) had also sent Seba drawings of his excellent snake collection, with the intention of using them in a joint publication on reptiles. When that project fell through, Seba had the drawings copied before he sent them back to Leipzig. Linck complained in a letter to Scheuchzer that Seba had then included the drawings in his *Thesaurus*. Seba also availed himself of the existing literature on natural history to fill in gaps in his collection and to obtain pictorial material. If we compare a plate from Blasius (fig. 12) with one in the *Thesaurus* (I, 98–100), and one from Merian (fig. 11) with another in the *Thesaurus* (I, 69), it becomes clear that a substantial portion of the plates in his first volume are based on older works. Such borrowings were made for the sake of completeness and were quite commonplace. They nevertheless carried a certain risk, especially when the original sources were drawings made or provided by sailors. Many of these were of mediocre quality and dubious authenticity (I, 101).

Whether or not originally in colour, whether or not based on existing illustrations, the *Thesaurus* remains an impressive example of a Baroque book. The artistic composition of every plate is particularly remarkable in the first volume, with all the pictorial elements combined into an overall composition. In emulation of Merian, the animals and plants are skilfully positioned and often arranged in little scenes, which adds considerably to their life-like effect as well as to their informative value. A snake, for example, is depicted in the process of swallowing its prey (II, 17); another is in a threatening position in front of a lizard (II, 20). The illustrations in the second, third and fourth volumes, which rely much less on previously published sources, increasingly follow contemporary conventions in scientific literature. Thus the animals are arranged in neat rows, properly separated by genus. In the last two volumes, which were completed after Seba's death, there is no interaction between the depicted animals. For best possible visual clarity, the animals are portrayed without any overlapping and with their size ratios correct – albeit in mirror image, which in the case of snail shells spiralling counter-clockwise became the source of some confusion. What was retained, though, was an ornamental arrangement of the objects on the plates, which is demonstrated by the symmetrically arranged snake plates (II, 37; II, 67) as well as by artistically arranged shells (III, 35; III, 56) and insects (IV, 25; IV, 77). That the display of a collection was aimed as much at satisfying the eye as the mind is illustrated by a surviving drawer full of shells from 1725 (fig. 5). The shells form a mosaic of diverse shapes and brilliant colours that is comparable to some of Seba's seashell plates (cf. III, 35-37). Seba presumably simply had the existing layouts in his storage boxes reproduced on the plates, just as Vincent Levin had done before him (fig. 2). Just as with the collection, there were thus always two aspects to the illustrations: they served both scientific instruction and aesthetic appreciation.

Most of the illustrations in the *Thesaurus* are limited to the external image of animals and plants. Besides the leaf skeletons, only a few anatomical dissections are represented. Nor does microscopy, which became very popular at the beginning of the 18th century, make any noticeable impact on the illustrations in the *Thesaurus*. Seba was a collector in the tradition of descriptive natural history, which was far removed from analytic approaches. Besides investigating and documenting the diversity of the earth's species, this descriptive method could also demonstrate developmental processes in nature, such as the metamorphosis of insects. Following Goedaert's example (fig. 9), the plates in the fourth volume depict, side by side, caterpillars, larvae and butterflies or moths.

The style of illustration adopted in the first two volumes elicited the particular criticism of some of its purchasers. The aesthetic and scenic arrangements of the natural specimens satisfied scientific purposes no better than did the mixing of animals and plants in one plate. There was criticism, too, of the sometimes bizarre differences in scale. The reproach that the snakes, marine animals, and insects were not arranged according to the latest classificatory system, however, ignored the fact that when Seba died in 1736, a good portion of the plates were already finished and did not yet reflect the findings of Linnaeus, only published a year earlier in 1735. The foreword to Volume IV of the *Thesaurus* was almost apologetic in emphasizing that its aim was not to serve as a comprehensive handbook of natural history but only as a description of an individual collection. That this was itself of great value was underlined by Herman Boerhaave (1668–1738) in his foreword to Volume I. He emphasized the richness and uniqueness of Seba's collection and praised the usefulness of the work. At a time when knowledge of the diversity of nature was still very incomplete and satisfactory pictorial material was a scarce commodity, Seba's *Thesaurus* provided an enormous fund of information. Although the scientific utility of Seba's collection had its clear limitations, the *Thesaurus* nevertheless served as a point of departure for further research. Linnaeus, for instance, used the illustrations of Seba's collection to improve and supplement later editions of his *Systema Naturae*. A new edition of Seba's work was published in the second half of the 18th century, and the illustrations were still considered valuable enough to be reprinted again in the following century. The *Thesaurus* treated an important collection of natural specimens of the early 18th century. As a book, the actual stationary collection became mobile and permanently accessible to many interested persons – even when the collection itself had long been scattered to the four winds.

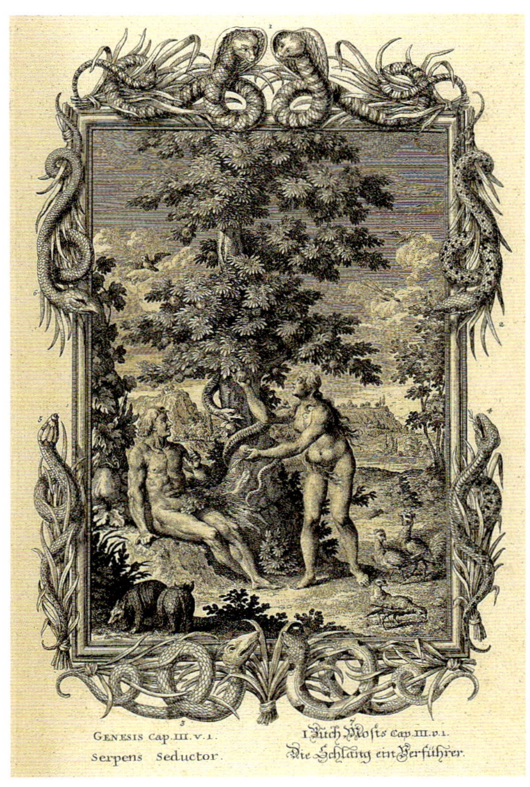

14

Fig. 14
Johann Jakob Scheuchzer: *Kupfer-Bibel*, 1731–1735
Göttingen, Niedersächsische Staats- und Universitätsbibliothek

Fig. 15
Albertus Seba: *Locupletissimi Rerum Thesauri Accurata Descriptio*, 1734–1765
Volume 1, frontispiece: Industria

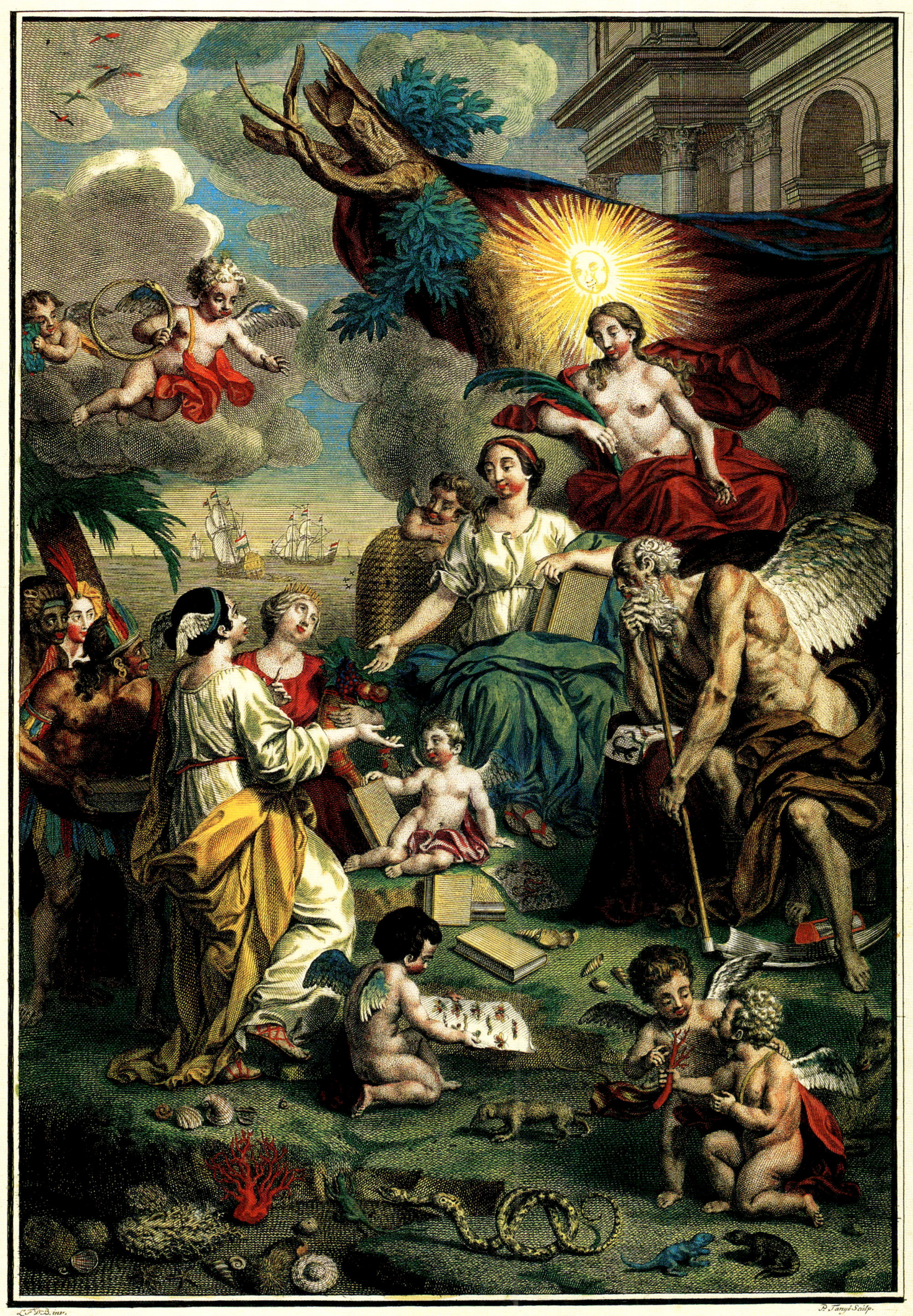

L.F.D.B. inv. P. Tanjé Sculp.

INDUSTRIA

Præsidio VERITATIS *munita,* SCIENTIARUM *incitata* AMORE, *adjuta* TEMPORE, *suam Sibi undequaque, instar* APUM, *colligens Supellectilem, cum* PHYSICA *disserit de variis Naturæ operibus, admiratione dignis, quæ in triplicis Animantium, Vegetantium, Fossiliumque Regni divitiis, ex omni* ORBIS TERRARUM *plaga, Mercaturæ ac Navigationis adminiculo, comparatis, detexit: nonnullis interim* GENIIS *adsidentibus, qui, admirandorum intenti Spectaculo, de his inter se conferunt; dum alii duo, ex alto delapsi, indefessos* INDUSTRIAE *labores Laureo Serto, et immortali Gloria, remunerari gestiunt.*

15

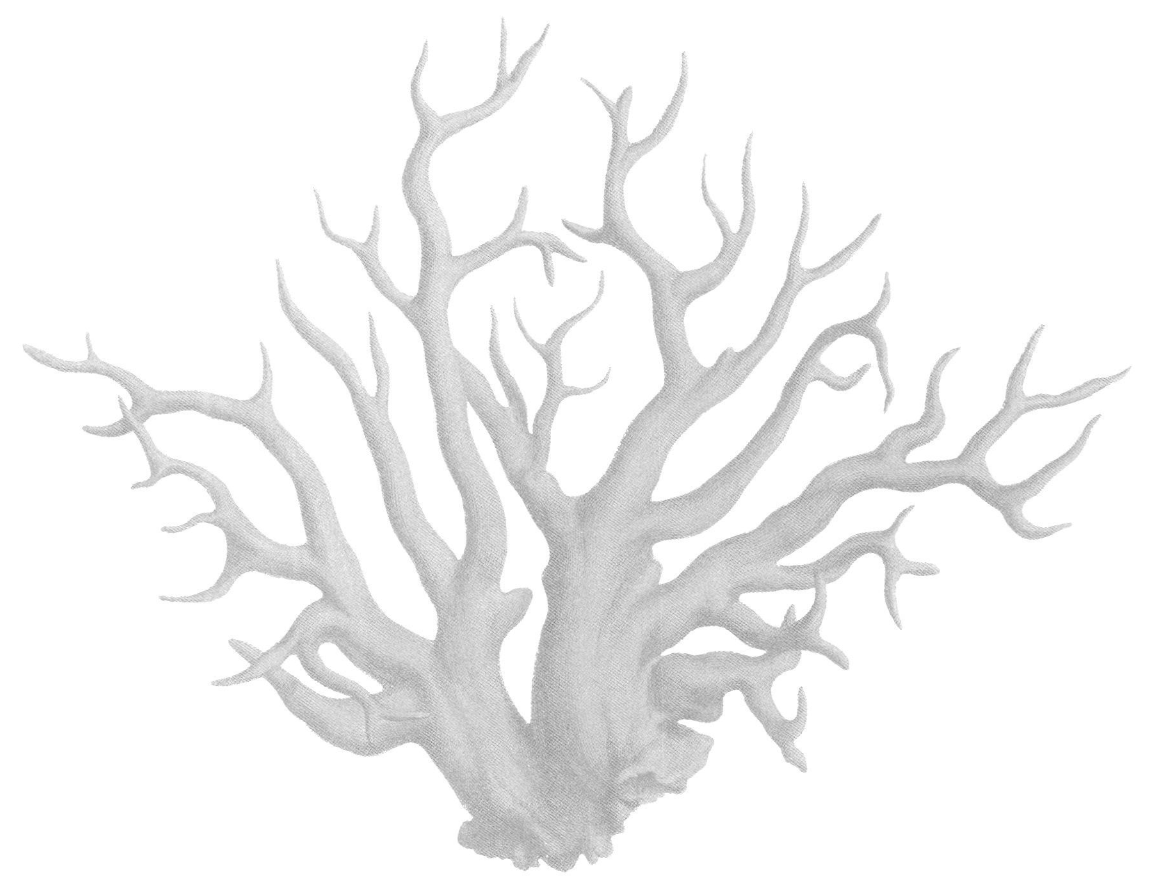

The Zoology and Botany in
ALBERTUS SEBA'S THESAURUS

Albertus Seba's *Thesaurus* was composed during a period of great change, which is what makes this work particularly interesting from today's point of view. In the first half of the 18th century, the study of biology were thriving, making its first strides towards becoming the true science. Even though the term "biology" itself was occasionally already in use by the close of the 17th century, it had to await the beginning of the 19th century to become officially introduced. The longstanding links to medicine and the healing arts meant that scientific concepts in this field were quite well evolved. But the boundary with the arts was not yet sharply defined, and the Christian world view remained a pervasive influence. The prevailing view was that all of God's creations, including plants and animals, fulfilled a specific purpose. Ultimately, everything in nature was of use to humankind, the crowning achievement of Creation. Some plants were put to use as medicinal herbs, other organisms served for human consumption or supplied materials for clothing. If all of God's creations fulfilled a purpose, then, evidently, a divine order must exist, a harmony of the cosmos. Thus an important aspect of the natural sciences, which incorporated what we would call the biosciences today, was to decipher and understand this order. This, in turn, would bring man closer to God, for God was to be understood above all through His works.

Socially and politically, the era in which the *Thesaurus* was compiled was hallmarked by the great voyages of discovery and the budding trade between the continents. Interest in novelties and goods from distant lands also extended to exotic animals and plants, of course. One consequence was a proliferation of cabinets of curiosities, which had first blossomed in the 17th century. Many now took on the character of natural history collections. Beside royal and princely cabinets, a series of private collections appeared, among which Seba's took a prominent place. It encompassed to a certain extent the whole animal kingdom, with many groups represented by an unusually large abundance of species and individual specimens.

The emergence of such collections was paralleled by the publication of books likewise aimed at reflecting the diversity of organisms. The comprehensiveness and quality of the *Thesaurus* thereby makes Seba's work virtually unique. It presents an exceptionally rich assortment of species, contains detailed facts and descriptions of individual species, and offers many illustrations of excellent quality. Furthermore, it was published in two separate bilingual editions – one in Latin and Dutch, and the other in Latin and French. It thus offers an unrivalled insight into the state of biological knowledge in its own day.

The THESAURUS *in the history of science*

Seba's compendium appeared during a transitional period in the history of science. Superficial observation of nature was being increasingly replaced by close examination of the diversity of biological forms; comparative anatomy and morphology became the new tools of study, and empiricism began to gain the upper hand. In the first half of the 16th century, plants and animals were still categorized primarily by their uses to man, or were simply sorted alphabetically, as in the *Historia Stirpium* by Leonhart Fuchs (1501–1566), a botanical work published in 1542 which names about 500 different species, and the mighty *Historia Animalium* by Conrad Gesner (1516–1565), a splendid tome of over 4000 pages. For the most part, it was not deemed practical to evolve a more sophisticated system of classification based on similarity. A very early exception appeared in a publication of 1555 by Pierre Belon (1517–1569), in which parts of a bird's skeleton were displayed next to the corresponding human ones for comparison. Only much later, in 1699, would Edward Tyson (1651–1703) portray the great similarity between chimpanzees and human beings in his anatomical work *Orang Outan, sive Homo sylvestris.*

Caspar Bauhin (1560–1624), in his *Pinax theatri botanici* of 1623, presented about 6000 plant species arranged into numerous groups according to similarity. Microscopes subsequently opened the way to observing the finer anatomical details: with this new tool, Robert Hooke (1635–1702), Marcello Malpighi (1628–1694) and Jan Swammerdam (1637–1680), for instance, were able to provide detailed descriptions of plant structures and insects. In 1674 Antoni van Leeuwenhoek (1632–1723) started to examine the many different types of unicellular organisms.

This growing interest in the physical composition of animals and plants elicited questions about the functions of the different structures discovered. Closer observations of plant and animal behaviour led to more accurate knowledge about their organisms and thus to new information about the functions of their bodily structures. As an almost natural consequence, morphological and anatomical descriptions of animals grew increasingly detailed. Nevertheless, the recommendation by the famous botanist John Ray (1627–1705) in his *Methodus Plantarum* of 1703 was still far from self-evident: *The best arrangement of plants is that in which all genera, from the highest to the subordinate and lowest, have several common attributes or agree in several parts or accidents.* Unlike plants, animals were much easier to identify and order into groups because of their greater diversity. Here, too, John Ray made important contributions with his treatises on mammals, reptiles, insects, birds and fish, some of which were only published posthumously in 1713.

Ray's interpretation of species, which signalled the way to addressing the multifariousness of living organisms, also left its mark on the *Thesaurus*, such as in Seba's presentation of a number of varieties of a single species. Ray was a friend of Sir Hans Sloane (1660–1753), a wealthy London doctor, whose collection from the same period as Seba's was considered the largest ever to have been amassed by a private individual. It was managed in a highly scientific manner, thanks to his personal connections and advanced level of education. Sloane had studied botany and anatomy under Guichard Duverney (1648–1731) and Joseph Pitton de Tournefort (1656–1708) and published botanical and zoological works about the West Indies and Madeira. In 1748 the Swede Pehr Kalm visited Sloane's collection and was impressed by the birds (including many humming birds), which were stuffed and mounted in a natural way, and by the numerous jars containing snakes, lizards, fish, birds, caterpillars, etc., conserved in "spirits of wine". Sloane's enormous herbarium and his library of 48,000 volumes were an important supplement to the collection. Volumes of hand-coloured illustrations of every conceivable natural specimen were stored in a separate room containing *such valuable works as the ones by Merian, Catesby, Seba, [and] Madame Blackwell.* Sloane's collection became the cornerstone of the collections of the British Museum.

It was not Sloane's friend John Ray, but a personal acquaintance of Seba's who designed the generally accepted classificatory method that still forms the basis of modern taxonomy. Carolus Linnaeus (1707–1778, granted a patent of nobility in 1762 from which time he was styled Carl von Linné) devised a consistent binomial nomenclature for species and introduced a number of hierarchical levels with specific names assigned to individual orders. For example, he coined the term "primates" for the ape-like animals that include humans. Linnaeus was very familiar with Albertus Seba's collection and used the *Thesaurus* as a source in his research. In the first edition of his *Systema Naturae* of 1735, Linnaeus records 549 species and in many cases makes reference to the fact that they are illustrated in Seba's work; in total, he cites the *Thesaurus* 284 times. By the tenth edition, which appeared in 1758, he had expanded his work to catalogue some 4390 species, yet the goal of circumscribing the variety of organisms had come no closer. If one considers that about 1.5 million species have been identified today, in a diversity that continues to amaze even the experts, it is no wonder that during the first half of the 18th century naturalists and collectors were often uncertain about exactly what type of animal they had in front of them, especially ones brought back from the farthest corners of the earth. Their underestimation of the scope of biodiversity made them slow to develop a more refined classificatory system of living organisms. Linnaeus estimated that there were probably about 10,000 species of plants and just as many of animals. Under the assumption of such low numbers, a relatively simple classification of the species seemed entirely workable.

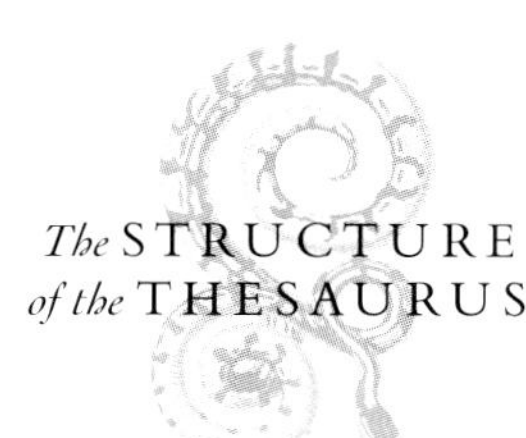

The STRUCTURE *of the* THESAURUS

Seba could not have suspected the immense range of existing life forms, but that did not diminish the task before him of organizing his large assortment of specimens. The Linnaean system was not yet available to him as a guideline since, even by the time of Seba's death in 1736, it had not yet become generally known. Irrespective of this, the apothecary and collector was clearly concerned to draw upon the known resemblances between organisms in his publication. The labels he assigned to animals and plants document that he saw more in these similarities than something merely superficial. Volume I depicts, next to millipedes, ringed worms which live in the sea (Polychaeta), which Seba refers to as marine millipedes. According to today's terminology, these species are not very closely related at all, but Seba deemed them largely comparable from a morphological point of view.

Seba described the four moray eels on Plate 69 in Volume II as sea serpents ("Serpents de mer"), while the gill openings of the two "Brazilian" chain morays (*Echidna catenata*) are missing from the illustration. Thus it is very likely that Seba was unclear about their actual classification and considered them true snakes. By contrast, other passages in the *Thesaurus* identified very subtle characteristic relations between the species that are still considered valid today.

Overall, however, the *Thesaurus* classifies its material under a different system than is employed today. Many plates unite organisms from entirely different orders and base their arrangement – probably deliberately – on criteria other than "systematic" factors. Many of the illustrations strive to give a life-like impression of the animals and their behaviour whilst adhering to the most stringent aesthetic criteria.

Although the first 29 plates of Volume I are primarily devoted to plants, they also contain butterflies, snakes and lizards, and even an armadillo. Plates 30 to 58 take mammals as their focus, but birds and snakes are depicted there besides. Spiders and scorpions are represented on Plate 69. Then follow seven plates with frogs and toads. The last part of Volume I closes with a colourful assortment of organisms – among them such curiosities as a seven-headed hydra on Plate 102 and an elephant embryo on Plate 111.

Volume II is chiefly devoted to snakes, a subject of particular interest to Seba. Even before he took up publication of the *Thesaurus* he had intended to write a book about snakes with another apothecary from Leipzig, Johann Heinrich Linck (1674–1734). That project never materialized, however, because of disagreements about the shape the work should take. Seba nevertheless copied the illustrations of snakes which he had received from Linck on loan and included them in the second volume of his *Thesaurus*.

Volume III treats marine organisms such as snails, shellfish and sea urchins, as well as fish. Seba had originally asked Linnaeus to assist with the section on fish, but Linnaeus was already busy conducting a botanical analysis of the gardens of the banker George Clifford. Moreover, fish were not by any means one of his main fields of interest, so Linnaeus recommended an expert in this zoological class, his impoverished friend Petrus Artedi (1705–1735). Artedi started working with Seba's collection in July 1735 but died unexpectedly in an accident just a few weeks later, on 28 September – while walking home from Seba's house at night he fell into a canal and drowned. Artedi's comprehensive manuscript about fish, which includes his examination of the samples from Seba's collection, was eventually published by Linnaeus under the general title *Ichthyologia*.

On 2 May 1736 – with the third volume of his *Thesaurus* still incomplete and only partially in print – Albertus Seba died. Since his estate first had to be settled before publication could continue, Volume III did not appear until 1758. Its production was supervised by Arnout Vosmaer, director of the collections of the Prince of Orange.

The fourth volume of the *Thesaurus* finally appeared in 1765, almost 30 years after Seba's death. It is dedicated primarily to insects, fossils and minerals.

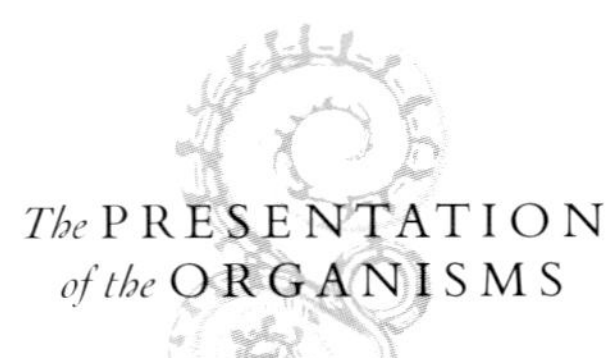

The PRESENTATION *of the* ORGANISMS

The animals in particular in Seba's collection are frequently depicted in life-like, seemingly natural poses. It was often left to the imagination of the artist to "bring back to life" a completely unfamiliar preserved creature, since only in the rarest of cases did any of the animals arrive in Holland alive. Snakes, lizards and frogs, for example, were generally conserved in alcohol and transported in jars. But they frequently arrived in poor condition, especially if the alcohol evaporated during the long voyage. Evaporation was not the only problem: the high-proof spirits were evidently an irresistable temptation for crew members as well.

Until the end of the 19th century, lack of relevant knowledge about exotic animals made depicting them in a natural pose a difficult exercise. The *Thesaurus* nevertheless succeeds in mastering this problem in many cases. There are, for example, several plates illustrating how marsupials carry their young in pouches on their abdomen, something at that time known only by a few experts. A particularly instructive illustration shows an opossom sitting upright with its pouch wide open to reveal the nipples on the back wall (I, 39).

This species – then still virtually unknown – is also depicted, very true to life, carrying its already quite large young on its back, their tails wrapped around their mother's (I, 31). Only the way that the mother is holding her tail is unnatural, but that is how it in places continued to be rendered even up to the beginning of the 20th century.

The endeavour to place the animals in a natural setting also produced illustrations that from today's vantage-point seem bizarre. Some dwarf opossums (I, 31) are shown "sitting up" and the two-toed sloth (I, 34) is even walking upright like a primate on a branch. Linnaeus too had assumed that sloths were monkeys.

There is often a tendency in Seba's illustrations to humanize the animals, especially the mammals. The ears of the monkey on Plate 48 (Fig. 3), the anteater (Fig. 1) and civet (Fig. 2) on Plate 40, and the porcupine (Figs. 1-2) on Plate 52 of Volume I, all bear a remarkable resemblance to the human auricle and even the eyes of some animals (I, 30, Figs. 1-2 and I, 31) are styled after those of *Homo sapiens*. This anthropomorphization in the *Thesaurus* followed the tradition of the animal books by Conrad Gesner (1516–1565) and Ulisse Aldrovandi (1522–1605) from the 16th century.

The arrangement of the animals on the individual plates evidently arose in part from the attempt to produce attractive symmetrical compositions. Thus, for instance, the snake on Plate 72 in Volume I was placed there because not enough room was left for another type of animal. It is also looped to accentuate the symmetrical composition of the page. This penchant for symmetry is particularly obvious in Plate 97 in Volume 1. In the upper middle portion of the picture, the tails of two lizards are arranged to form a loop, each identical – in mirror image – to the figure formed by the tail of the animal in the other half of the picture. This artistic purpose reaches its climax in the composition of lizards, snakes and birds (I, 110).

Strange as it may seem to modern scientists, aesthetic considerations play an important role throughout the work. But they also lend the *Thesaurus* its particular attractiveness, not least in its compositional variety. For artistic reasons alone, relations that do not exist in nature were drawn between plants and animals. On Plate 75 in Volume I, for instance, a snake is looping itself among the stems of a plant and at the opposite edge a lizard is seen – or least suggested – doing the same, simply for reasons of symmetry. On Plate 7 in Volume II, a bird is boldly perched on the coiled body of a snake. The illustrations of birds in flight are also artificially staged – strictly speaking, these birds are not in flight at all. In other cases, the bodies of birds were reproduced in the state in which they arrived in Holland: some without feet and often even missing wings (1, 60). The scarlet ibis (I, 62), by contrast, is stalking very naturally among the reeds.

Seba rarely took bio-geographical aspects into consideration while compiling the plates. This is particularly apparent in Plate 41 of Volume II; its unrealistic tropical scenario combines animals that, according to Seba's own indications, occur in completely different parts of the world. Thus snakes from Brazil are depicted with a small lizard from Ceylon (now Sri Lanka). It was not yet known that the distributions of individual species are regionally delimited, many of them quite narrowly – and necessarily so, as we now know from Darwin's theory of evolution. It was merely taken as self-evident that certain tropical species did not live in cooler regions. It was also known that species from aquatic environments, such as dragonflies, mayflies, fish and crocodiles, were not to be found in desert regions. The general principle that different regions are inhabited by different organisms was only formulated in 1776 by the French naturalist Georges Louis Leclerc de Buffon (1707–1788).

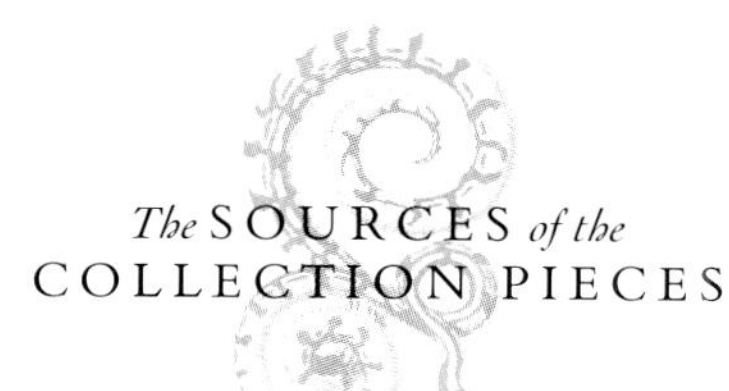

The SOURCES *of the* COLLECTION PIECES

The illustrations in the *Thesaurus* are essentially based on the pieces comprising Seba's collection. In a few cases, however, illustrations were copied out of other works, although without giving due acknowledgment to the original authors.

The exhibits in Seba's collection came from all parts of the then known world, and above all the islands of modern-day Indonesia, the northern regions of South America, the Caribbean, Central America, eastern North America, India and Sri Lanka, North Africa and the West African coast. They originated in particular from the Dutch colonies of the day; along the northern coast of South America, the Netherlands had acquired Essequibo in 1625, Curaçao in 1634 and Surinam in 1667. In North America, New Holland had counted among the Dutch possessions since 1612. Its capital city, New Amsterdam, was founded in 1626, only to be renamed New York by the British in 1667. In Asia, Ceylon (now Sri Lanka) at the tip of the Indian subcontinent had been a part of the Dutch empire since 1658, and there were numerous Dutch settlements throughout the Indonesian archipelago.

Seba's collection was not restricted to "exotic" items, however, but also included natural specimens from central Europe, whereby relatively well-known local species were only included in the *Thesaurus* in a small number of instances. When it came to the origins of less familiar specimens, the apothecary in many cases had to rely for his information on the dealers and sailors from whom he had bought or swapped a piece. Needless to say, these travellers' accounts were not always reliable. Thus Plate 102 in Volume II clearly depicts a royal python from Africa, but Seba gives the snake's origin as Brazil and even adds a locally used name for it. Many other suspect examples could be mentioned as well. Seba evidently made some interesting acquisitions for his collection without knowing anything at all about where they had come from.

The fish in the *Thesaurus* offer a useful opportunity to elucidate the sources of one group of organisms, since they are featured in only 13 plates in the *Thesaurus* and hence are easily surveyable. Seba provides very little information about the origins of his fish. The electric eel (III, 34, Fig. 6) is an exception, because it was shipped home by the director of the Dutch colony of Esséquébo (Essequibo, Guyana). Electric eels produce electric shocks of up to 500 volts to stun their prey – fishes and mammals. Although it would be the end of the 18th century before it was confirmed, through experiments, that this really was an electrical phenomenon, the effects of these electric shocks on the eel's prey are already described in Seba.

Explicit statements in the *Thesaurus* about the distribution of a fish species are made only in conjunction with the few European varieties and the porcupine fish depicted on Plate 23 of Volume III.

All the fish included in Seba's collection normally live in shallow waters of no more than 20 metres in depth and could have been easily caught using the fishing methods of the day. 83 of the 88 fish varieties identified by Seba are restricted to tropical or subtropical climates. Only five species also live in the more temperate European waters of the eastern North Atlantic, the North Sea and the Baltic. Only 15 are freshwater fish and, with the exception of the sturgeon, are all found in the South American Amazon basin. All but one of these freshwater fish are still commonly known in Surinam. The other species inhabit the marine regions or the brackish waters of the estuaries.

The majority of shellfish and snails in the *Thesaurus* also came from tropical and subtropical regions. As a rule they were inhabitants of tidal zones and shoals, although some species, like the *Glossus humanus* (Linnaeus, 1758) depicted on Plate 86 in Volume III (Fig. 1), occur at greater depths as well – in this case, down to 3000 metres. Truly deep-sea forms were only brought to the surface with the advent of modern fishing techniques, such as seines and trawl nets, and there are snail species such as *Cyprea fultoni* (Sowerby, 1903), which until just a few decades ago could only be retrieved from the stomachs of deep-sea fish. Such species obviously do not feature in Seba's collection, since they and the fish who preyed on them were beyond the reach of the fishing nets of his day.

In the 18th century it was quite commonplace for sailors to barter with native peoples for unusually large and beautiful shells to take home and sell at a good price. That is probably how many of the exhibits found their way into Seba's collection.

The marsupials depicted in the *Thesaurus* all originate from the Americas, since only very rarely did any such specimens reach Europe from Australia, the home of most living marsupial species.

CURIOSITIES *and* SPECIAL ATTRACTIONS *in the* THESAURUS

Strange and rare abnormalities formed special attractions in cabinets of natural curiosities and wonders. Such so-called deformities were also a part of Seba's collection. The *Thesaurus* depicts Siamese-twin deer (I, 45) and goats (I, 46), as well as lizards with cleft or double tails (I, 90). One repeatedly observed anomaly, a two-tailed scorpion, is also represented. Invertebrates with unusual characteristics, such as starfishes with severed or split arms as a result of injury (III, 6, 8), were likewise considered curiosities in the collection.

Mammals

A particular rarity in the *Thesaurus* are the so-called "Fliegende Katzen" (flying cats) and "Fliegende Hunde" (flying dogs) from tropical regions, although – contrary to what their names imply – they are not related to feline or canine species. *Flughund* (lit. flying dog) nevertheless remains the German designation for the fruit bat even today (in English it is also called a flying fox). Amongst the animals which Seba describes as "flying dogs" is a true fruit bat and a tropical American false vampire bat (*Vampyrum spectrum*, I, 58, Fig. 1). Among the "flying cats" in the *Thesaurus* (I, 58, Figs. 2-3) we find the giant flying lemur of the Philippines (*Cynocephalus volans*), which together with another species forms a separate group of mammals.

Snails and shellfish

Compared with other collections of the time, Seba's selection of molluscs from virtually every one of the world's oceans was enormous and comprised a particularly valuable part of the collection. At the beginning of the 18th century the fashion for collecting snail and seashells was at its height among wealthy citizens and nobility throughout Europe. Seba used this passion to good advantage and regularly sold duplicate specimens and less perfect pieces from his collection. In an advertisement, for example, he offered *a barrelful of conches of sorts for grottoes*. Such shells were incorporated into ornamental garden "grottoes" in line with the tastes of the day. Varieties particularly sought after for their extreme rarity, like the "precious wentletrap" (*Epitonium scalare* Linnaeus, 1758), do not number among the apothecary's exhibits, however. A French countess is purported to have given away an entire manor estate in exchange for one.

The magnificent arrangements of snail and seashells on Plates 35-37 in Volume III, which include some fossorial varieties and corals, satisfied the aesthetic tastes of contemporary cabinet visitors. Such gastropod mosaics continued to be a favourite gift item even into the 19th century, brought home from foreign harbours by mariners and whale hunters for their wives and sweethearts.

The echinoderms

The "prickle-skinned" marine animals of the phylum *Echinodermata*, including sea urchins, starfish, brittle stars ("snake-tails"), sea lilies and sea cucumbers, are among the special attractions of Seba's collection. Some of the species depicted in the *Thesaurus* come from colder waters of the upper latitudes, among them the giant sea star *Hymenaster pellucidus* (Thomson, 1873) from the Arctic oceans (III, 8, Fig. 1). The snaky-armed starfish variety *Gorgonocephalus caput medusae* (Linnaeus, 1758; III, 9, Figs. 1-2; III, 11, Fig. 1) inhabits the European North Sea. When – in 1818 – the polar naturalist Sir John Ross subsequently caught one of them, together with other organisms, in waters over 1.8 kilometres deep in Baffin Bay, it constituted important proof that life also exists in the oceanic depths.

Another remarkable echinoderm from Seba's collection is the feather star (*Comanthina,* III, 9, Figs. 3-4) from the West Indian Pacific. The first living specimens of feather stars were gathered from the Mediterranean at the end of the 16th century. Their relatives, the sea lilies, whose stalked calyxes resemble flowers, belong in the same phylum and, accordingly, are likewise animals. It was thought that sea lilies had been extinct for millions of years and so it was a great surprise when a modern specimen was presented to the French Academy of Science in 1755. The fact that fixed sea lilies were systematically related to motile feather stars was not known for a long time. Only in 1834 did the English naturalist John Vaughan Thompson manage to demonstrate that the sea lily he had examined was a feather star in a larval state and it finally became clear that all motile feather stars only detach from their stalked larval forms in the course of their development. Thus the close relation between sea lilies and feather stars was proven.

The seven-headed hydra

Strange and fabulous creatures are also included among the curiosities in the *Thesaurus*. Seba was by no means the only apothecary to believe that they really existed: in the first half of the 18th century mythological beings were the subject of serious research, and as late as 1784 one anonymous author tried to prove that unicorns and giant sea serpents did not exist. For historians of science, one particularly interesting mythical creature is undoubtedly Seba's seven-headed "hydra" (I, 102). Its dentition indicates a very aggressive carnivore that dragged its sack-shaped body about on two clawed extremities. Seba reported that he had copied an illustration of a specimen from a collection in Hamburg. But he was still a little doubtful about the genuineness of the hydra at first: *I do admit, though, that not absolutely trusting it, I wrote to my friend Mr. Jean Freder from Notorp near Hamburg. This very judiciously curious natural historian, who had seen the same hydra with his own eyes, assured me that it was definitely not the work of art but truly that of Nature.* Thus convinced of the authenticity of the "seven-headed serpent", Seba also cited earlier authorities such as Conrad Gesner, Ulisse Aldrovandi, and Athanasius Kircher (1602–1680), who had supplied vivid descriptions and illustrations of this hydra in their publications. It ought to have occurred to Seba, though, that his own hydra shared suspiciously many similarities with the one in the illustration by Aldrovandi from 1639. We can only assume that an enterprising forger had used Aldrovandi's illustration as a basis for the drawing Seba had taken as his source.

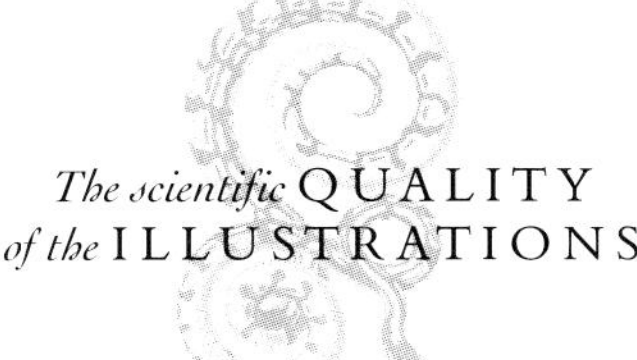

The scientific QUALITY *of the* ILLUSTRATIONS

The example of the hydra begs the basic question of whether the illustrations and texts in the *Thesaurus* have any scientific merit or reliability from today's point of view. Only in the very rarest of cases were artists able to draw their animal subjects from life, a limiting factor which from the very start compromised the accuracy of their illustrations. The limbs of the animals are thus often incorrectly positioned, and the overall postures of many organisms are unnaturally rendered. The tail of the crocodile (I, 106), for example, is contorted in a way that could never occur naturally. Such illustrations recall medieval illustrations of dragons with writhing, lashing tails to dramatize their terrifying character – all these "beasts" were, of course, lumped together under the archaic term "worm".

Insect wings are, in many cases, inaccurately reproduced, reflecting the ignorance about the importance of their veined structure. The body segmentation of the insects is sometimes incorrect as well. A few lacewing flies have an inordinately long abdomen (e.g. IV, 86), because the artist drew more segments than the insects actually had; in other cases the abdomen is too short.

Not infrequently, the illustrations contain errors that might well have been avoided with better attention to the morphological traits of the animals. Thus the ants on Plate 40 in Volume I have eight legs, and not the correct number of six.

Prior to publication, the drawings first had to be transferred onto the copper plate. For this purpose, the engraver received an additional copy of the drawing in mirror image so that the final print would come out the proper way round. In some cases such copies were not made, so a few of the illustrations were reproduced in reverse. While this did not affect bilaterally symmetrical organisms, it had an unfortunate consequence for snails, whose shell openings lies either to the left or right of their vertical axis; many of these snails thus appear in the *Thesaurus* with their shell openings on the wrong side.

In the wake of Seba's publication, and in particular following the widespread embrace of Linnaeus' system of classification, zoological research began to develop rapidly. A century later, Johann Georg Wagler (1800–1832) had some harsh words for the illustrations of reptiles and amphibians in the *Thesaurus*. In his posthumously published work of 1833, Wagler faulted in particular the quality of the lizard illustration in Figure 5 of

Plate 72 in Volume I: *The artist's very unsuccessfully rendered, albeit still recognizable figure is assigned quite correctly by Merrem* [Balsius Merrem, who published a commentary on the reptiles and amphibians in the *Thesaurus* in 1820] *among his Agama versicolor, which, by the way, is not native to Brazil but to India.* According to Wagler, other illustrations could not be related to any animal whatsoever. Figure 3 on Plate 92 in Volume I was *in every respect a monstrous, unidentifiable figure*; and Figure 1 on Plate 7 in Volume II was no more instructive: *Which? Entirely indeterminable figure.* The biologist is even stronger in his condemnation of the water snakes depicted in Plate 10 in Volume II: "*Coluber natrix* Linn[aeus]. Three figures gone badly wrong by the artist, which should never be cited elsewhere." This criticism was not always fair; although scientific understanding of organisms had progressed enormously in 100 years, there were still many species with which Seba may have been familiar but of which Wagler had no knowledge. But it is indicative that even Linnaeus hesitated to cite Seba's work in the tenth and twelth editions (1758, 1767) of his *Systema Naturae,* preferring instead books by other authors. Apparently, the illustrations in the *Thesaurus* often no longer met his requirements.

The *Thesaurus* nevertheless retains special importance through the manner in which it depicted the collection pieces. Going beyond mere presentations of isolated specimens, some illustrations establish interconnections and have an explanatory character. Butterflies are frequently depicted together with their corresponding caterpillars, for example. Anteaters are shown licking up ants with their long, slender tongues. Other plates (I, 103–104) illustrate how a young crocodile hatches out of its egg. Impressive, too, is the illustration of a snake (II, 17) demonstrating how wide its mouth can open while swallowing bigger chunks of food. On Plate 56 in Volume I there is a bat climbing about in the branches with its wings half folded. Thus the reader is shown not just the animals themselves, but provided with additional information about how they live.

In his attempt to characterize the animals and show them in their natural habitats, Seba would occasionally transgress the boundary into fiction, however, particularly in his explanatory texts. He describes one animal from the family *Felidae* (I, 30) as follows: *Wild cat from America, resembling the tiger. This beast is so ferocious and mean that it hunts down other animals, pounces on their faces, gouges out their eyes with its long and sharp claws, peels off their skin, and feeds itself on their blood…* Such characterizations led to the demonization of animals generally harmless to humans.

IDENTIFICATION *of the* ANIMALS *in the* THESAURUS

In order to gain as accurate a picture as possible of the breadth of species illustrated in the *Thesaurus,* an attempt was made to classify, using modern taxonomy, the animals it portrays. Although the pictures themselves often seem to the reader to be very true to life, in many cases it proved difficult to identify exactly which animal they represented. The reason for this lay not just in the inaccuracies in many of the illustrations, arising – as we have already seen – out of the fact that very few of the animals were drawn from living specimens. Above all, it lay in the sheer variety of species. If one considers that about 8900 types of birds are known, 3100 types of snakes, and almost 200,000 species of butterflies, it is understandable how exact identification may pose a problem.

Snake species, for example, show very little differences in their body shape, and unrelated species frequently share the same colouration. Since the snakes were generally drawn from specimens preserved in alcohol, whose skins had already discoloured or faded, their true colours and patterning could not be reproduced faithfully. Identification is complicated further by the fact that many species vary greatly in colour both depending on where they come from geographically and even just from one individual to another. The males and females of a species also frequently differ, and many creatures change their colour as they pass through different stages of maturity. It is frequently unclear whether Seba's plates depict a juvenile or an adult animal.

The identification of certain mammals is complicated by the fact that they are in some cases attributed, as mentioned earlier, with anthropomorphic characteristics. In a similar process, animals of which Seba and his artists had no precise visual idea were often attributed with body parts belonging to more familiar species. In describing an anteater in Figure 2 of Plate 40(I), Seba compared its head with that of a sheep: *Tamandua from Mexico, called Yzquiepatl, which means little fox … Its head is like that of a sheep, and agrees otherwise as well with the Tamandua illustrated here, if you just except the head, which is differently shaped, much smaller, and strongly resembling that of dogs from the North* ... Two long teeth are shown protruding from the animal's lower jaw – the only two, according to Seba. Attaching any family classification, let alone any mammalian order, to such a mysterious creature would be sheer speculation.

Geoffroy St. Hilaire from France had already pointed out in the 19th century that one of the armadillos on Plate 30 in Volume I (Fig. 4) was a construct from two different species, perhaps the giant armadillo (*Priodontes maximus)* and the six-banded armadillo (*Euphractus sexcinctus*).

Notwithstanding such composites and animals created on the basis of analogy, the possibility remains that some of the species depicted in the *Thesaurus* have since become extinct, without ever having been mentioned by other authors.

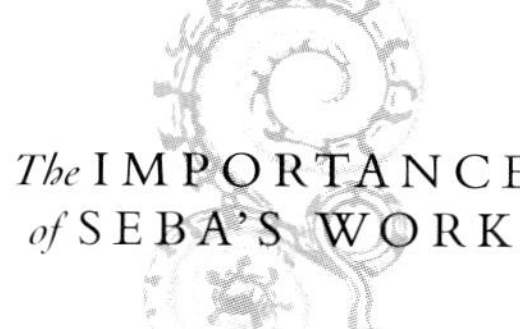

The IMPORTANCE *of* SEBA'S WORK

No other work at the beginning of the 18th century offered such a comprehensive survey of the diversity of living beings as Seba's *Thesaurus*. This fact alone justifies calling it a scientific work, in spite of the weaknesses outlined above. A good indicator of the profound influence of Seba's work is the considerable number of authors who cited the *Thesaurus* and described species with reference to its illustrations. First and foremost of these is Linnaeus. He was followed by Laurenti (1768), Gmelin (1789), Blumenbach (1779), Fabricius, and many others who all referred to Seba's famous work in their descriptions of a whole range of new species.

Seba's *Thesaurus* also exerted an influence of a more indirect nature: travel accounts and natural history books are known to have inspired many naturalists, Charles Darwin included, to make their own contribution toward the detailed exploration of the world. Seba's cabinet and *Thesaurus* surely served as such a stimulus by presenting the nature of exotic regions so vividly, as few other works of the period. Such collections must likewise have attracted leading naturalists to join expeditions. The famous sailor James Cook (1728–1779) was accompanied on his circumnavigation of the world of 1768–1771 by scientific authorities of the highest calibre, Joseph Banks (1743–1820) and Daniel Solander (1736–1782). They were supported by a young illustrator, Sydney Parkinson (1745–1771), who put to paper excellent and very detailed representations of the fauna and flora encountered along the way.

It was only at the beginning of the 19th century, when Linnaeus' *Species Plantarum* and *Systema Naturae* – works which duly acknowledged earlier publications in the field – became generally accepted as the basis for biological classification and taxonomy, that interest in Seba's *Thesaurus* began to wane. While Linnaeus' work has remained the subject of intense scientific study, his sources predating 1735 have received scant attention, even though they had opened the way for the Swedish naturalist to become what he is held as today: a meticulous archivist of nature, whose efforts laid the groundwork of modern biology. Seba's collection and his *Thesaurus* are undoubtedly among these earlier sources.

Even a hundred years after the publication of the *Thesaurus*, Albertus Seba was still a familiar name. His importance to the science of his day is reflected in the number of species that had been named after him by the second half of the 19th century. Thus the lizard *Oplurus sebae*, known as the Madagascan swift, bears his name, as does the African rock python (*Python sebae*, Gmelin, 1789). A dozen fish species were named after Seba between 1800 and 1860. The descriptions of these species usually refer back to illustrations in the *Thesaurus*. Three of these twelve species names are still valid today: the sebae anemonefish (*Amphiprion sebae* Bleeker, 1853); the emperor red snapper (*Diacope sebae* Cuvier, 1816, which is equivalent to *Lutjanus sebae* Cuvier, 1916); and the seba mono see or African moony (*Psettus sebae,* also referred to as *Monodactylus sebae* Cuvier, 1829). But numerous other organisms, such as the snail, seba's moon (*Polinices sebae* Récluz, 1844), also continue to keep his name alive.

LOCUPLETISSIMI RERUM NATURALIUM THESAURI

ACCURATA DESCRIPTIO,

ET

ICONIBUS ARTIFICIOSISSIMIS

EXPRESSIO,

PER

UNIVERSAM PHYSICES HISTORIAM.

OPUS,

CUI, IN HOC RERUM GENERE, NULLUM PAR EXSTITIT.
EX TOTO TERRARUM ORBE COLLEGIT,
DIGESSIT, DESCRIPSIT, ET DEPINGENDUM CURAVIT

ALBERTUS SEBA,

ETZELA OOSTFRISIUS,

ACADEMIÆ CÆSAREÆ LEOPOLDINO CAROLINÆ NATURÆ CURIOSORUM
COLLEGA XENOCRATES DICTUS; SOCIETATIS REGIÆ ANGLICANÆ,
ET INSTITUTI BONONIENSIS, SODALIS.

TOMUS I.

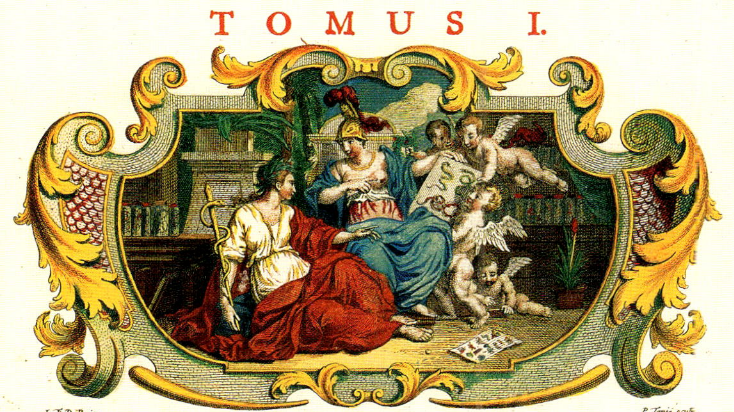

AMSTELAEDAMI,
Apud JANSSONIO-WAESBERGIOS,
& J. WETSTENIUM, & GUL. SMITH.
MDCCXXXIV.

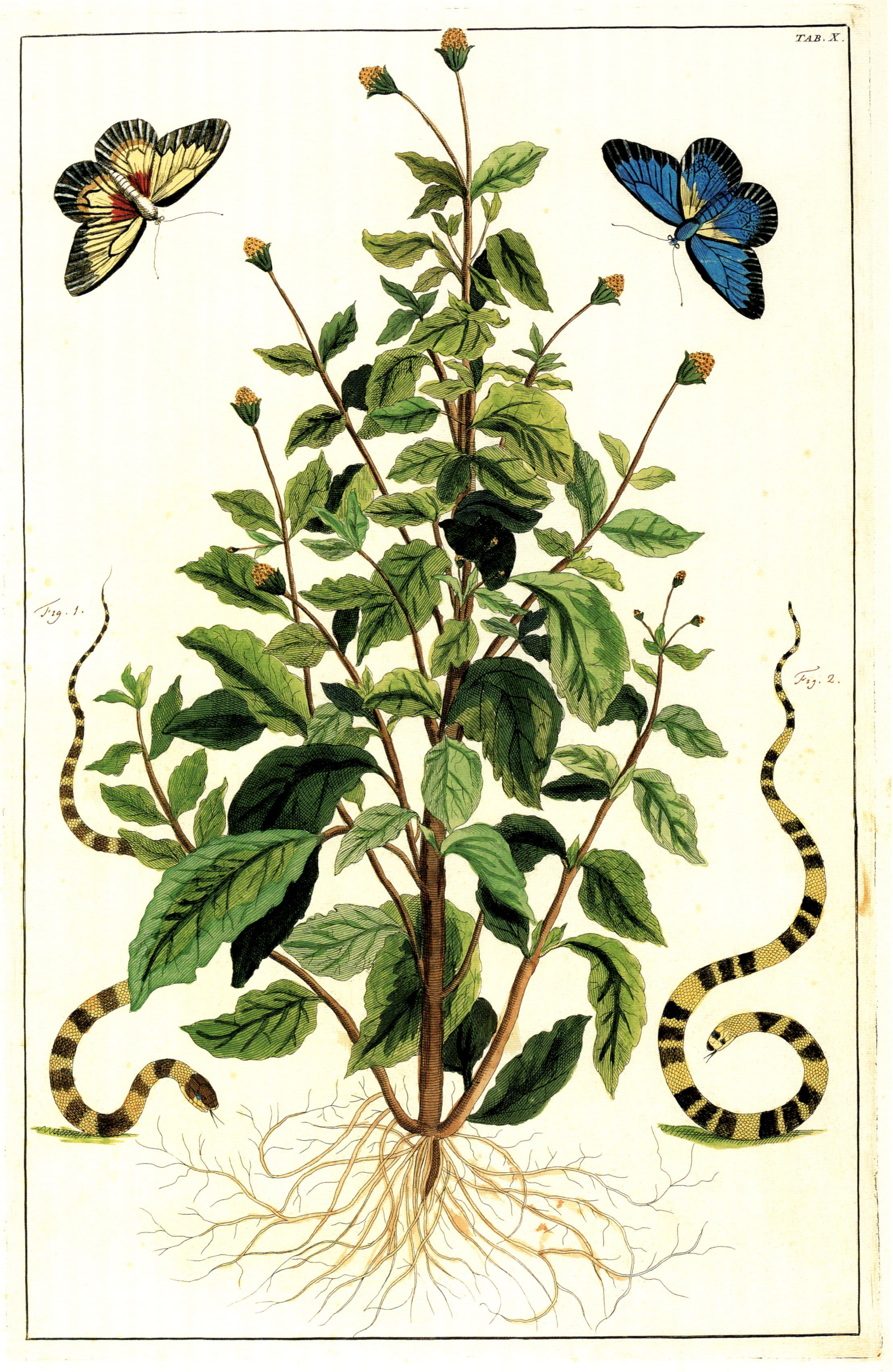

Lepidoptera, *Acmella et Serpentes* **1** *Bungarus fasciatus*
Butterflies, plant and snakes · Tagfalter, Pflanze und Schlangen · Papillons diurnes, plante et serpents **1** Banded krait · Gelber Bungar · Bongare annelé
2 Snake, according to Seba from Ceylon · Schlange, nach Seba aus Ceylon · Serpent, de Ceylan selon Seba

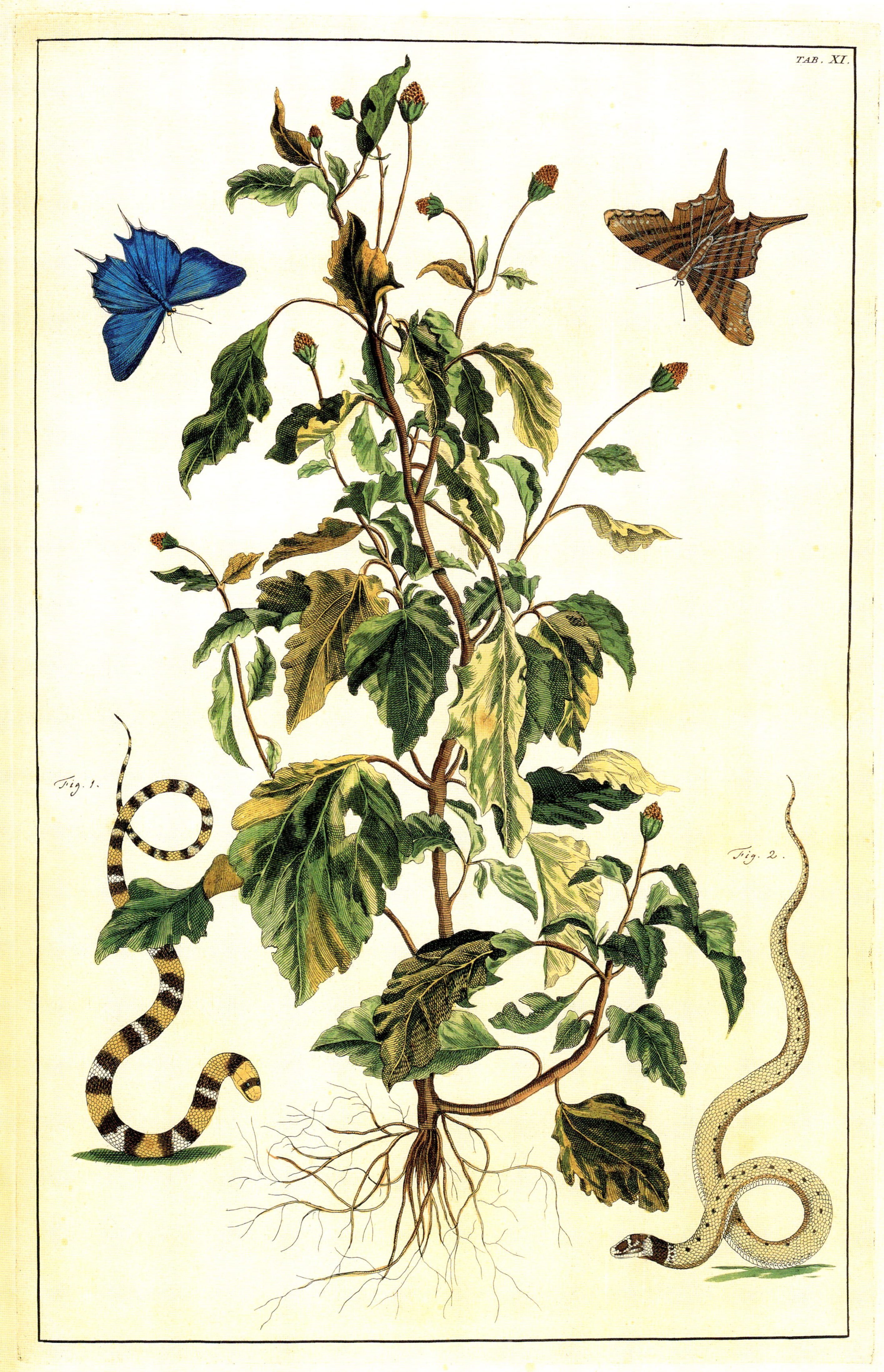

Papilionidae et *Acmella* 1 Serpentes 2 *Oligodon?*
Tropical butterflies and plant · Tropische Tagfalter und Pflanze · Papillons diurnes tropicaux et plante
1 Snake, according to Seba from Ceylon · Schlange, nach Seba aus Ceylon · Serpent, de Ceylan selon Seba 2 Kukuri snake · Oligodon · Oligodon

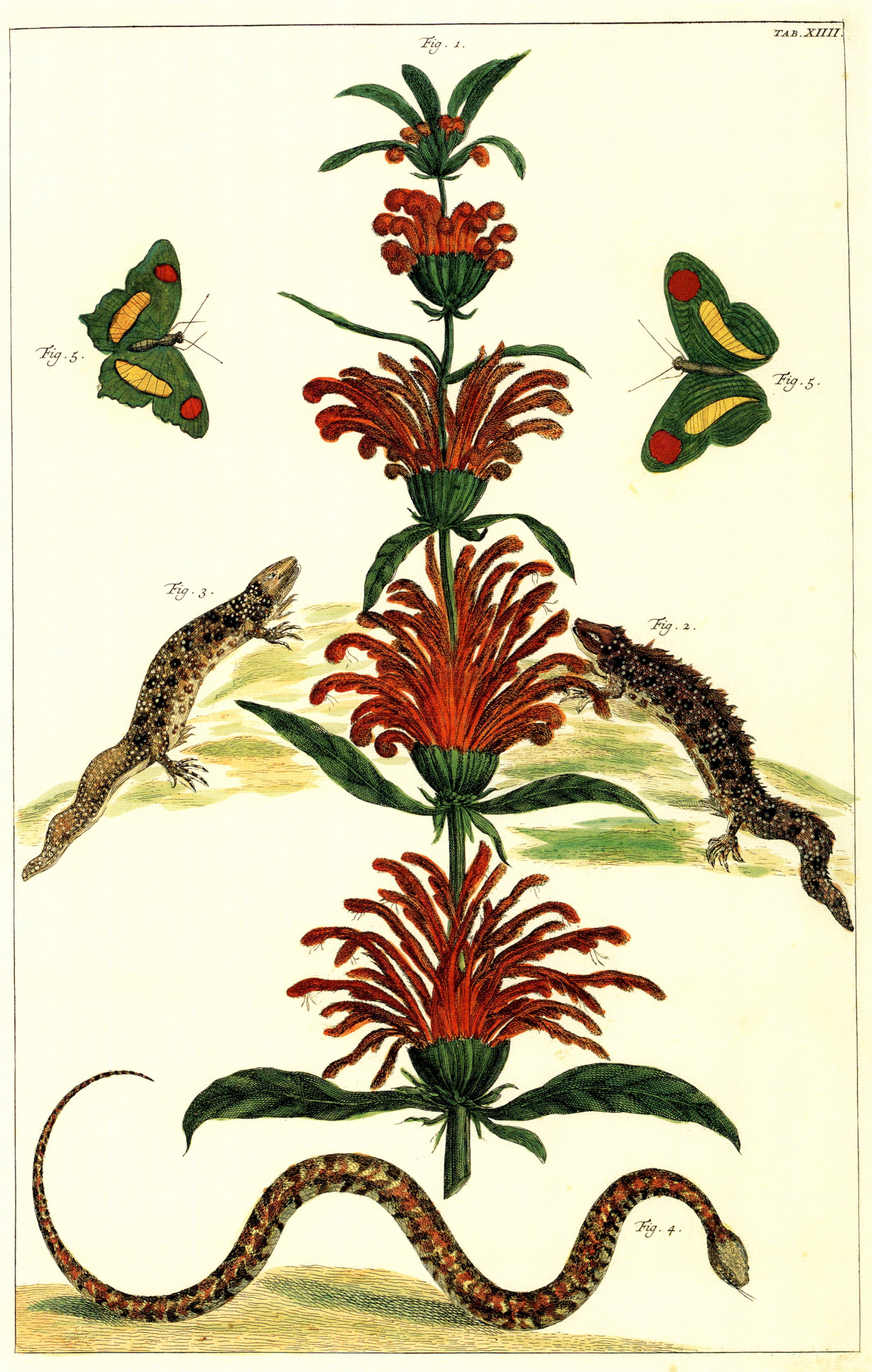

1 *Leonotis leonurus* 2-3 *Salamandridae* 4 Serpentes 5 Lepidoptera
1 Lion's ear · Löwenohr · Queue-de-lion 2-3 Newts · Molche · Urodèles 4 Snake, according to Seba from Africa · Schlange, nach Seba aus Afrika · Serpent, d'Afrique selon Seba
5 Tropical butterflies · Tagfalter · Papillons diurnes

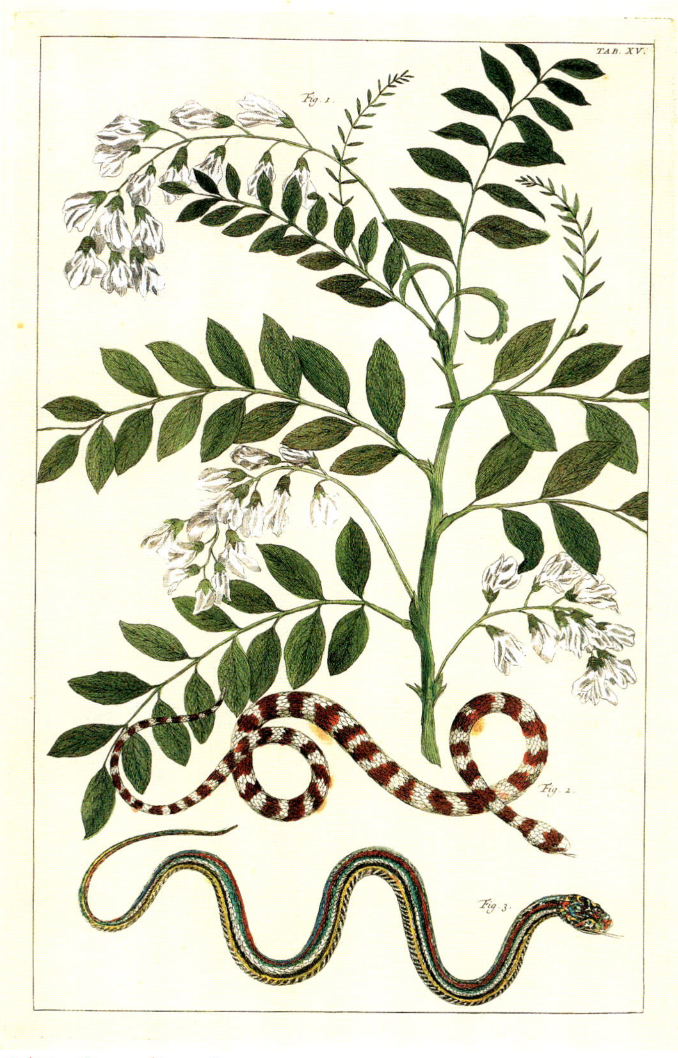

1 *Robinia* **2** *Lampropeltis sp.* **3** Serpentes
1 False acacia · Robinie · Robinier faux-acacia **2** King snake · Königsnatter · Serpent roi **3** Snake, according to Seba from Africa · Schlange, nach Seba aus Afrika · Serpent, d'Afrique selon Seba

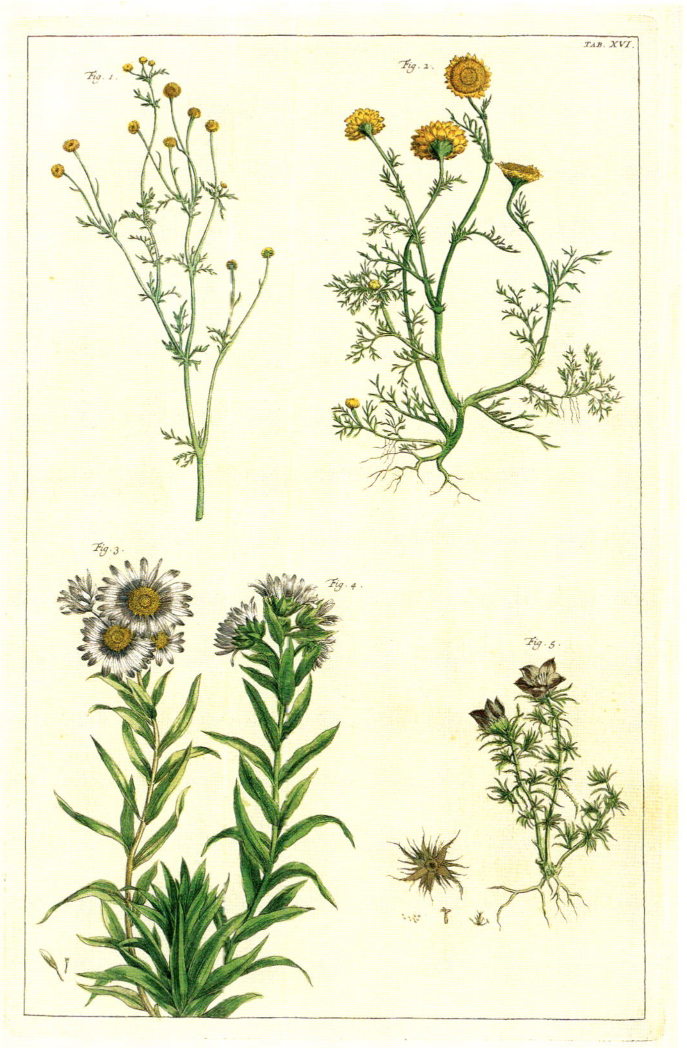

1, 3-4 Compositae **2** *Anacyclus* **5** *Campanulaceae*
1, 3-4 Sunflower family · Korbblütler · Composées **2** Mount Atlas daisy · Ringblume · Pyrèthre d'Afrique **5** Bluebell family · Glockenblumengewächse · Campanulacées

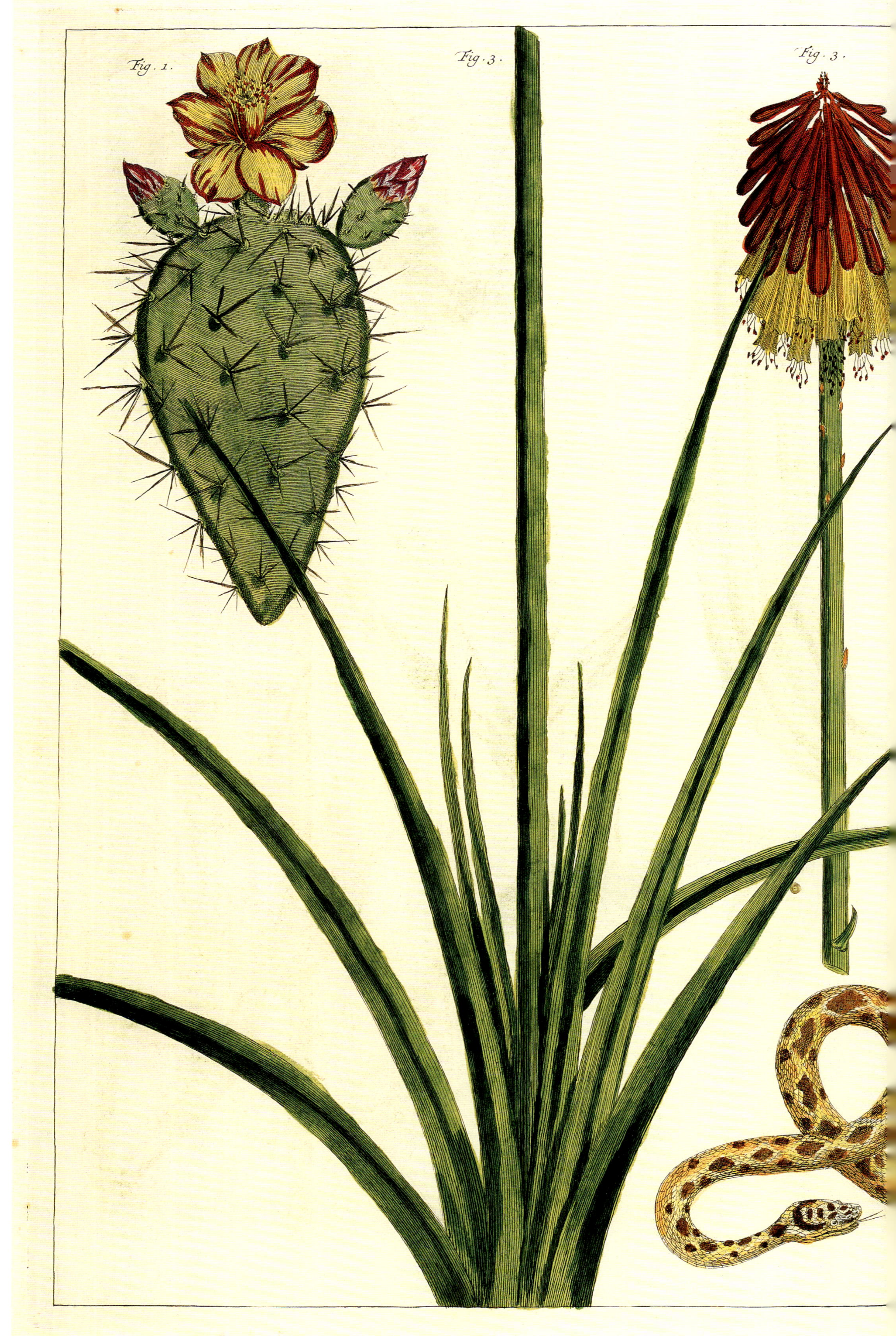

1 *Opuntia ficus-indica* 2 *Euphorbia sp.* 3 *Kniphovia uvaria* 4 *Agapanthus africanus* 5 Mesembryanthemaceae 6 *Carpobrotus edulis* 7 Serpentes
1 Prickly pear · Echter Feigenkaktus · Figuier d'Inde 2 Spurge · Wolfsmilch · Euphorbe 3 Red-hot poker · Fackellilie · Tritorne 4 African lily · Schmucklilie · Agapanthe 5 Ice plant · Eiskrautgewächse · Mésembryanthémacée 6 Sour fig · Pferdefeige · Ficoïde 7 Snake, according to Seba from Africa · Schlange, nach Seba aus Afrika · Serpent, d'Afrique selon Seba

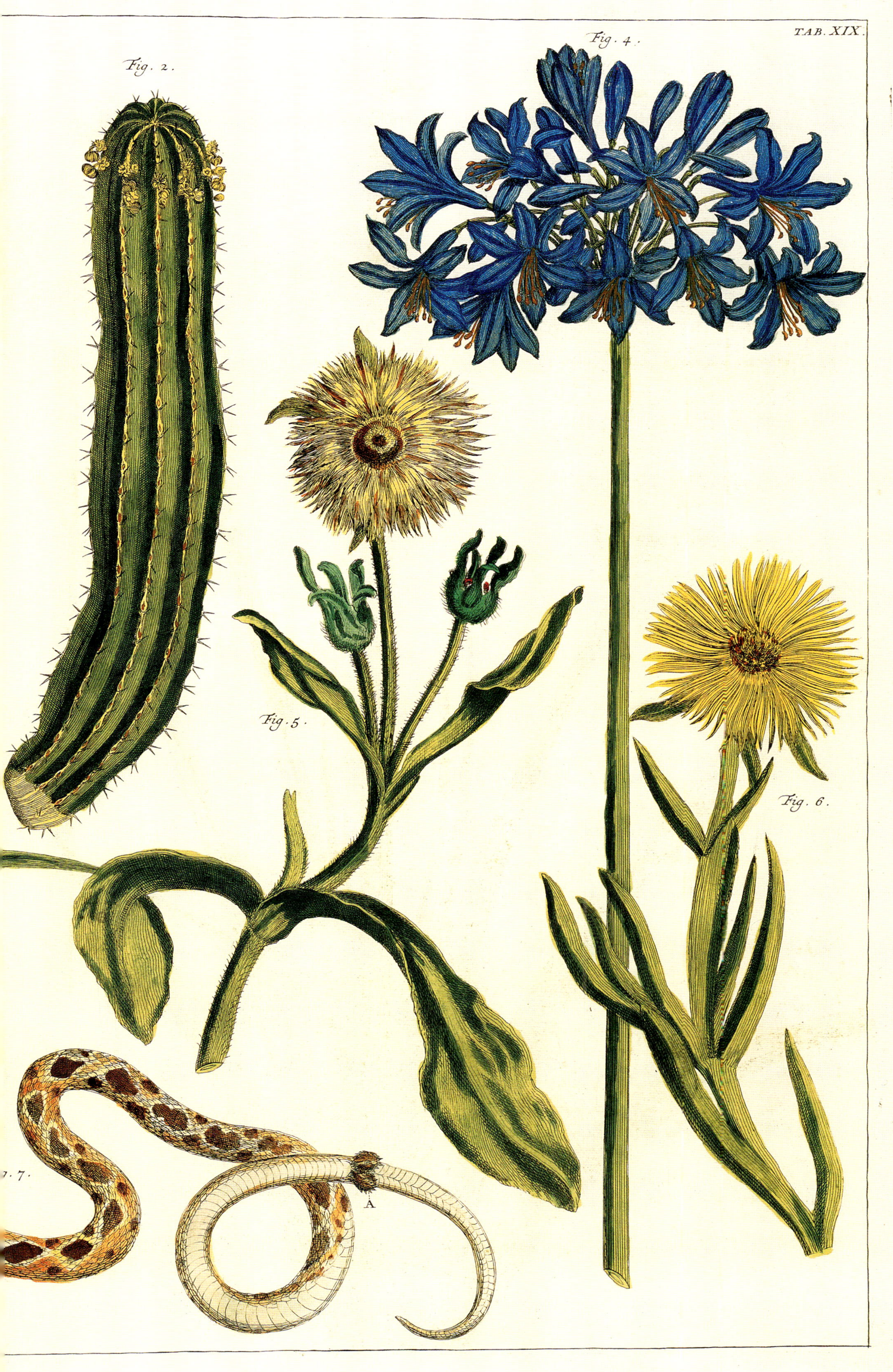
TAB. XIX.
Fig. 2.
Fig. 4.
Fig. 5.
Fig. 6.
A

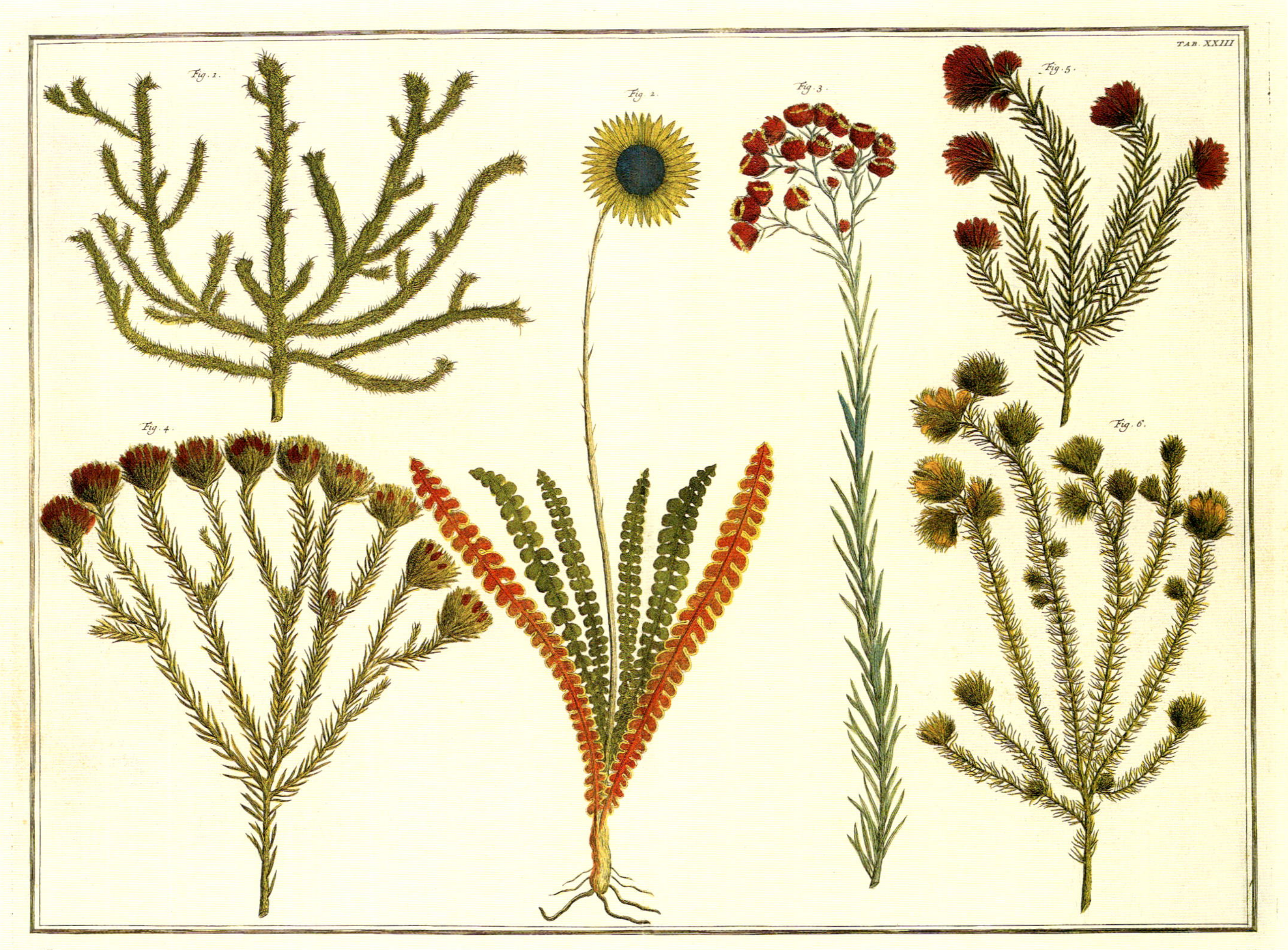

2 Compositae 3 *Helichrysum* 4-5 Proteaceae 6 *Genista*
2 Sunflower family · Korbblütler · Composées **3** Everlasting flower · Strohblume · Hélichryse **4-5** Protea family · Silberbaumgewächse · Protéacées **6** Greenweed · Ginster · Genêt

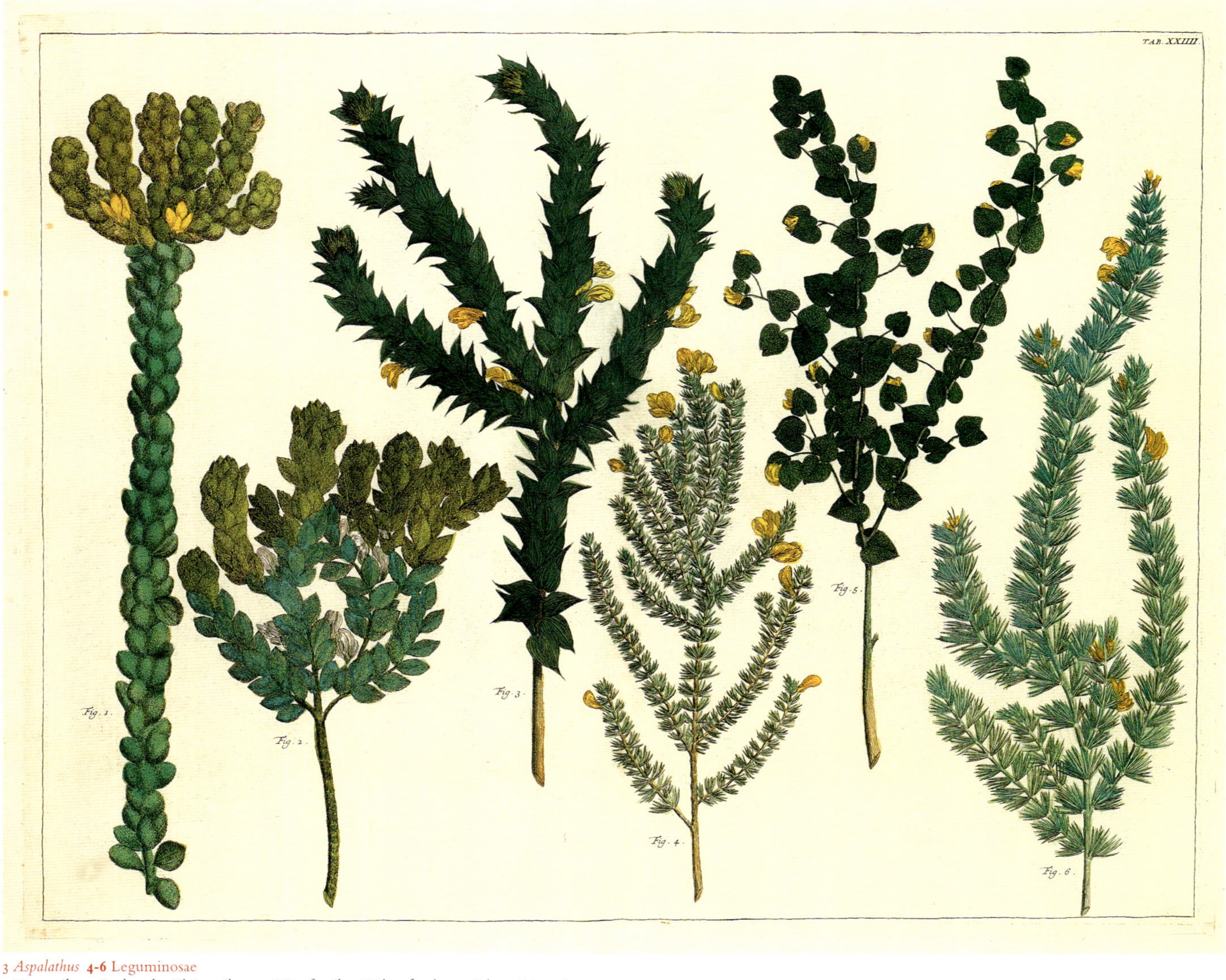

3 *Aspalathus* 4-6 Leguminosae
3 Tea rooibos · Rotbusch · Thé rooibos **4-6** Pea family · Hülsenfruchtgewächse · Légumineuses

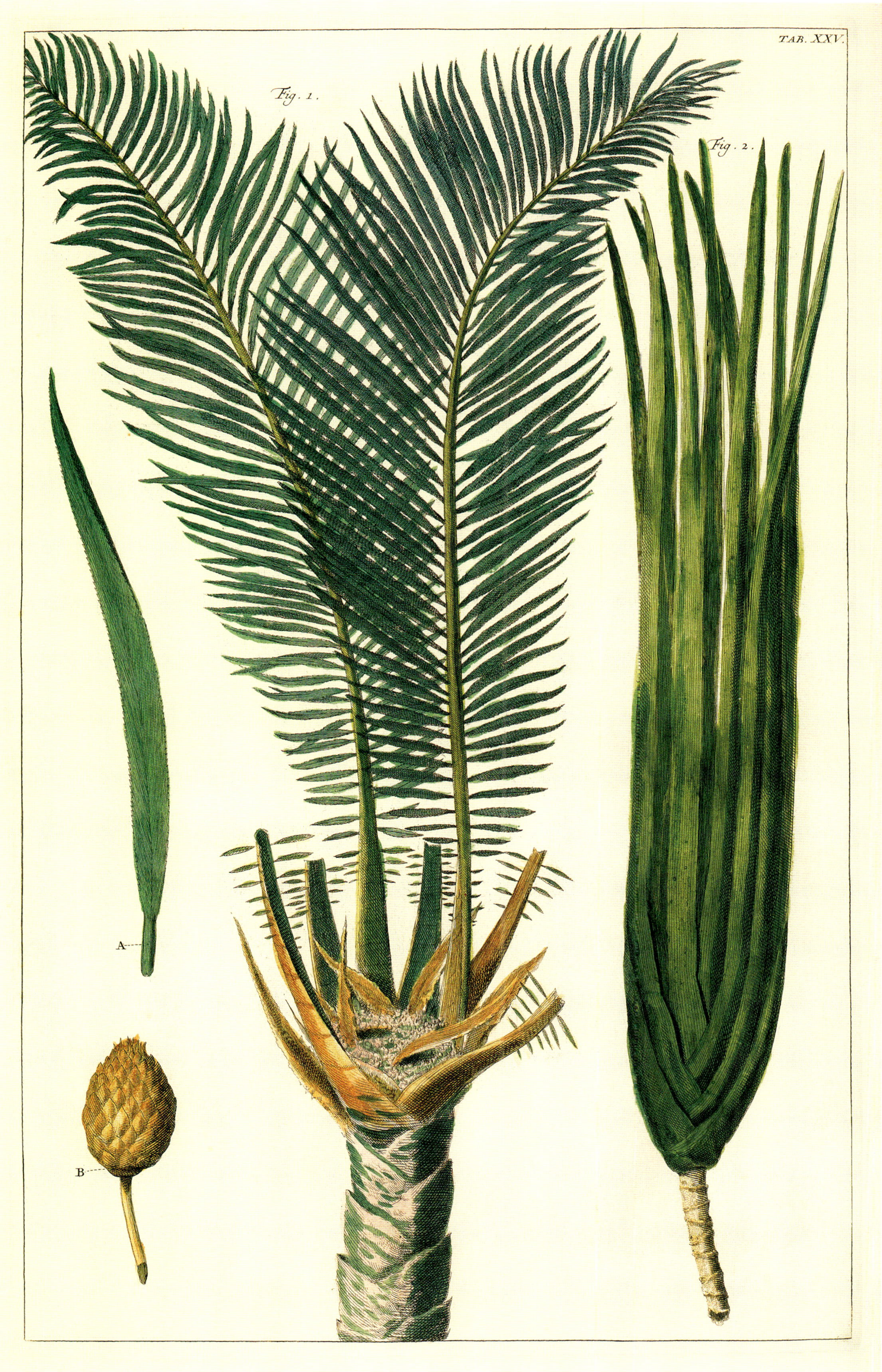

1-2 *Palmae*
1-2 Palm family · Palmengewächse · Palmacées

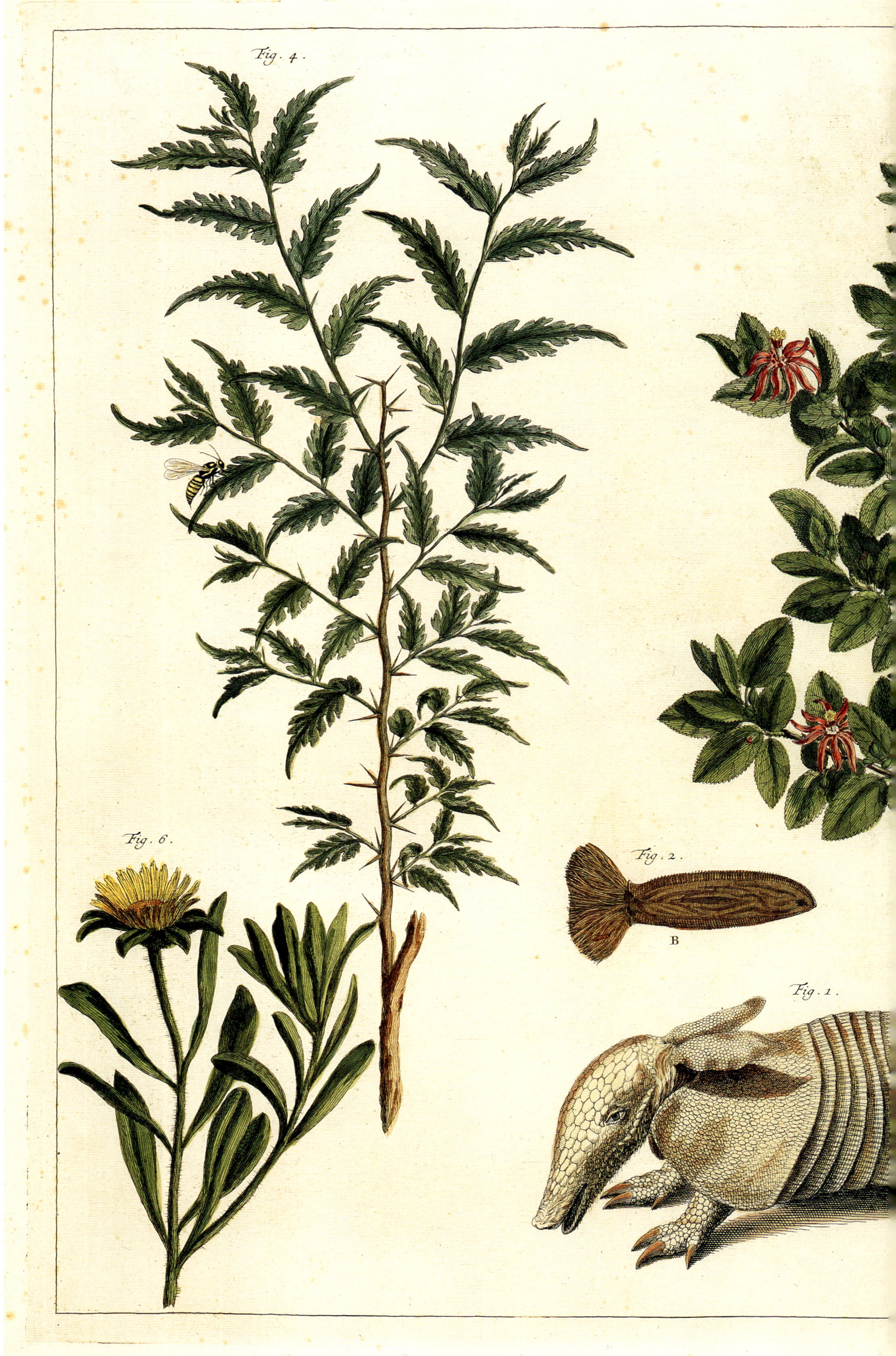

1 *Dasypus novemcinctus* 3 *Grewia occidentalis* 6 Mesembryanthemaceae 7 *Asteriscus sp.*
1 Nine-banded armadillo · Neunbinden-Gürteltier · Tatou à neuf bandes 3 Crossberry · Grewie · Greuvier 6 Ice plant · Eiskrautgewächse · Mésembryanthémacée
7 Asteriscus · Asteriskus · Astérolide

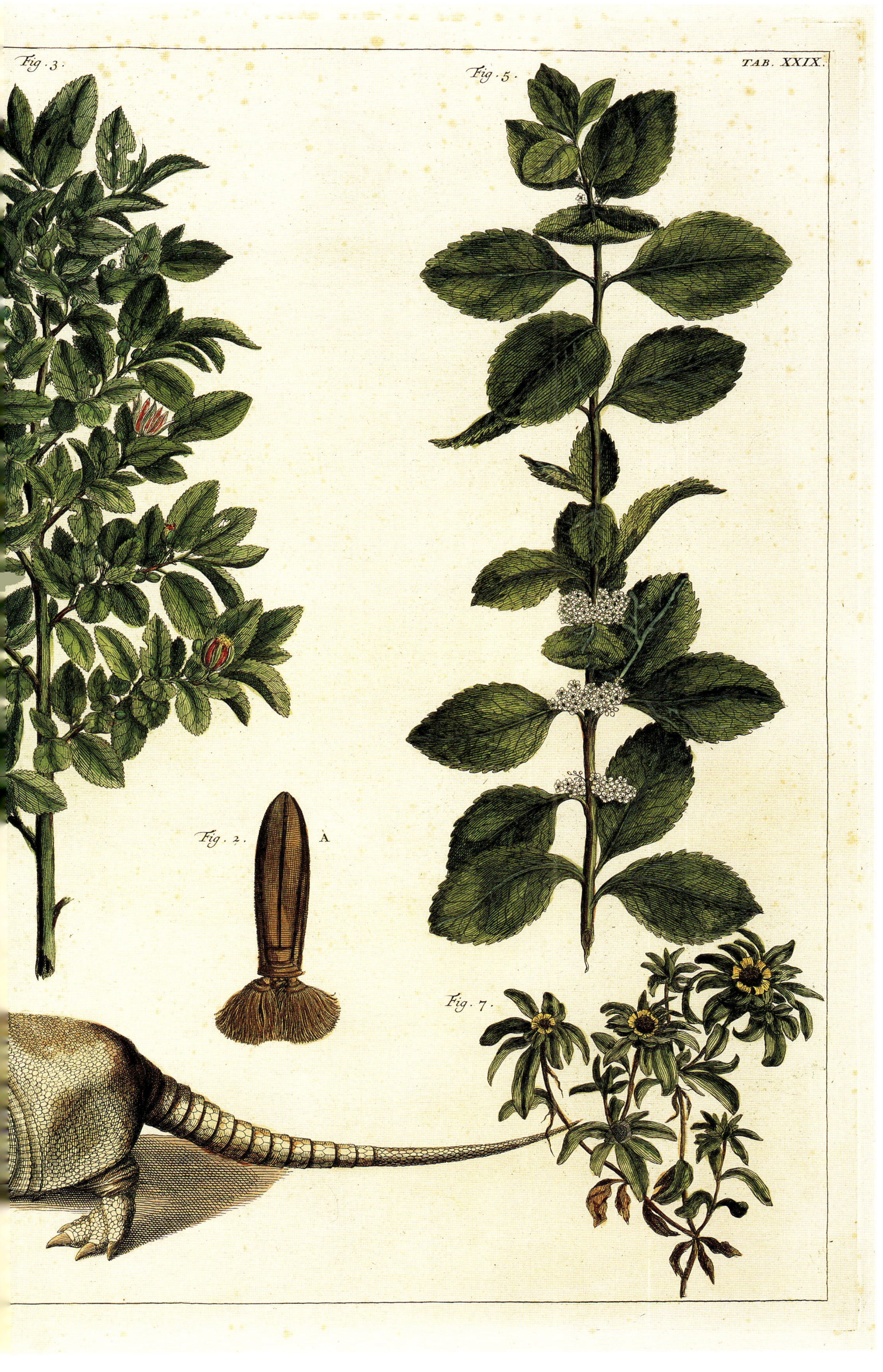
Fig. 3.
Fig. 5.
TAB. XXIX.
Fig. 2.
A
Fig. 7.

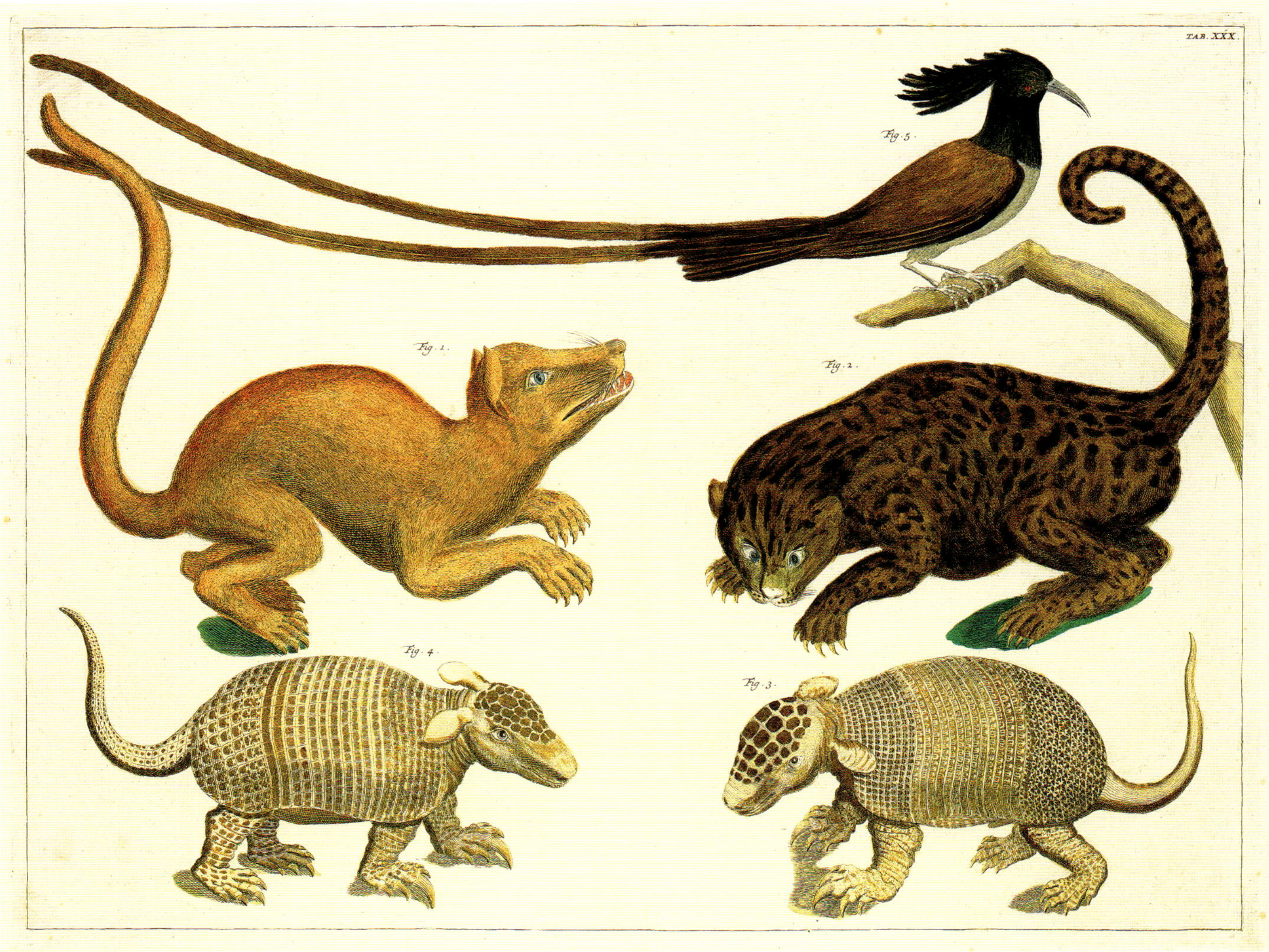

1 Herpestidae? **2** Felidae **3** *Cabassous unicinctus* **4** *Dasypodidae* **5** *Terpsiphone paradisi*
1 Mongoose · Mungo · Mangouste **2** Felines · Katzenartige · Félidés **3** Northern naked-tailed armadillo · Nacktschwanz-Gürteltier · Tatou à onze bandes **4** Armadillo · Gürteltier · Tatou **5** Asian paradise-flycatcher (dark variety) · Fahlbauchparadiesschnäpper (dunkle Form) · Tchitrec de Paradis (espèce sombre)

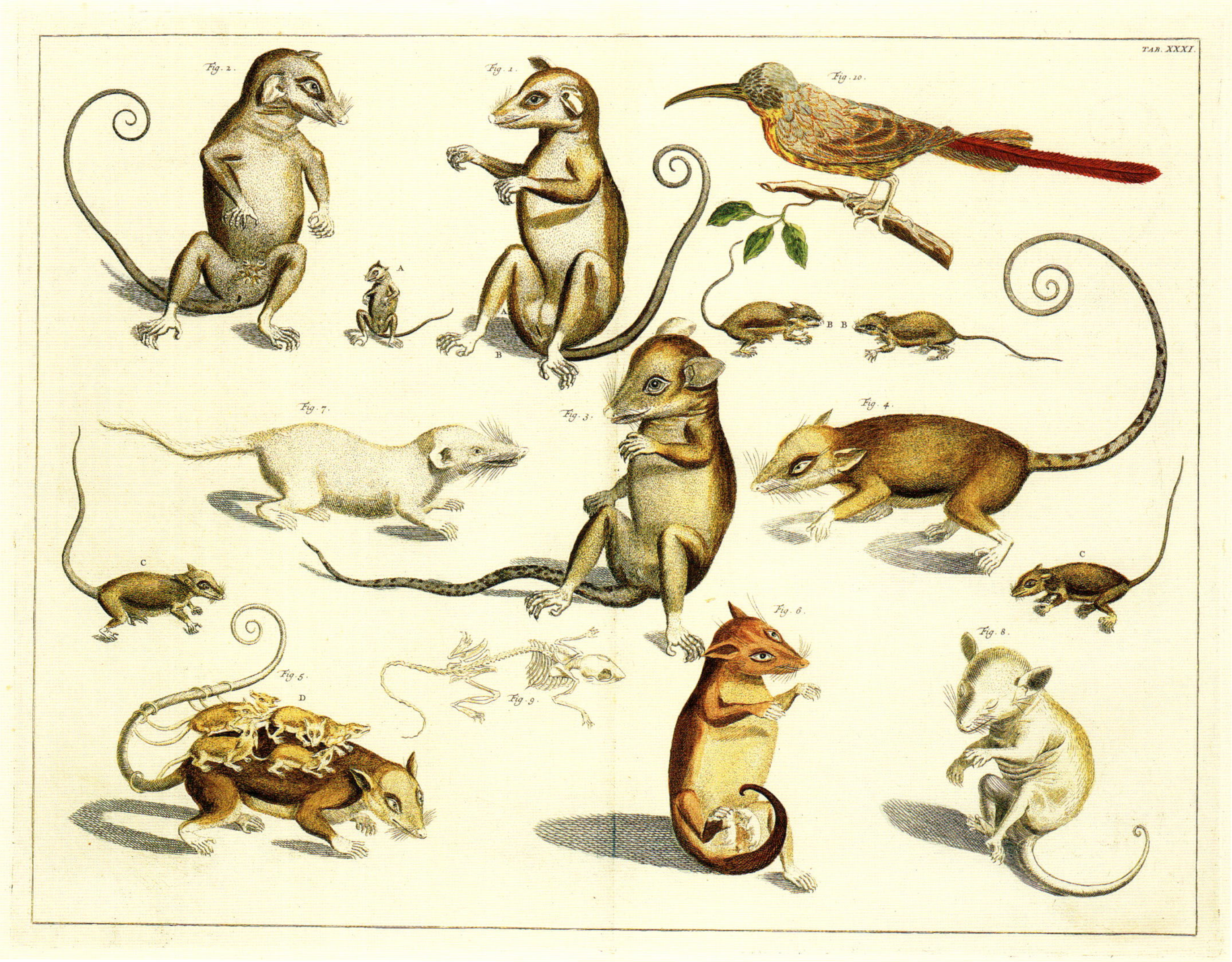

1-8 *Marmosa sp.* **9** *Rattus rattus* **10** *Merops nubicus*
1-8 Mouse opossums · Mauszwergbeutelratten · Sarigues **9** House rat · Skelett der Hausratte · Rat noir **10** Carmine bee-eater · Scharlachspint · Guêpier superbe

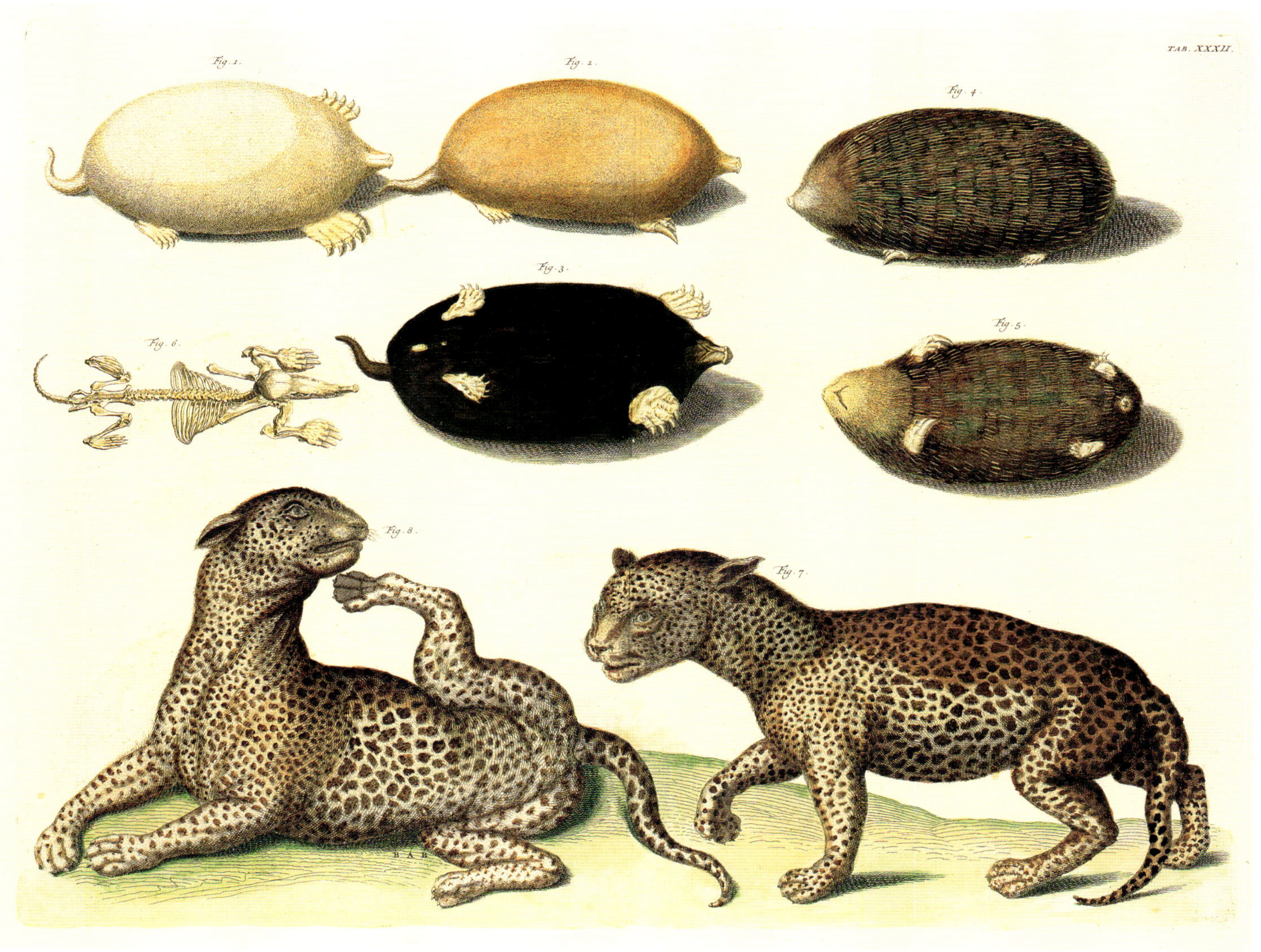

1, 6 *Talpa europaea* **2** *Talpa sp.* **3** *Scalopus aquaticus* **4-5** *Chrysochloris sp.* **7-8** *Acinonyx jubatus*
1, 6 Eurasian common mole · Maulwurf · Taupe commune **2** Mole · Maulwurf · Taupe **3** Eastern American mole · Ostamerikanischer Maulwurf · Taupe à queue glabre
4-5 Golden mole · Goldmull · Chrysochloridé **7-8** Cheetahs · Geparde · Guépards

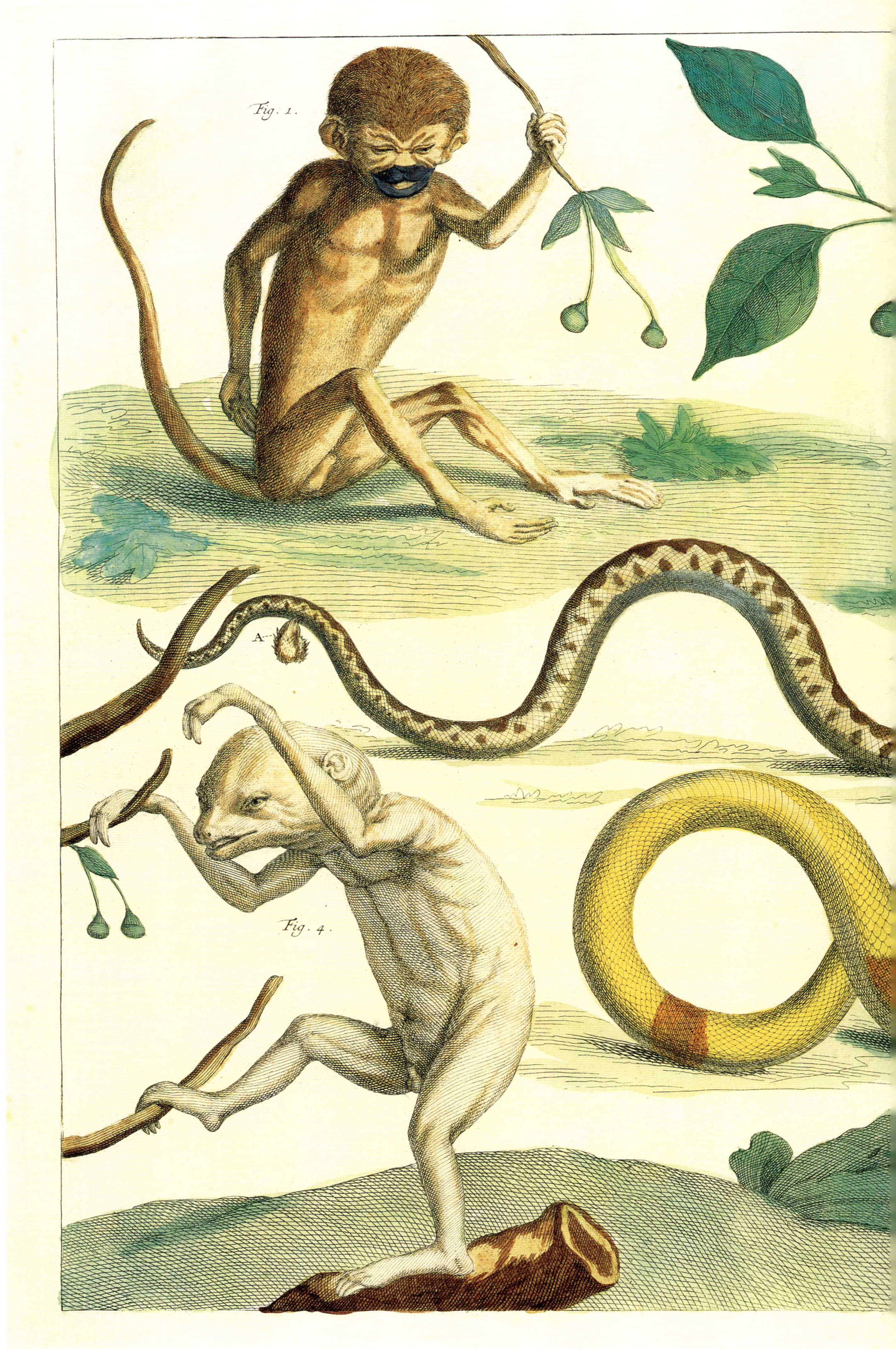

1 *Saimiri sciureus* 2 *Bradypus tridactylus* 3 *Camphora* 4 *Choloepus didactylus* 5 *Vipera berus* 6 Serpentes
1 Squirrel monkey · Totenkopfäffchen · Sapajou jaune 2 Three-toed tree sloth · Dreizehen-Faultier · Paresseux à trois doigts 3 Camphor tree · Kampferbaum · Cannelier camphrier
4 Two-toed tree sloth · Zweizehen-Faultier · Paresseux à deux doigts 5 Common viper · Kreuzotter · Vipère péliade 6 Snake, according to Seba from Ceylon · Schlange, nach Seba aus Ceylon · Serpent, de Ceylan selon Seba

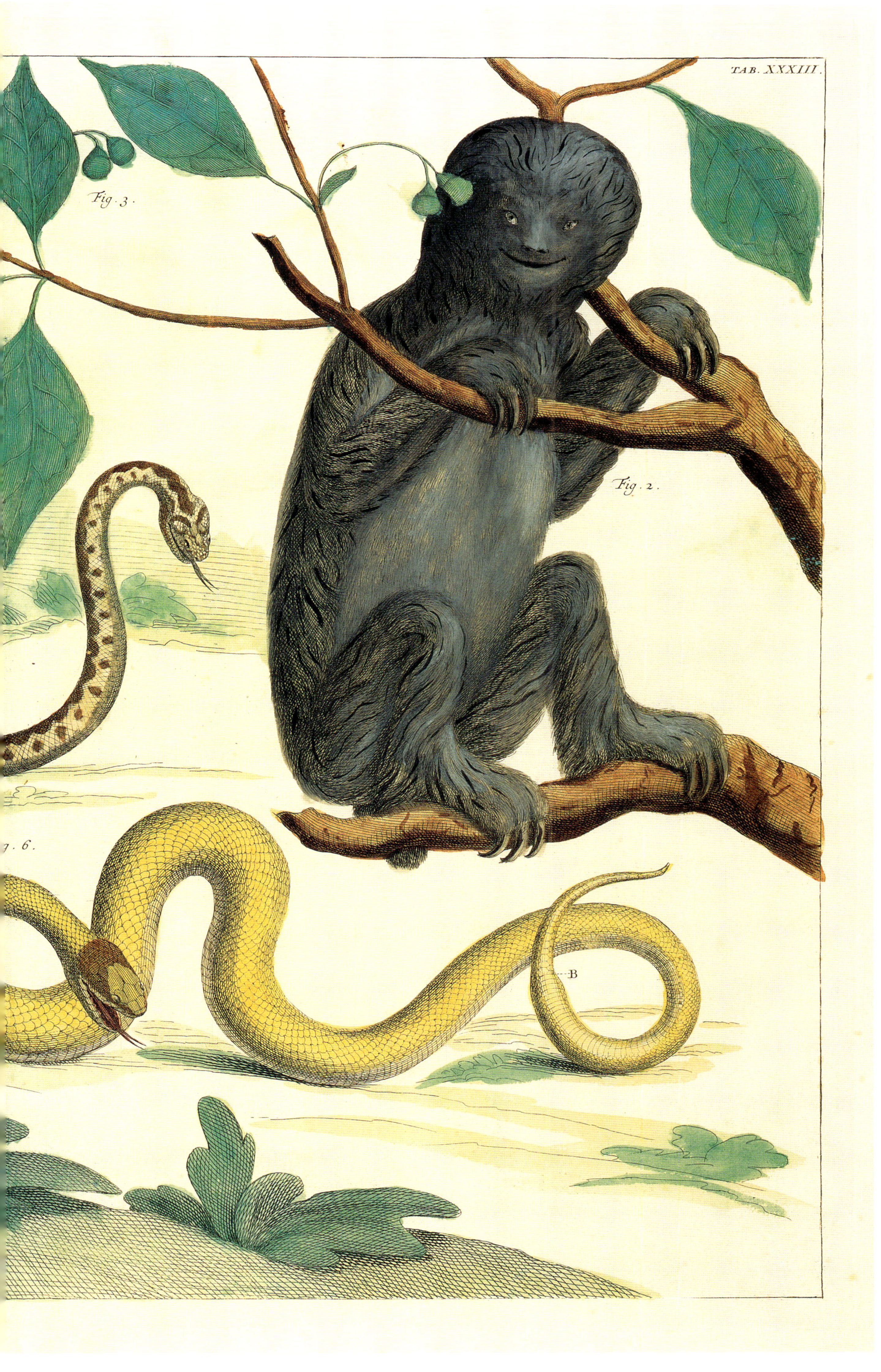
TAB. XXXIII.
Fig. 3.
Fig. 2.
B

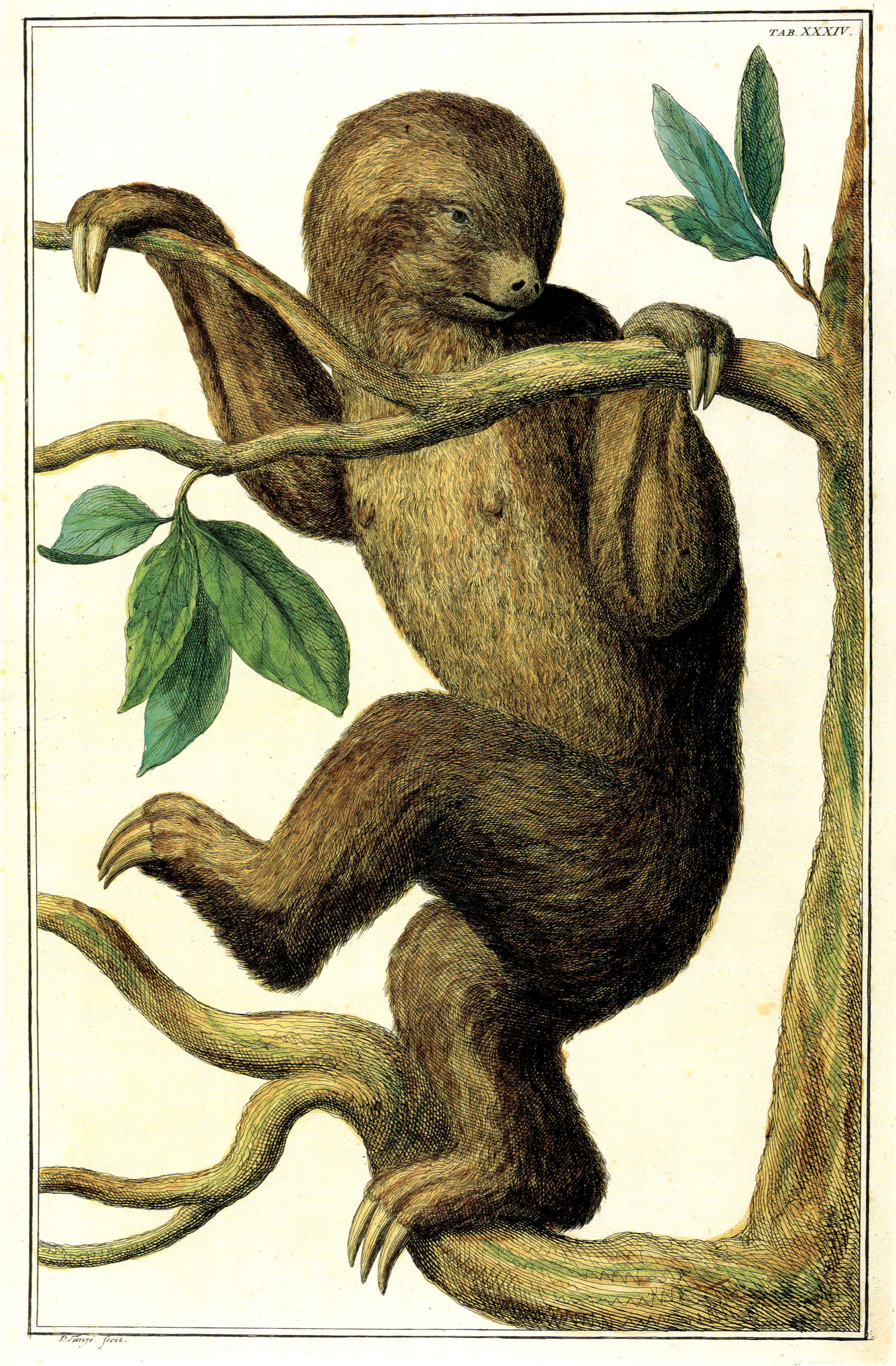

1 *Choloepus didactylus*
1 Two-toed tree sloth · Zweizehen-Faultier · Paresseux à deux doigts

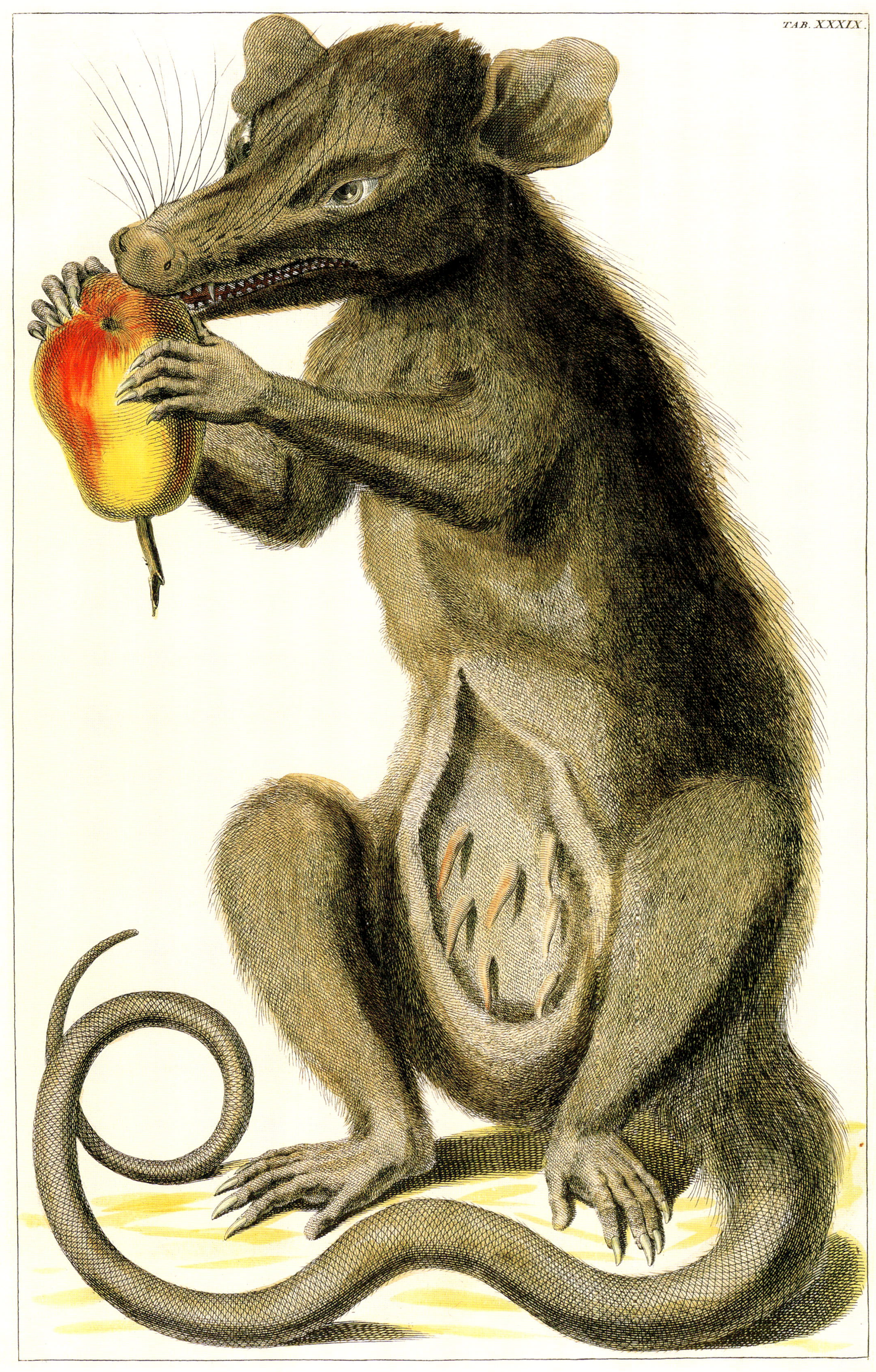

1 *Didelphis marsupialis*
1 Southern common opossum · Beutelratte · Opossum commun

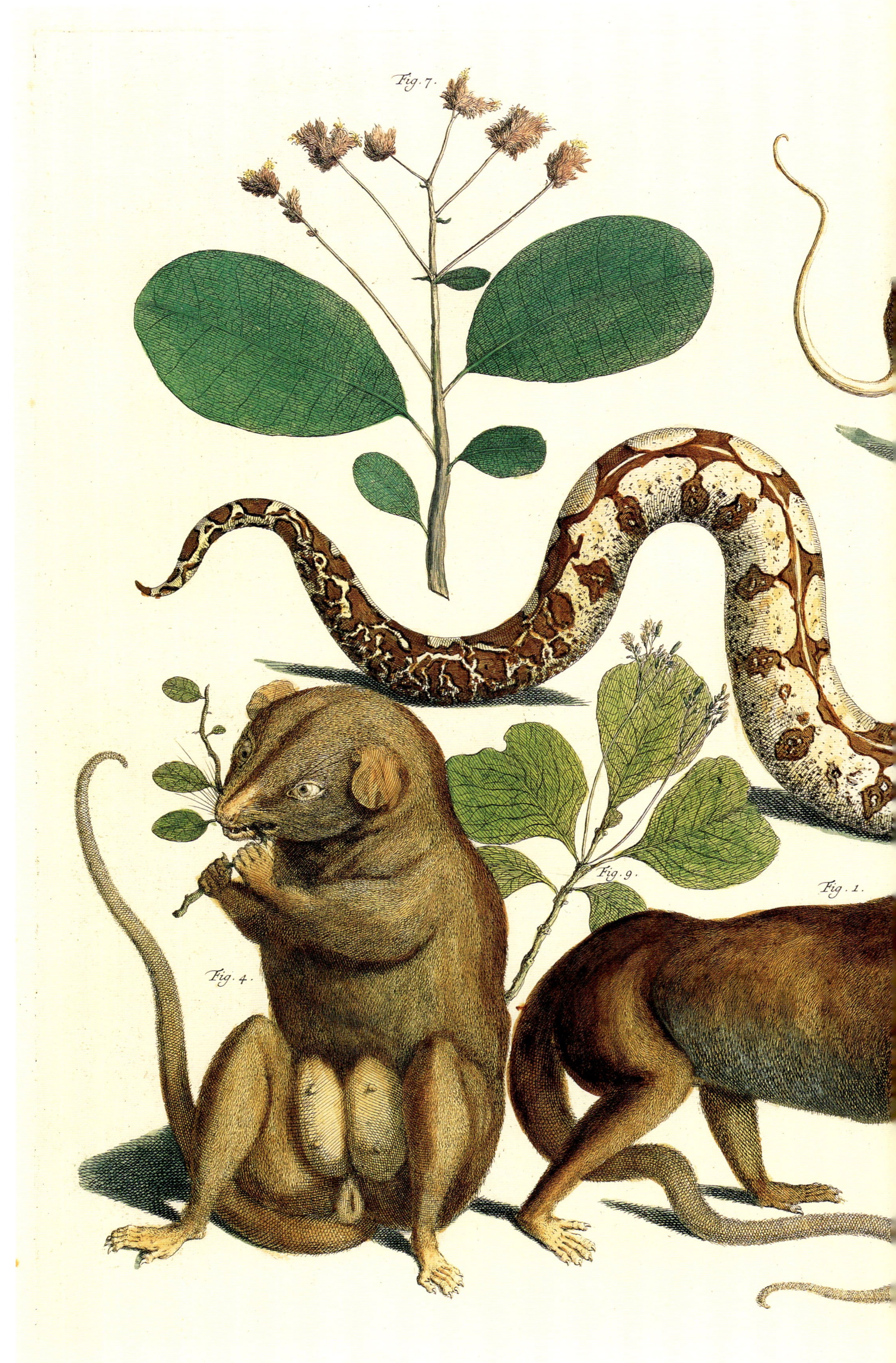

1-3 Philander opossum 4 Caluromys philander 5 Boa constrictor 7 Cotinus
1-3 Gray four-eyed opossum · Graue Vieraugenbeutelratte · Sarigue à quatre yeux 4 Woolly opossum · Wollhaarbeutelratte · Opossum jaune 5 Common boa · Abgottschlange · Boa constricteur 7 Smoke-tree · Perückenstrauch · Arbre à perruque

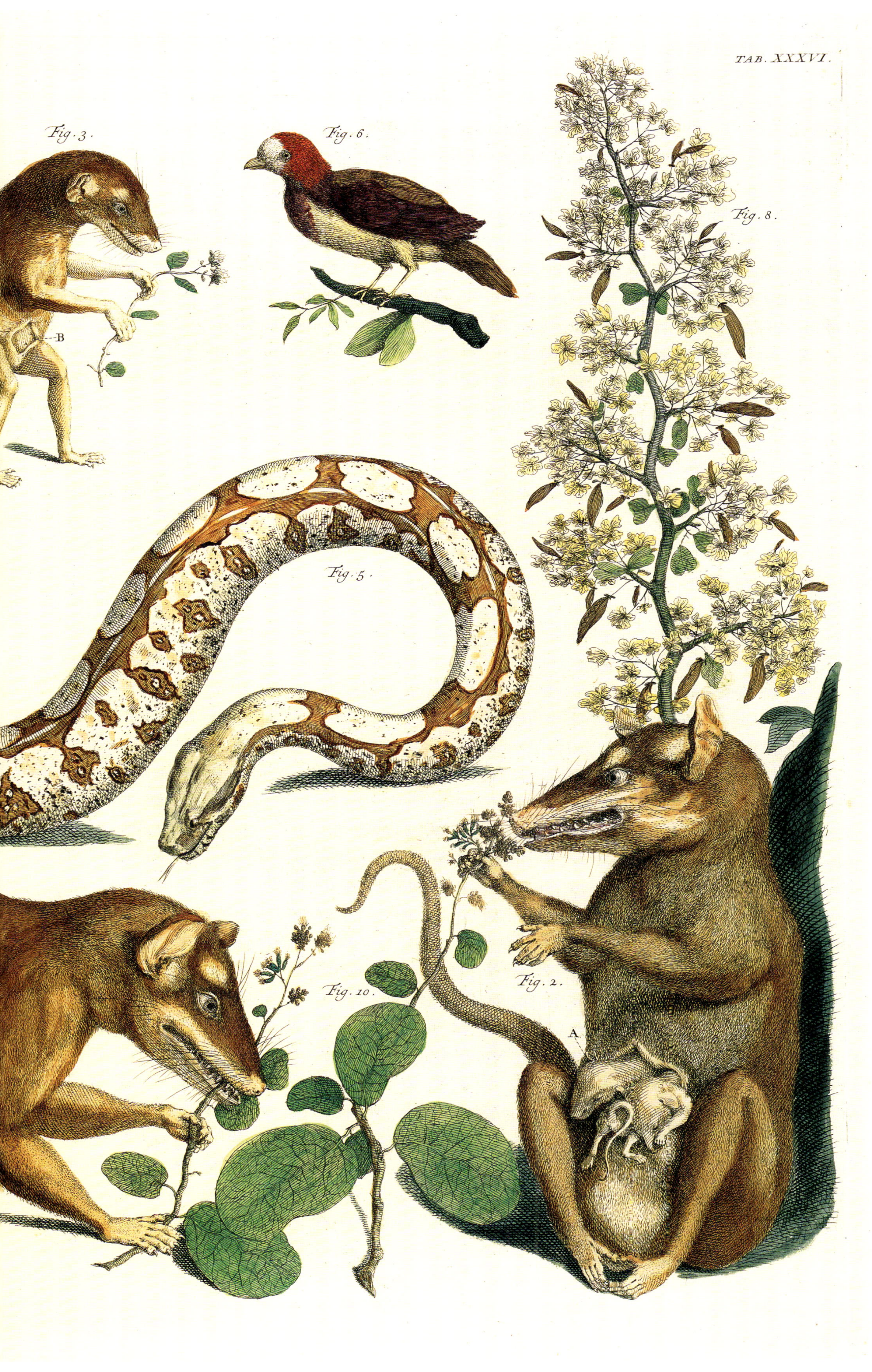

Fig. 3.
Fig. 6.
Fig. 8.
B
Fig. 5.
Fig. 10.
Fig. 2.
A

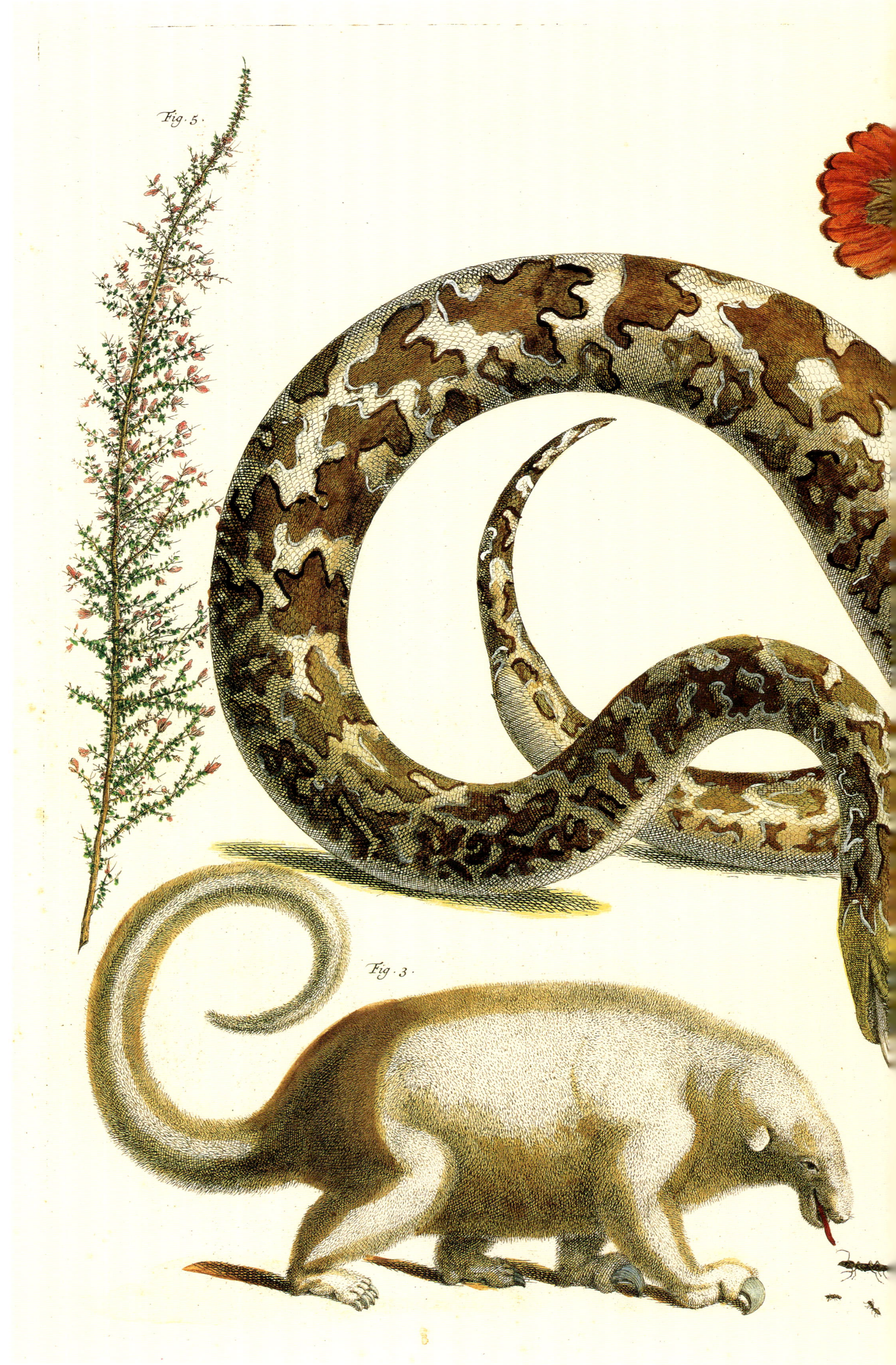

1 Pythonidae 2 *Tamandua tetradactyla* 3 *Cyclopes didactylus* 4 *Chrysolampis mosquitus* 5 *Erica sp.*
1 Python · Python · Python 2 Lesser anteater · Kleiner Ameisenbär · Tamandua à quatre doigts 3 Silky anteater · Zwergameisenbär · Fourmilier didactyle 4 Ruby-topaz hummingbird · Moskitokolibri · Colibri rubis-topaze 5 Heath · Heide · Bruyère

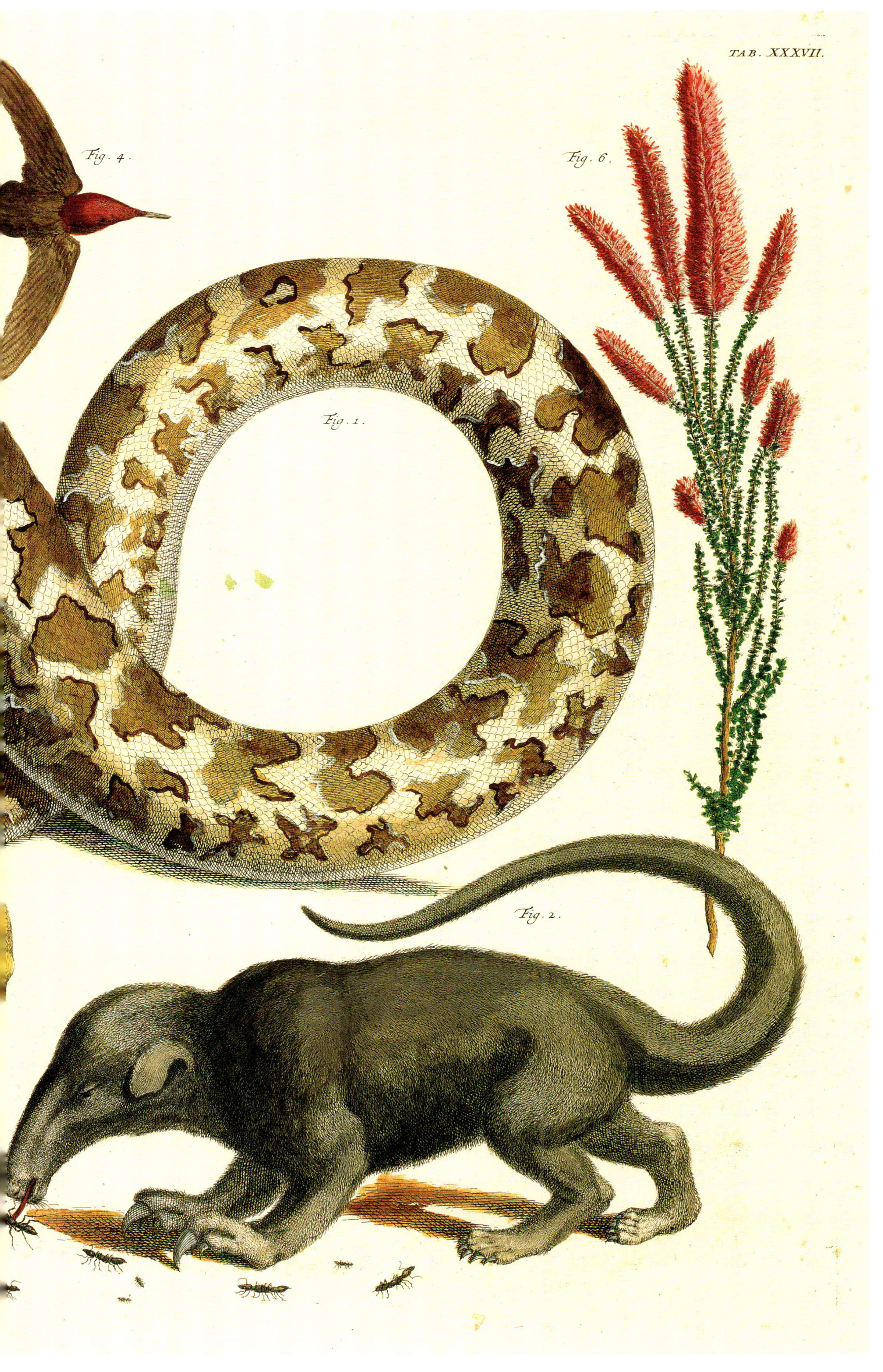
TAB. XXXVII.
Fig. 4.
Fig. 6.
Fig. 1.
Fig. 2.

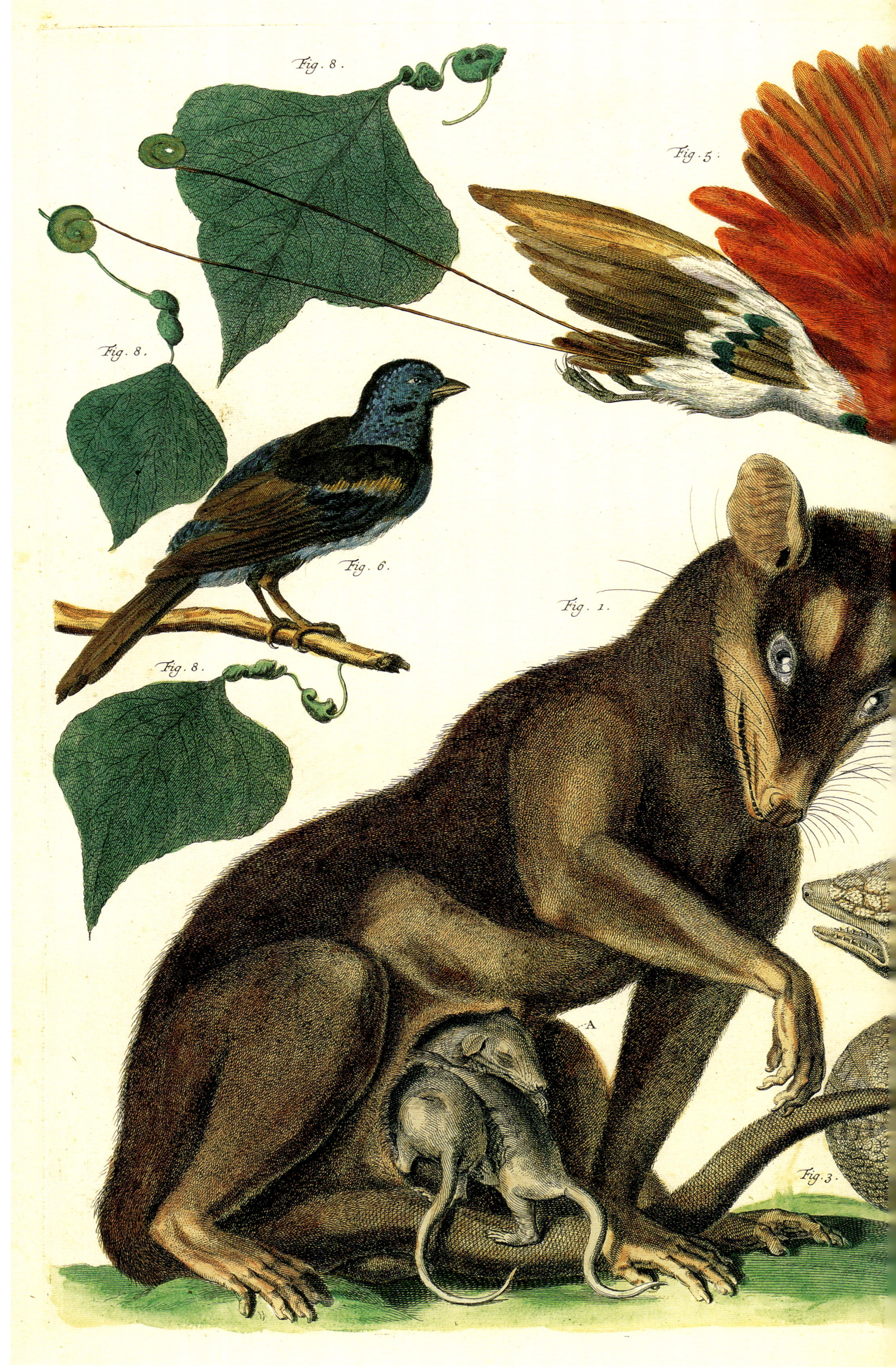

1 *Metachirus nudicaudatus* 2-3 *Tolypeutes tricinctus* 4 *Lorius lory* 5 *Cicinnurus regius*
1 Brown four-eyed opossum · Braune Vieraugenbeutelratte · Sarigue à quatre yeux 2-3 Three-banded armadillo · Kugelgürteltier · Tatou à trois bandes 4 Black-capped Lory · Frauenlori · Lori tricolore 5 King bird of paradise · Königsparadisvogel · Paradisier royal

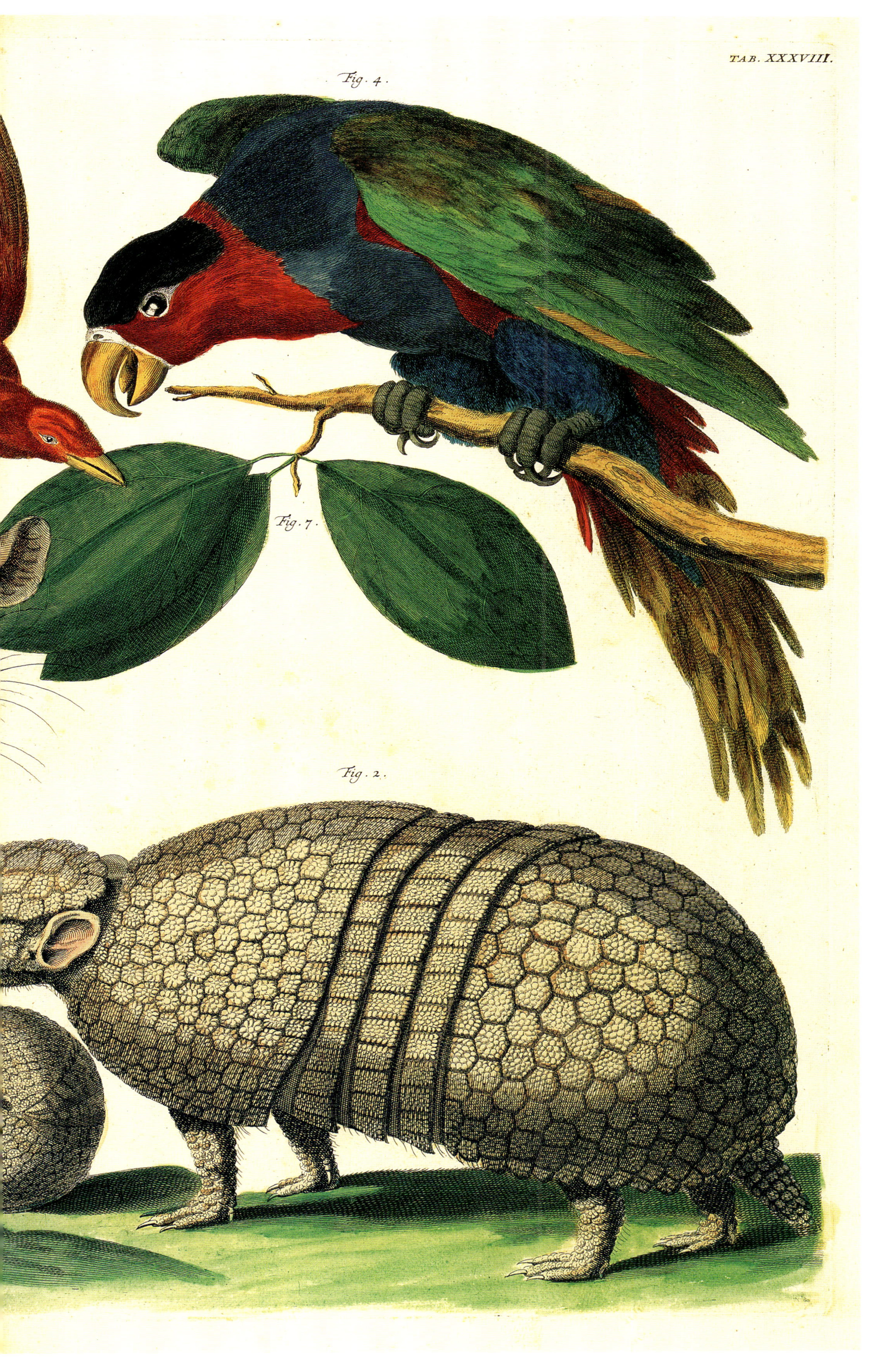
TAB. XXXVIII.
Fig. 4.
Fig. 7.
Fig. 2.

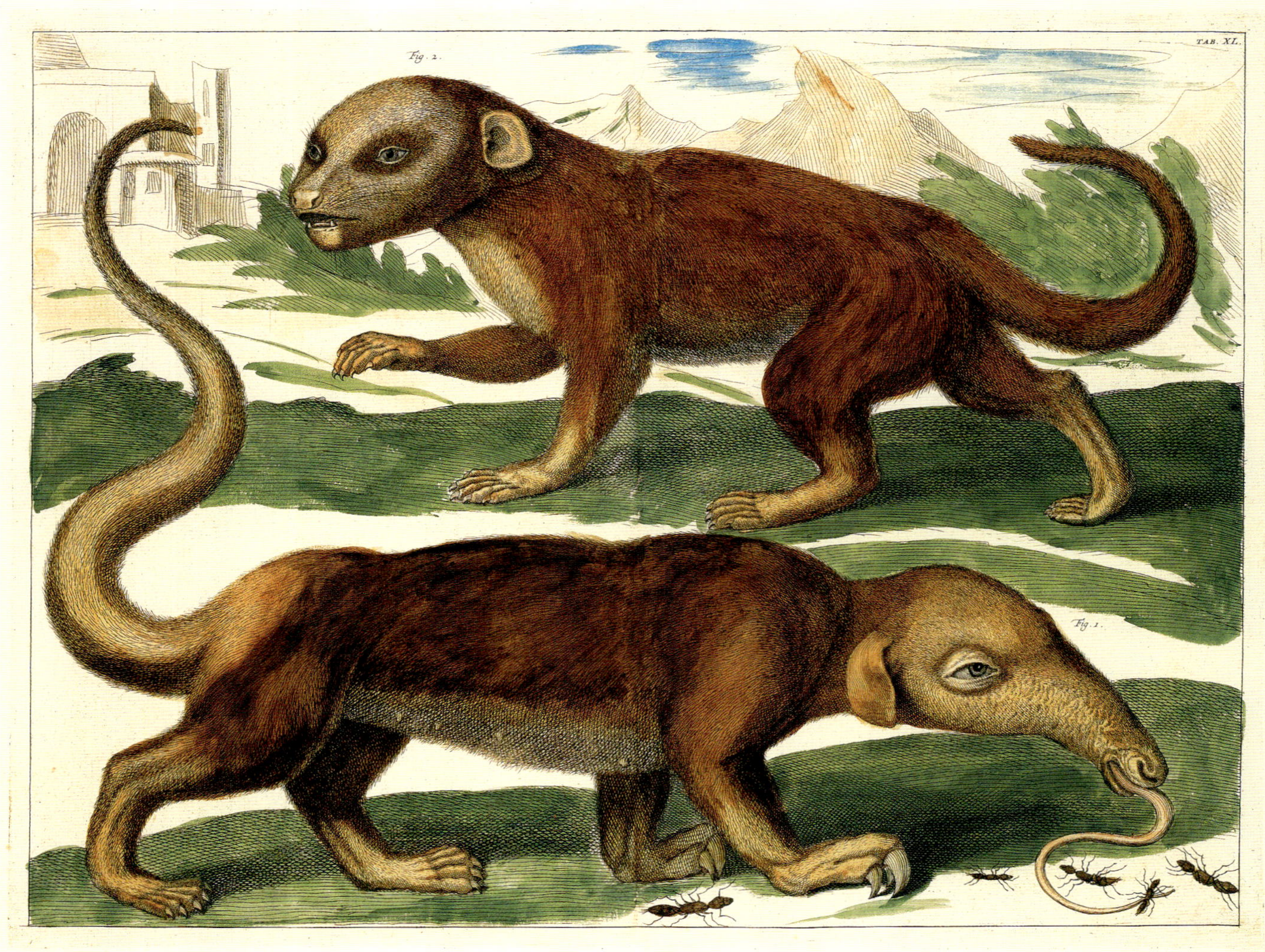

1 *Tamandua tetradactyla* 2 Herpestidae/Viveridae?
1 Lesser anteater · Kleiner Ameisenbär · Tamandua à quatre doigts 2 Mongoose: Slender-tailed meerkat · Schleichkatze: Erdmännchen · Viverridé: Suricate

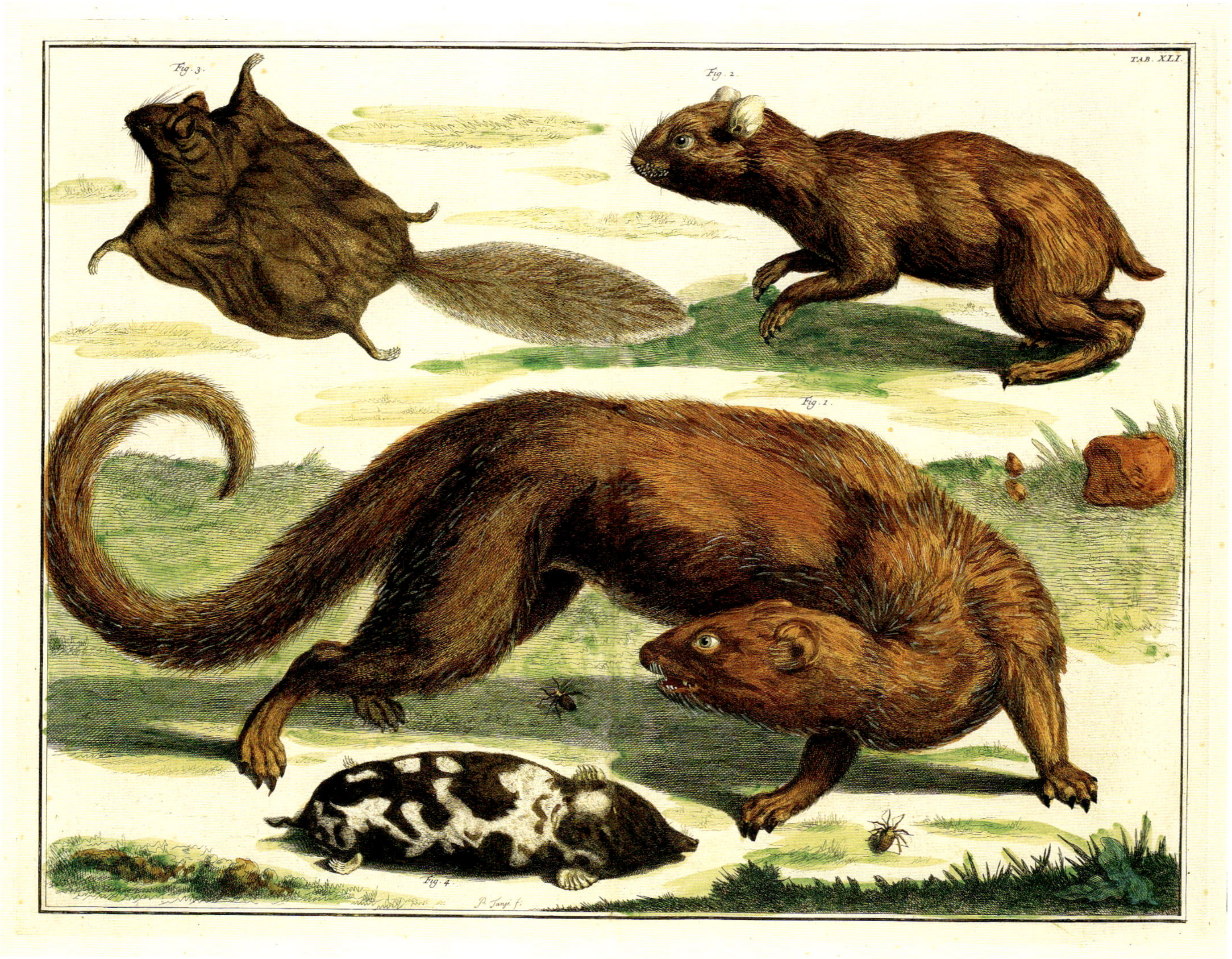

1 Herpestidae 2 *Myoprocta exilis* 3 *Glaucomys volans* 4 *Talpa europaea*
1 Mongoose · Mungo · Mangouste 2 Red acouchi · Acouchi · Acouchi 3 Southern flying squirrel · Gleithörnchen · Ecureuil volant du Sud
4 Eurasian common mole · Maulwurf · Taupe commune

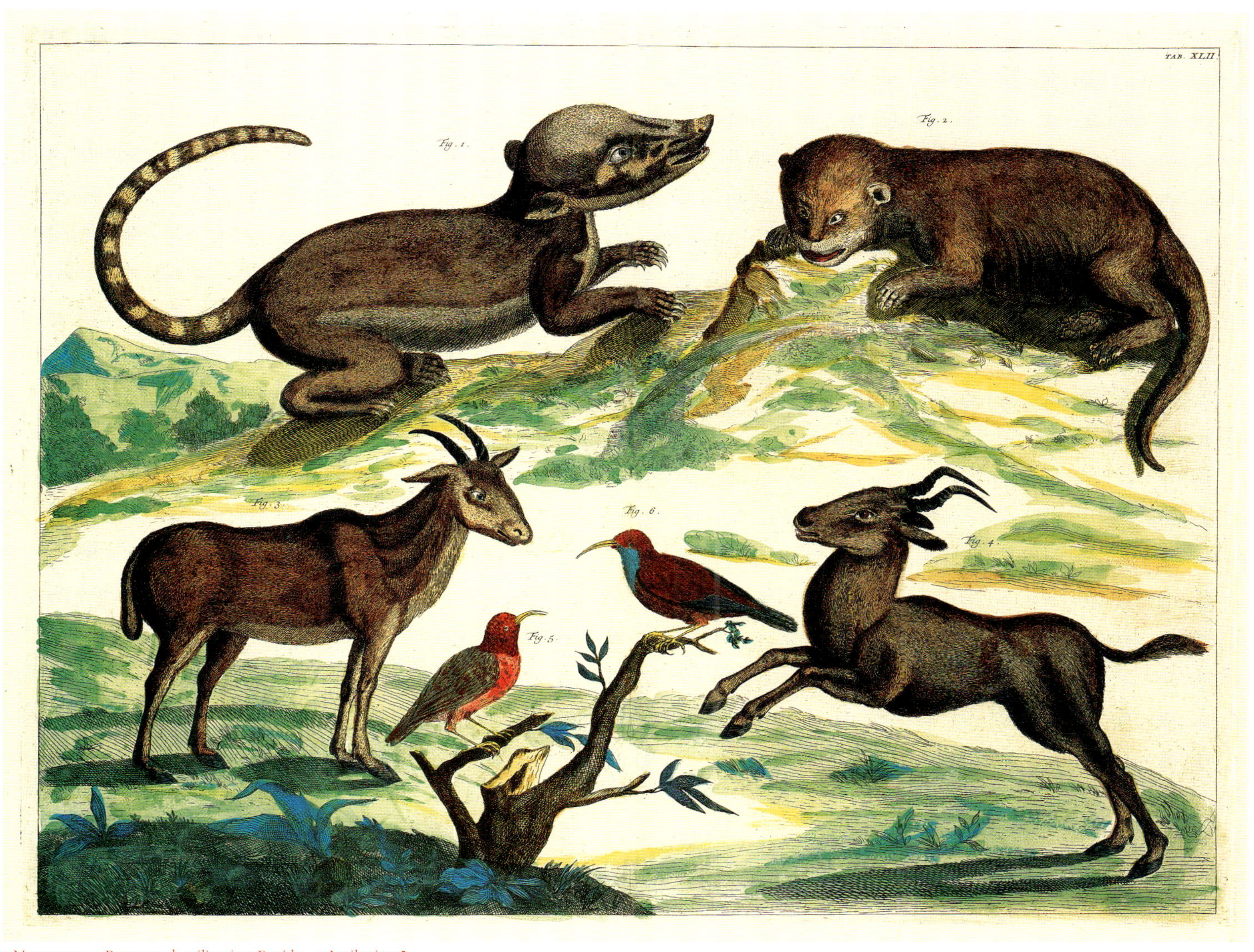

1 *Nasua nasua* 2 Pteronura brasiliensis 3 Bovidae 4 Antilopinae?
1 Coati · Nasenbär · Coati roux 2 Giant otter · Riesenotter · Loutre géante du Brésil 3 Bovides · Bovide · Boviné 4 Antilopine · Antilope · Antilopiné

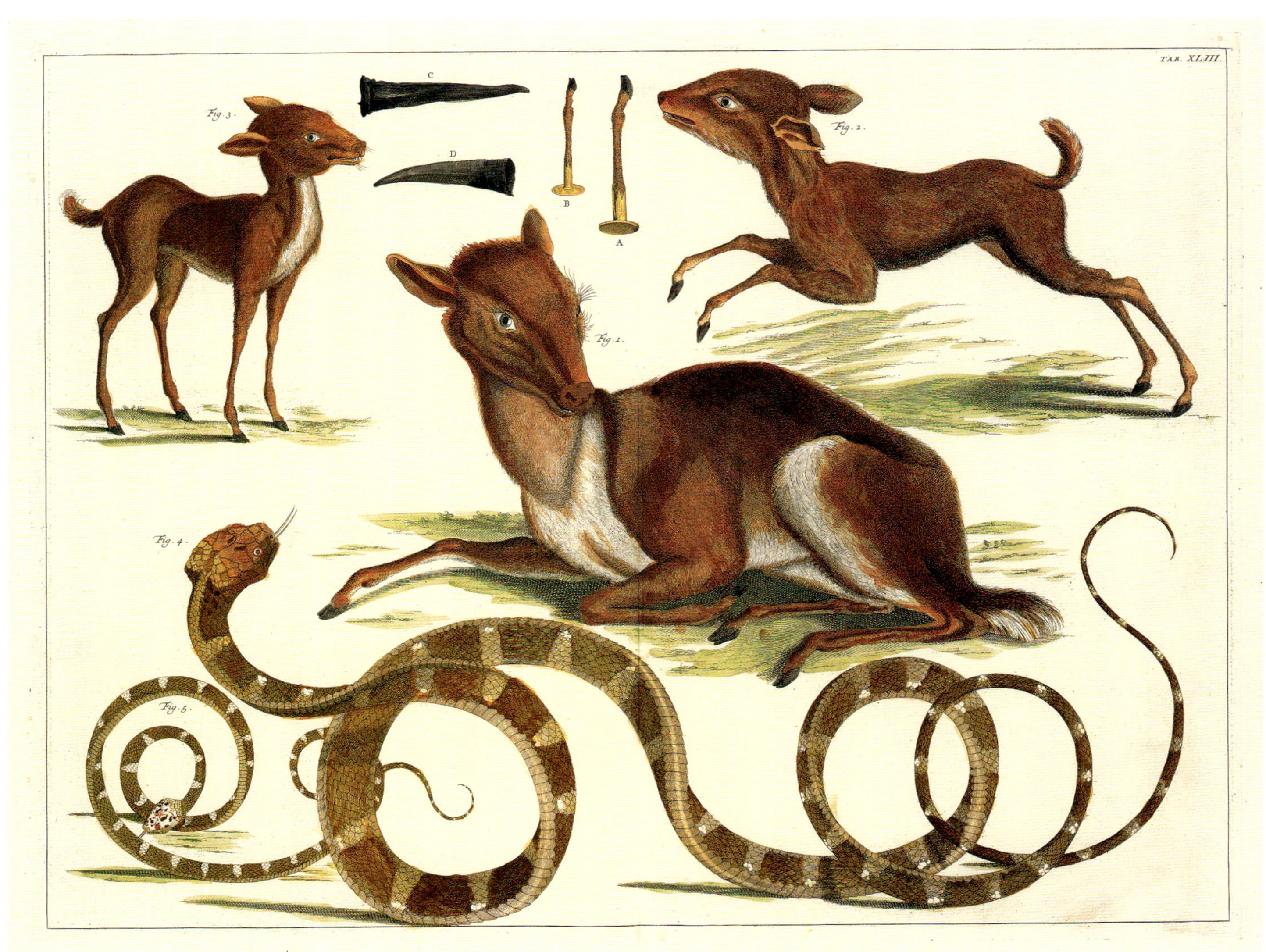

1, 3 Cervidae **2** Bovidae (Caprinae? Antelopinae?) **4-5** *Dipsas indica*
1, 3 Deers · Hirsche · Cerfs **2** Bovide (Caprine? Antelopinae?) · Rinderartiges Säugetier (Caprinae? Antelopinae?) · Bovidé (Capriné? Antilopiné?)
4-5 Snail-eating snakes · Dipsas-Schlangen · Dipsas, serpents mangeurs d'escargots

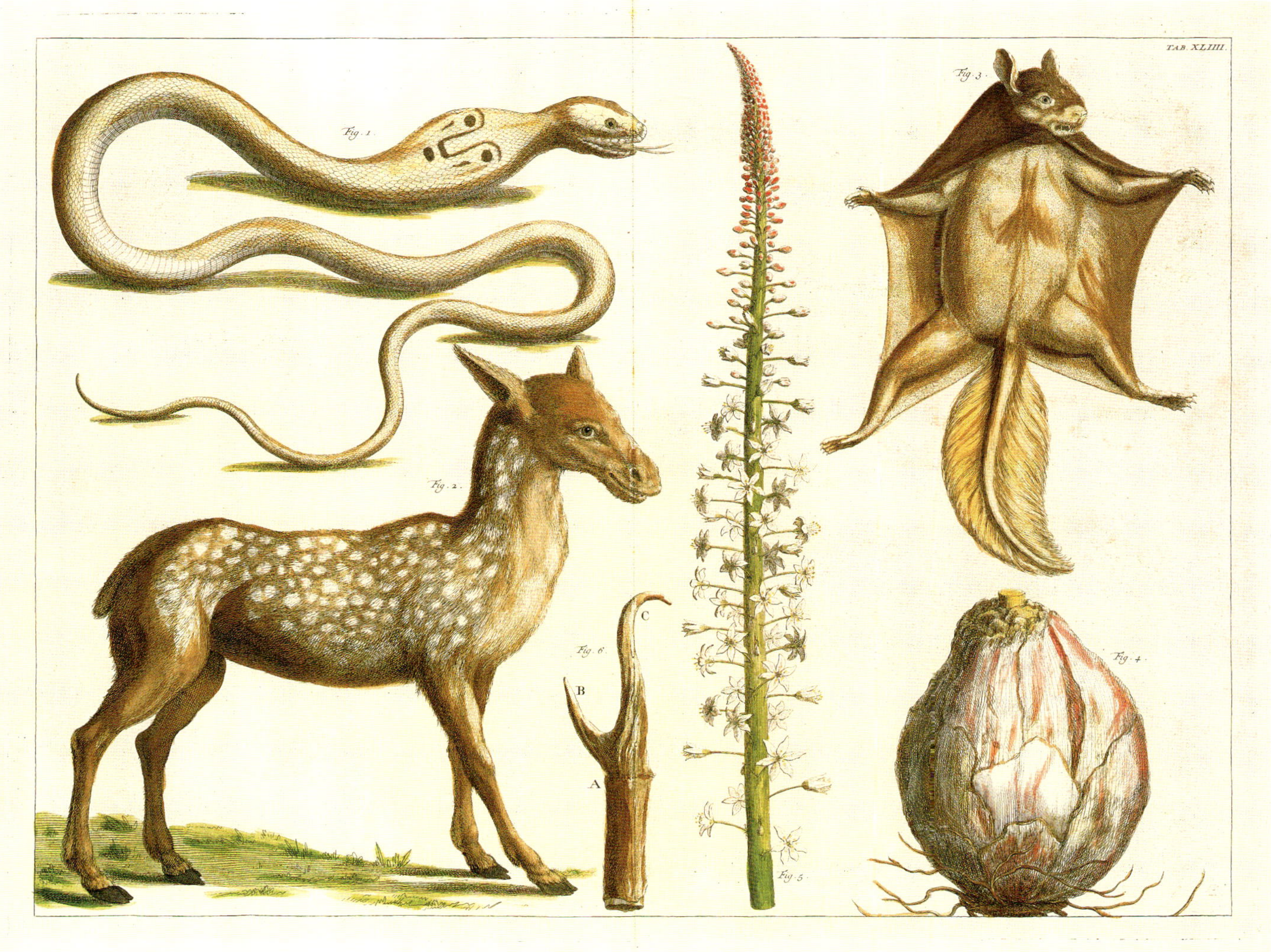

1 *Naja naja* 2 Cervidae 3 *Hylopetes* 4-5 *Urginea maritima*
1 Indian cobra · Brillenschlange · Cobra des Indes 2 Deer · Hirsch · Cerf 3 Arrow-tailed flying squirrel · Gleithörnchen · Ecureuil volant 4-5 Squill · Meerzwiebel · Scille

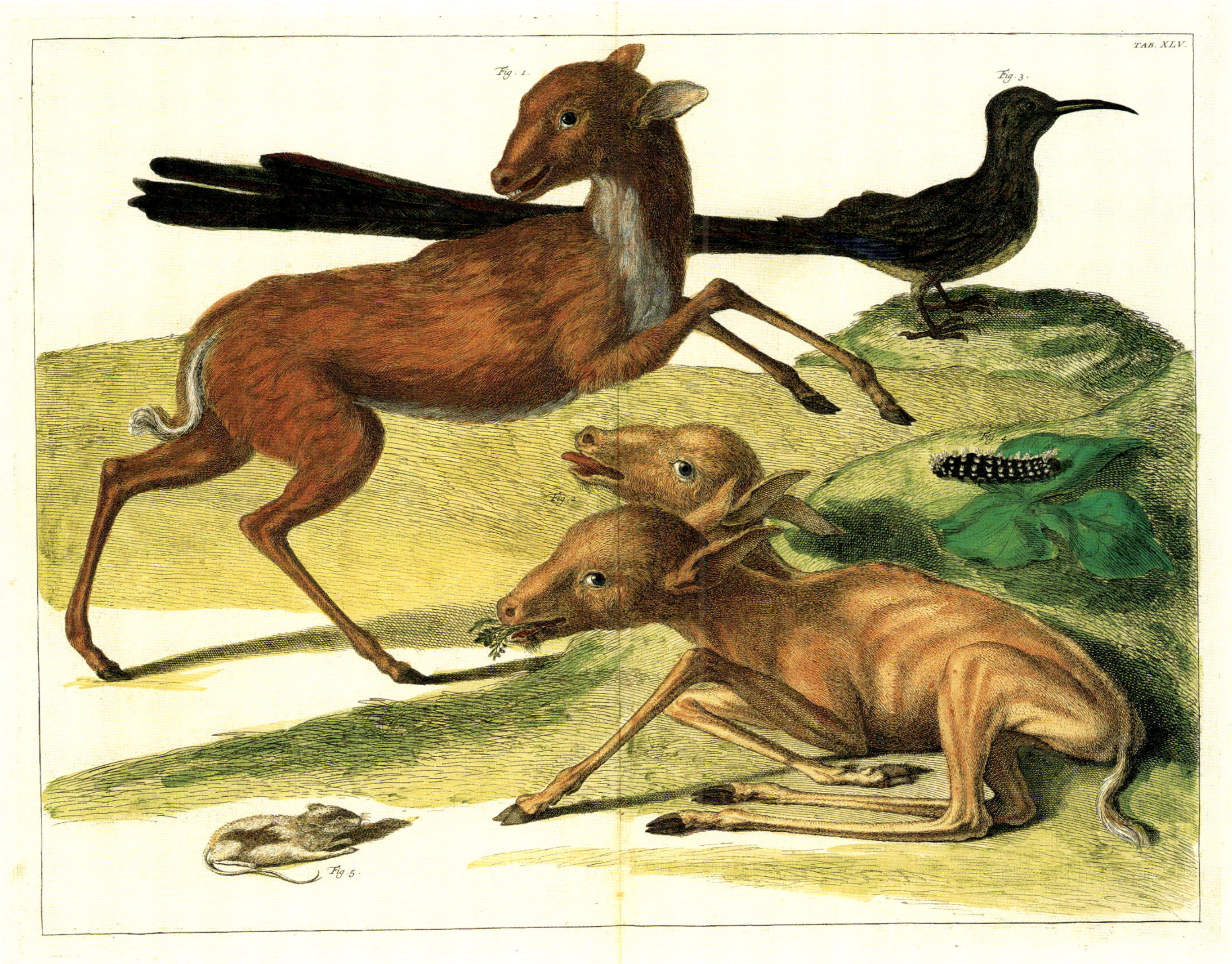

1-2 Cervidae 3 Cuculiformes 4 Lepidoptera 5 *Mus sp.*
1 Deer · Hirsch · Cerf 2 Siamese deer twins · Siamesische Zwillinge von Hirschen · Frères siamois de cerfs 3 Cuculiform bird · Kuckucksvogel · Oiseau cuculiforme
4 Lepidopteran caterpillar · Schmetterlingsraupe · Larve de papillon 5 Mouse · Maus · Souris

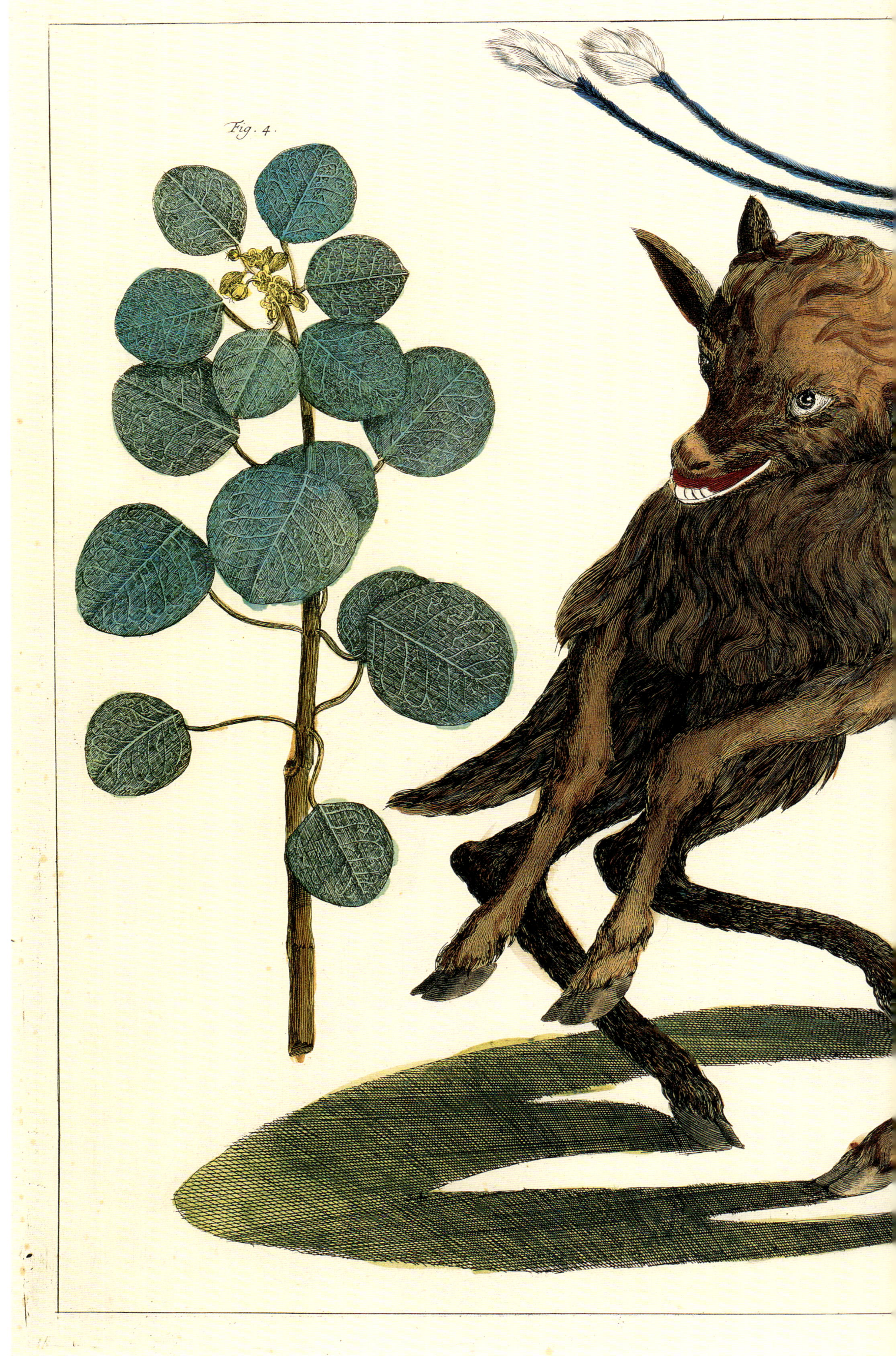

1 *Capra* 2 *Felis* 3 *Tanysiptera galatea* 4 Euphorbiaceae
1 Siamese goat twins · Siamesische Zwillinge von Ziegen · Frères siamois de chèvres 2 Siamese twins of young small cats · Siamesische Zwillinge von jungen Katzenartigen · Frères siamois de chats 3 Common paradise-kingfisher · Spatelliest · Martin-chasseur à longs brins 4 Spurge family · Wolfsmilchgewächs · Euphorbiacées

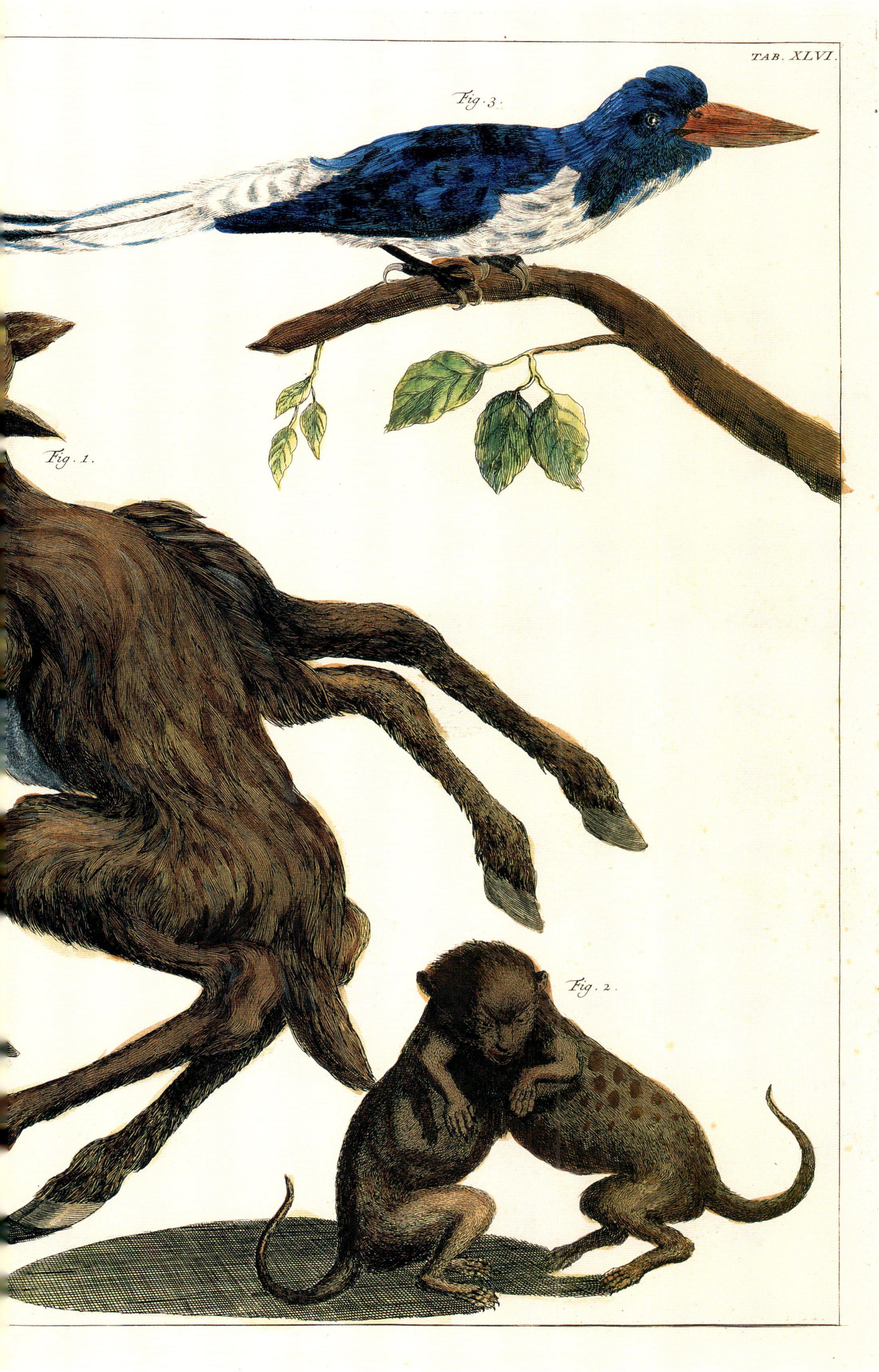
TAB. XLVI.
Fig. 3.
Fig. 1.
Fig. 2.

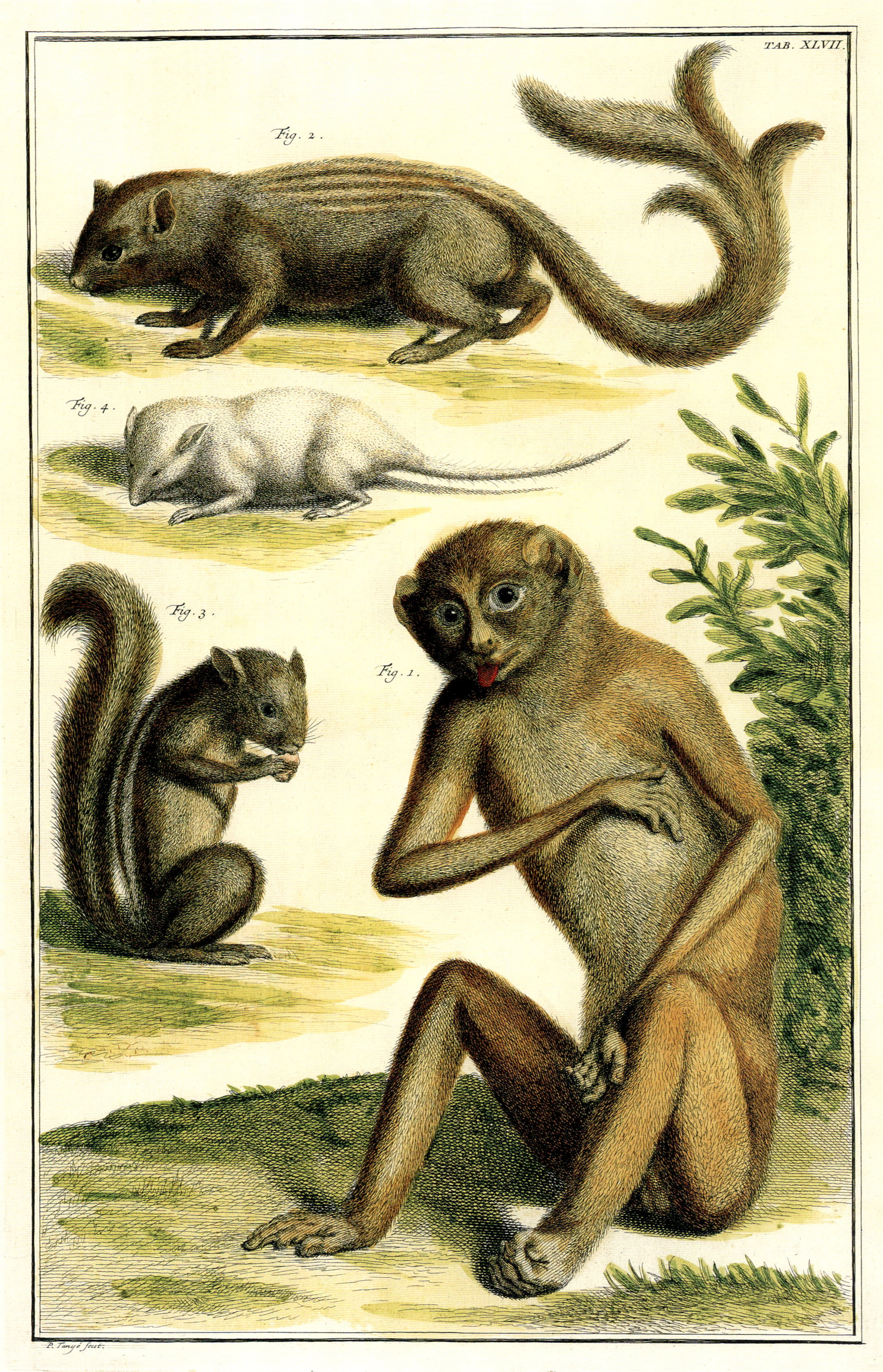

1 *Loris tardigradus* 2 Sciuridae 3 *Funambulus tristriatus* 4 *Mus sp.*
1 Slender loris · Schlanklori · Loris grêle 2 Tree squirrel · Hörnchen · Ecureuil 3 Asiatic striped palm squirrel · Palmenhörnchen · Ecureuil palmiste 4 Mouse · Maus · Souris

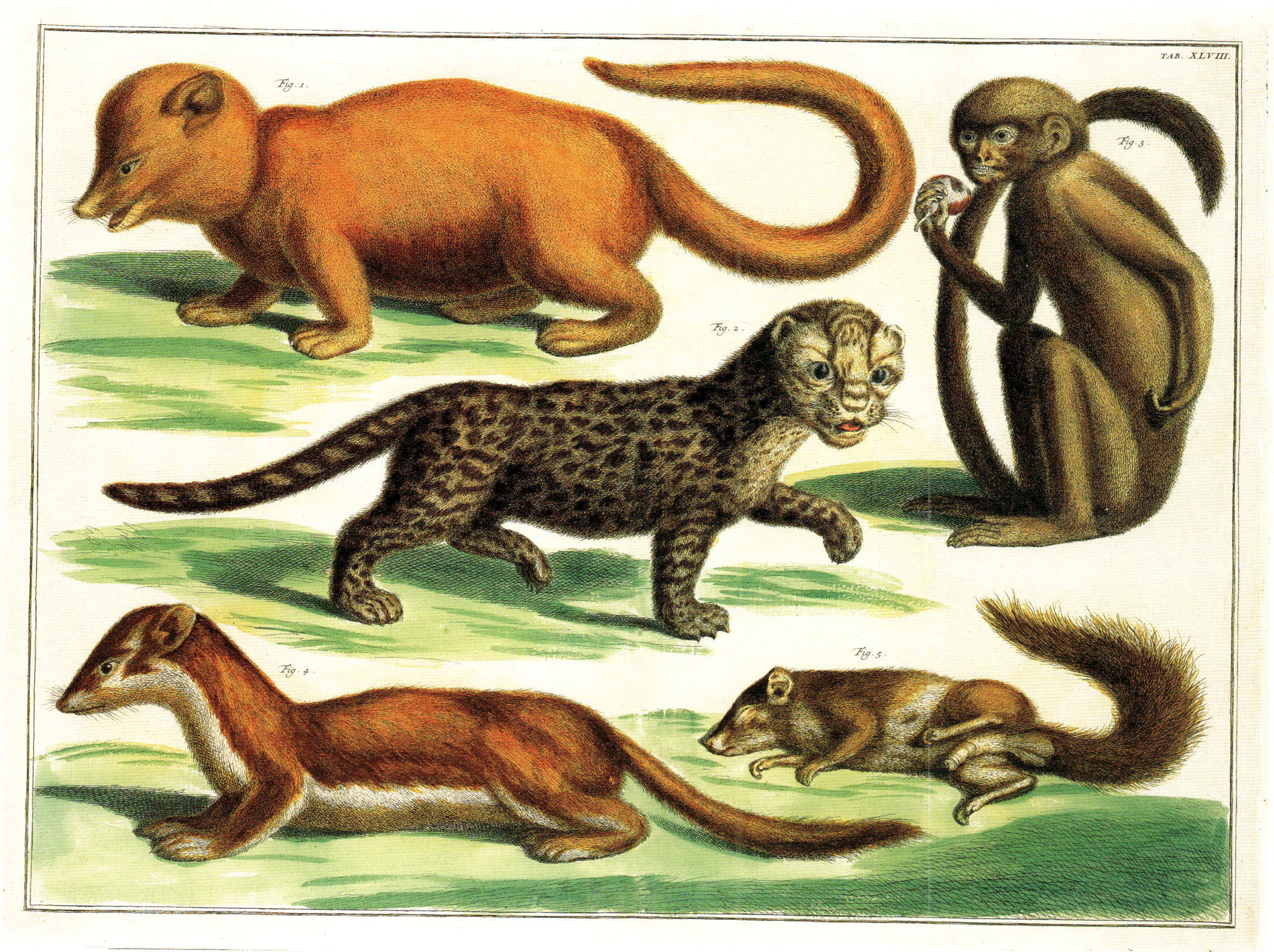

1 Viverridae 2 *Felis* 3 *Cercopithecus mitis* 4 *Mustela erminea* 5 *Sciurus*
1 Civet · Zibetkatze · Civette 2 Small cat · Katzenartige · Chat 3 Blue monkey · Diademmeerkatze · Cercopithèque diadème 4 Ermine · Hermelin · Hermine 5 Tree squirrel · Hörnchen · Ecureuil

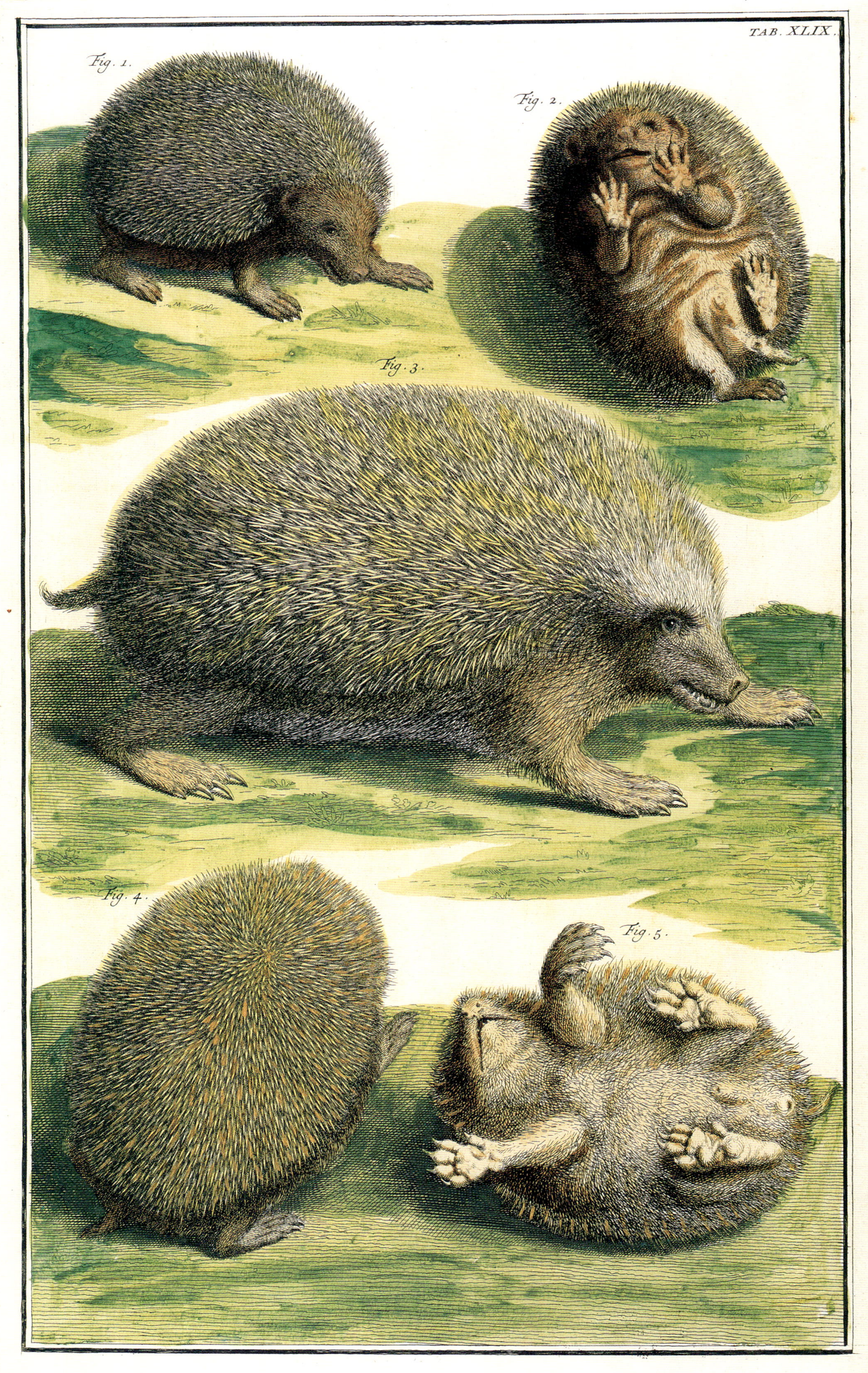

1-2 *Erinaceus europaeus* **3-5** *Erinaceus sp.*
1-2 Hedgehogs · Igel · Hérissons communs **3-5** Hedgehogs · Igel · Hérissons

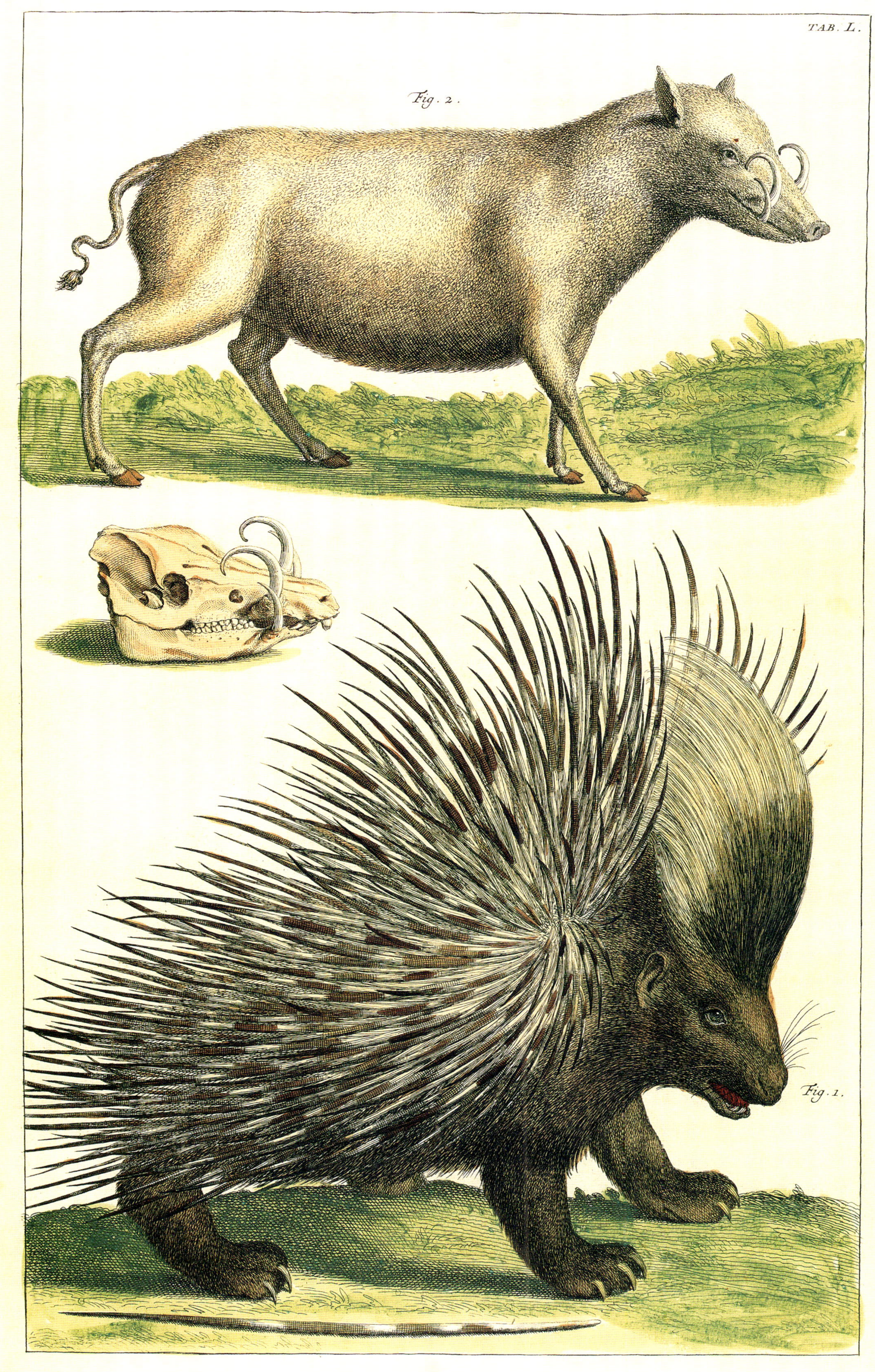

1 *Hystrix cristata* 2-3 *Babyrousa babyrussa*
1 Porcupine · Stachelschwein · Porc-épic à crête 2-3 Babirussa · Hirscheber · Babiroussa

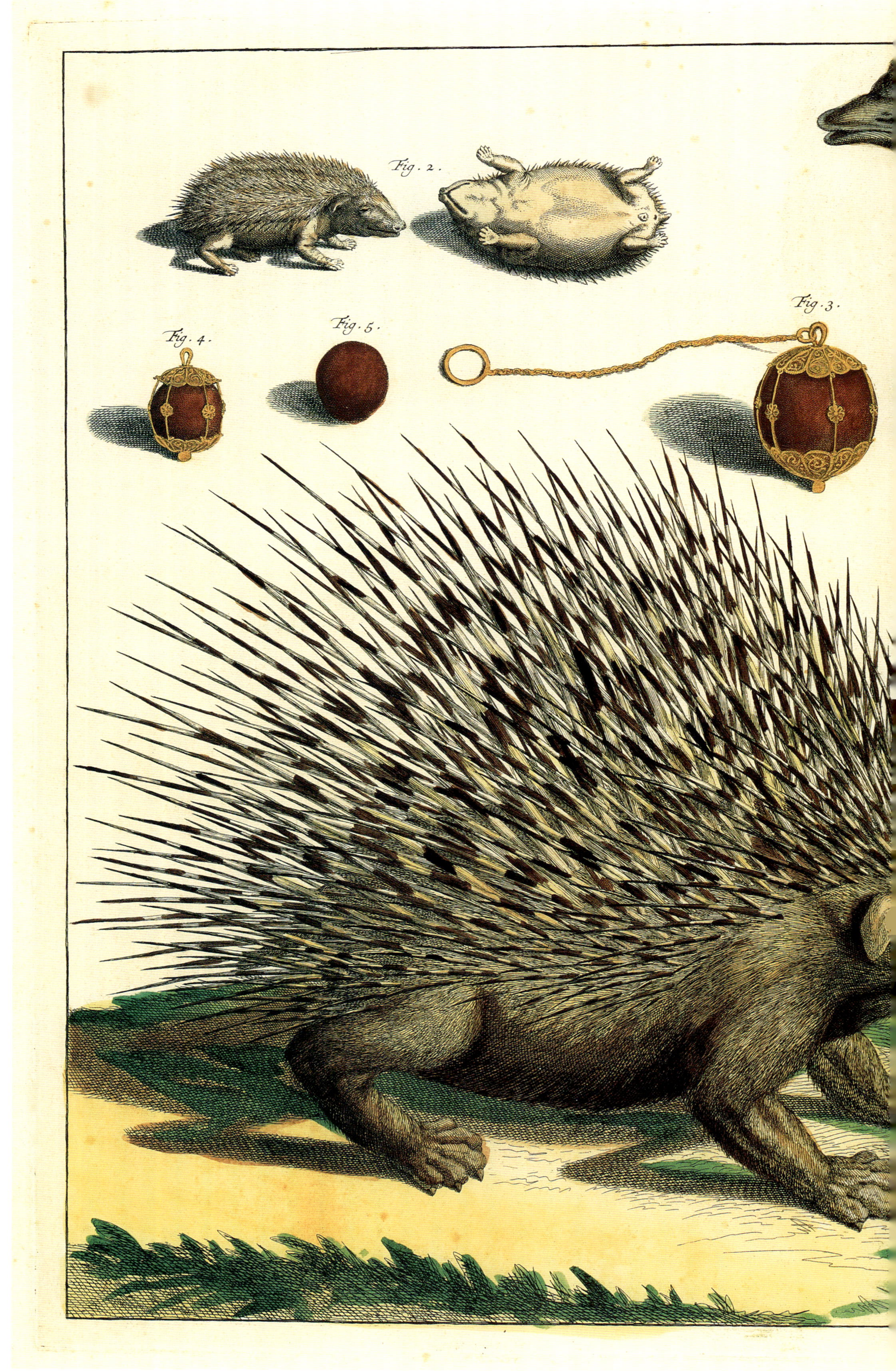

1-2 *Hystrix brachyura* 6 *Struthio camelus*
1-2 Malayan porcupines · Stachelschweine · Porcs-épics 6 Ostrich · Strauß · Autruche d'Afrique

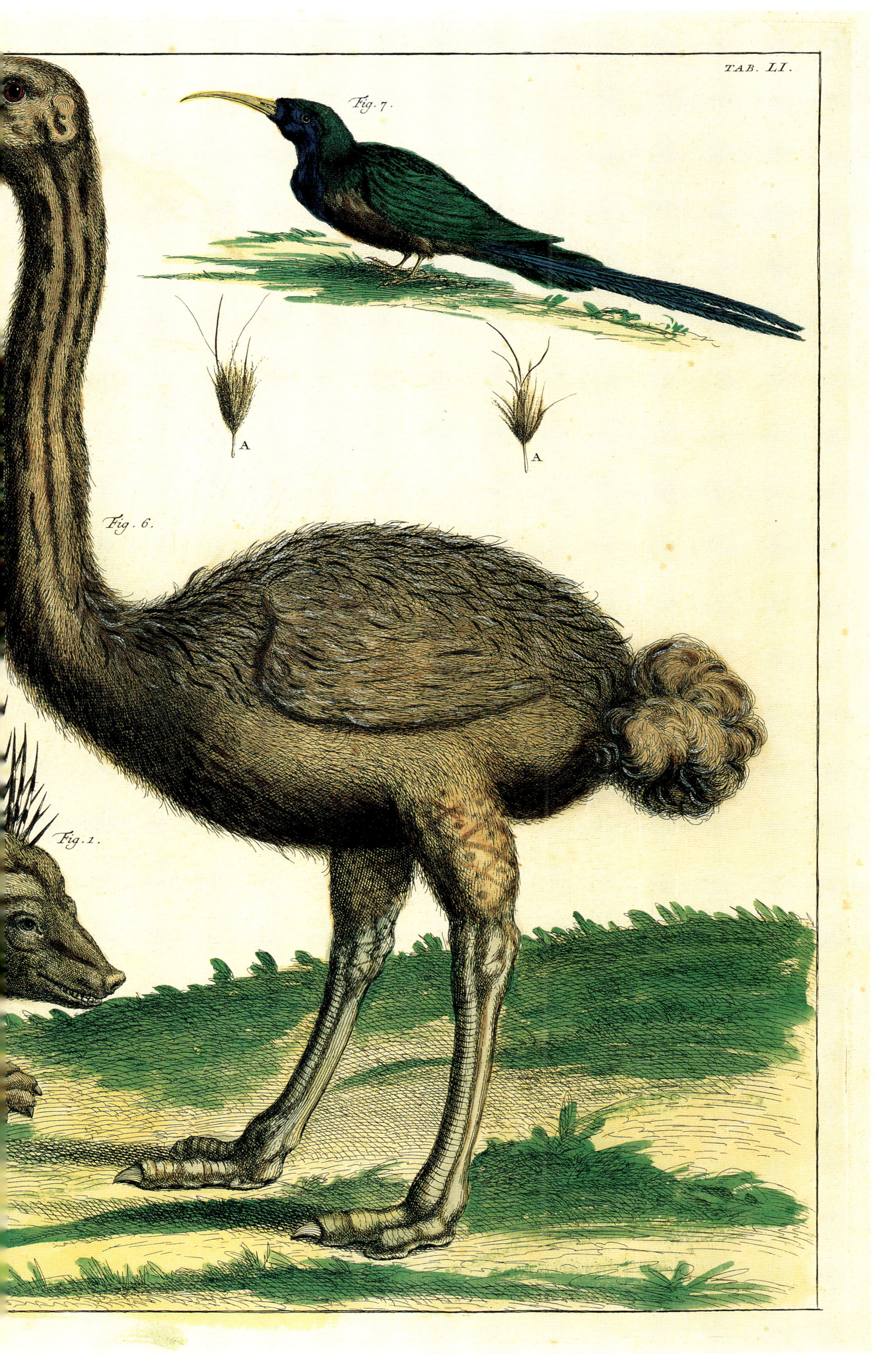
TAB. LI.
Fig. 7.
A
A
Fig. 6.
Fig. 1.

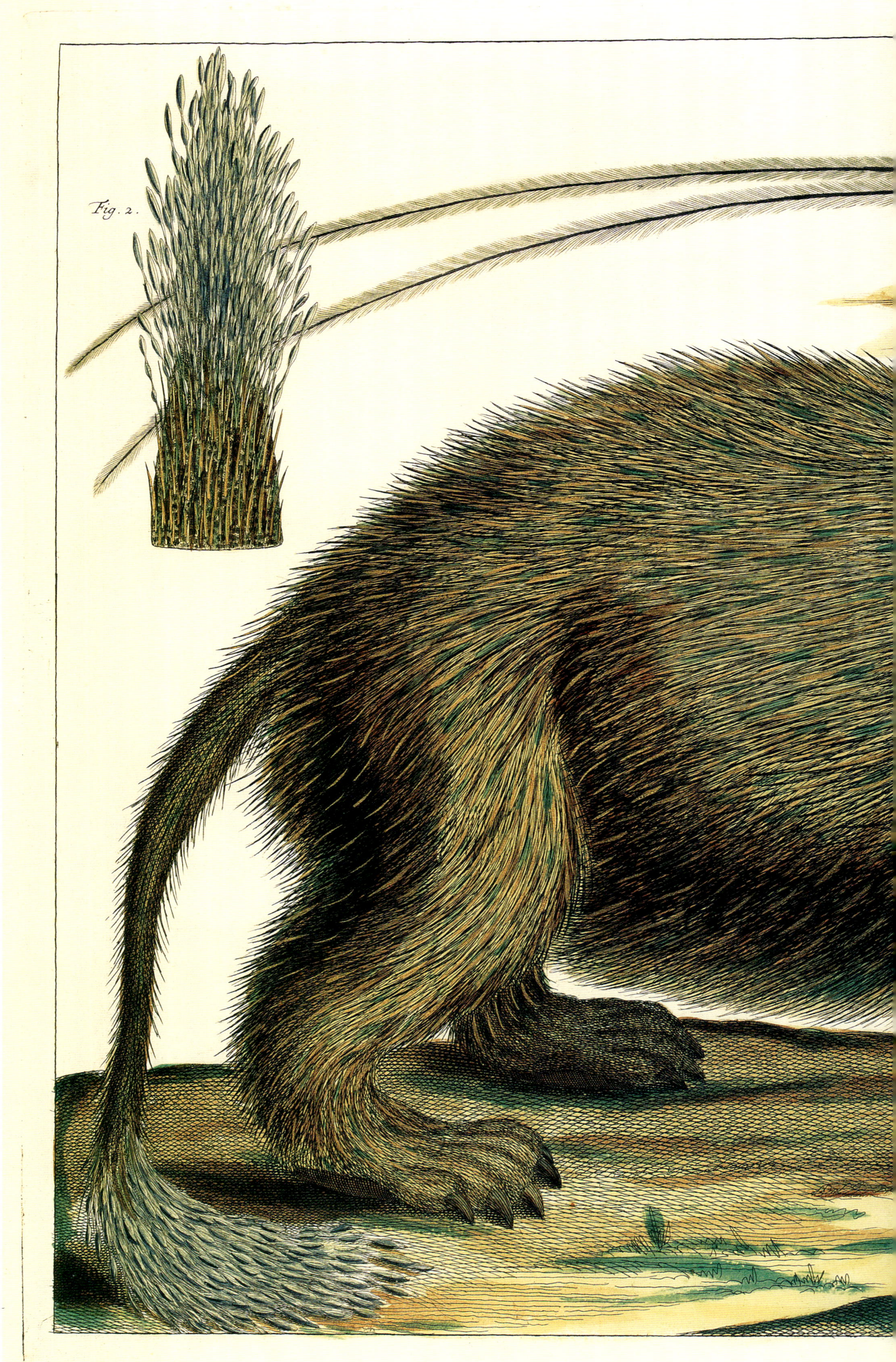

1-2 *Trichys fasciculata* 3 *Terpsiphone paradisi* 4 Crotalus
1-2 Long-tailed porcupine · Malayischer Pinselstachler · Porc-épic à longue queue 3 Asian paradise-flycatcher (dark version) · Fahlbauchparadiesschnäpper (dunkle Form) · Tchitrec de Paradis (plumage sombre) 4 Red diamond rattlesnake · Rote Diamantklapperschlange · Crotale rouge

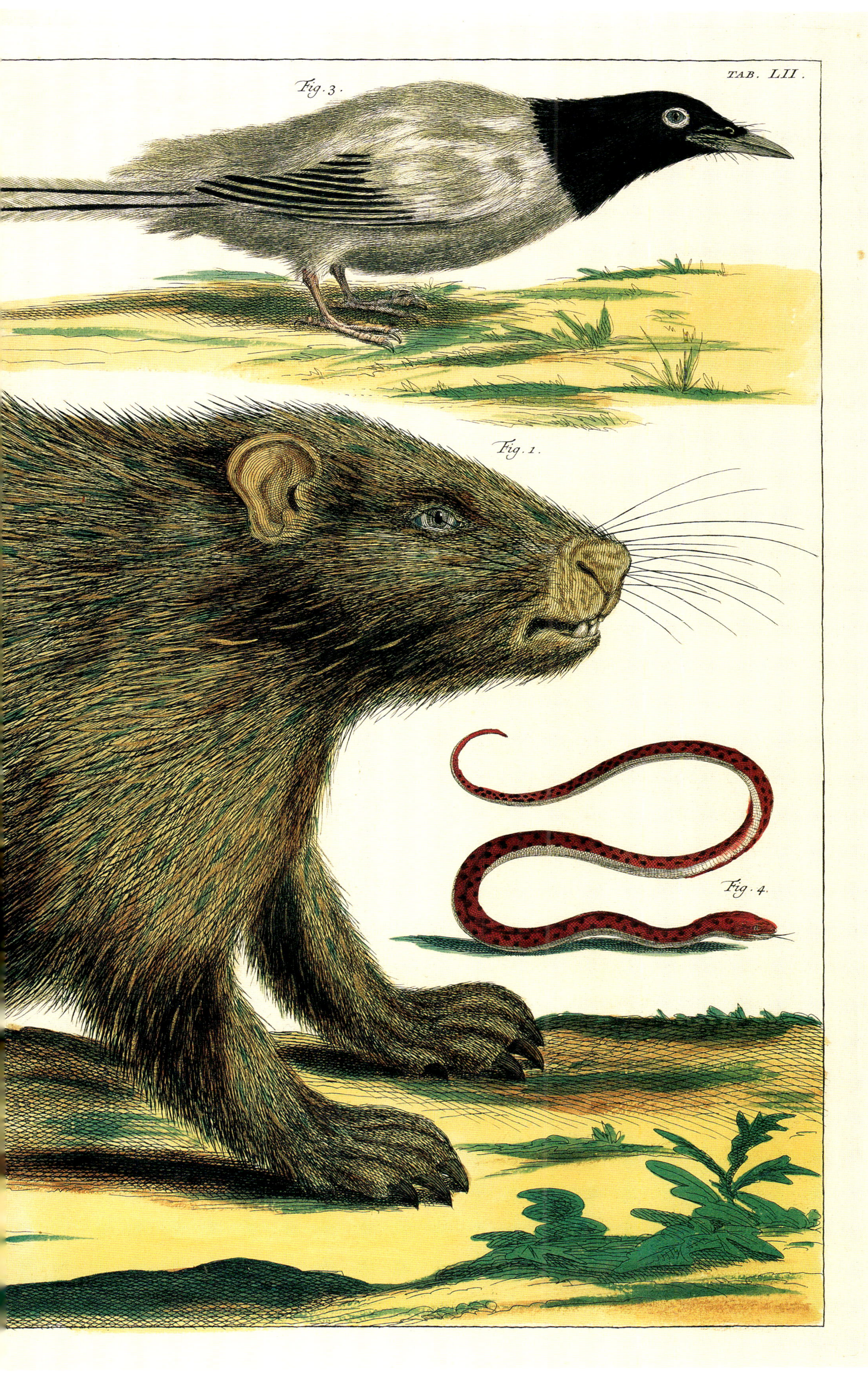
Fig. 3.
TAB. LII.
Fig. 1.
Fig. 4.

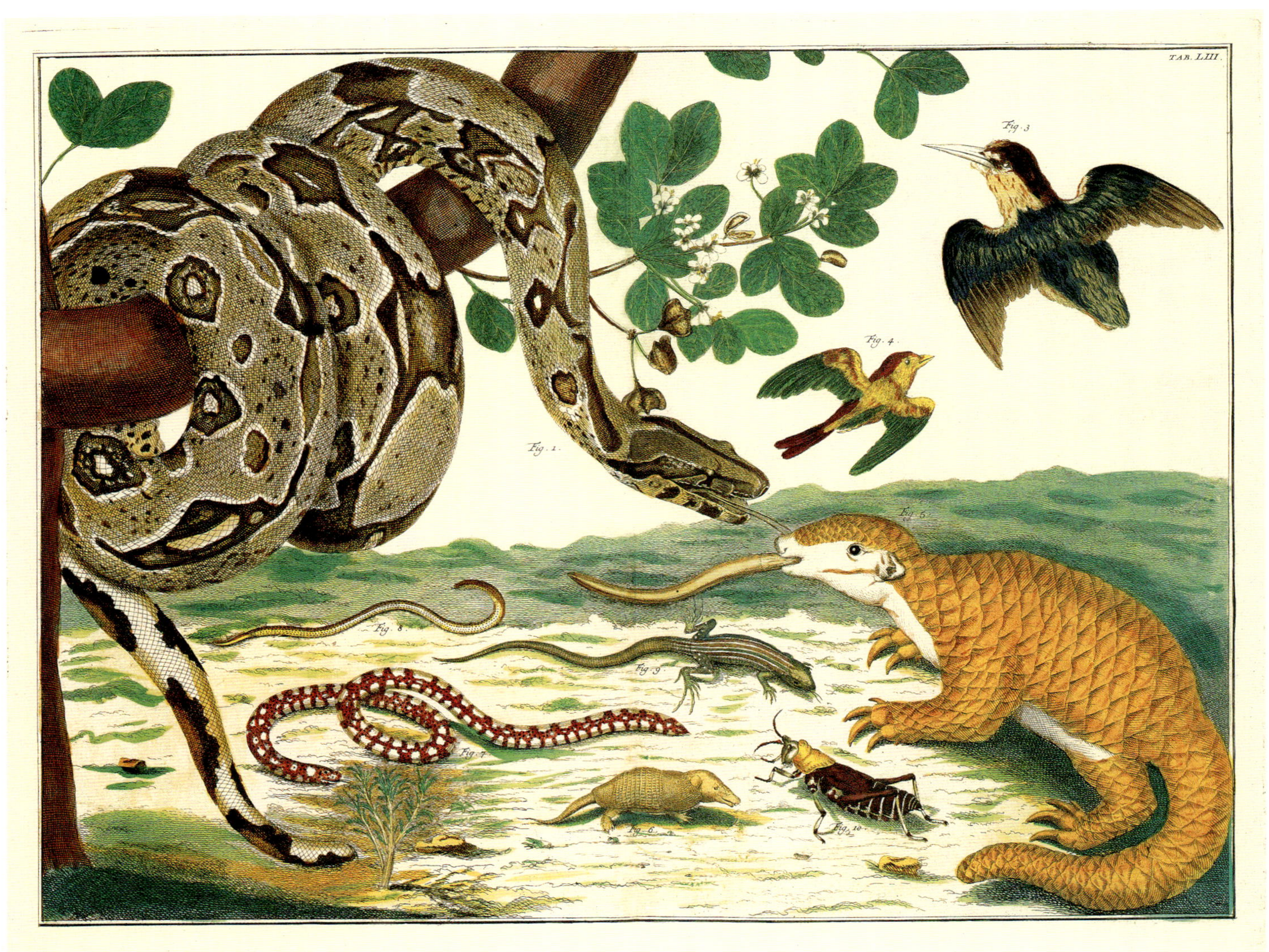

1 *Boa constrictor* **2** *Guaiacum sp.* **3** Alcedinidae **5** *Manis sp.* **6** *Dasypus novemcinctus* **7** Amphisbaenia sp.? **8** Serpentes **9** Lacertidae **10** Saltatoria: Caelifera
1 Common boa · Abgottschlange · Boa constricteur **2** Lignum vitae · Guajakbaum · Bois de gaïac **3** Kingfisher · Eisvogel · Martin-pêcheur **5** Pangolin · Schuppentier · Pangolin **6** Nine-banded armadillo · Neunbinden-Gürteltier · Tatou à neuf bandes **7** Worm lizard · Doppelschleiche · Amphisbène **8** Snake, according to Seba from the Orient · Schlange, nach Seba aus dem Orient · Serpent, d'Orient selon Seba **9** Lizard · Eidechse · Lézard **10** Saltatorian · Kurzfühlerschrecke · Sauterelle à antennes courtes

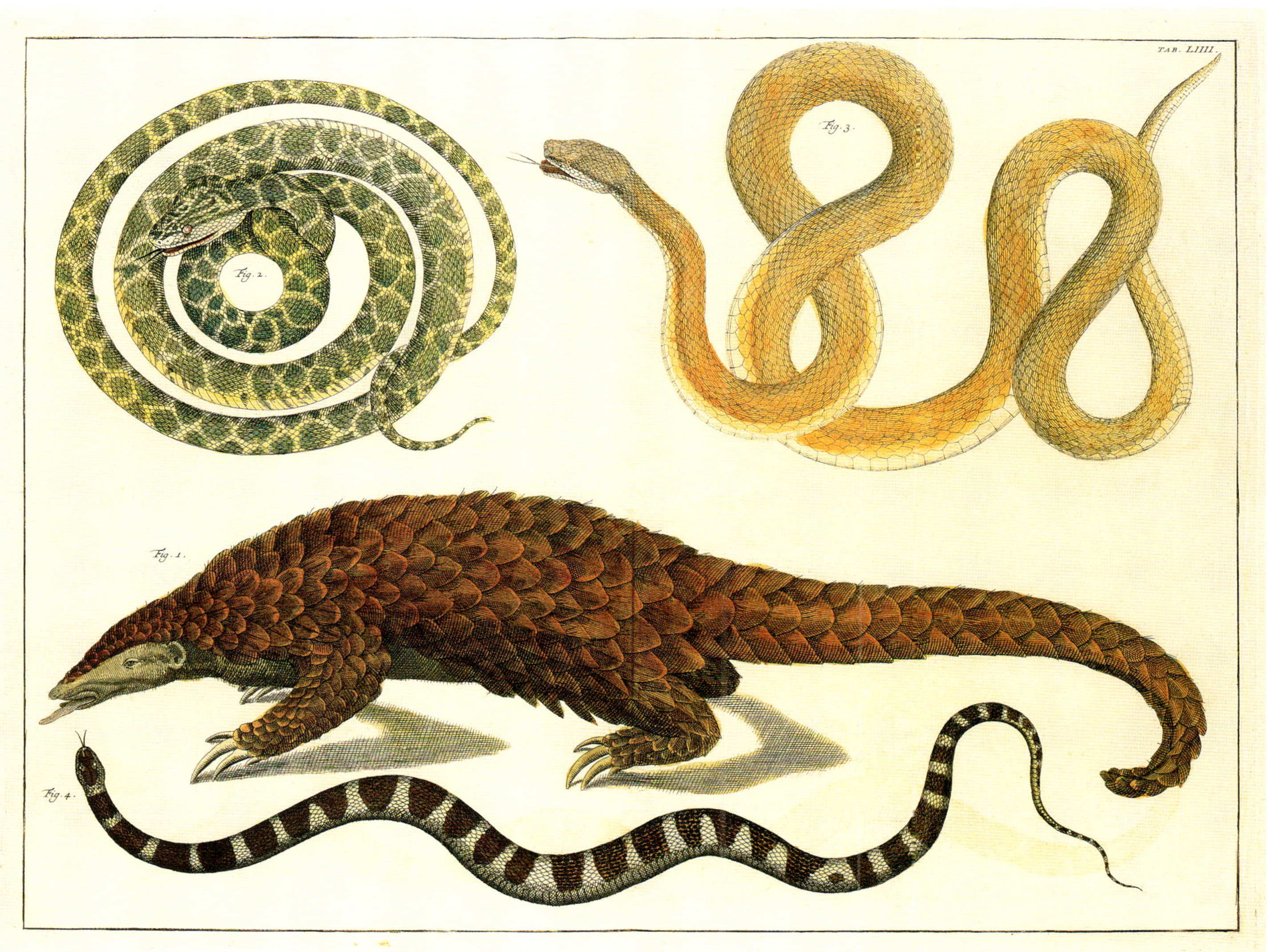

1 Manis sp. 2 Corallus hortulanus 3 Psammophis schokari? 4 Serpentes
1 Pangolin · Schuppentier · Pangolin 2 Amazon tree boa · Gewöhnliche Hundskopfboa · Boa canin 3 Forskål's sandsnake · Schlanke Sandrennnatter · Couleuvre des sables
4 Snake, according to Seba from Africa · Schlange, nach Seba aus Afrika · Serpent, d'Afrique selon Seba

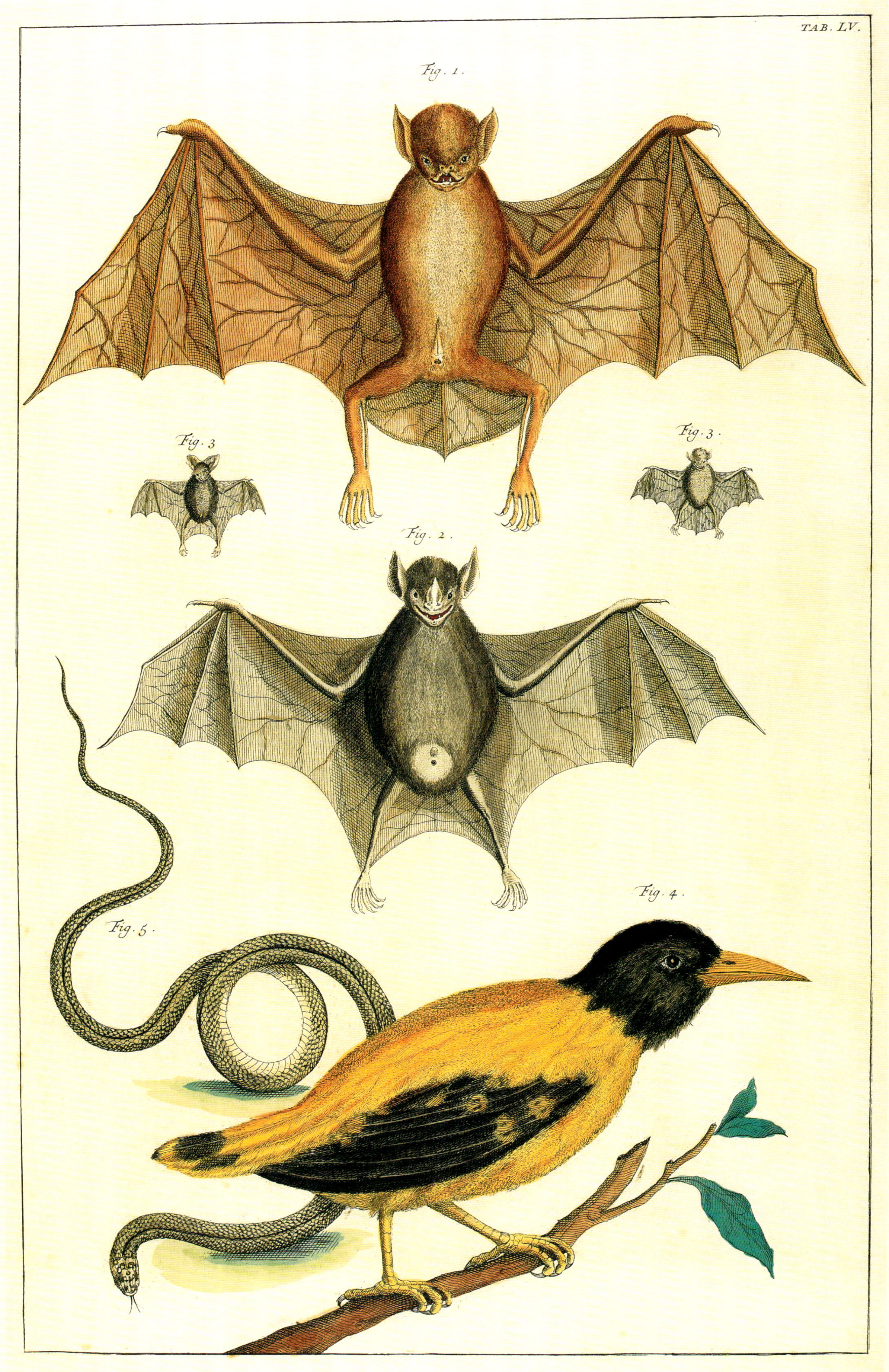

1 *Noctilio sp.* 2 *Carollia perspicillata* 3 Chiroptera 4 *Icterus granduacauda* 5 Serpentes
1 Bulldog bat · Bulldoggen-Fledermaus · Noctilion pêcheuse 2 Seba's short-tailed bat · Blattnase · Vespertilion à nez plat 3 Bats · Fledermäuse · Chauve-souris
4 Black-headed oriole (Audubon's Oriole) · Schwarzkopftrupial · Oriole d'Audubon 5 Snake, according to Seba from America · Schlange, nach Seba aus Amerika · Serpent, d'Amérique selon Seba

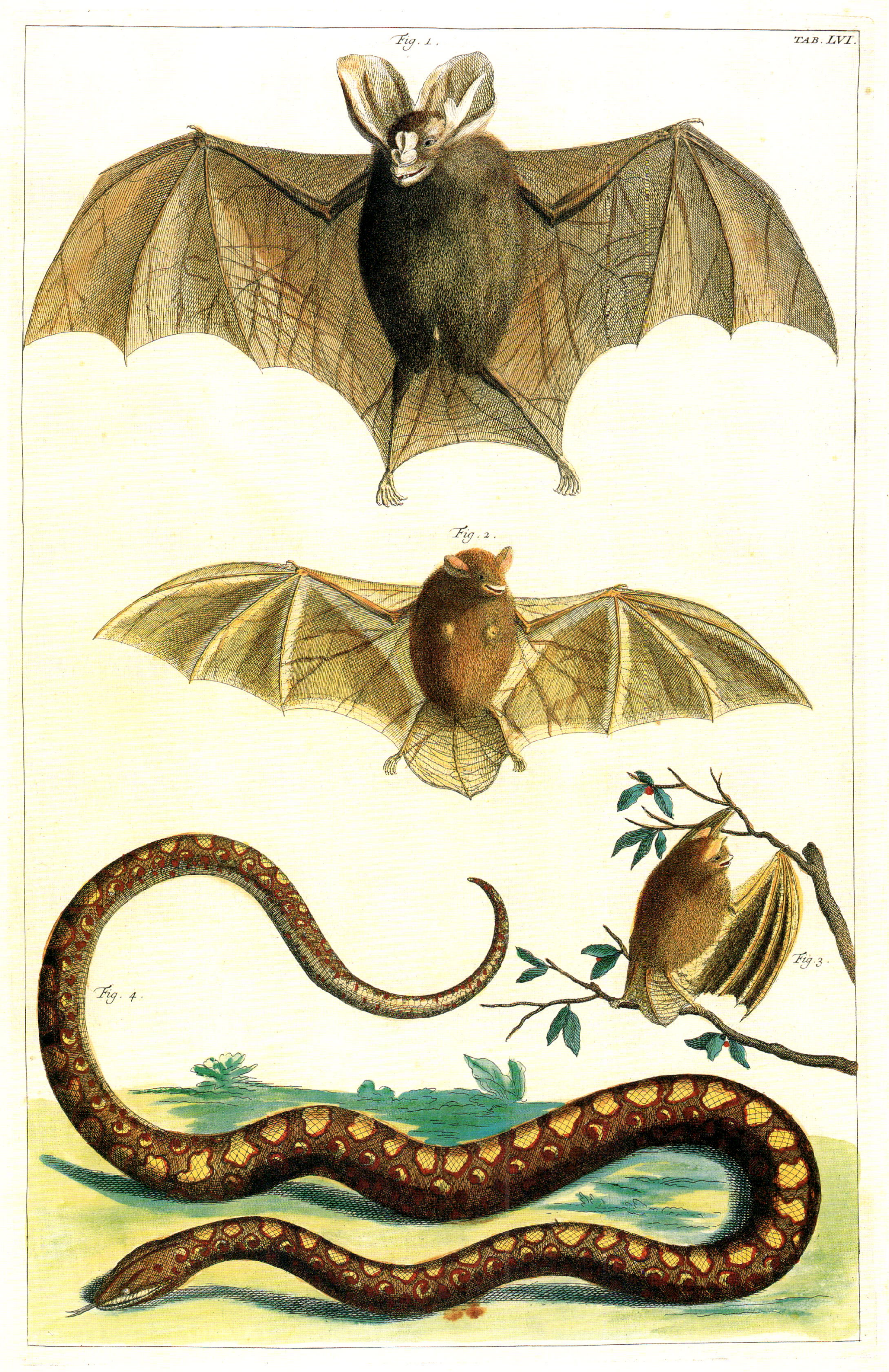

1 Megadermatidae **2-3** *Kerivoula picta* **4** Serpentes
1 False vampire bats · Falscher Vampir · Mégaderme **2-3** Long-winged bats · Langflügel-Fledermäuse · Kerivoules **4** Snake, according to Seba from Ternate · Schlange, nach Seba aus Ternate · Serpent, de Ternate selon Seba

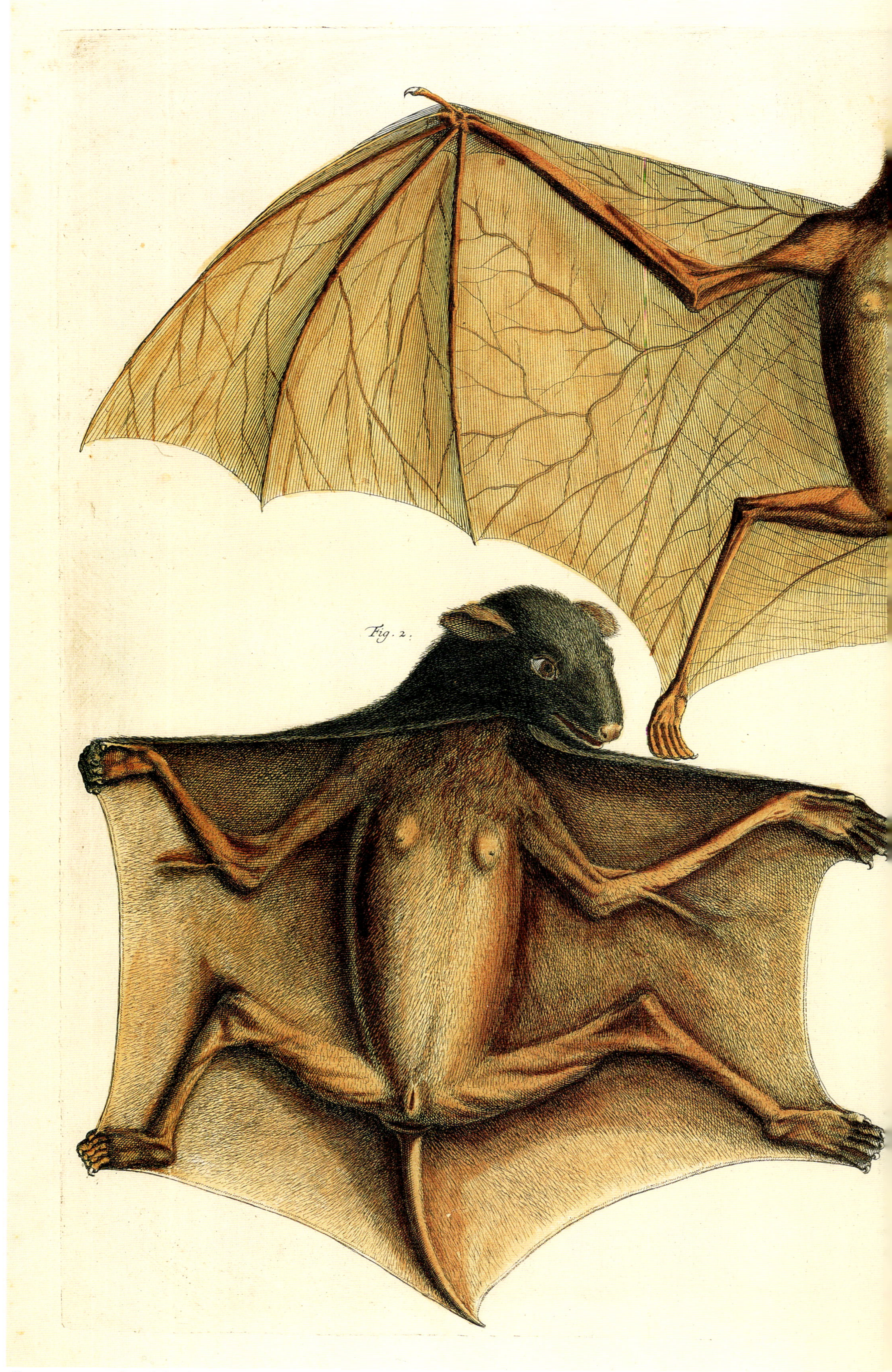

1 *Vampyrum spectrum* 2-3 *Cynocephalus volans*
1 Spectral bat · Vampir-Fledermaus · Vampire commun 2-3 Philippine flying lemur · Philippinen-Gleitflieger · Galéopithèque volant

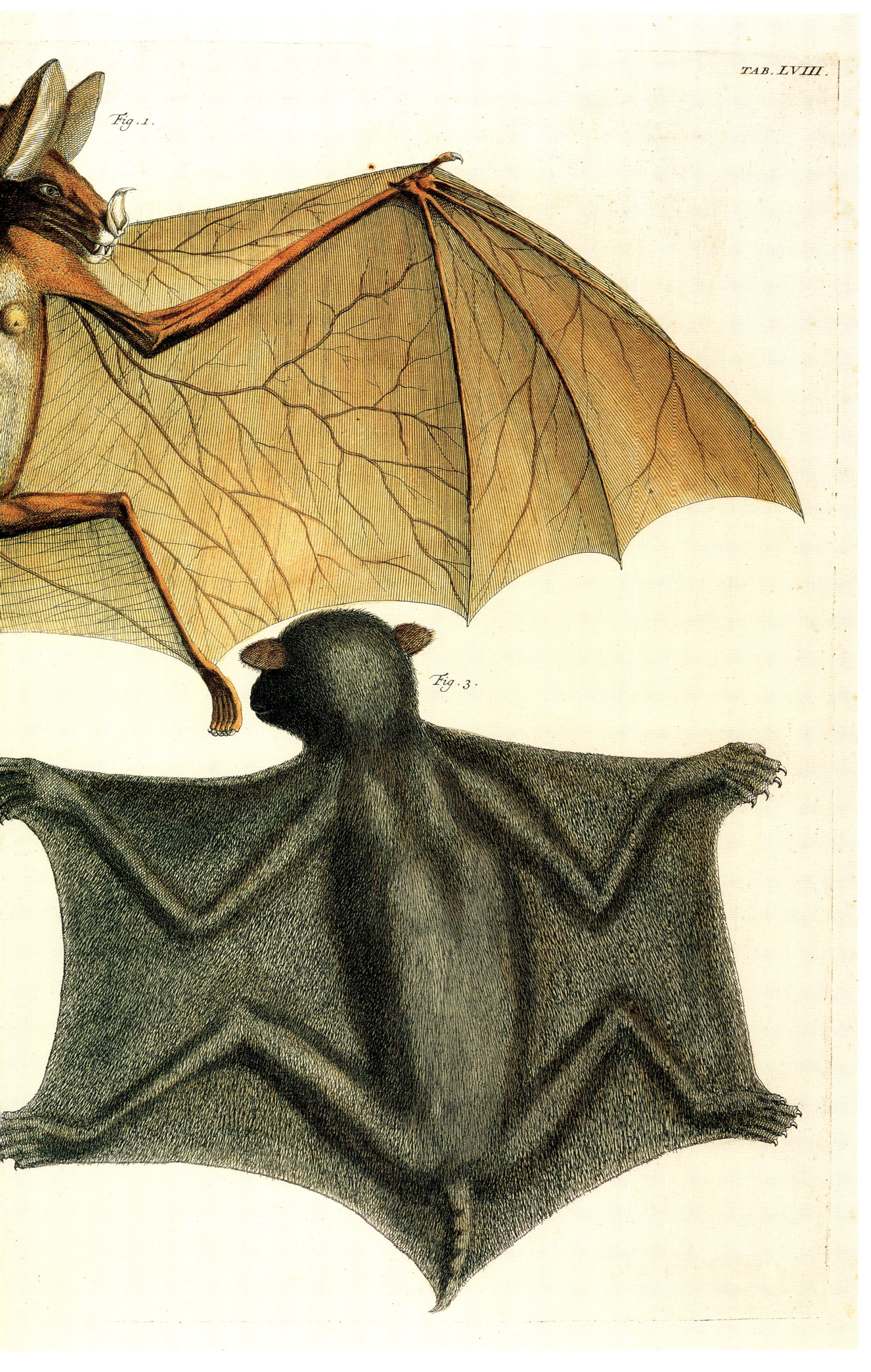
TAB. LVIII.
Fig. 1.
Fig. 3.

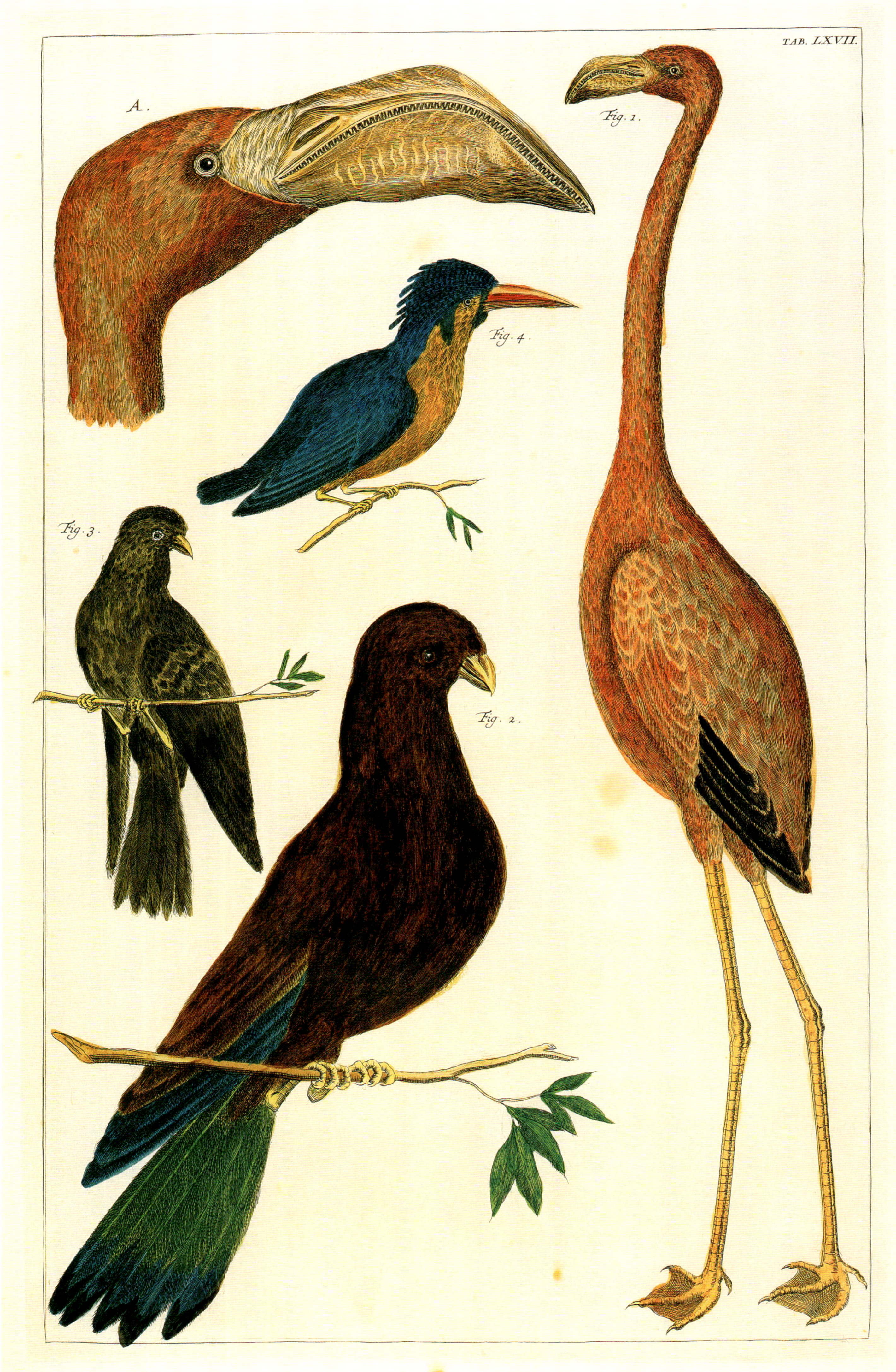

1 *Phoenicopterus ruber* 2 Columbidae 4 Alcedinidae
1 Greater flamingo · Flamingo · Flamant rose 2 Pigeons & doves · Taube · Pigeon 4 Kingfisher · Eisvogel · Martin-pêcheur

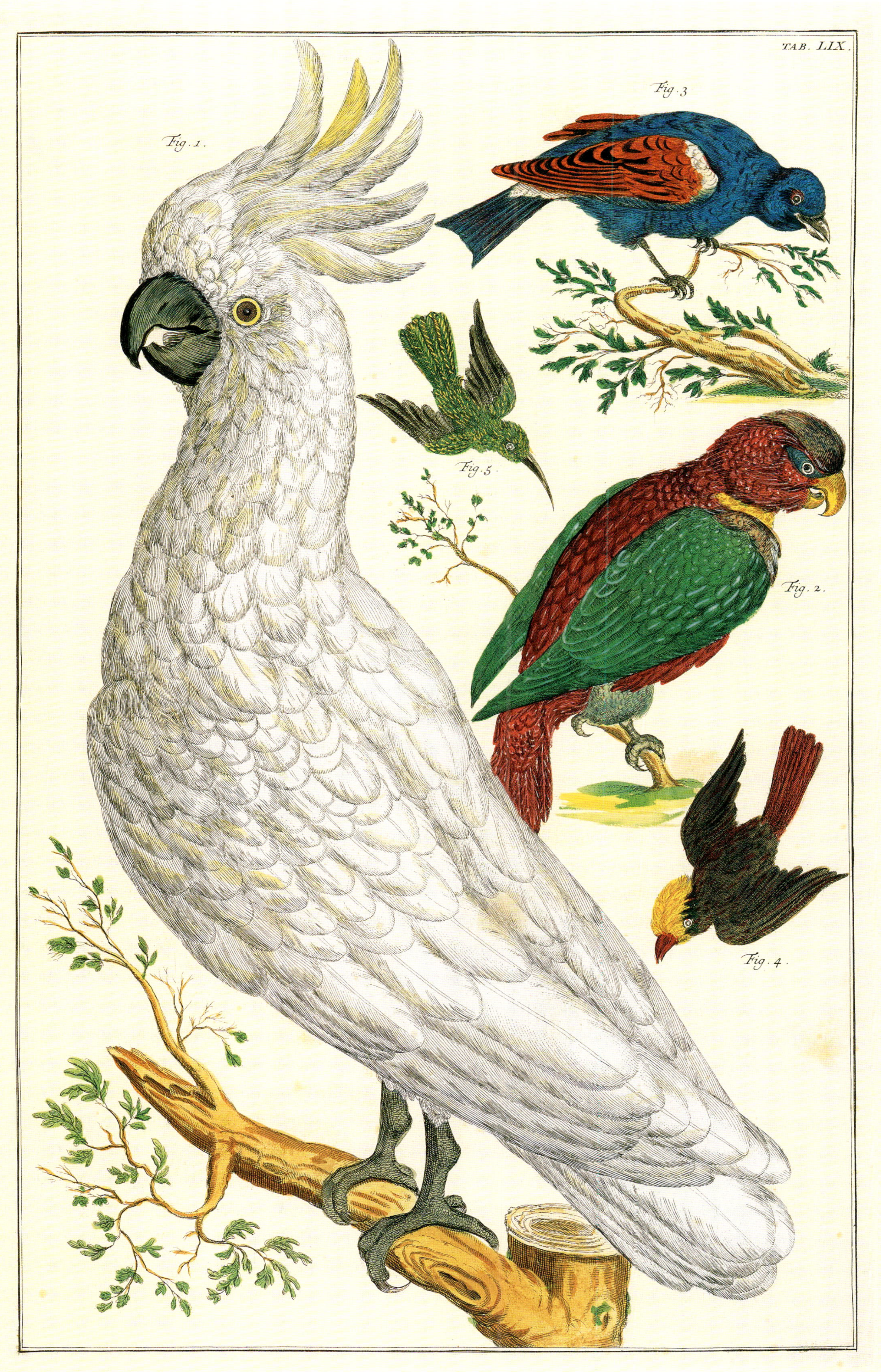

1 *Cacatua sulphurea* 2 *Deroptys accipitrinus* 3 *Agelaius tricolor* 4 *Antilophia galeata* 5 Trochilidae
1 Lesser sulphur-crested cockatoo · Gelbwangenkakadu · Cacatoès soufré 2 Hawk-headed parrot · Fächerpapagei · Papegeai maillé 3 Tricolored blackbird · Dreifarbenstärling · Carouge de Californie 4 Helmeted manakin · Helmpipra · Manakin casqué 5 Hummingbird · Kolibri · Colibri

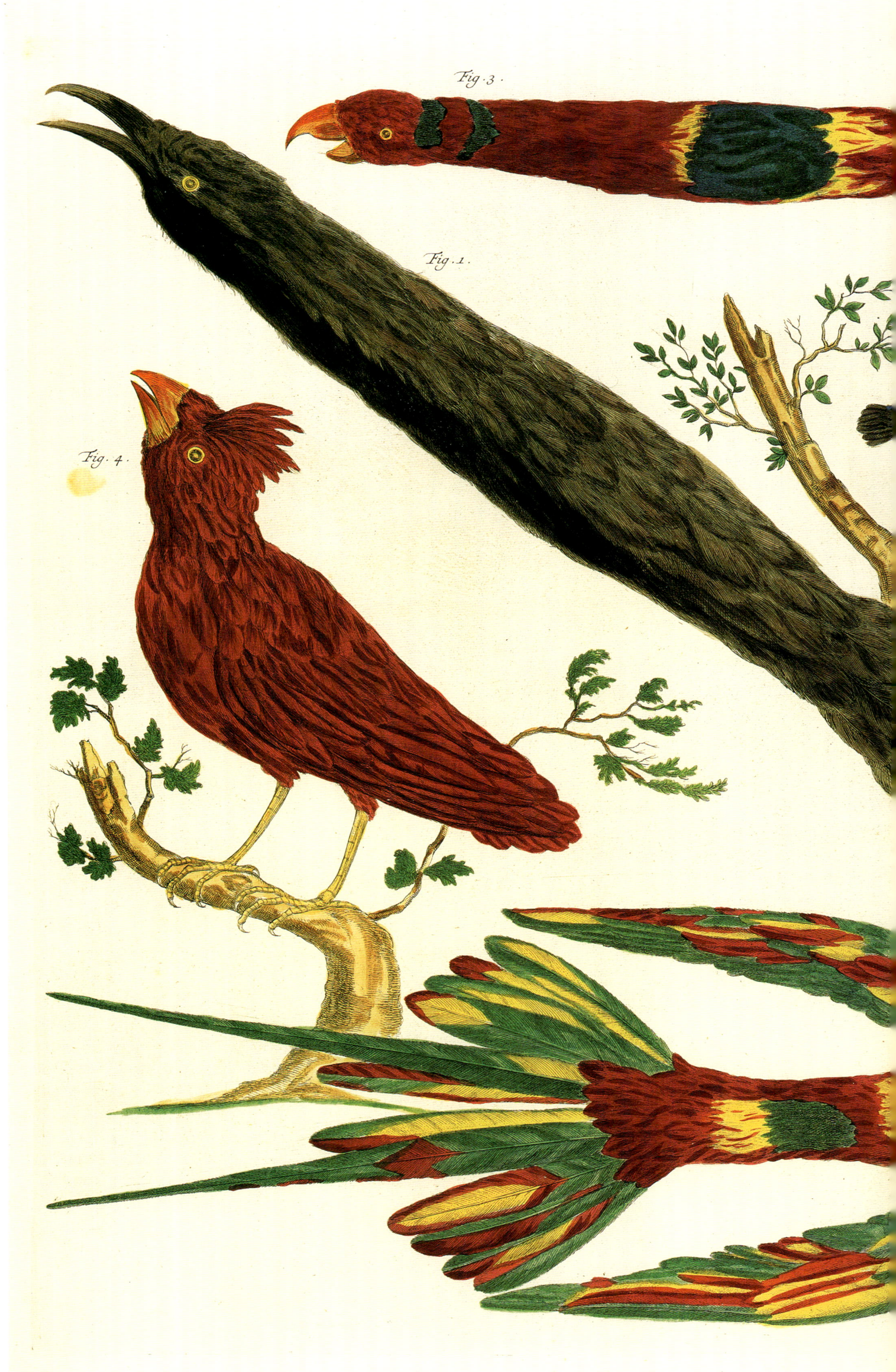

1 Quiscalus sp. 2-3 Psittaculidae 4 *Cardinalis cardinalis* 5 *Cyanerpes cyaneus* 6 *Tangara guttata* 7 *Pipra erythrocephala* 8 *Pipra rubrocapilla*
1 Grackle · Grackel · Quiscale bronzé 2-3 Parrots · Edelpapageien · Perroquets 4 Common cardinal · Rotkardinal · Cardinal rouge 5 Red-legged honeycreeper · Türkisnaschvogel · Guit-guit sai 6 Speckled Tanger · Tropfentangare · Calliste tiqueté 7 Golden-headed manakin · Goldkopfpipra · Manakin à tête d'or 8 Red-headed manakin · Rotkopfpipra · Manakin à tête rouge

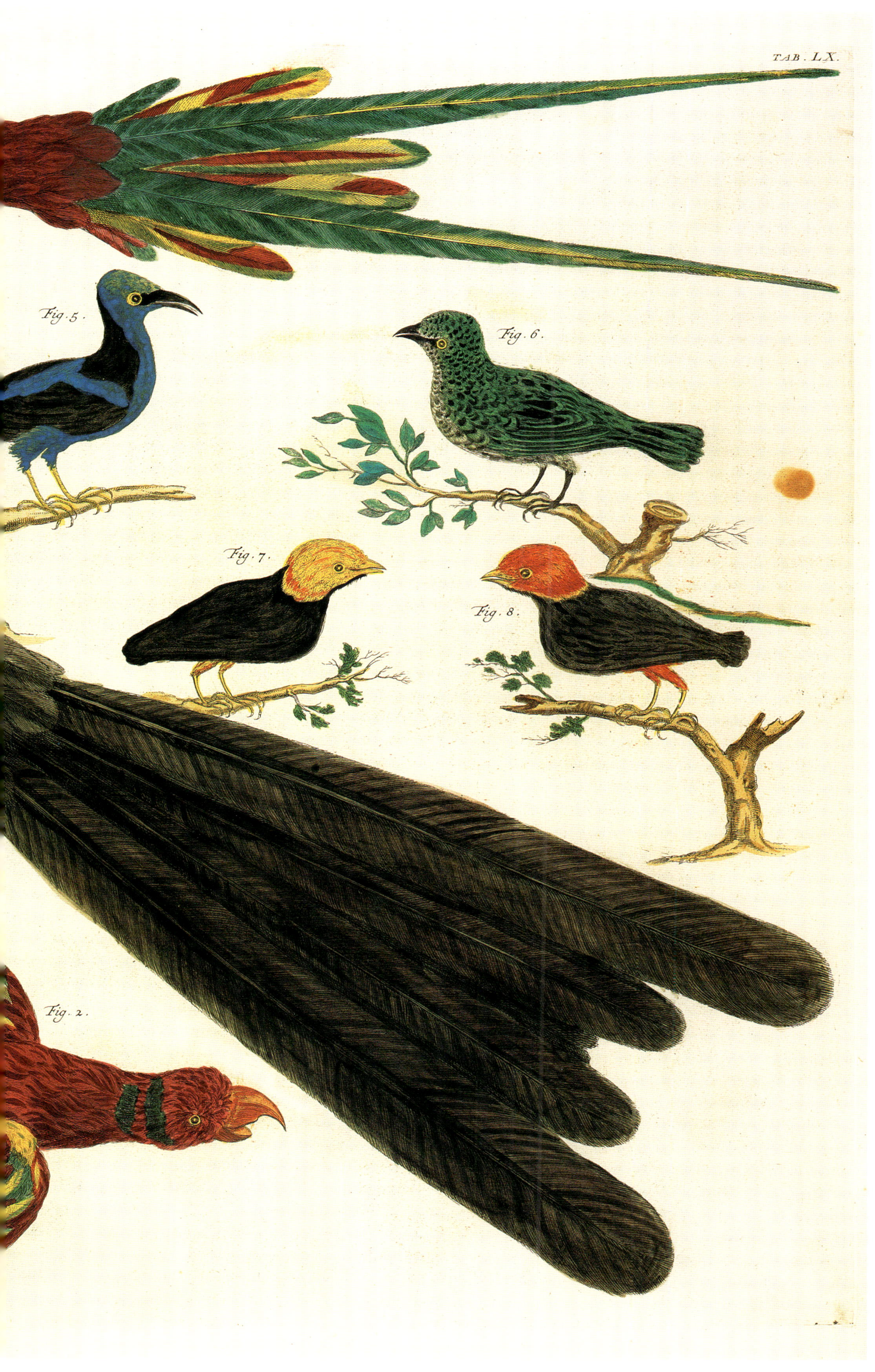
TAB. LX.
Fig. 5.
Fig. 6.
Fig. 7.
Fig. 8.
Fig. 2.

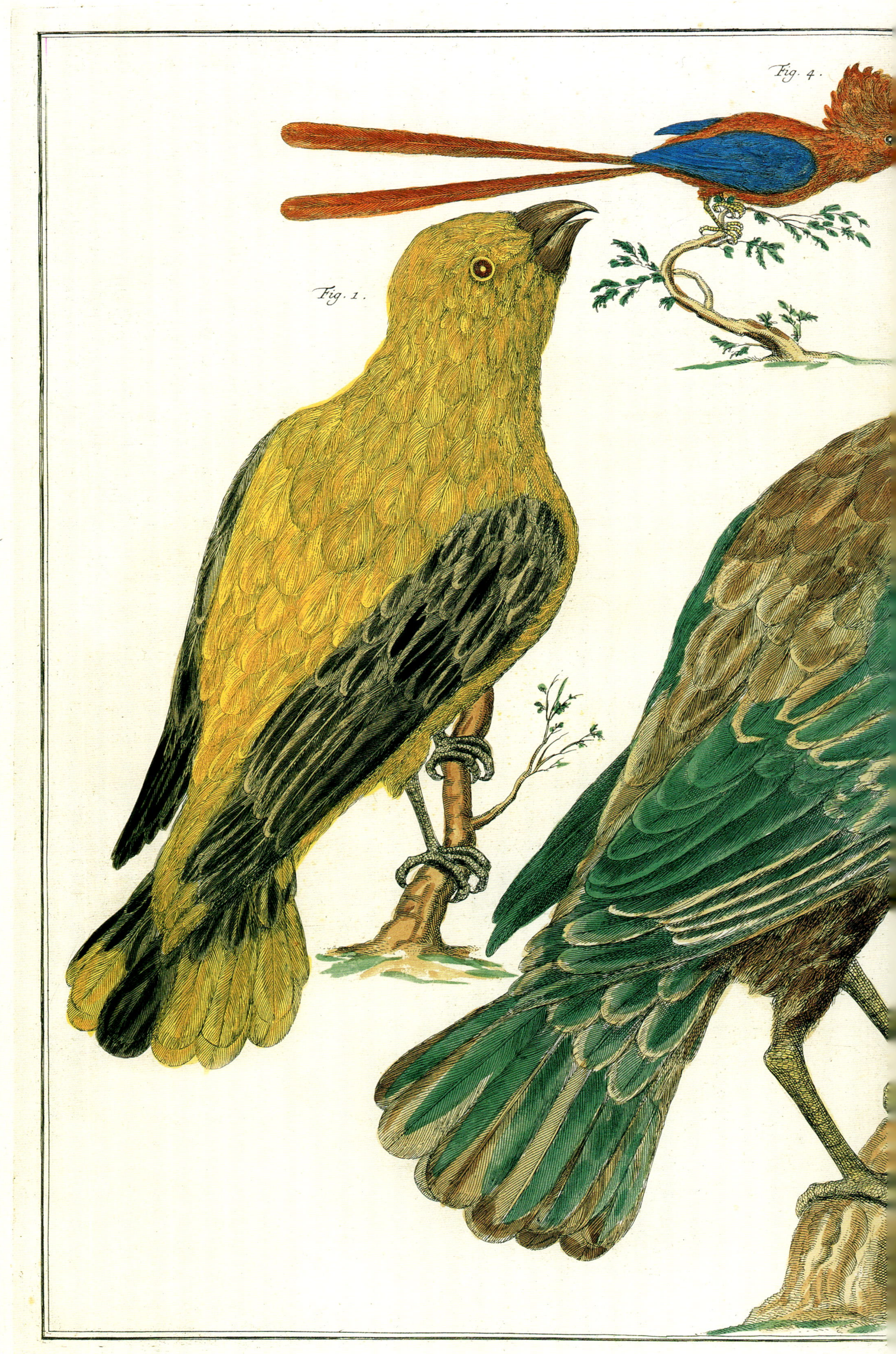

Aves 3 Oriolidae 5 Trochilidae
Various birds · Verschiedene Vögel · Oiseaux divers 3 Oriol · Pirol · Merle doré 5 Hummingbird · Kolibri · Colibri

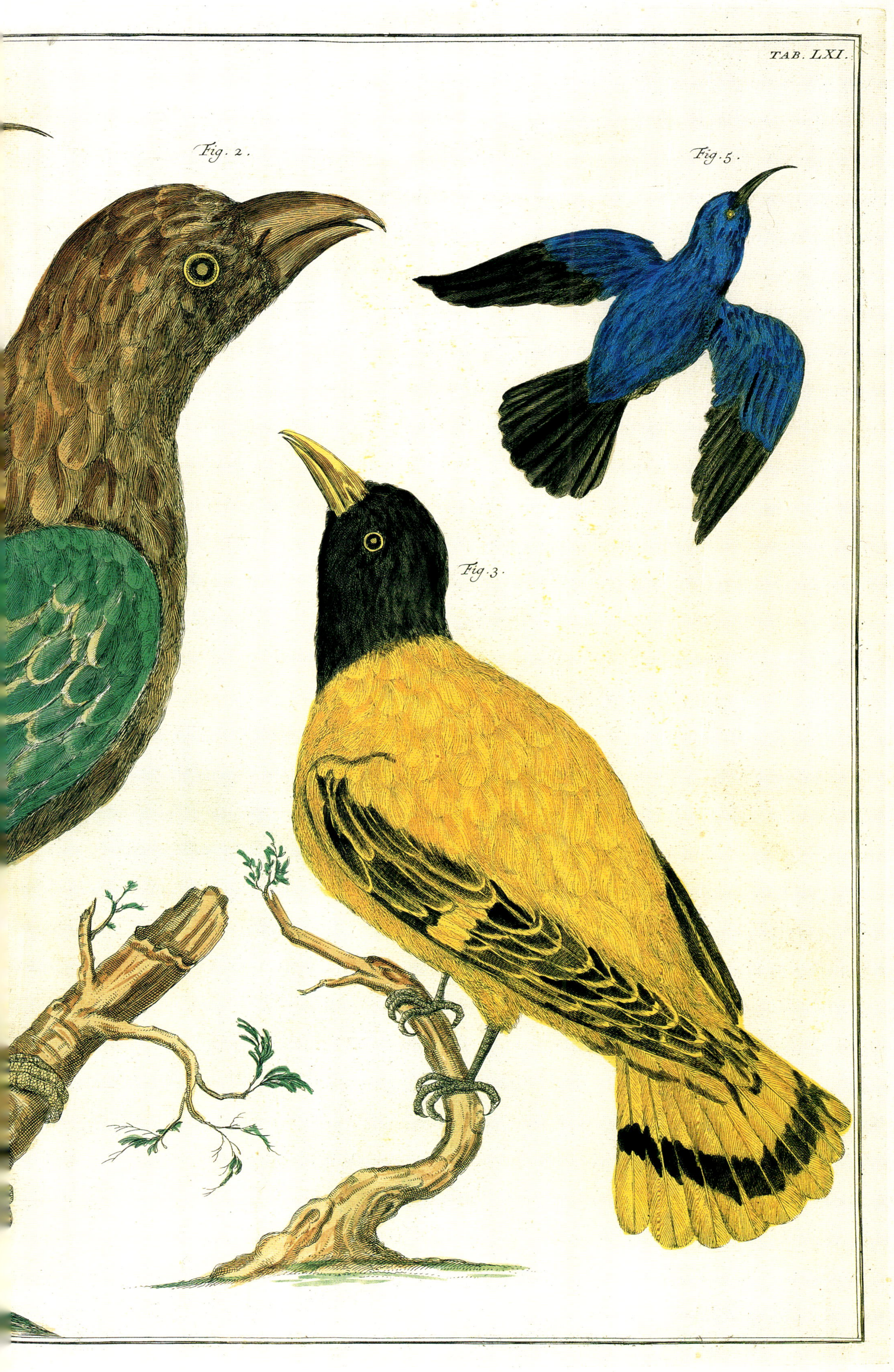
TAB. LXI.
Fig. 2.
Fig. 5.
Fig. 3.

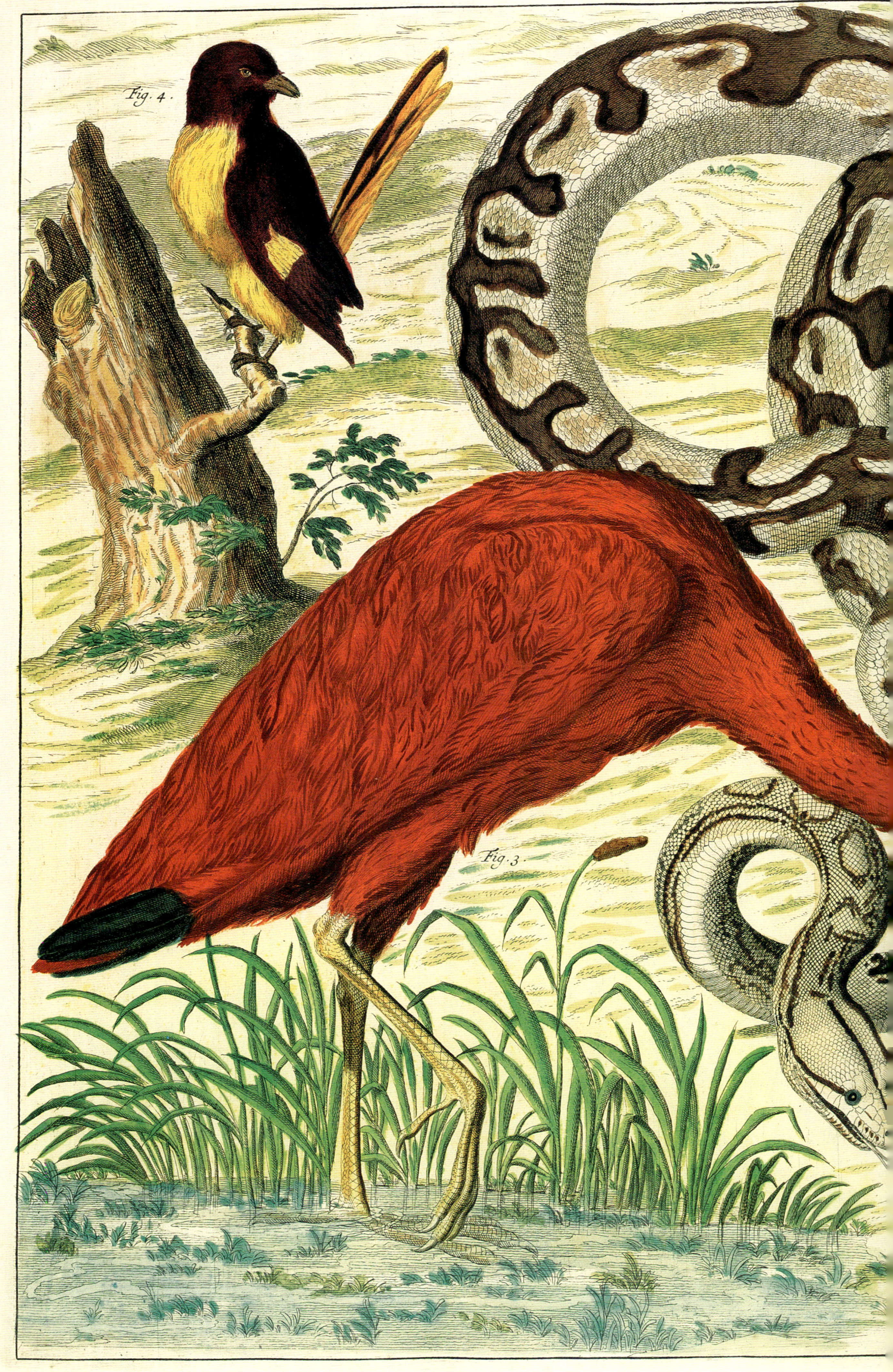

1 *Python regius* 2 *Python reticulatus* 3 *Eudocimus ruber* 4 *Trichixos pyrrhopyga*
1 Royal python · Königspython · Python royal 2 Reticulated python (pale specimen) · Netzpython (helles Exemplar) · Python réticulé (exemplaire clair) 3 Scarlet ibis · Scharlachsichler · Ibis rouge 4 Rufous-tailed shama · Feuerschwanzschama · Shama à queue rousse

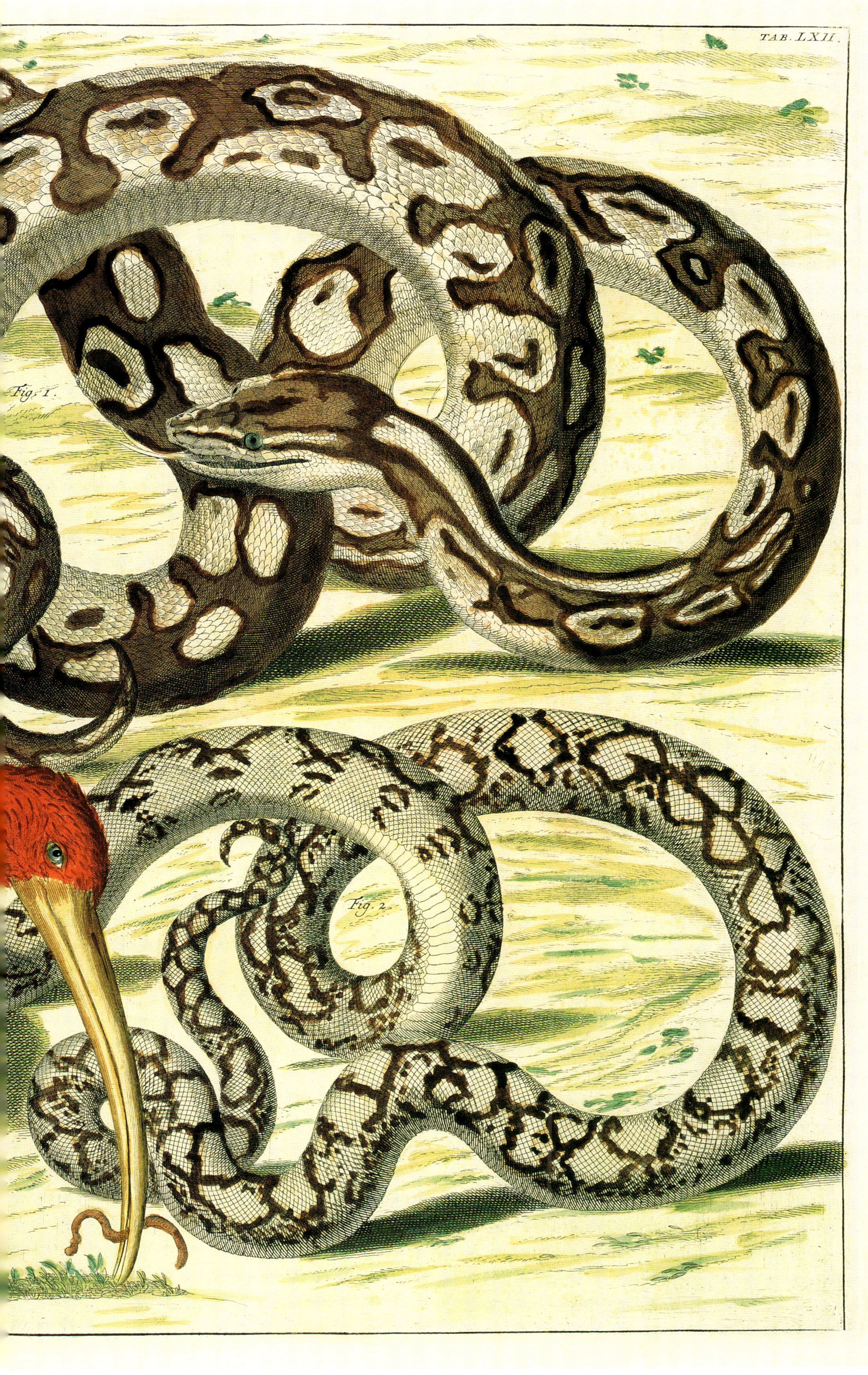
TAB. LXII.
Fig. 1.
Fig. 2.

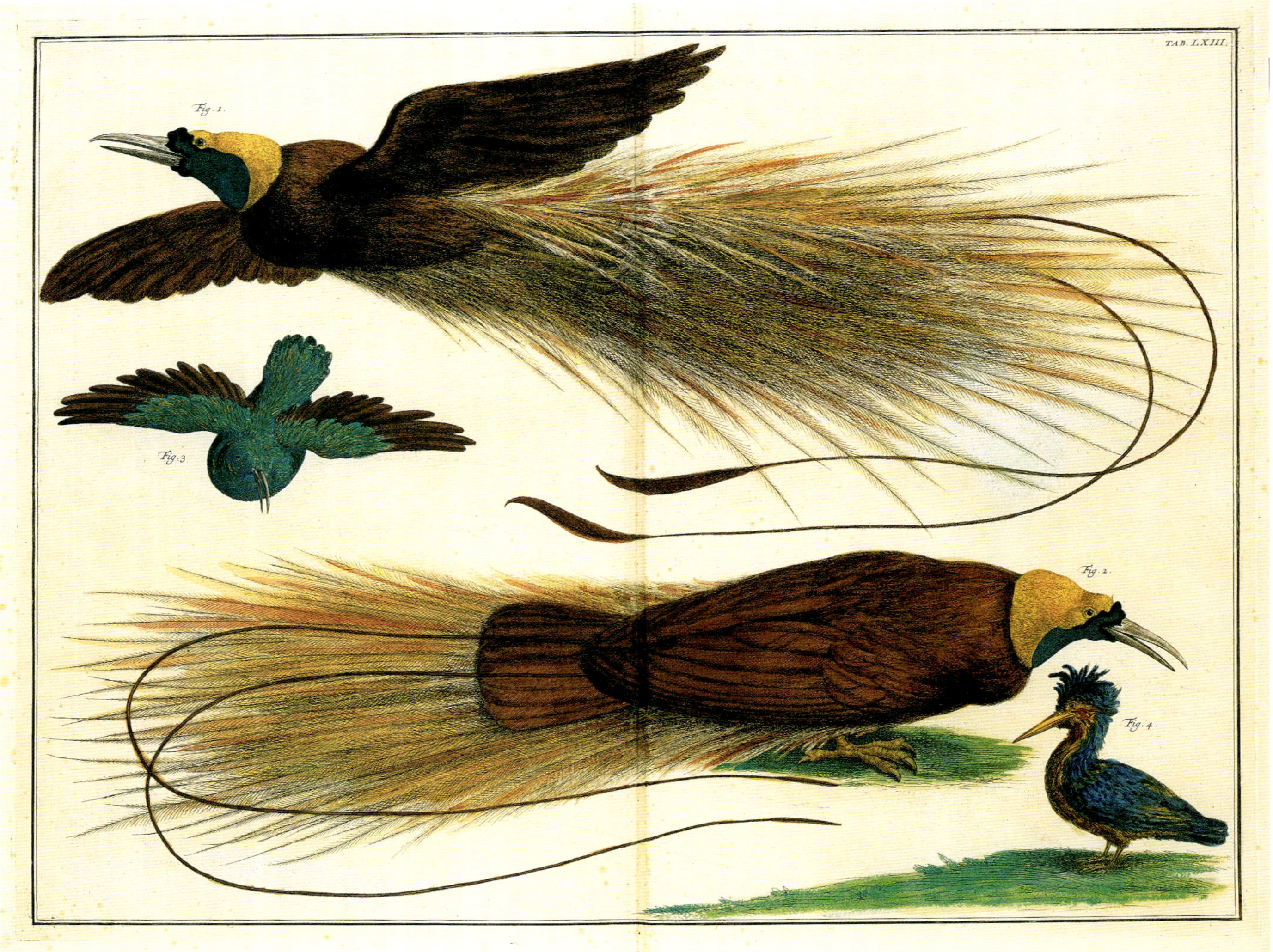

1-2 *Paradisea apoda* **3** Dicaeinae **4** Alcedinidae
1-2 Greater birc of paradise · Großer Paradiesvogel · Paradisier grand-émeraude **4** Kingfisher · Eisvogel · Martin-pêcheur

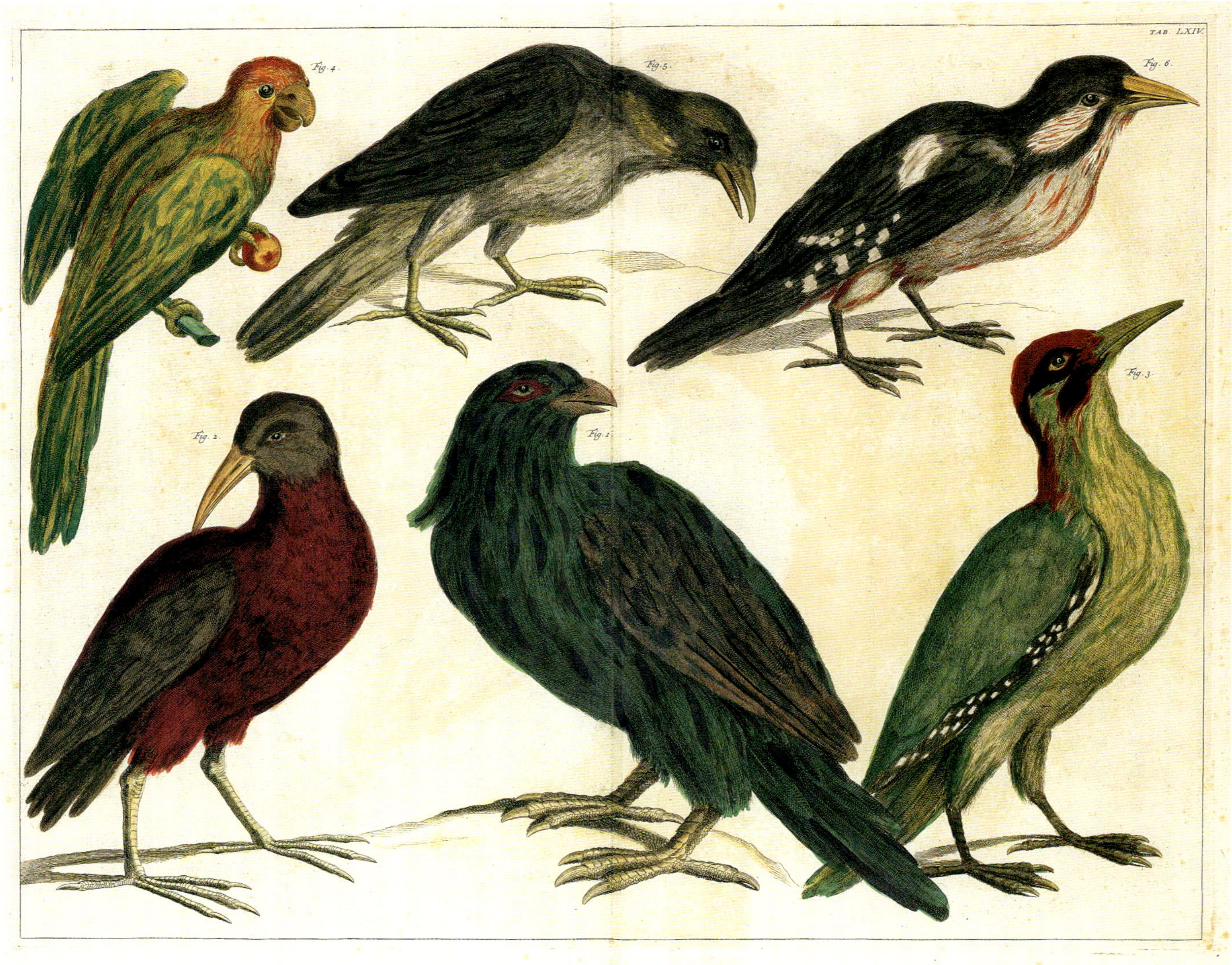

1, 5 *Aves* **2** Rallidae **3** *Picus viridis* **4** *Eupsittula pertinax* **6** Picidae sp.
1, 4-5 Birds · Vögel · Oiseaux **2** Rail · Ralle · Rallidé **3** European green woodpecker · Grünspecht · Pic vert **6** Woodpecker · Specht · Pic vert

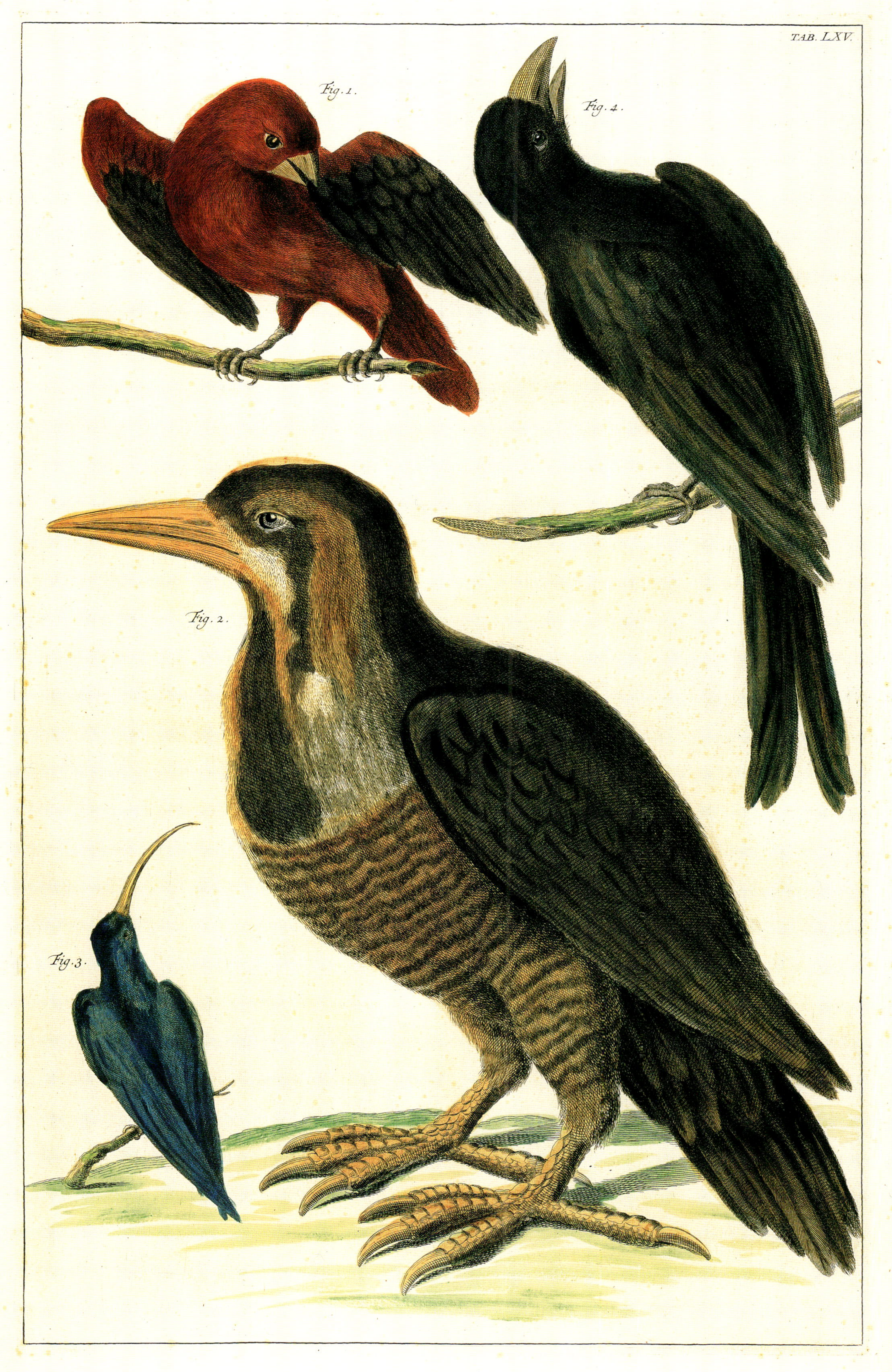

1 *Cyanocompsa brissonii* 2 Picidae 3 Trochilidae
1 Ultramarine grosbeak · Ultramarinbischof · Evêque de Brisson 2 Woodpecker · Specht · Pic vert 3 Hummingbird · Kolibri · Colibri

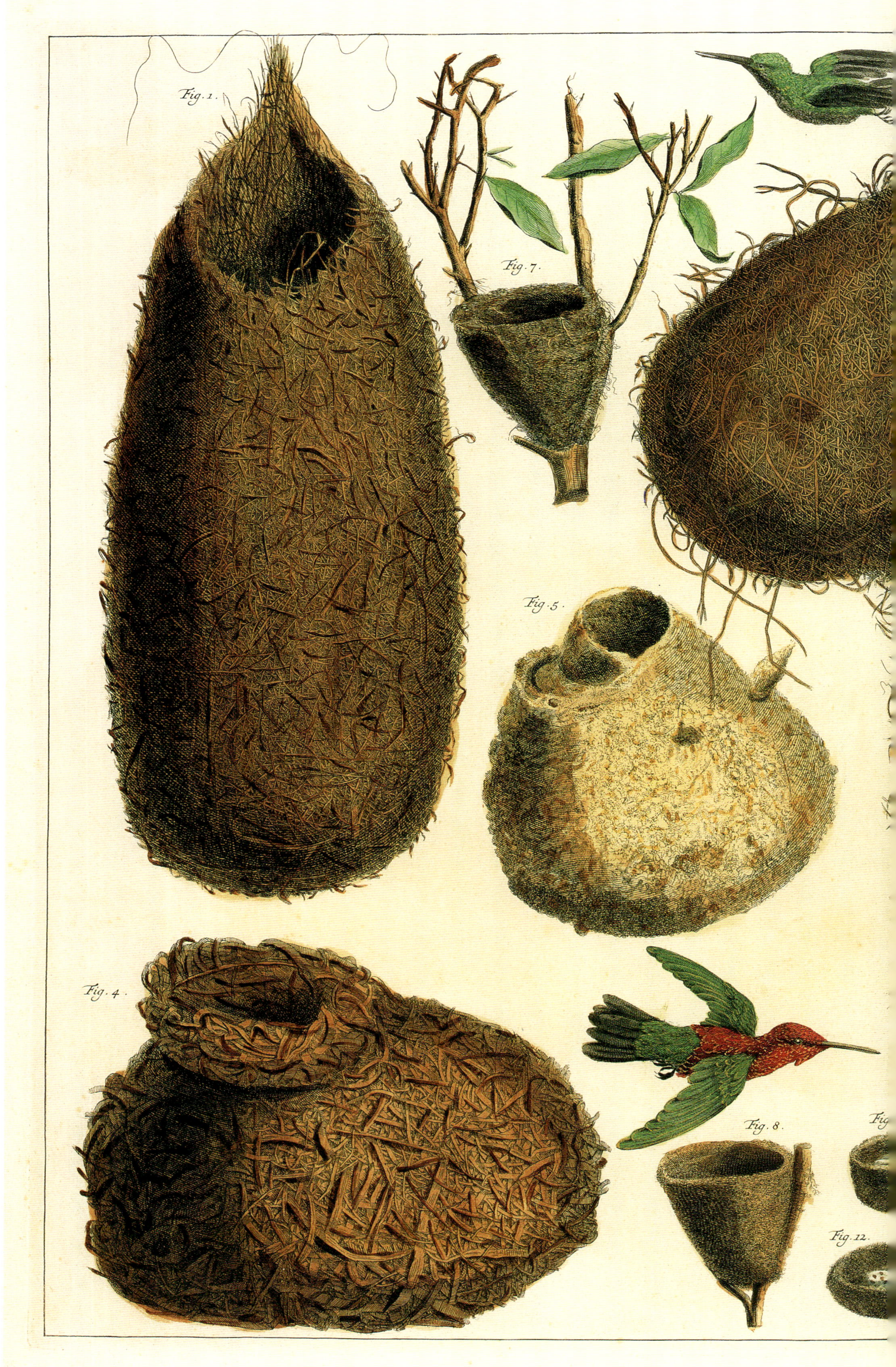

Aves
Bird nests · Nester verschiedener Vogelarten · Nids d'oiseaux

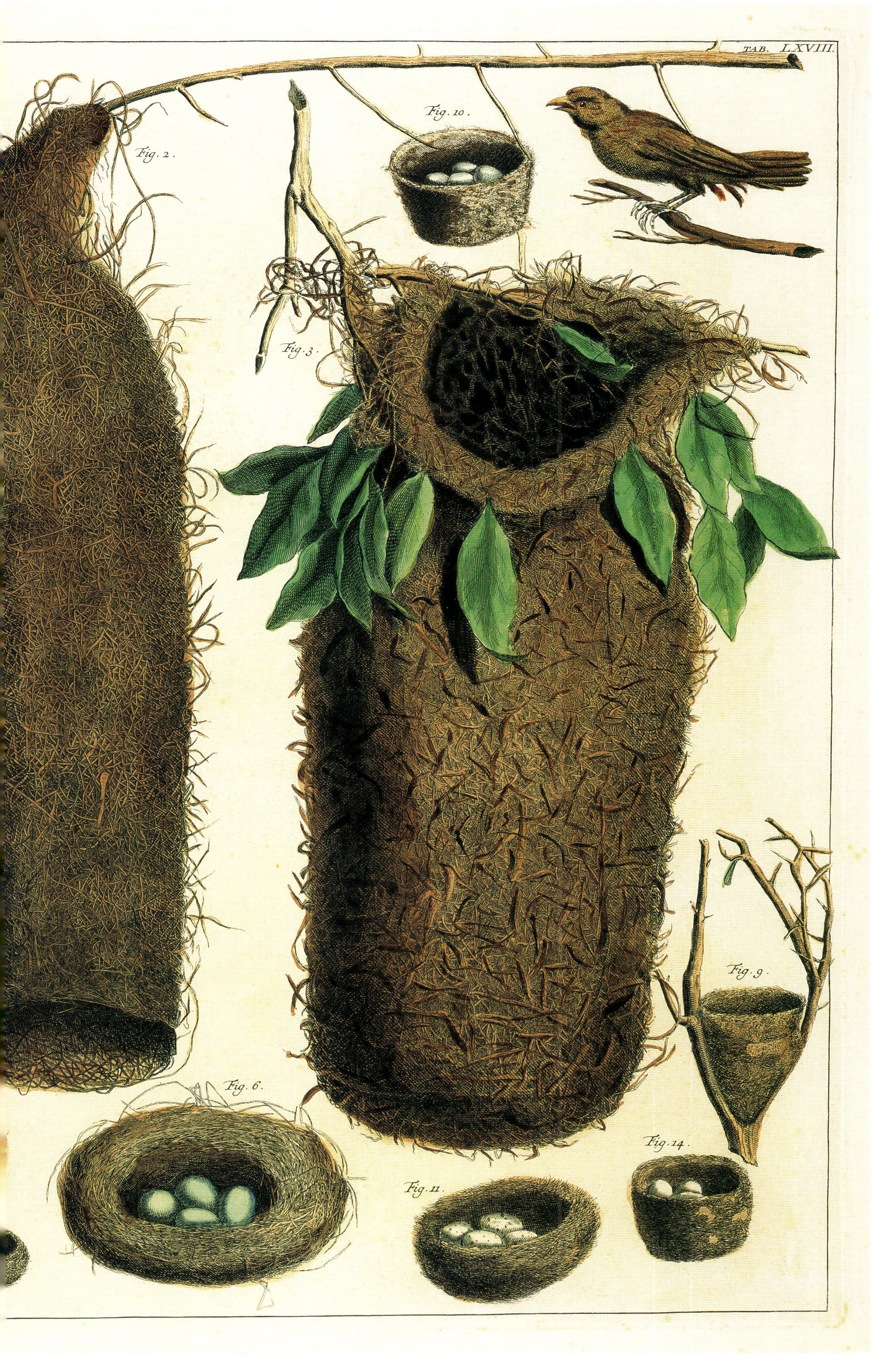
TAB. LXVIII.
Fig. 2.
Fig. 10.
Fig. 3.
Fig. 9.
Fig. 6.
Fig. 14.
Fig. 11.

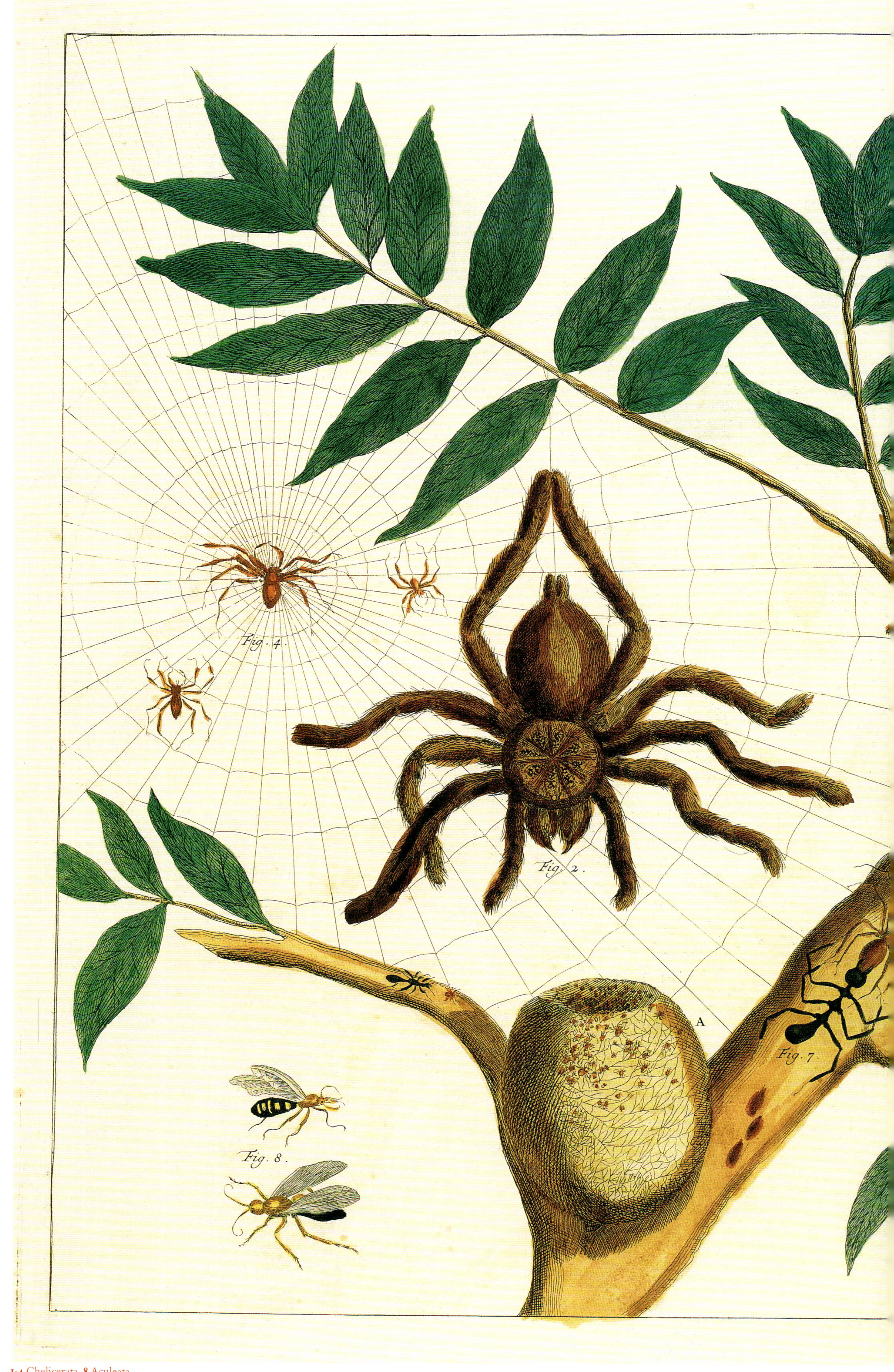

1-4 Chelicerata 8 Aculeata
1-4 Chelicerates · Spinnentiere · Chélicérates **8** Aculeate hymenopterans · Stechimmen · Guêpes piqueuses

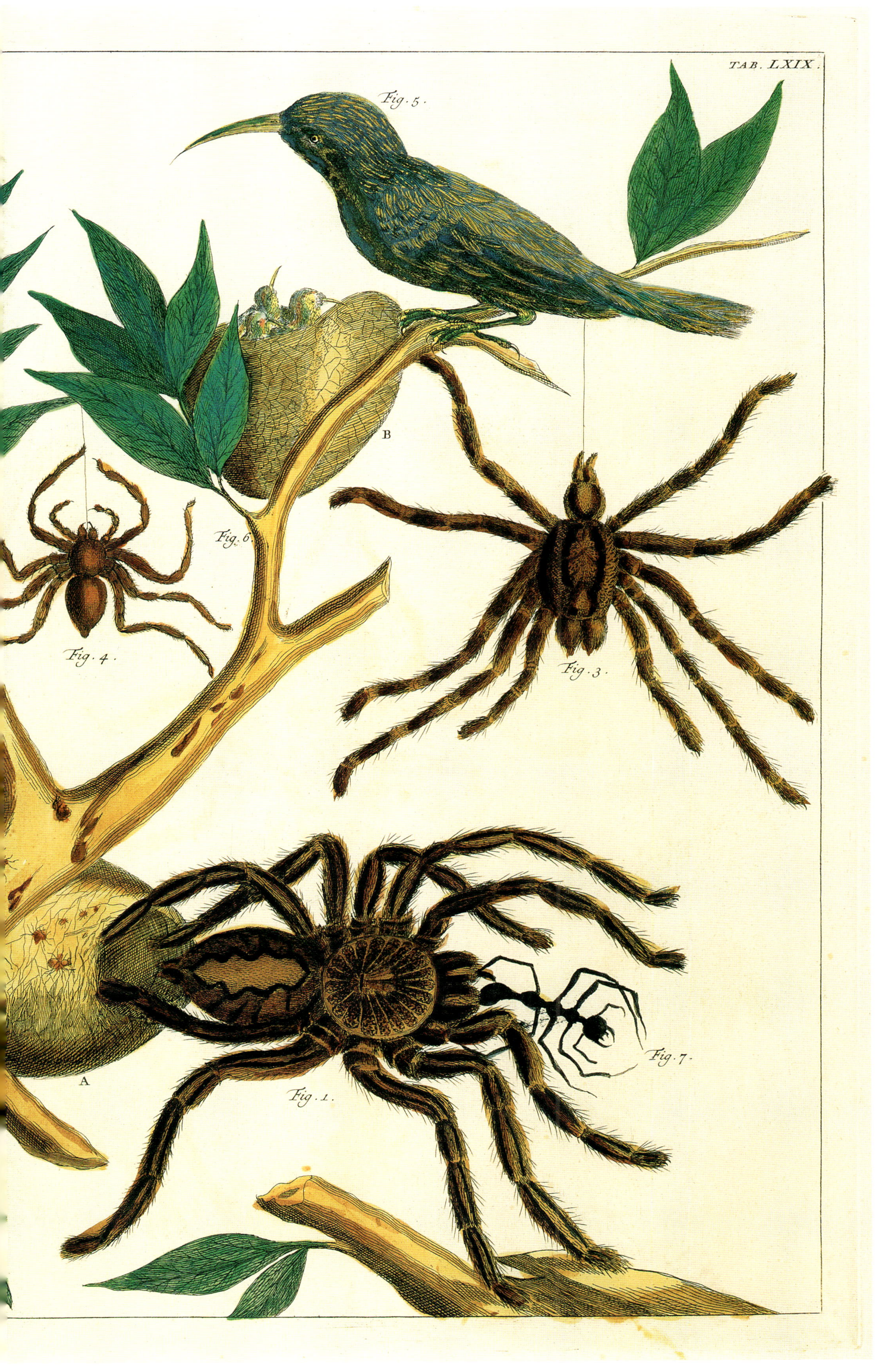
TAB. LXIX.
Fig. 5.
B
Fig. 6.
Fig. 4.
Fig. 3.
Fig. 7.
A
Fig. 1.

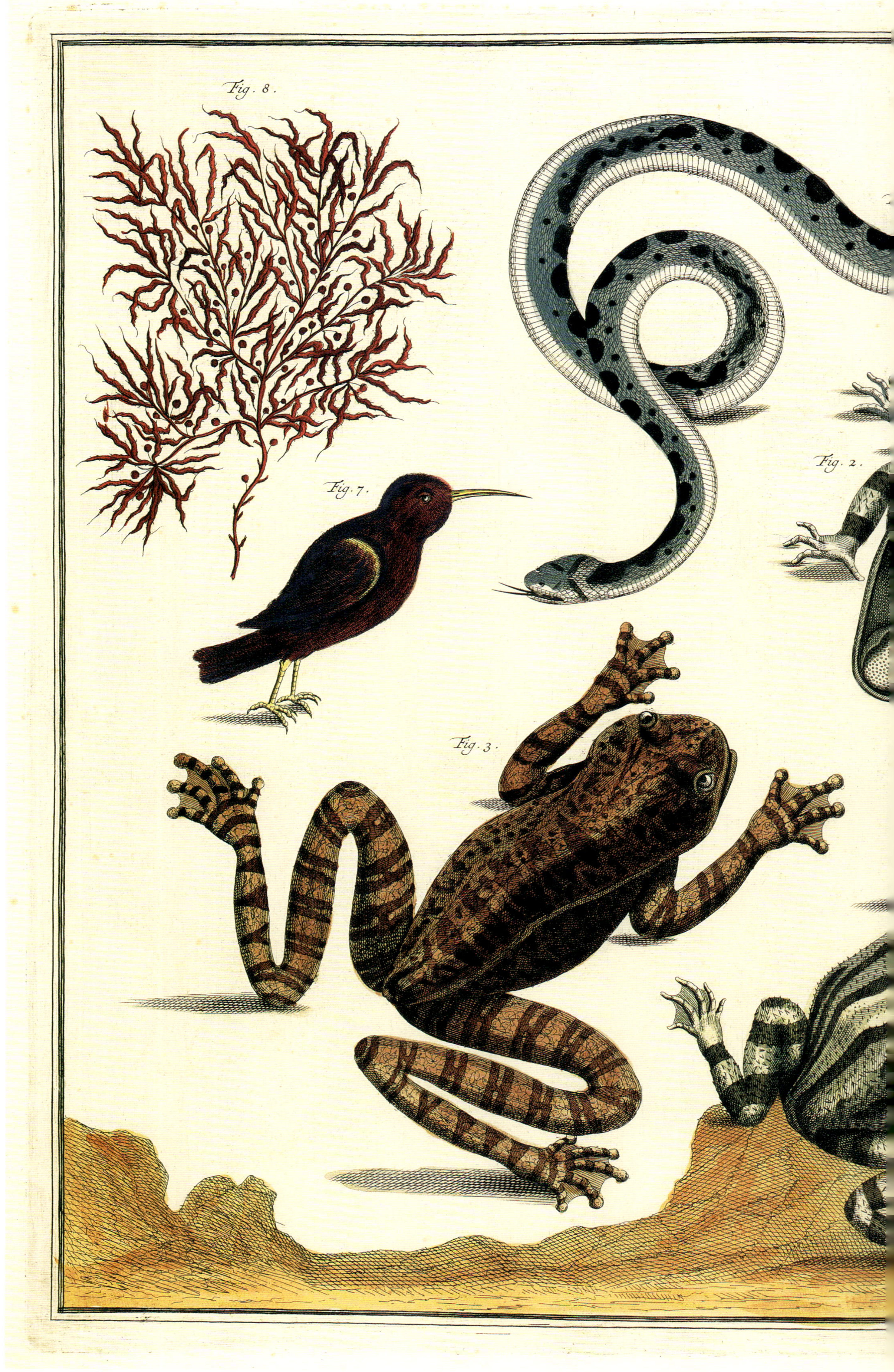

1-4 Anura 5 Lacertidae 6 Serpentes
1-4 Frogs · Froschlurche · Grenouilles 5 Lizard · Eidechse · Lézard 6 Snake, according to Seba from Virginia · Schlange, nach Seba aus Virginia · Serpent, de Virginie selon Seba

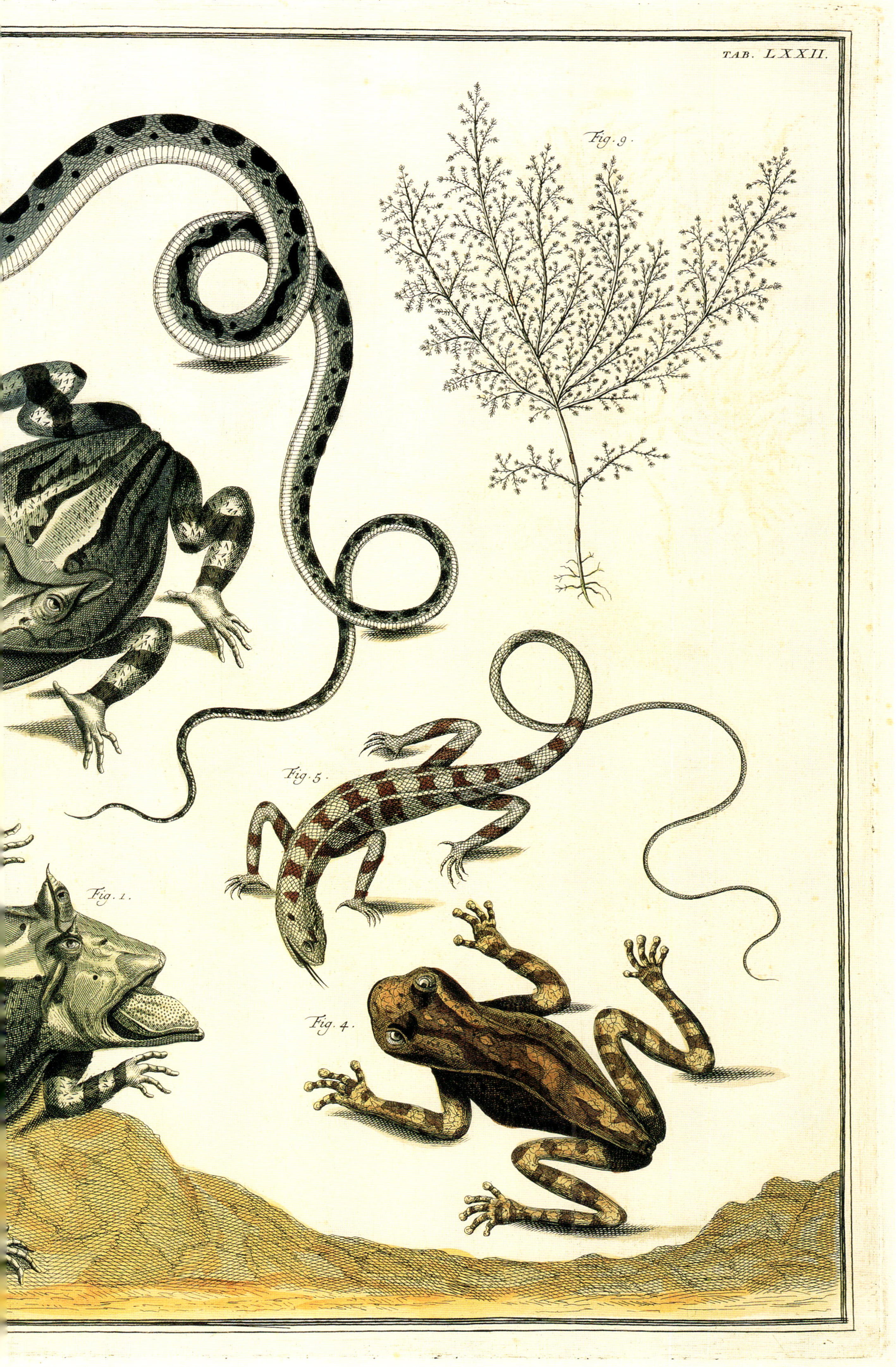
TAB. LXXII.
Fig. 9.
Fig. 5.
Fig. 1.
Fig. 4.

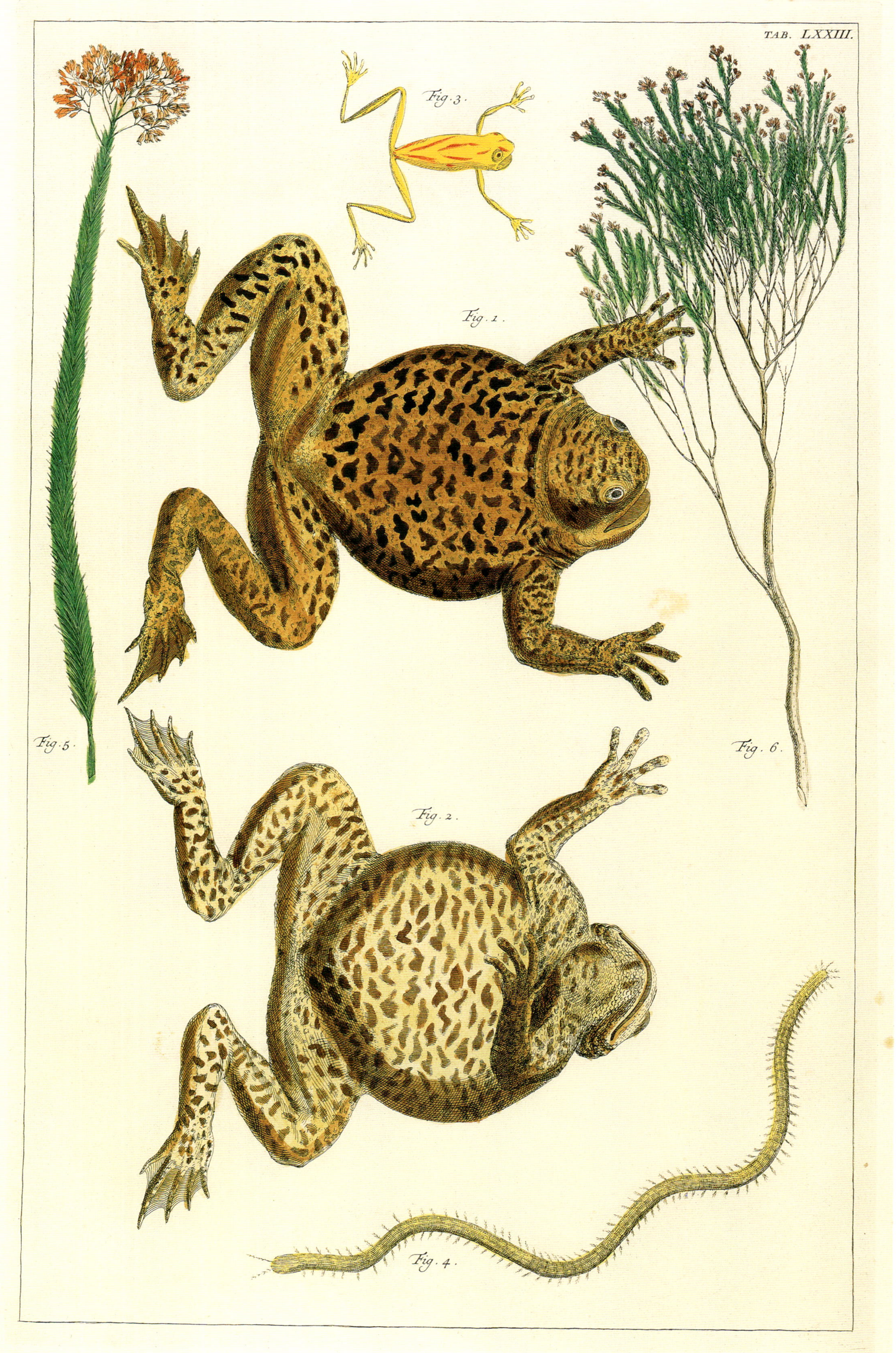

1-2 *Bufo marinus* **3** *Epipedobates tricolor* **4** Chilopoda
1-2 Giant toad · Aga-Kröte · Crapaud géant **3** Tree frog · Baumfrosch · Grenouille arboricole **4** Centipede · Hundertfüßer · Centipède

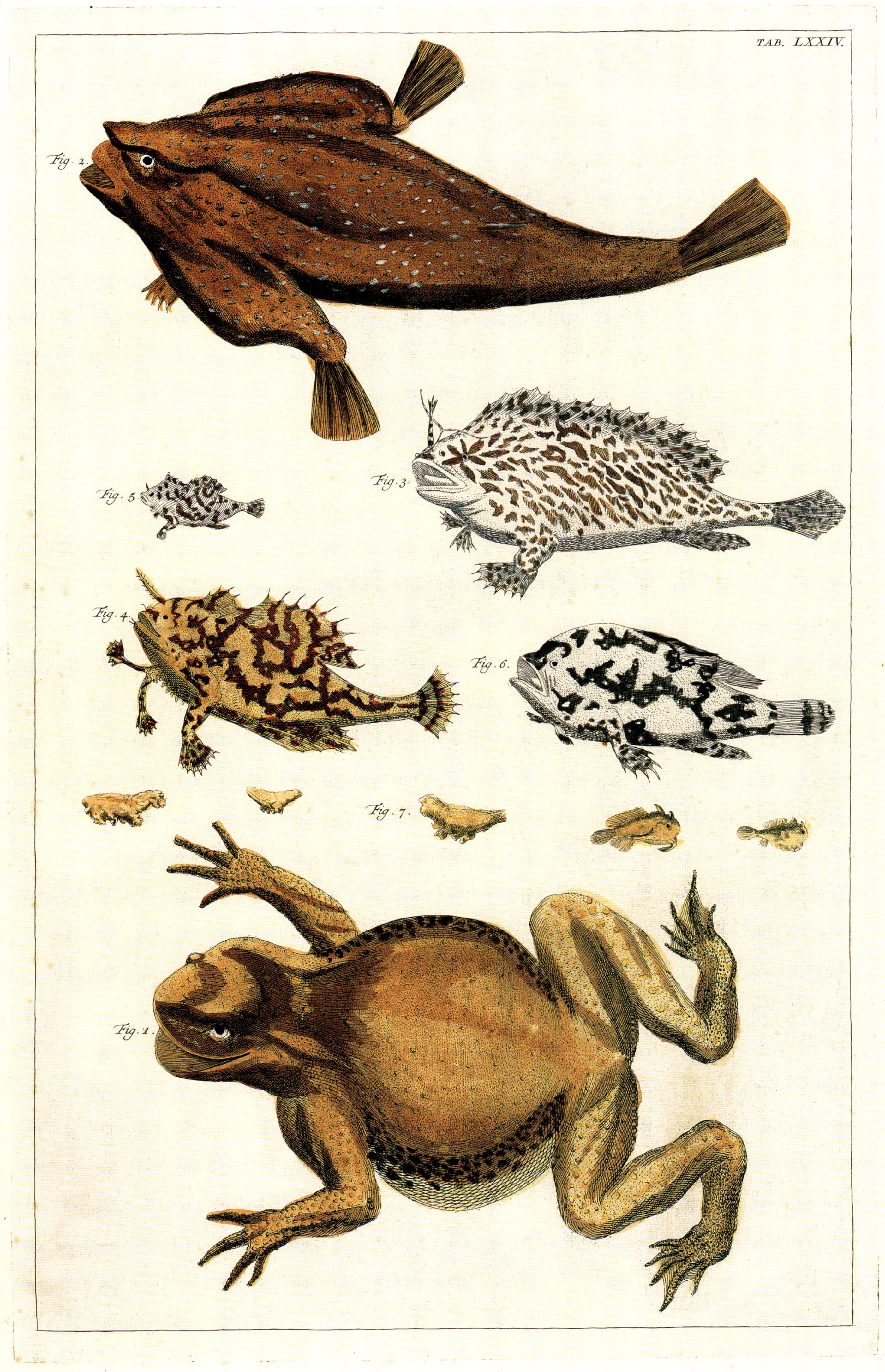

1 Anura **2** *Ogcocephalus vespertilio* **3-6** *Histrio histrio* **7** Partem Mollusca?
1 Toad · Froschlurch · Crapaud **2** Longsnout batfish · Langnasen-Seefledermaus · Chauve-souris de mer **3-6** Sargassumfishes · Sargasso-Fische · Pêcheurs des Sargasses
7 Marine snails (partly) · Meeres-Nacktschnecken (zum Teil) · Gastéropodes de mer sans coquille (partiellement)

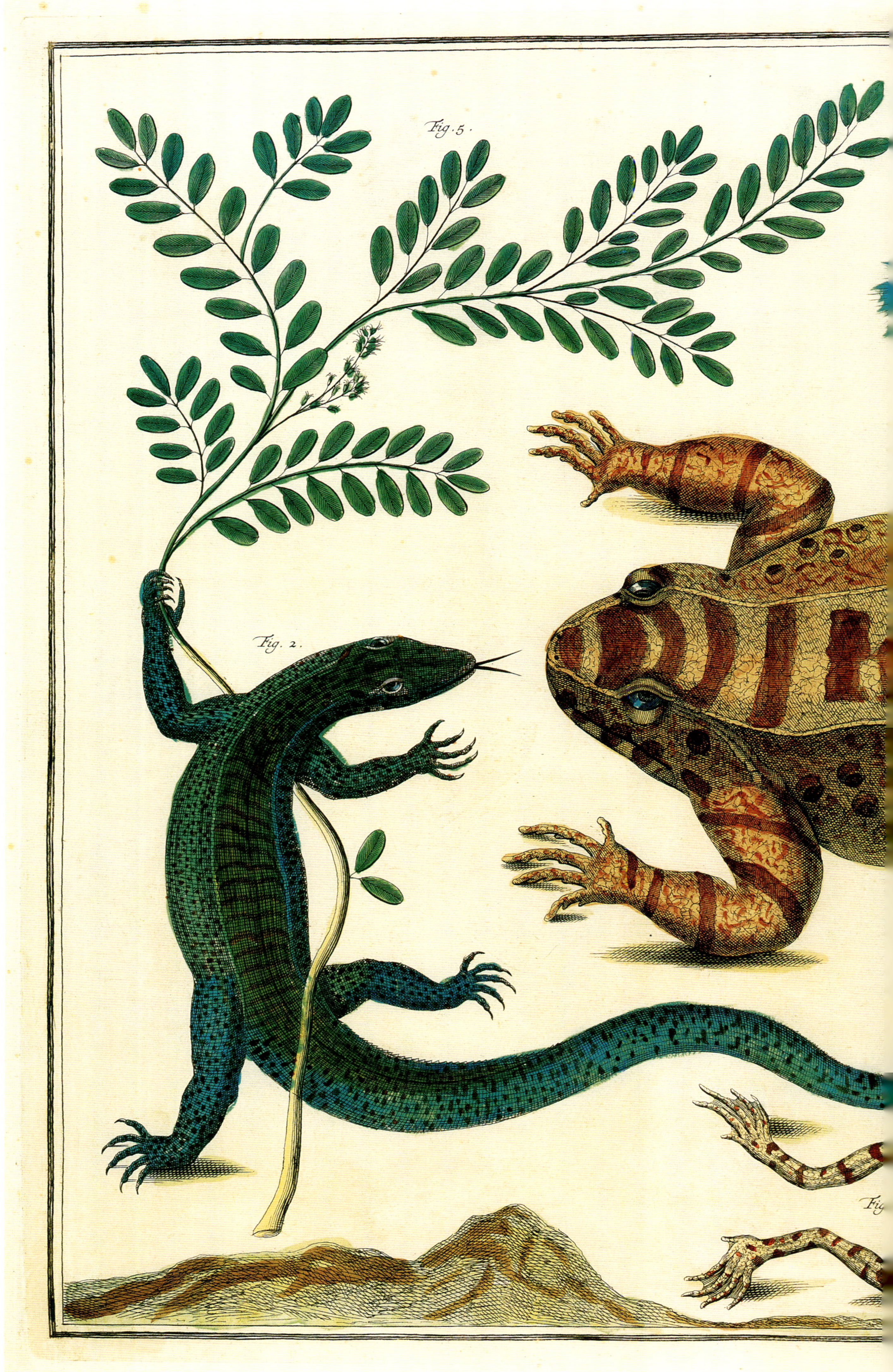

1, 4 Anura 2 Lacertidae 3 Serpentes 5 Plantae 6 Capparaceae
1 Toad · Kröte · Crapaud 2 Lizard · Eidechse · Lézard 3 Snake, according to Seba from Virginia · Schlange, nach Seba aus Virginia · Serpent, de Virginie selon Seba
6 Caper family · Kaperngewächse · Capparidacées

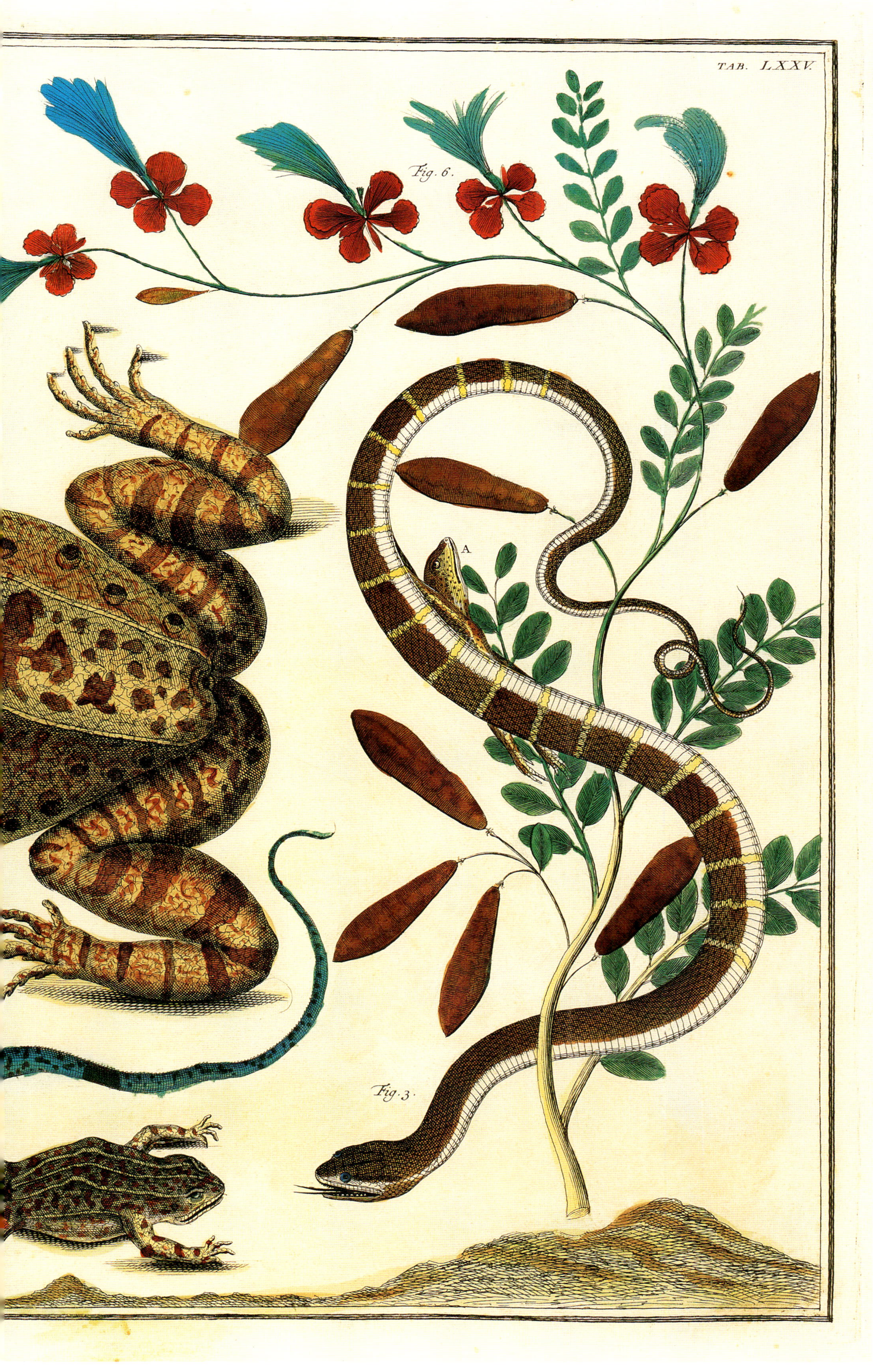
TAB. LXXV.
Fig. 6.
A
Fig. 3.

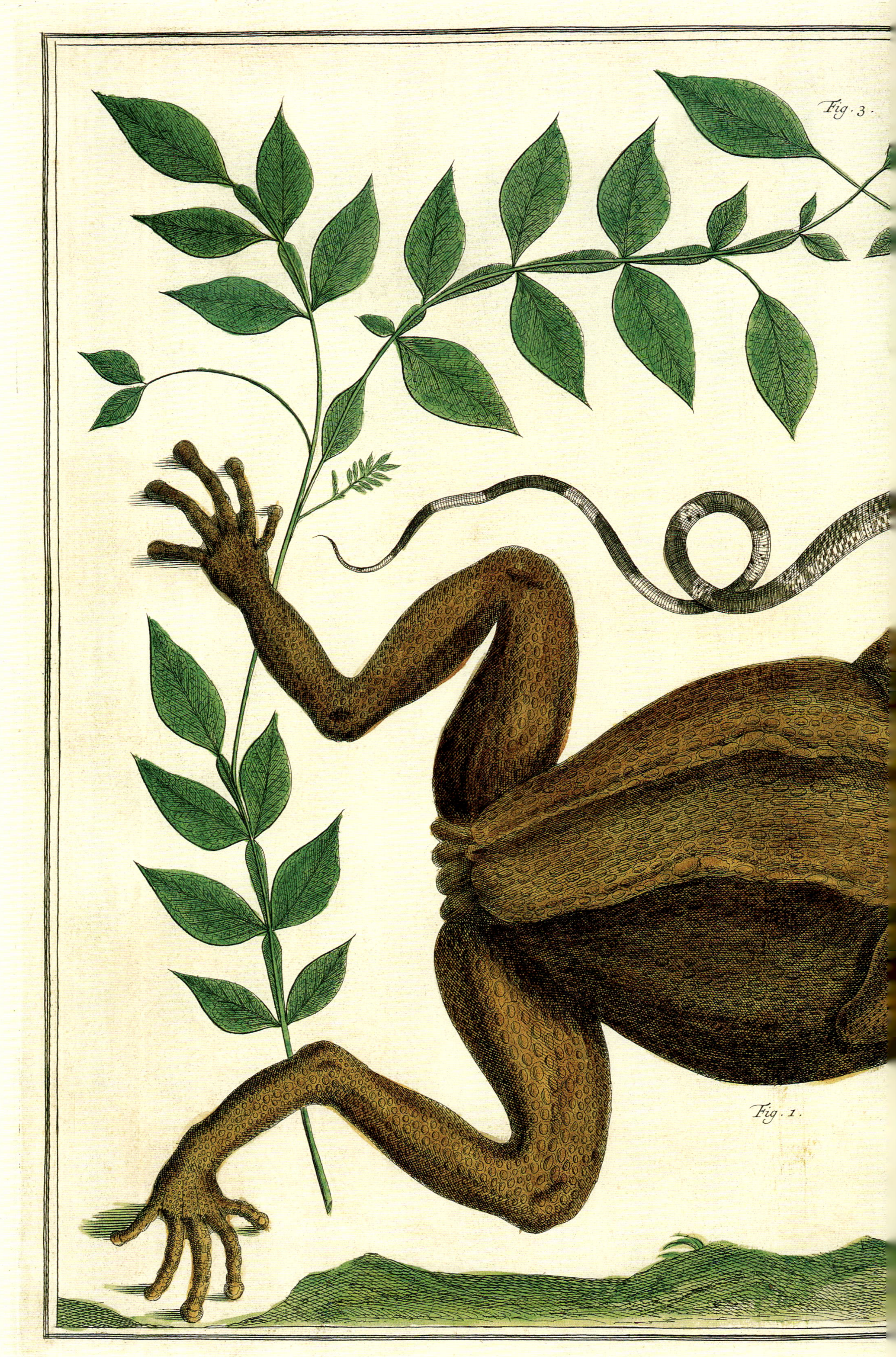

1 *Bufo marinus* 2 Lacertidae
1 Giant toad · Aga-Kröte · Crapaud géant 2 Lizard · Eidechse · Lézard

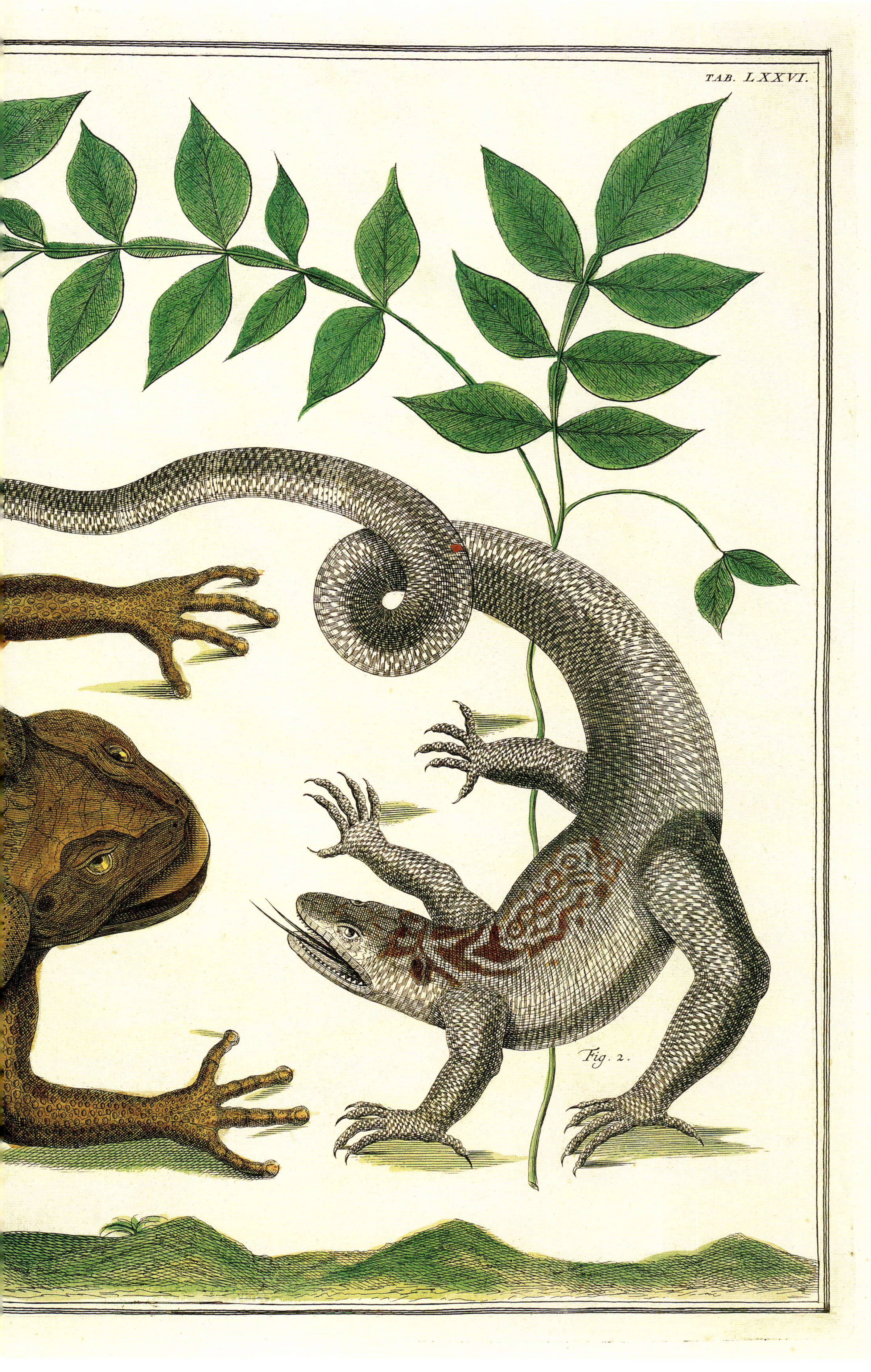
TAB. LXXVI.
Fig. 2.

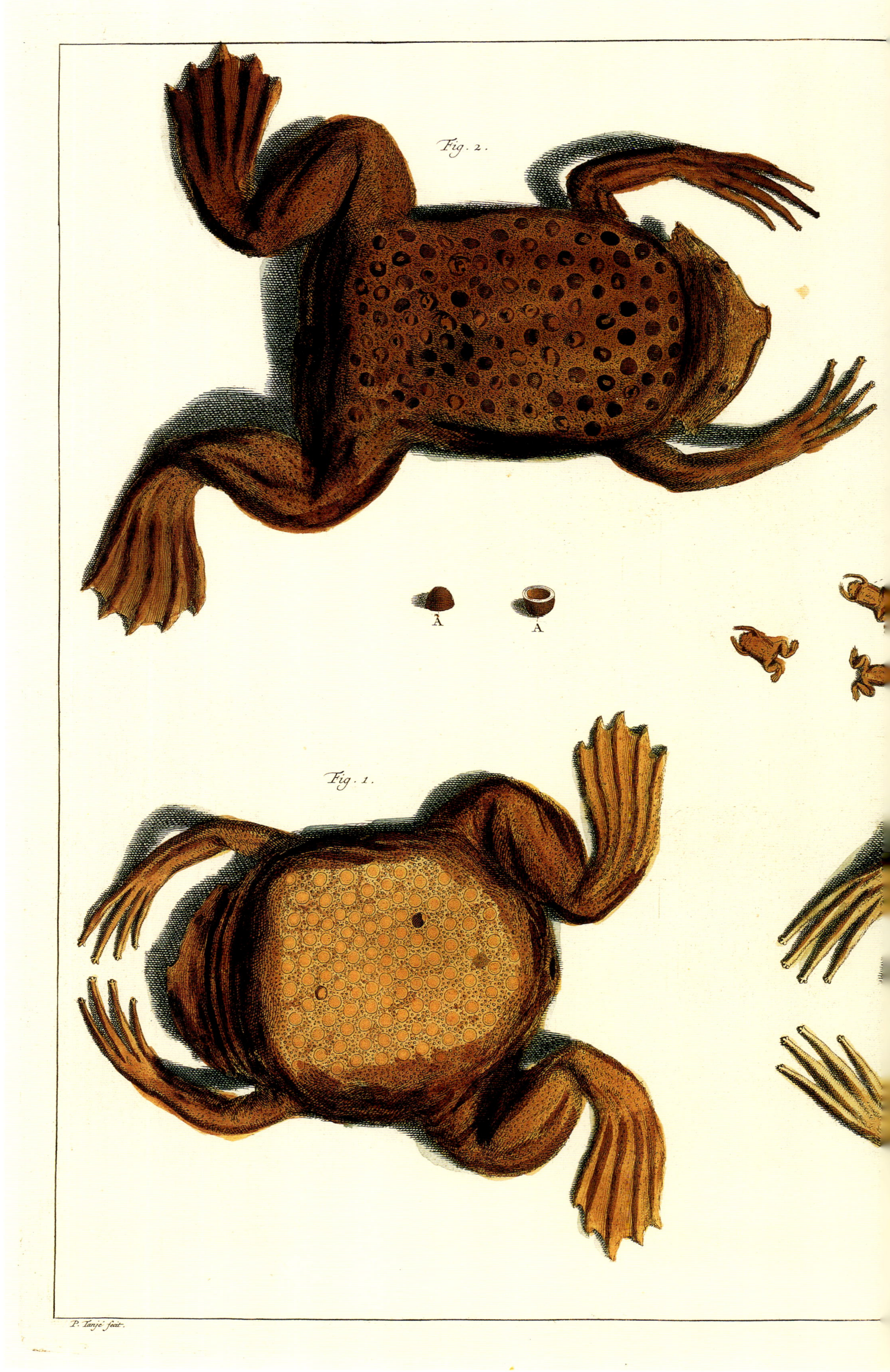

1-4 *Pipa pipa*
1-4 Surinam toad · Wabenkröte · Pipa américain du Surinam

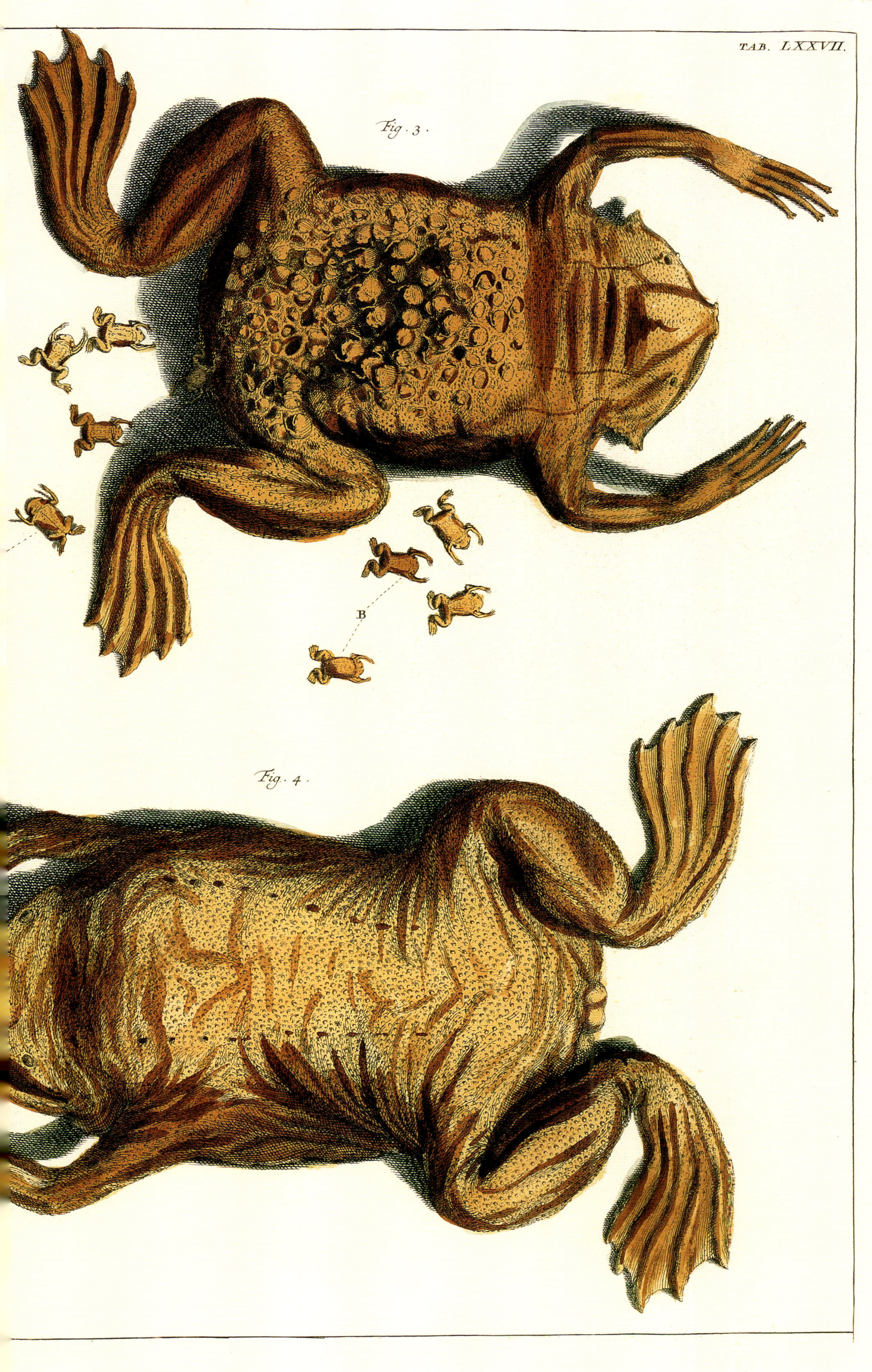
TAB. LXXVII.
Fig. 3.
B
Fig. 4.

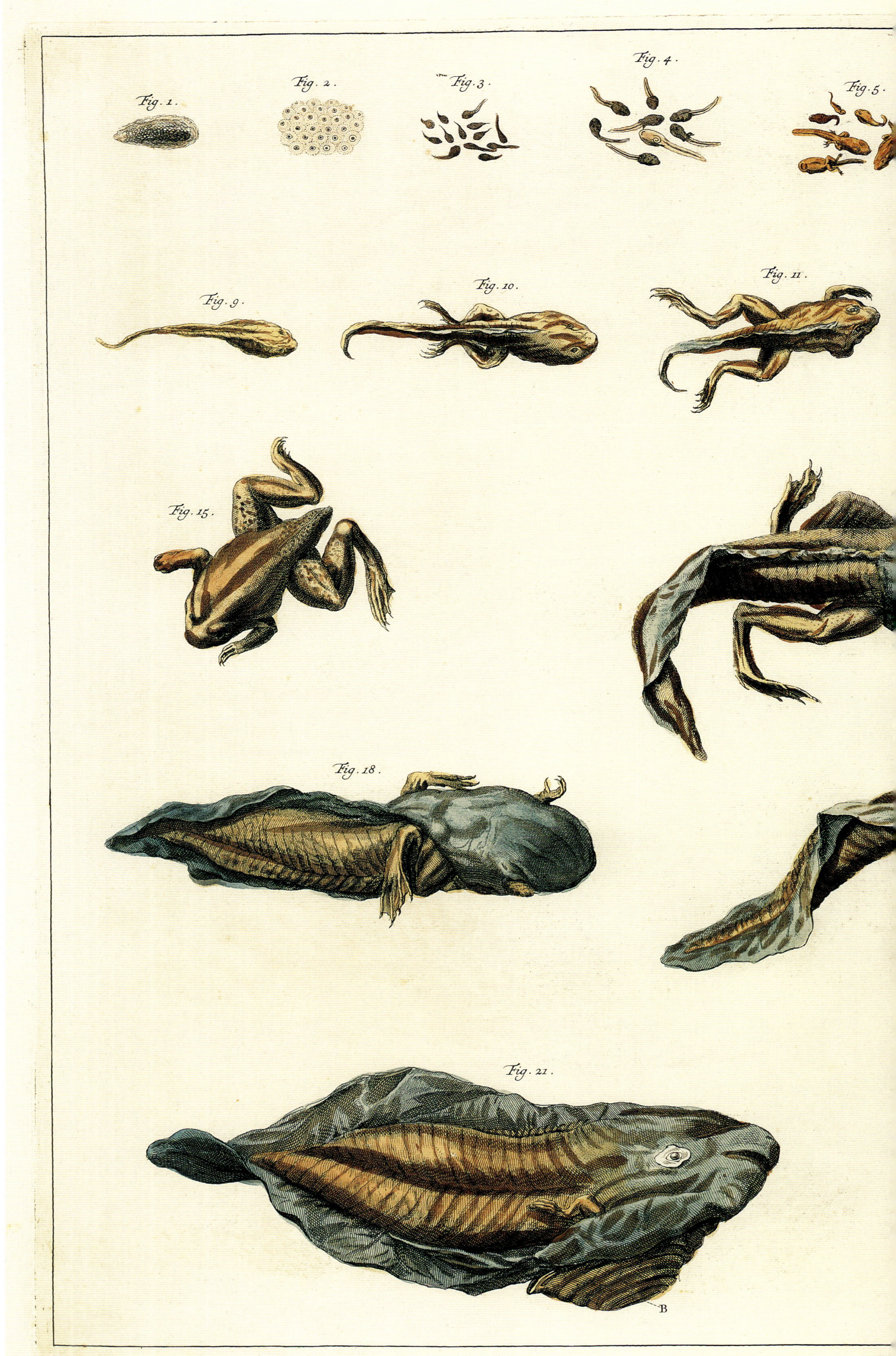

1-15 Anura **16-21** Anura et pisces
1-15 Metamorphosis of frogs · Metamorphose von Fröschen · Métamorphose des grenouilles **16-21** Fictive metamorphosis of American frogs into fishes · Fiktive Umwandlung amerikanischer Frösche in Fische · La métamorphose fictive des grenouilles en poissons

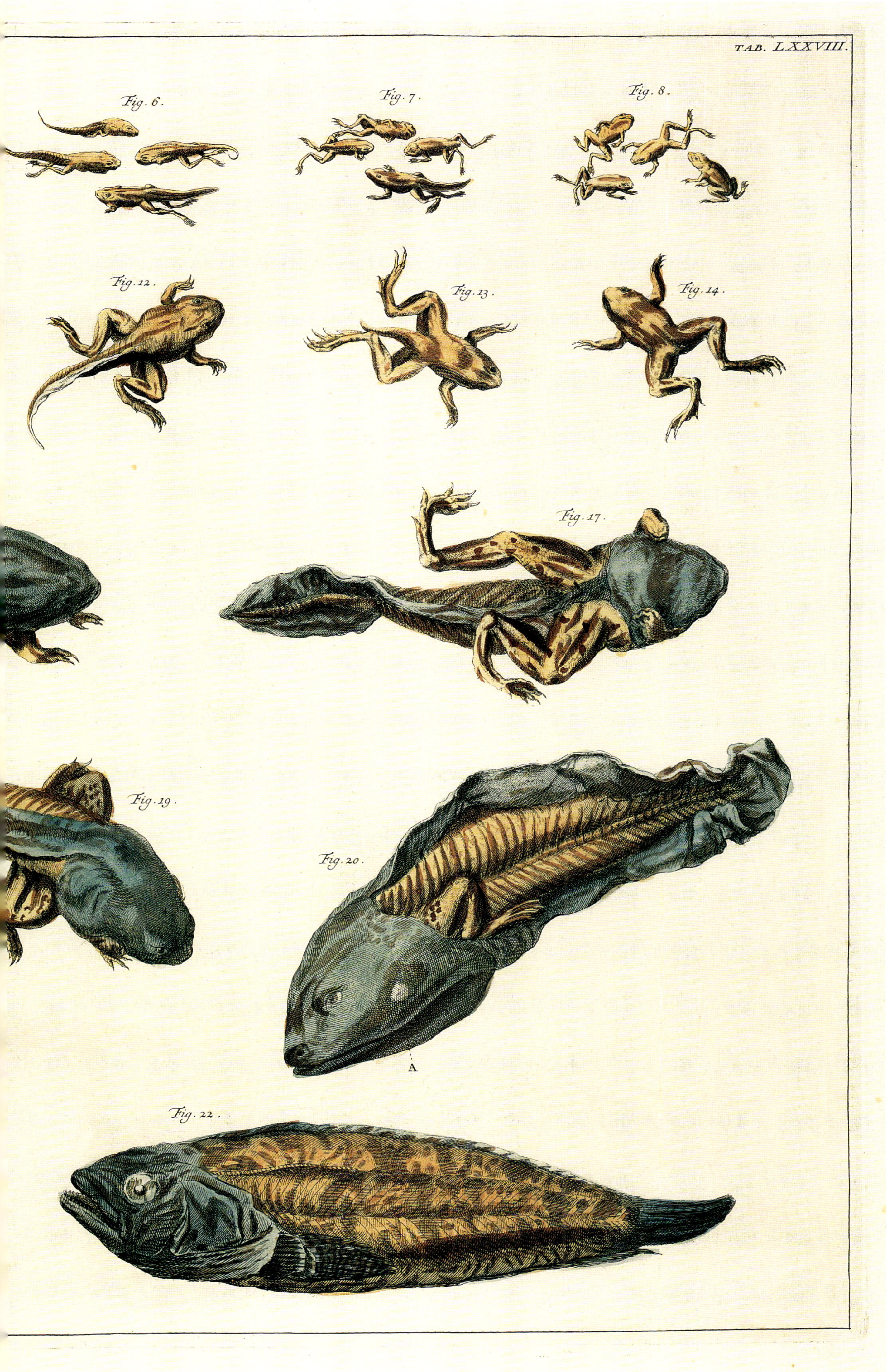
TAB. LXXVIII.
Fig. 6.
Fig. 7.
Fig. 8.
Fig. 12.
Fig. 13.
Fig. 14.
Fig. 17.
Fig. 19.
Fig. 20.
A
Fig. 22.

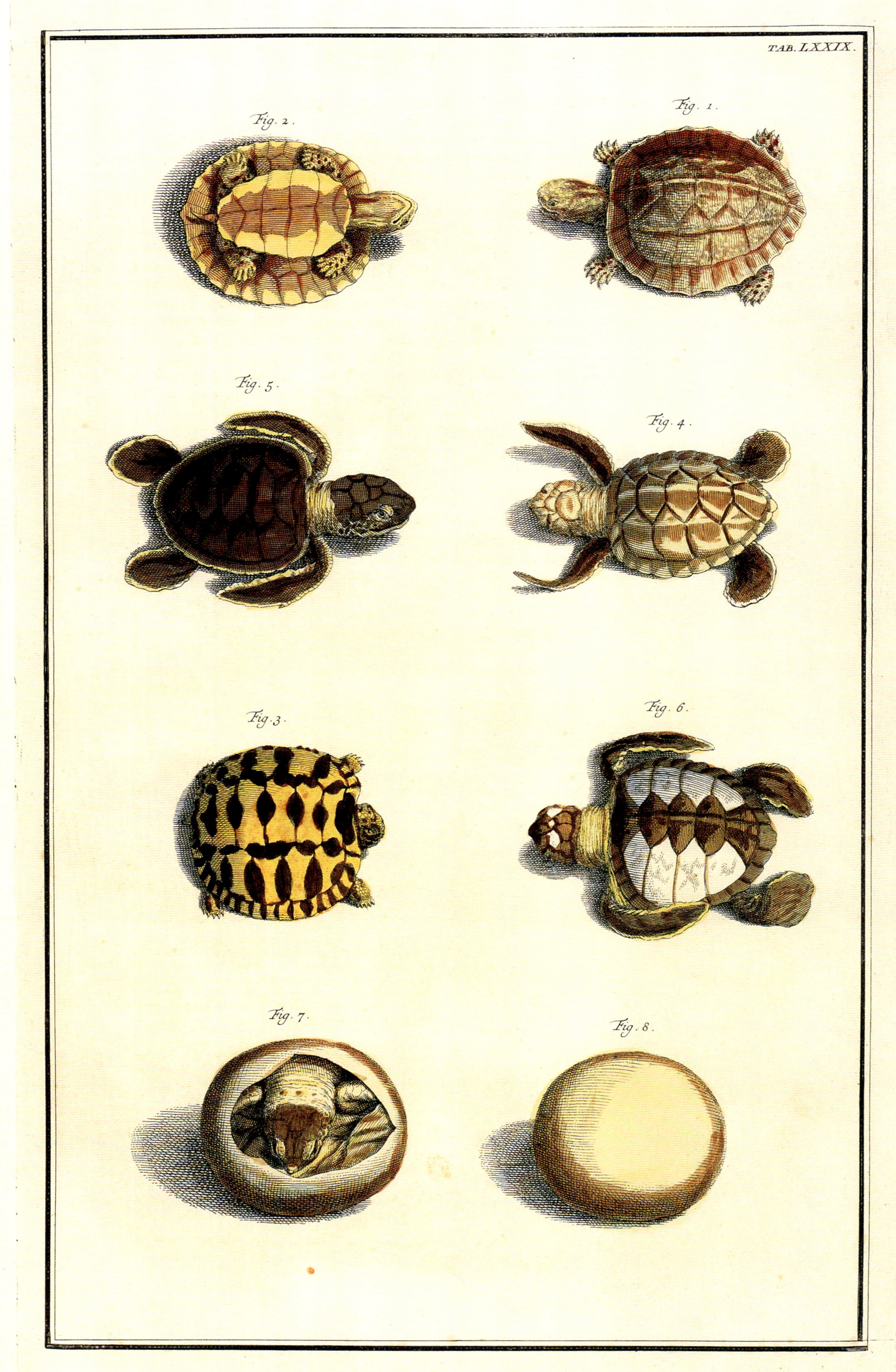

1-2 *Melanochelys tricarinata* 3 *Geochelone elegans* 4-7 *Chelonia mydas* 8 Ovum
1-2 Three-keeled land tortoise · Landschildkröte · Tortue carinée 3 Star tortoise · Sternschildkröte · Tortue carinée 4-7 Green turtles · Suppenschildkröten · Tortues vertes 8 Egg · Ei · Œuf

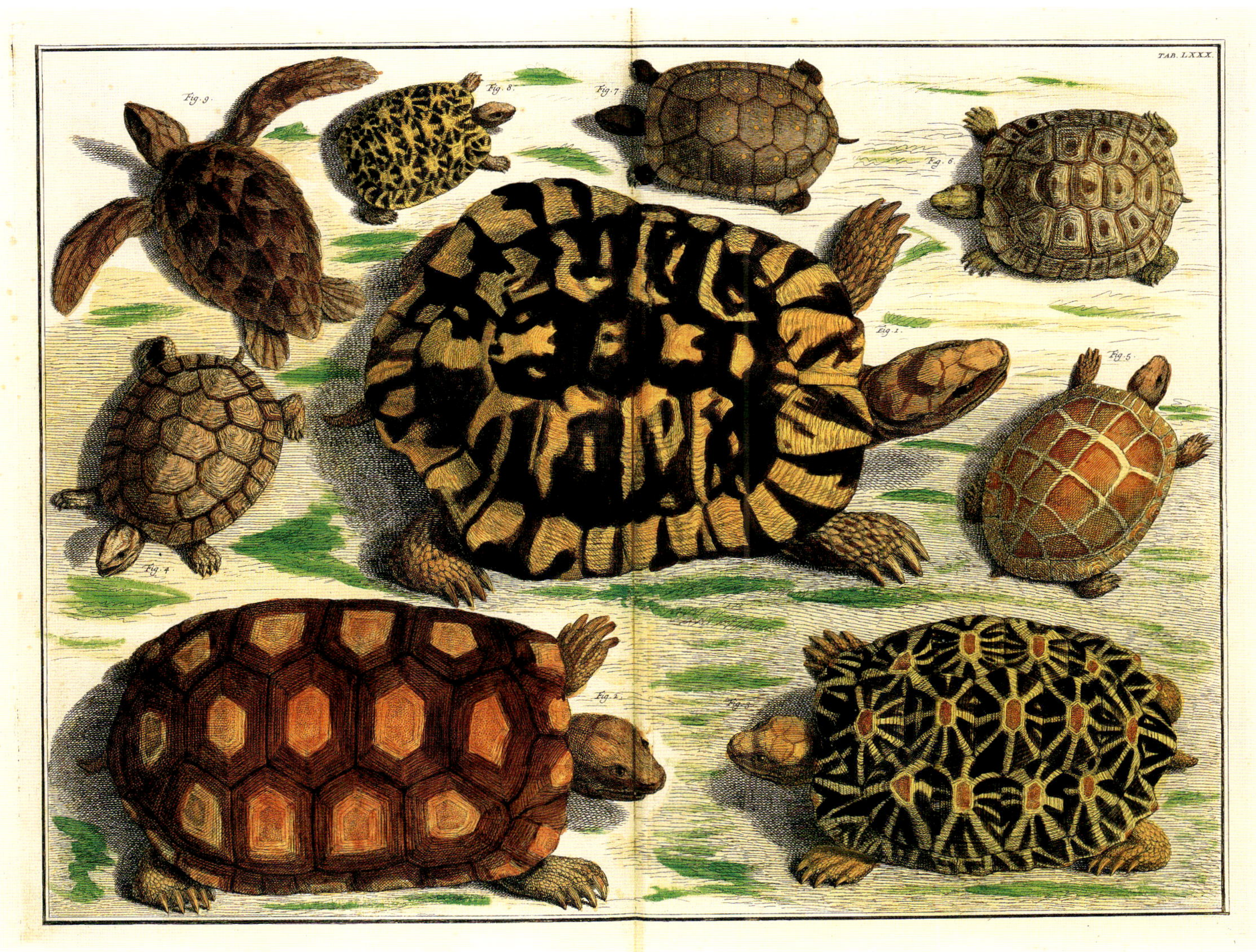

1 Testudo hermanni *2 Geochelone carbonaria* *3 Geochelone elegans* 4 Chelonia *5 Chrysemys picta* *6 Homopus areolatus* *7 Clemmys guttata* *8 Homopus sp.* *9 Eretmochelys imbricata*
1 Greek tortoise · Griechische Landschildkröte · Tortue d'Hermann 2 Red-footed tortoise · Köhlerschildkröte · Tortue charbonnière 3 Star tortoise · Sternschildkröte · Tortue étoilée de l'Inde 4 Tortoise · Schildkröte · Tortue 5 Painted turtle · Zierschildkröte · Tortue peinte 6 Beaked cape tortoise · Papageischnabel-Flachschildkröte · Homopode aérolé 7 Spotted turtle · Tropfenschildkröte Clemmyde à gouttelettes 8 Cope turtle · Flachschildkröte · Homopode 9 Hawksbill turtle · Karettschildkröte · Tortue imbriquée

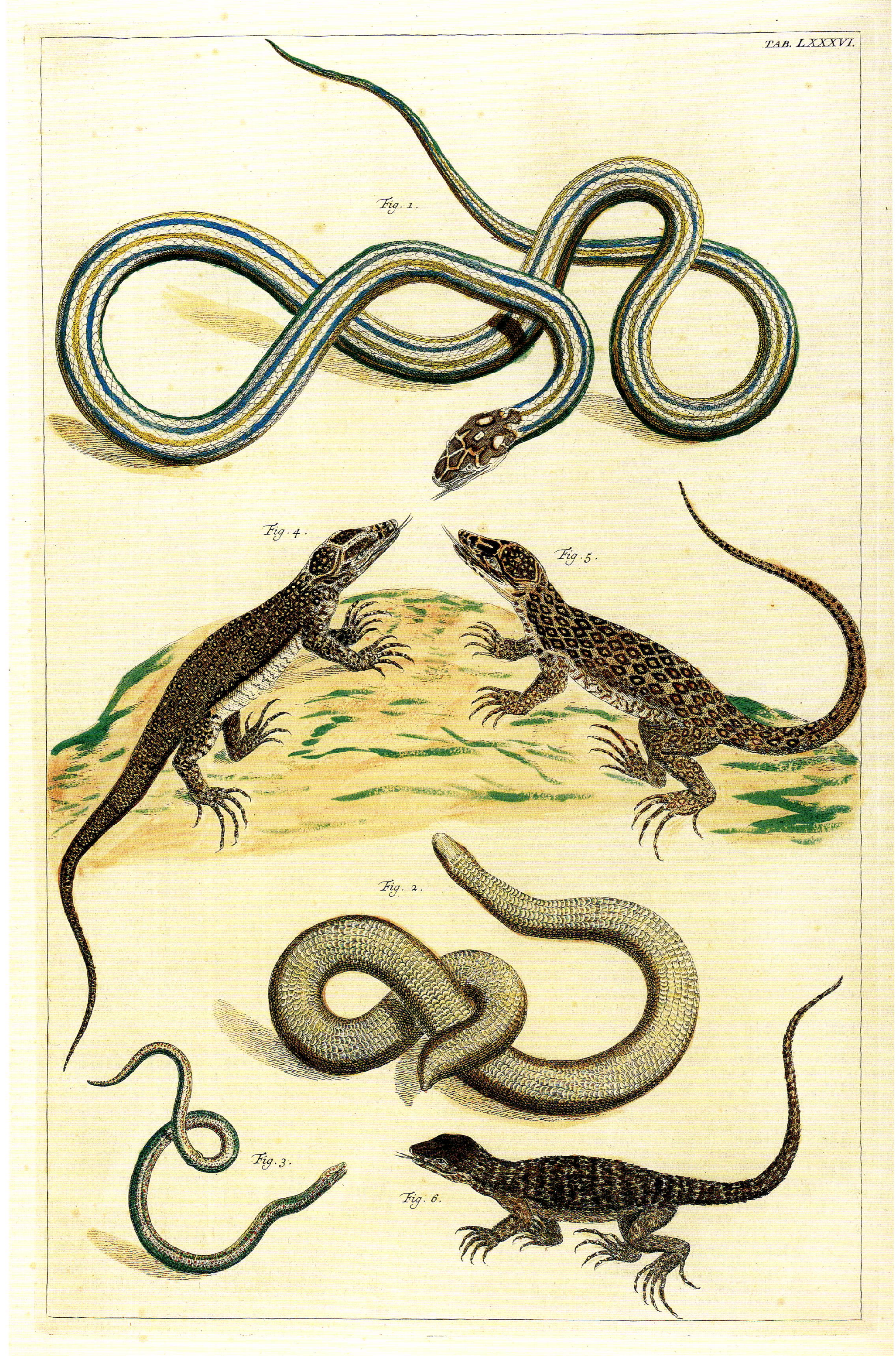

1 Serpentes 2 Typhlopidae 4-6 Squamata
1 Snake, according to Seba from Mauritania · Schlange, nach Seba aus Mauretanien · Serpent, de Mauritanie selon Seba **2** Blind snake · Blindschlange · Typhlopidé
4-6 Squamata · Echsen · Squamates

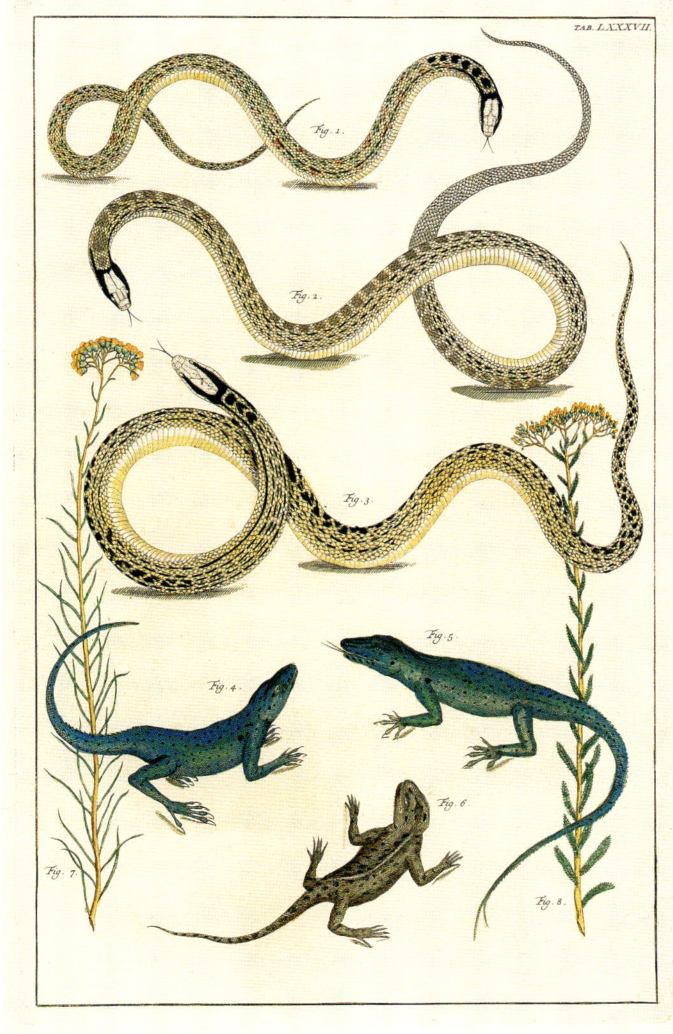

1-3 Serpentes **4-6** Lacertidae **7** Compositae
1-3 Snakes, according to Seba from Brazil · Schlangen, nach Seba aus Brasilien · Serpents, du Brésil selon Seba **4-6** Lizards · Eidechsen · Sauriens
7 Sunflower family · Korbblütler · Composées

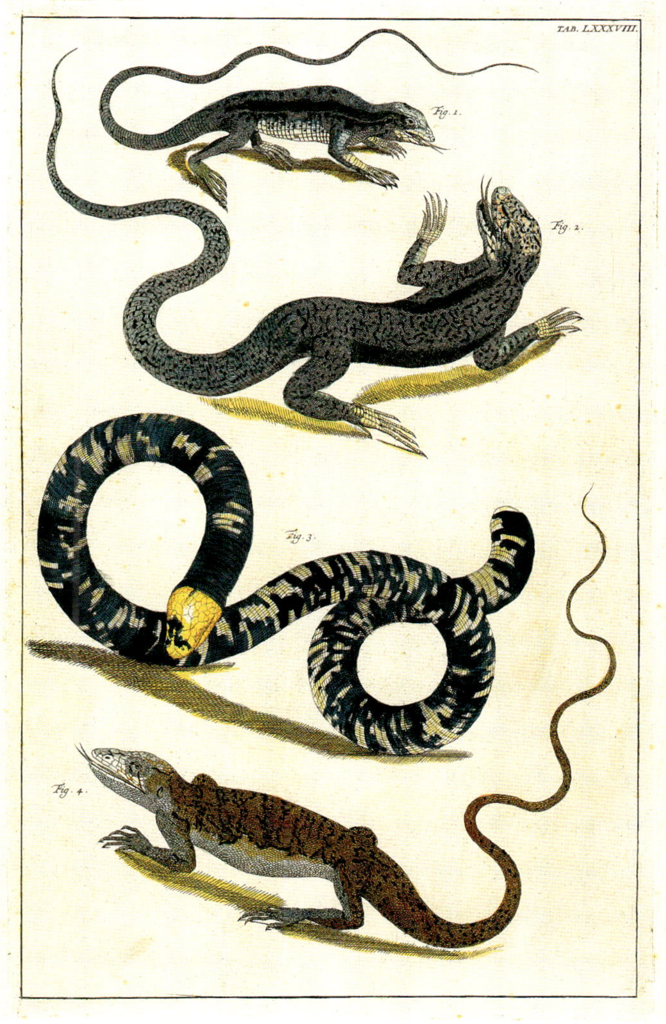

1-2, 4 Sauria **3** Amphisbaenia
1-2, 4 Lizards, iguanas or anoles · Eidechsen, Iguanas oder Anolis · Sauriens, iguanes ou anolis
3 Worm lizard · Doppelschleiche · Amphisbène

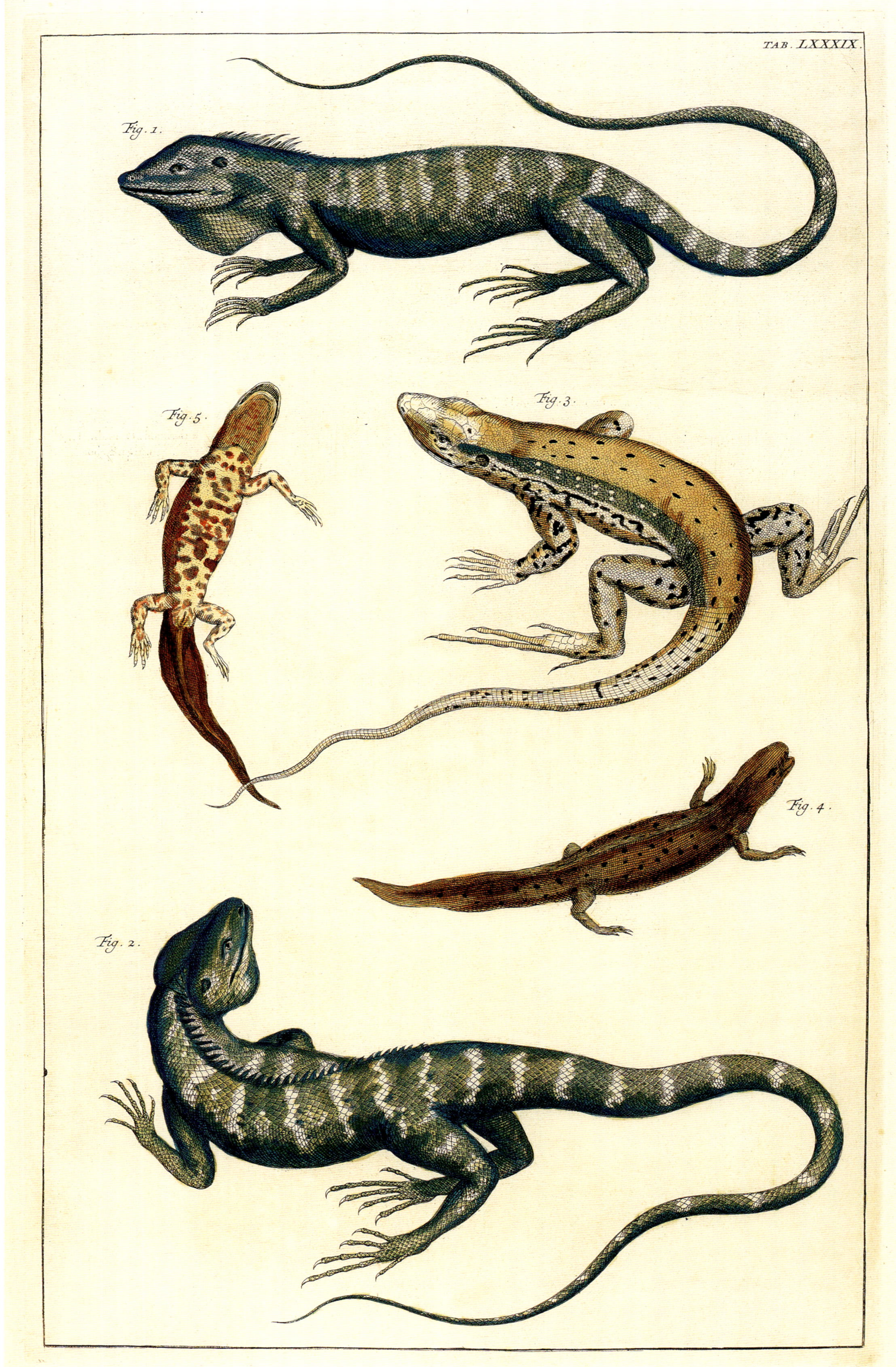

1-2 Iguanidae 3 Sauria 4-5 Salamandridae
1-2 Iguanas or anoles · Leguane oder Anolis · Iguanes ou anolis 3 Lizard · Eidechse · Saurien 4-5 Newts · Molche · Tritons

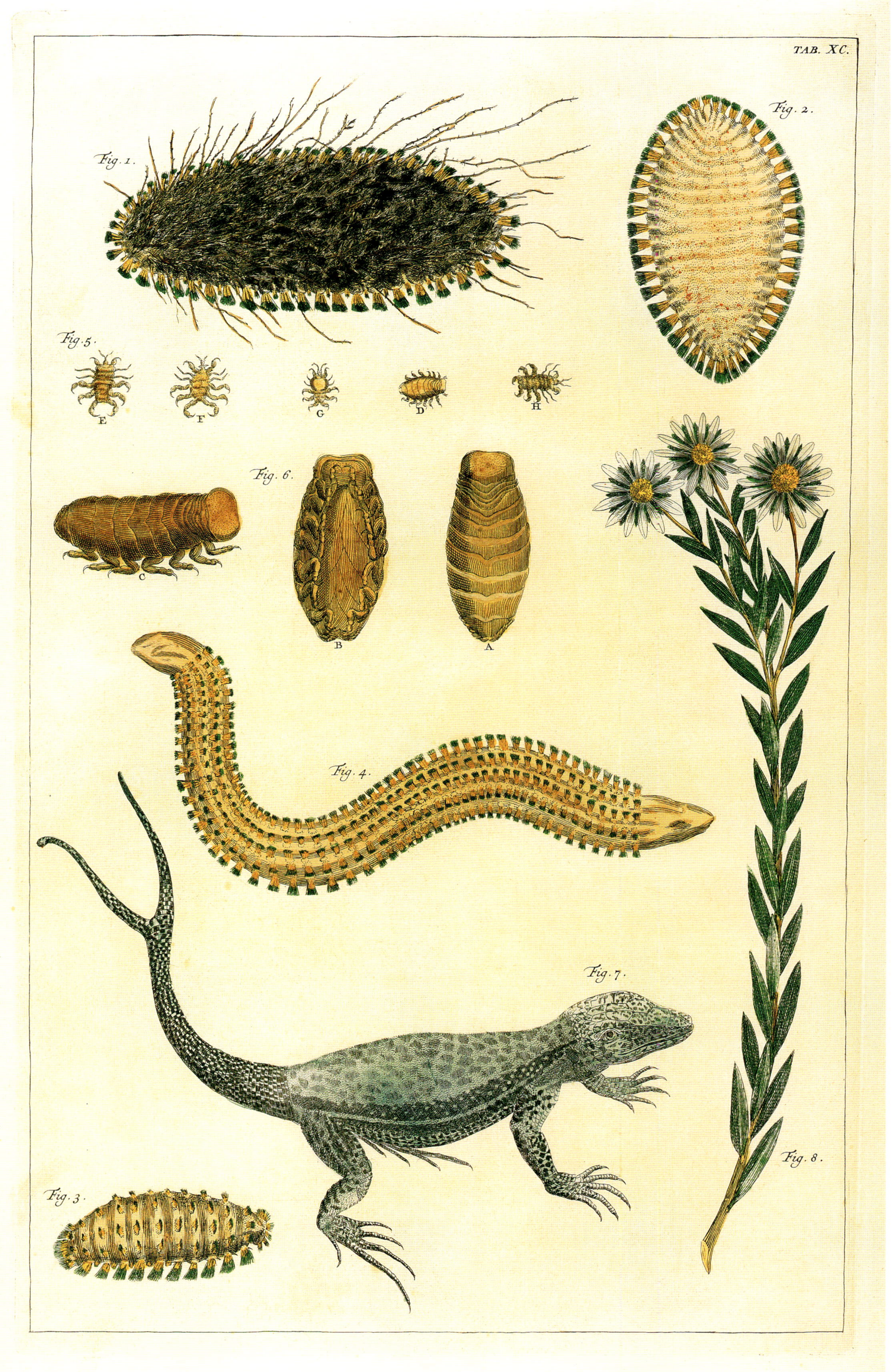

1-4 Polychaeta 5 Cyamidae 6 Isopoda: Cymothoida 7 Sauria 8 Compositae
1-4 Sea mice · Seemäuse · Aphrodites épineuses 5 Whale-lice · Wal-Läuse · Crustacéens 6 Isopod · Marine Assel · Crustacéens 7 Lizard · Eidechse · Saurien
8 Sunflower family · Korbblütler · Composées

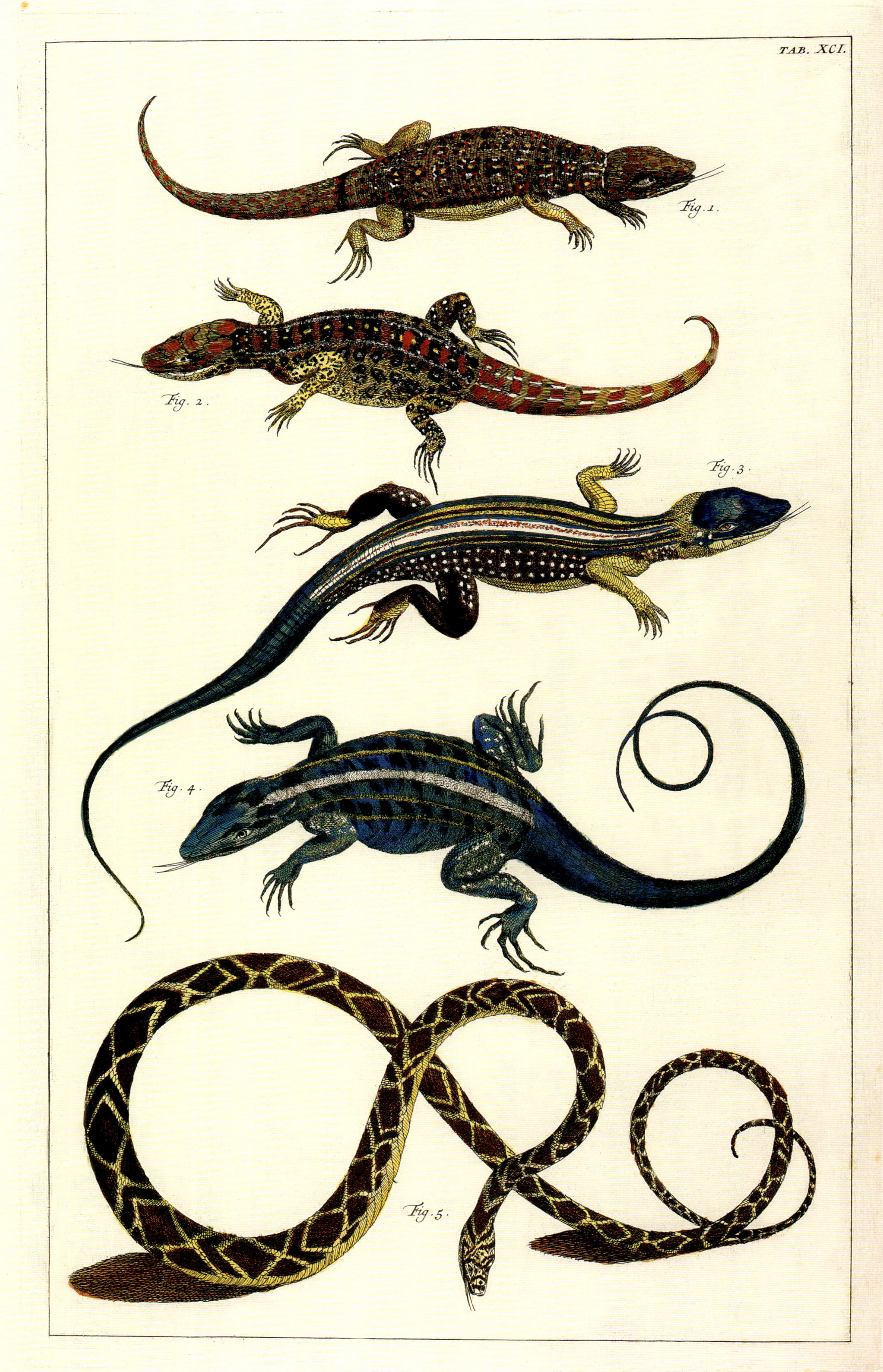

1-4 Sauria 5 Serpentes
1-4 Lizards · Eidechsen · Lézards 5 Snake, according to Seba from Brazil · Schlange, nach Seba aus Brasilien · Serpent, du Brésil selon Seba

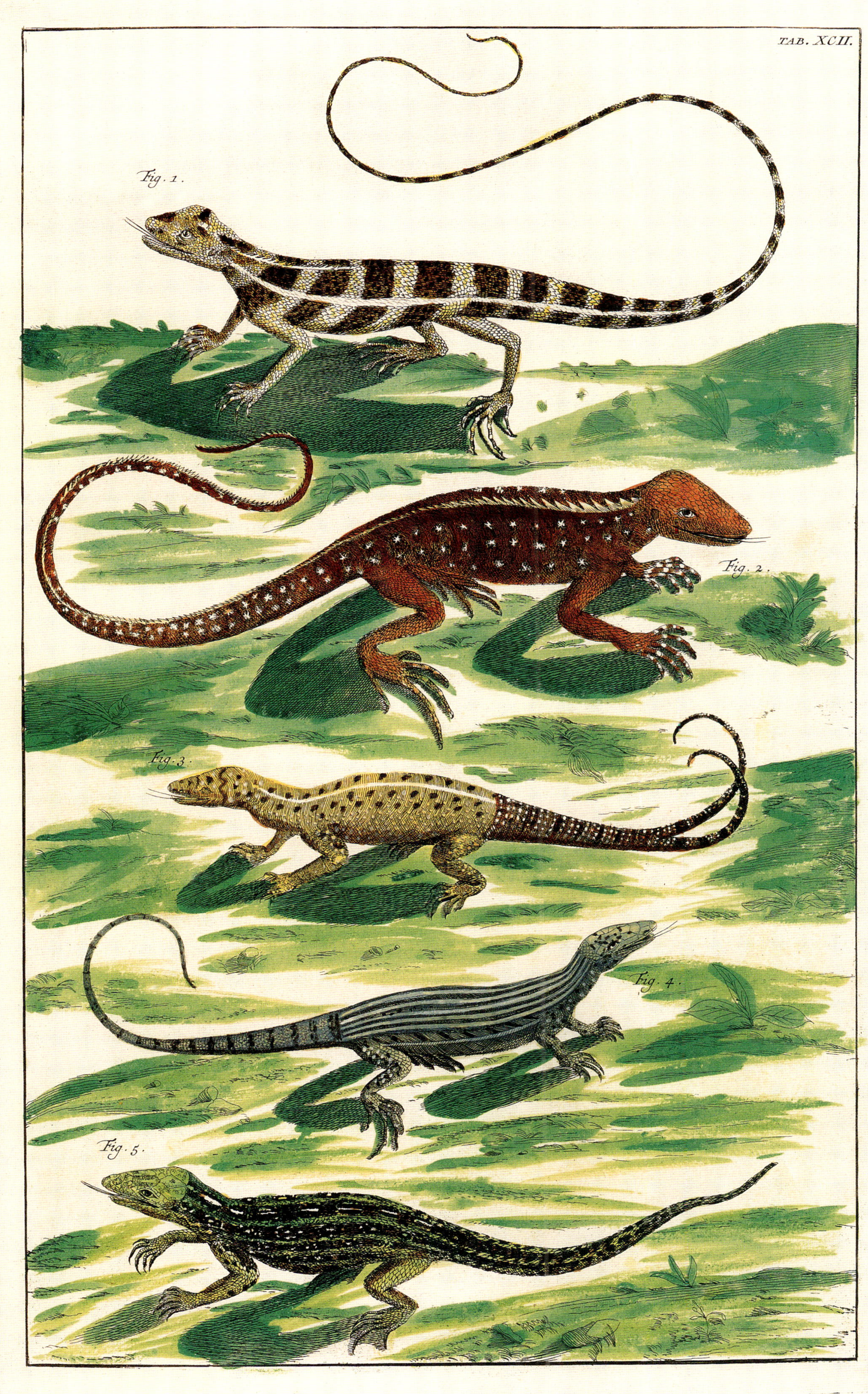

1-5 Sauria
1-5 Lizards and anoles · Eidechsen und Anolis · Lézards et anolis

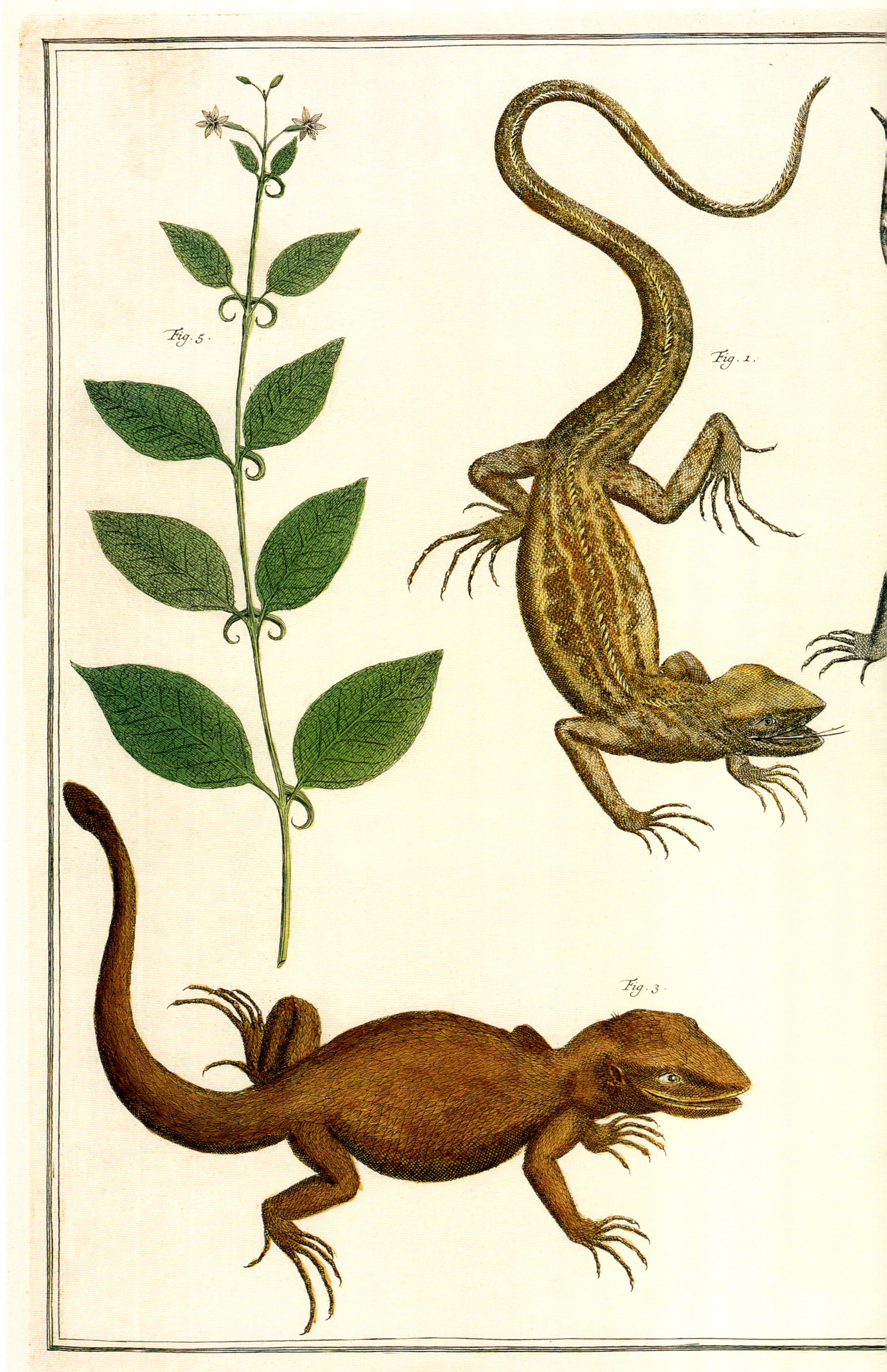

1-4 Sauria
1-4 Lizards · Eidechsen · Lézards

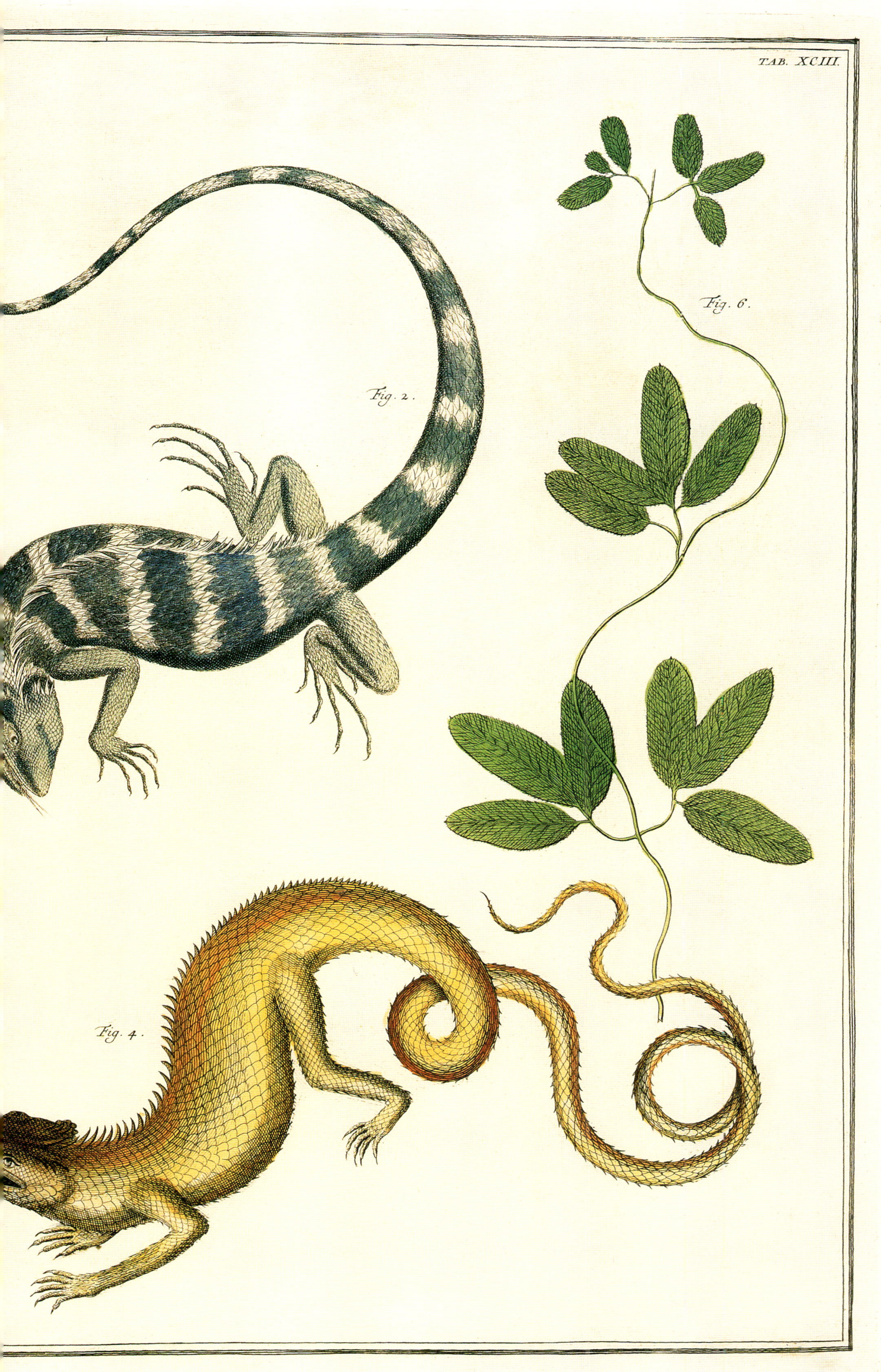
TAB. XCIII.
Fig. 2.
Fig. 6.
Fig. 4.

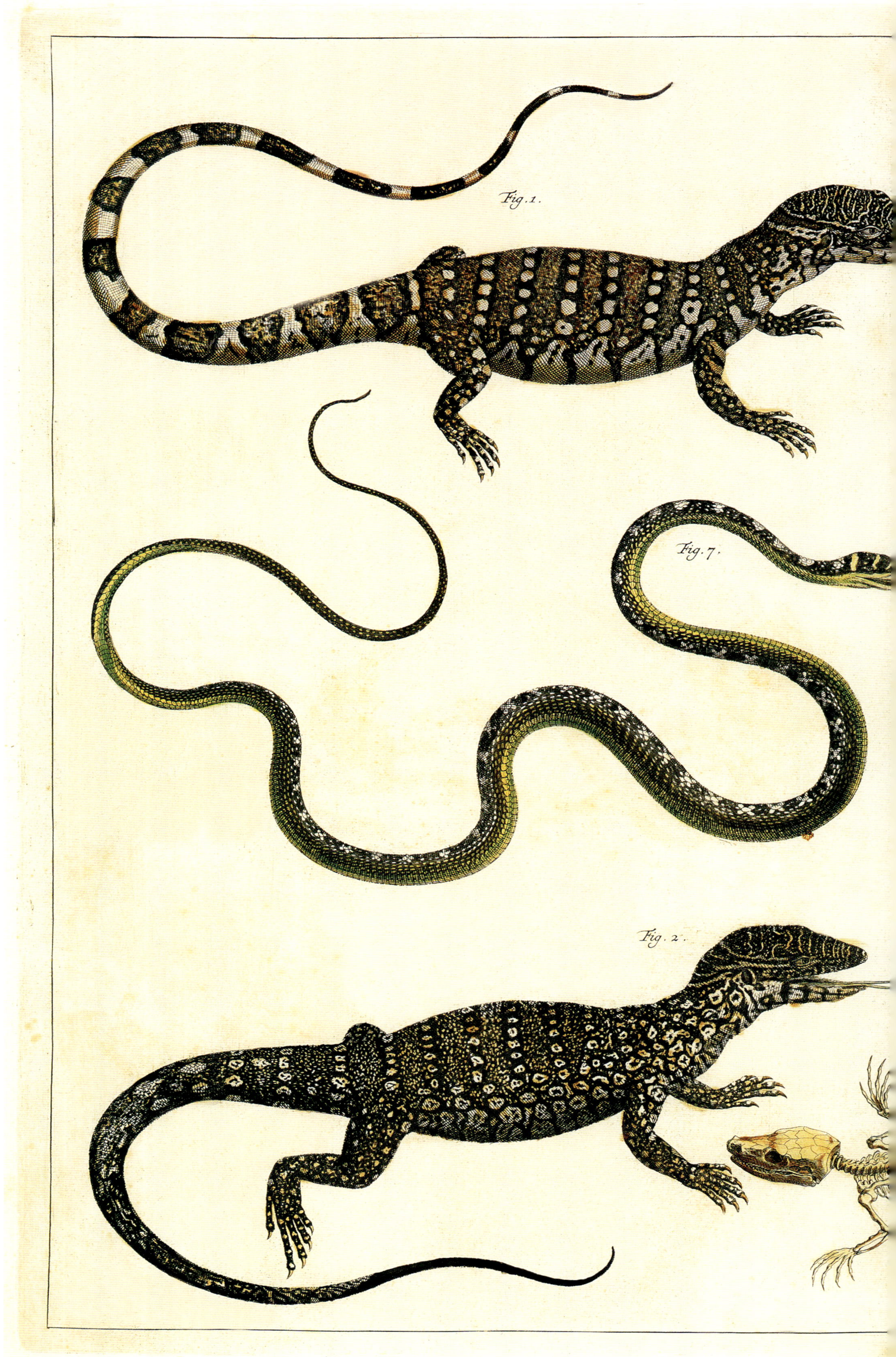

1-3 *Varanus* **4** Agamidae **5-6** Sauria **7-8** Serpentes
1-3 Monitors · Warane · Varanidés **4** Agama · Agame · Agamidé **5-6** Lizards and anoles · Eidechsen und Anolis · Lézards et anolis **7** Snake, according to Seba from Ceylon · Schlange, nach Seba aus Ceylon · Serpent, de Ceylan selon Seba

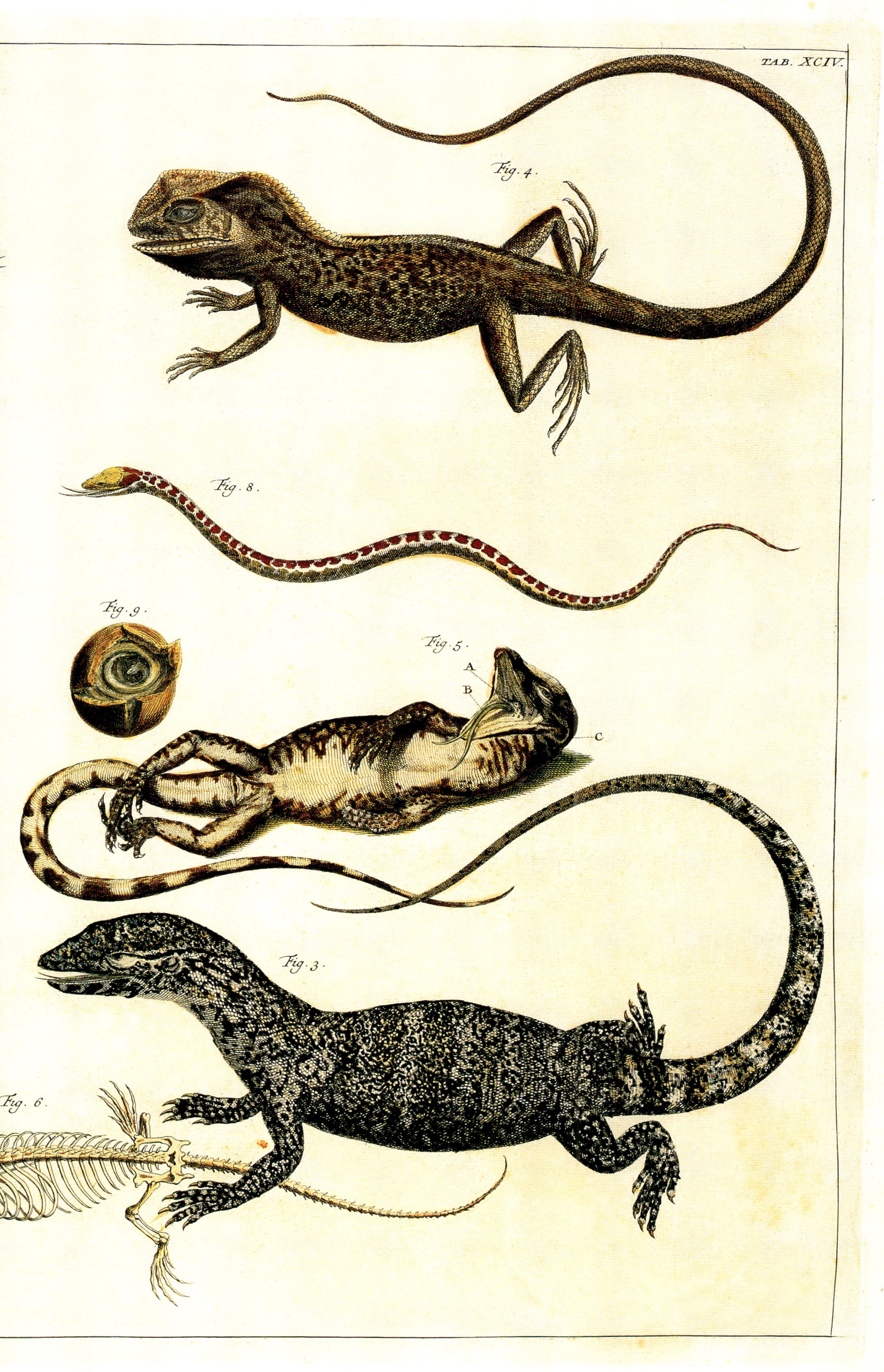
TAB. XCIV.
Fig. 4.
Fig. 8.
Fig. 9.
Fig. 5.
A
B
C
Fig. 3.
Fig. 6.

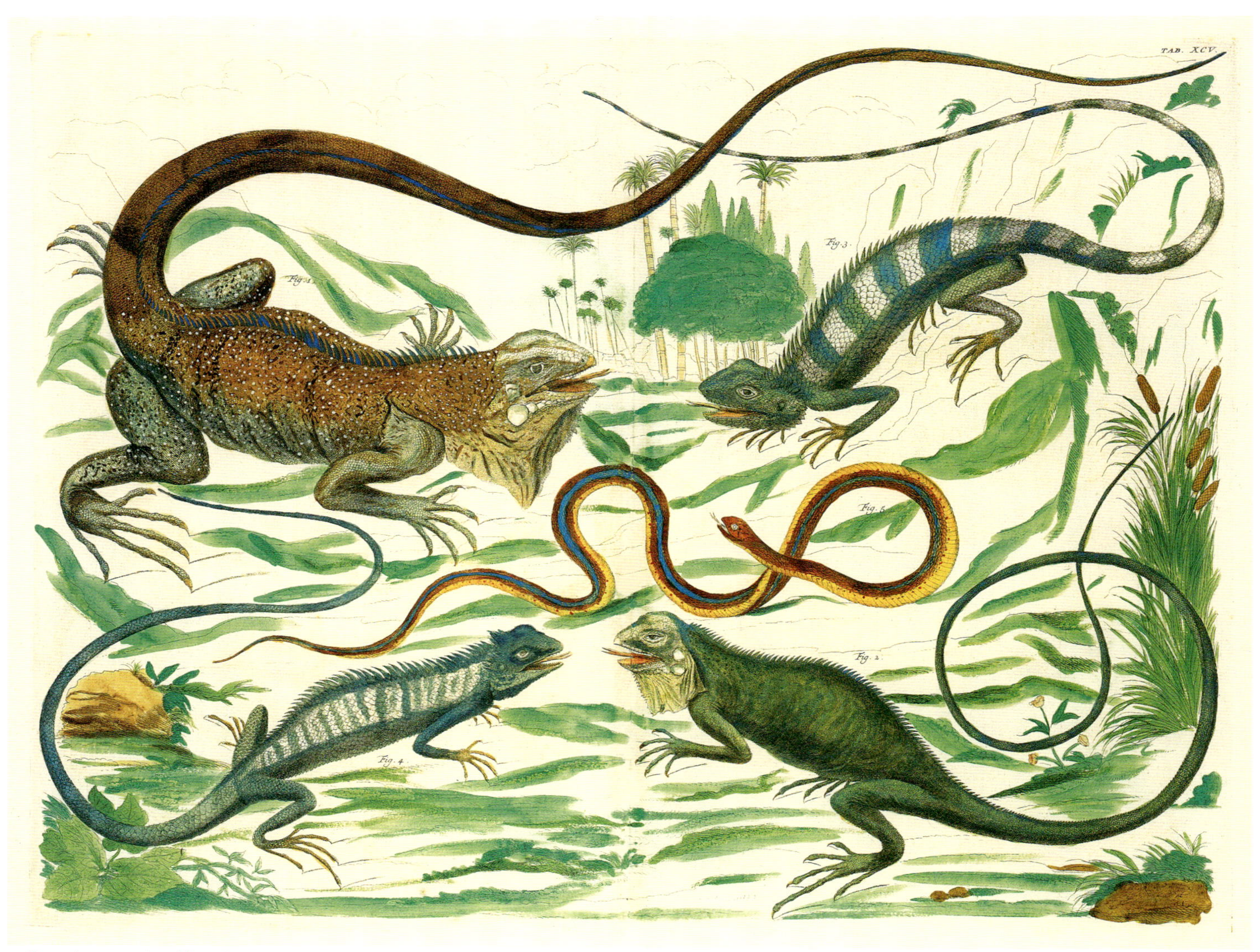

1-2 *Iguana iguana* **3-4** Agamidae **5** Serpentes
1-2 Green iguanas · Grüne Leguane · Iguanes communs **3-4** Agamas · Agamen · Agamidés

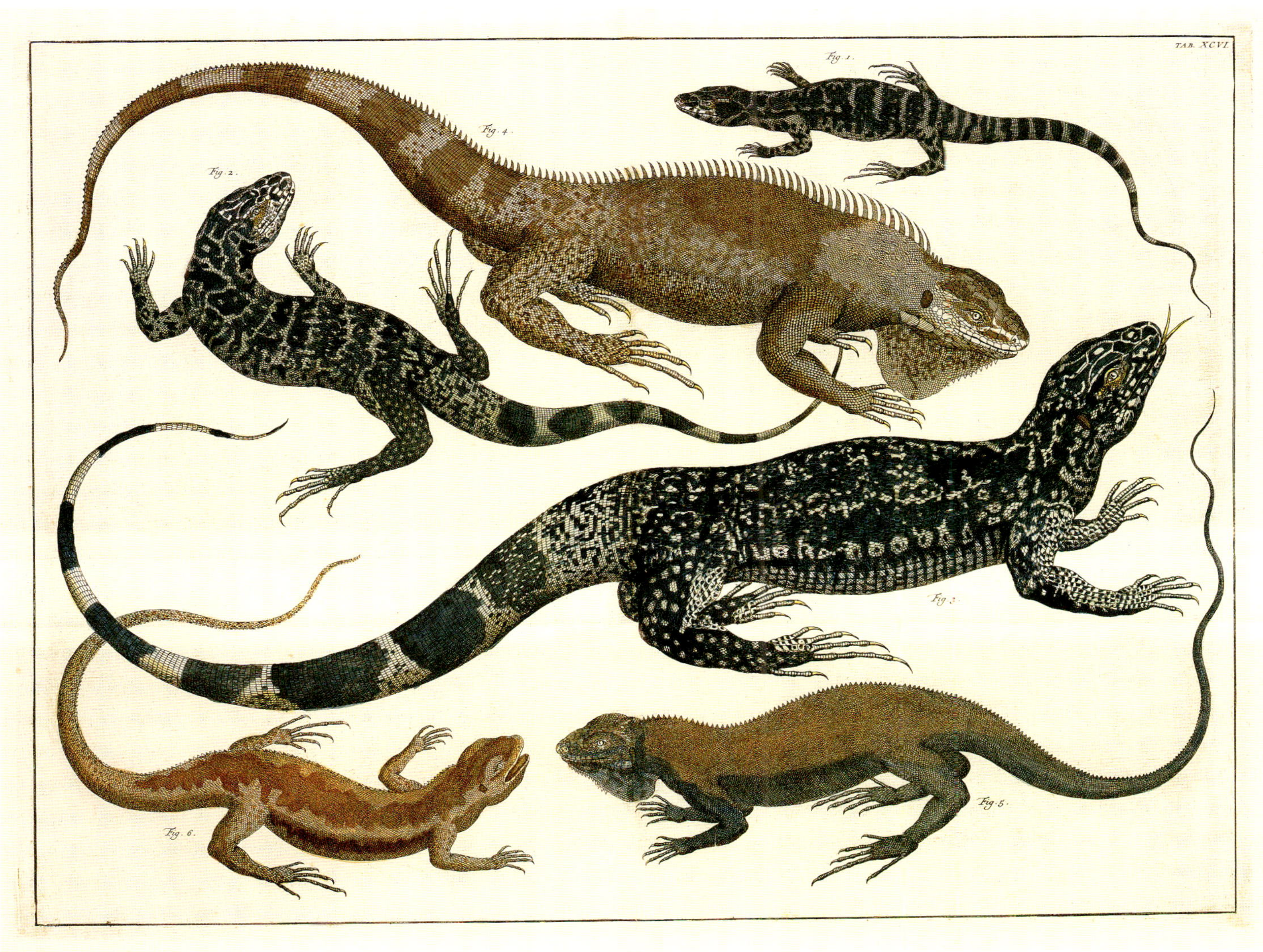

1-3 *Tupinambis teguixin* **4-6** Sauria
1-3 Common tegus · Tejus · Tégus communs **4-6** Lizards · Eidechsen · Sauriens

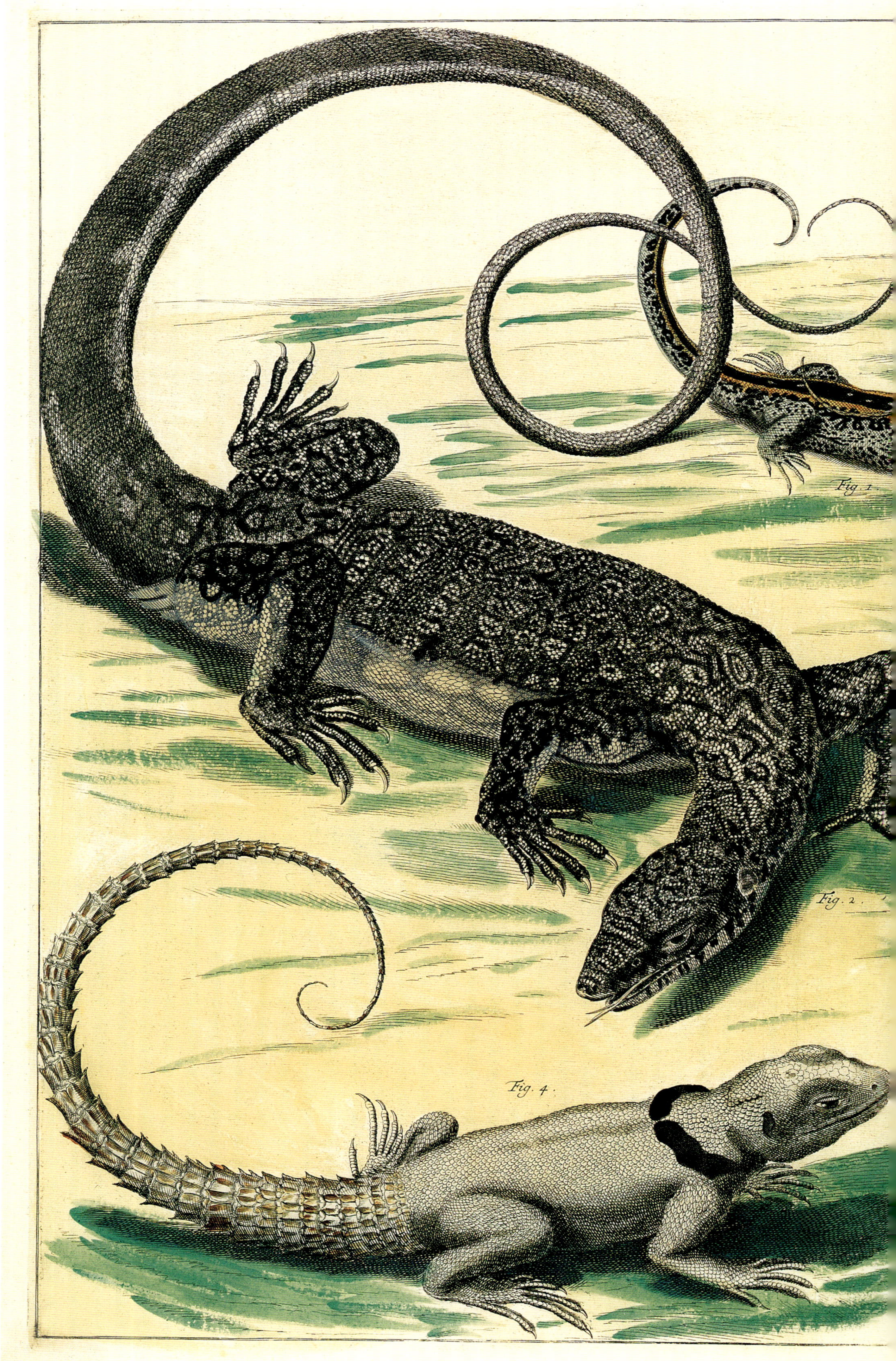

1-5 Squamata 3 *Iguana iguana*
1-5 Squamata from South America · Echsen aus Südamerika · Squamates d'Amérique du Sud 3 Green iguana · Grüner Leguan · Iguane vert

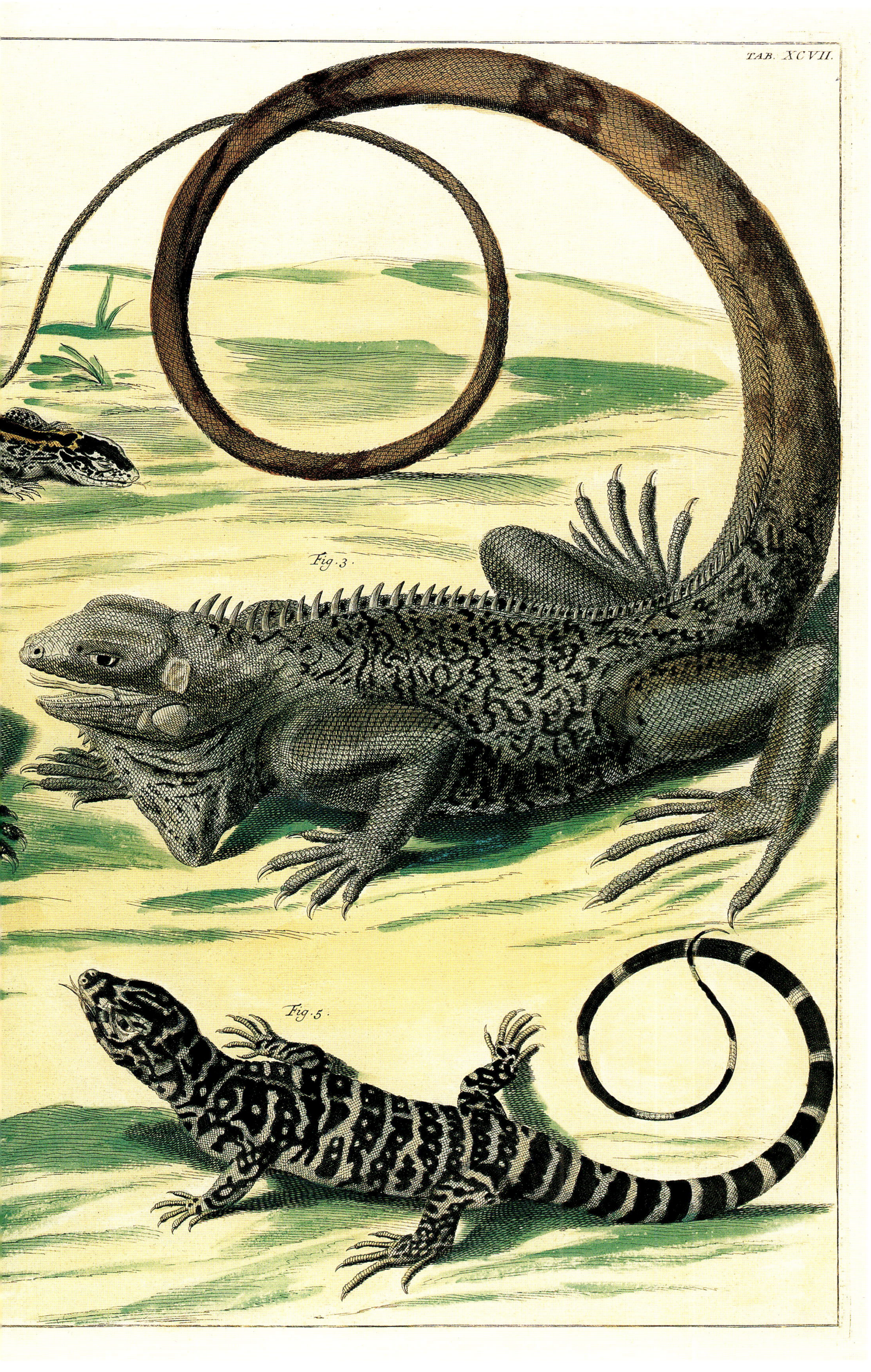
TAB. XCVII.
Fig. 3.
Fig. 5.

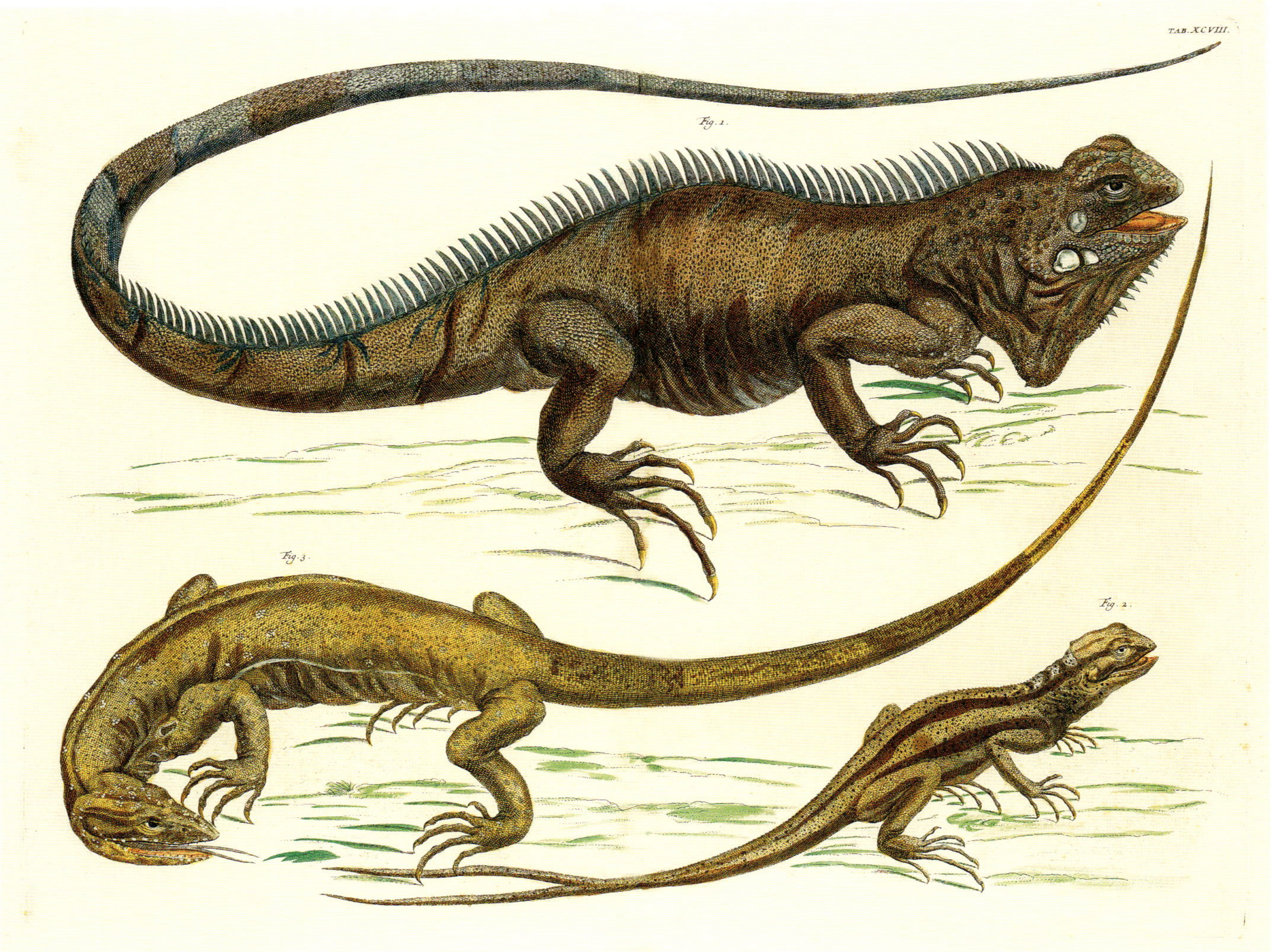

1 *Iguana iguana* 2 Polychrotidae 3 *Tupinambis teguixin*
1 Green iguana · Grüner Leguan · Iguane vert 3 Common tegu · Teju · Tégu commun

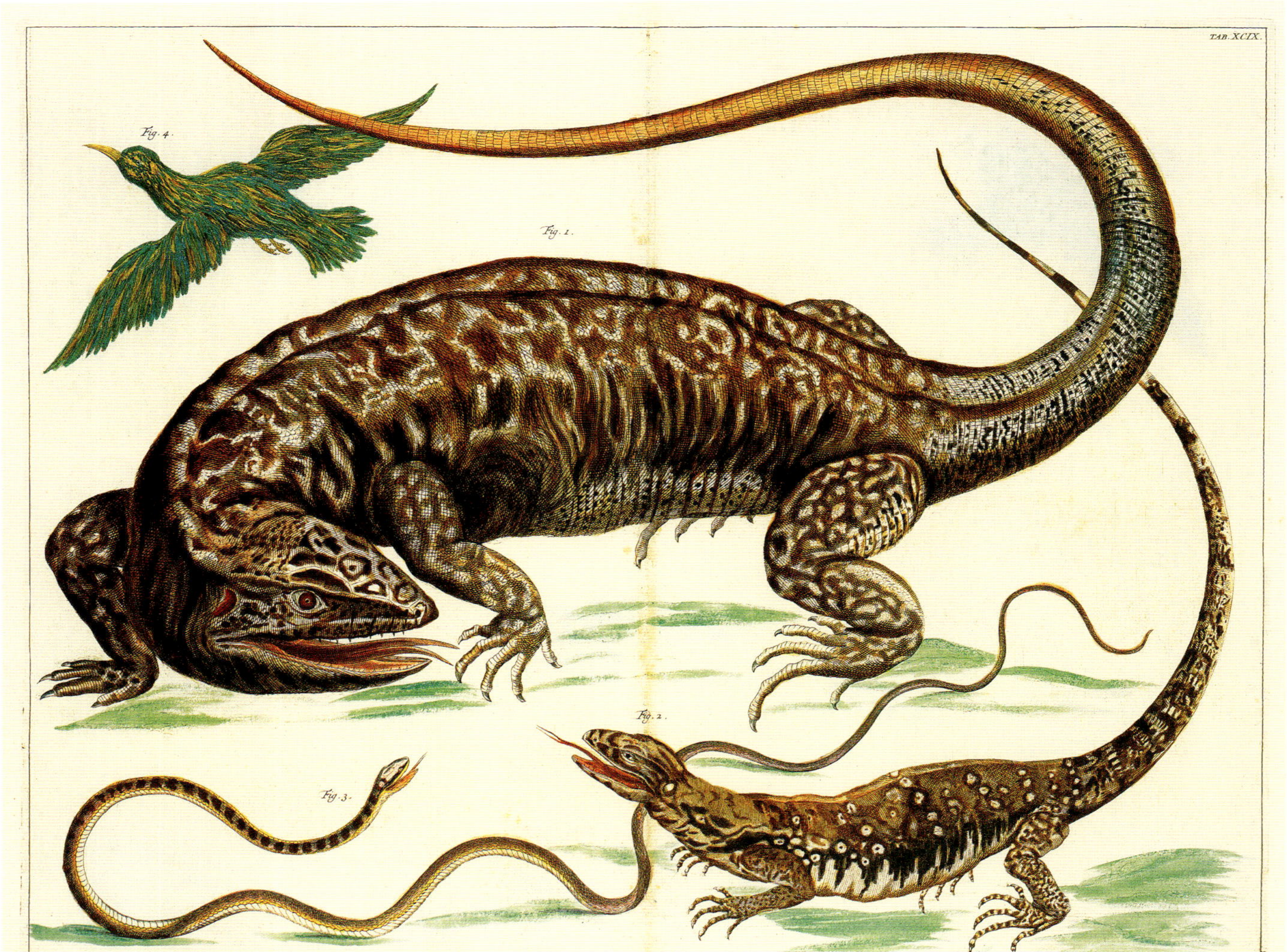

1 *Tupinambis teguixin* 2 Varanus 3 Serpentes 4 Trochilidae
1 Common tegu · Teju · Tégu commun 2 Monitor from South East Asia · Waran aus Südostasien · Varanidé de l'Asie du Sud-Est 3 Snake, according to Seba from Madeira · Schlange, nach Seba von Madeira · Serpent, de Madère selon Seba 4 Hummingbird · Kolibri · Colibri

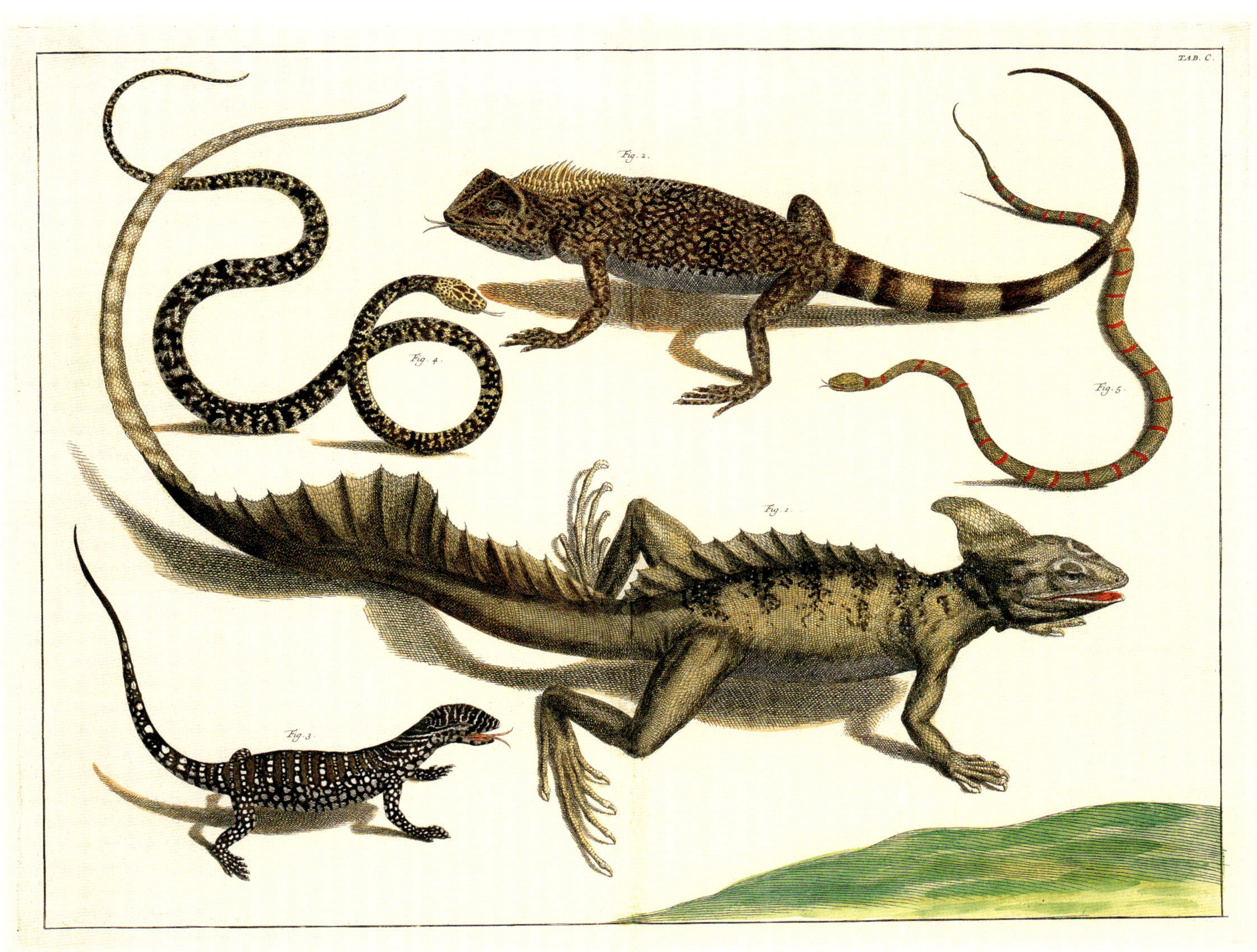

1 *Basiliscus basiliscus* 2-3 Squamata 4-5 Serpentes
1 Common basilisk · Basilisk · Basilic 2-3 Squamata · Schuppenkriechtiere · Squamates 4-5 Snakes, according to Seba from Ceylon · Schlangen nach Seba aus Ceylon · Serpents, de Ceylan selon Seba

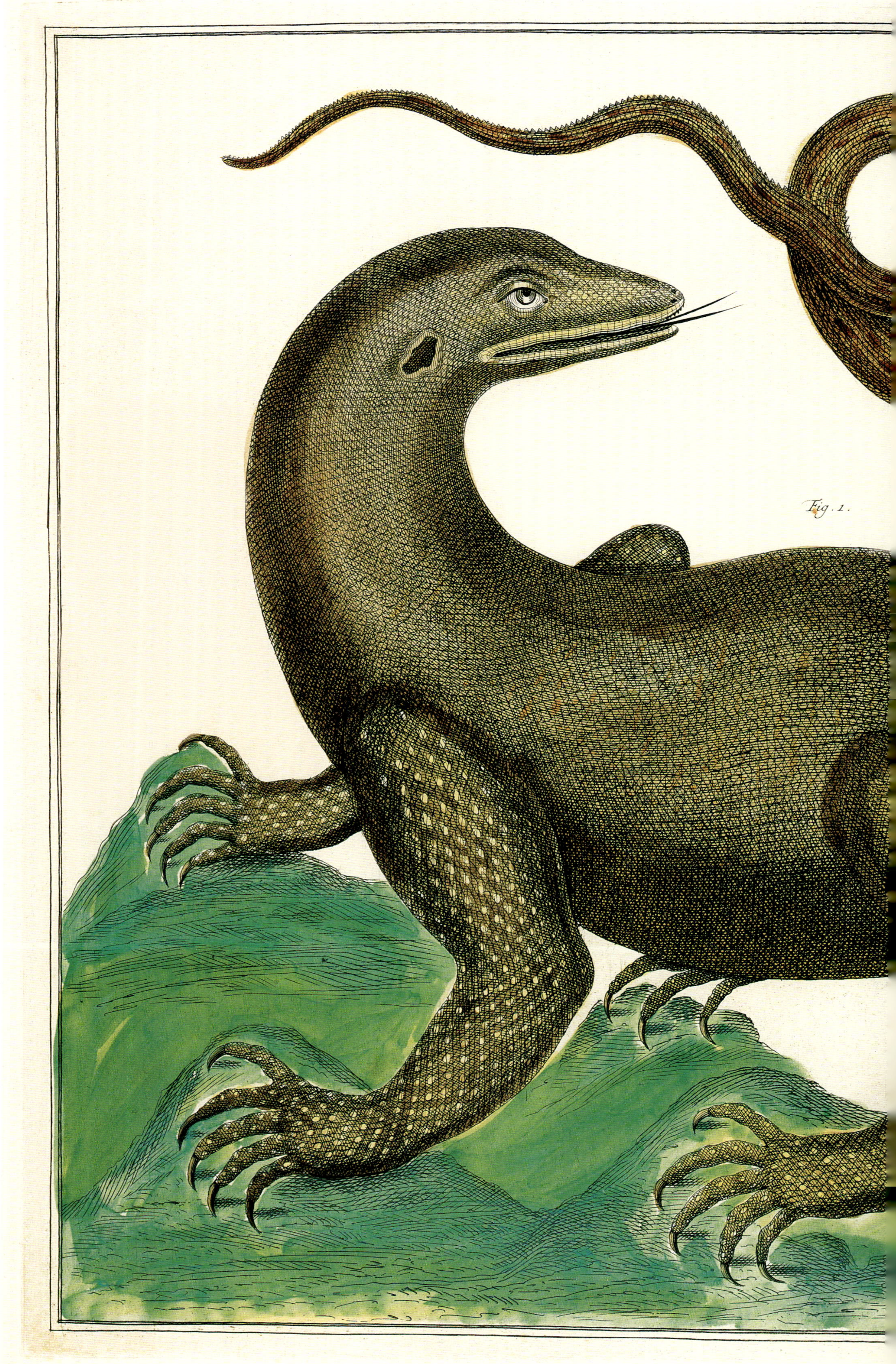

Squamata
Squamata · Echse · Squamate

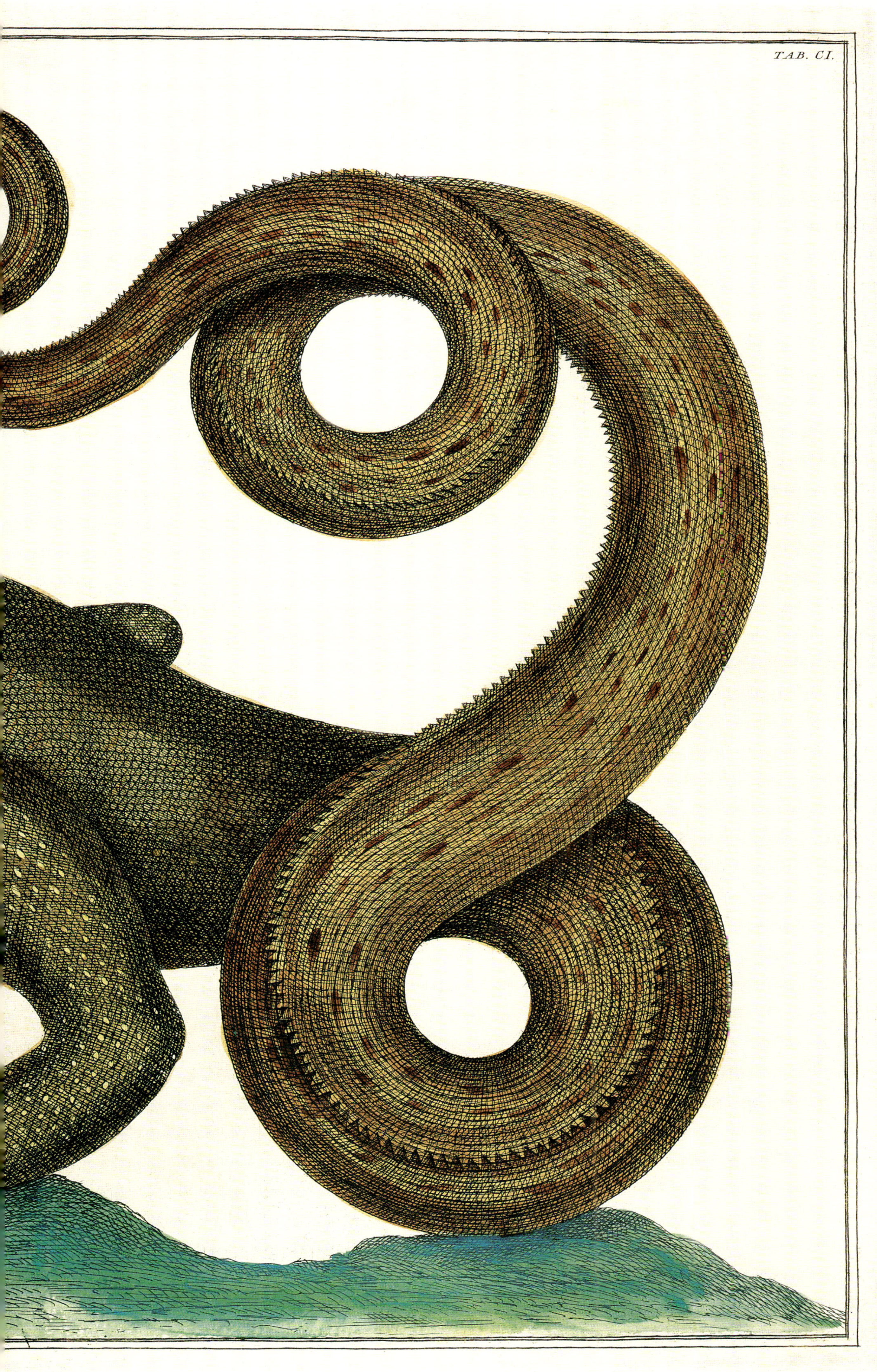
TAB. CI.

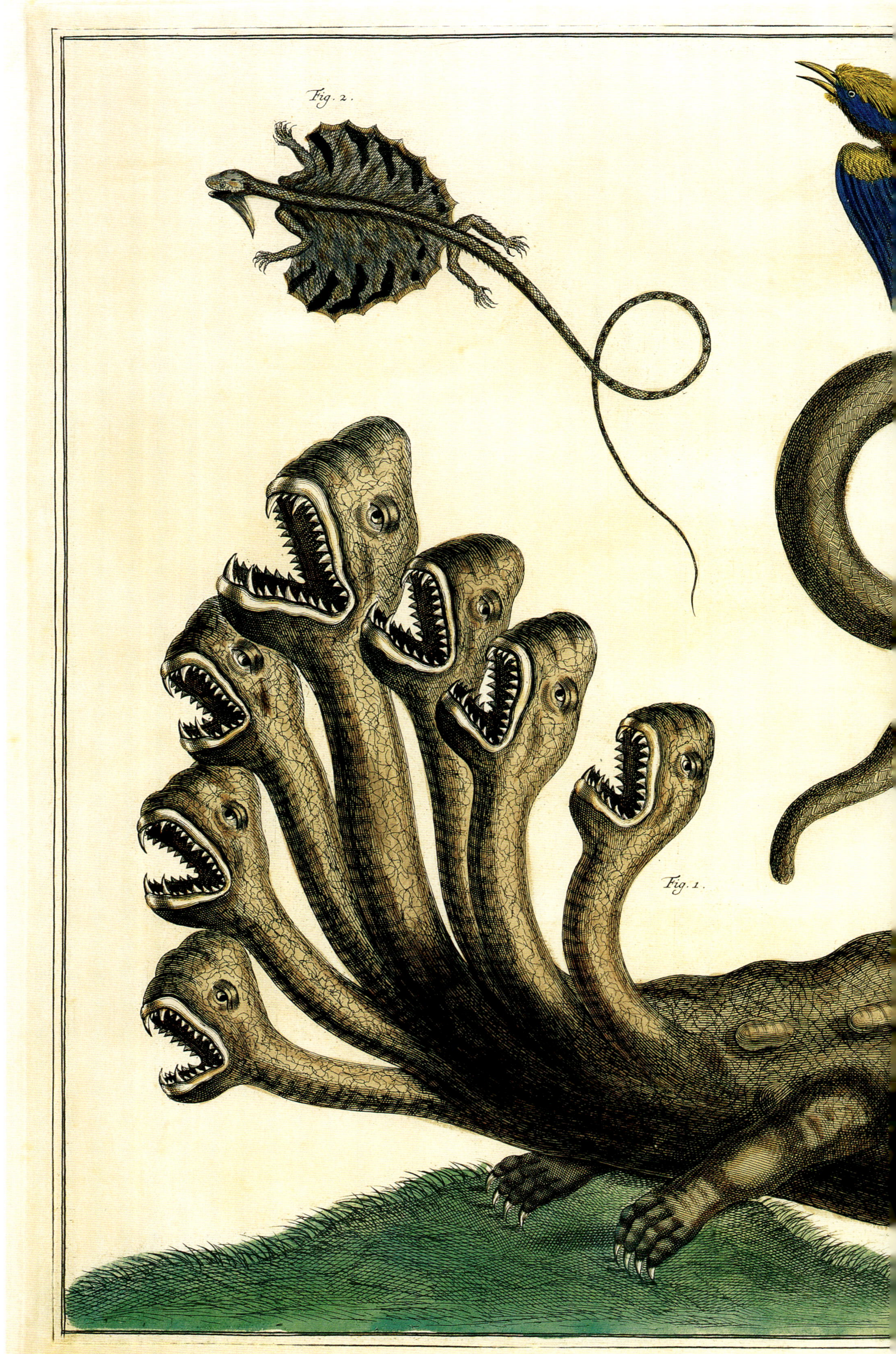

1 "Hydra" 2 Draco sp.
1 Fantasy animal · Fantasietier · Animal fabuleux 2 Flying dragon · Flugdrachen · Dragon volant

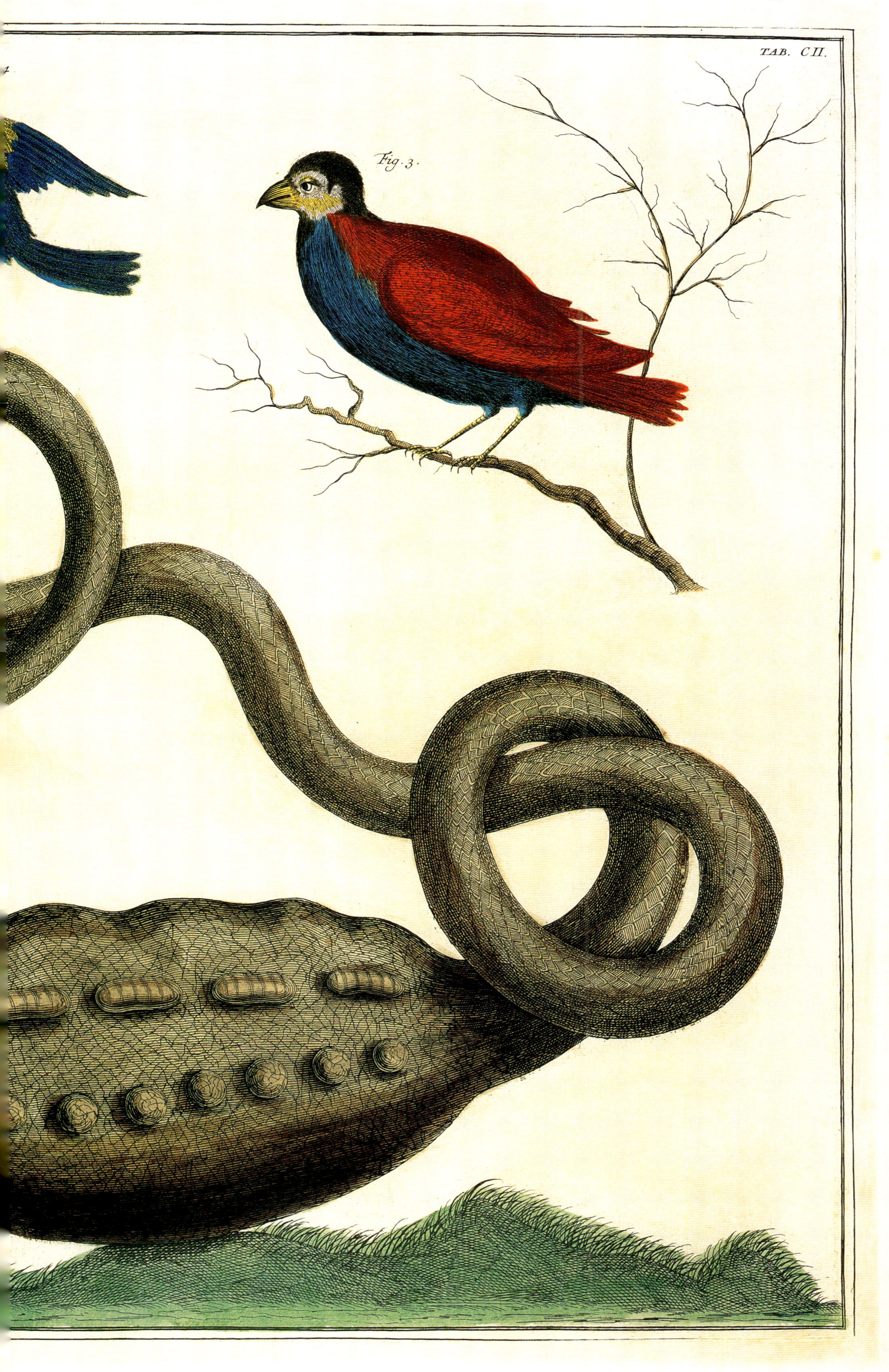
TAB. CII.
Fig. 3.

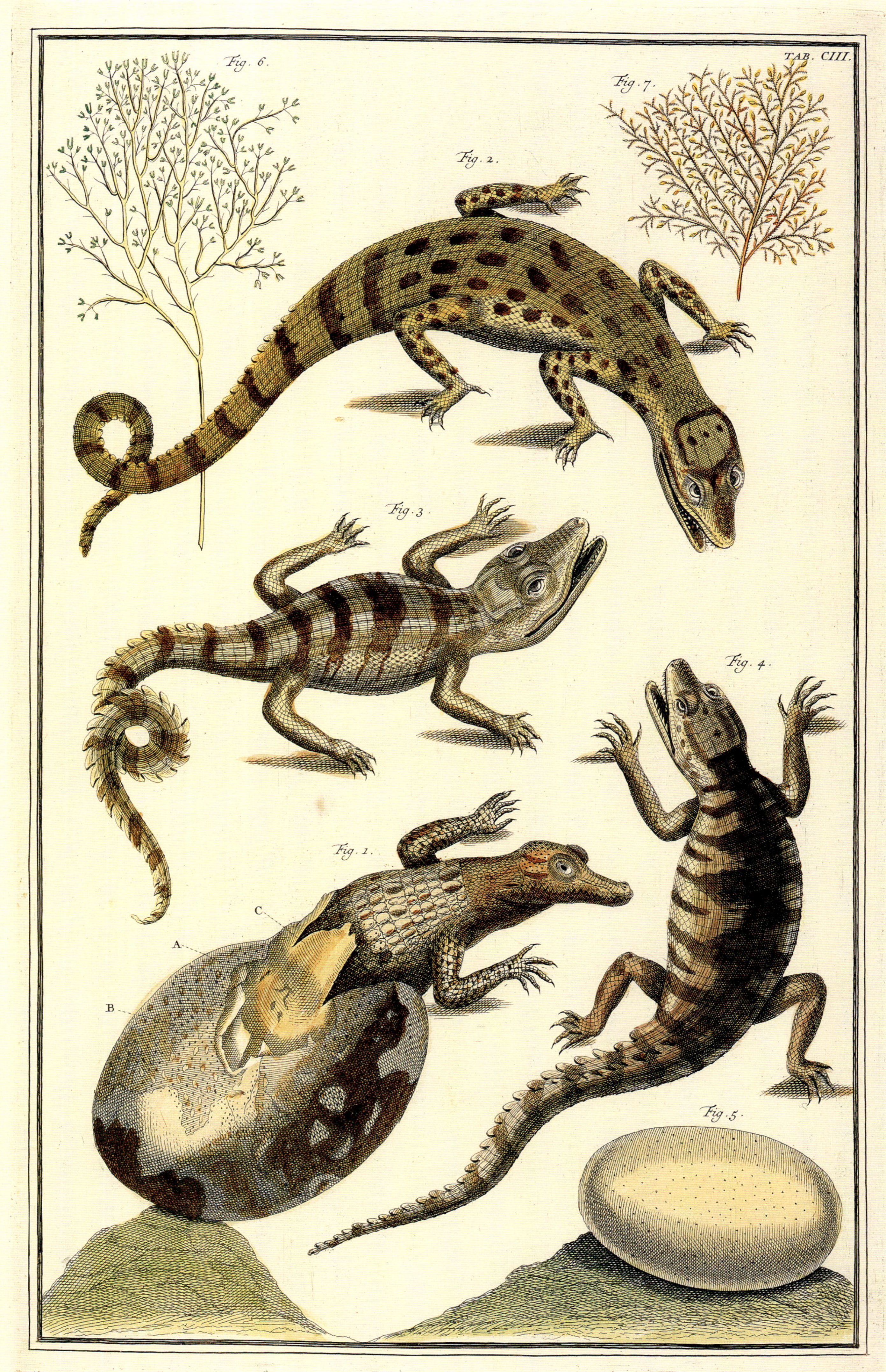

1-5 Crocodilia
1-5 Crocodiles · Krokodile · Crocodiliens

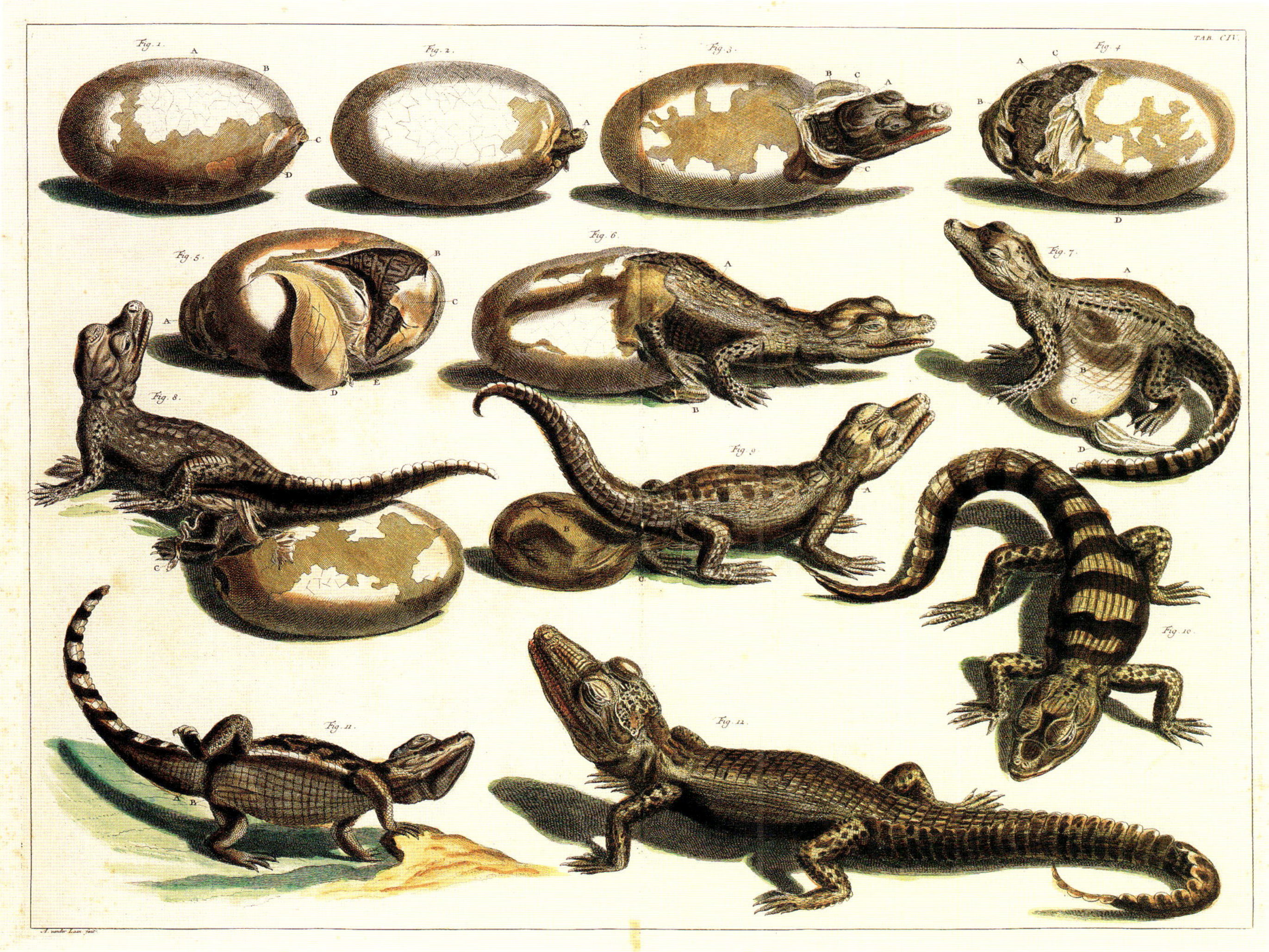

1-12 *Crocodilia*
1-12 Crocodiles · Krokodile · Crocodiliens

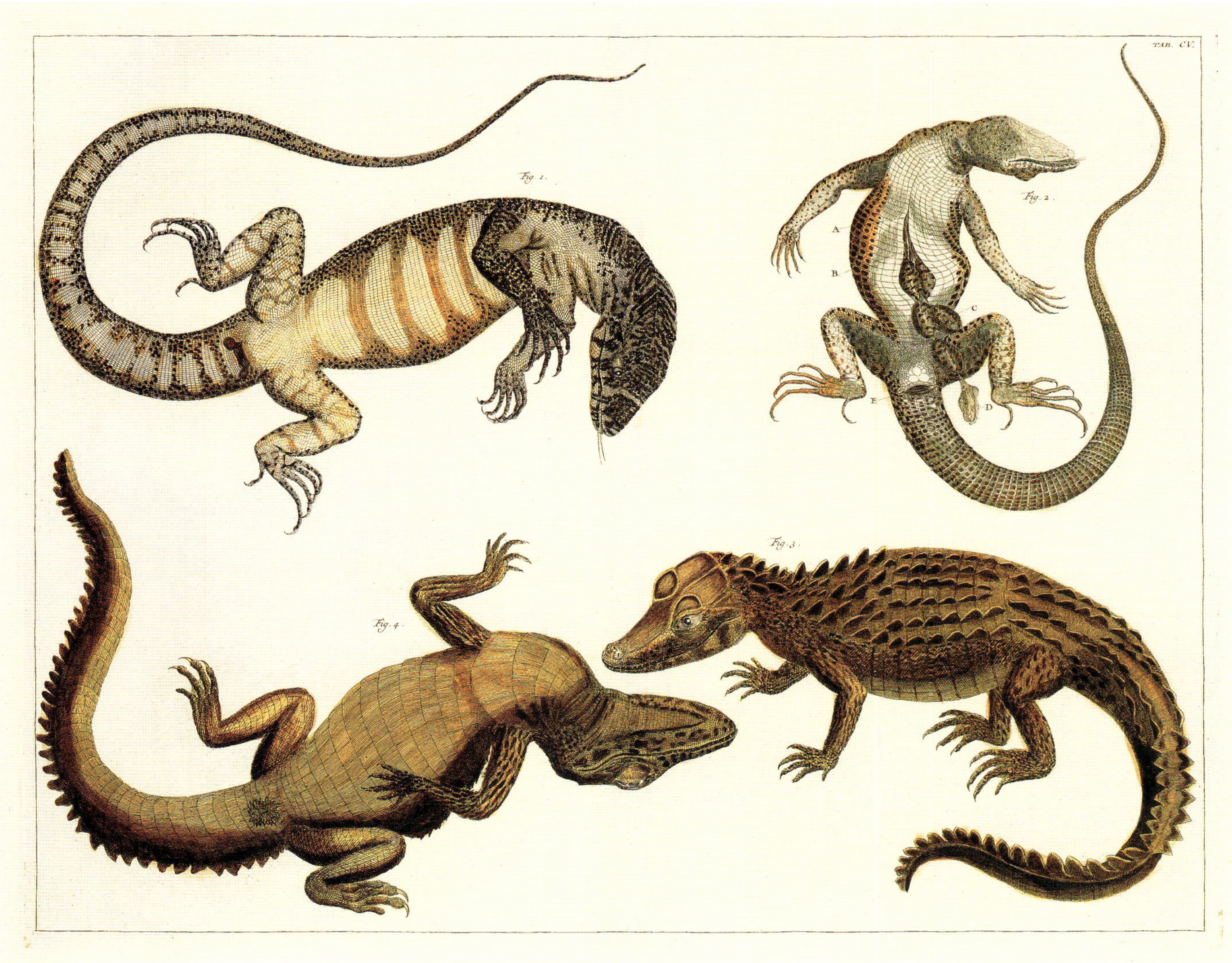

1-2 *Varanus sp.* **3-4** *Paleosuchus sp.*
1-2 Monitors from South East Asia · Warane aus Südostasien · Varanidés de l'Asie du Sud-Est **3-4** Dwarf caimans · Glattstirnkaimane · Paléosuches

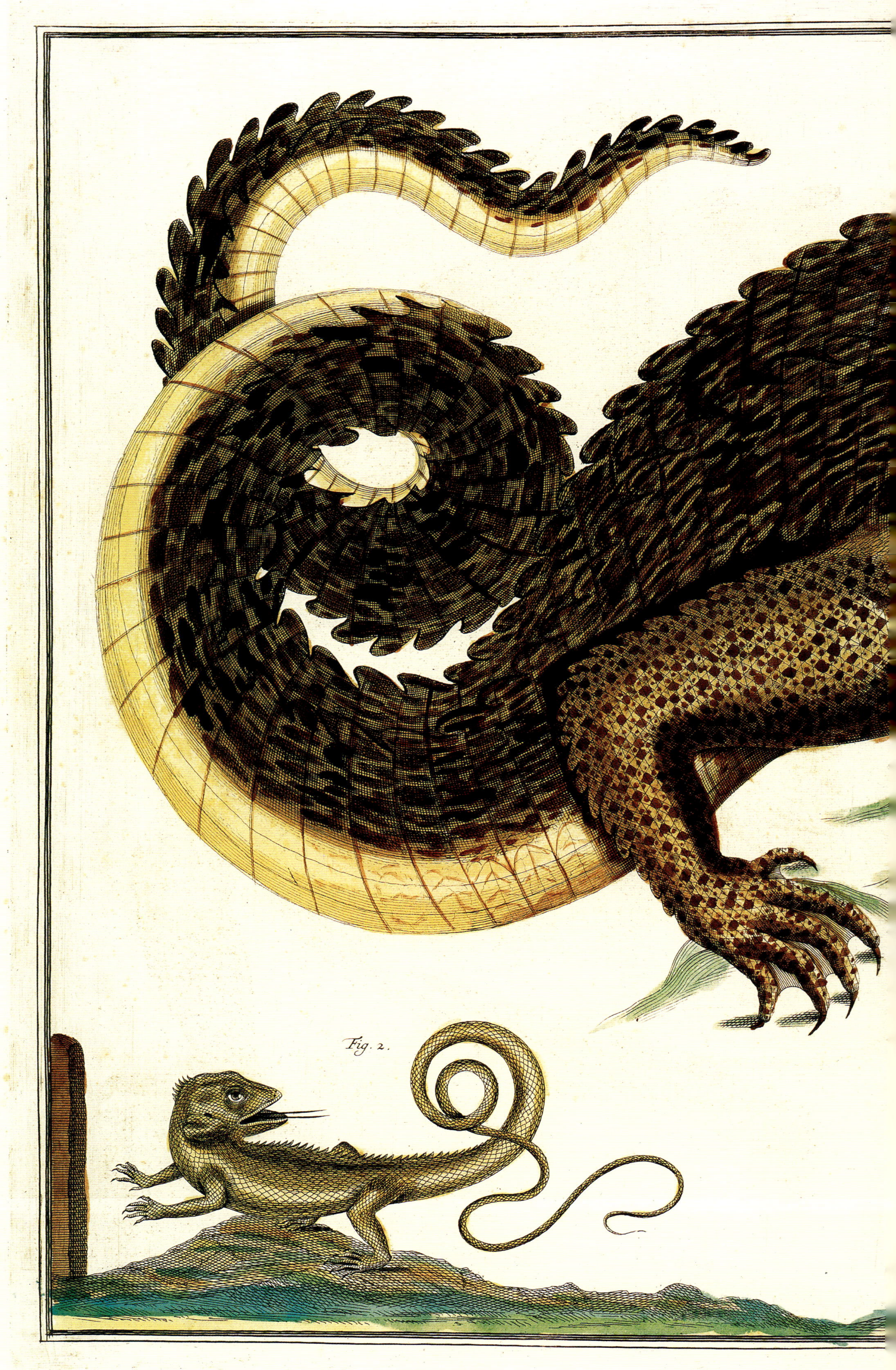

1 Squamata 2 Squamata
1 Crocodile · Krokodil · Crocodilien 2 Lizard · Kleine Echse · Petit lézard

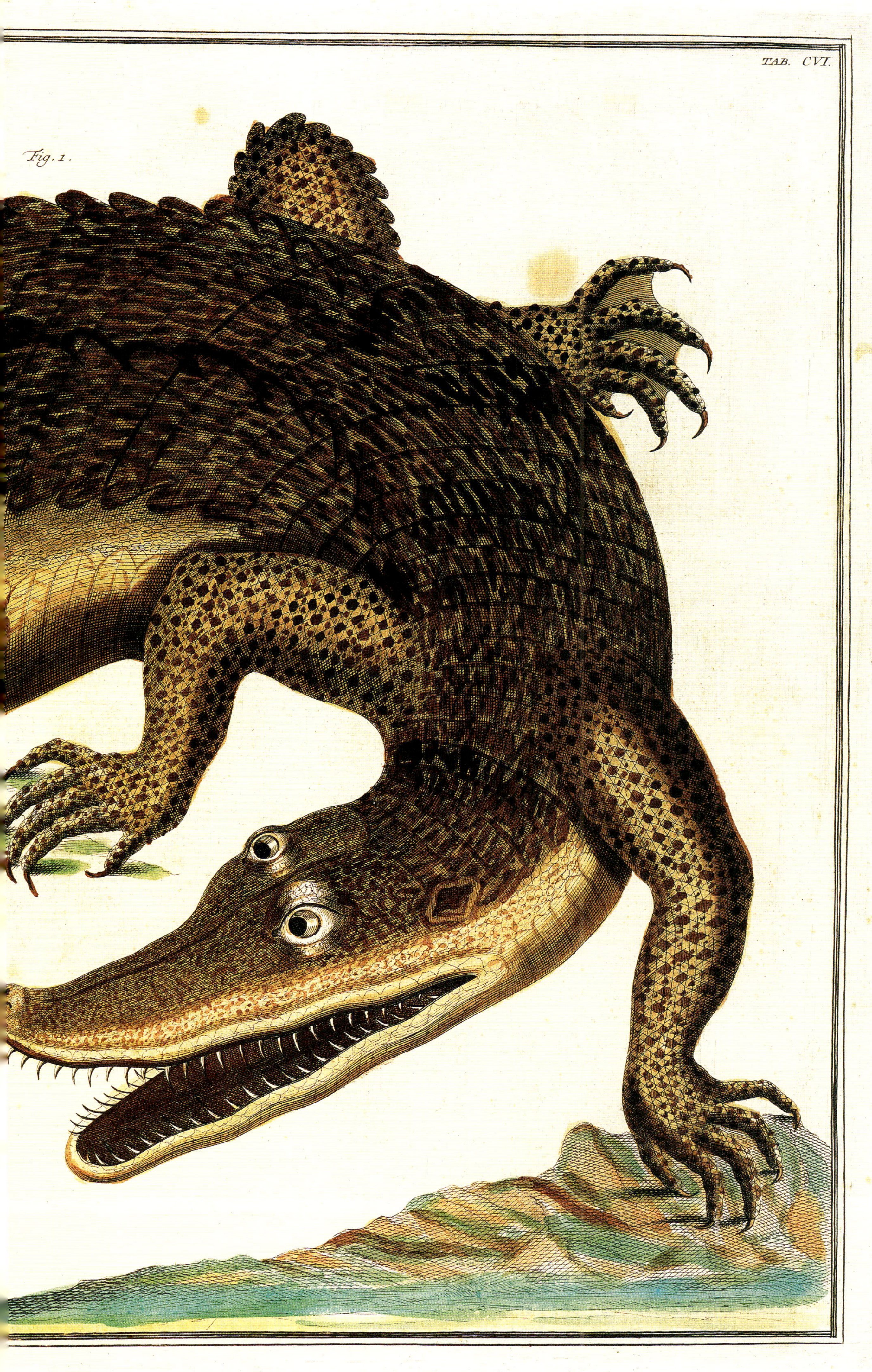
TAB. CVI.
Fig. 1.

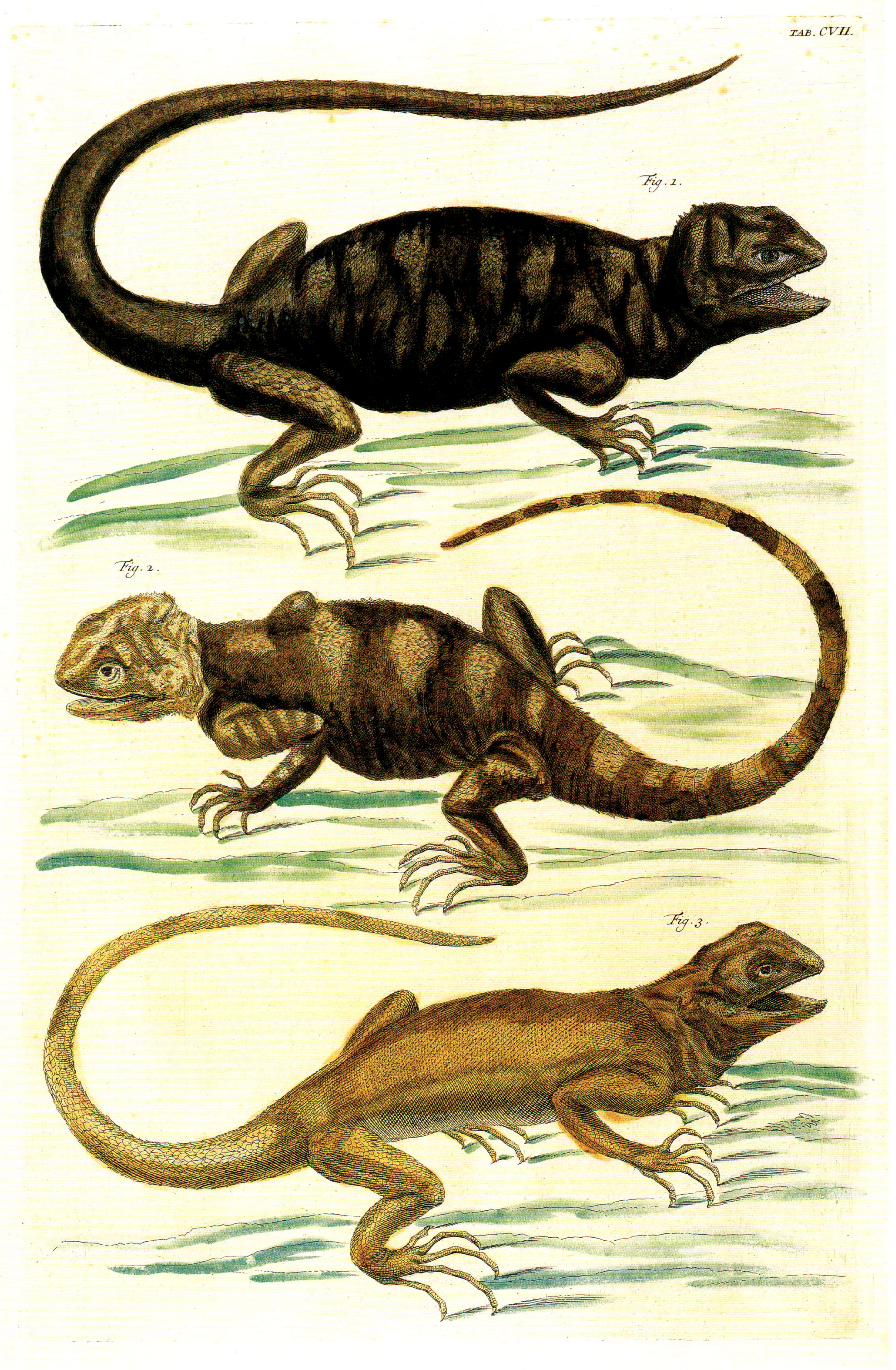

1-3 Iguanidae
1-3 Iguanas · Leguane · Iguanidés

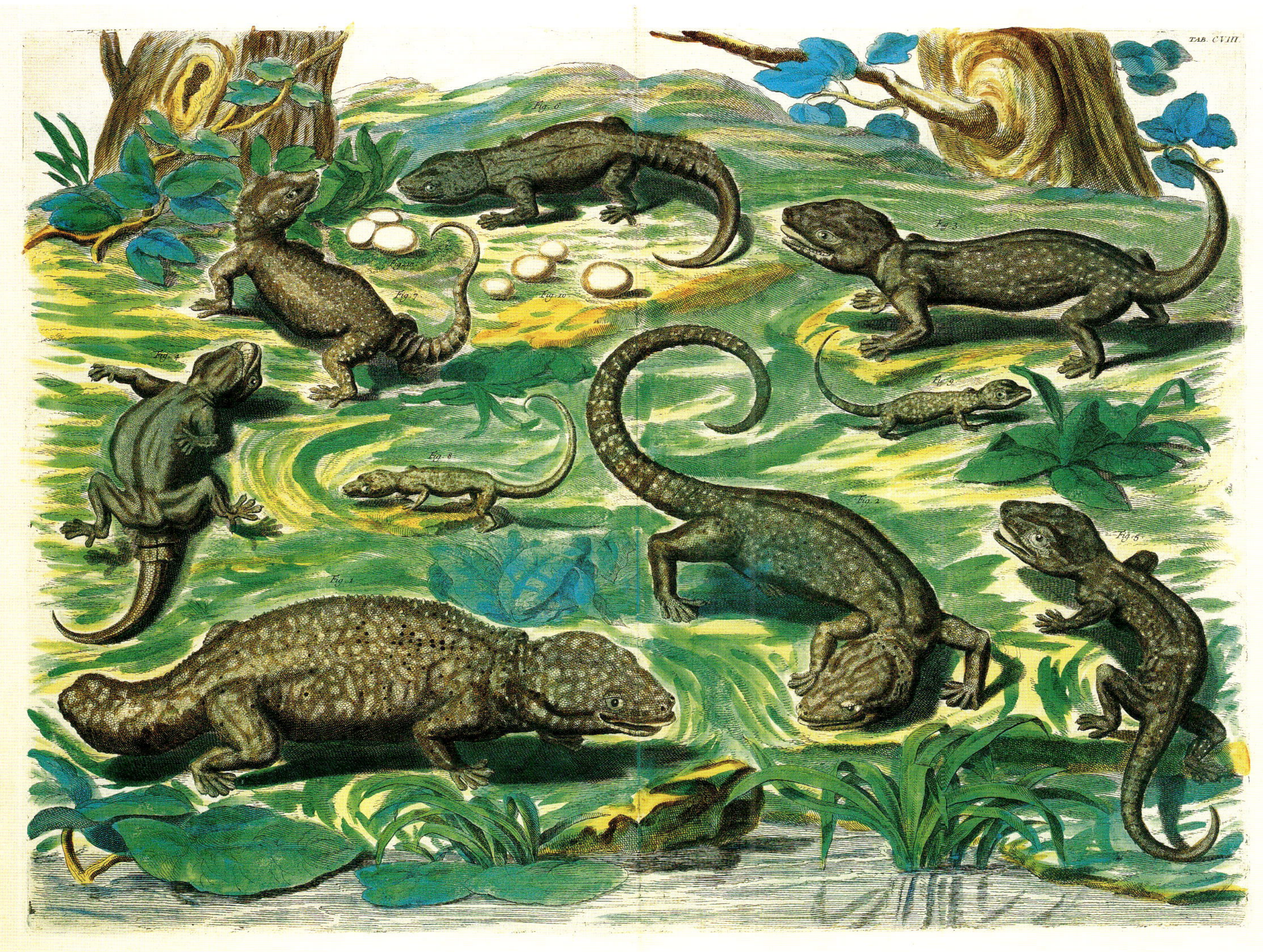

1-10 Gekkonidae
1-10 Gekkos · Geckos · Gekkonidés

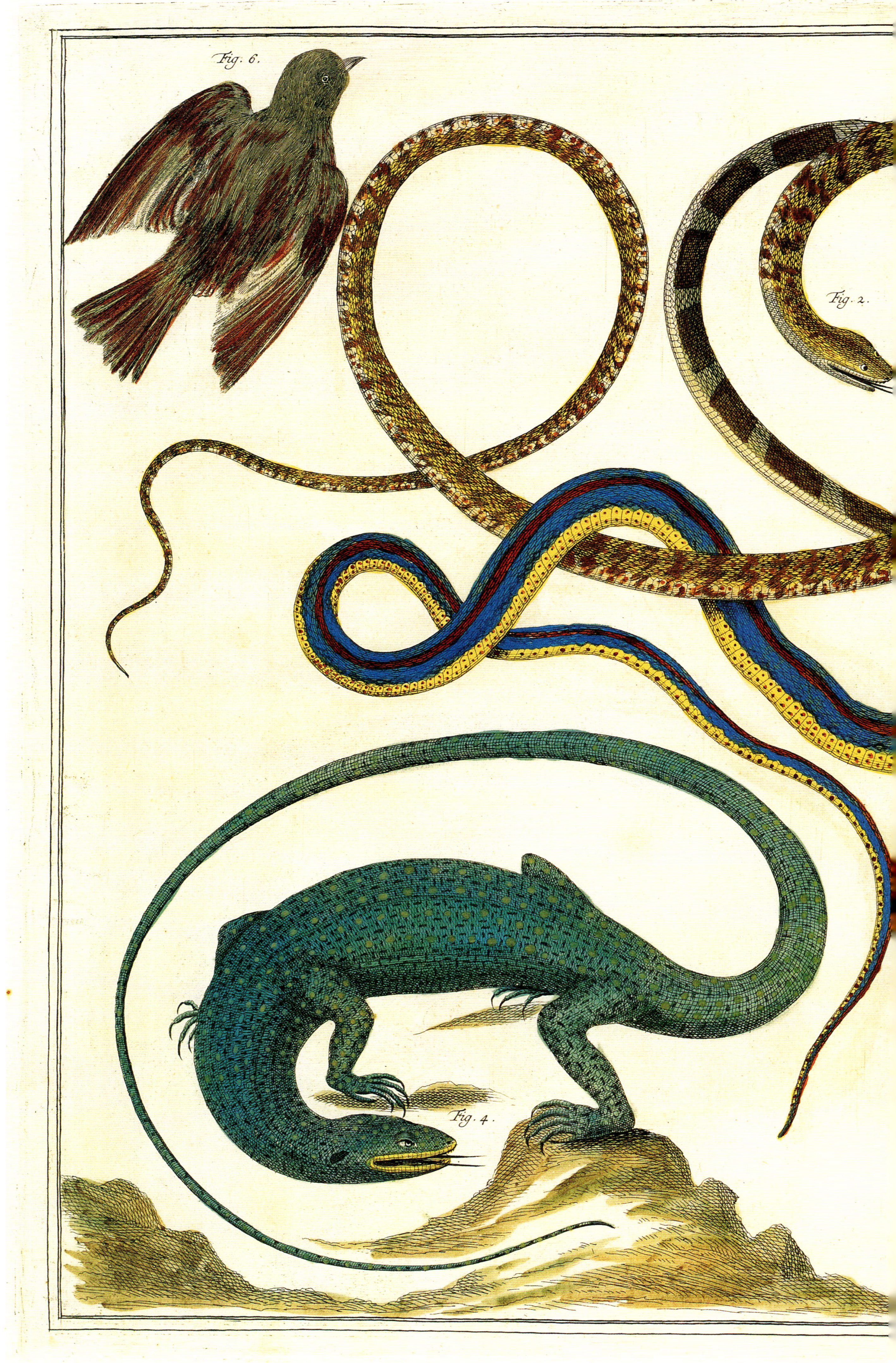

1-3 Serpentes 4-5 Sauria
1-3 Various snakes · Verschiedene Schlangen · Serpents divers 4-5 Lizards · Eidechsen · Lézards

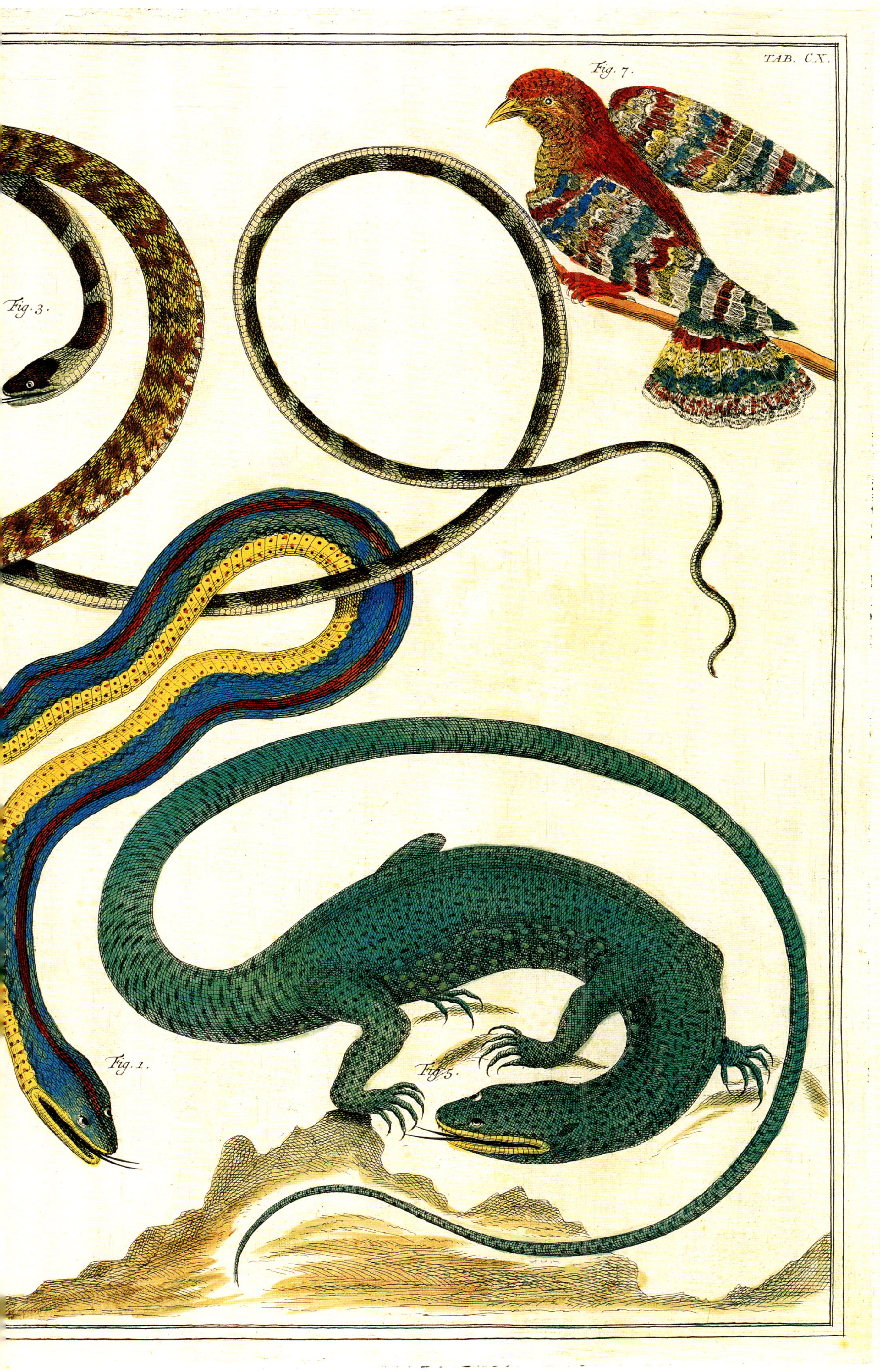
TAB. CX.
Fig. 7.
Fig. 3.
Fig. 1.
Fig. 5.

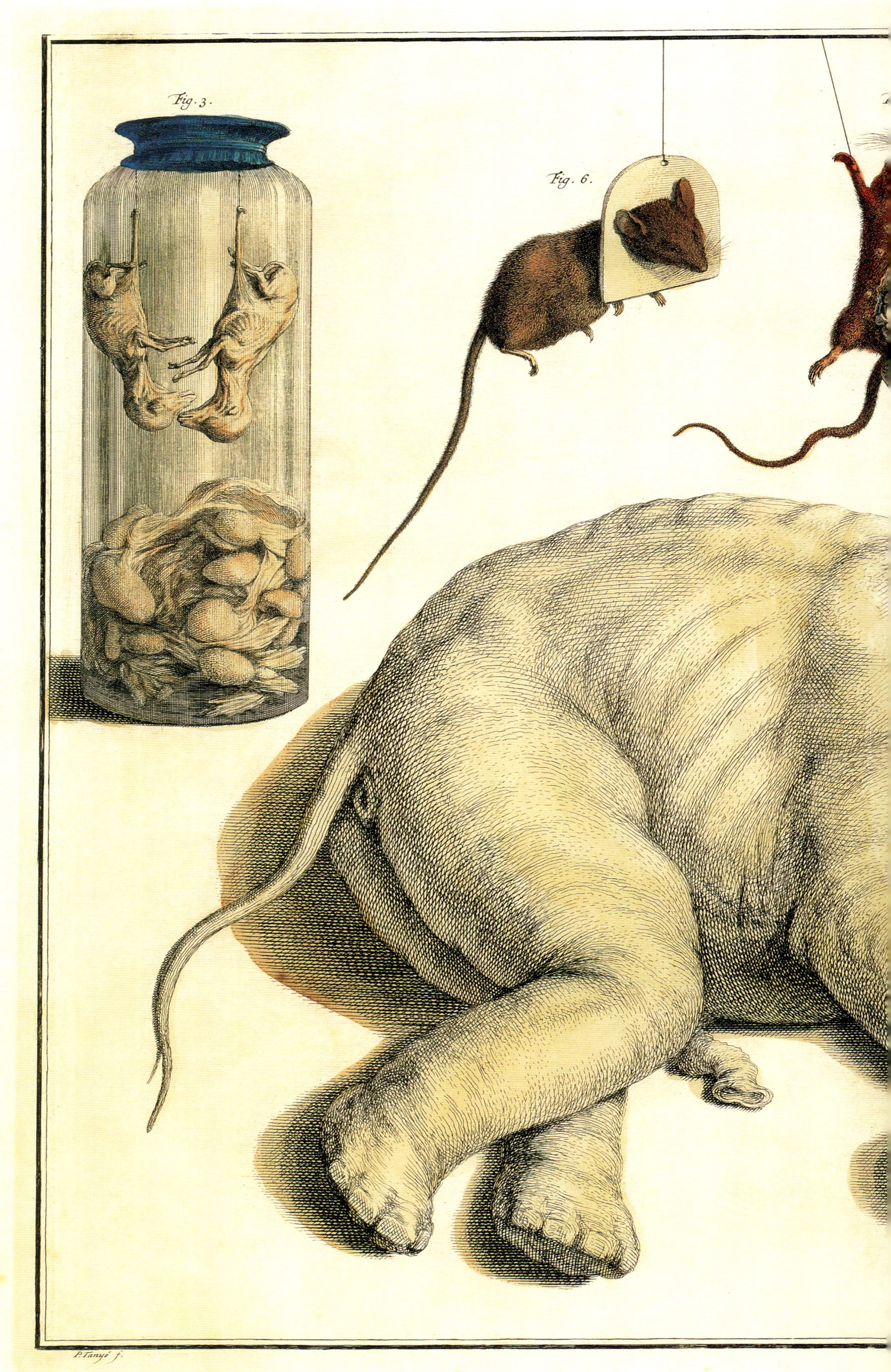

1 Elephas maximus 2 Homo sapiens 3 Ovis 4 Sus 5-6 Mus
1 Asiatic elephant (foetus) · Indischer Elefant (Fötus) · Eléphant d'Asie (fœtus) **2** Human (foetus) · Mensch (Fötus) · Homme (fœtus) **3** Sheep (embryo) · Schaf (Embryo) · Mouton (embryon) **4** Pig (embryo) · Schwein (Embryo) · Porc (embryon) **5-6** Mice · Mäuse · Souris

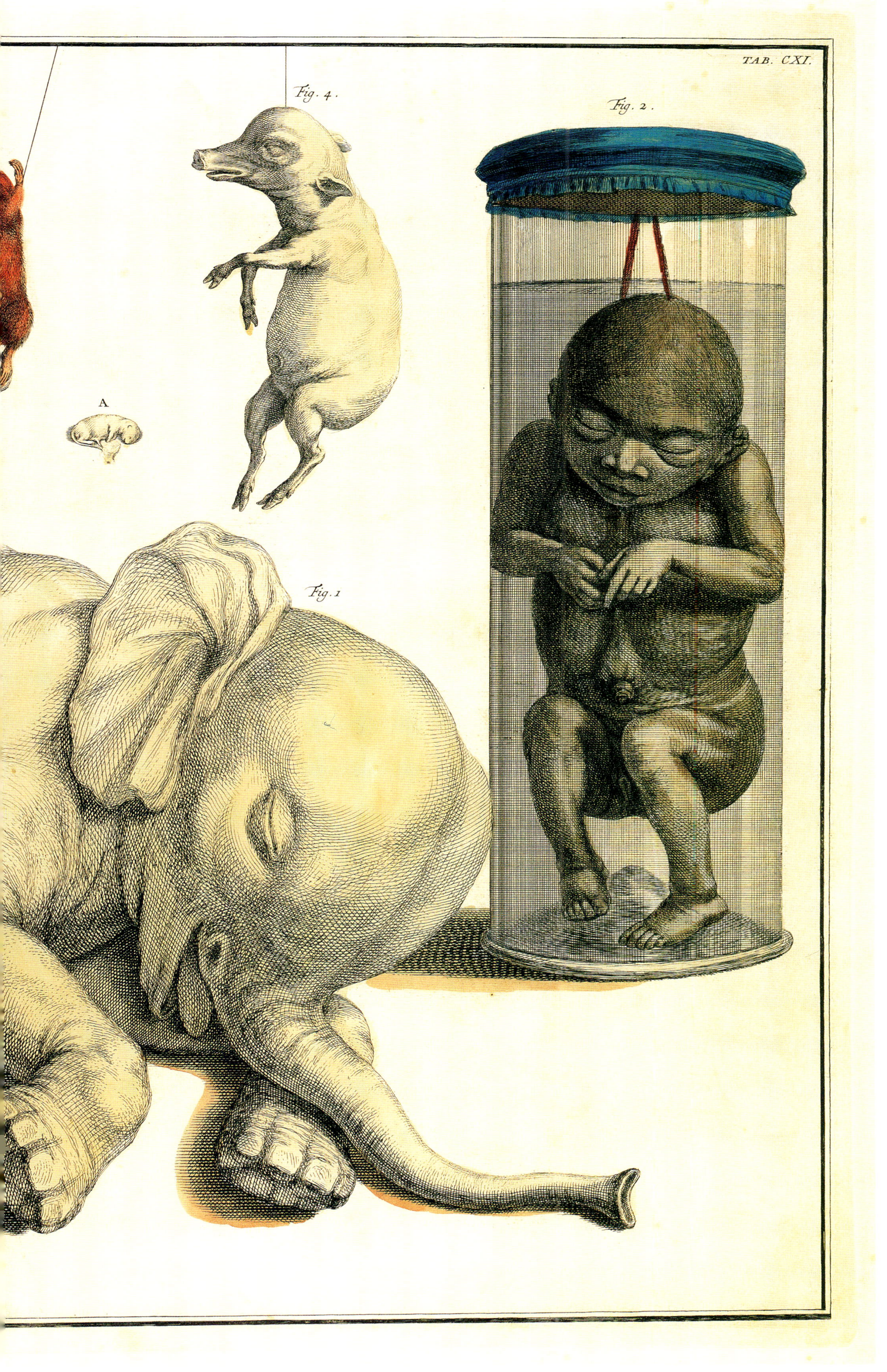
TAB. CXI.
Fig. 4.
Fig. 2.
A
Fig. 1

LOCUPLETISSIMI RERUM NATURALIUM THESAURI

ACCURATA DESCRIPTIO,
ET
ICONIBUS ARTIFICIOSISSIMIS
EXPRESSIO,
PER
UNIVERSAM PHYSICES HISTORIAM.

OPUS,

CUI, IN HOC RERUM GENERE, NULLUM PAR EXSTITIT.
EX TOTO TERRARUM ORBE COLLEGIT,
DIGESSIT, DESCRIPSIT, ET DEPINGENDUM CURAVIT

ALBERTUS SEBA,
ETZELA OOSTFRISIUS,
ACADEMIÆ CÆSAREÆ LEOPOLDINO CAROLINÆ NATURÆ CURIOSORUM
COLLEGA XENOCRATES DICTUS; SOCIETATIS REGIÆ ANGLICANÆ,
ET INSTITUTI BONONIENSIS, SODALIS.

TOMUS II.

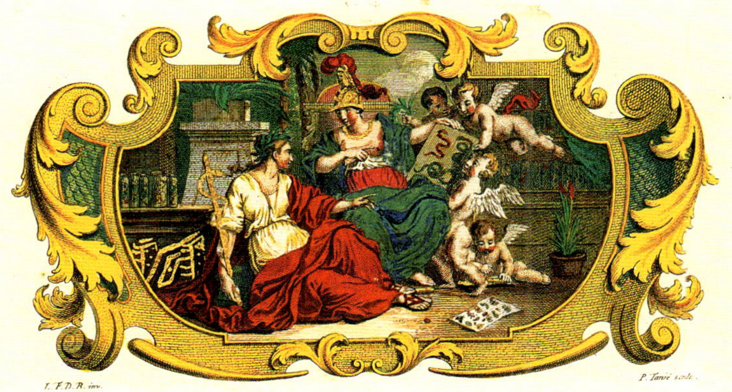

AMSTELAEDAMI,
Apud J. WETSTENIUM, & GUL. SMITH,
& JANSSONIO-WAESBERGIOS.
MDCCXXXV.

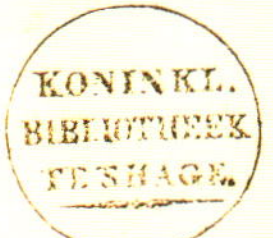

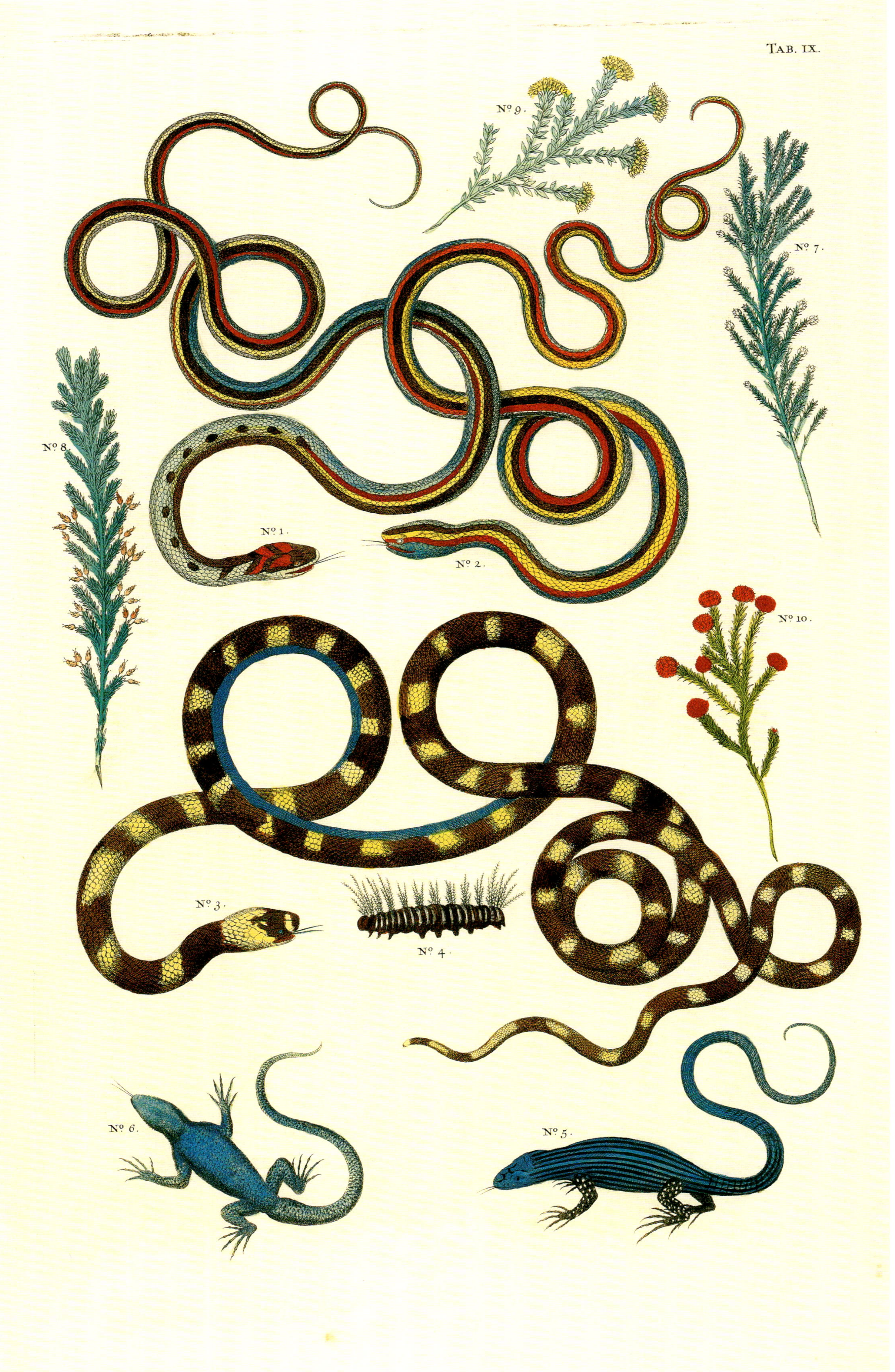

1-3 Serpentes 4 Lepidoptera 5-6 Squamata: Sauria 7-10 Ericaceae
1 Snake, described by Seba as a species known by the Portuguese as *Chayquarona* · Schlange, nach Seba eine Art, die von den Portugiesen *Chayquarona* genannt wird · Serpent, d'après Seba une espèce qui fut appelée *Chayquarona* par les Portugais **3** Snake, according to Seba from Africa · Schlange, nach Seba aus Afrika · Serpent, d'Afrique selon Seba **4** Caterpillar · Schmetterlingsraupe · Larve de papillon **5-6** Lizards · Echsen · Sauriens **7-10** Heath family · Heidekrautgewächse · Ericacées

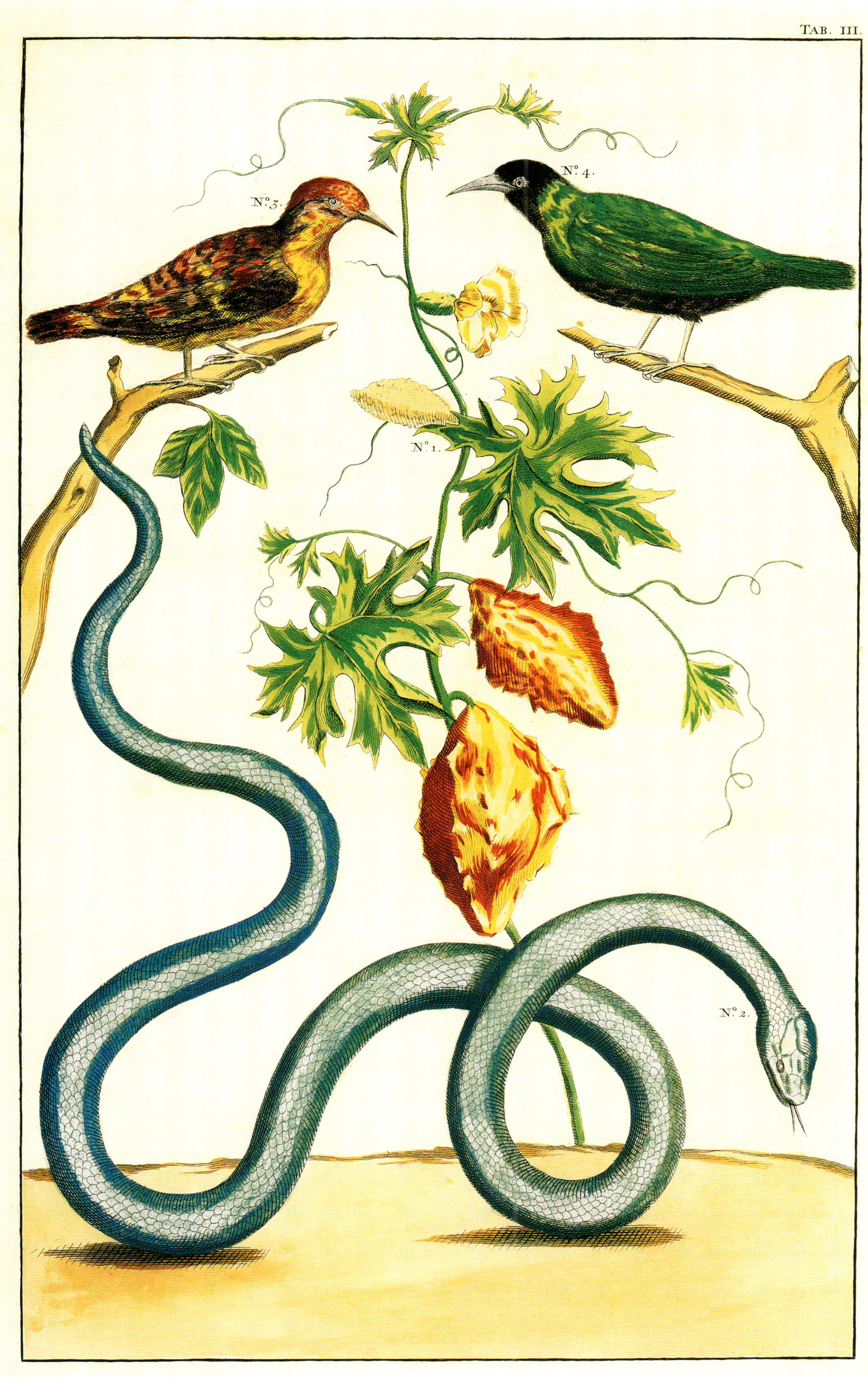

2 Serpentes 3-4 Aves
2 Snake, according to Seba from America · Schlange, nach Seba aus Amerika · Serpent, d'Amérique selon Seba
3-4 Birds, according to Seba from America · Vögel, nach Seba aus Amerika · Oiseaux, d'Amérique selon Seba

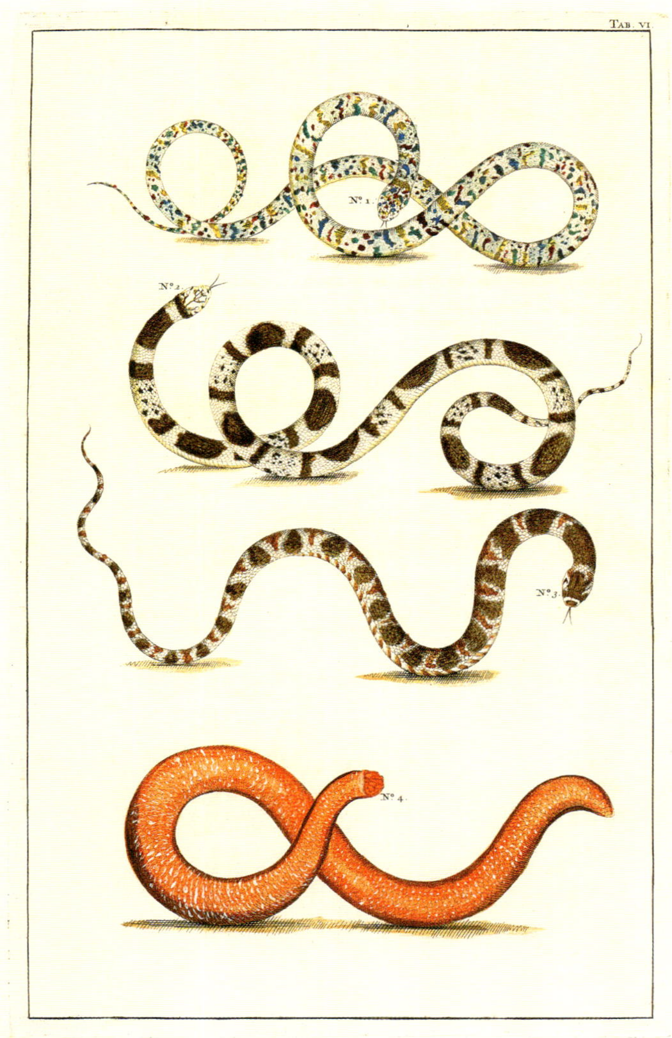

1-3 Serpentes 4 *Amphisbaena alba*
1-3 Snakes, according to Seba from Brasil (1), Senegal (2) and America (3) · Schlangen, nach Seba aus Brasilien (1), dem Senegal (2) und Amerika (3) · Serpents, du Brésil (1), du Sénégal (2) et d'Amérique (3), selon Seba **4** White-bellied worm lizard · Rote Doppelschleiche · Amphisbène blanche

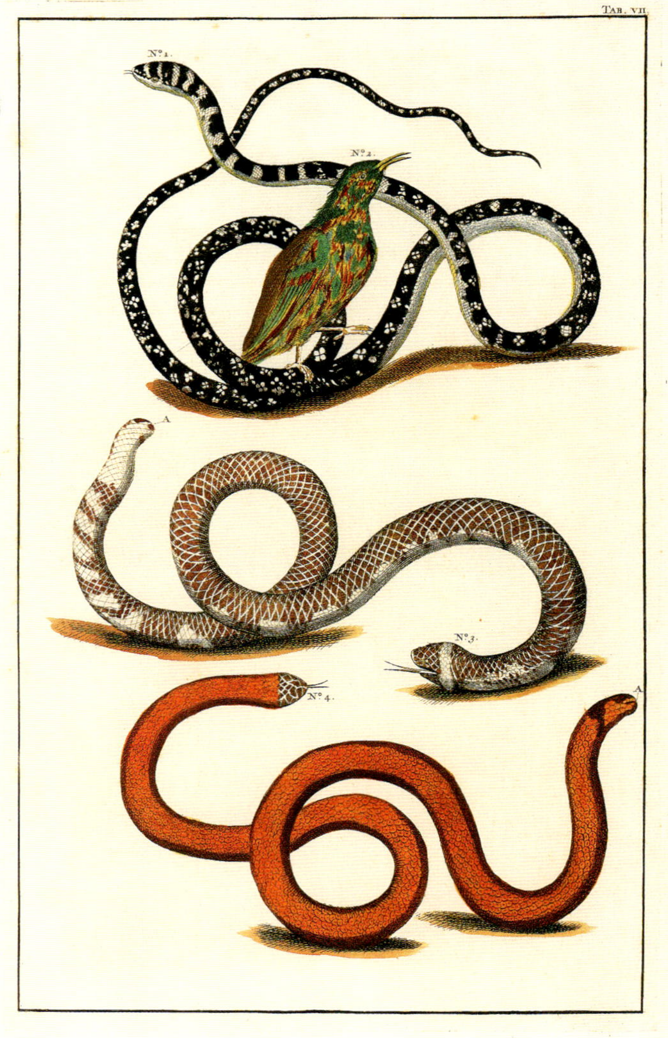

1 Serpentes 2 Aves 3-4 Amphisbaenia sp.
1 Snake, described by Seba as a *flying snake from Ambon* · Schlange, nach Seba *Fliegende Schlange aus Ambon* · Serpent, Seba l'appelle *Serpent volant d'Amboine* **2** Bird · Vogel · Oiseau
3-4 Worm lizards · Doppelschleichen · Amphisbénidés

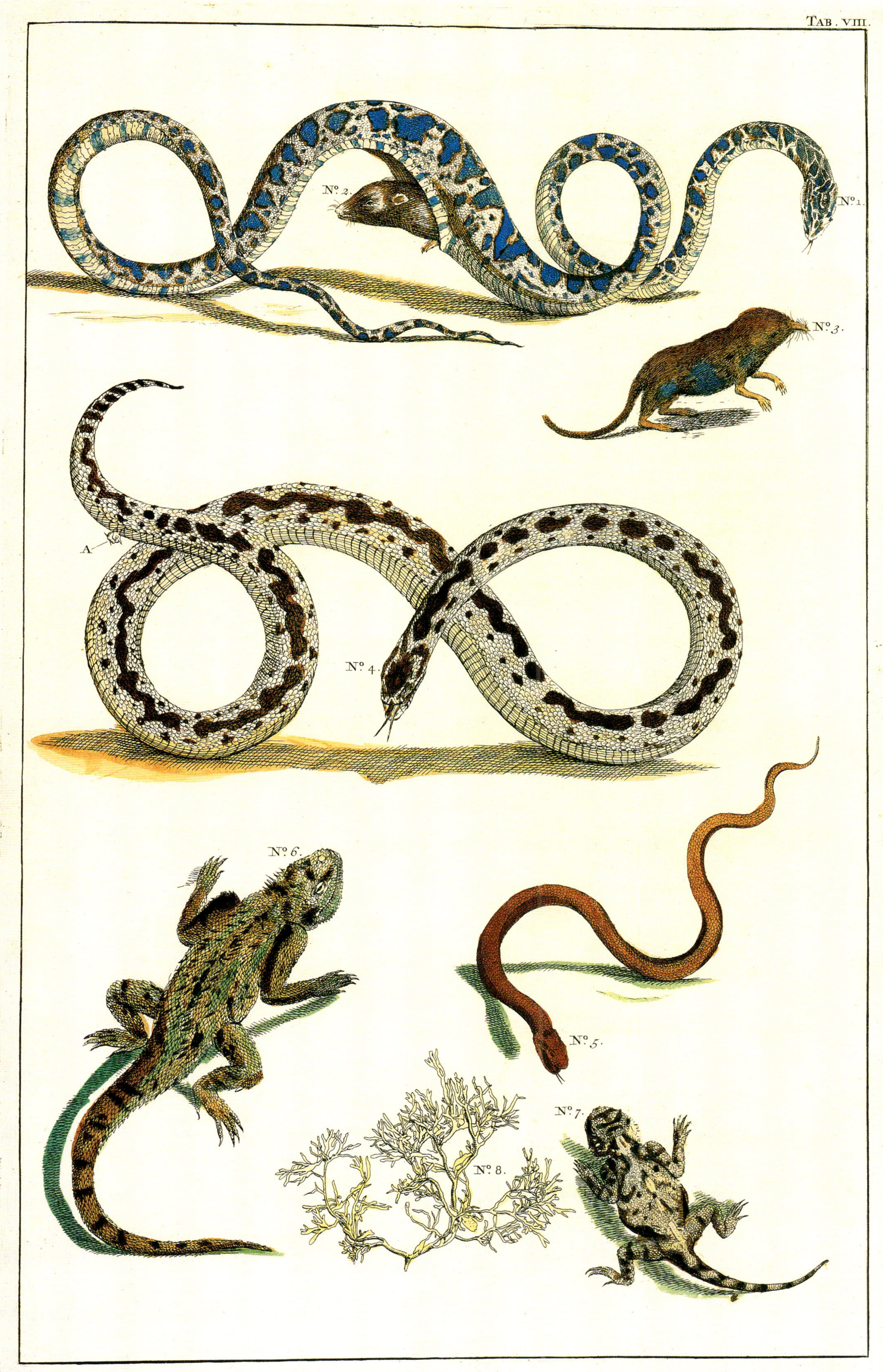

1, 5 Serpentes **2** Muridae **3** Soricidae **4** *Vipera berus* **6-7** Squamata

1 Snake, according to Seba from Ceylon · Schlange, nach Seba aus Ceylon · Serpent, de Ceylan selon Seba **2** Rat · Ratte · Rat **3** Shrew · Spitzmaus · Musaraigne **4** Adder/Common viper · Kreuzotter · Vipère péliade **5** Snake, according to Seba from Surinam · Schlange, nach Seba aus Surinam · Serpent, du Surinam selon Seba **6-7** Lizards · Echsen · Sauriens

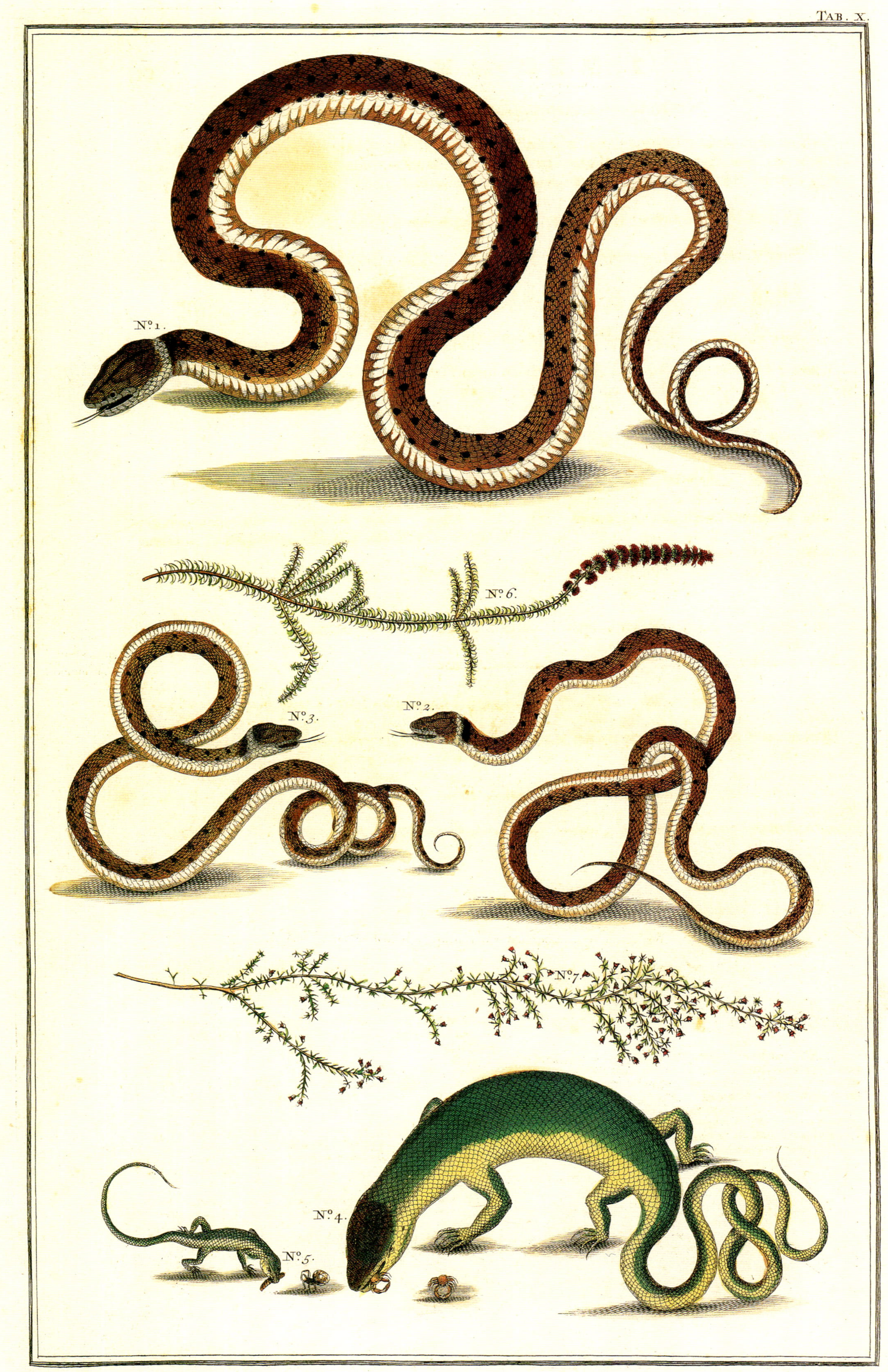

1-3 *Natrix natrix* 4-5 Squamata: Scincidae 6-7 Ericaceae
1-3 Grass snakes · Ringelnattern · Couleuvres à collier **4-5** Skink · Skink · Scinque **6-7** Heath family · Heidekrautgewächse · Ericacées

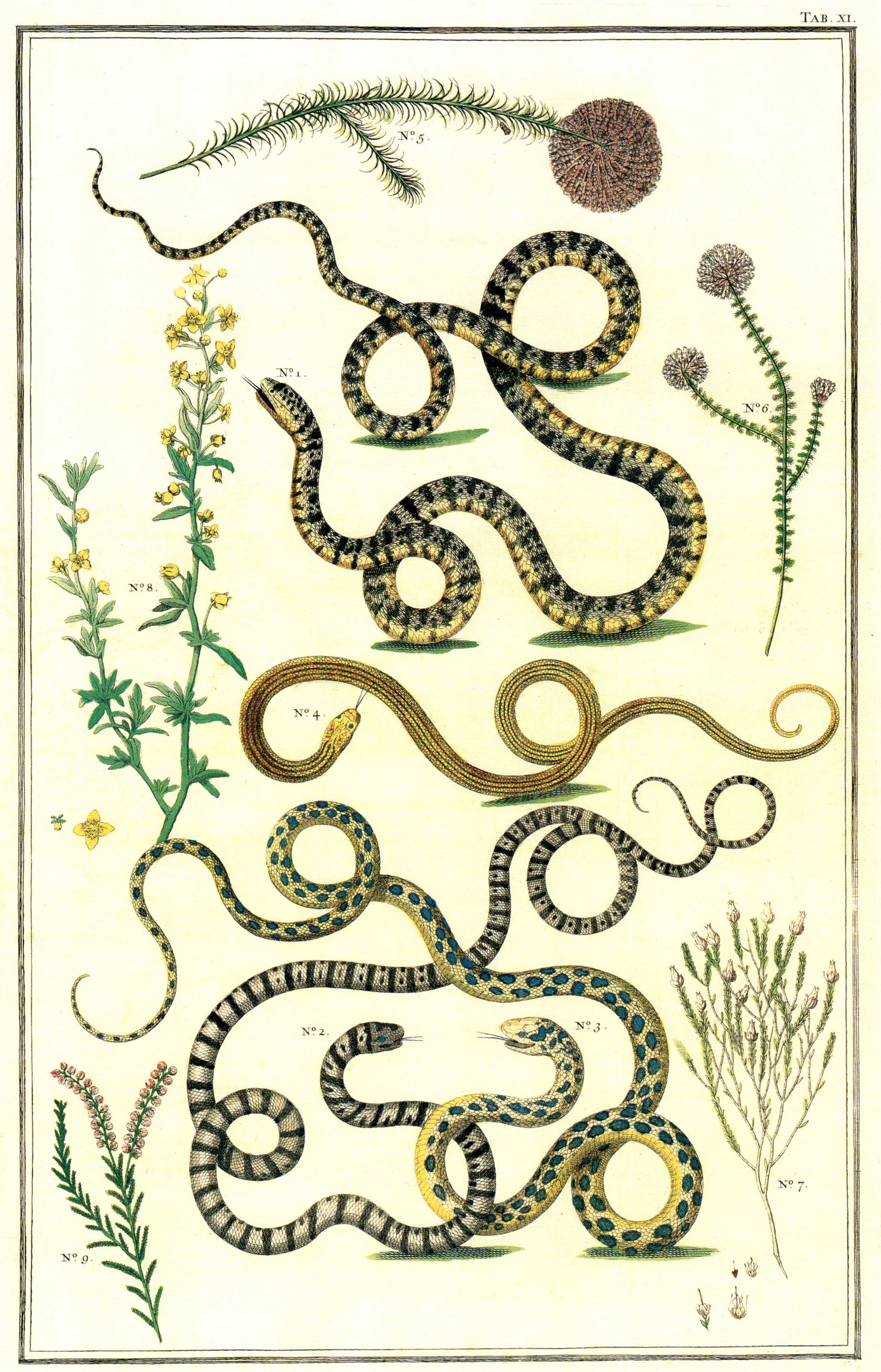

1, 3 Serpentes 2 *Chionactis occipitalis?* 4 *Stenorrhina freminvillil* 9 *Erica carnea*
1, 2 Western shovelnose snake · Schaufelnasennatter · Serpent corail 3 Snake, according to Seba from America · Schlange, nach Seba aus Amerika · Serpent, d'Amérique selon Seba
4 Scorpion eater/Scorpion eating snake · Schlange · Serpent mangeur de scorpions 9 Spring heath · Schneeheide · Bruyère incarnat

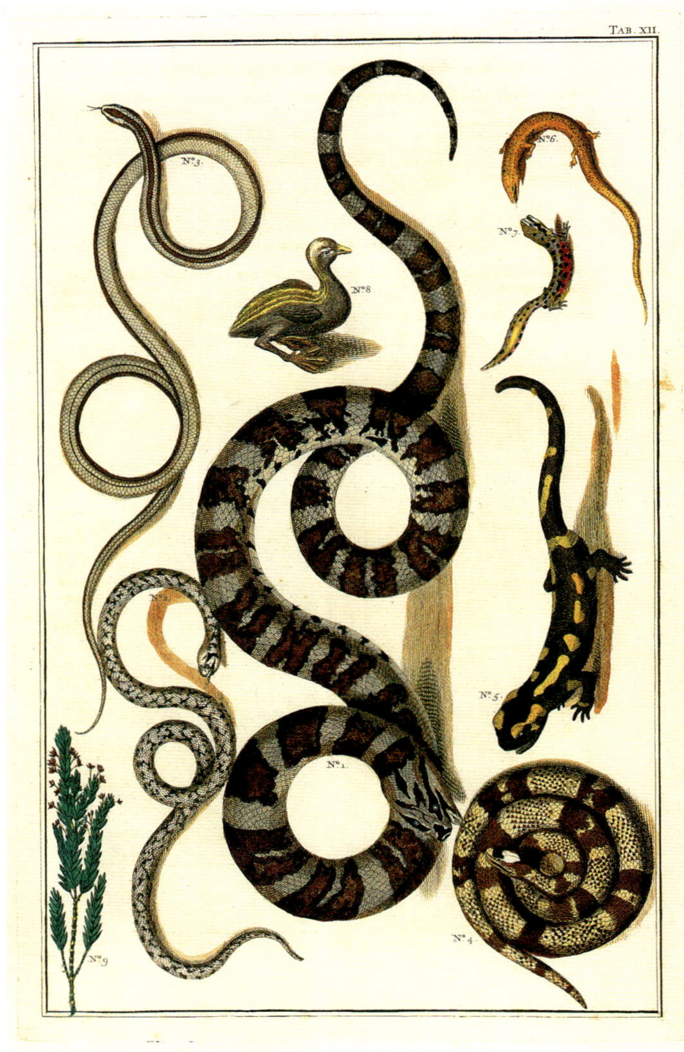

1-4 Serpentes **5** Caudata, Salamandridae: *Salamandra salamandra* **6** Squamata **7** *Triturus alpestris?* **8** Podicepidae

1-4 Snakes, according to Seba from America · Schlangen, nach Seba aus Amerika · Serpents, d'Amérique selon Seba **5** Fire salamander · Feuersalamander · Salamandre terrestre/ Salamandre tachetée **6** Lizard · Echse · Saurien **7** Alpine newt · Bergmolch · Triton alpestre **8** Grebe · Lappentaucher · Grèbe

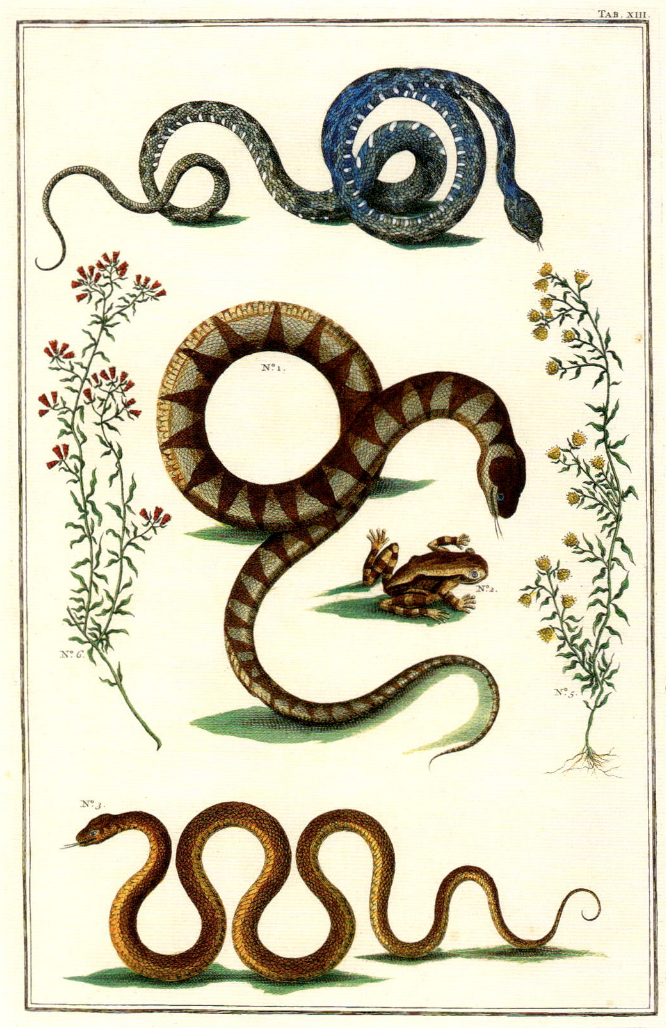

1 *Vipera ammodytes* **2** *Hyla arborea*? **3-4** Serpentes **5-6** *Helichrysum*

1 Nose-horned viper · Sandotter · Vipère des sables **2** Tree frog · Laubfrosch · Grenouille arboricole **3-4** Snakes, according to Seba from America (3) and Africa (4) · Schlangen, nach Seba aus Amerika (3) und Afrika (4) · Serpents, d'Amérique (3) et d'Afrique (4), selon Seba **5-6** Everlasting flower · Strohblume · Hélichryse

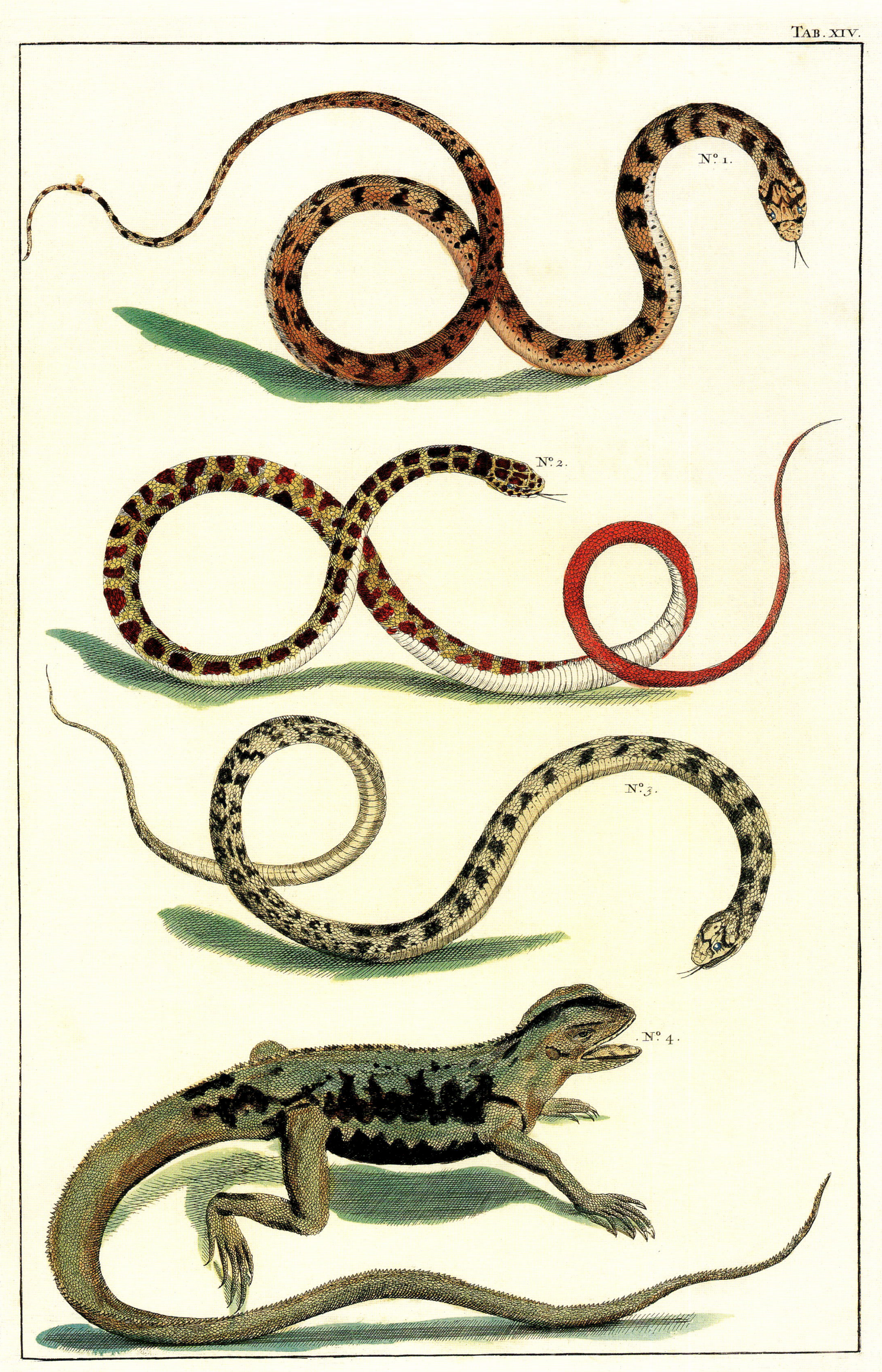

1-3 Serpentes **4** Agamidae
1-3 Snakes, according to Seba from America and Ambon · Schlangen, nach Seba aus Amerika und Ambon · Serpents, d'Amérique et d'Amboine selon Seba **4** Agama · Agame · Agame

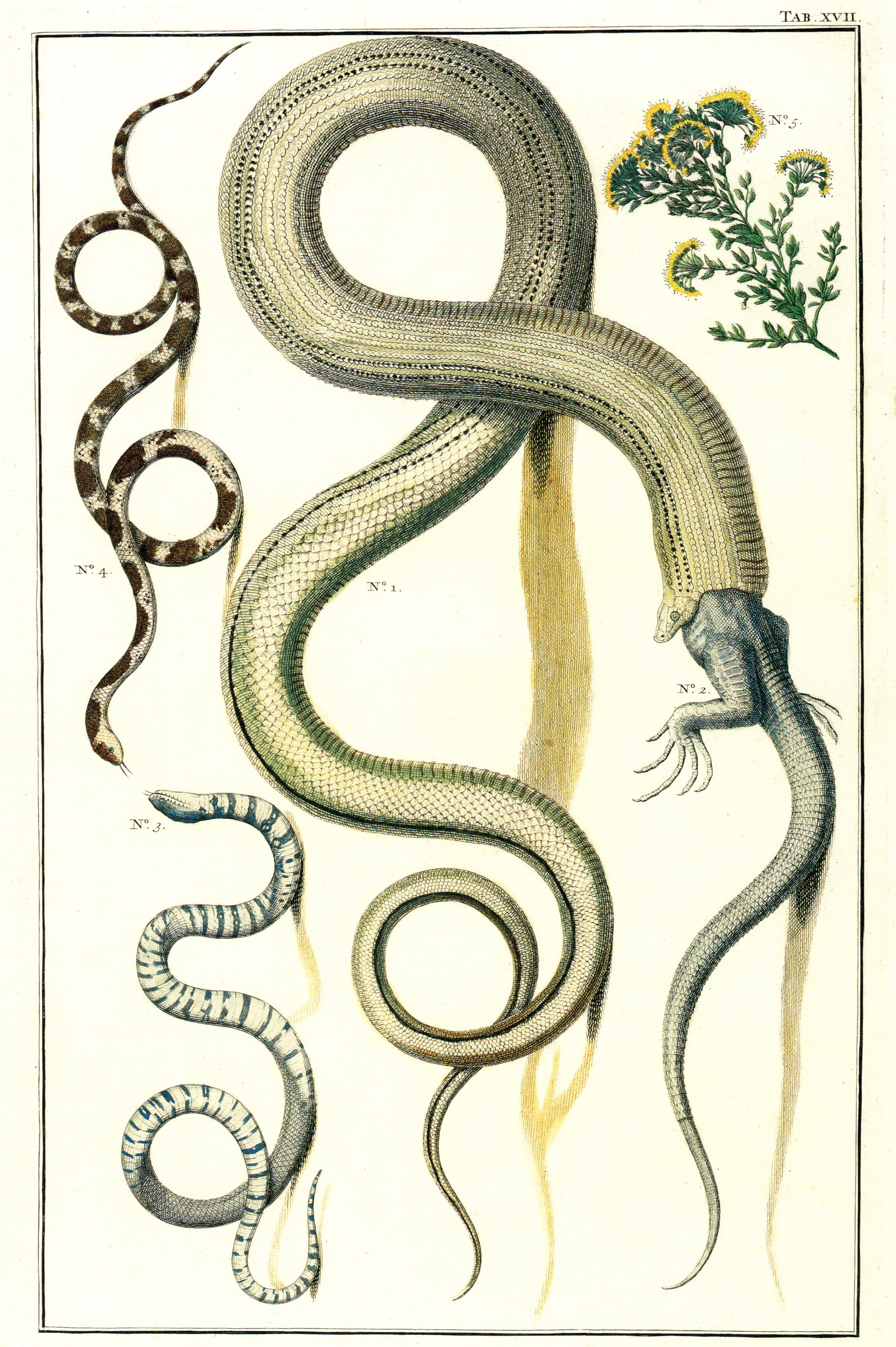

1, 3-4 Serpentes **2** Squamata

1, 3-4 Snakes, according to Seba from Ambon (1), Africa (3), and America (4) · Schlangen, nach Seba aus Ambon (1), Afrika (3) und Amerika (4) · Serpents, d'Amboine (1), d'Afrique (3) et d'Amérique (4), selon Seba **2** Lizard · Echse · Saurien

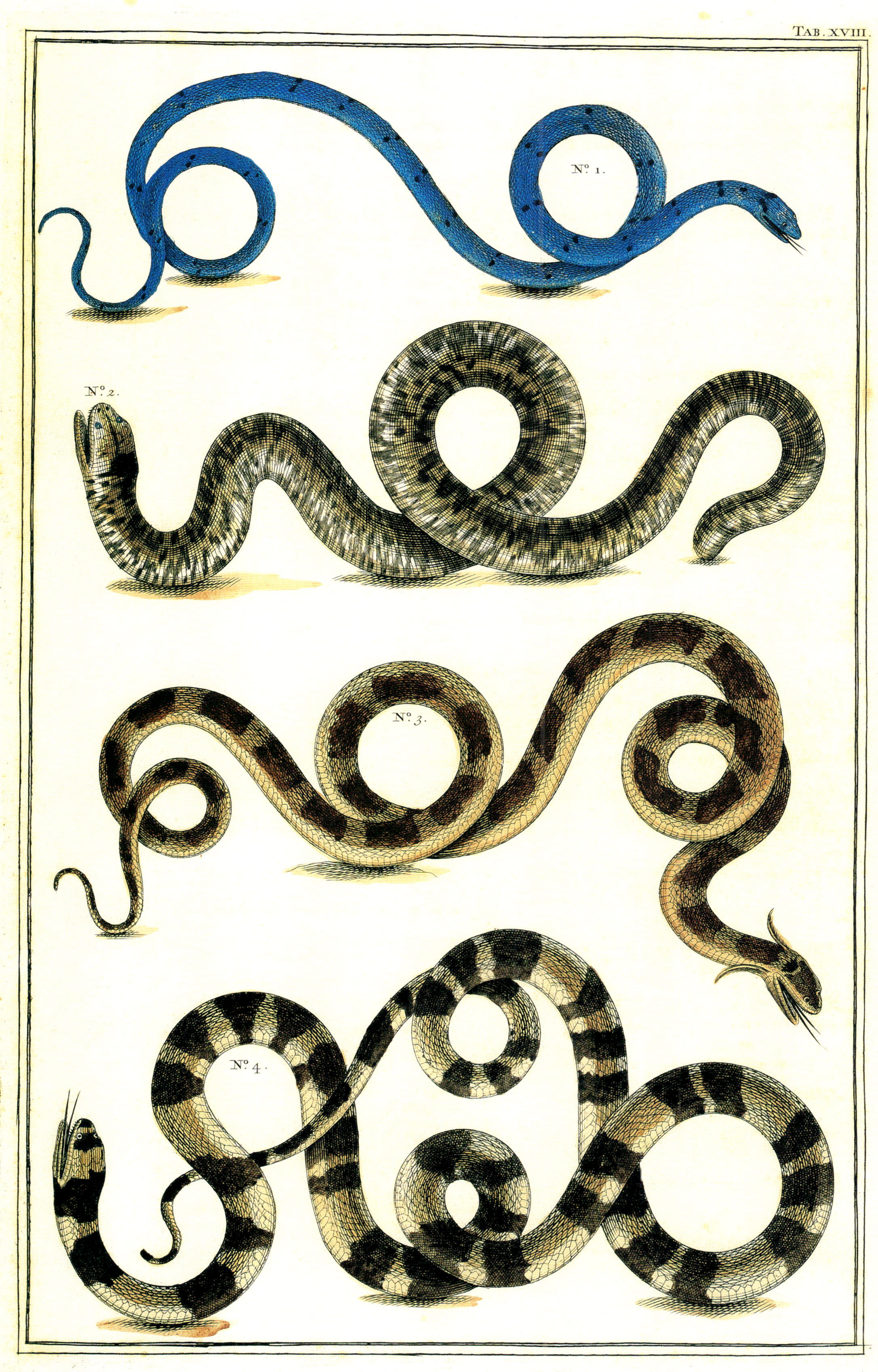

1-4 Serpentes 2 Erycinae?
1-4 Snakes from various regions · Schlangen aus verschiedenen Regionen · Serpents de différentes régions 2 Sand boa · Sandboa · Boa des sables

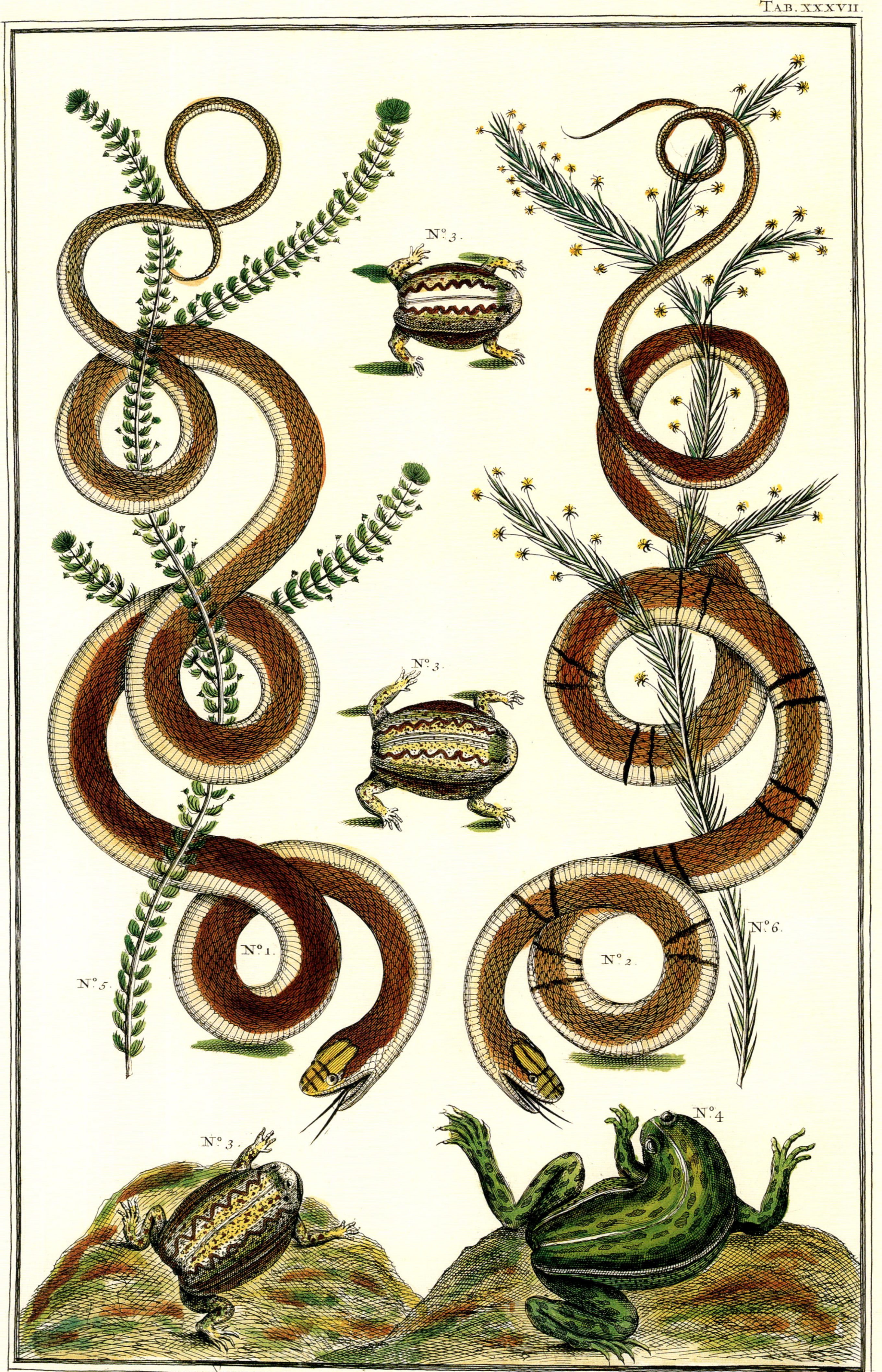

1-2 Serpentes 3 Microhylidae 4 Anura
1-2 Snakes, according to Seba from Africa · Schlangen, nach Seba aus Afrika · Serpents, d'Afrique selon Seba 3 Narrow-mouthed toad · Engmaulfrosch · Microhylidé
4 Frog · Froschlurch · Grenouille

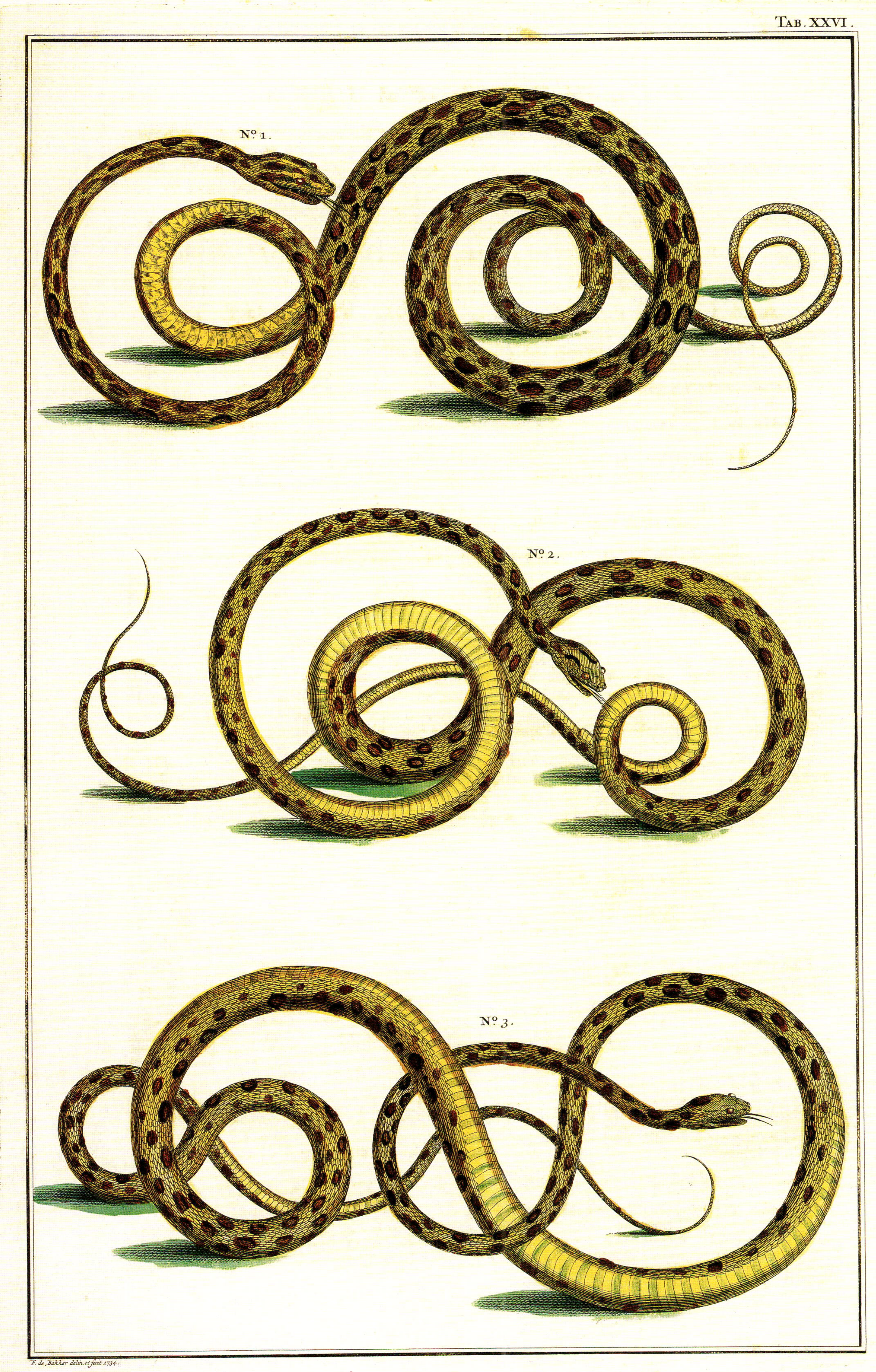

1-3 Serpentes
1 Snake, according to Seba from Nova Hispania · Schlange, nach Seba aus Nova Hispania · Serpent, de Nova Hispania selon Seba **2-3** Snakes from different continents · Schlangen von verschiedenen Kontinenten · Serpents de différents continents

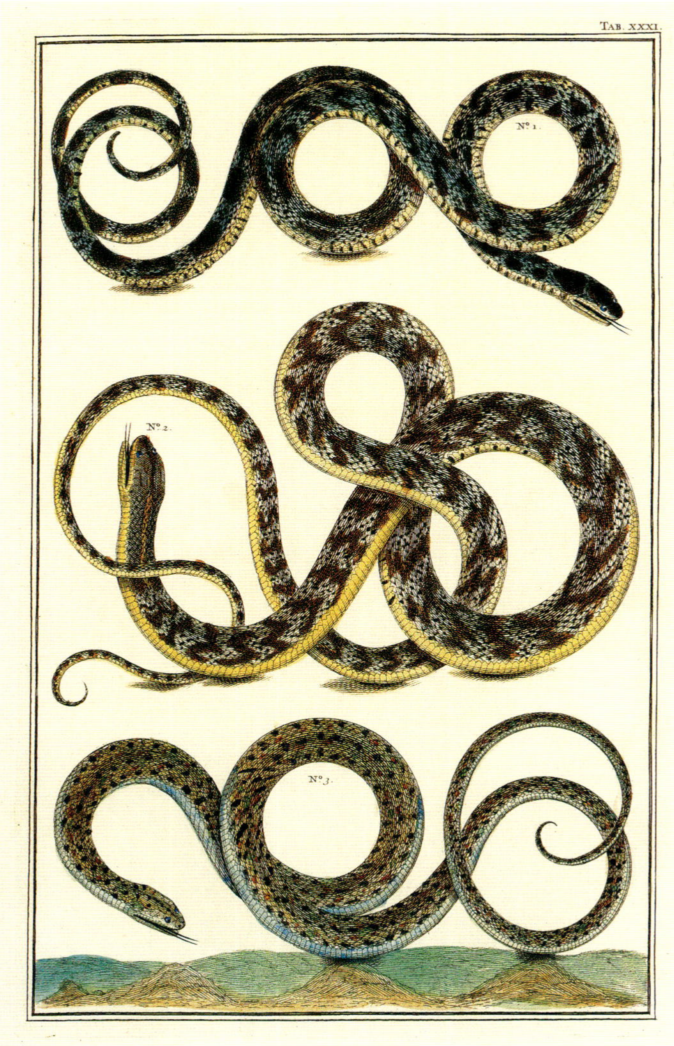

1-3 Serpentes
1-2 Snakes, according to Seba from America · Schlangen, nach Seba aus Amerika · Serpents, d'Amérique selon Seba **3** Snake, according to Seba from the Cape of Good Hope · Schlange, nach Seba vom Kap der Guten Hoffnung · Serpent, du cap de Bonne-Espérance selon Seba

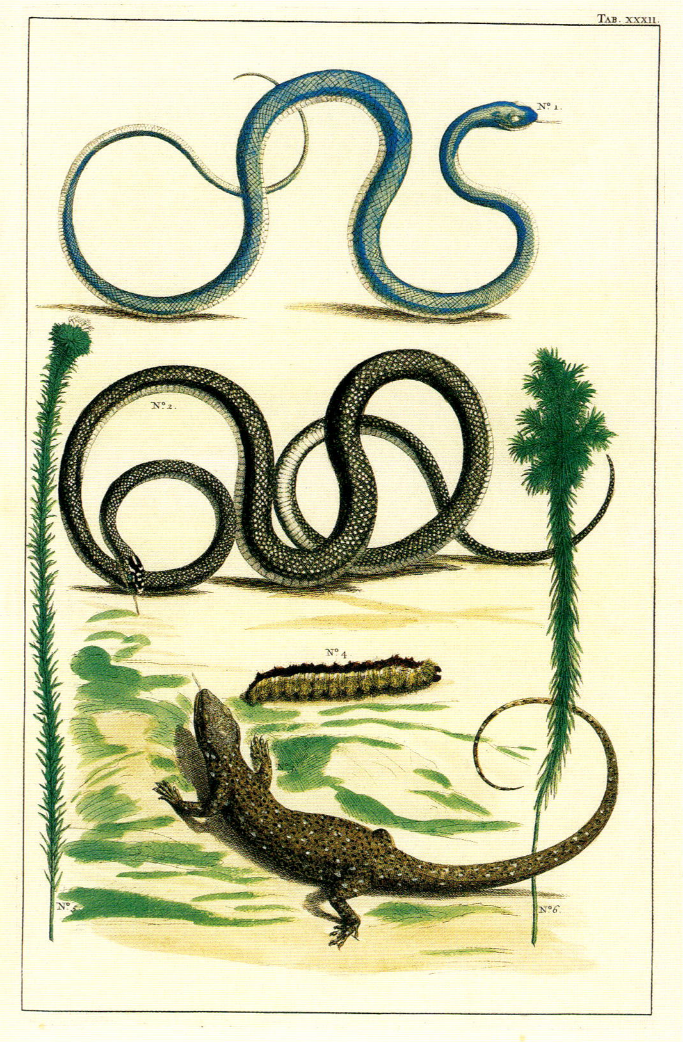

1, 2 Serpentes **3** Squamata **4** Lepidoptera
1 Snake, according to Seba from Surinam · Schlange, nach Seba aus Surinam · Serpent, du Surinam selon Seba **2** Snake, according to Seba from Ceylon · Schlange, nach Seba aus Ceylon · Serpent, de Ceylan selon Seba **3** Lizard · Echse · Saurien **4** Caterpillar · Schmetterlingsraupe · Larve de papillon

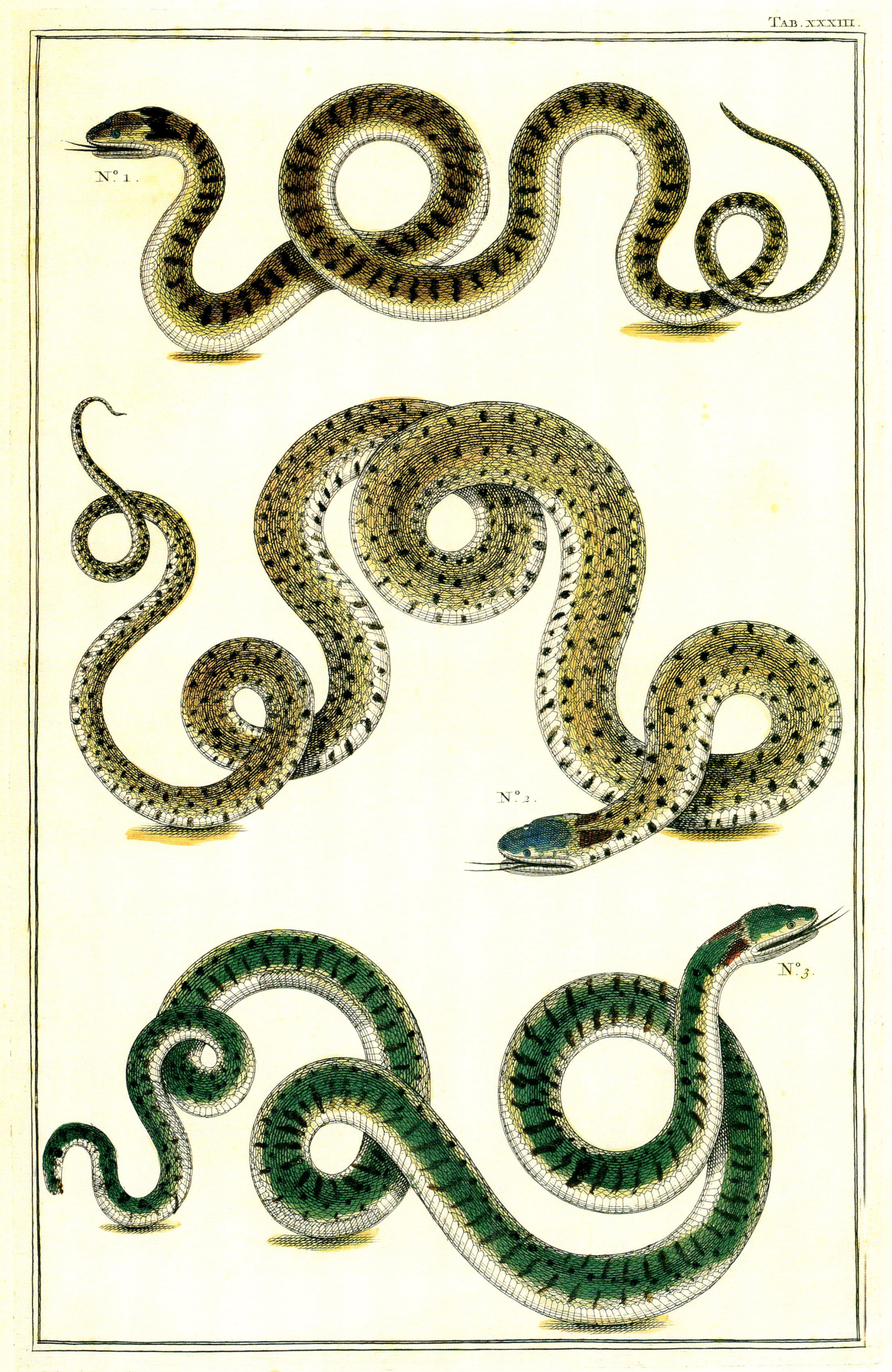

1 Coluber sp.? 2-3 Colubridae
1 Whip snake · Zornnatter · Couleuvre **2-3** Colubrine snakes · Nattern · Couleuvres

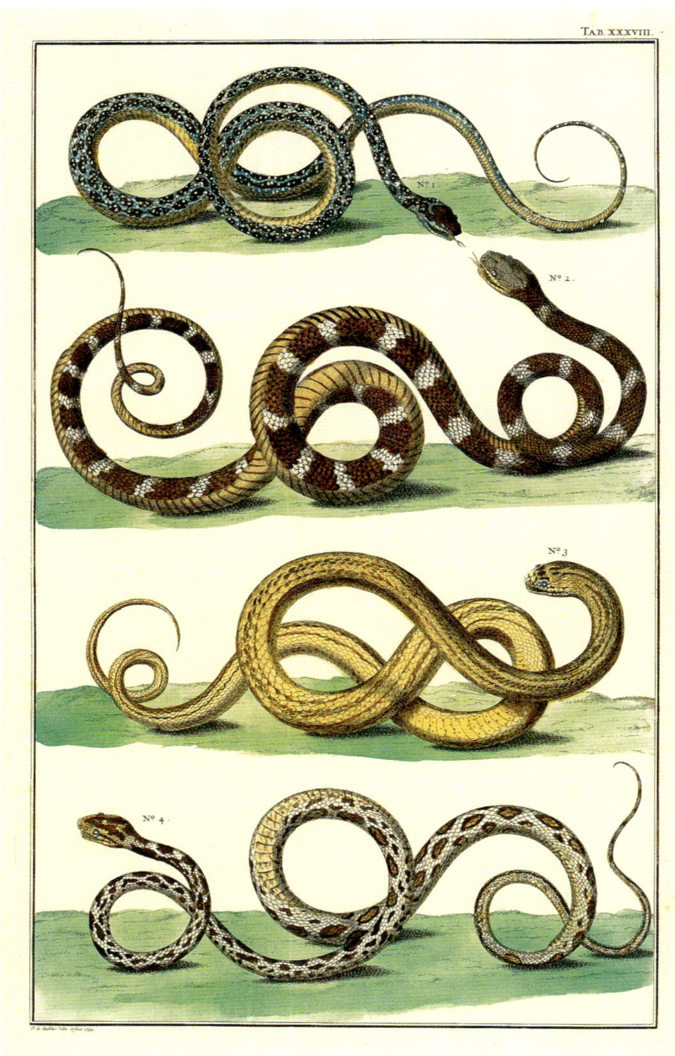

1-4 Serpentes
1-2, 4 Snakes, according to Seba from America · Schlangen, nach Seba aus Amerika · Serpents, d'Amérique selon Seba **3** Snake, according to Seba from Egypt · Schlange, nach Seba aus Ägypten · Serpent, d'Egypte selon Seba

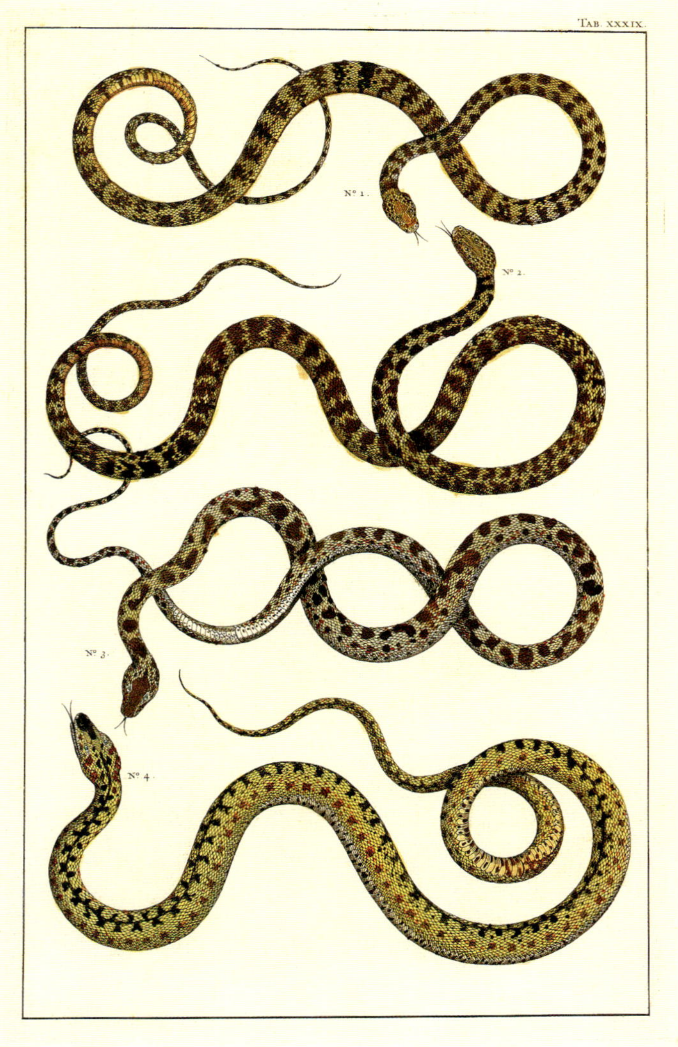

1-4 Serpentes
1-2 Snakes, according to Seba from Arabia · Schlangen, nach Seba aus Arabien · Serpents, d'Arabie selon Seba **3-4** Snakes, according to Seba from Ceylon · Schlangen, nach Seba aus Ceylon · Serpents, de Ceylan selon Seba

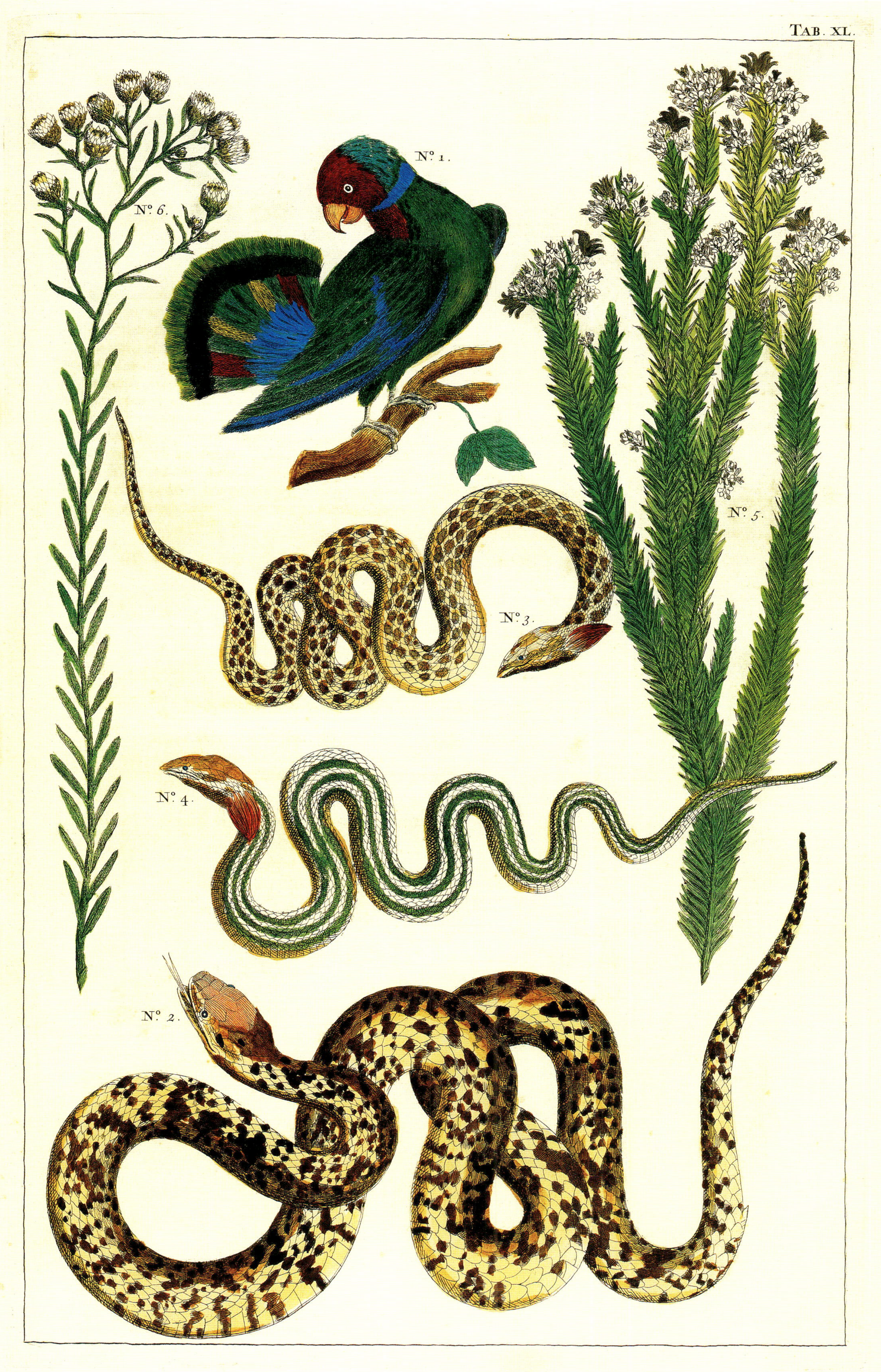

1 Aves 2-4 Serpentes 5 Compositae
1 Bird, according to Seba from America · Vogel, nach Seba aus Amerika · Oiseau, d'Amérique selon Seba 2-4 Various Snakes · Verschiedene Schlangen · Serpents divers
6 Sunflower family · Korbblütler · Composées

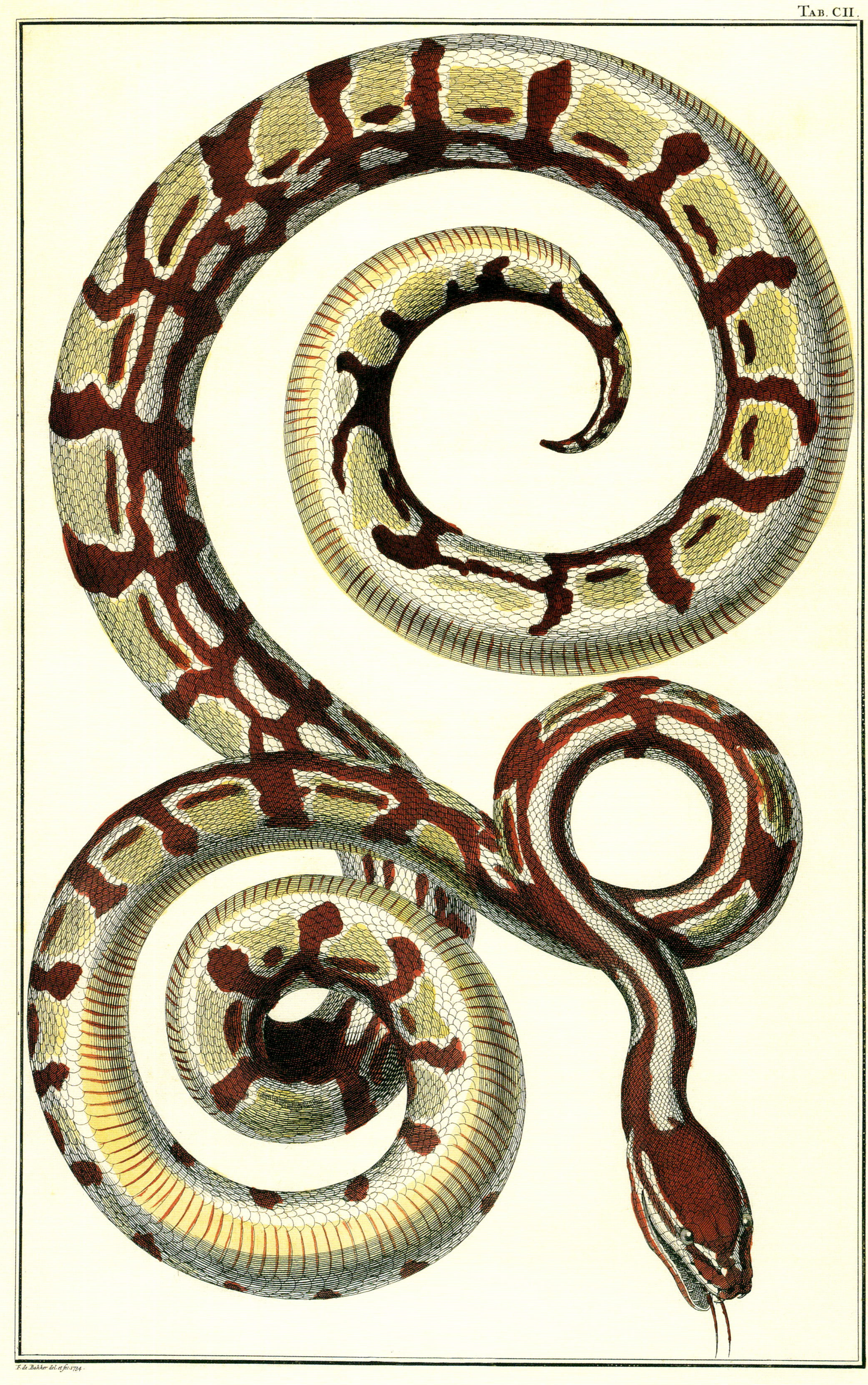

1 *Python regius*
1 Royal python · Königspython · Python royal

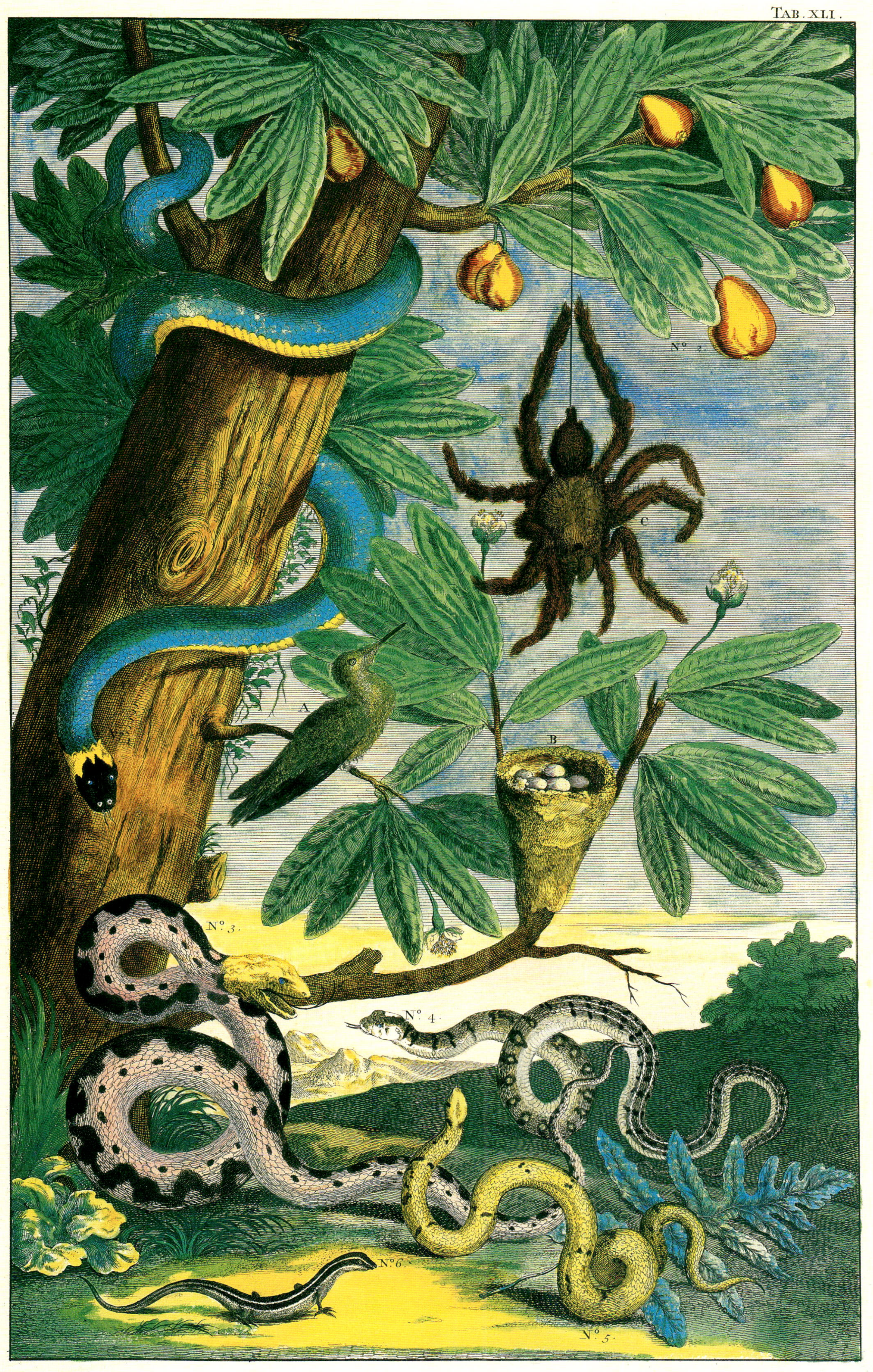

1, 3-4 Serpentes **2** *Psidium guajava* **6** Squamata **C** Mygalomorphae
1, 3-4 Snakes, according to Seba from America · Schlangen, laut Seba aus Amerika · Serpents, d'Amérique selon Seba **2** Guava · Guave · Goyavier **6** Lizard · Echse · Saurien
C Mygalomorph spider · Vogelspinne · Mygalomorphe

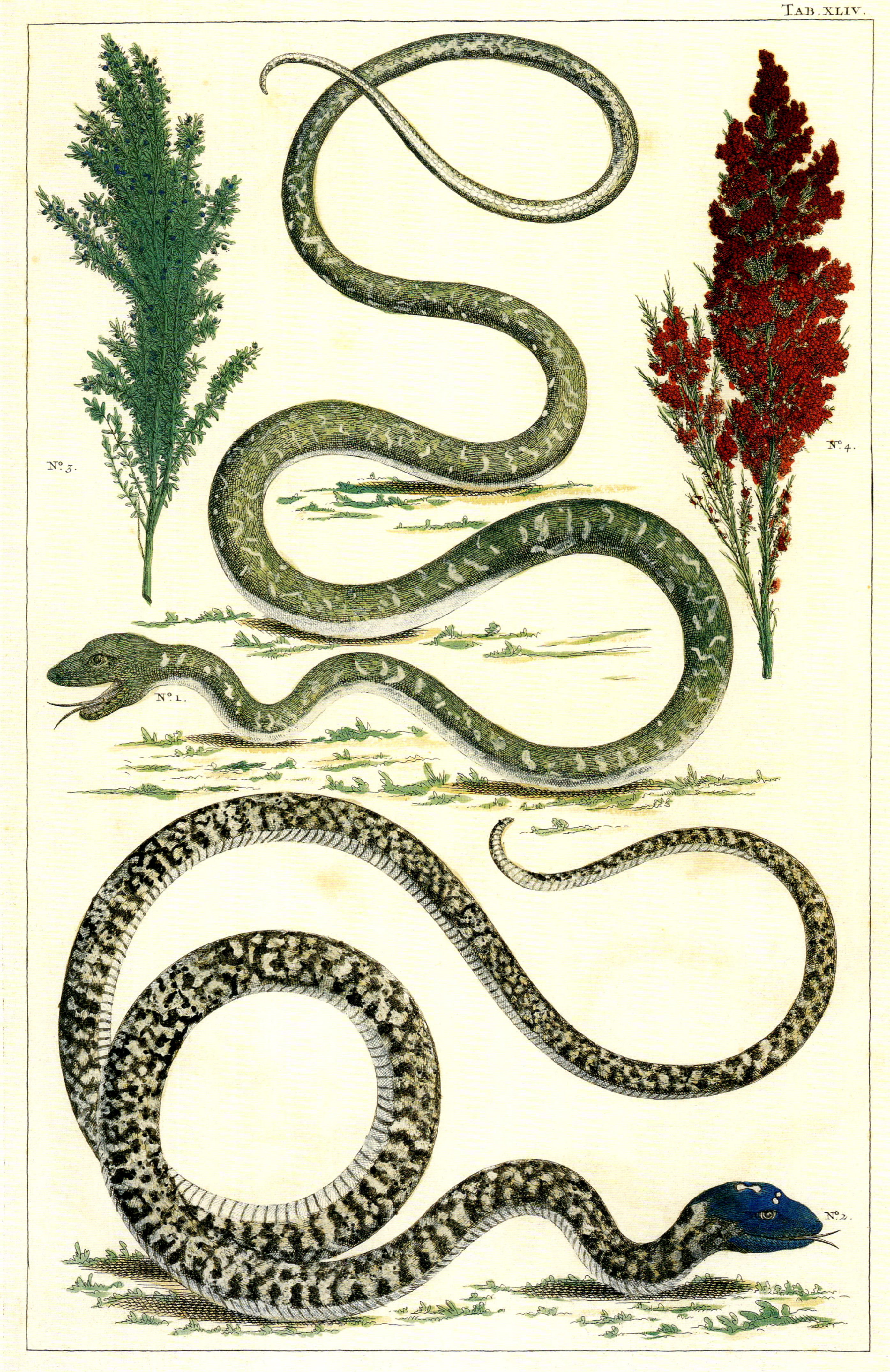

1 *Chrysopelea?* 2 Serpentes

1 Flying snake · Flugschlange · Serpent volant 2 Snake, according to Seba from Ambon · Schlange, nach Seba aus Ambon · Serpent, d'Amboine selon Seba

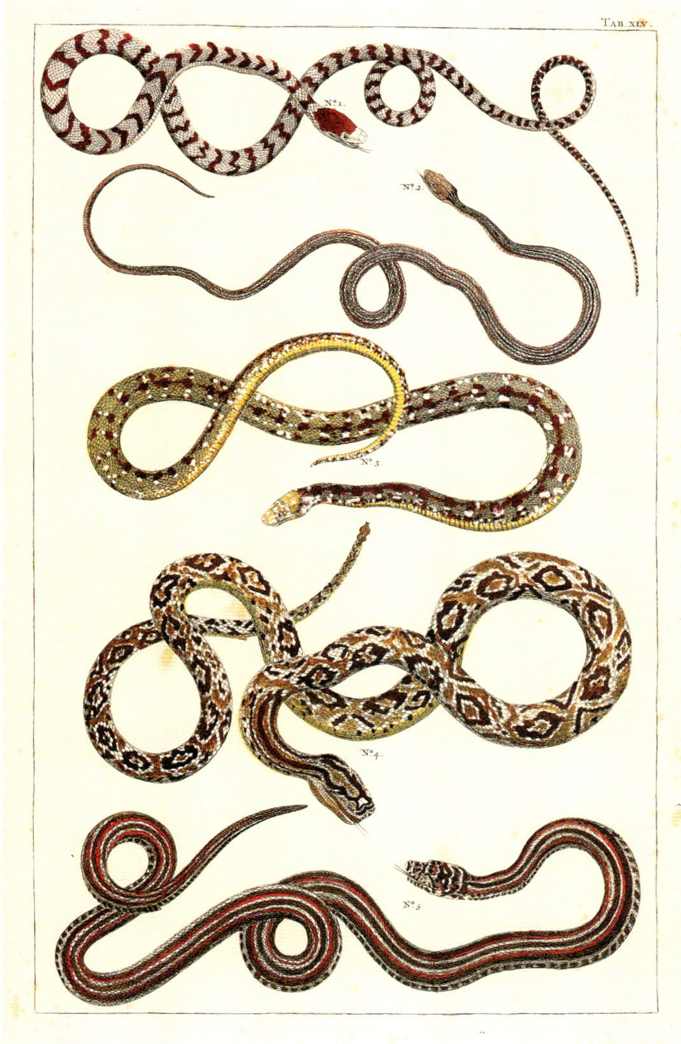

1-5 Serpentes
1-5 Snakes, according to Seba from Ceylon · Schlangen, nach Seba aus Ceylon · Serpents, de Ceylan selon Seba

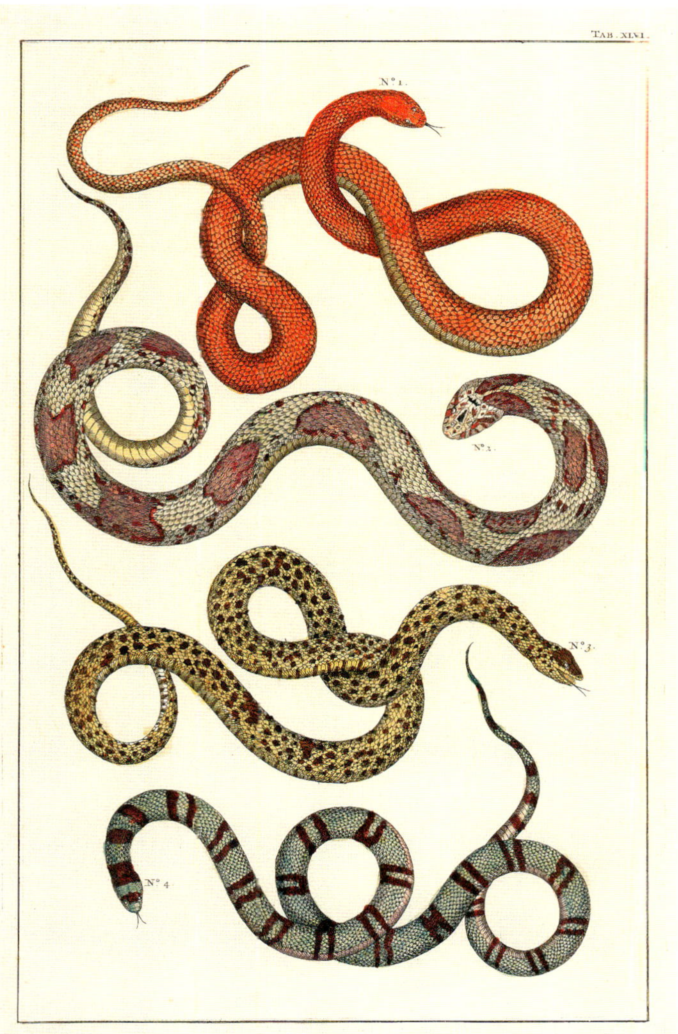

1-4 Serpentes
1-4 Snakes from different continents · Schlangen aus verschiedenen Kontinenten · Serpents de différents continents

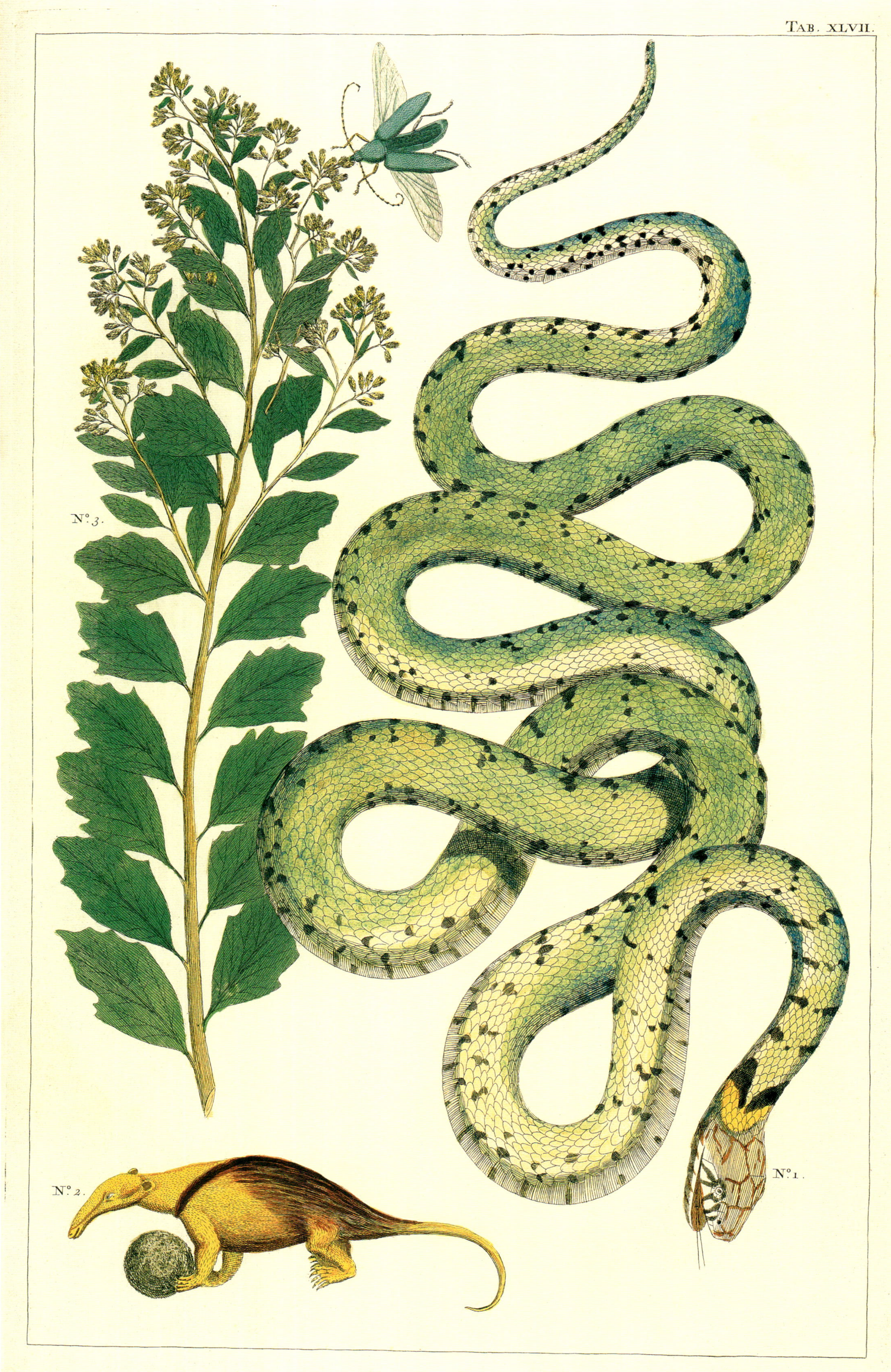

1 *Natrix natrix* 2 *Myrmecophaga tridactyla* 3 *Baccharis halinifolia* • *Cerambycidae*
1 Grass snake · Ringelnatter · Couleuvre à collier 2 Giant anteater (young) · Ameisenbär (Jungtier) · Grand fourmilier · (jeune animal) 3 Tree groundsel · Kreuzstrauch · Séneçon en arbre · • Long horned beetle · Bockkäfer · Capricorne

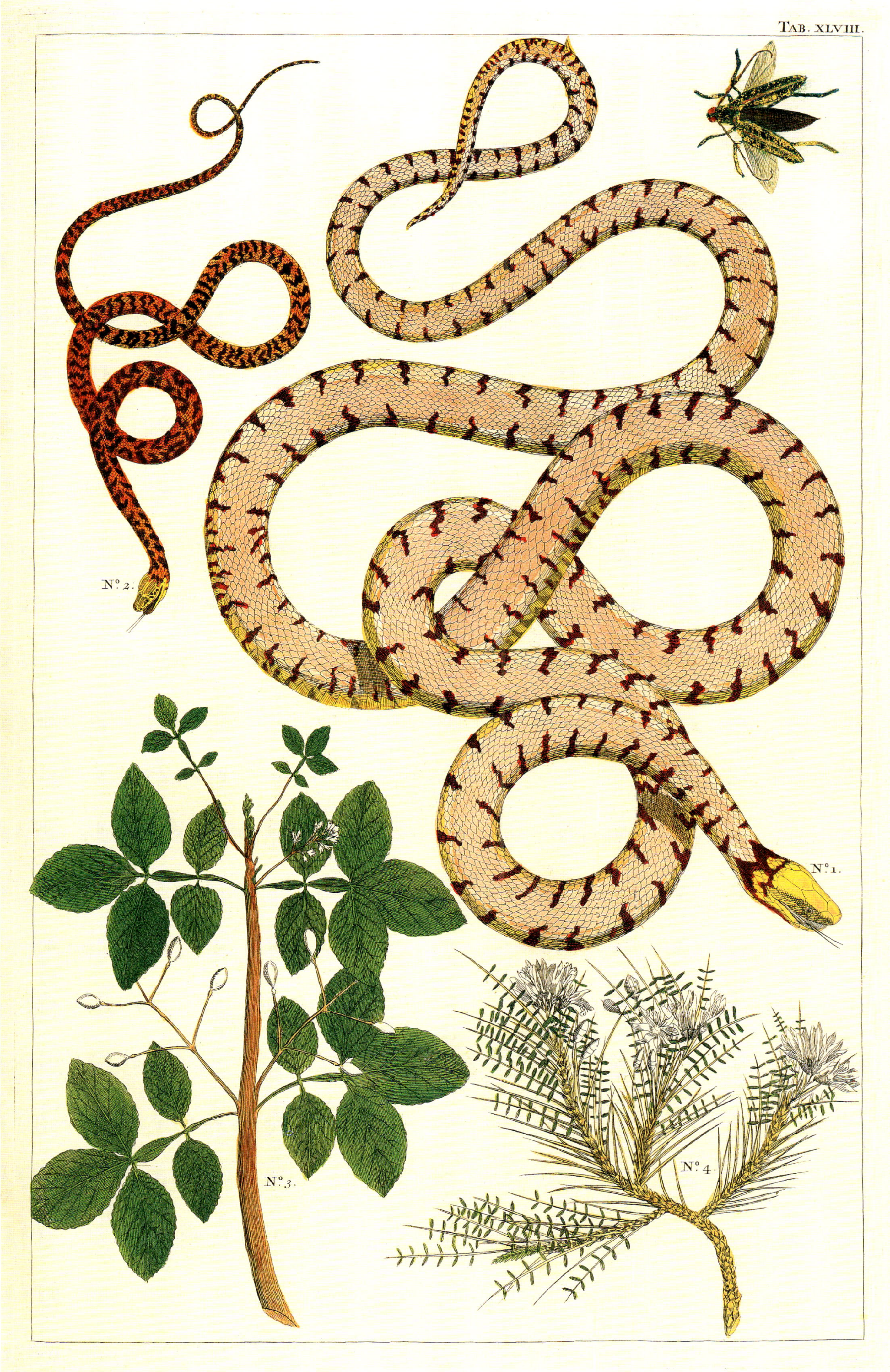

1 *Natrix natrix* 2 Serpentes 3 *Pistacia sp.* 4 *Astragalus sp.* • *Cerambycidae*
1 Grass snake · Ringelnatter · Couleuvre à collier 2 Snake, according to Seba from Ceylon · Schlange, nach Seba aus Ceylon · Serpent, de Ceylan selon Seba 3 Pistache · Pistazie · Pistachier
4 Milk vetch · Tragant · Astragale • Long horned beetle · Bockkäfer · Capricorne

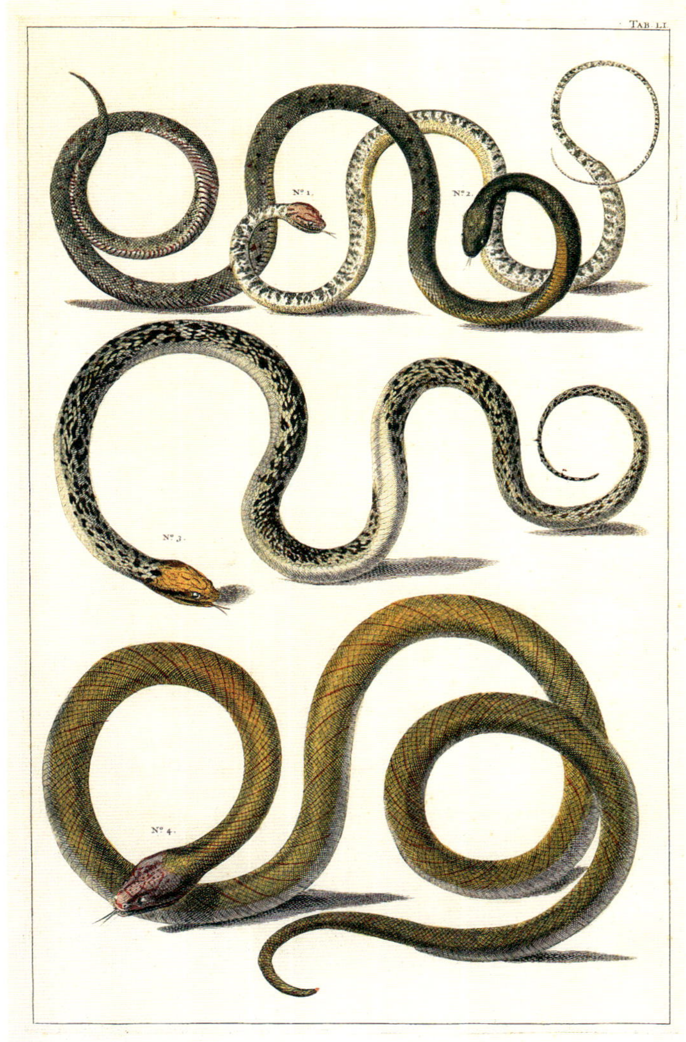

1, 3-4 Serpentes **2** *Virginia striatula*
1 Snake, according to Seba from Armenia · Schlange, nach Seba aus Armenien · Serpent, d'Arménie selon Seba **2** Rough earth snake · Erdschlange · Serpent fouisseur **3-4** Snakes, according to Seba from Brazil · Schlangen, nach Seba aus Brasilien · Serpents, du Brésil selon Seba

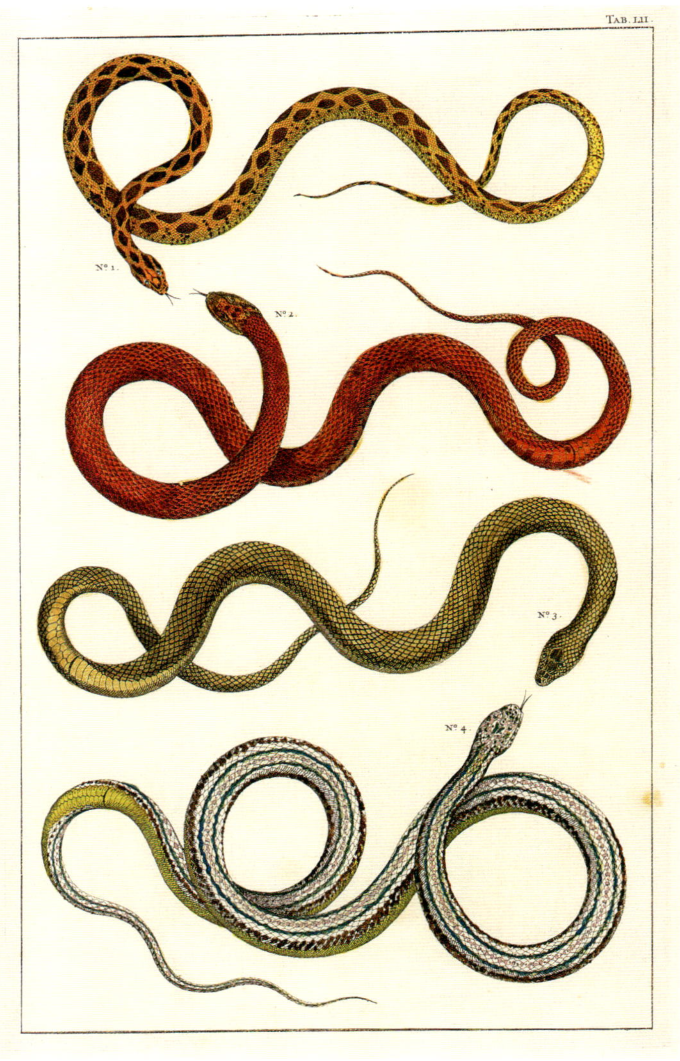

1-4 Serpentes
1-4 Various Snakes · Verschiedene Schlangen · Serpents divers

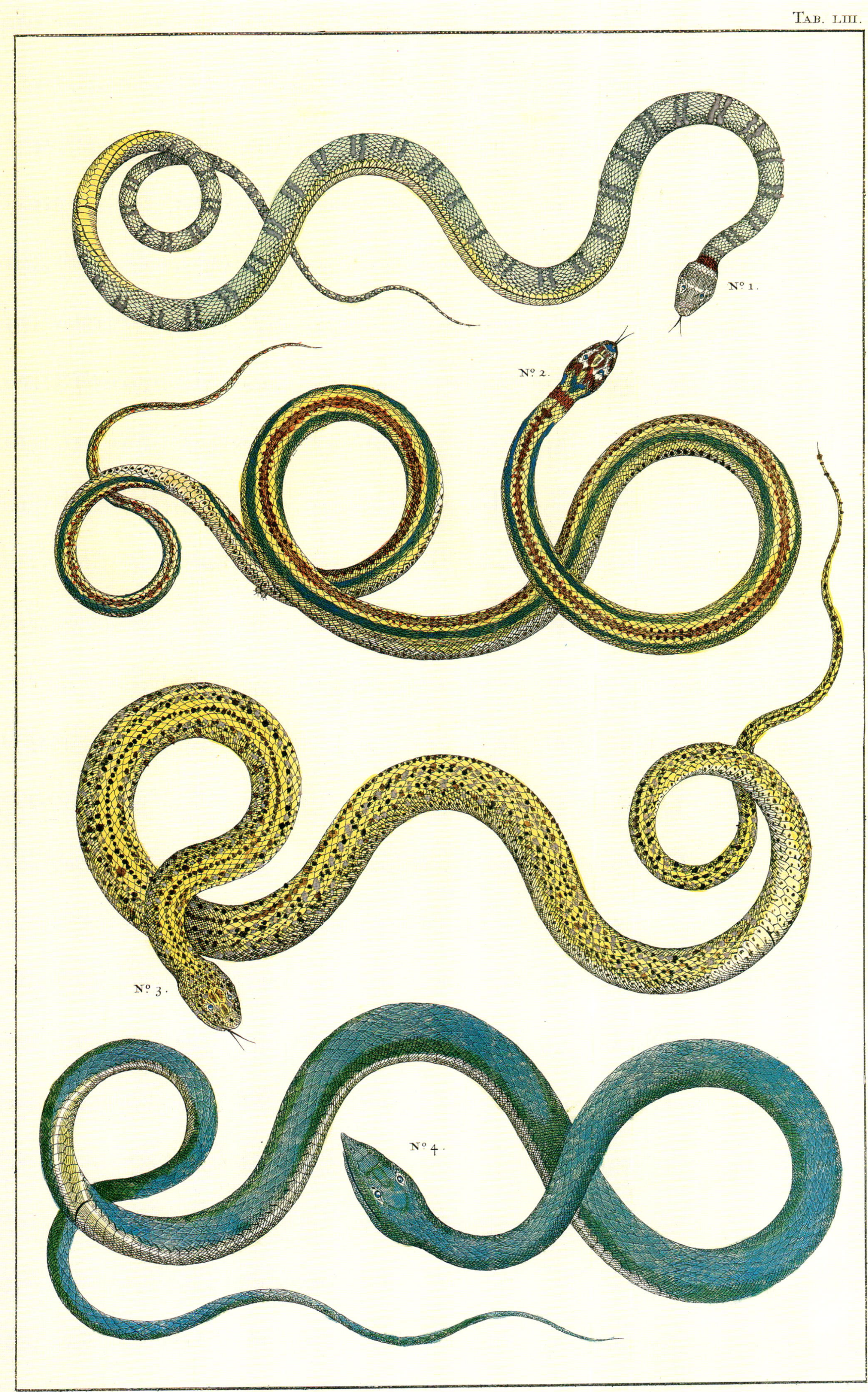

1-3 Serpentes **4** *Ahaetulla sp.?*
1-3 Snakes, according to Seba from Java (1), Martinique (2) and Cuba (3) · Schlangen, nach Seba von Java (1), Martinique (2) und Kuba (3) · Serpents, de Java (1), de la Martinique (2) et de Cuba (3), selon Seba **4** Asian longnose whipsnake · Baumschleicher · Serpent arboricole

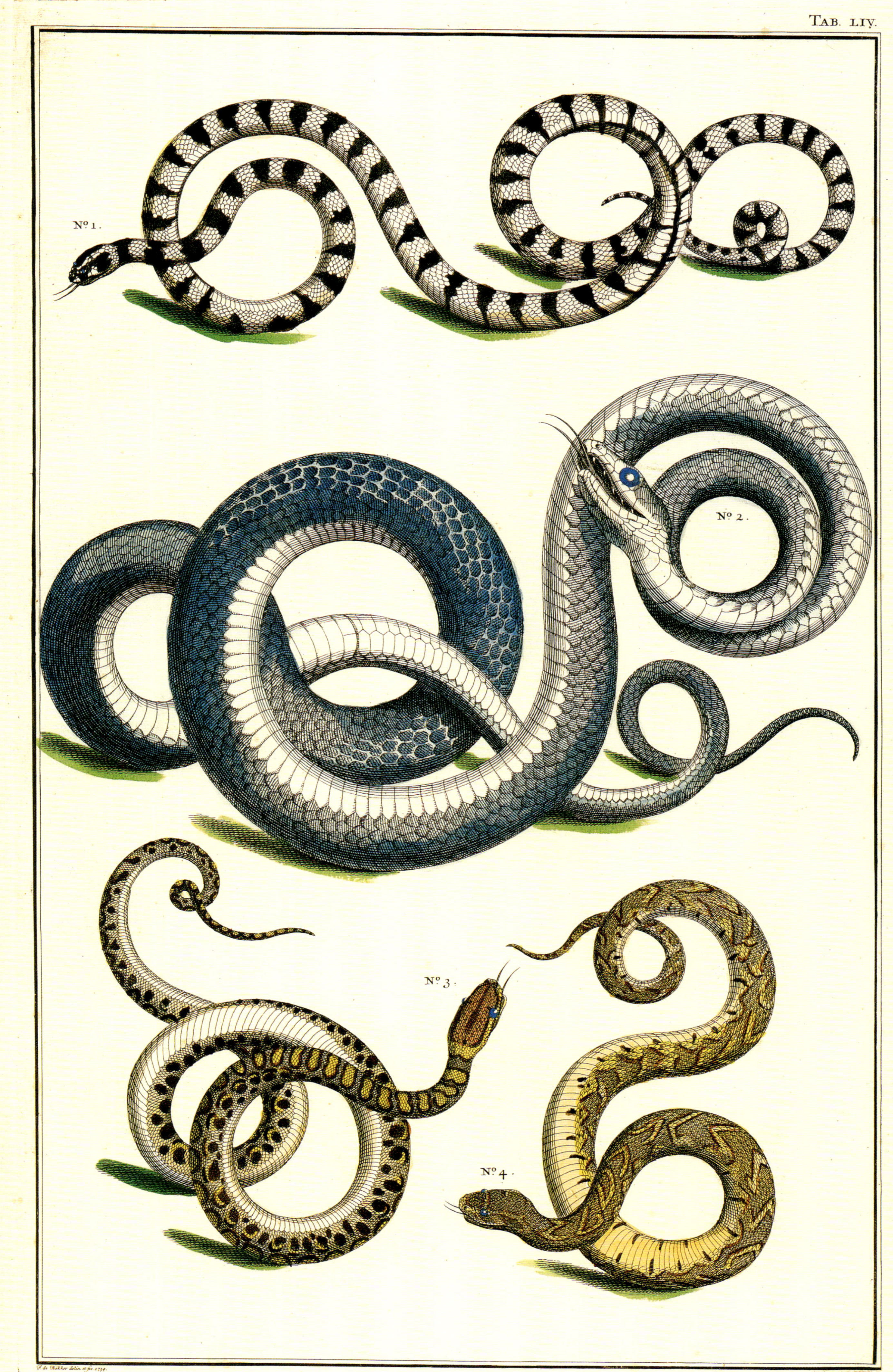

1-4 Serpentes
1-2 Snakes, according to Seba from Ambon · Schlangen, nach Seba aus Ambon · Serpents, d'Amboine selon Seba **3-4** Snakes, according to Seba from Africa · Schlangen, nach Seba aus Afrika · Serpents, d'Afrique selon Seba

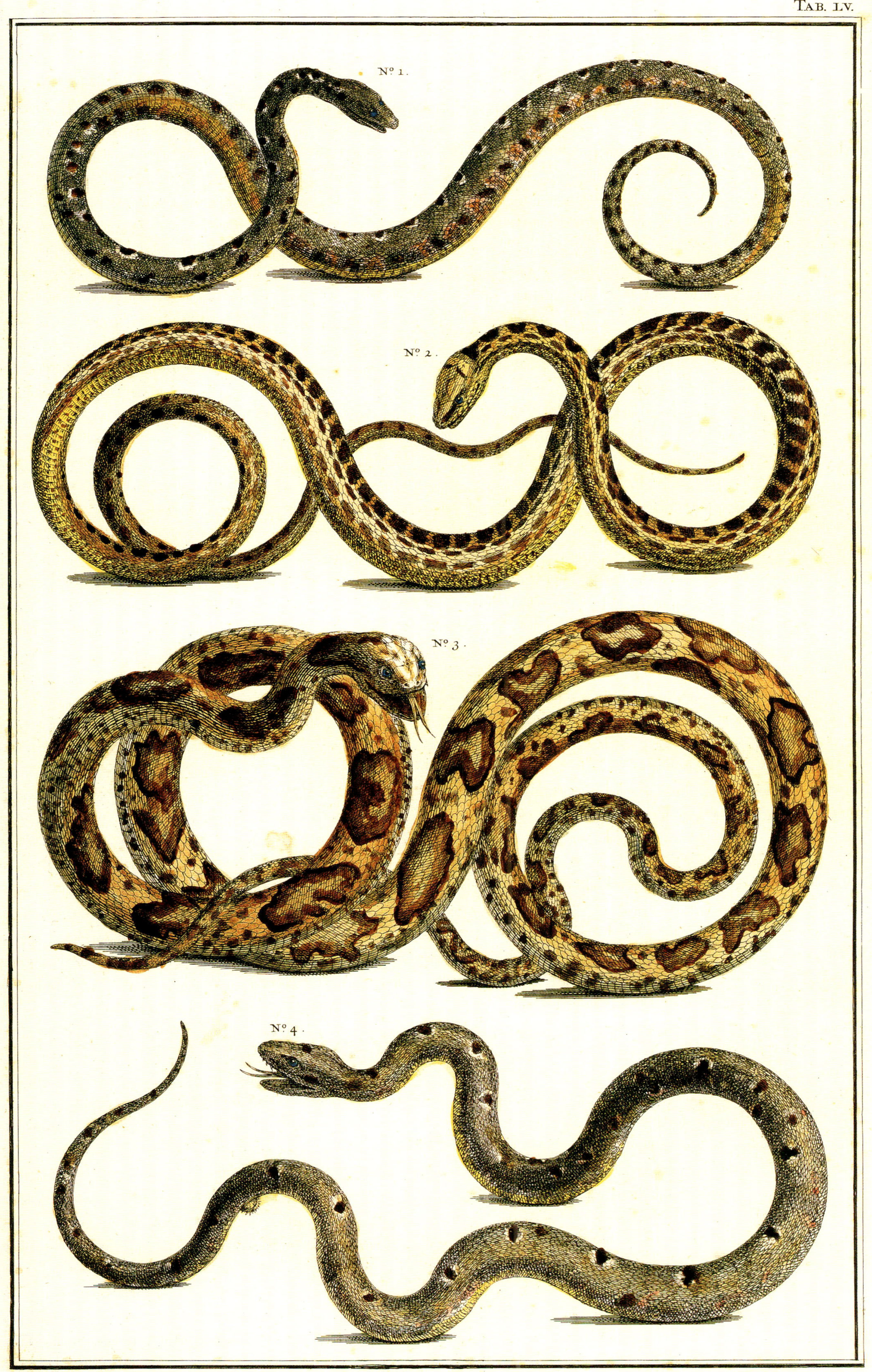

1-2, 4 Serpentes 3 *Vipera ammodytes?*
1-2, 4 Snakes, according to Seba from Ceylon · Schlangen, nach Seba aus Ceylon · Serpents, de Ceylan selon Seba **3** Nose-horned viper · Sandotter · Vipère des sables

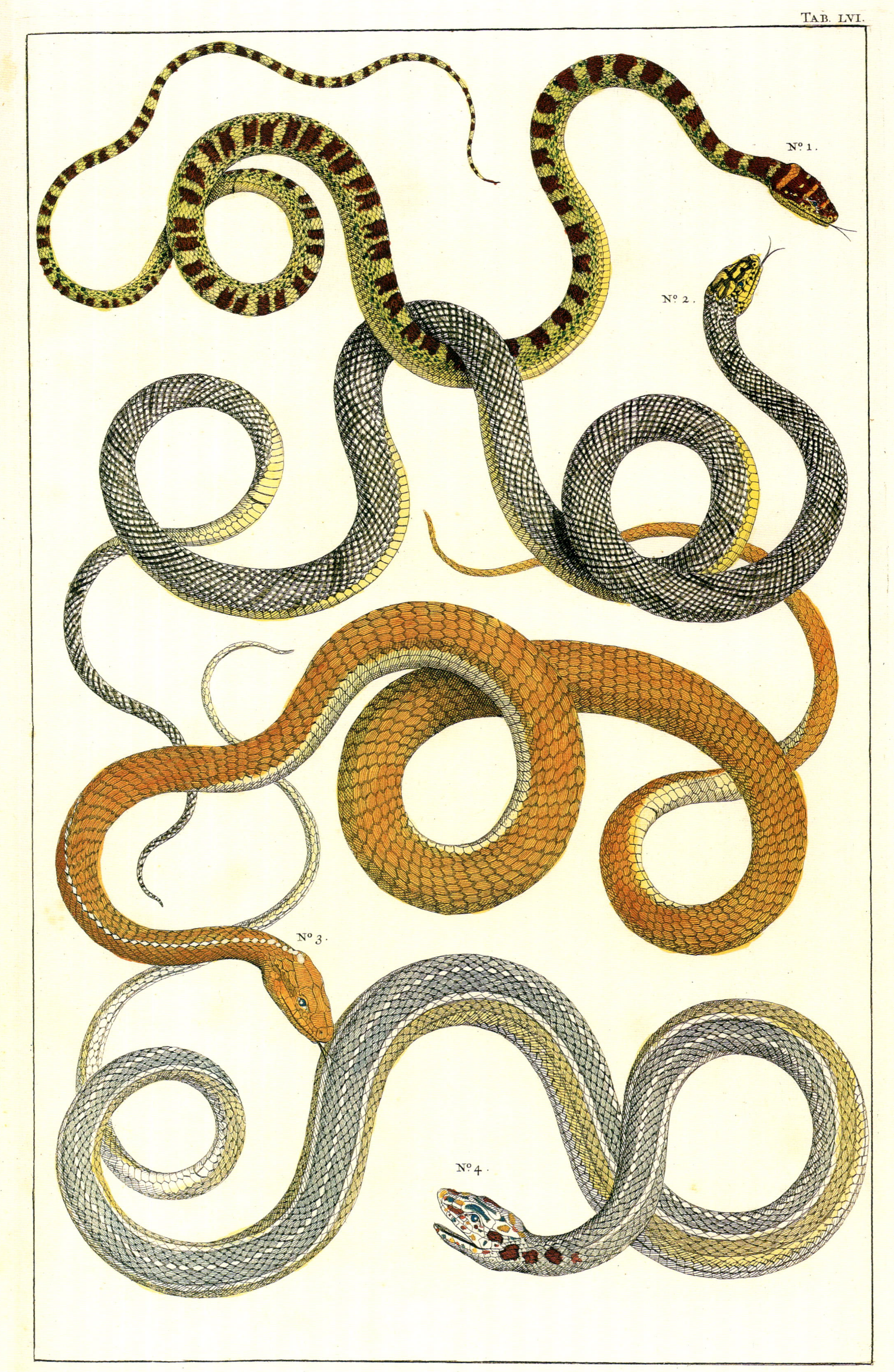

1-4 Serpentes
1-4 Snakes, according to Seba from Ambon, Ceylon, Bali and the Cape of Good Hope · Schlangen, nach Seba aus Ambon, Ceylon, Bali und vom Kap der Guten Hoffnung · Serpents, d'Amboine, de Ceylan, de Bali et du cap de Bonne-Espérance selon Seba

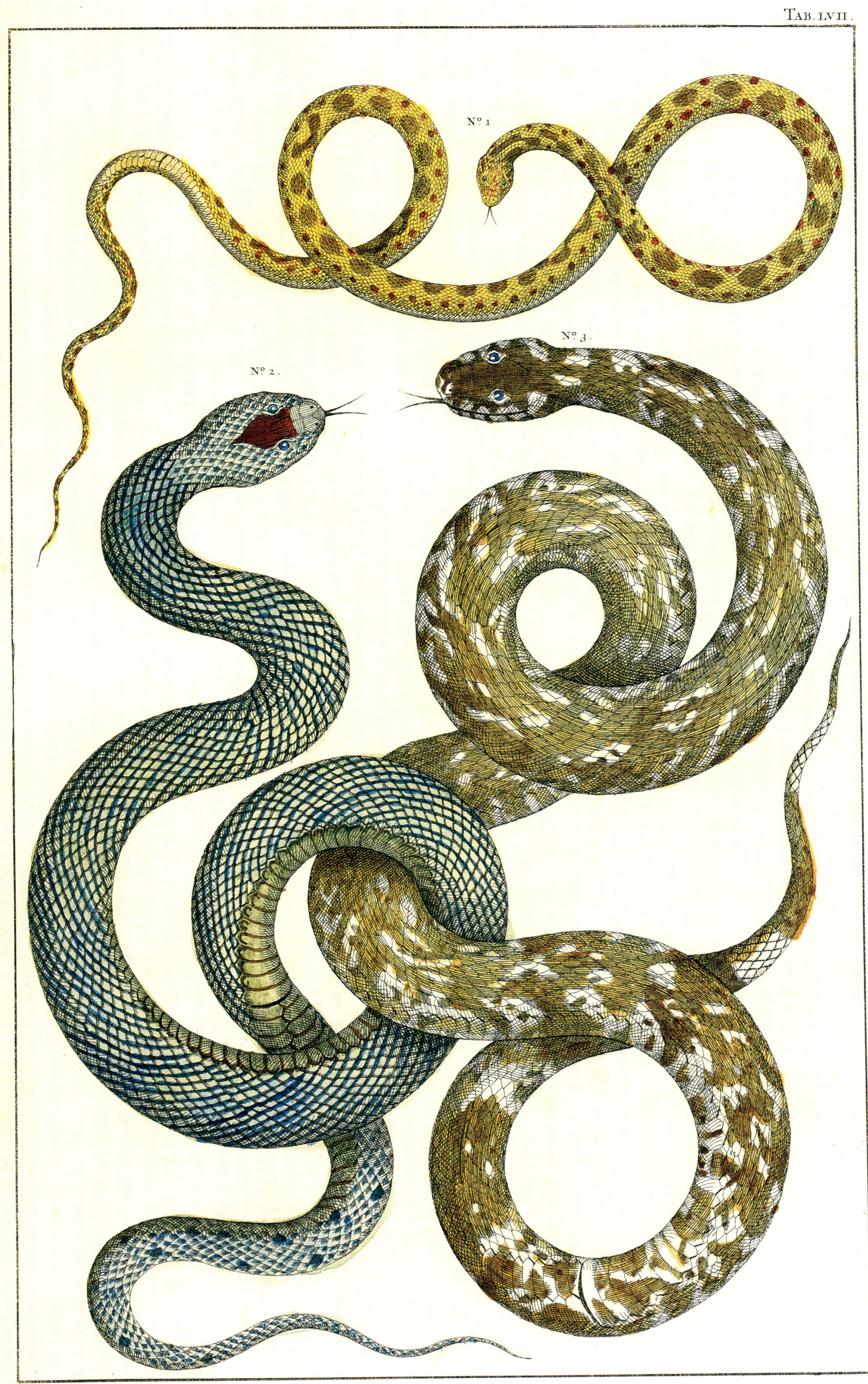

1-3 Serpentes
1-3 Various Snakes · Verschiedene Schlangen · Serpents divers

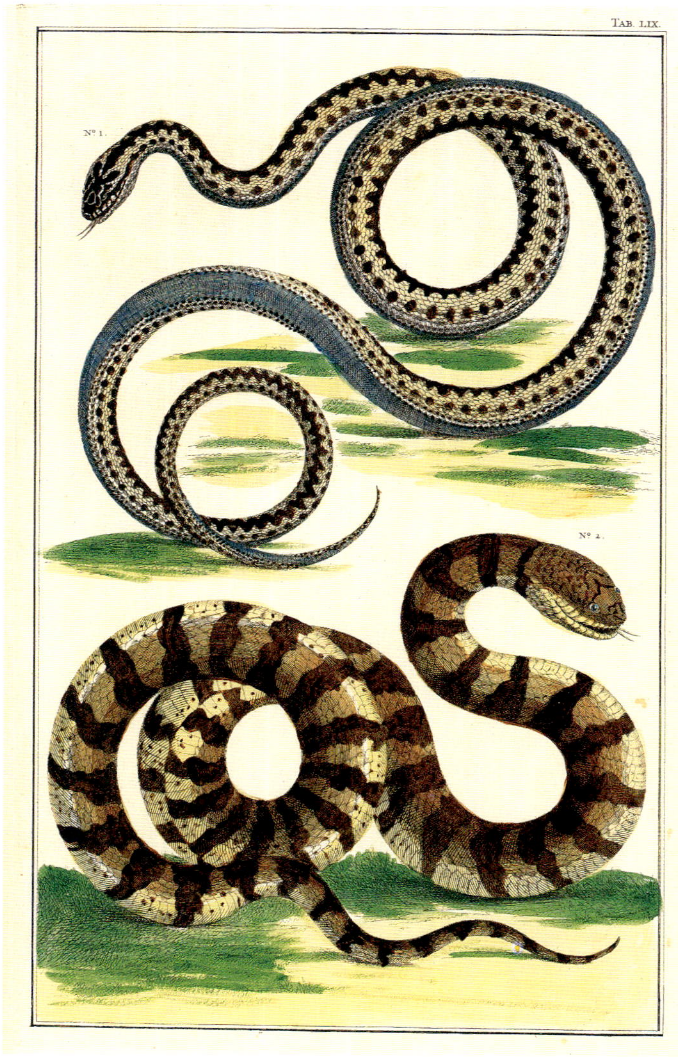

1-2 Serpentes
1-2 Snakes, according to Seba from Celebes (1) and Surinam (2) · Schlangen, nach Seba aus Celebes (1) und Surinam (2) · Serpents, de Célèbes (1) et du Surinam (2) selon Seba

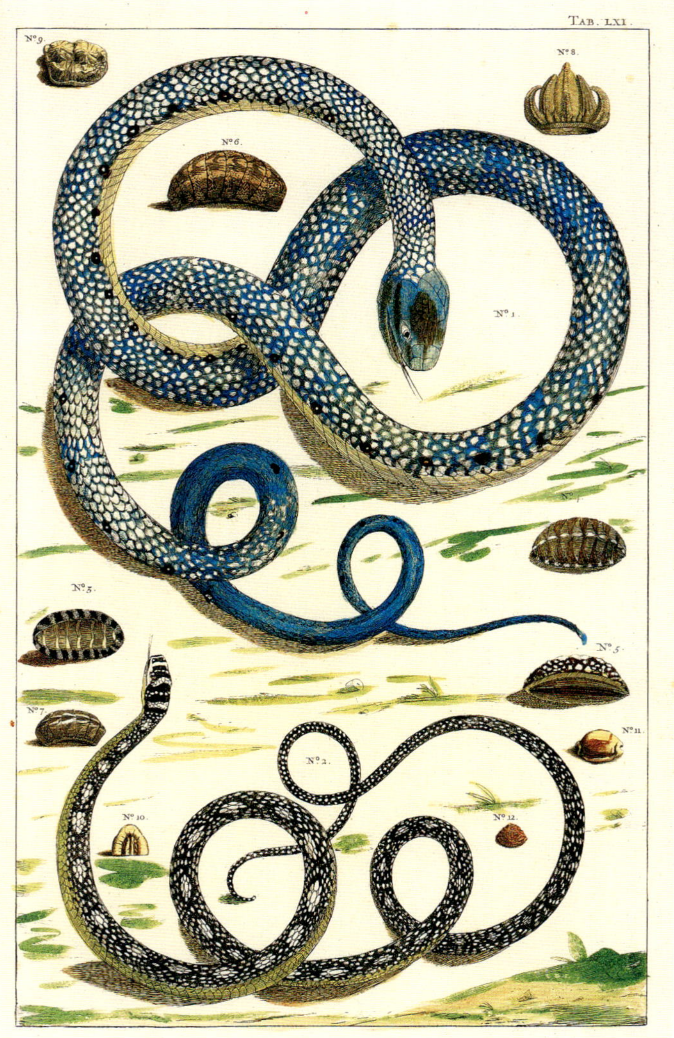

1-4 Serpentes **3-7** Polyplacophara
1 Snake, according to Seba from America · Schlange, nach Seba aus Amerika · Serpent, d'Amérique selon Seba **2** Snake, according to Seba from Ceylon · Schlange, nach Seba aus Ceylon · Serpents, de Ceylan selon Seba **3-7** Chitons · Käferschnecken · Placophores

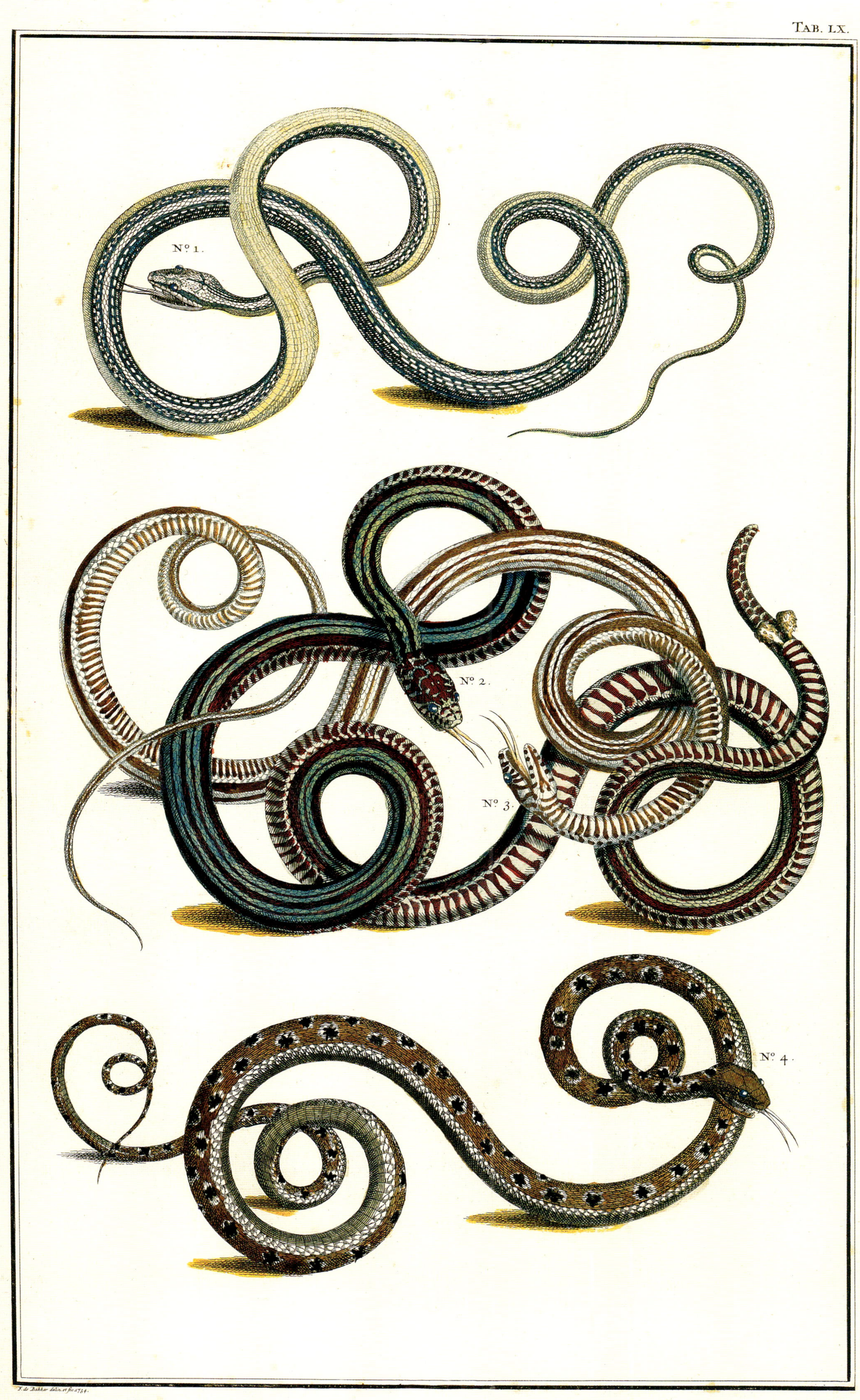

1-4 Serpentes
1-4 Various snakes · Verschiedene Schlangen · Serpents divers

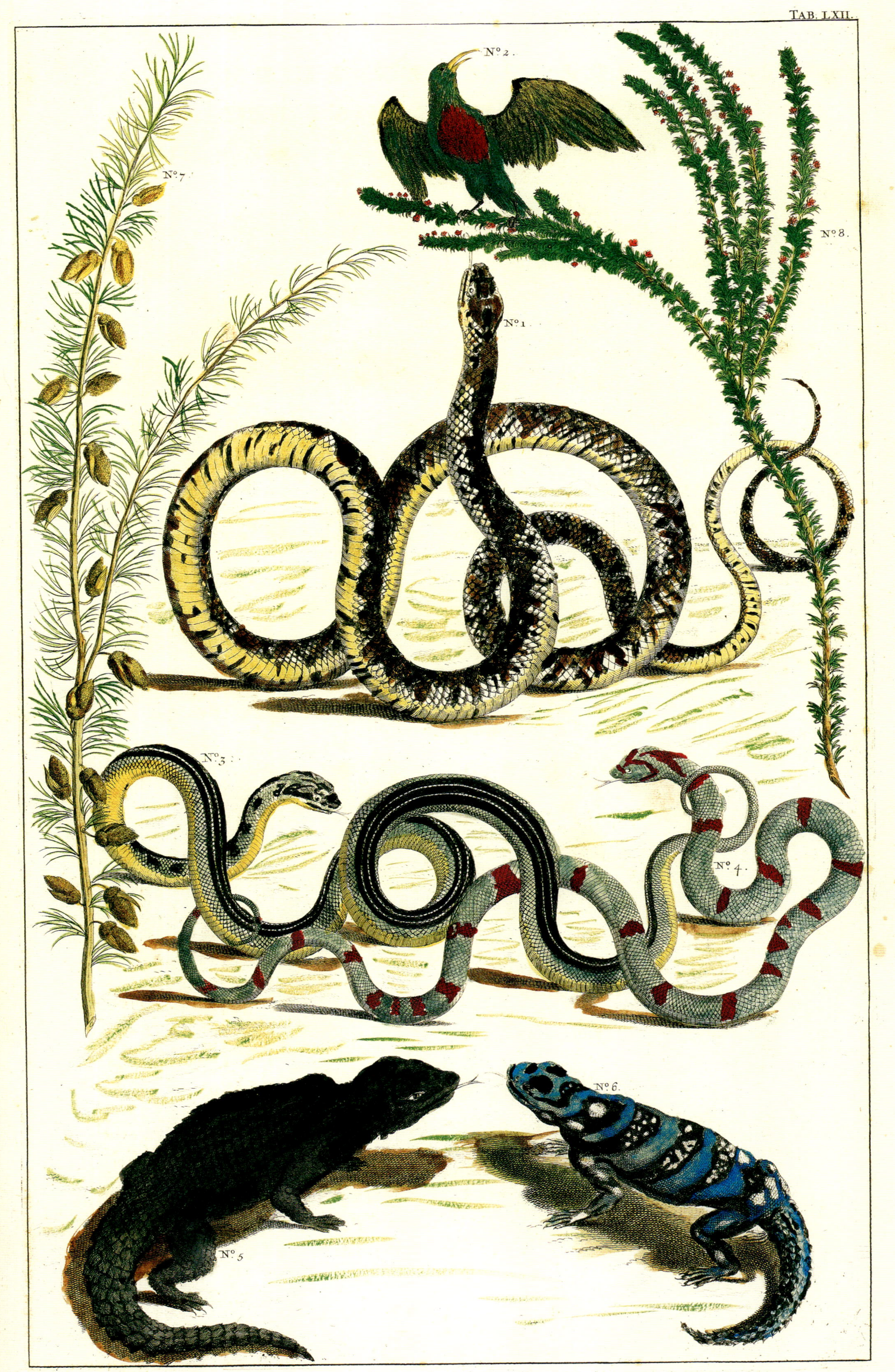

1, 3-4 Serpentes 2 Aves 5-6 Squamata
1, 3-4 Snakes from various regions · Schlangen aus verschiedenen Regionen · Serpents de différentes régions **2** Bird, according to Seba from Ambon · Vogel, nach Seba aus Ambon · Oiseau, d'Amboine selon Seba **5-6** Lizards · Echsen · Sauriens

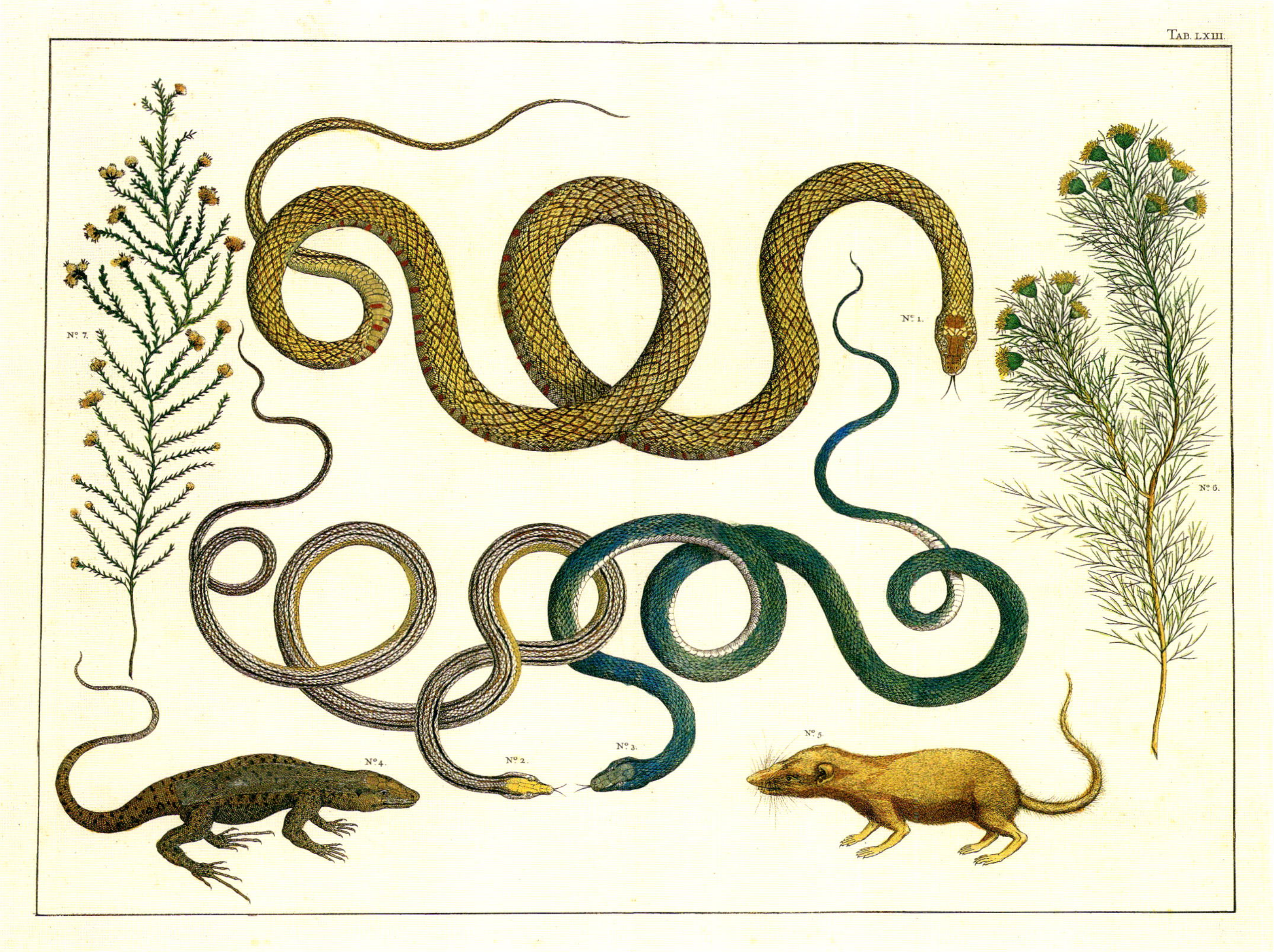

TAB. LXIII.

1-3 Serpentes **5** Soricidae **6** Compositae **7** Ericaceae
1 Snake, according to Seba from Mexico · Schlange, nach Seba aus Mexiko · Serpent, du Mexique selon Seba **2** Snake, according to Seba from Nova Hispania · Schlange, nach Seba aus Nova Hispania · Serpent, de Nova Hispania selon Seba **3** Snake, according to Seba from Africa · Schlange, nach Seba aus Afrika · Serpent, d'Afrique selon Seba **5** Shrew · Spitzmaus · Musaraigne **6** Sunflower family · Korbblütler · Composées **7** Heath family · Heidekrautgewächse · Ericacées

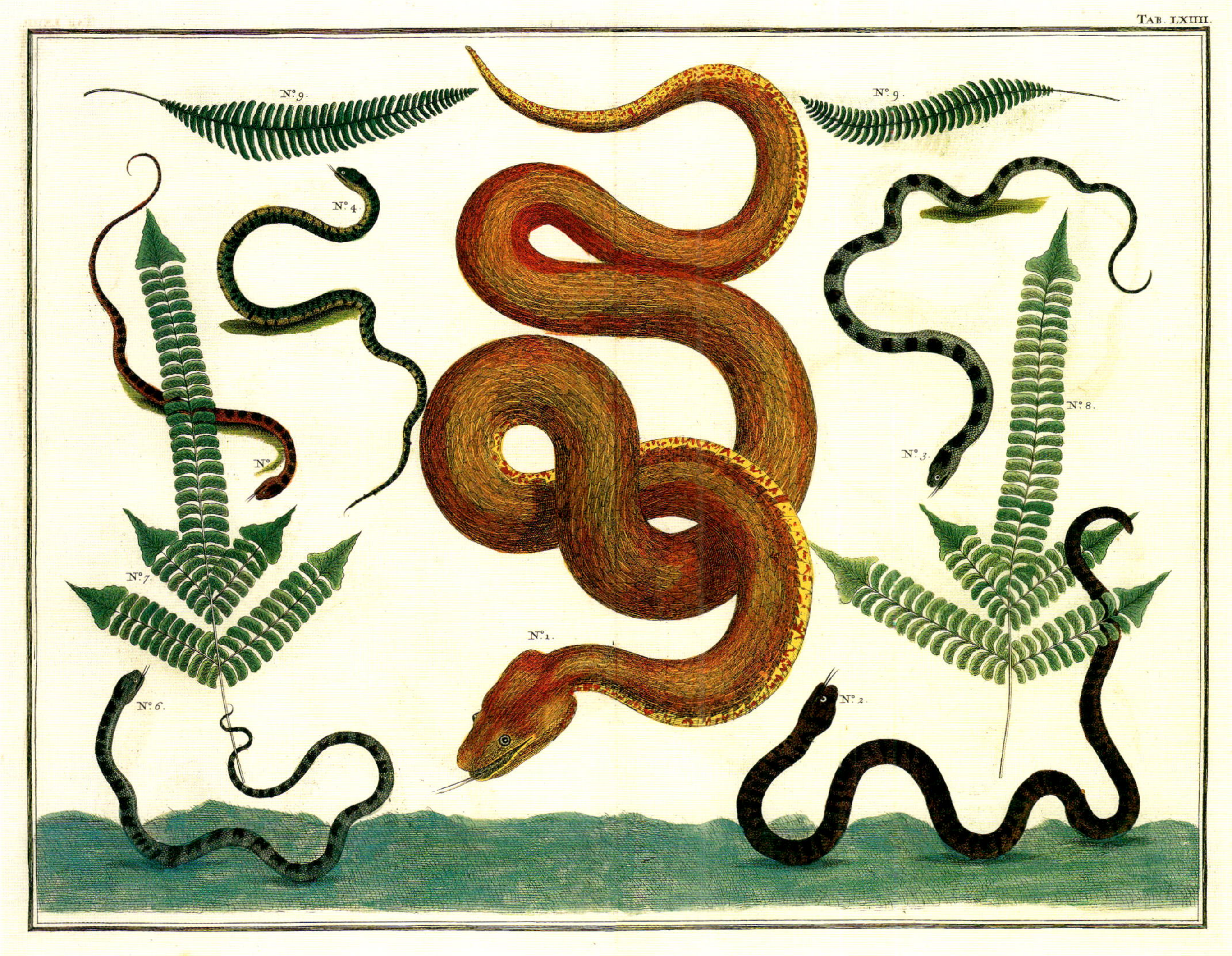

TAB. LXIIII.

1-3, 5-6 Serpentes **4** Squamata **7-9** *Adiantum*
1 Snake, according to Seba from St. Cruz · Schlange, nach Seba aus St. Cruz · Serpent, de Santa Cruz selon Seba **2-6** Snakes, according to Seba from America · Schlangen, nach Seba aus Amerika · Serpents, d'Amérique selon Seba **4** Lizard · Echse · Saurien **7-9** Maidenhair fern · Frauenhaarfarn · Cheveux-de-Vénus

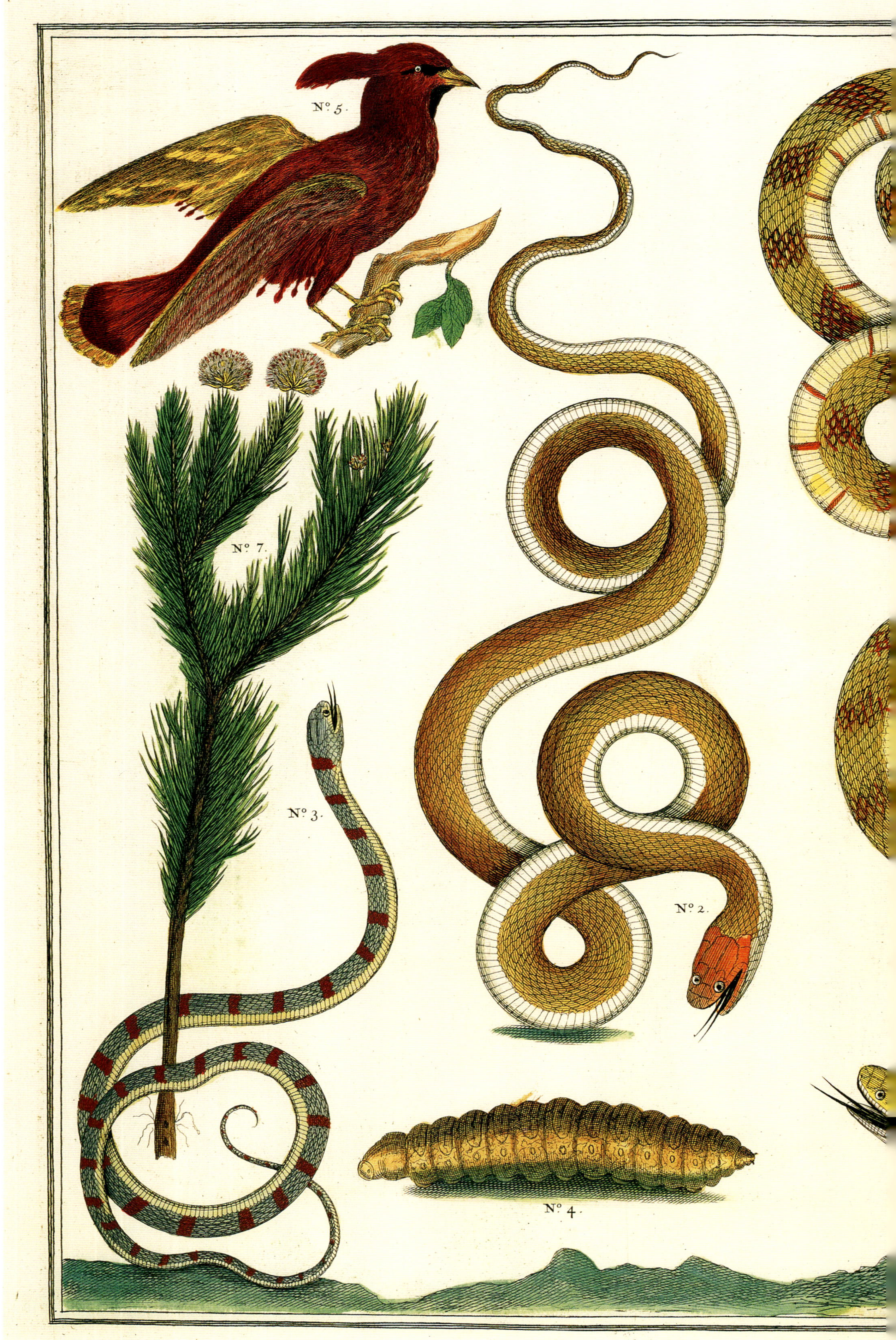

1-3 Serpentes 4 Larva insectorum 5 *Bombycilla garrulus* 6 Ploceidae
1 Snake, according to Seba from the Orient · Schlange, nach Seba aus dem Orient · Serpent, d'Orient selon Seba 2 Snake, according to Seba from Ambon · Schlange, nach Seba aus Ambon · Serpent, d'Amboine selon Seba 3 Snake, according to Seba from America · Schlange, nach Seba aus Amerika · Serpent, d'Amérique selon Seba 4 Insects found in snake no. 2 · In Schlange Nr. 2 gefundene Insektenlarve · Larve d'insecte trouvée dans le serpent n° 2 5 Bohemian waxwing · Seidenschwanz · Jaseur boréal 6 Weaver · Webervogel · Tisserin

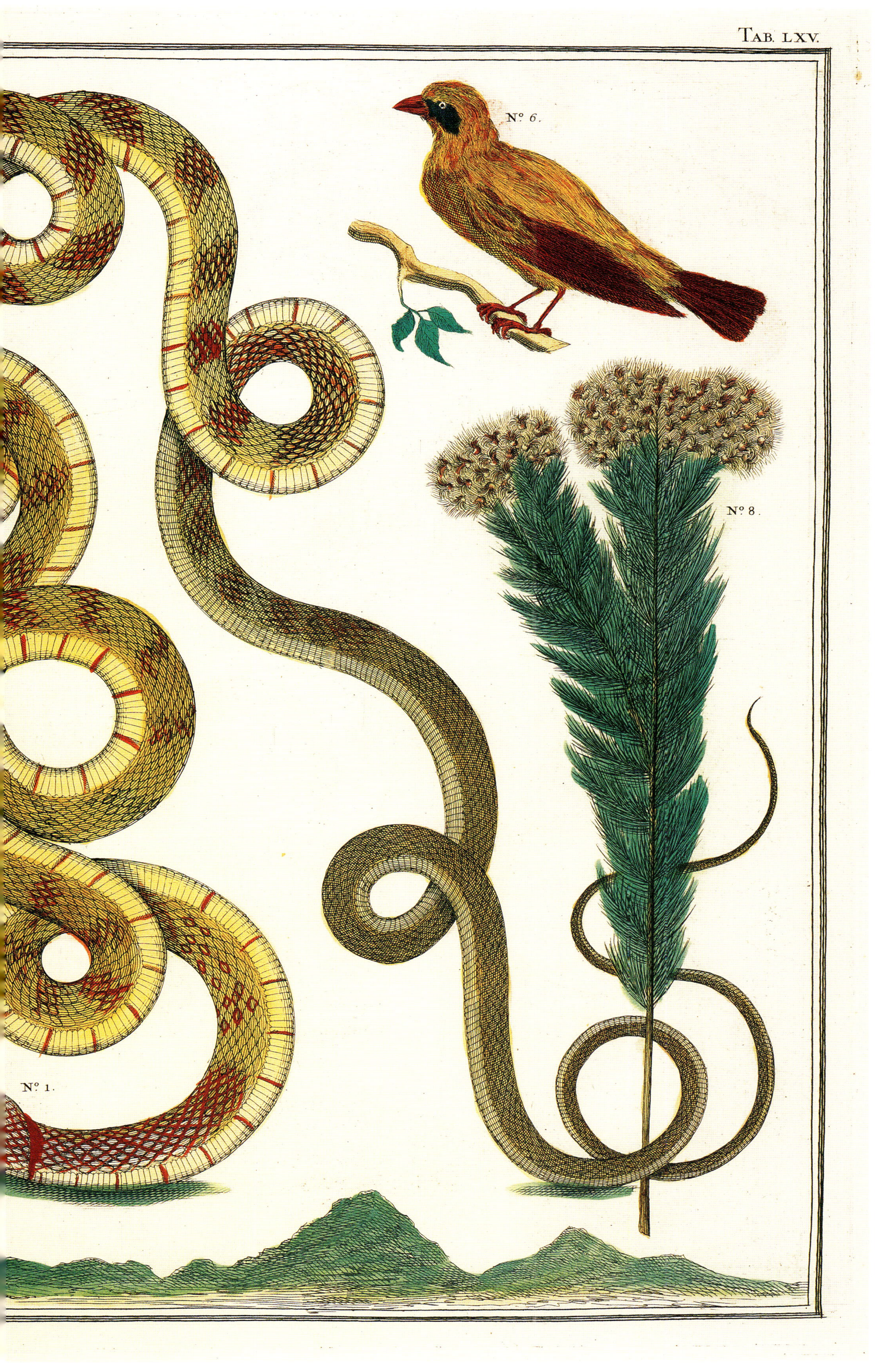
N°. 6.
N°. 8.
N°. 1.

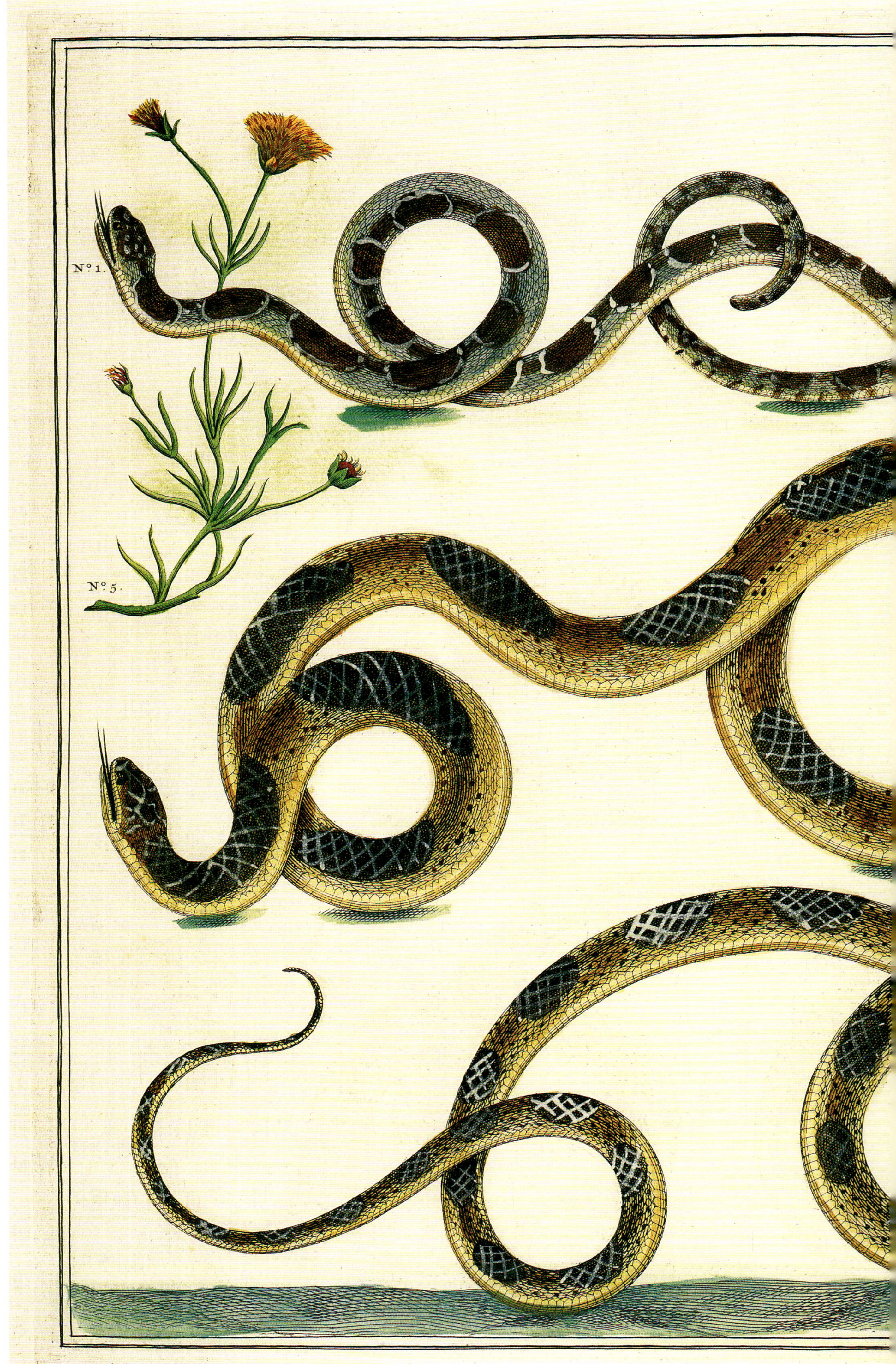

1-4 Serpentes **5-6** Compositae

1-4 Snakes, according to Seba from America · Schlangen, nach Seba aus Amerika · Serpents, d'Amérique selon Seba **5-6** Sunflower family · Korbblütler · Composées

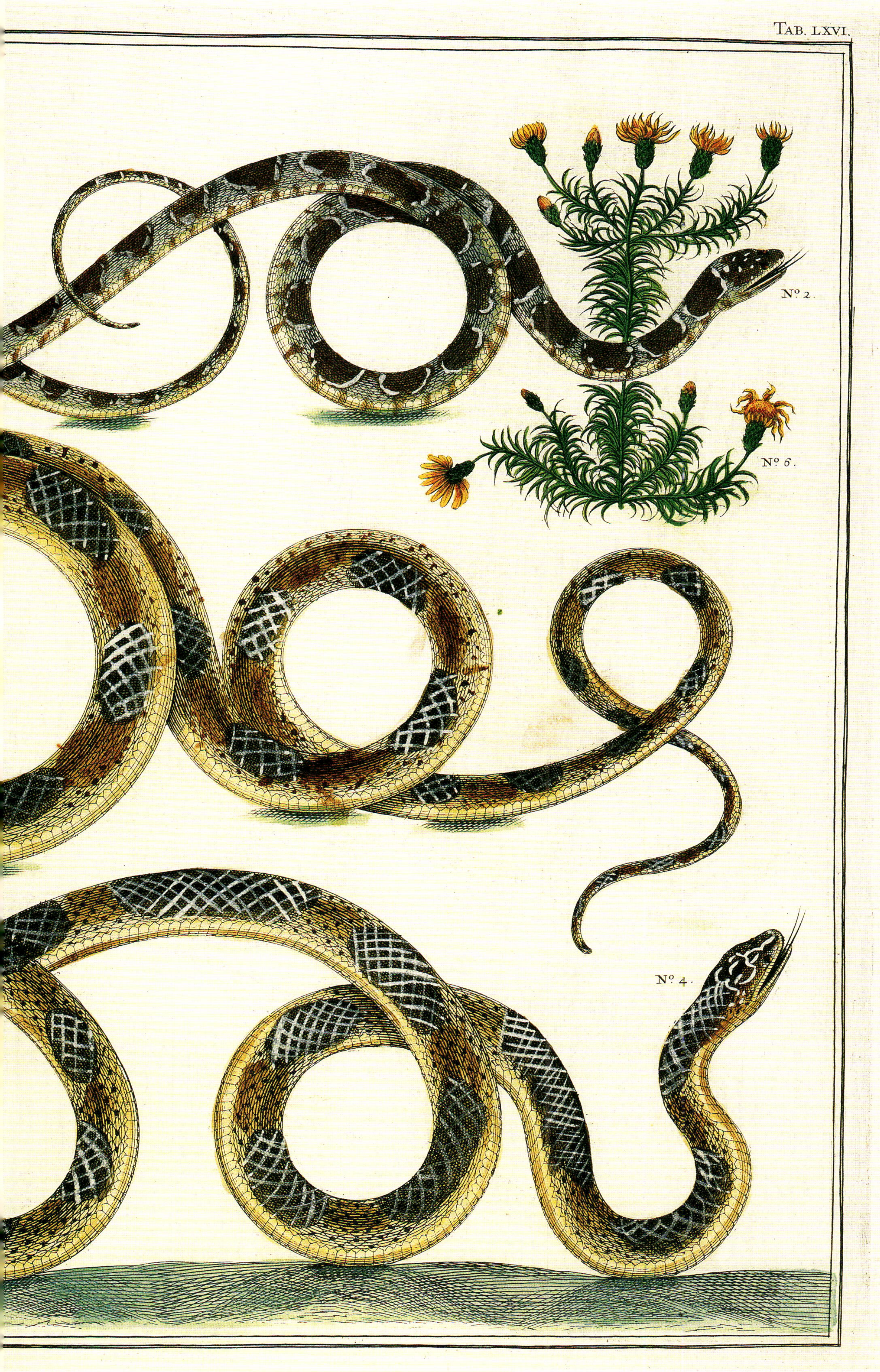
TAB. LXVI.
N° 2.
N° 6.
N° 4.

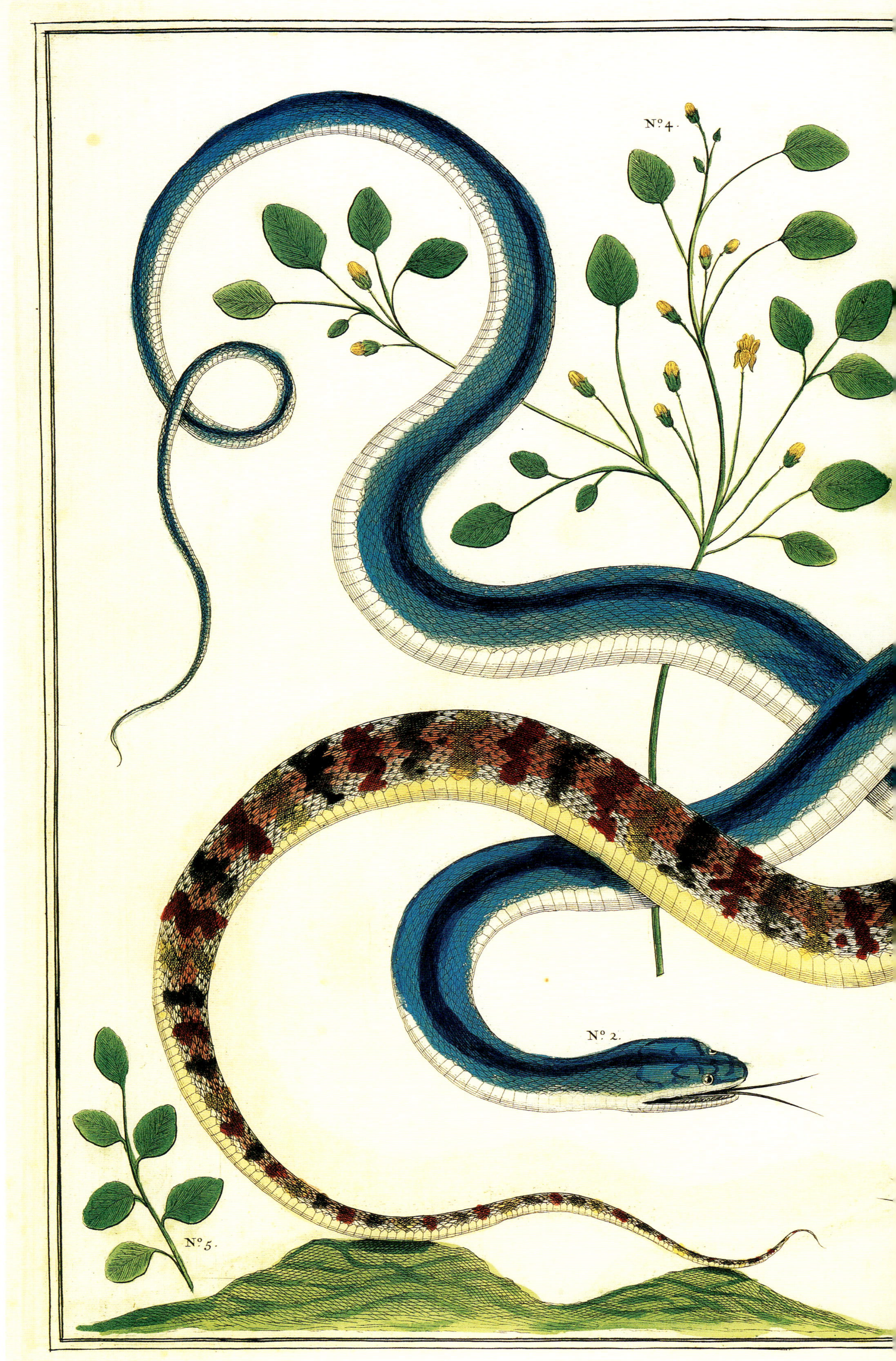

1-3 Serpentes
1-2 Snakes, according to Seba from Surinam · Schlangen, nach Seba aus Surinam · Serpents, du Surinam selon Seba **3** Snake, according to Seba from Brazil · Schlange, nach Seba aus Brasilien · Serpent, du Brésil selon Seba

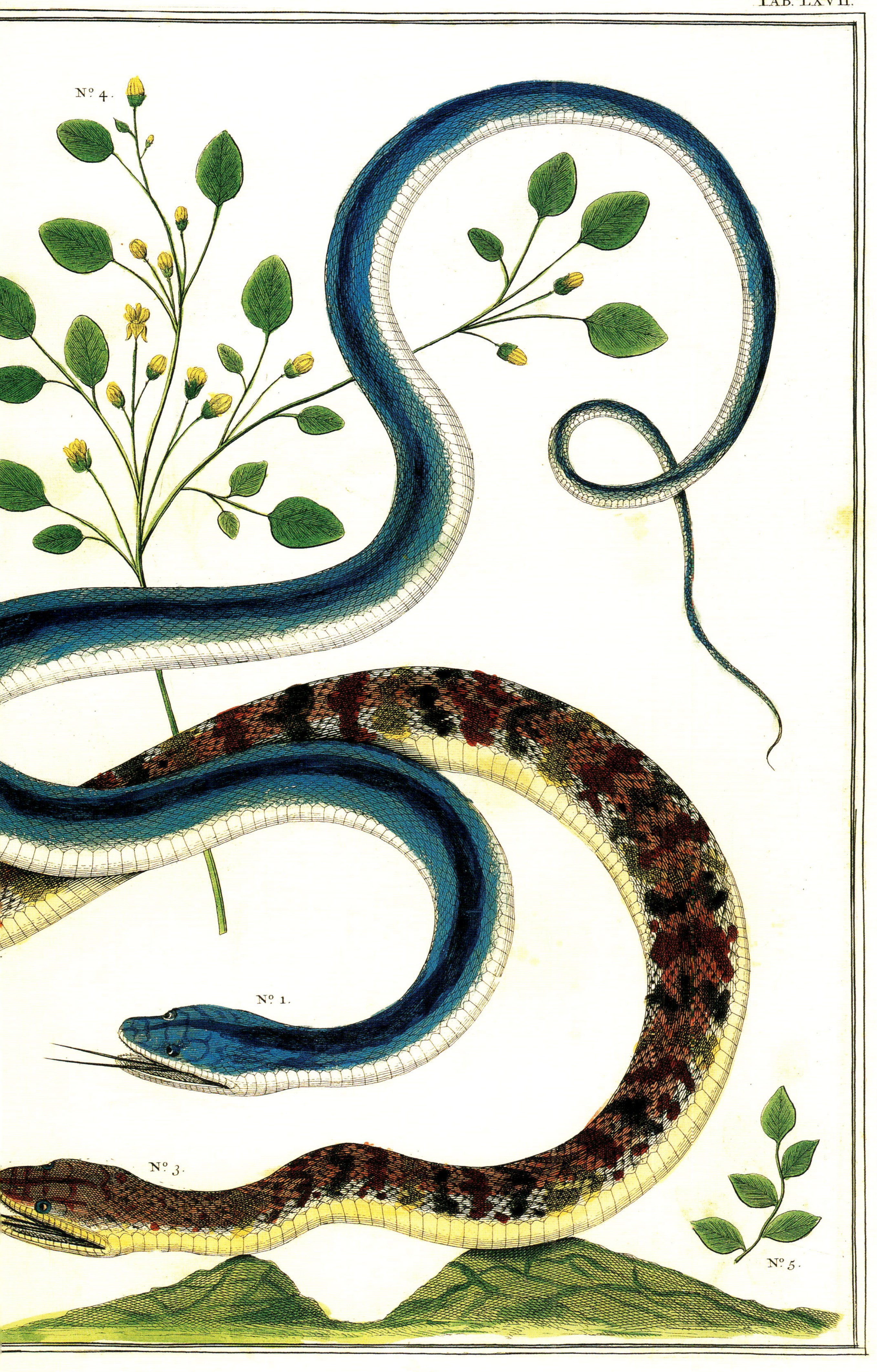
N°. 4.
N°. 1.
N°. 3.
N°. 5.

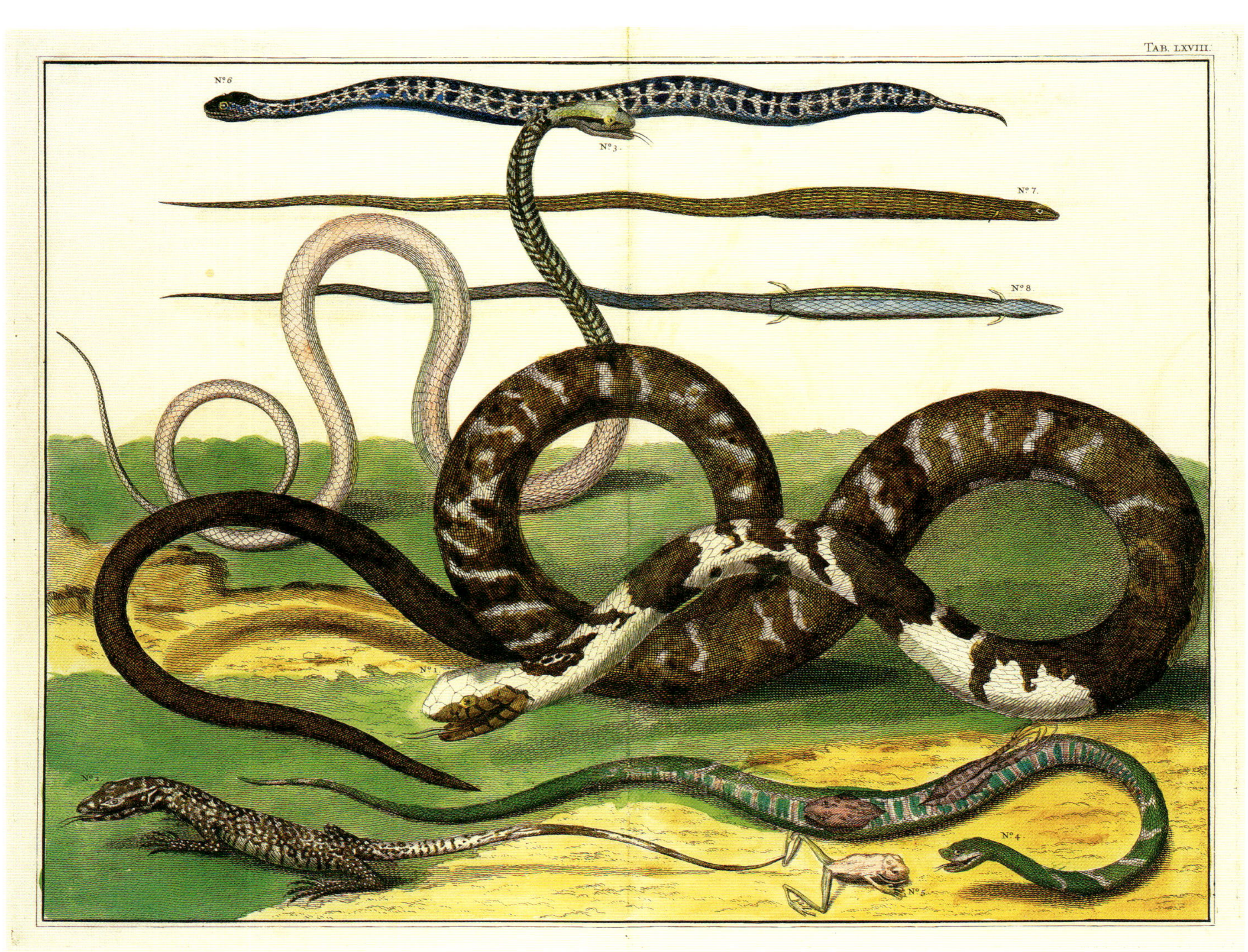

1, 3-4, 6 Serpentes **2** Squamata **5** Anura

1, 3 Snakes, according to Seba from Brazil · Schlangen, nach Seba aus Brasilien · Serpents, du Brésil selon Seba **2** Lizard · Echse · Saurien **4, 6** Snakes, according to Seba from America · Schlangen, nach Seba aus Amerika · Serpents, d'Amérique selon Seba **5** Frog · Frosch · Grenouille

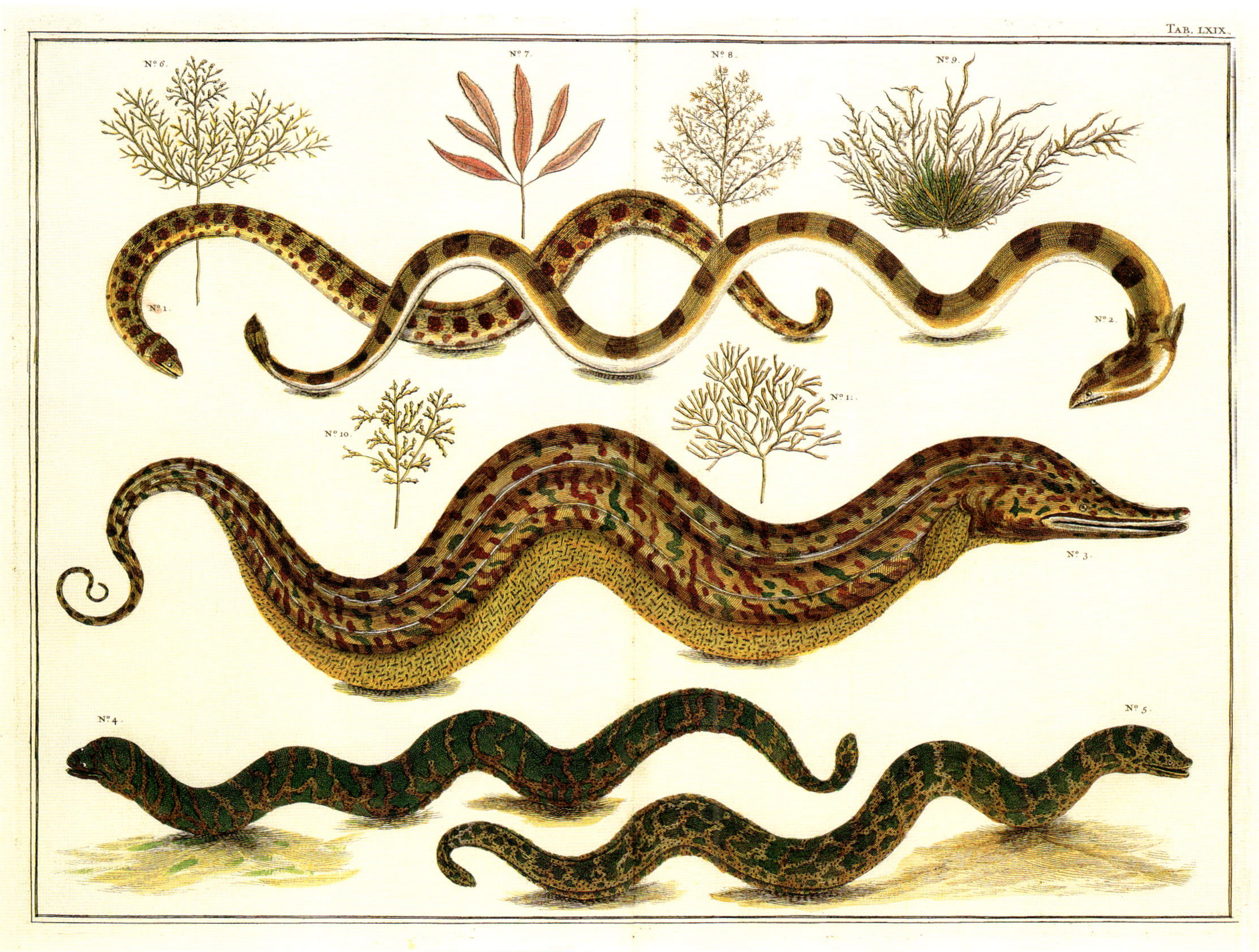

1-2 Muraenidae **3** *Gymnotus carapo* **4-5** *Echidna catenata* **6-11** Cnidaria: Anthozoa
1-2 Moray eels · Muränen · Murènes **3** Banded knifefish · Gebänderter Messerfisch · Gymnote rayée (Guyane française) **4-5** Chainlink moray eels · Schlangenmuränen · Murènes enchaînées
6-11 Corals · Korallen · Coraux

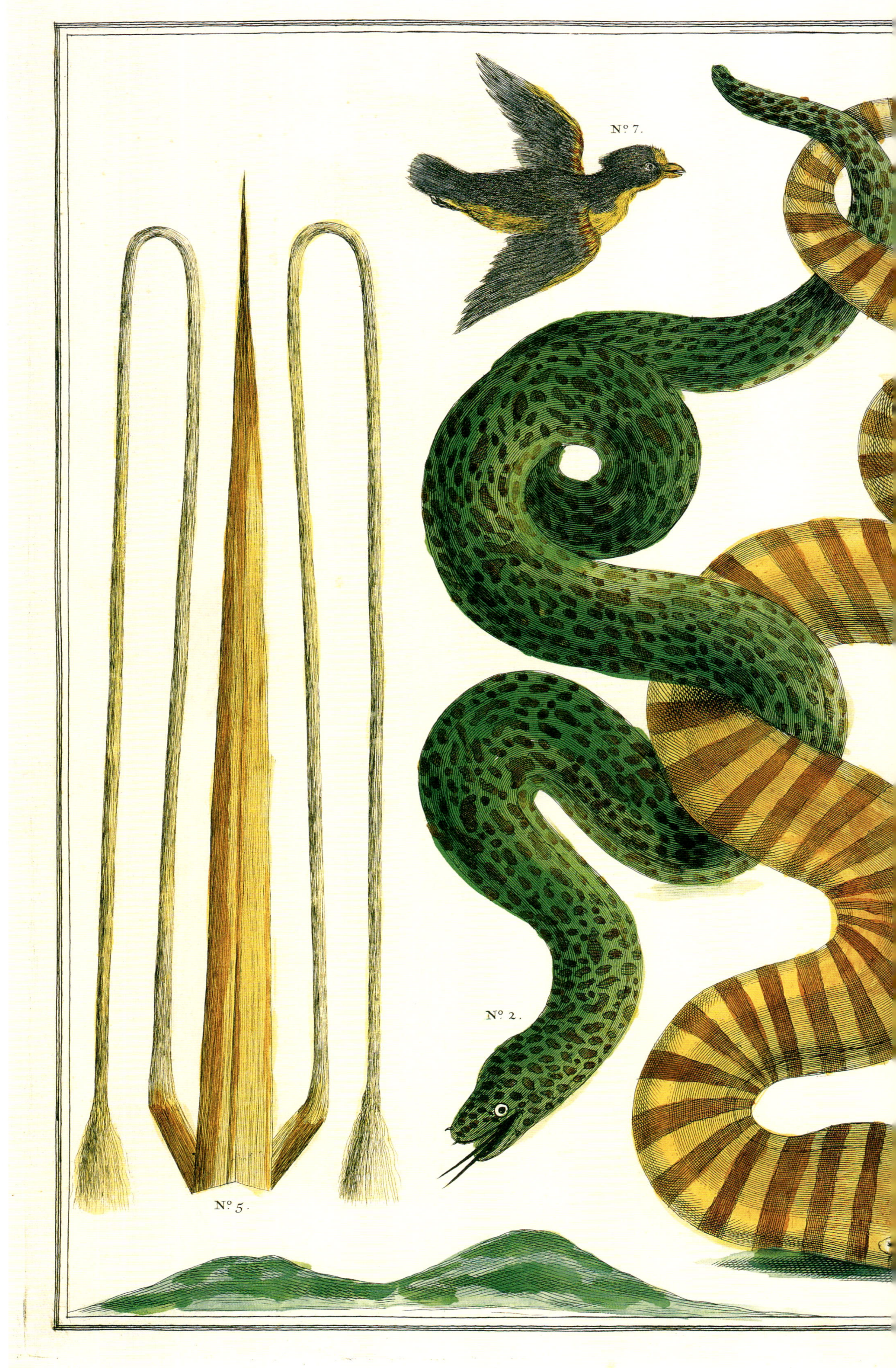

1 Muraenidae 2 Muraenidae 3 *Gymnomuraena zebra* 4 Hylidae
1-2 Moray eels · Muränen · Murènes 3 Zebra moray eel · Muräne · Murène zèbre 4 Tree frog · Laubfrosch · Grenouille verte

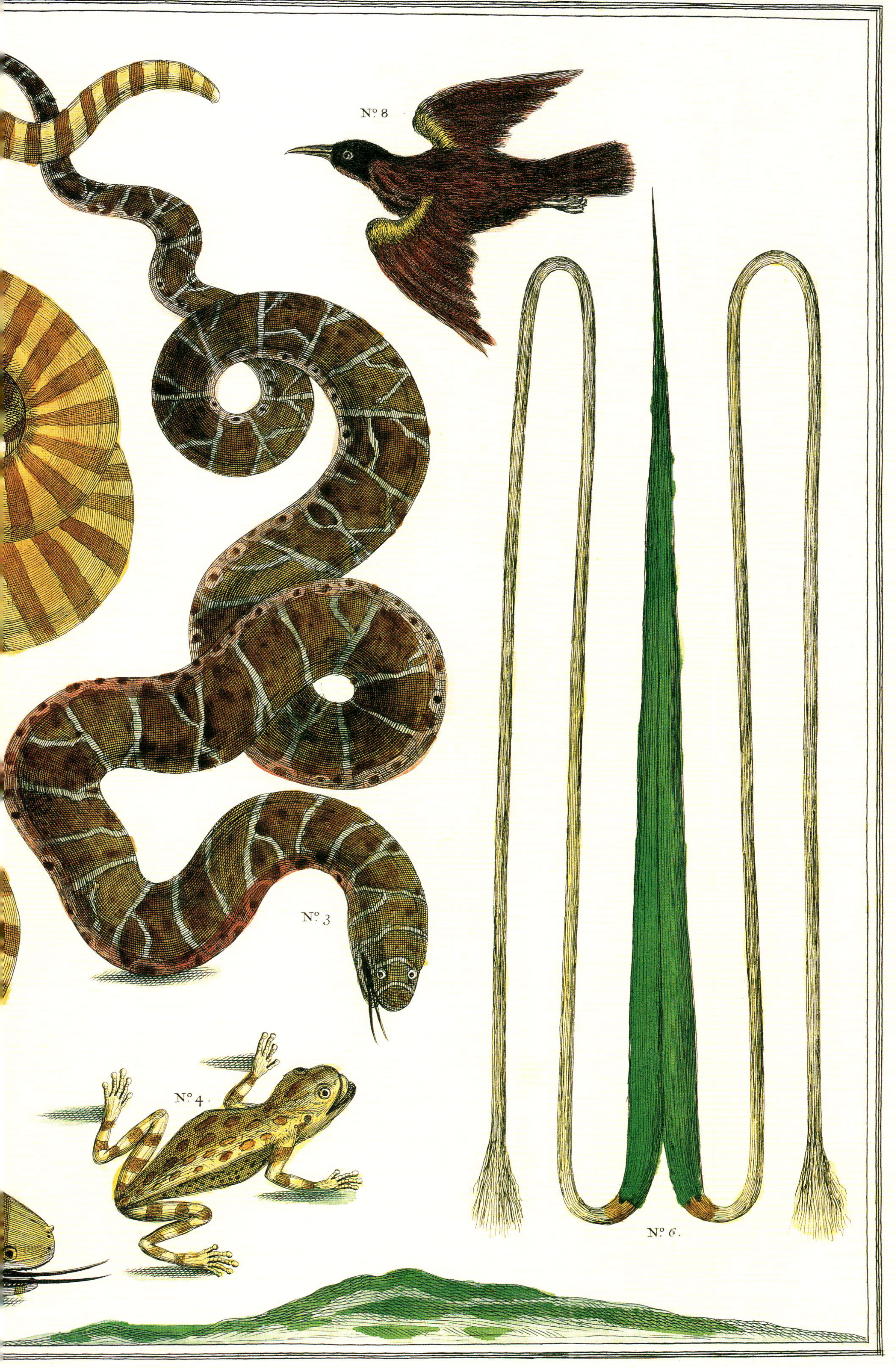
N° 8
N° 3
N° 4.
N° 6.

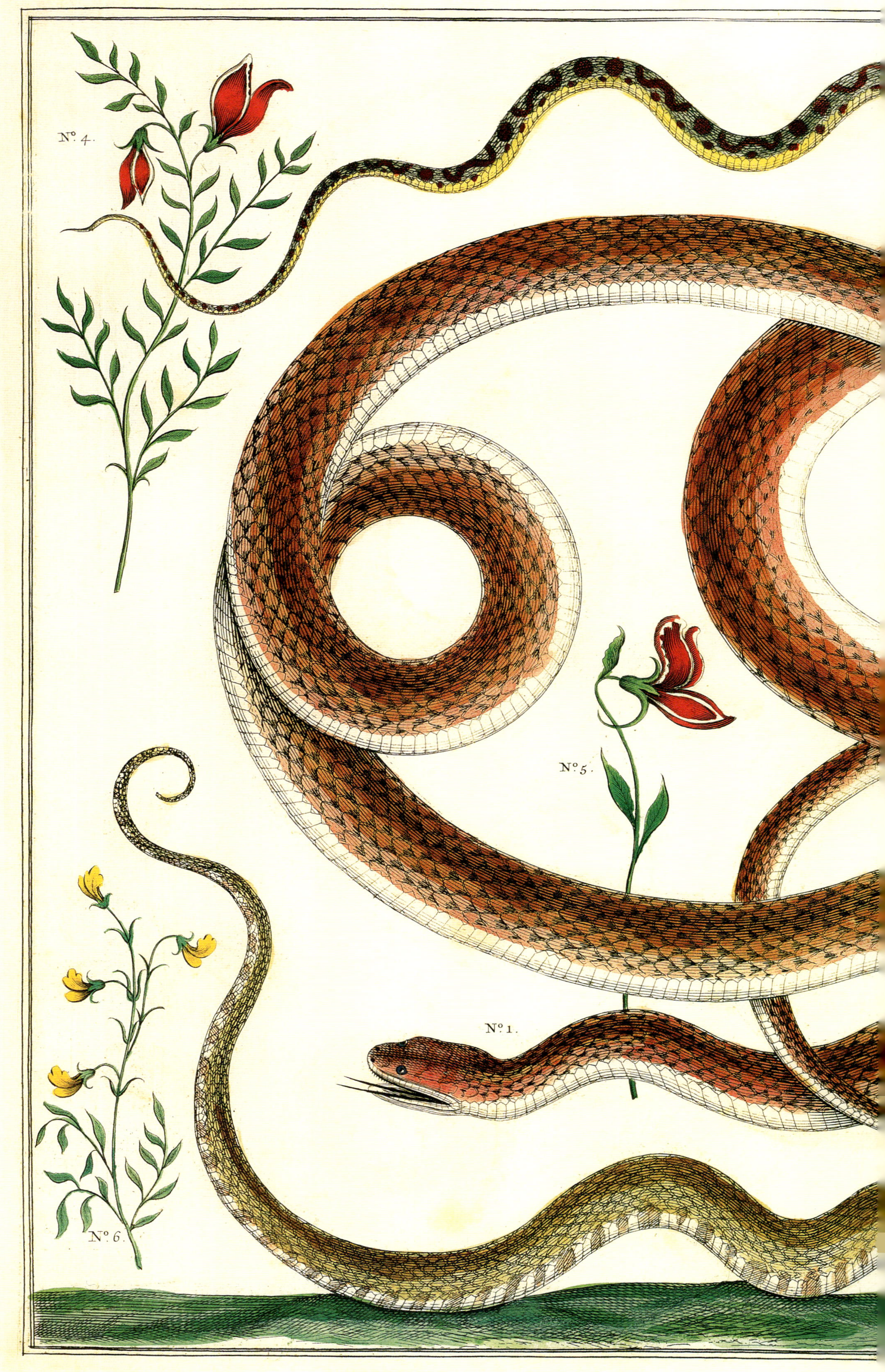

1-3 Serpentes 6-7 Leguminosae
1-3 Snakes, according to Seba from America · Schlangen, nach Seba aus Amerika · Serpents, d'Amérique selon Seba 6-7 Pea family · Hülsenfruchtgewächse · Légumineuses

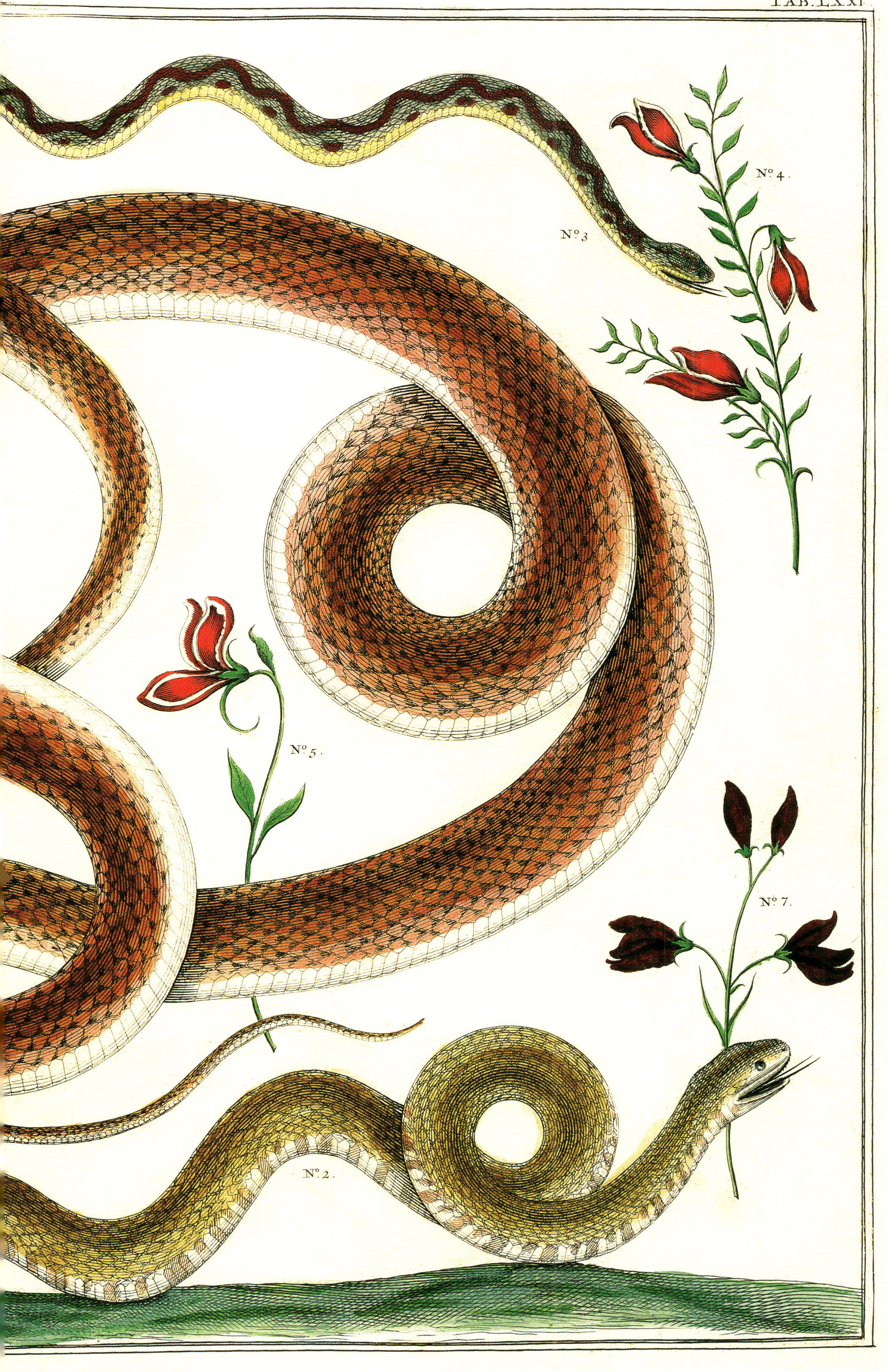
TAB. LXXI.
N.° 4.
N.° 3
N.° 5.
N.° 7.
N.° 2.

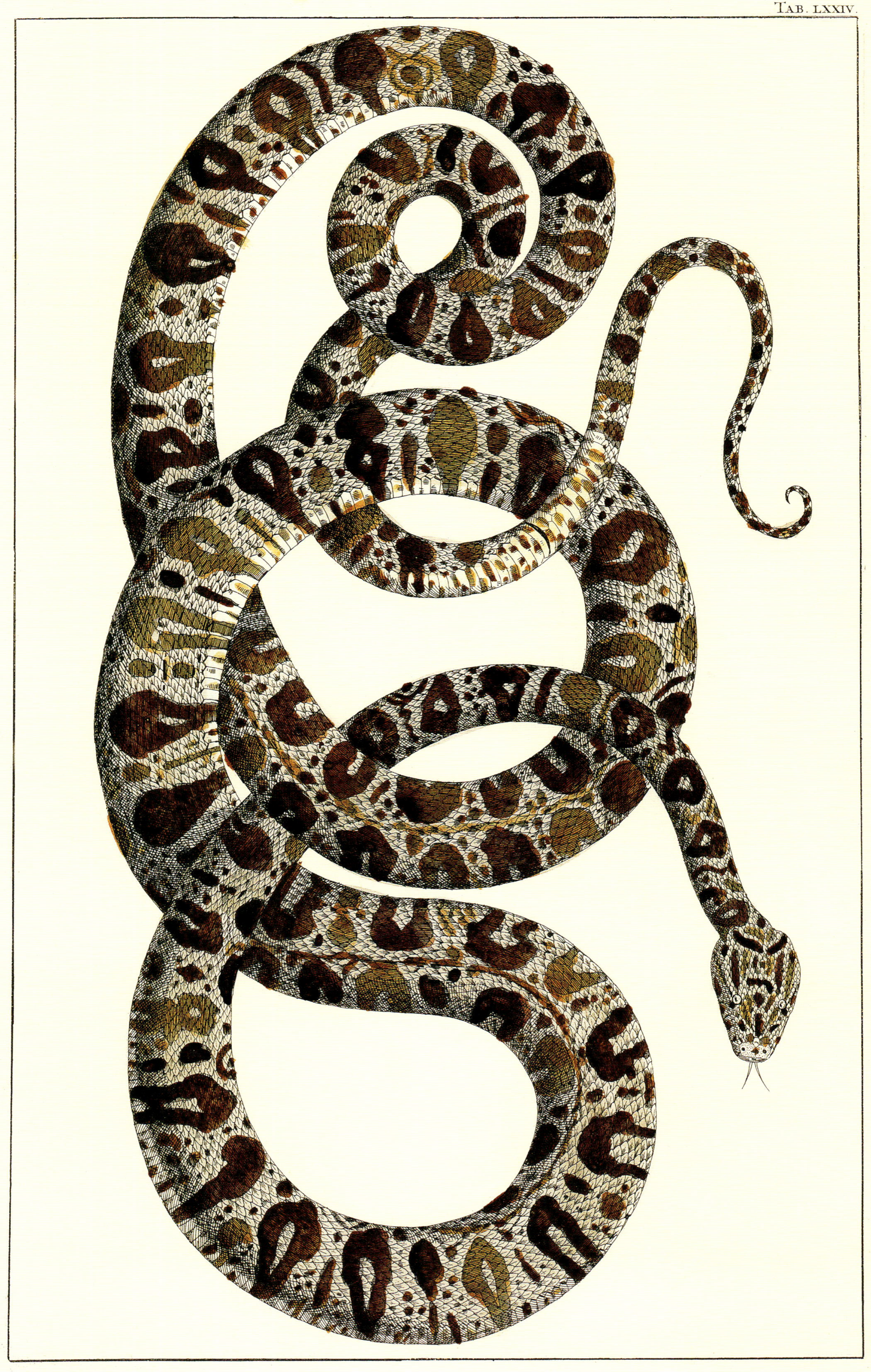

1 *Corallus enydris?*
1 Garden tree boa · Baumboa · Boa

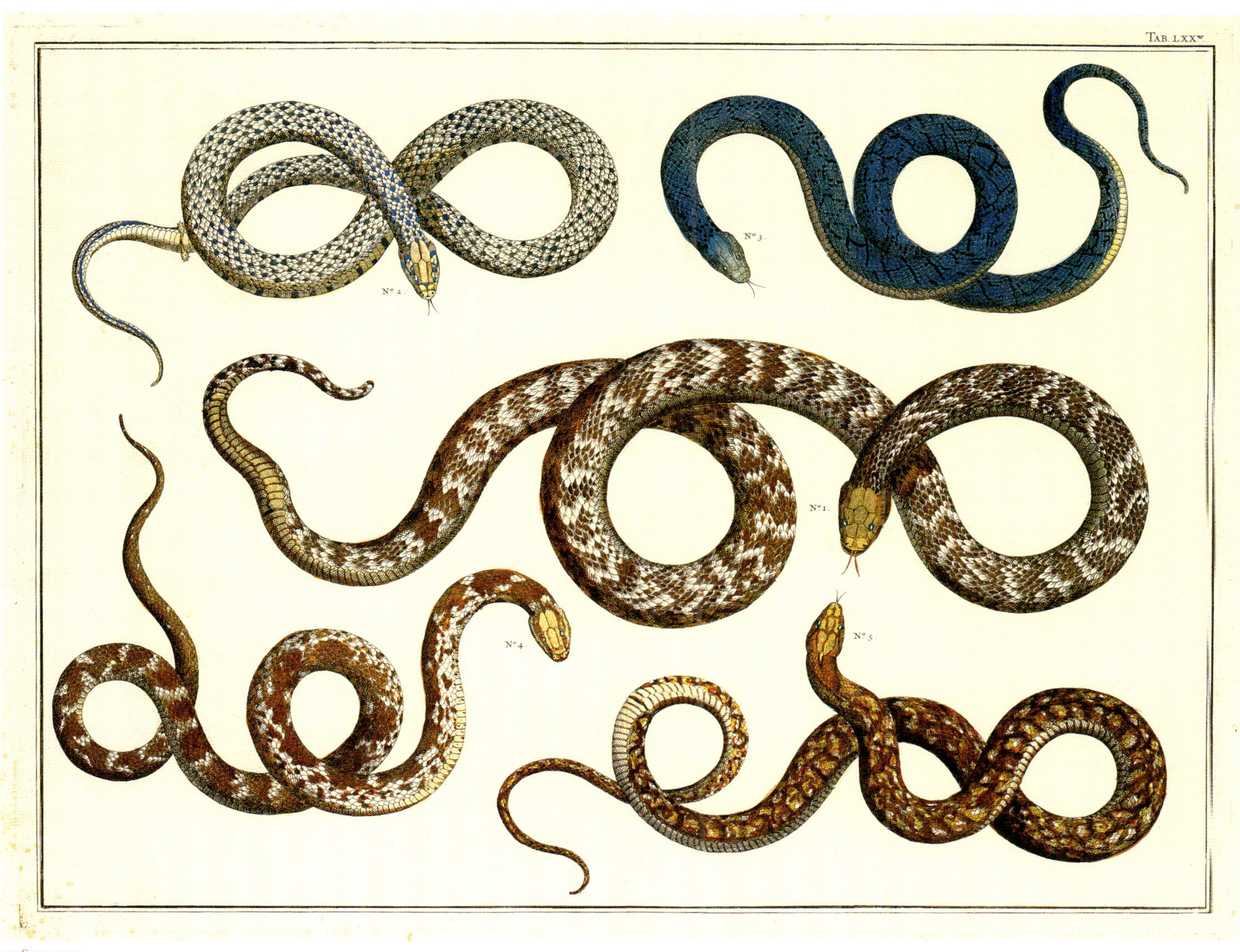

1-5 Serpentes
1-5 Snakes, according to Seba from America · Schlangen, nach Seba aus Amerika · Serpents, d'Amérique selon Seba

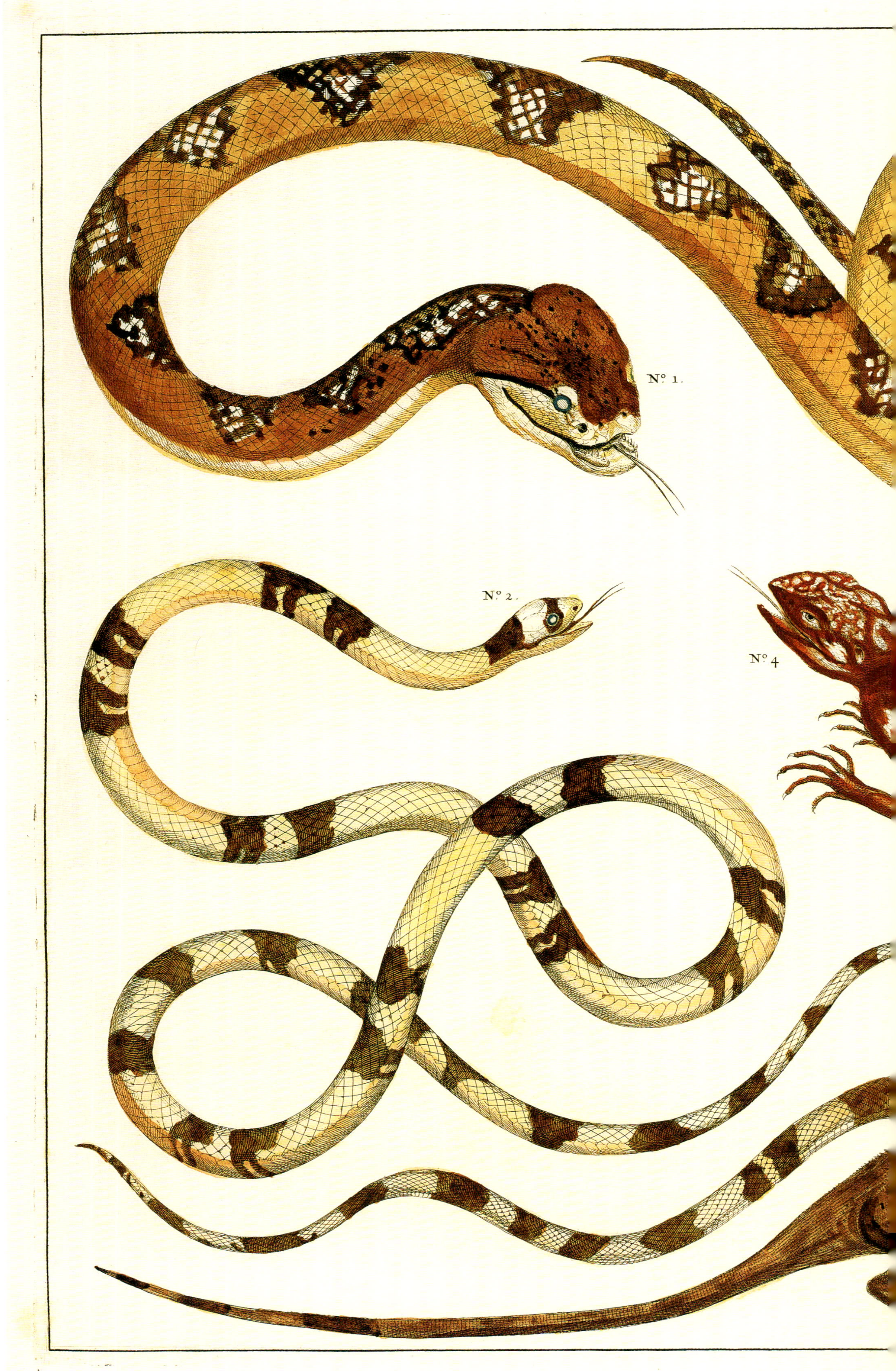

1 *Lachesis muta?* 2-3 Serpentes 4-5 Squamata
1 Bushmaster · Buschmeister · Surucucu 2-3 Snakes, according to Seba from Ceylon · Schlangen, nach Seba aus Ceylon · Serpents, de Ceylan selon Seba 4-5 Lizards · Echsen · Sauriens

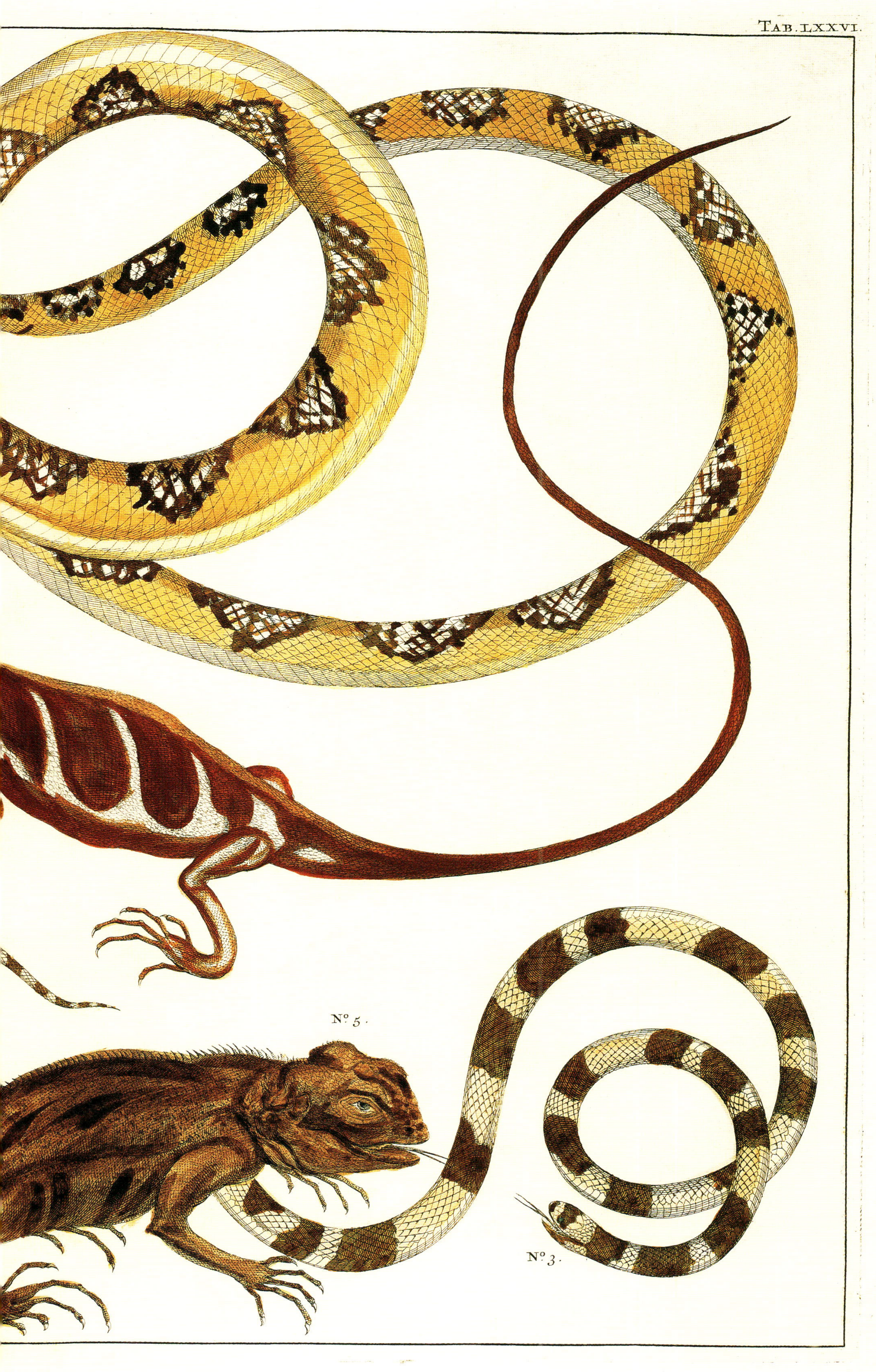
TAB. LXXVI.
N°. 5.
N°. 3.

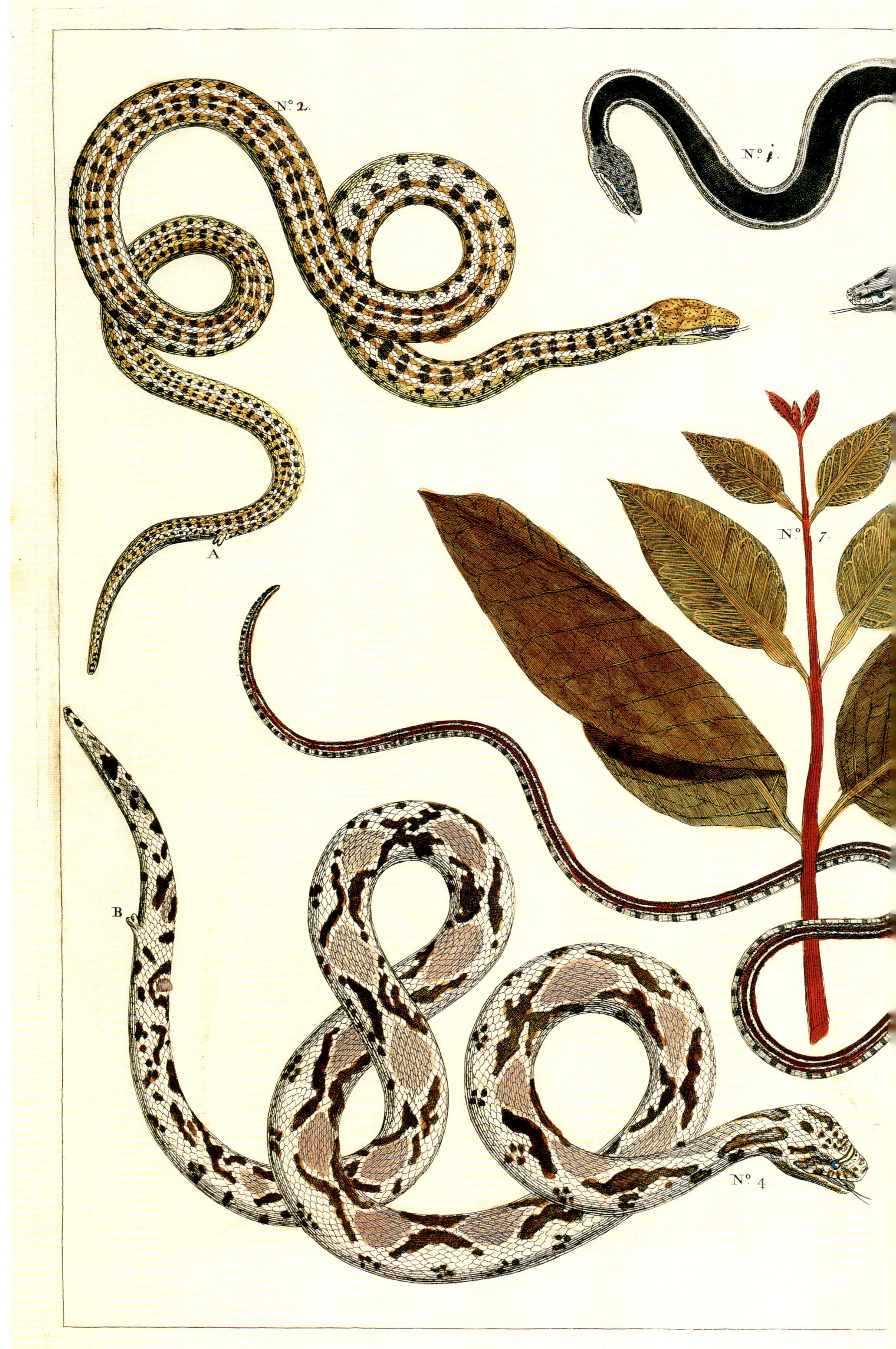

1-3, 6 Serpentes 4-5 *Epicrates?* 8 Melastomataceae
1-3, 6 Snakes, according to Seba from America · Schlangen, nach Seba aus Amerika · Serpents, d'Amérique selon Seba **4-5** Slender boa · Schlankboa · Boa
8 Melastoma family · Schwarzmundgewächse · Mélastomacées

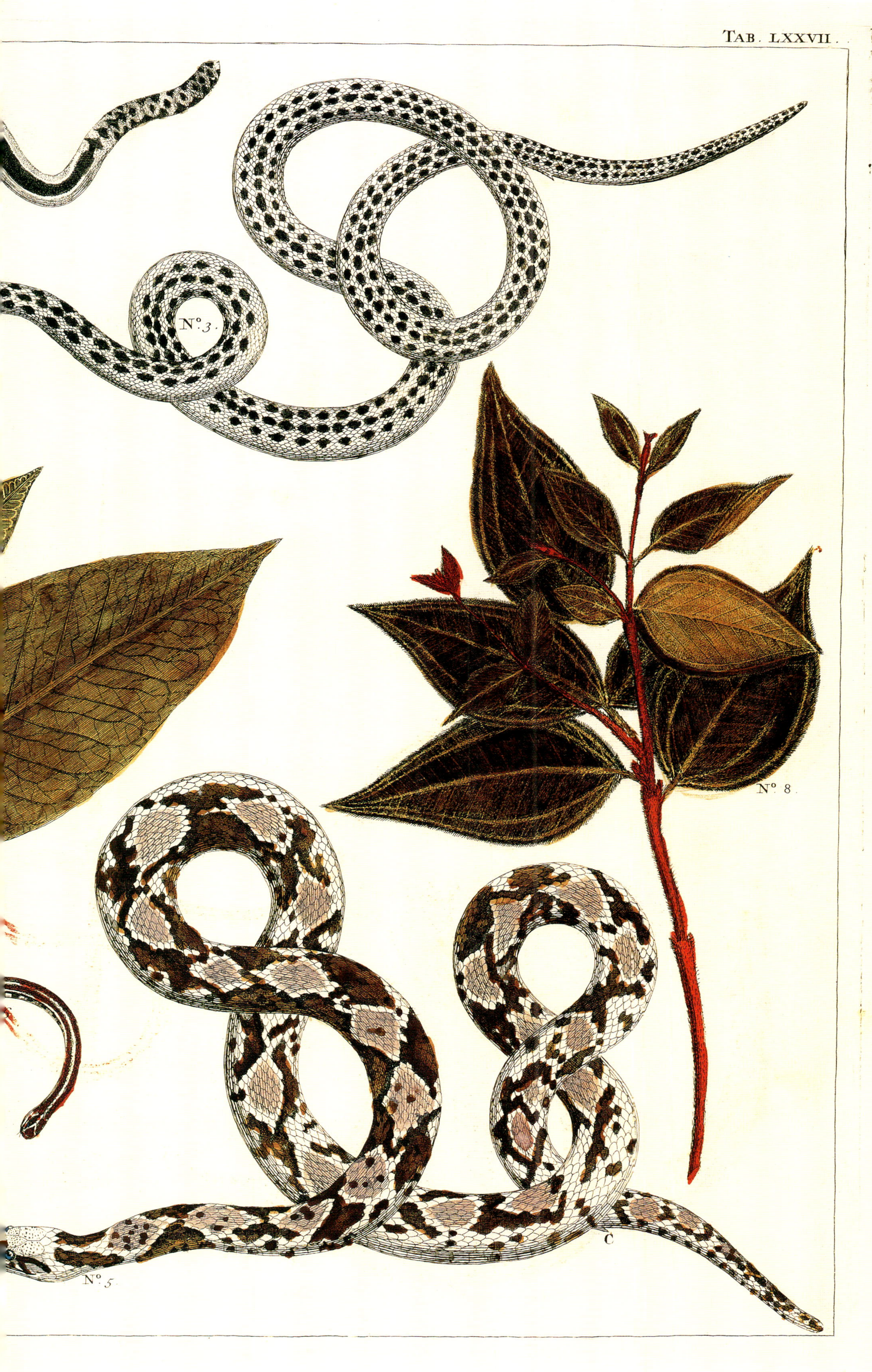
TAB. LXXVII.
N°. 3.
N°. 8.
N°. 5.
C

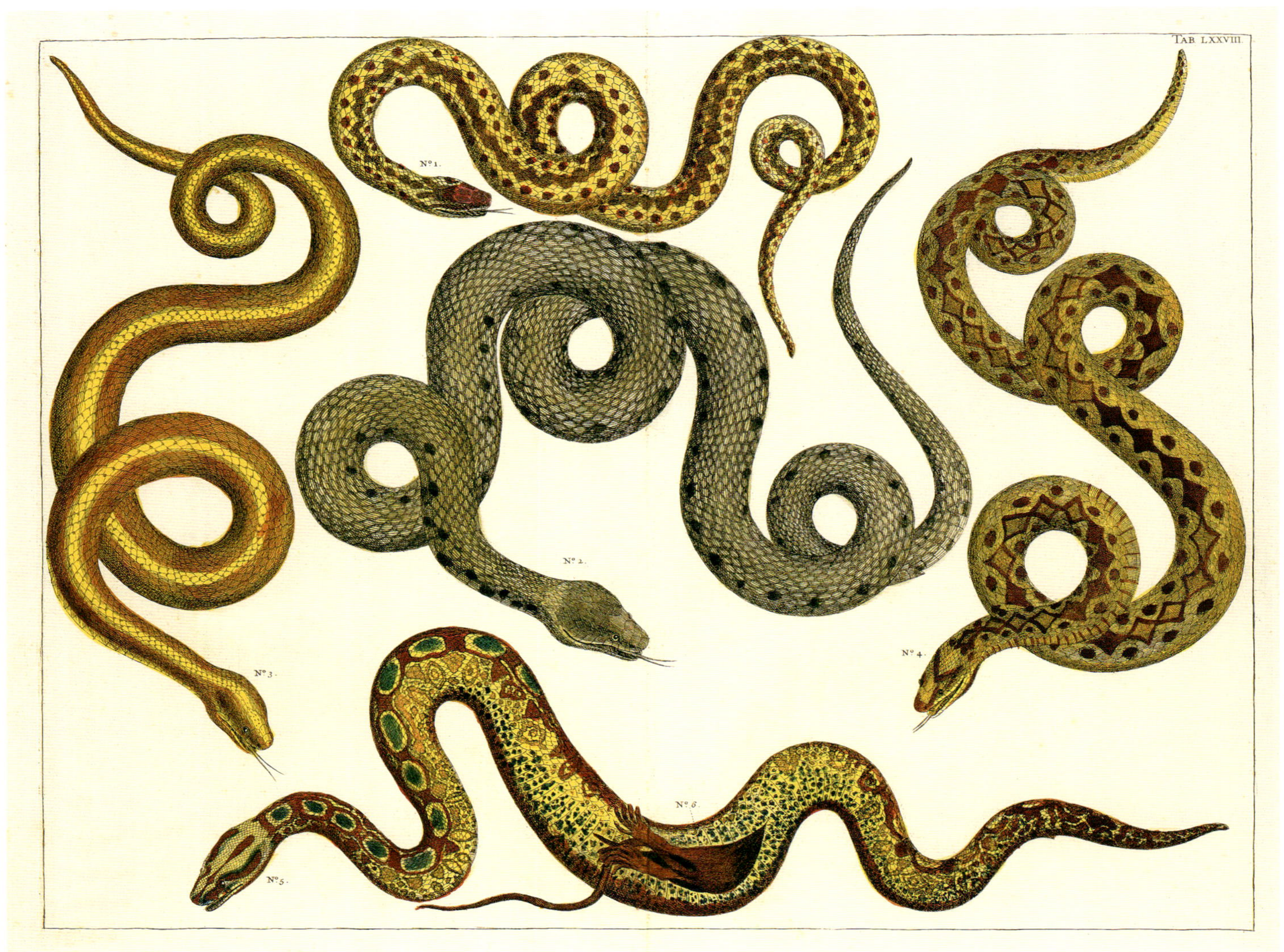

1 *Vipera berus?* 2, 4-5 Serpentes 3 *Lamprophis aurora* 6 Squamata
1 Adder/Common viper · Kreuzotter · Vipère péliade 2, 4-5 Snakes from different continents · Schlangen aus verschiedenen Kontinenten · Serpents de différents continents
3 Aurora house snake · Goldene Hausschlange · Serpent 6 Lizard · Echse · Saurien

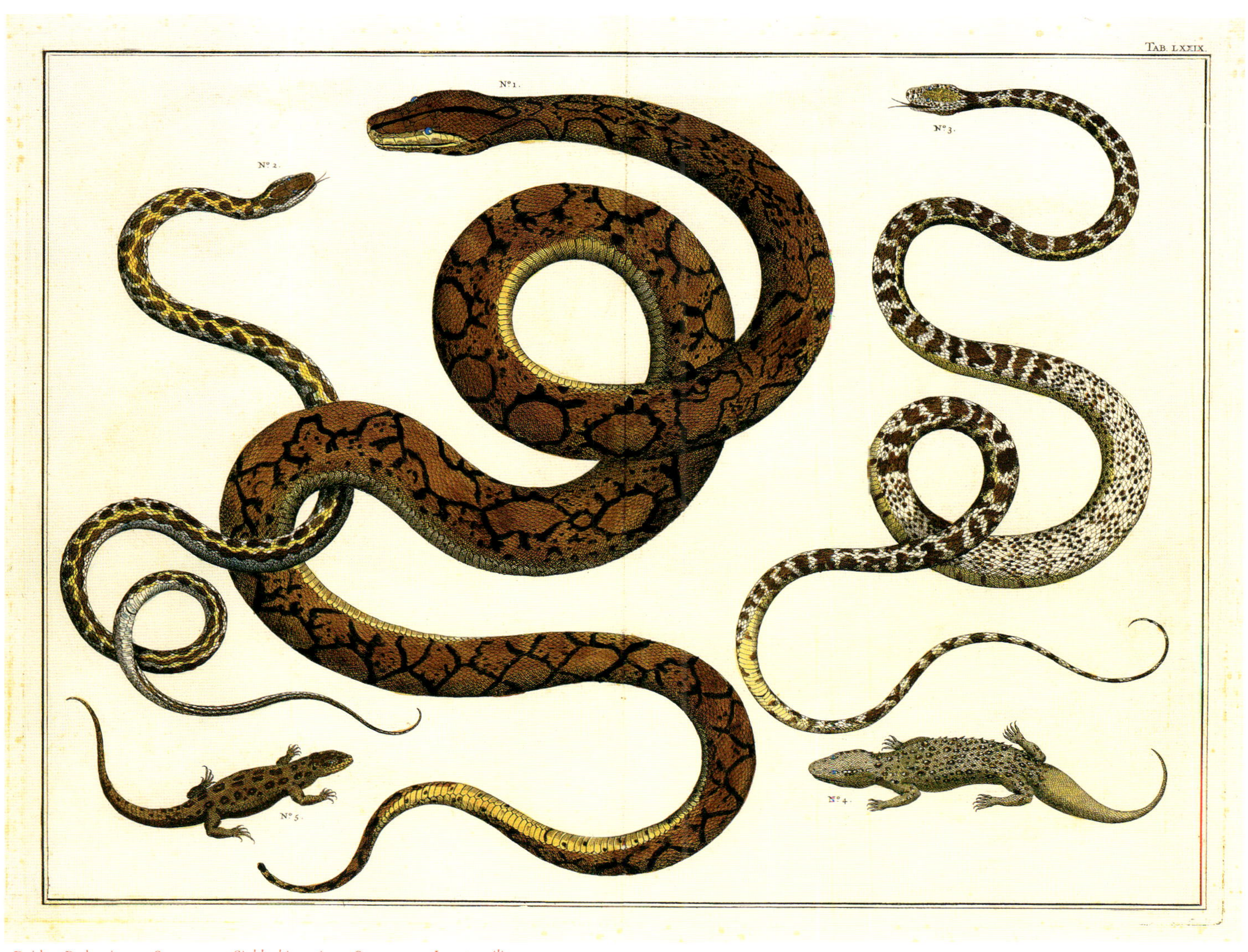

1 Boidae: Pythoninae 2 Serpentes 3 *Siphlophis cervina* 4 Squamata 5 *Lacerta agilis*
1 Python · Python · Python 2-3 Snakes, according to Seba from America · Schlangen, nach Seba aus Amerika · Serpents, d'Amérique selon Seba 4 Lizard · Echse · Saurien
5 Sand lizard · Zauneidechse · Lézard agile

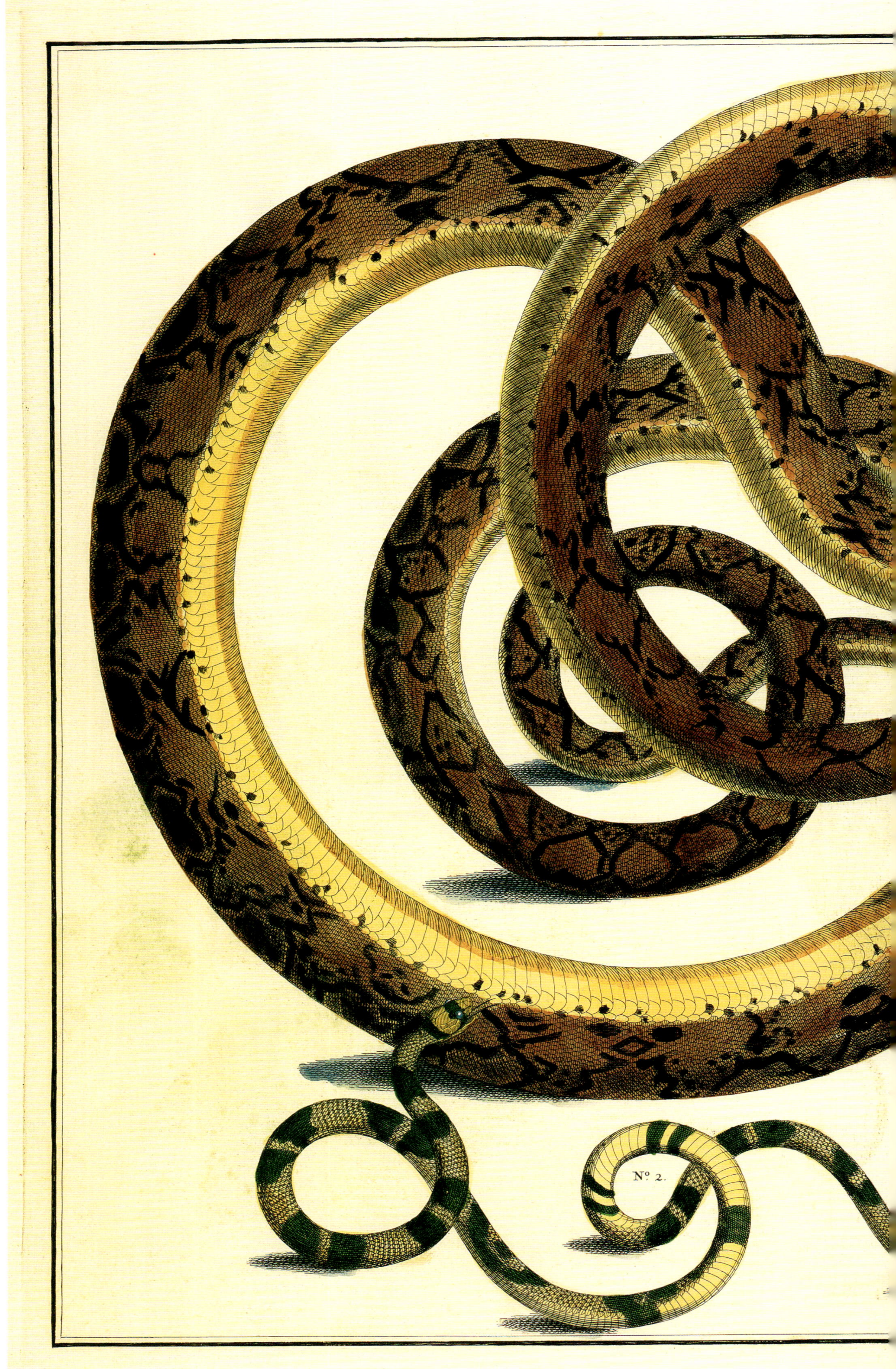

1 Boinae 2 Serpentes 3 *Ipomoea*
1 Boine snake · Riesenschlange · Boïné 2 Snake, according to Seba from Mexico · Schlange, nach Seba aus Mexiko · Serpent, du Mexique selon Seba
3 Morning-glory · Prunkwinde · Ipomée

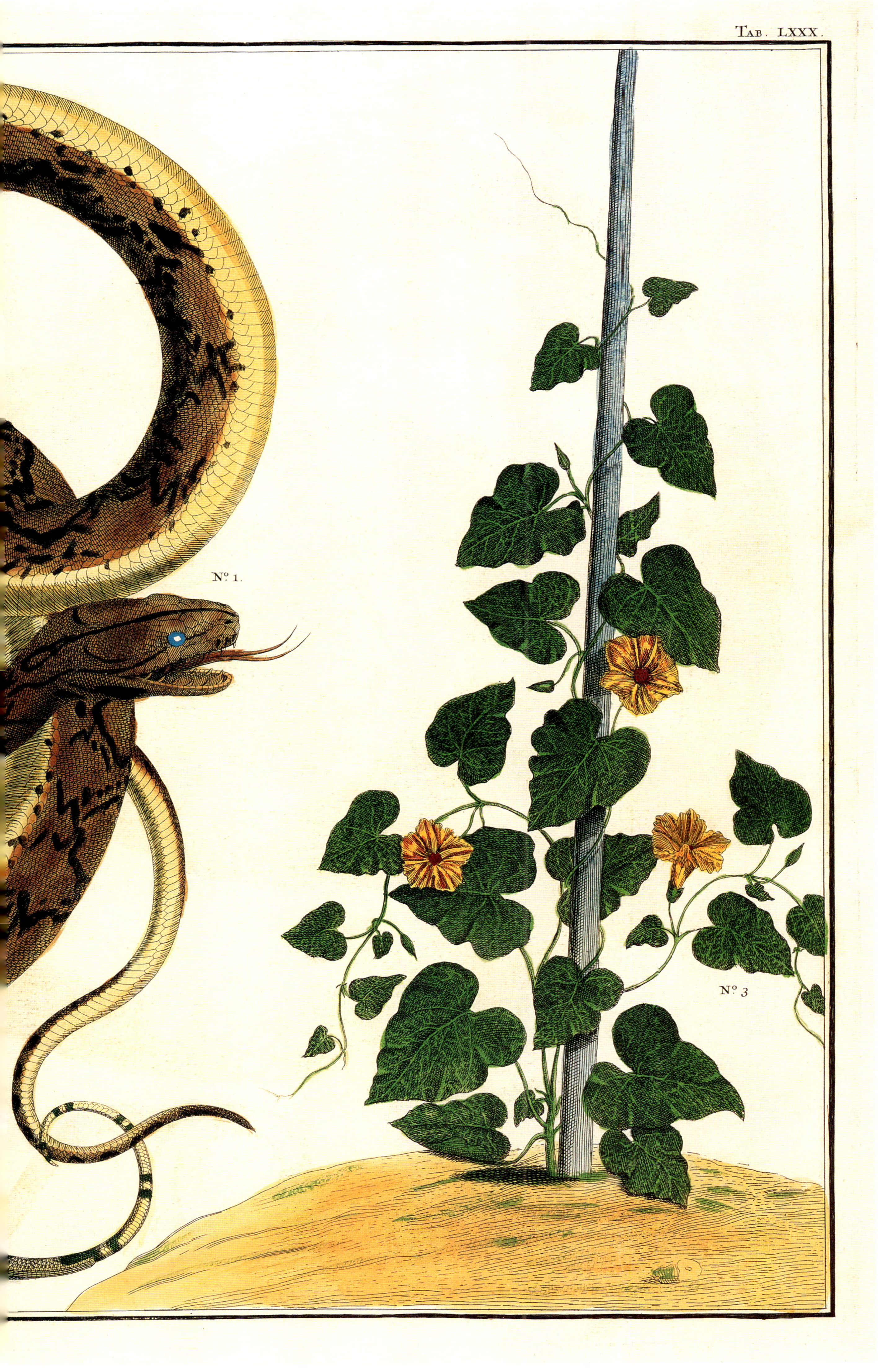
Tab. LXXX.
Nº 1.
Nº 3

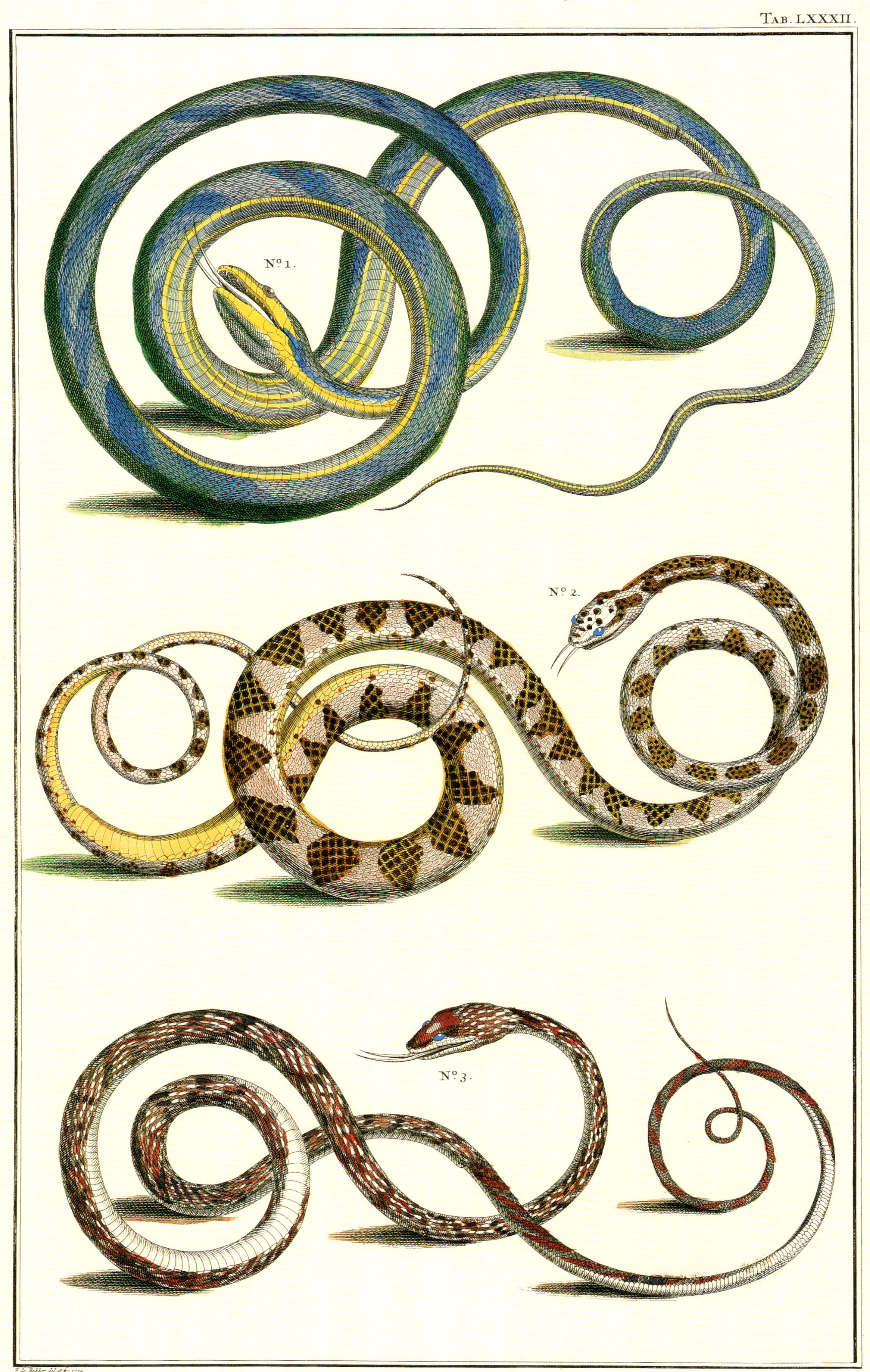

1 *Ahaetulla sp.* 2–3 Serpentes
1–3 Various snakes · Verschiedene Schlangen · Serpents divers

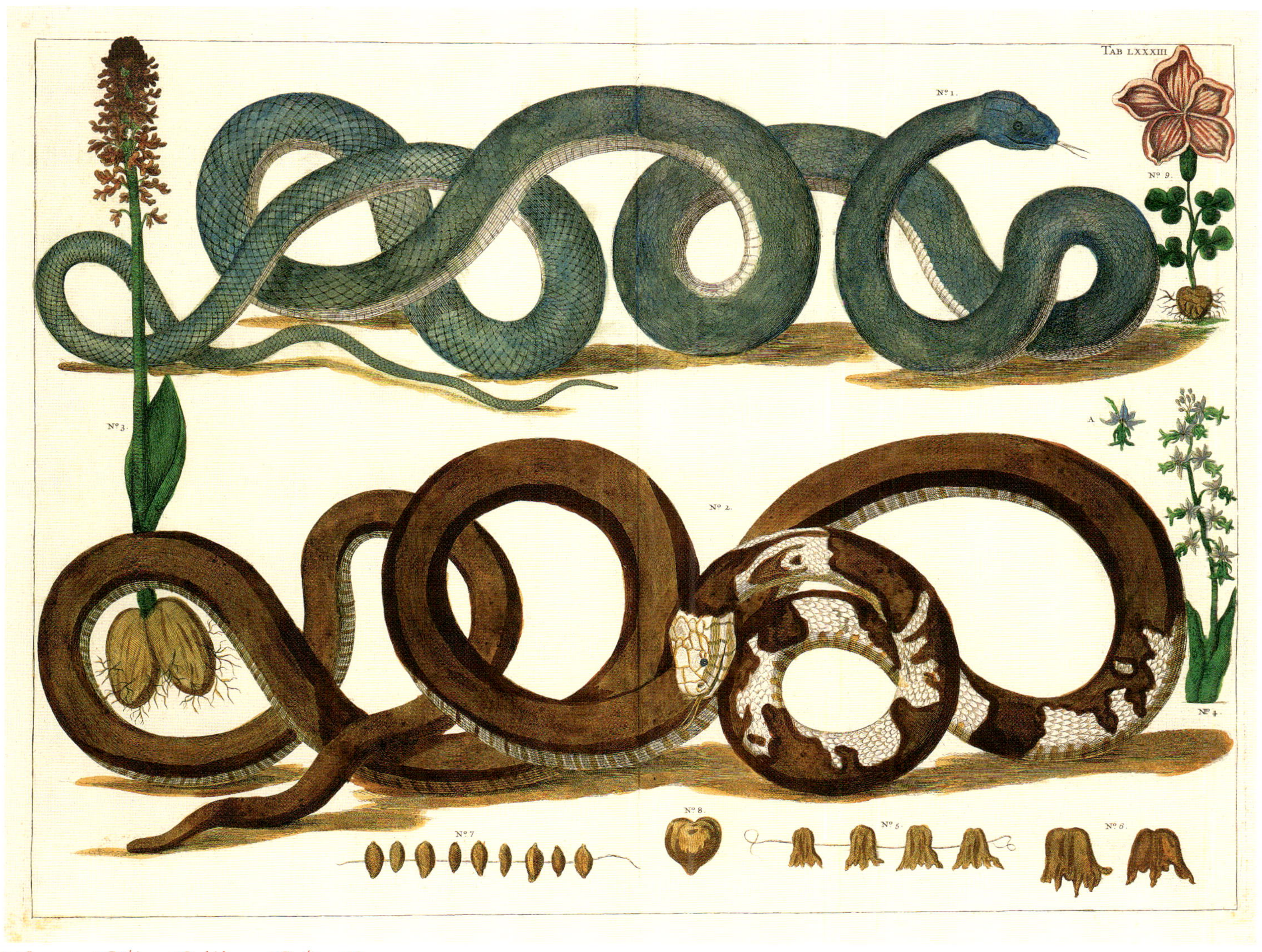

1-2 Serpentes 3 *Orchis sp.* 4 Orchidaceae 5 *Oxalis sp.* 6 Lauraceae

1 Snake, according to Seba from India · Schlange, nach Seba aus Indien · Serpent, de l'Inde selon Seba **2** Snake, according to Seba from Ceylon · Schlange, nach Seba aus Ceylon · Serpent, de Ceylan selon Seba **3** Orchis · Knabenkraut · Orchis **4** Orchid family · Orchideengewächse · Orchidacées **5** Wood sorrel · Sauerklee · Surelle **6** Laurel family · Lorbeergewächse · Lauracées

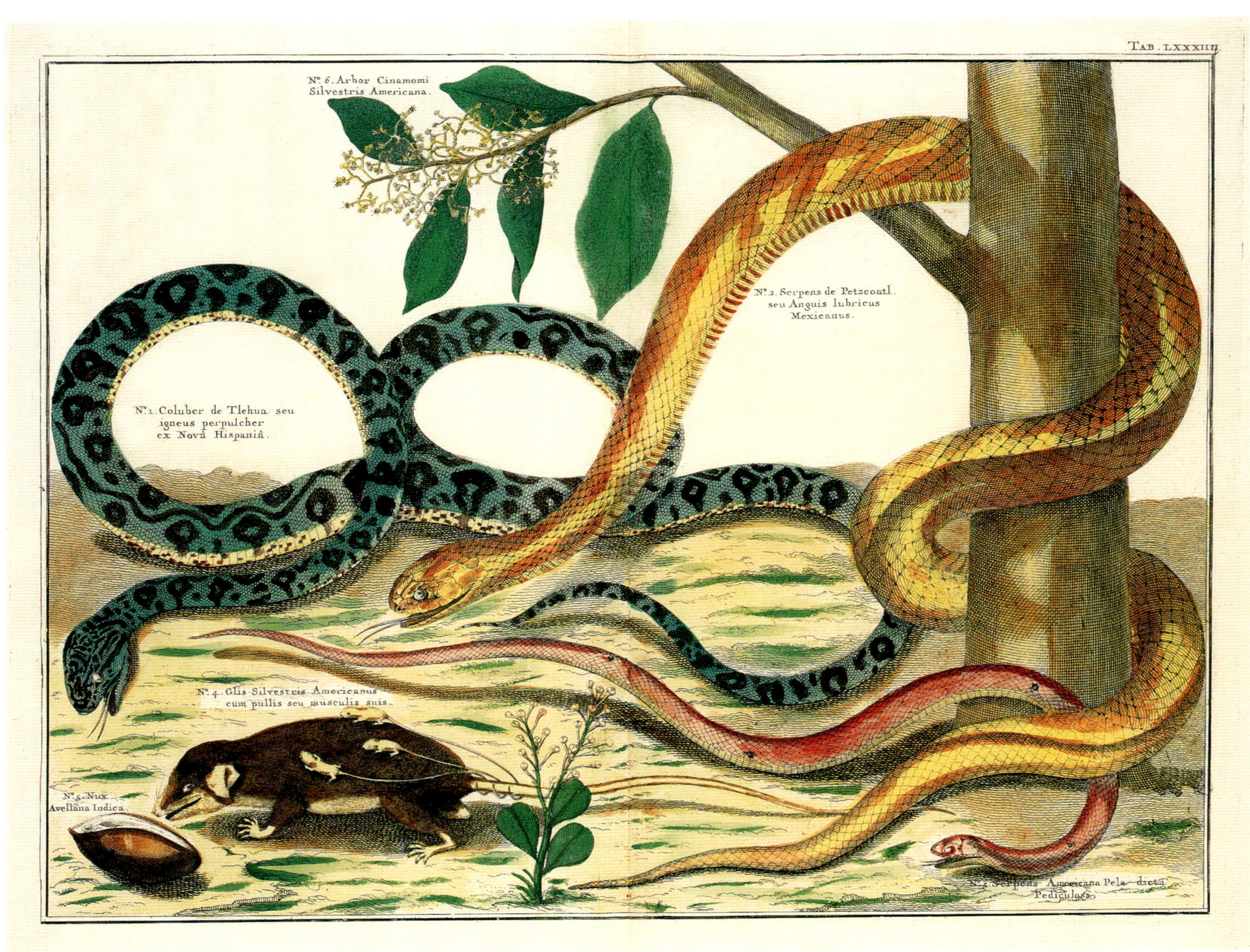

1 Boinae **2-3** Serpentes **4** *Myoxis glis* **5** »Nux Avelana, Indica« (Seba) **6** Lauraceae

1 Boine snake · Riesenschlange · Boïné **2-3** Snakes, according to Seba from America · Schlangen, nach Seba aus Amerika · Serpents, d'Amérique selon Seba **4** Fat dormouse · Siebenschläfer · Loir gris **5** "Nut from India" (Seba) · „Nuß aus Indien" (Seba) · « Noix d'Inde » (Seba) **6** Laurel family · Lorbeergewächse · Lauracées

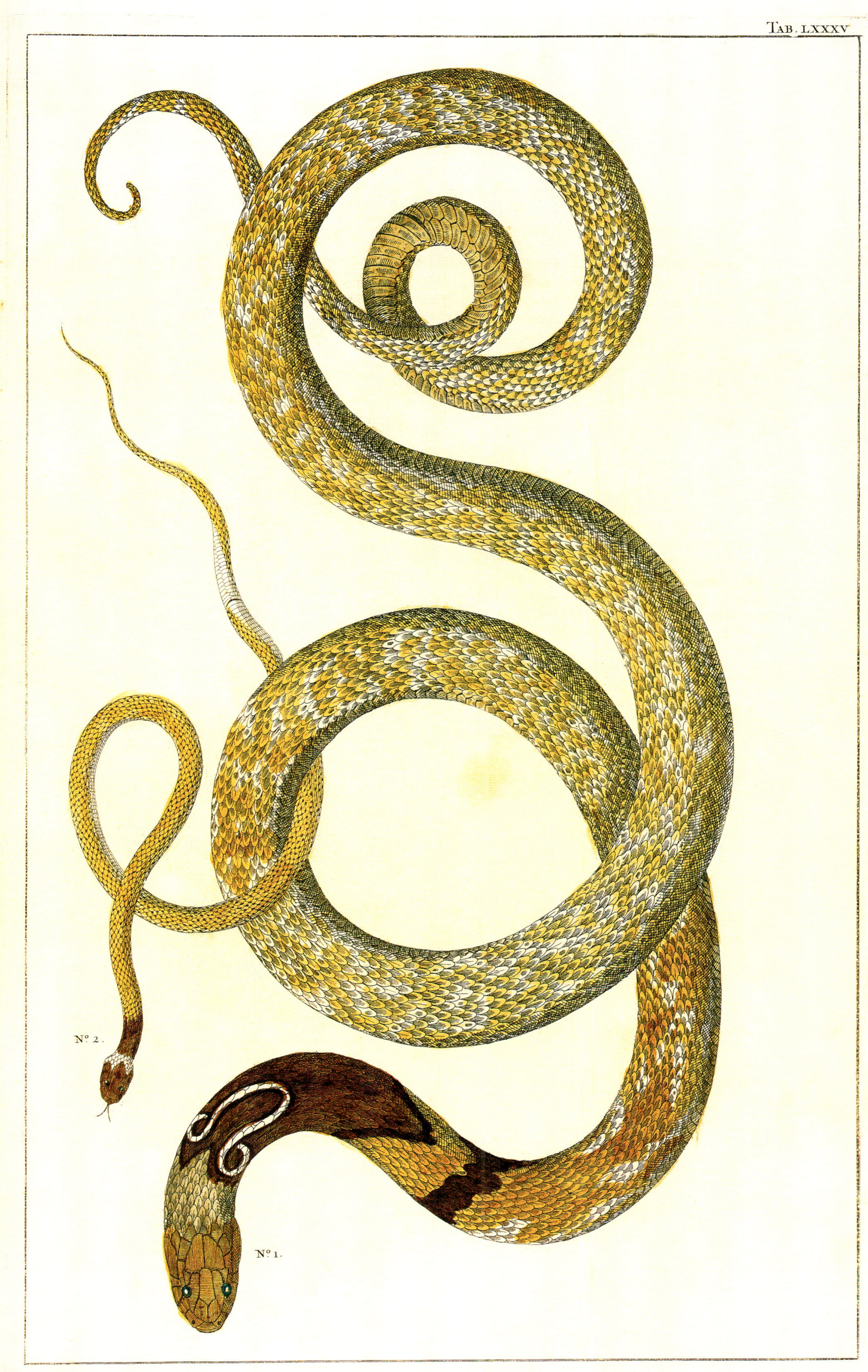

1 *Naja naja* 2 Serpentes
1 Common cobra · Brillenschlange/Kobra · Cobra indien 2 Snake, according to Seba from Peru · Schlange, nach Seba aus Peru · Serpent, du Pérou selon Seba

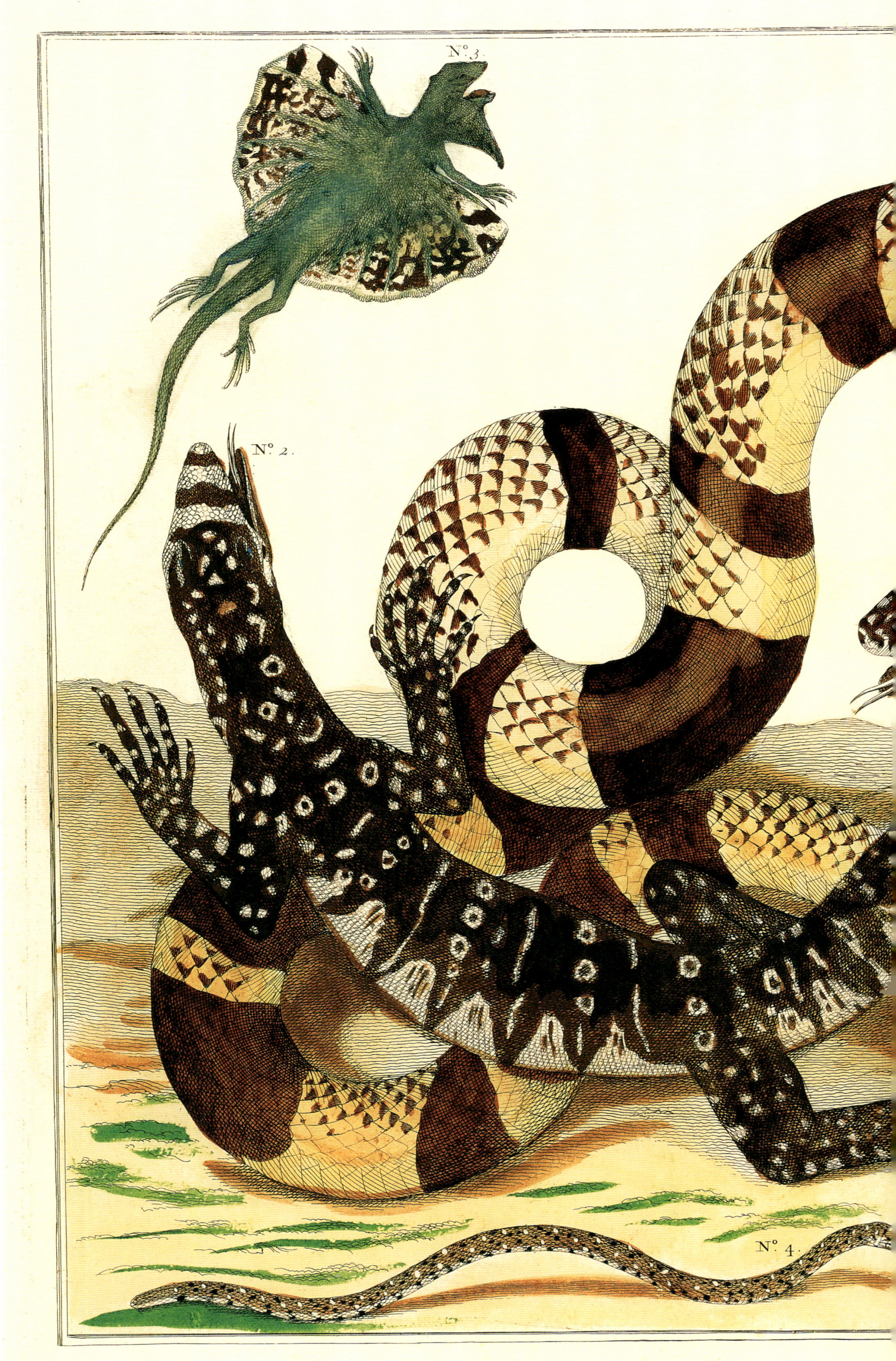

1 Serpentes 2 *Varanus sp.* 3 *Draco sp.* 4-5 Serpentes 6 Ericaceae
1 Snake, according to Seba from Asia · Schlange, nach Seba aus Asien · Serpent, d'Asie selon Seba 2 Monitor · Waran · Varanidé 3 Flying dragon · Flugdrache · Dragon volant
4-5 Snakes, according to Seba from Peru · Schlangen, nach Seba aus Peru · Serpents, du Pérou selon Seba 6 Heath family · Heidekrautgewächse · Ericacées

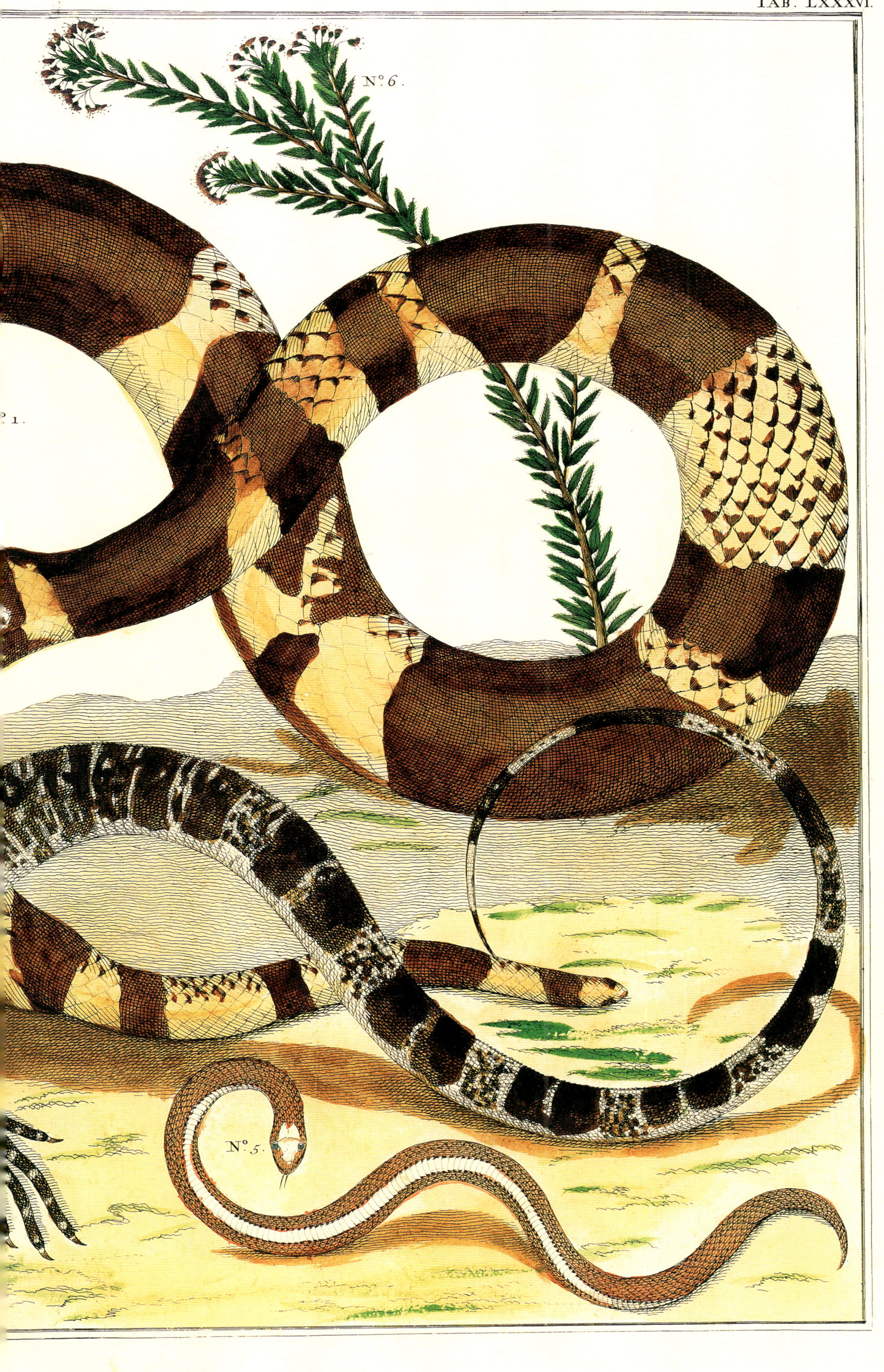
TAB. LXXXVI.
N°. 6.
° 1.
N°. 5.

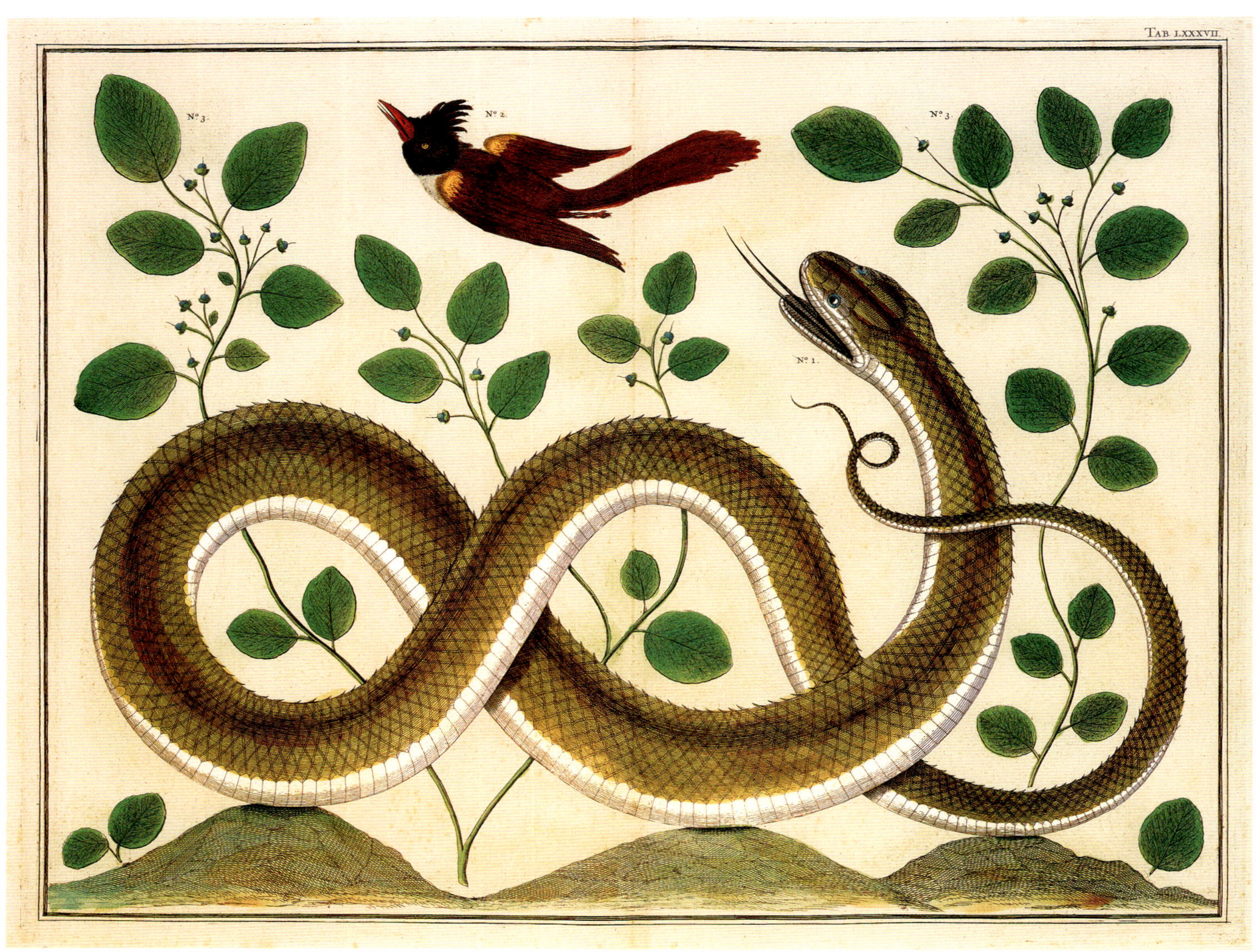

1 Serpentes 2 *Taeniotricus andrei*
1 Snake, according to Seba from Brazil · Schlange, nach Seba aus Brasilien · Serpent, du Brésil selon Seba 2 Black-crested tyrant · Schwarzkopftyrann · Tyranneau d'André

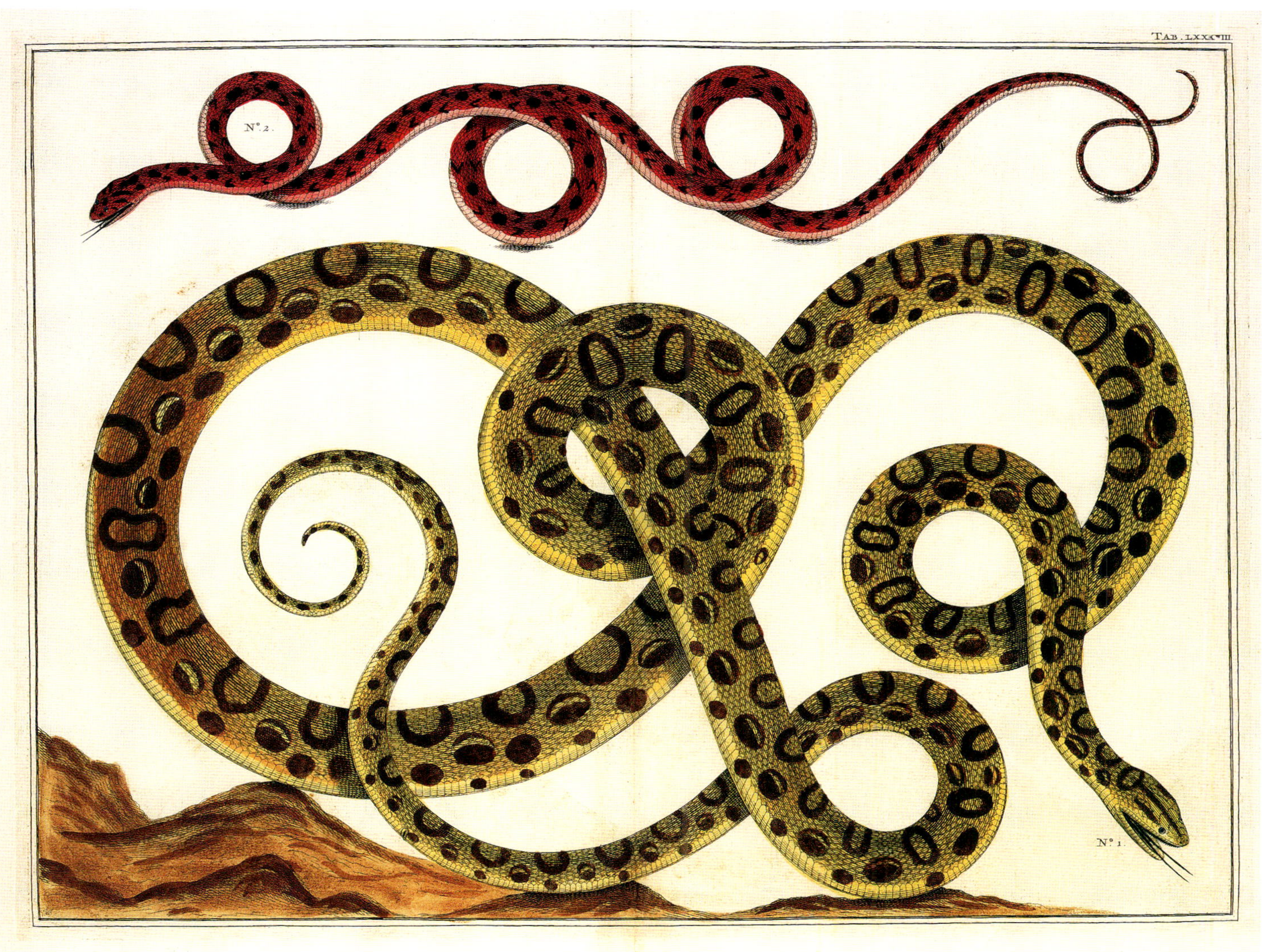

1 *Epicrates cenchria* 2 Serpentes
1 Rainbow boa · Regenbogenboa · Boa arc-en-ciel 2 Snake, according to Seba from Ceylon · Schlange, nach Seba aus Ceylon · Serpent, de Ceylan selon Seba

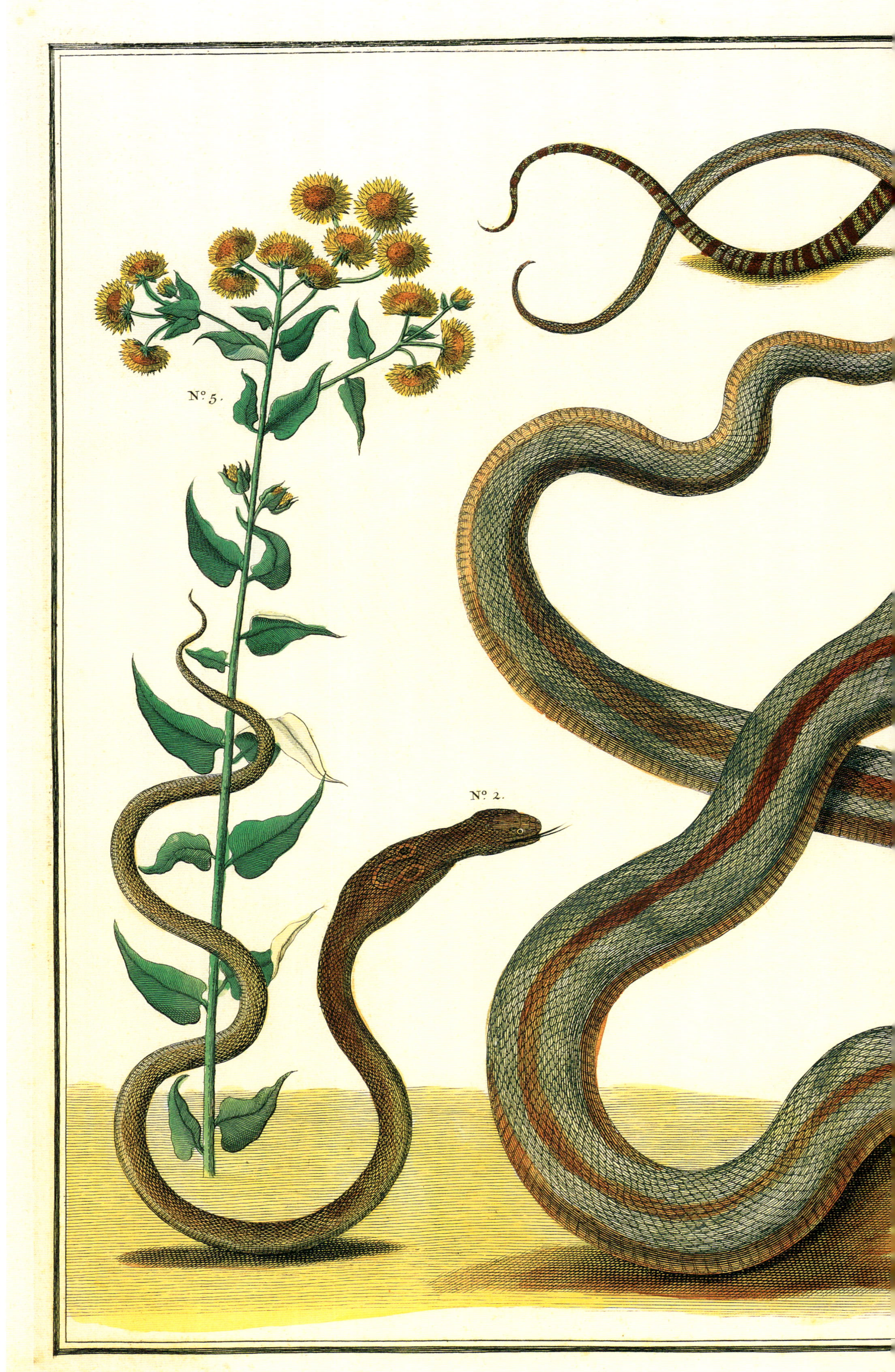

1-4 *Naja naja* **5** Compositae
1-4 Common cobra · Brillenschlange/Kobra · Cobra indien **5** Sunflower family · Korbblütler · Composées

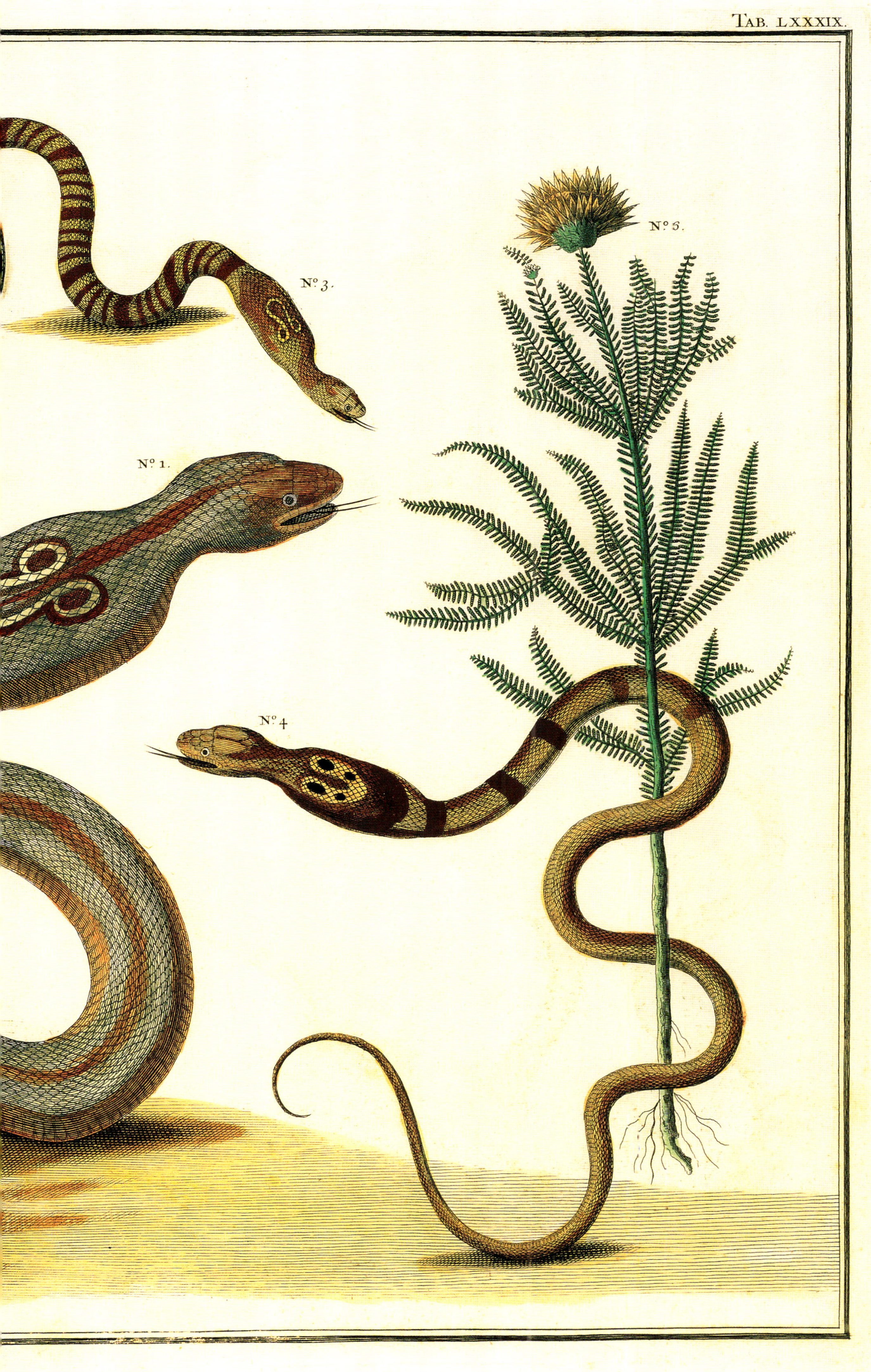
TAB. LXXXIX.
N° 5.
N° 3.
N° 1.
N° 4

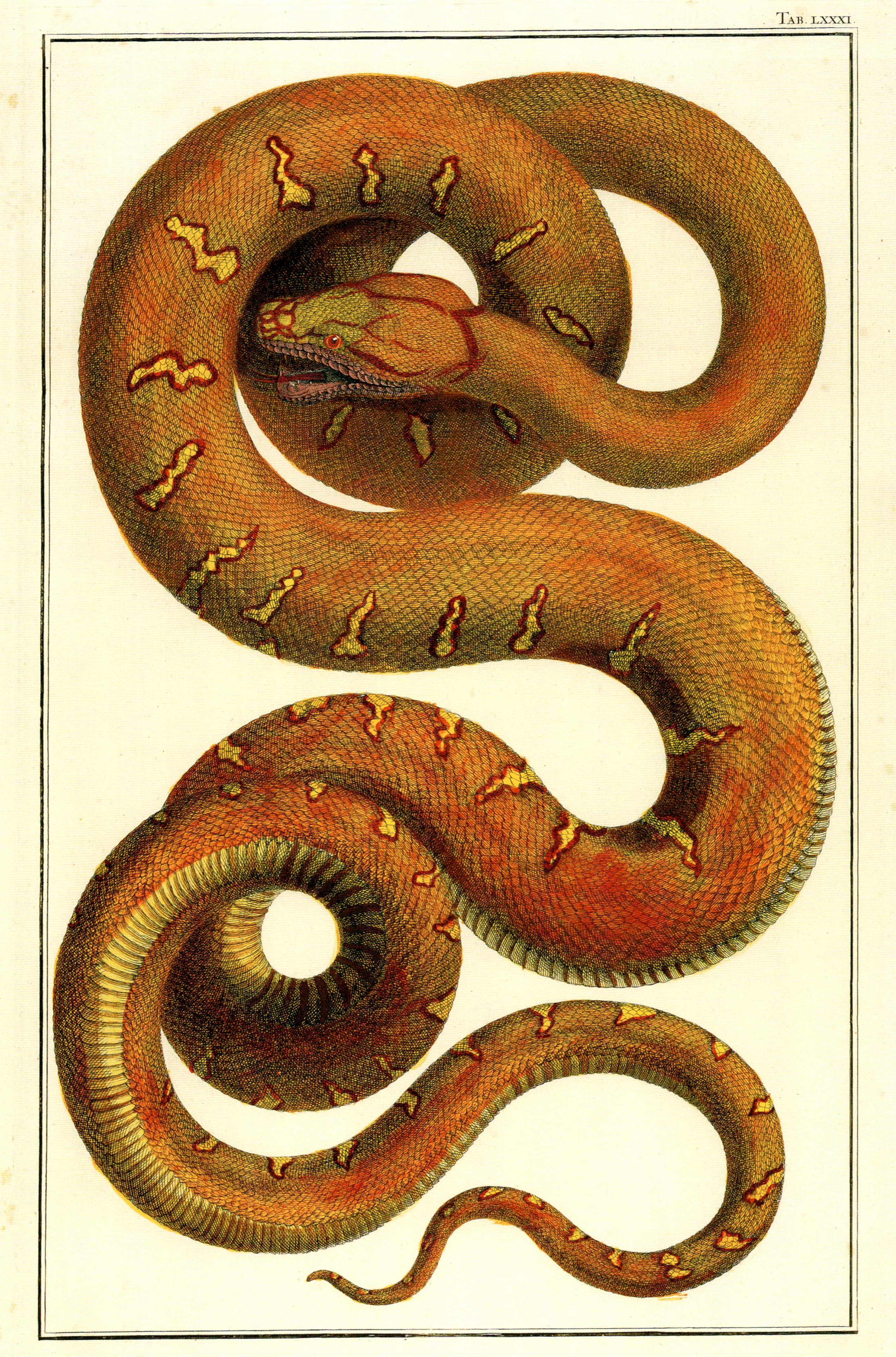

1 *Corallus caninus*
1 Emerald Tree Boa · Hundskopfboa · Boa canin

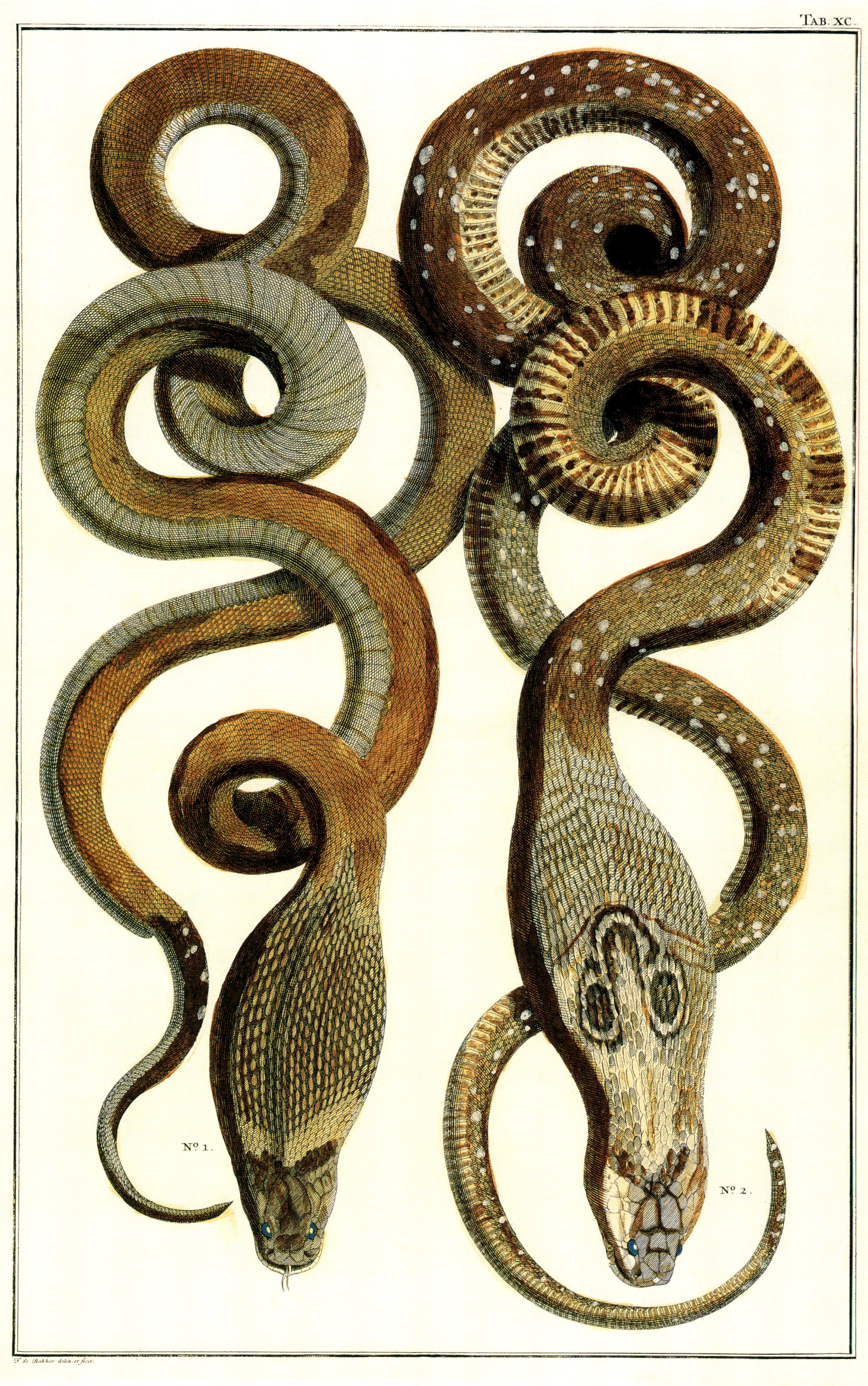

1-2 *Naja naja*

1-2 Common cobra · Brillenschlange/Indische Kobra · Cobra indien

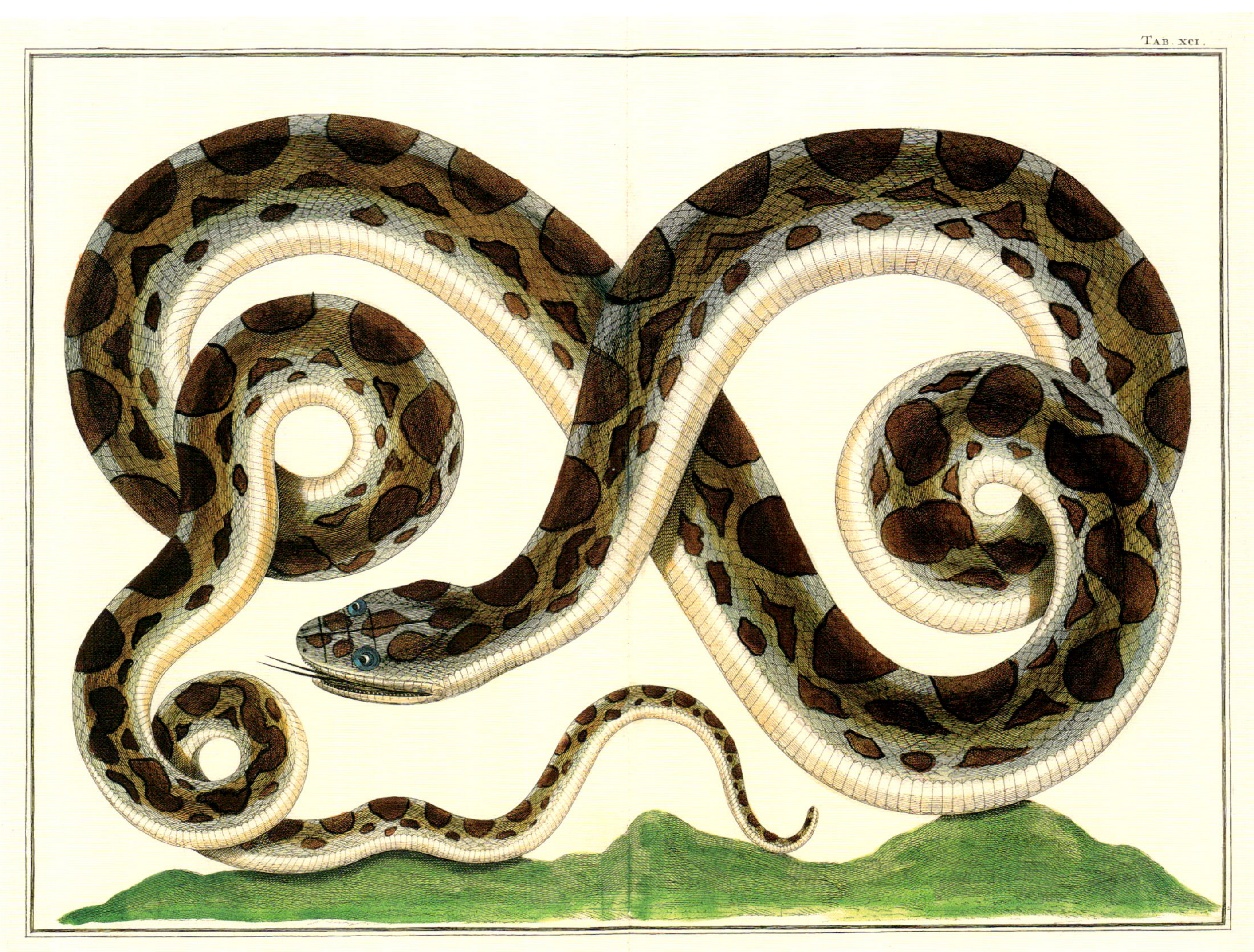

1 Boidae
1 Boid snake · Riesenschlange · Boïdé

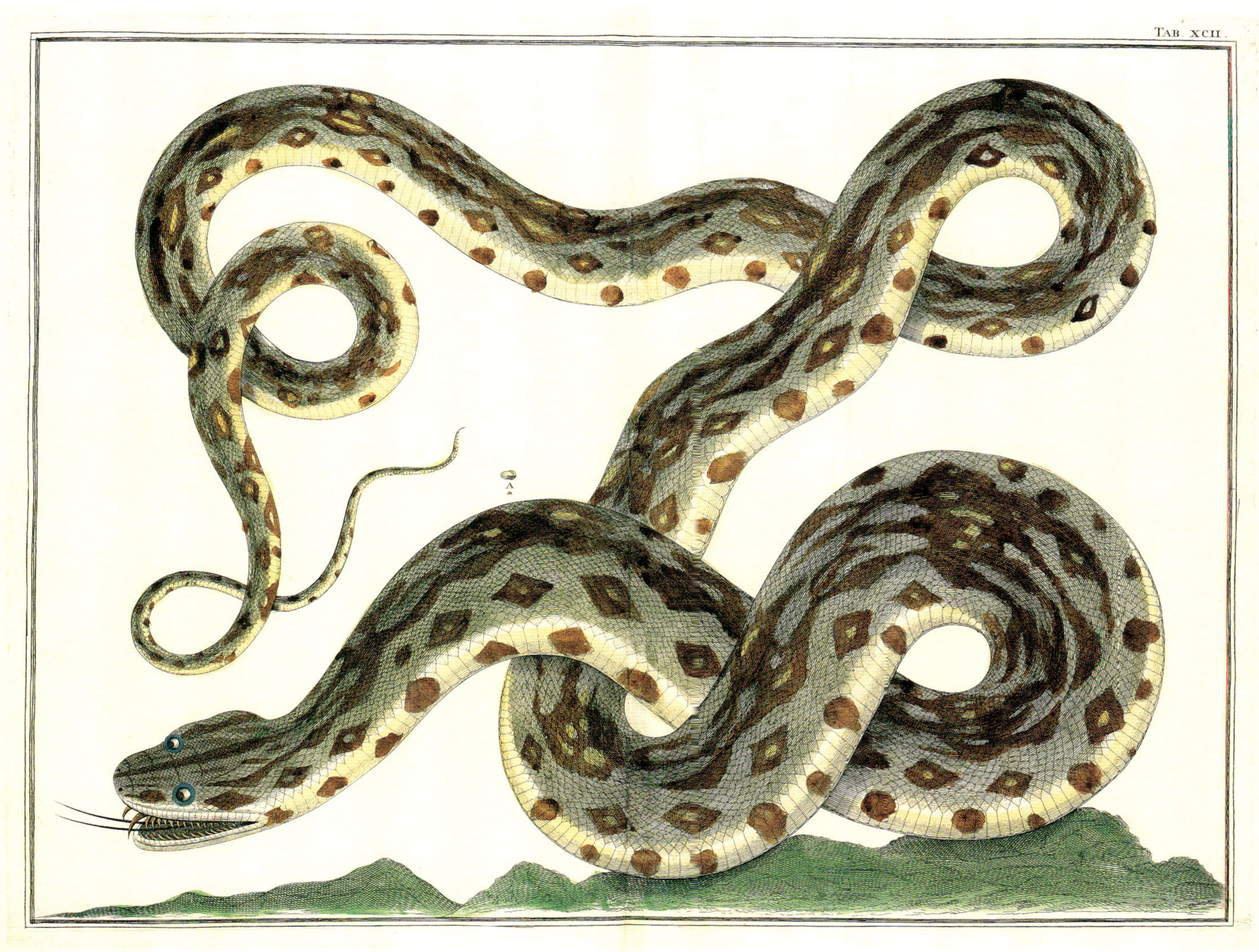

1 *Boa constrictor?*
1 Common boa · Abgottschlange · Boa constricteur

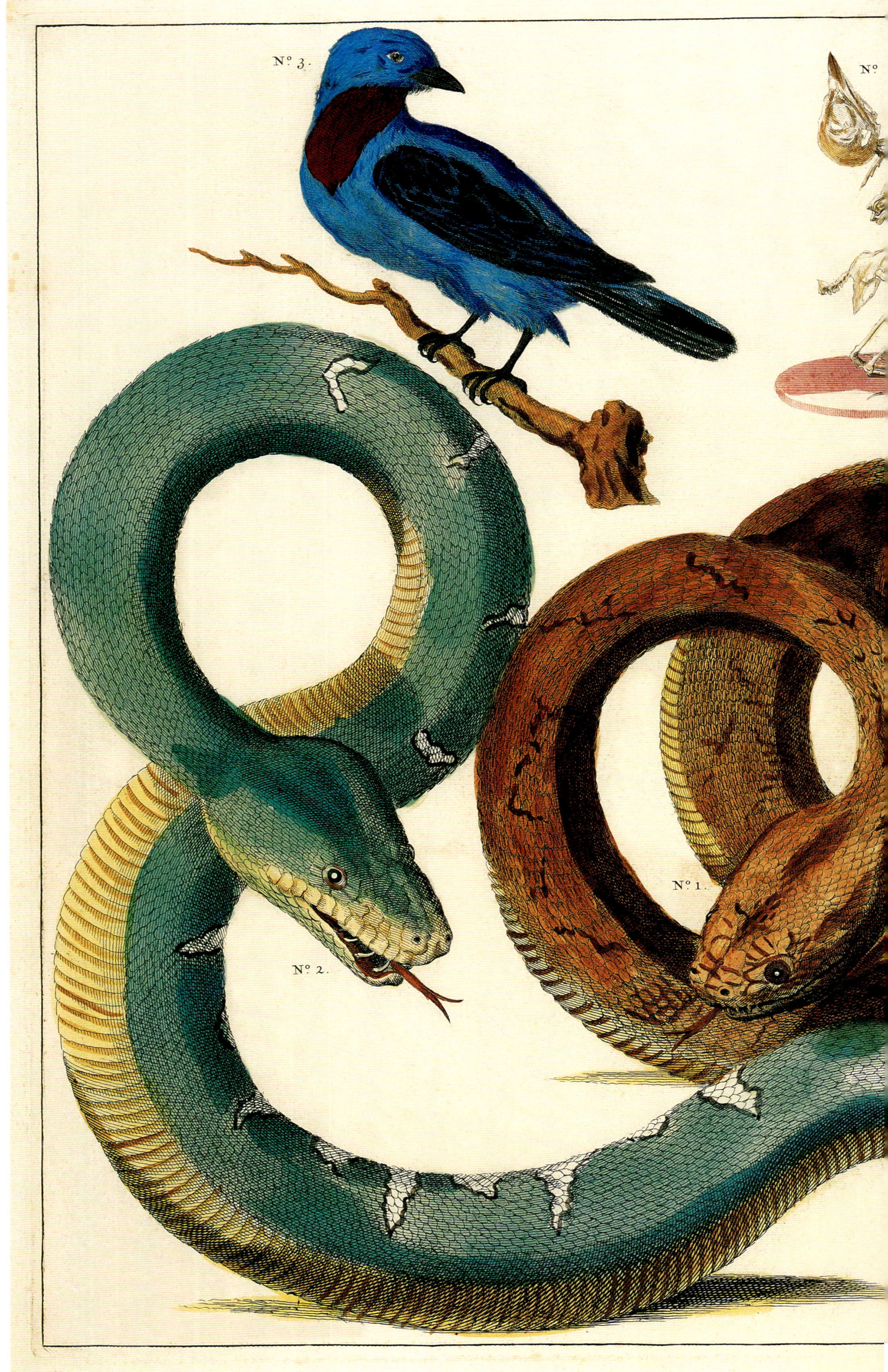

1 Serpentes 2 *Corallus caninus* 3 *Cotinga cayana* 4 *Icterus chrysater* 5 *Pipra pipra* 6 Aves
1 Snake, according to Seba from Asia · Schlange, nach Seba aus Asien · Serpent, d'Asie selon Seba 2 Emerald tree boa · Hundskopfboa · Boa canin 3 Spangled cotinga · Halsbandkotinga · Cotinga de Cayenne 4 Yellow-backed oriole · Schwarzflügeltrupial · Oriole noir et or 5 White-crowned manakin · Weißscheitelpipra · Manakin à tête blanche 6 Skeleton of a bird · Vogelskelett · Squelette d'oiseau

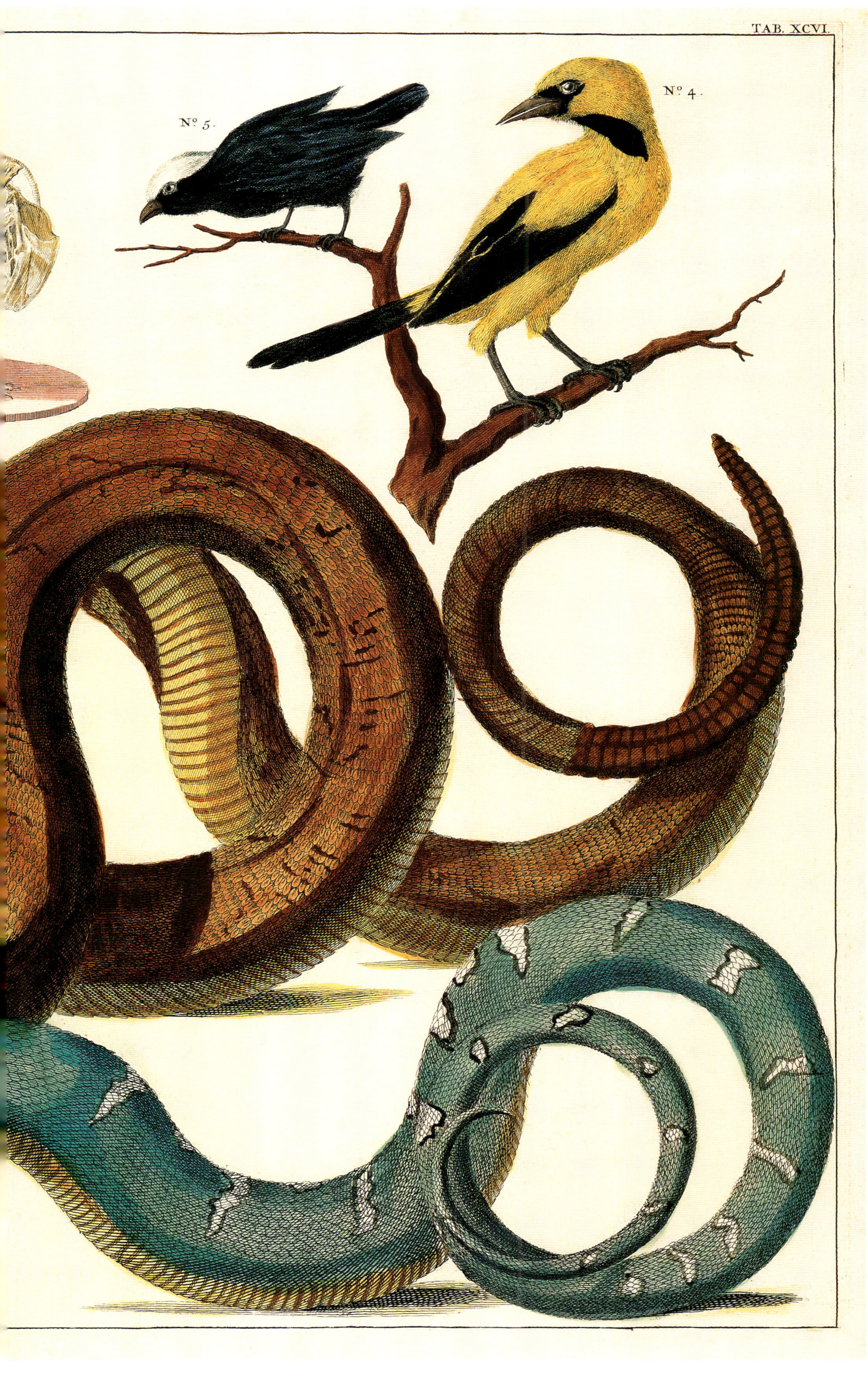
TAB. XCVI.
N°. 5.
N°. 4.

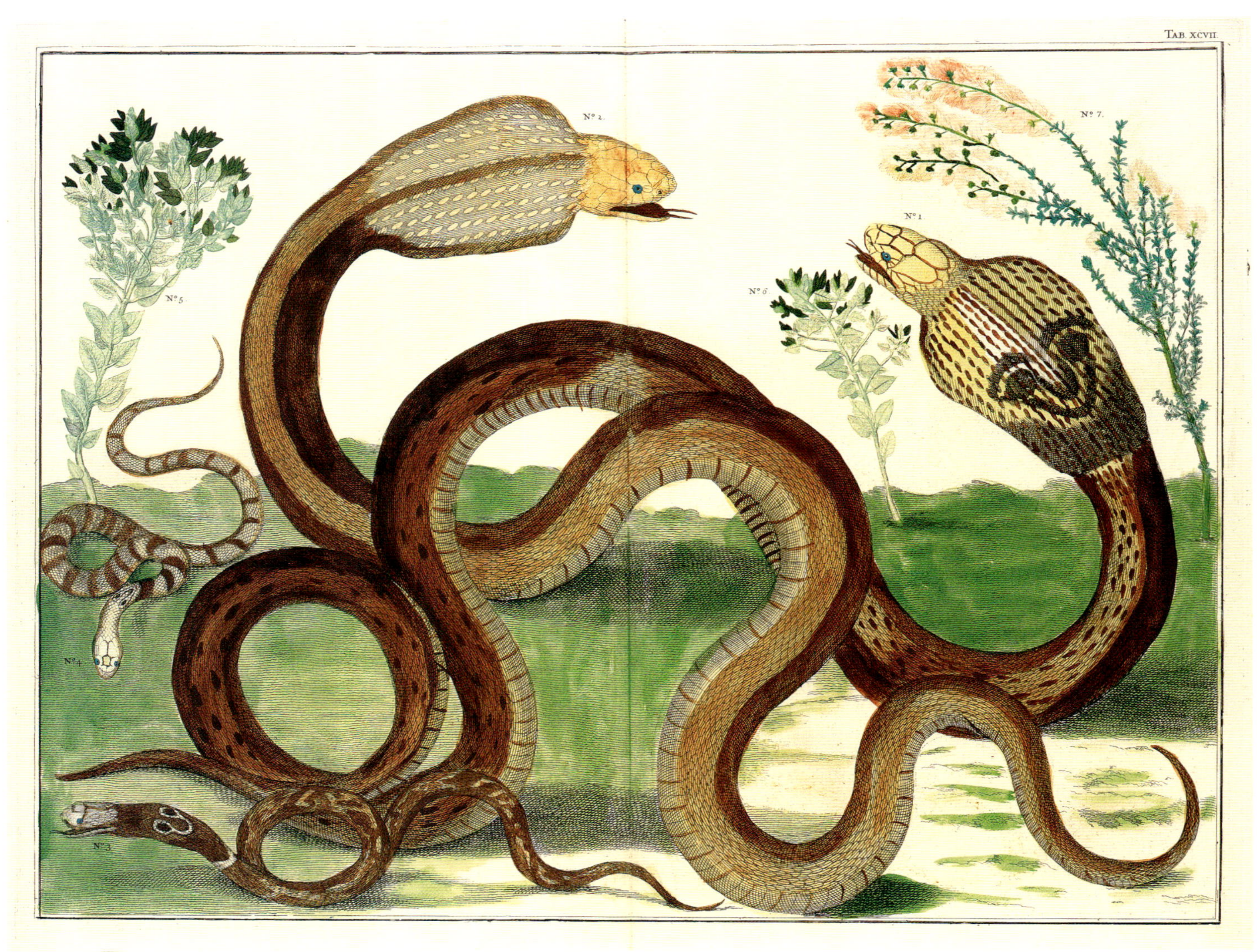

1-3 *Naja naja* **4** Serpentes
1-3 Common cobra · Brillenschlange/Indische Kobra · Cobra indien **4** Snake, according to Seba from Nova Hispania · Schlange, nach Seba aus Nova Hispania · Serpent, de Nova Hispania selon Seba

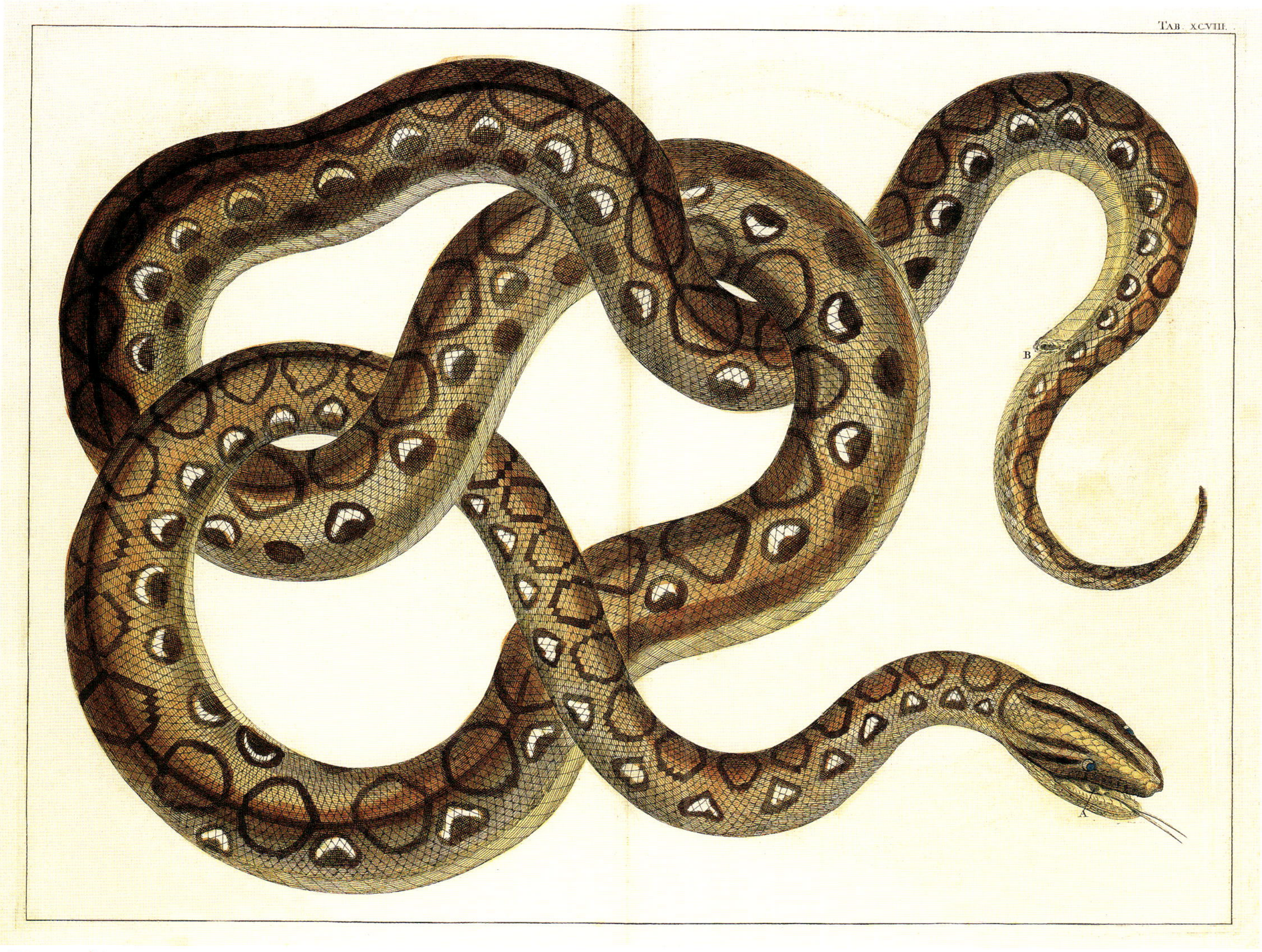

1 *Epicrates cenchria*
1 Rainbow boa · Regenbogenboa · Boa arc-en-ciel

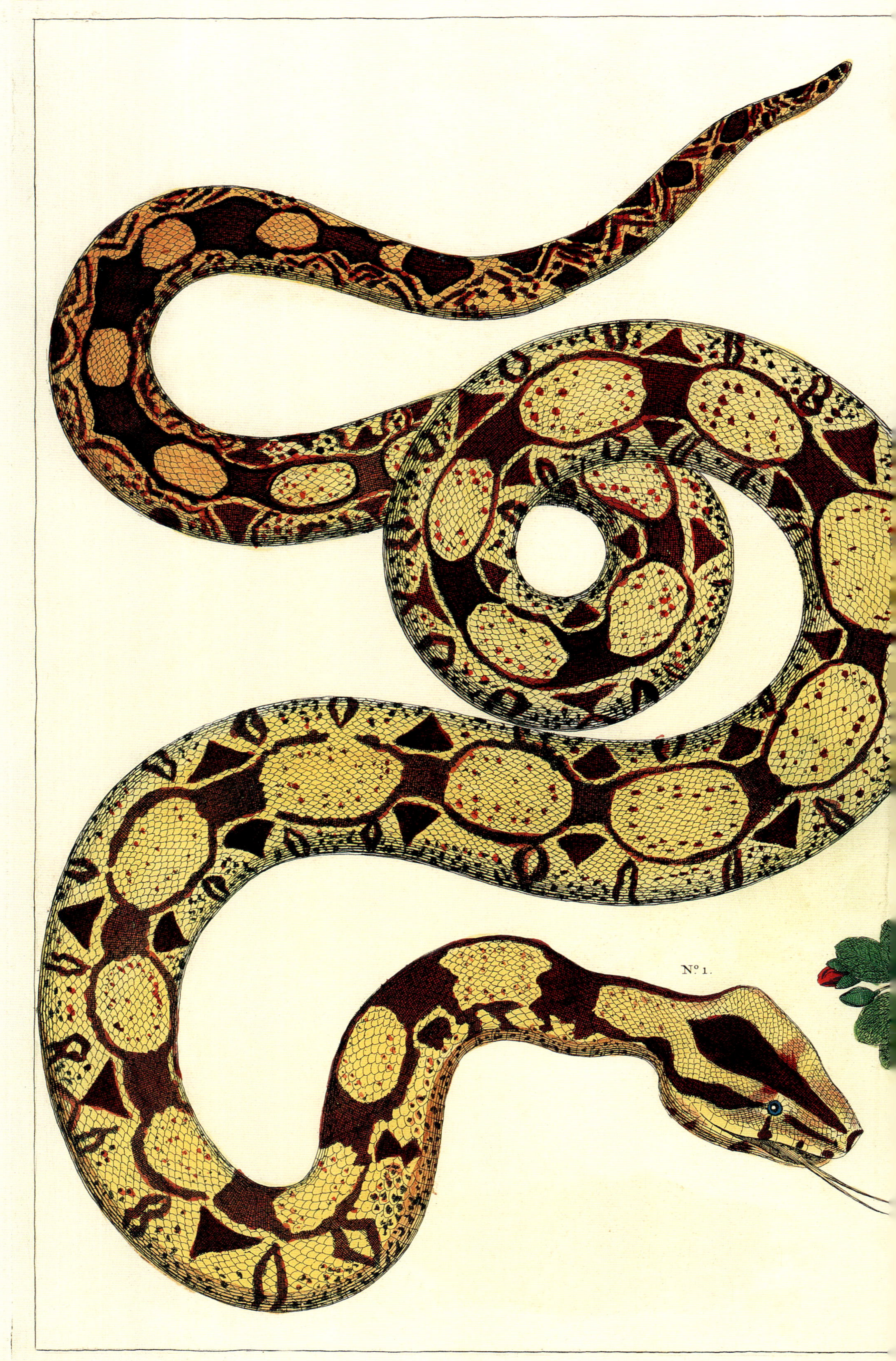

1 *Boa constrictor?* 2 Boinae
1 Common boa · Abgottschlange · Boa constricteur 2 Boine snake · Riesenschlange · Boïné

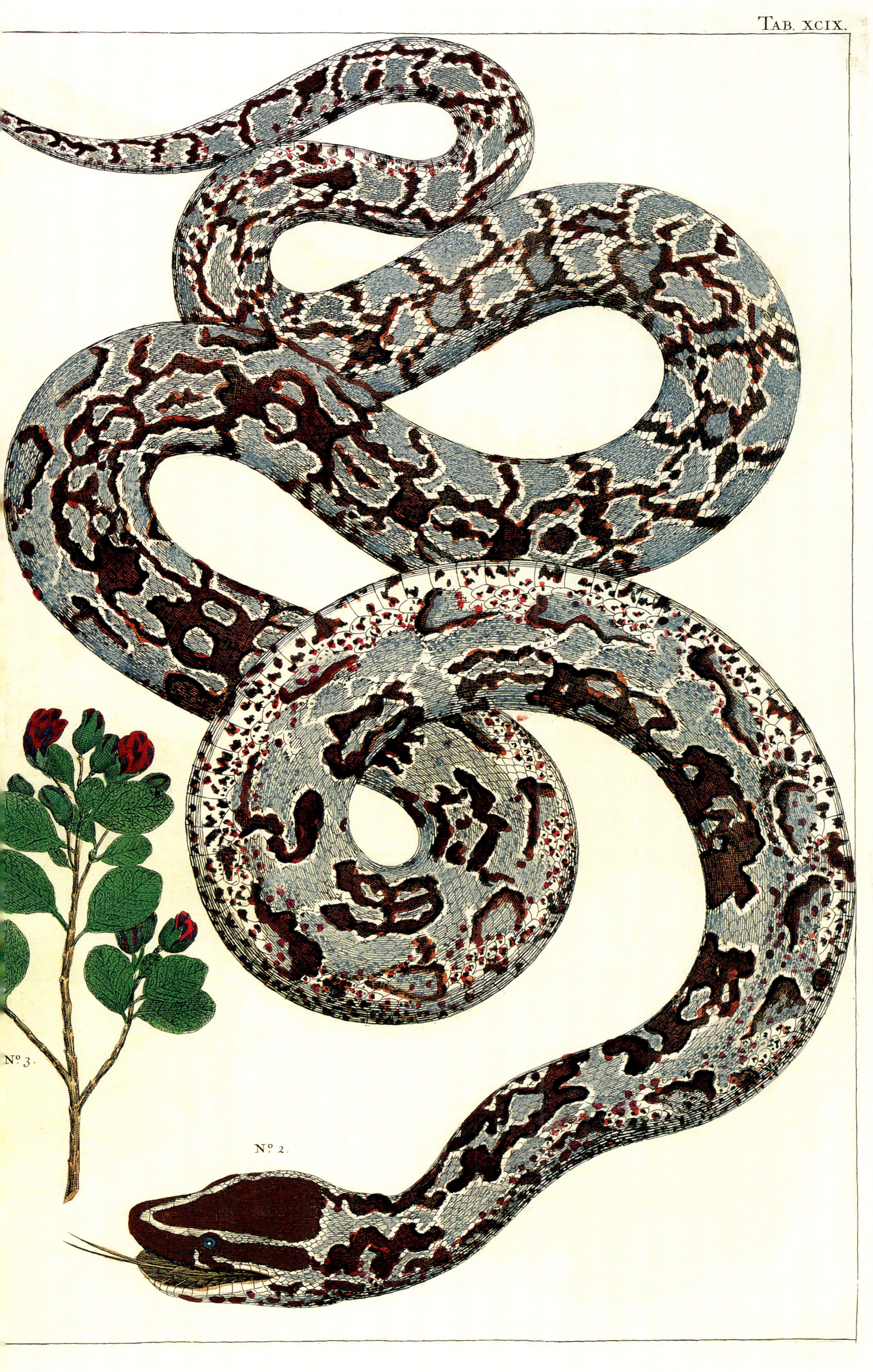
TAB. XCIX.
N.º 3.
N.º 2.

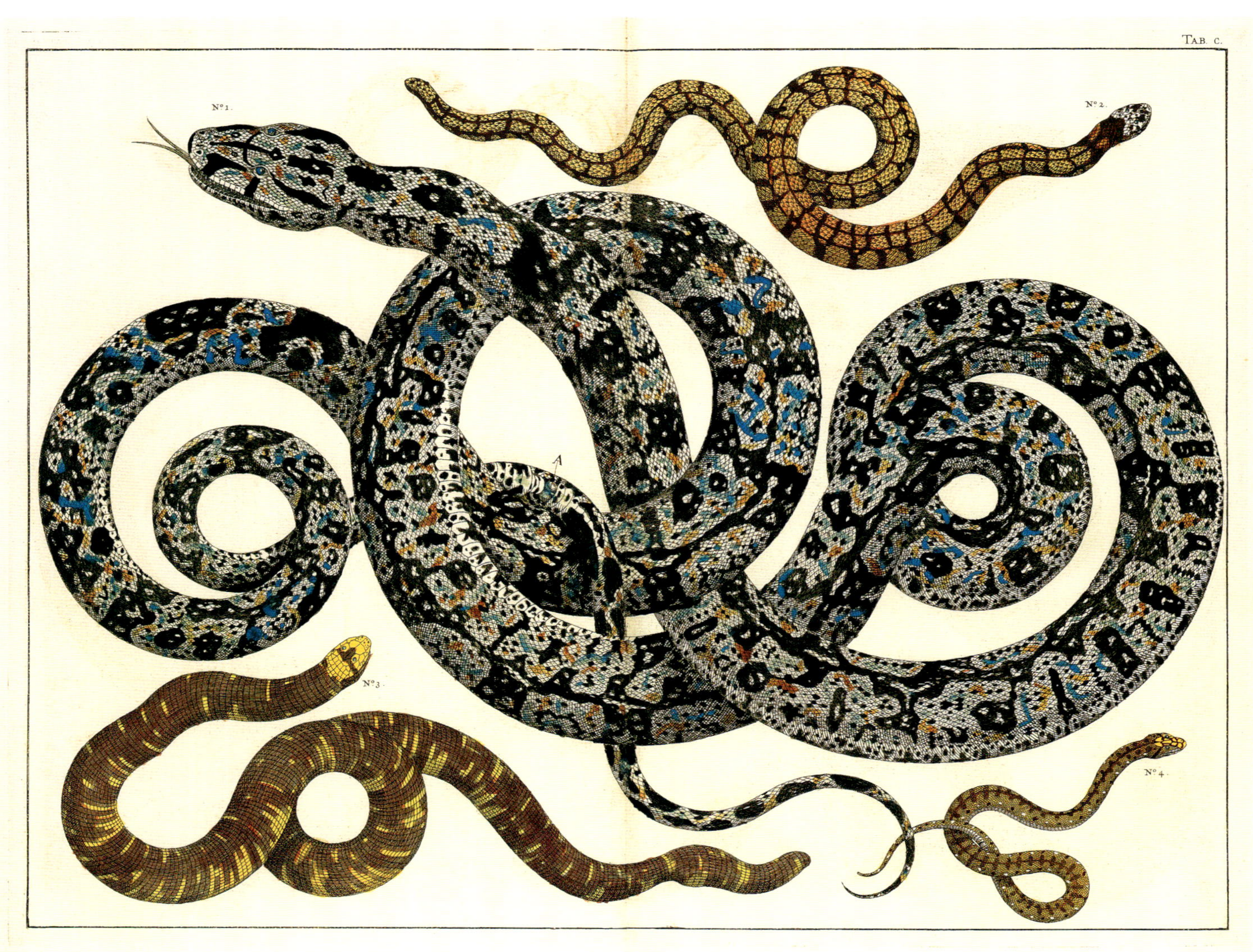

1 *Boa constrictor?* **2, 4** Serpentes **3** Amphisbaenia sp.
1 Common boa · Abgottschlange · Boa constricteur **2** Snake, according to Seba from Brazil · Schlange, nach Seba aus Brasilien · Serpent, du Brésil selon Seba
3 Ringed lizard · Doppelschleiche · Amphisbène **4** Snake, according to Seba from Ambon · Schlange, nach Seba aus Ambon · Serpent, d'Amboine selon Seba

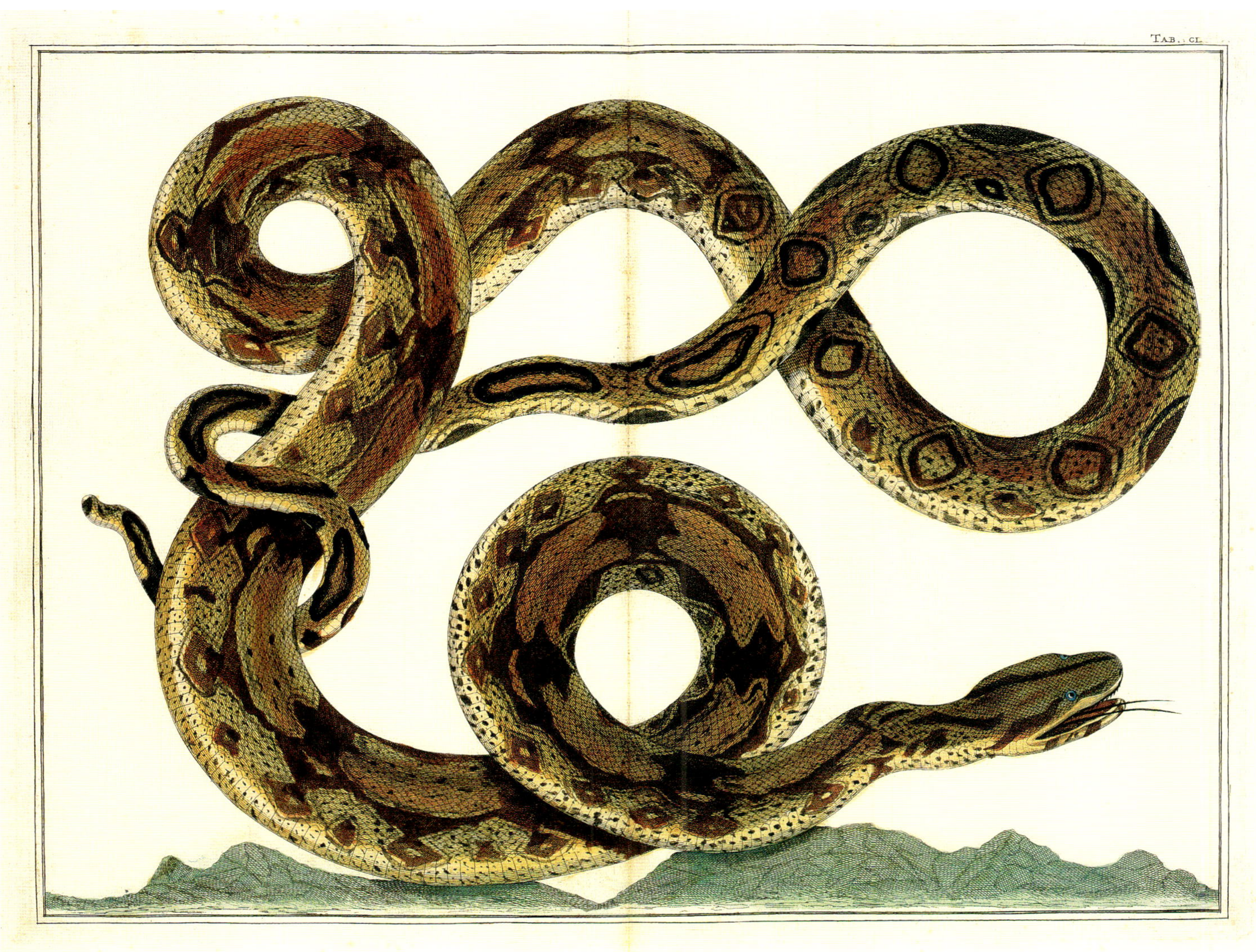

1 *Python molurus*
1 Indian python · Tiger Python · Python indien

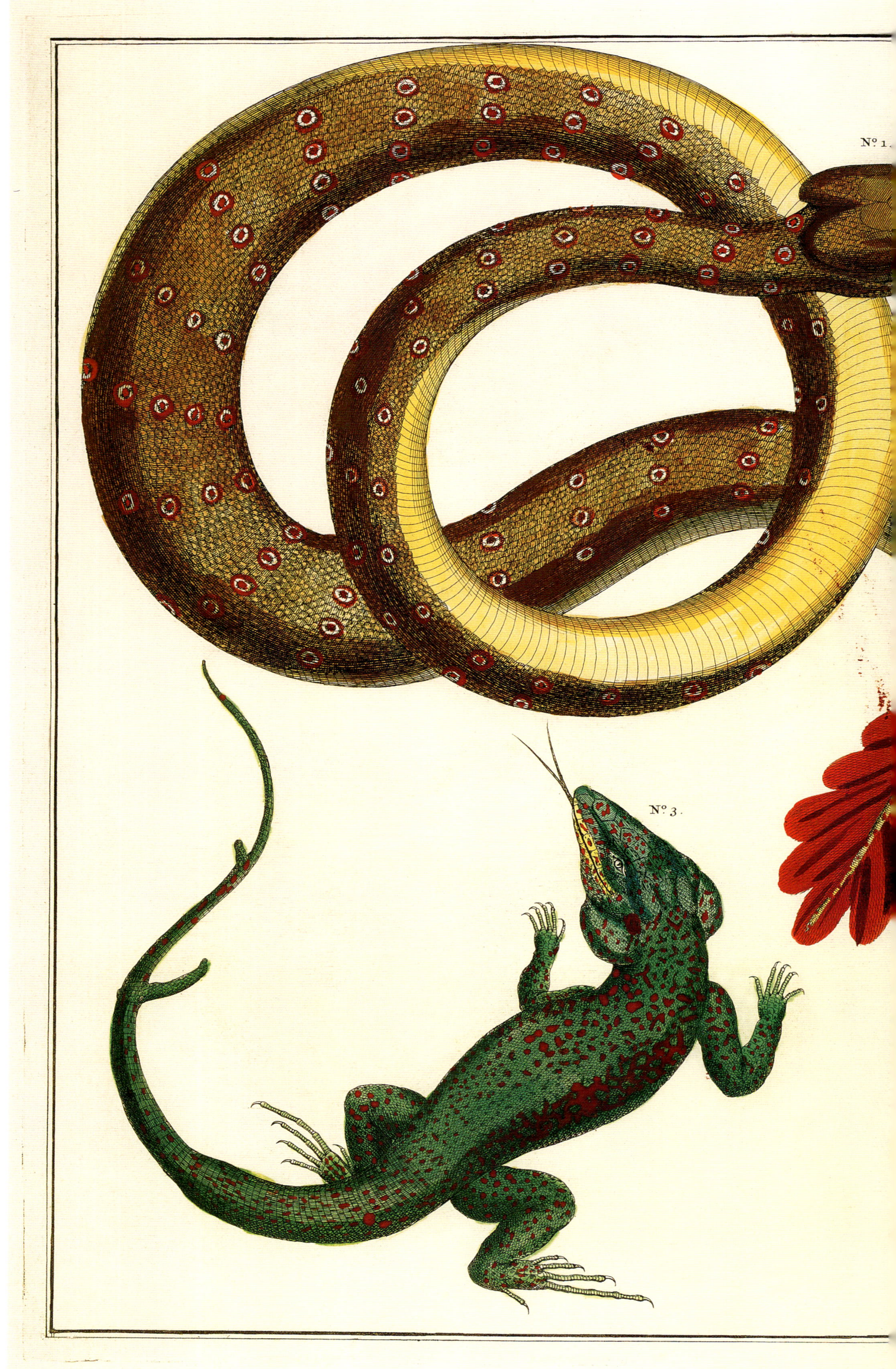

1 Serpentes 2-4 Squamata
1 Snake, according to Seba from Africa · Schlange, nach Seba aus Afrika · Serpent, d'Afrique selon Seba 2-4 Lizards · Echsen · Sauriens

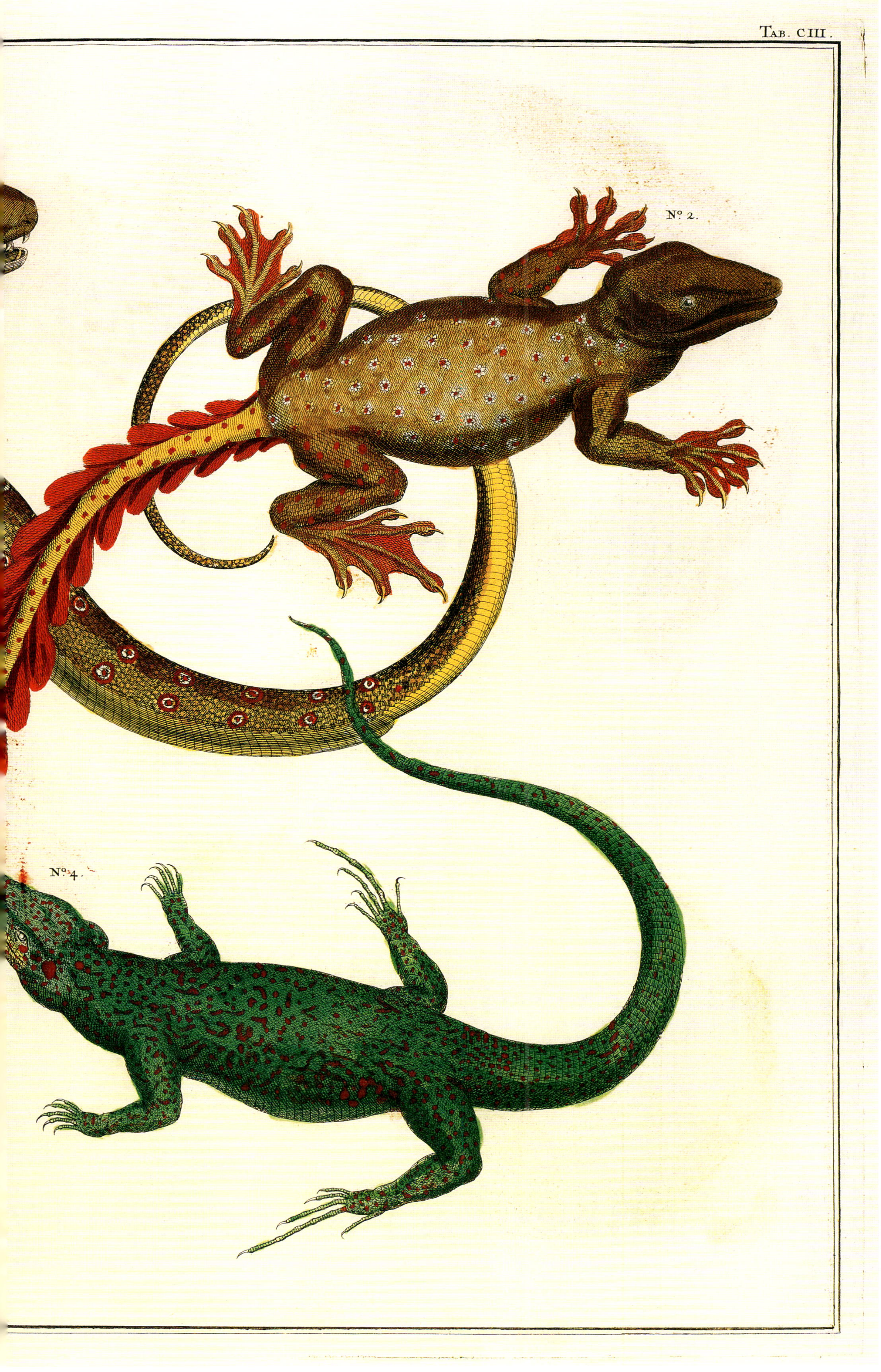
TAB. CIII.
N°. 2.
N°. 4.

LOCUPLETISSIMI RERUM NATURALIUM THESAURI

ACCURATA DESCRIPTIO

ET

ICONIBUS ARTIFICIOSISSIMIS

EXPRESSIO

PER

UNIVERSAM PHYSICES HISTORIAM.

OPUS,

CUI, IN HOC RERUM GENERE, NULLUM PAR EXSTITIT.
EX TOTO TERRARUM ORBE COLLEGIT,
DIGESSIT, DESCRIPSIT, ET DEPINGENDUM CURAVIT

ALBERTUS SEBA,

ETZELA OOSTFRISIUS,

ACADEMIÆ CÆSAREÆ LEOPOLDINO CAROLINÆ NATURÆ CURIOSORUM
COLLEGA XENOCRATES DICTUS; SOCIETATIS REGIÆ ANGLICANÆ,
ET INSTITUTI BONONIENSIS, SODALIS.

TOMUS III.

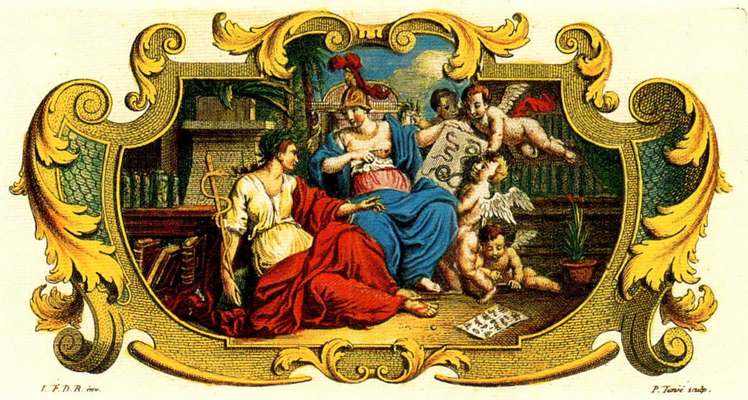

AMSTELAEDAMI,
Apud JANSSONIO-WAESBERGIOS.
MDCCLVIII.

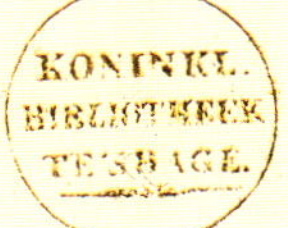

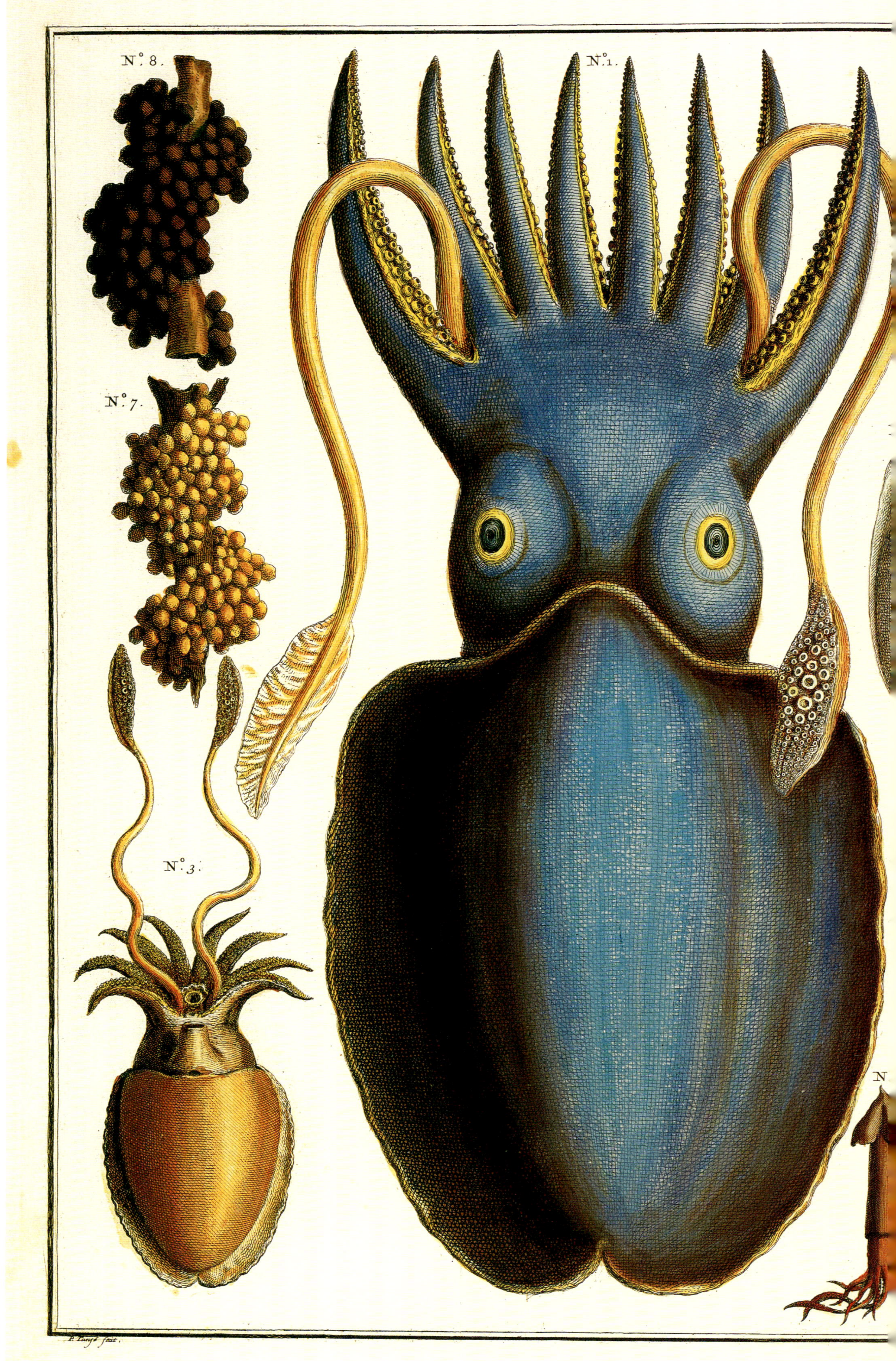

1-4 Sepiida 5-6 Teuthida 7-8 Ovum 9-10 Sepiidae
1-4 Sepias · Sepien · Seiches 5-6 Arrow squids/Flying squids · Pfeilkalmare · Encornets volants ou calmars 7-8 Sepia eggs · Sepia-Eier · Œufs de seiches
9-10 Cuttlebones of Sepia · Schulpe · Os de seiches

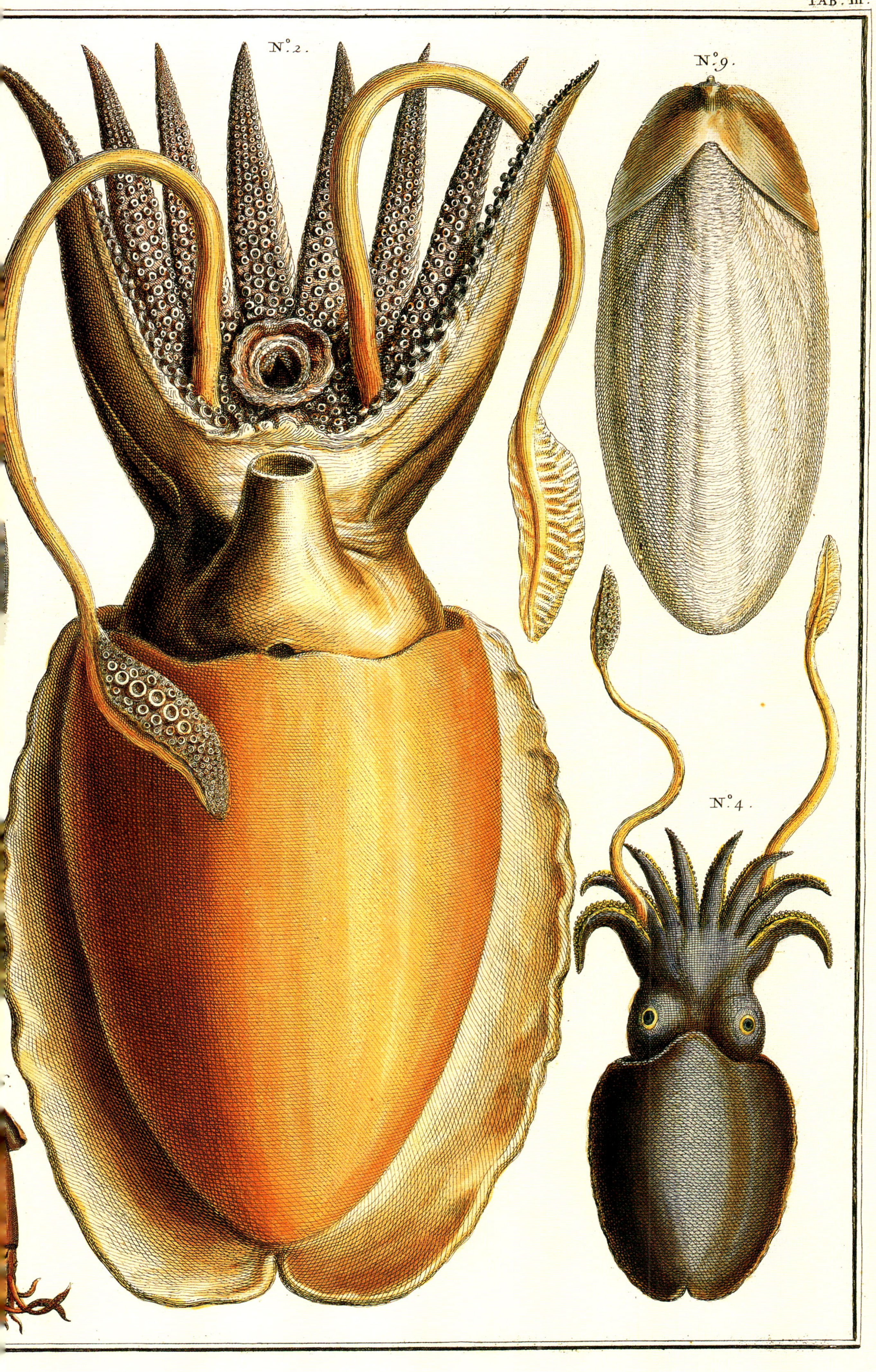
TAB. III.
N.° 2.
N.° 9.
N.° 4.

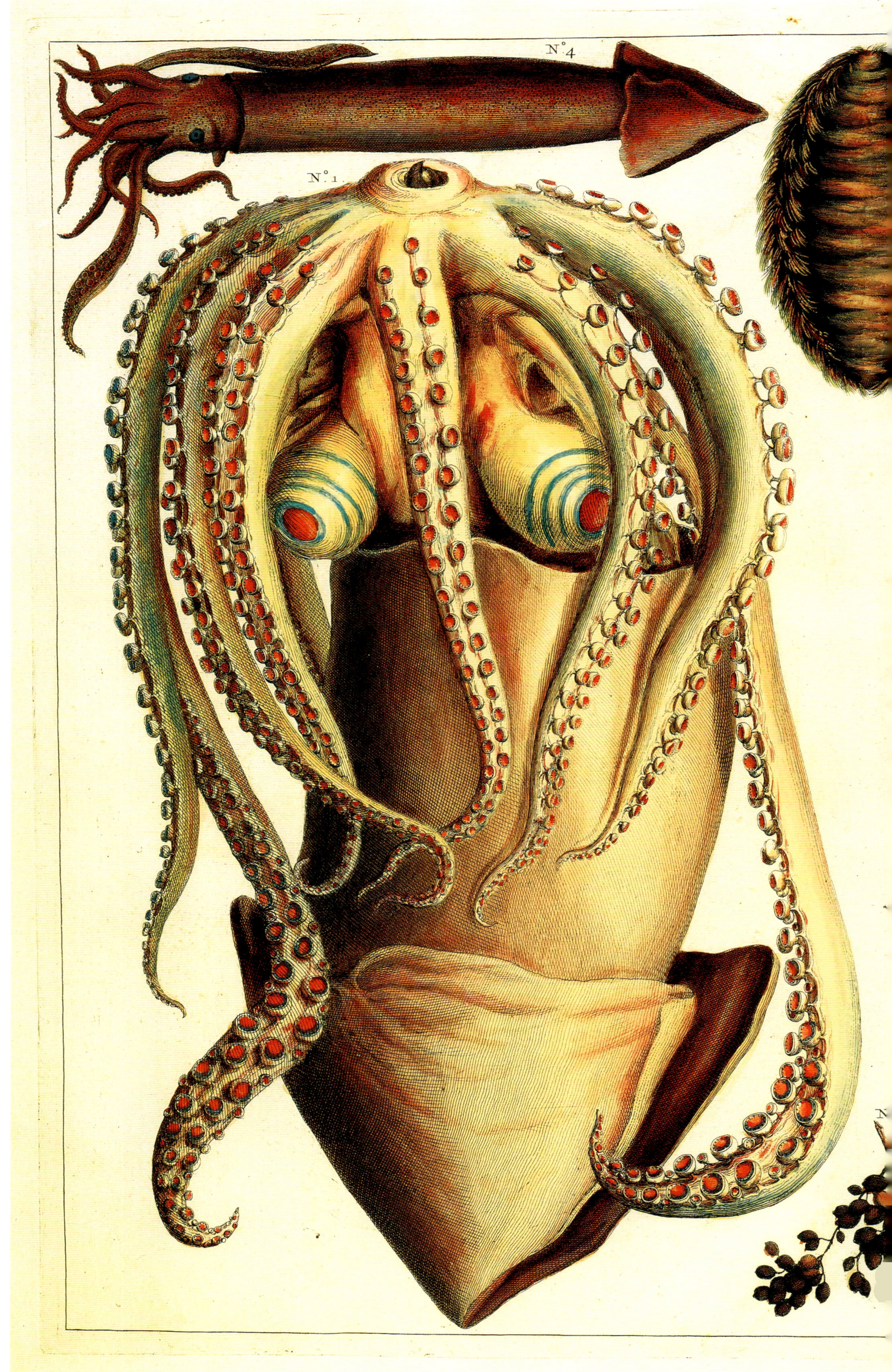

1-2 *Loligo?* 3-5 Teuthida 7-8 Annelida (Aphrodite)
1-2 Squids · Kalmare · Calmars **3-5** Arrow squids/Flying squids · Pfeilkalmare · Encornets volants ou calmars **7-8** Sea mice · Seemäuse · Aphrodites épineuses

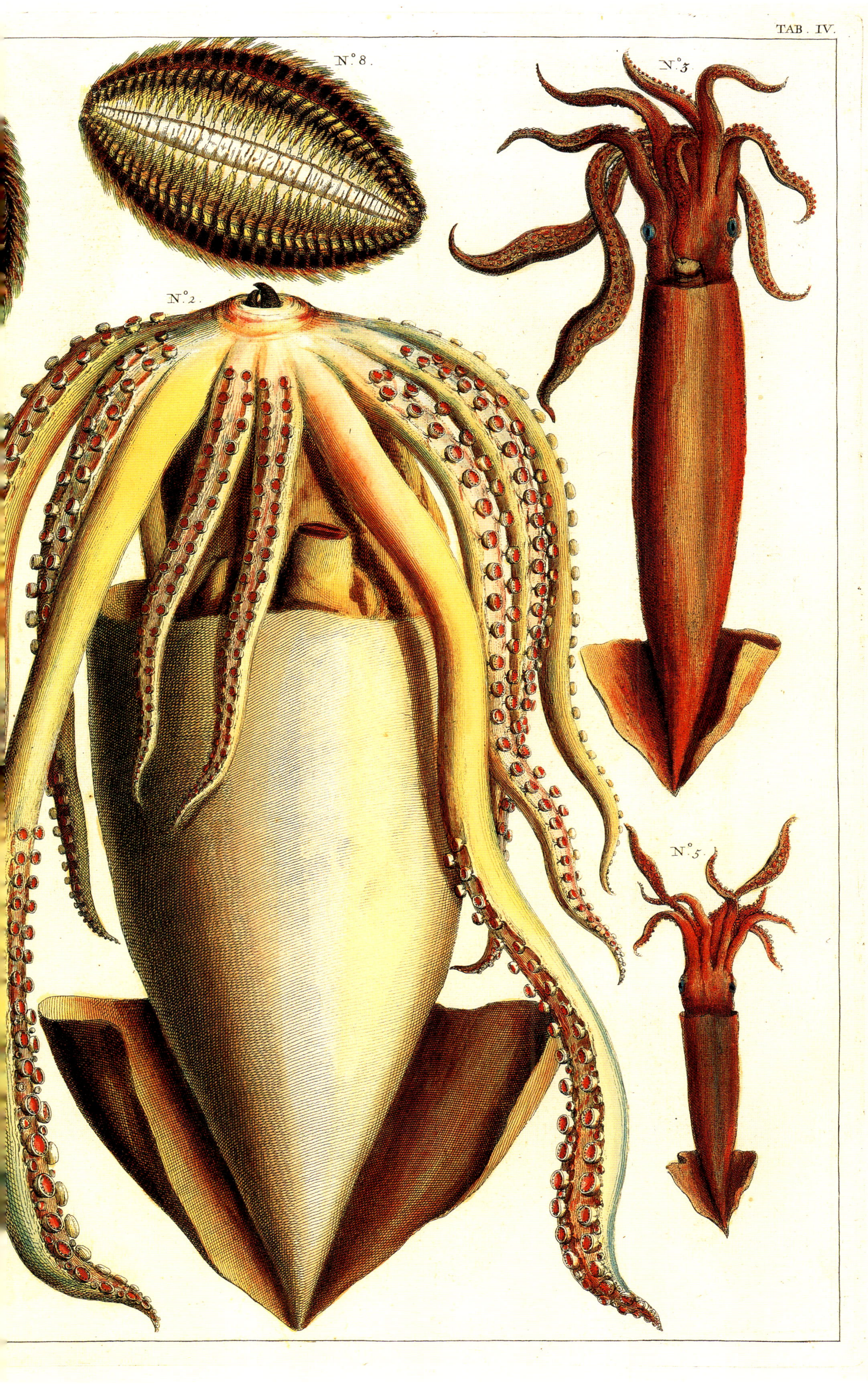
TAB. IV.
N.° 8.
N.° 3
N.° 2.
N.° 5.

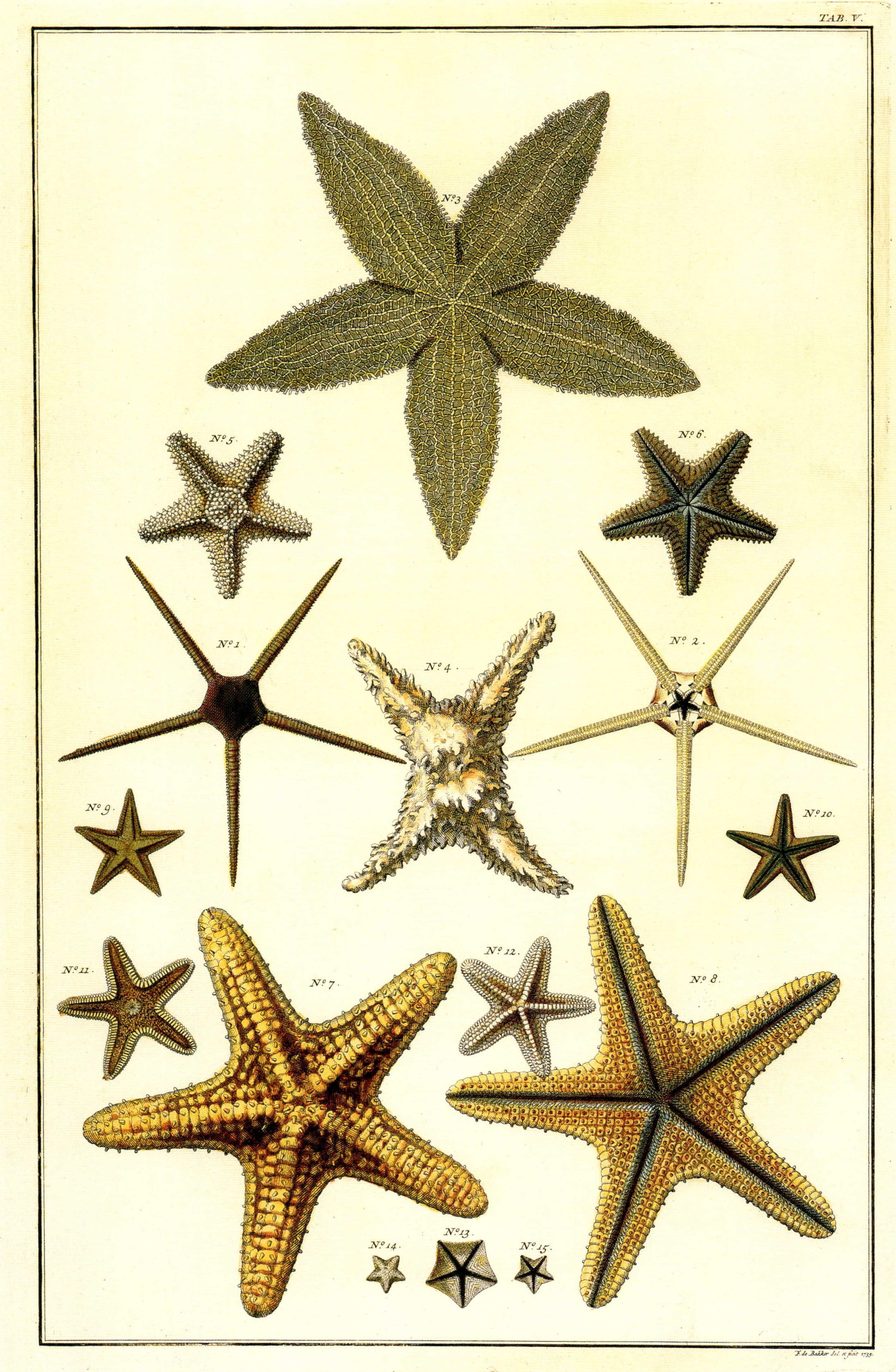

1-2 Phrynophiurida **3** *Asterias rubens* **9-10** *Astropecten aranciacus* **13-15** *Asterina gibbosa*
1-2 Serpent star · Krötenschlangenstern · Ophiure **3** Common starfish · Gewöhnlicher Seestern · Etoile de mer commune **9-10** Red comb stars · Große Kammseesterne · Grandes étoiles de mer
13-15 Common cushion stars · Kissenseesterne · Etoiles de mer pentagonales

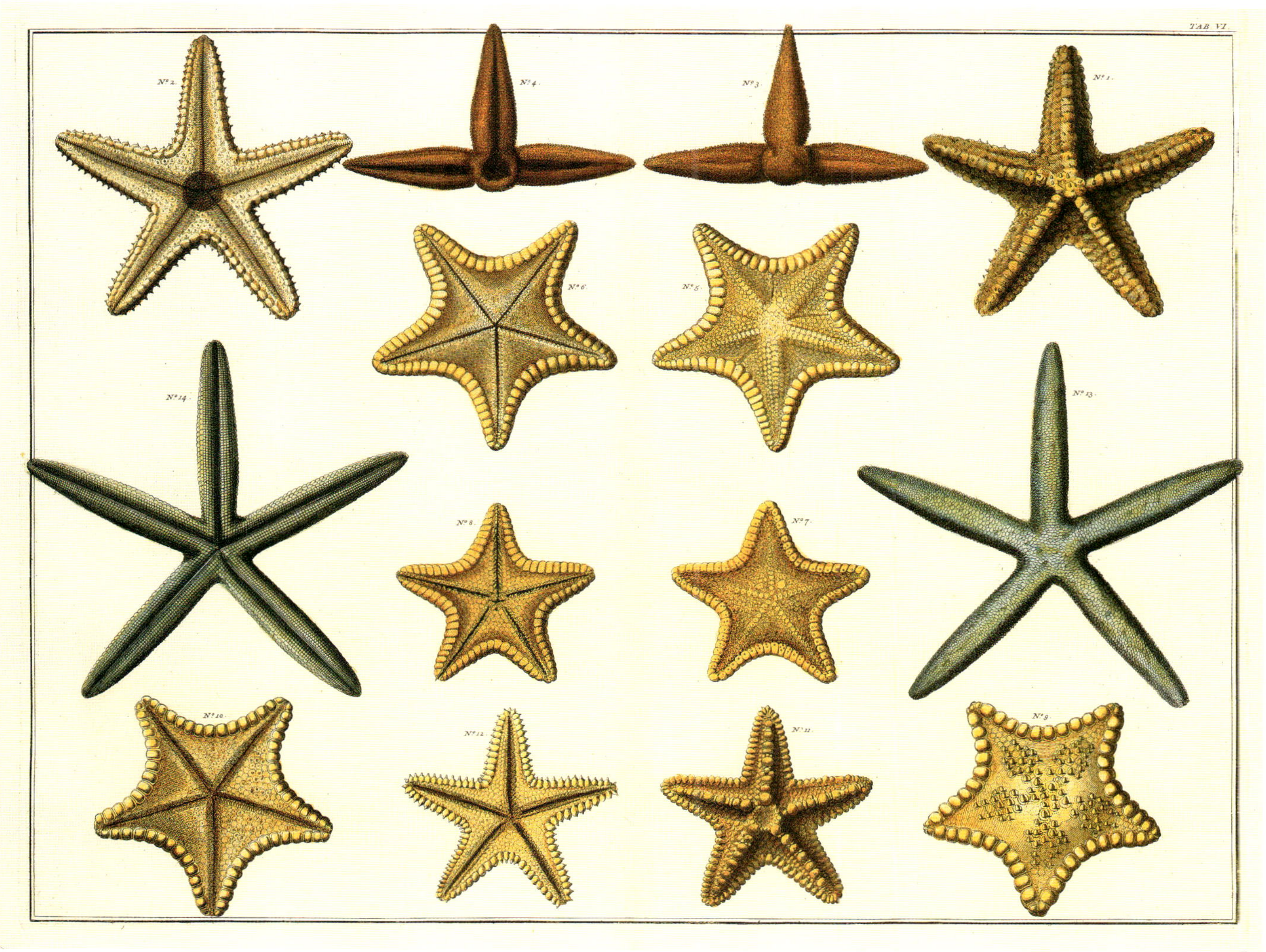

TAB. VI

N° 2. N° 4. N° 3. N° 1. N° 6. N° 5. N° 14. N° 13. N° 8. N° 7. N° 10. N° 12. N° 11. N° 9.

Asteroida **3-4** *Asterias rubens* **5-6, 9-10** *Ceramaster* **7-8** *Dipsacaster* **11-12** *Oreaster reticularis* **13-14** *Ophidiaster ophidianus*
Starfishes · Seesterne · Etoiles de mer **3-4** Common starfish · Gewöhnlicher Seestern · Etoile de mer commune
11-12 Cushion sea star · Kissenseestern · Etoile de mer **13-14** Purple sea star · Violettroter Seestern · Astérie pourpre

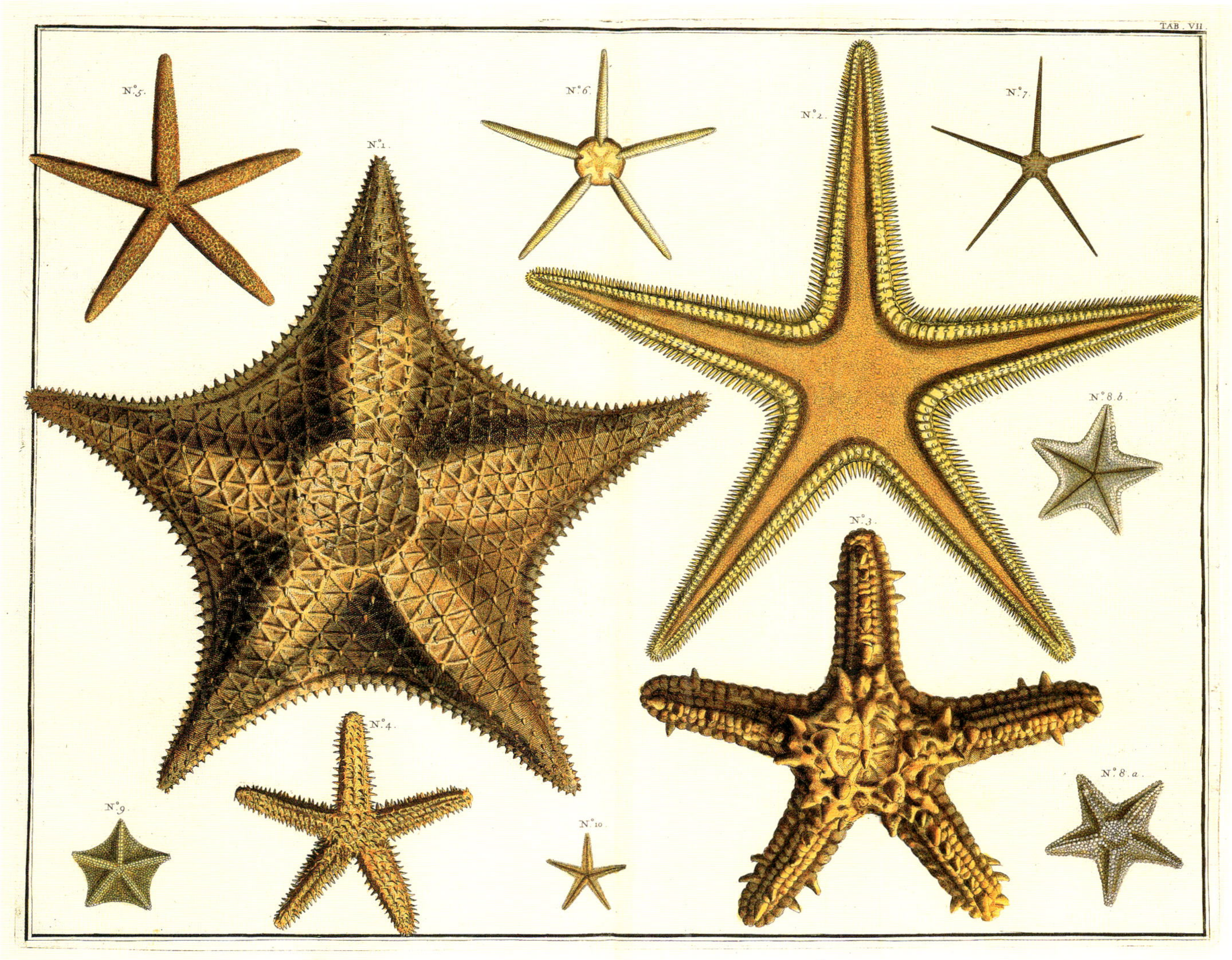

TAB. VII

N° 5. N° 6. N° 2. N° 7. N° 1. N° 8. b. N° 3. N° 4. N° 8. a. N° 9. N° 10

1-3, 8-10 Phanerozonia **4** Marthasterias glacialis **5** Spinulosa **6-7** Ophiurida
1-3, 8-10 Edged starfishes · Großplattenseesterne · Etoiles de mer **4** Spiny starfish · Eisseestern · Etoile de mer glaciaire **5** Orange starfish · Purpurseestern · Etoile de mer rouge
6-7 Serpent stars · Schlangensterne · Ophiures

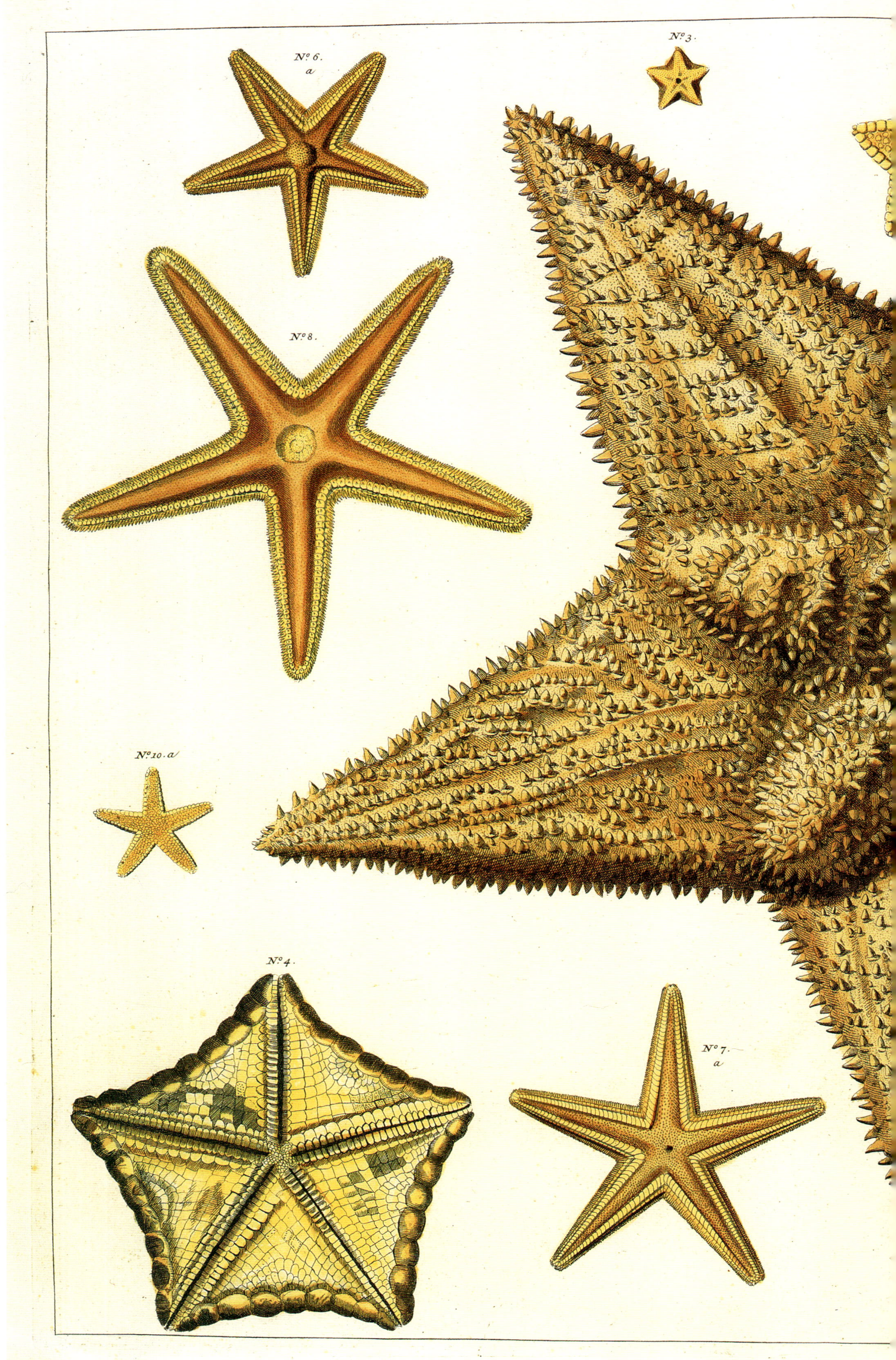

1 *Hymenaster pellucidus* 3 *Asterina gibbosa* 5 *Crossaster papposus* 6-7 *Astropecten aranciacus* 8-10 *Astropecten typicus*
1 Starfish · Seestern · Etoile de mer 3 Common cushion star · Polsterseestern · Etoile de mer pentagonale 5 Common sun star · Sonnenseestern · Soleil de mer épineux 6-7 Red comb stars · Große Kammseesterne · Grandes étoiles de mer 8-10 Sand stars · Kammseesterne · Etoiles des sables

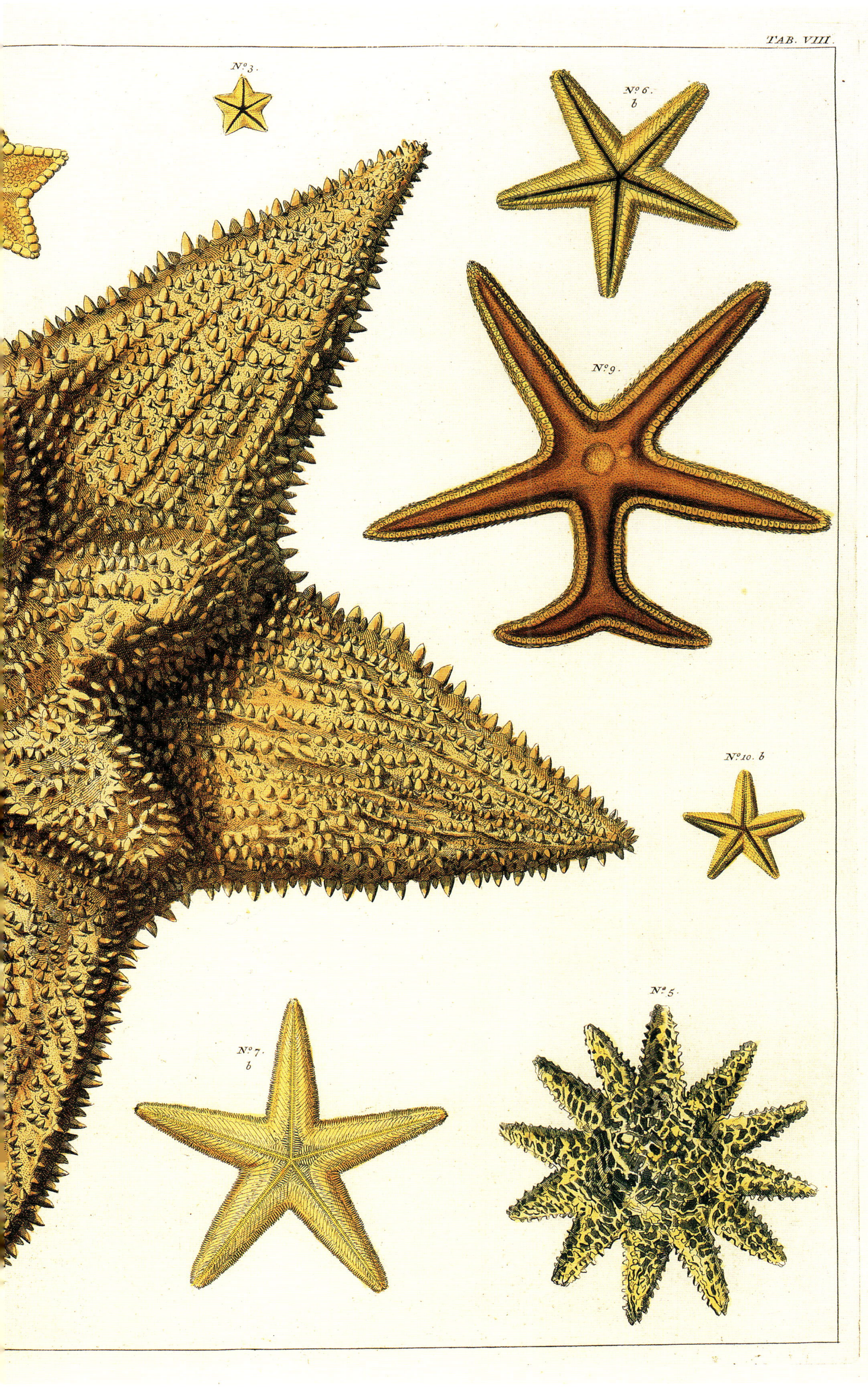
TAB. VIII.
N.º 3.
N.º 6.
b
N.º 9.
N.º 10. b
N.º 7.
b
N.º 5.

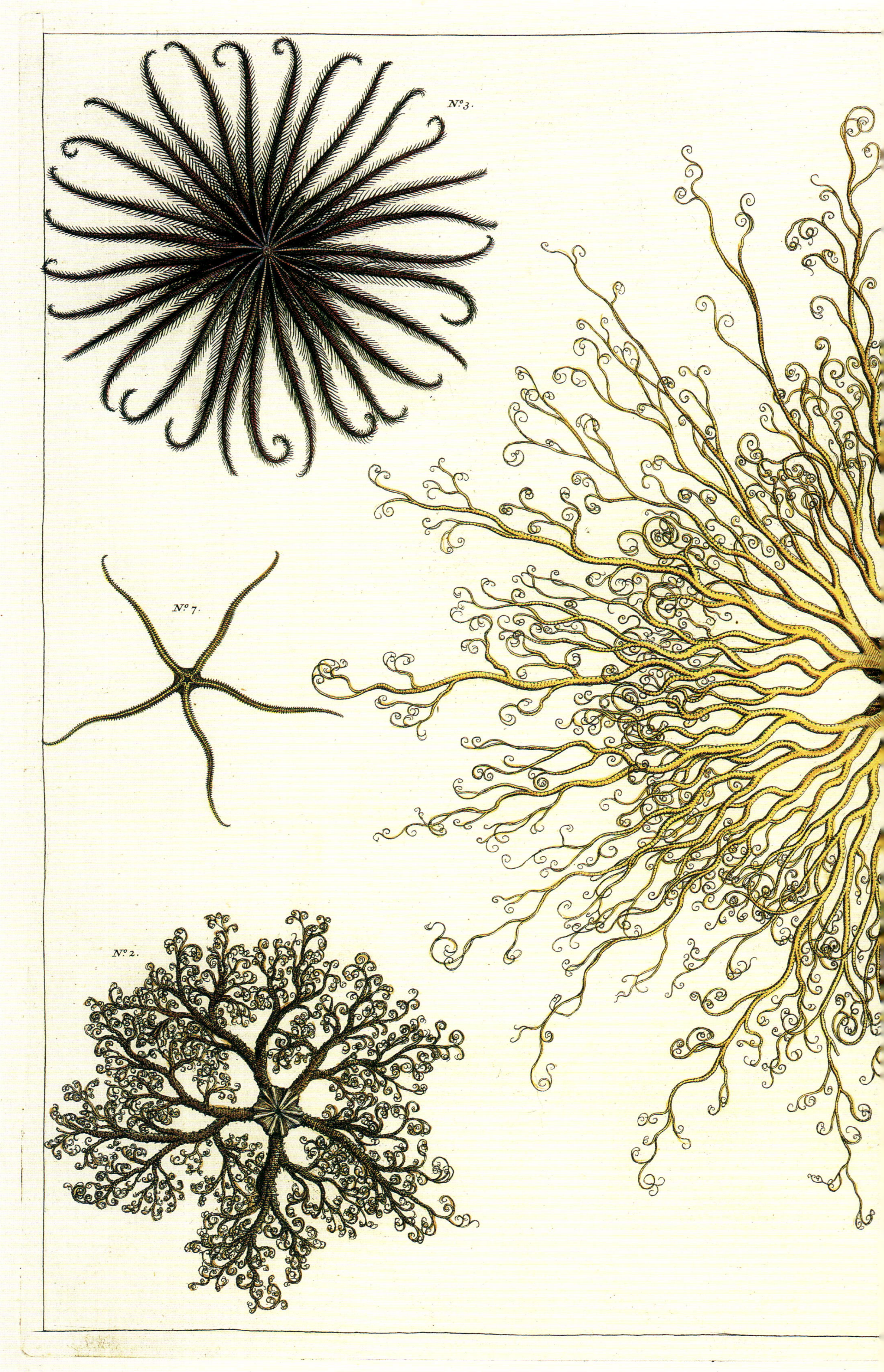

1-2 *Gorgonocephalus caput medusae* 3-4 *Comanthina* 5-6 *Ophiothrix* 7 *Ophioderma longicauda*
1-2 Gorgon's heads · Gorgonenhäupter · Gorgonocéphales (Crinoïdes) **3-4** Feather stars · Haarsterne · Lys de mer **5-6** Common brittle stars · Zerbrechliche Schlangensterne · Ophiures fragiles **7** Brown brittlestar · Brauner Schlangenstern · Ophiure lisse

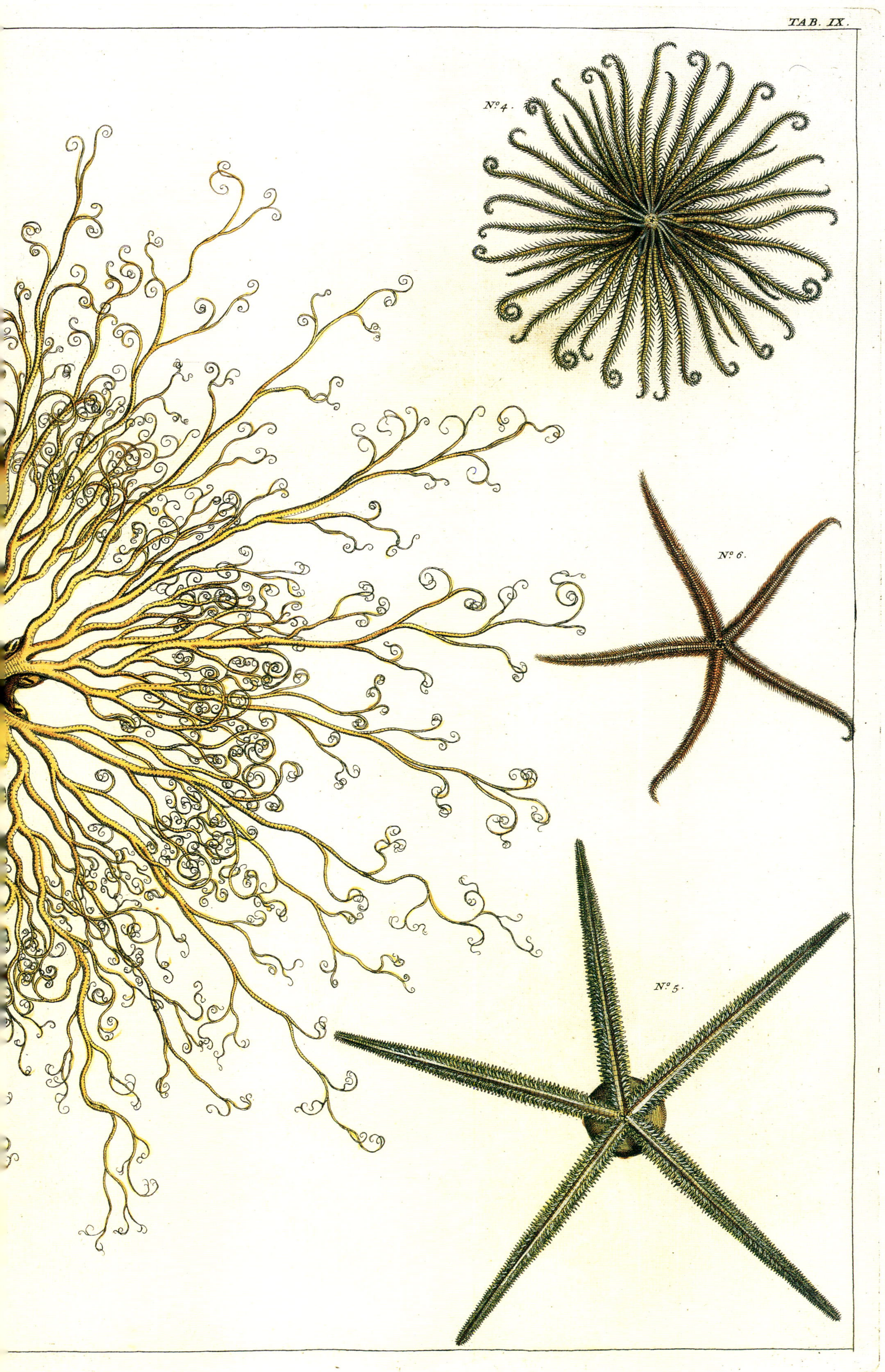
TAB. IX.
N.º 4.
N.º 6.
N.º 5.

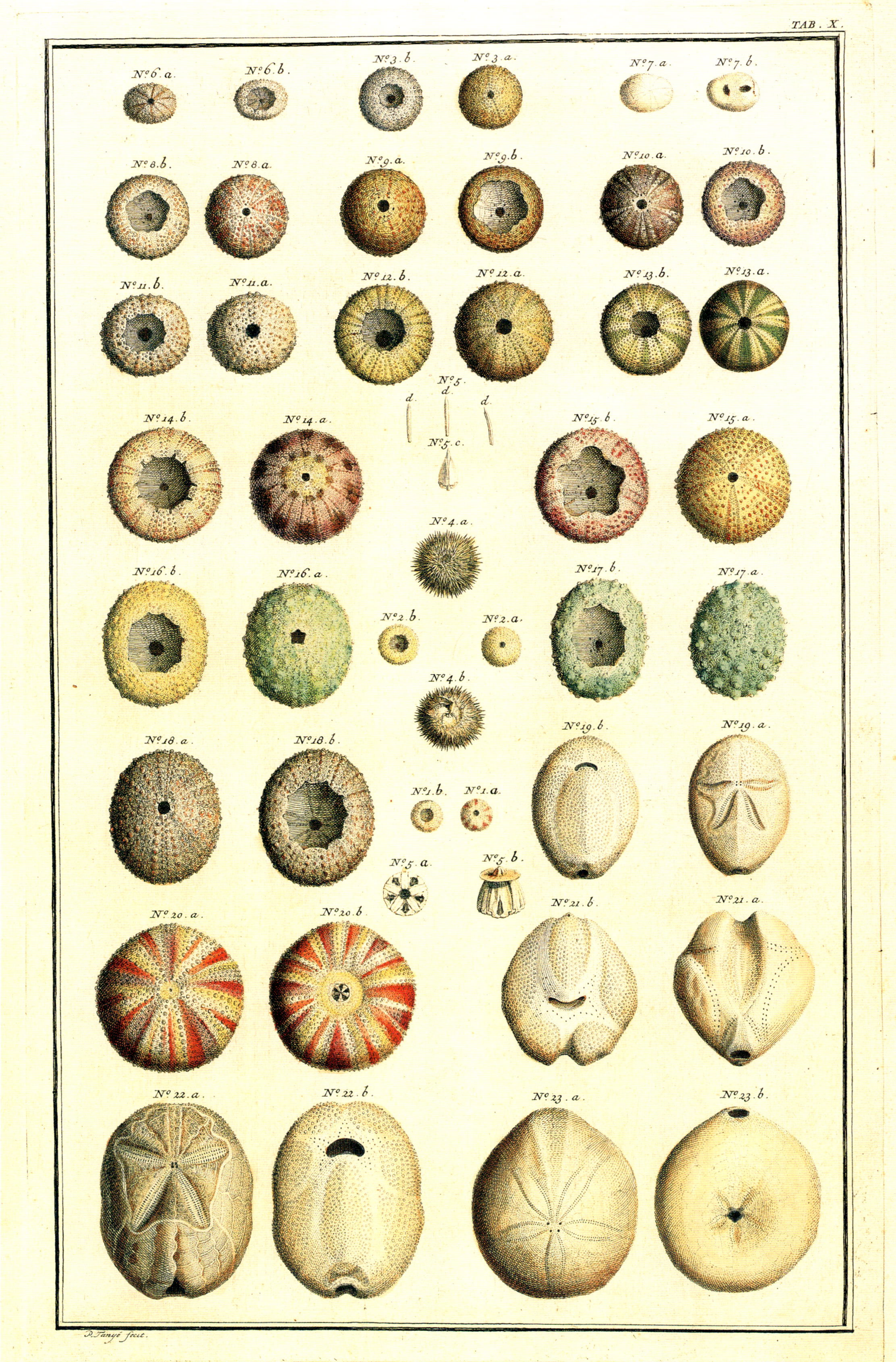

1-4, 6, 8-18 Echinacea 7 Echinoneus 19, 21-22 Spatangoida 20 Cidaroida
1-4, 6, 8-18 Sea urchins · Seeigel · Oursins **7** Sand dollar · Sanddollar · Dollar des sables **19, 21-22** Heart urchins · Herzseeigel · Oursins cœurs ou spatangues
20 Lance urchin · Lanzenseeigel · Oursin porte-lance

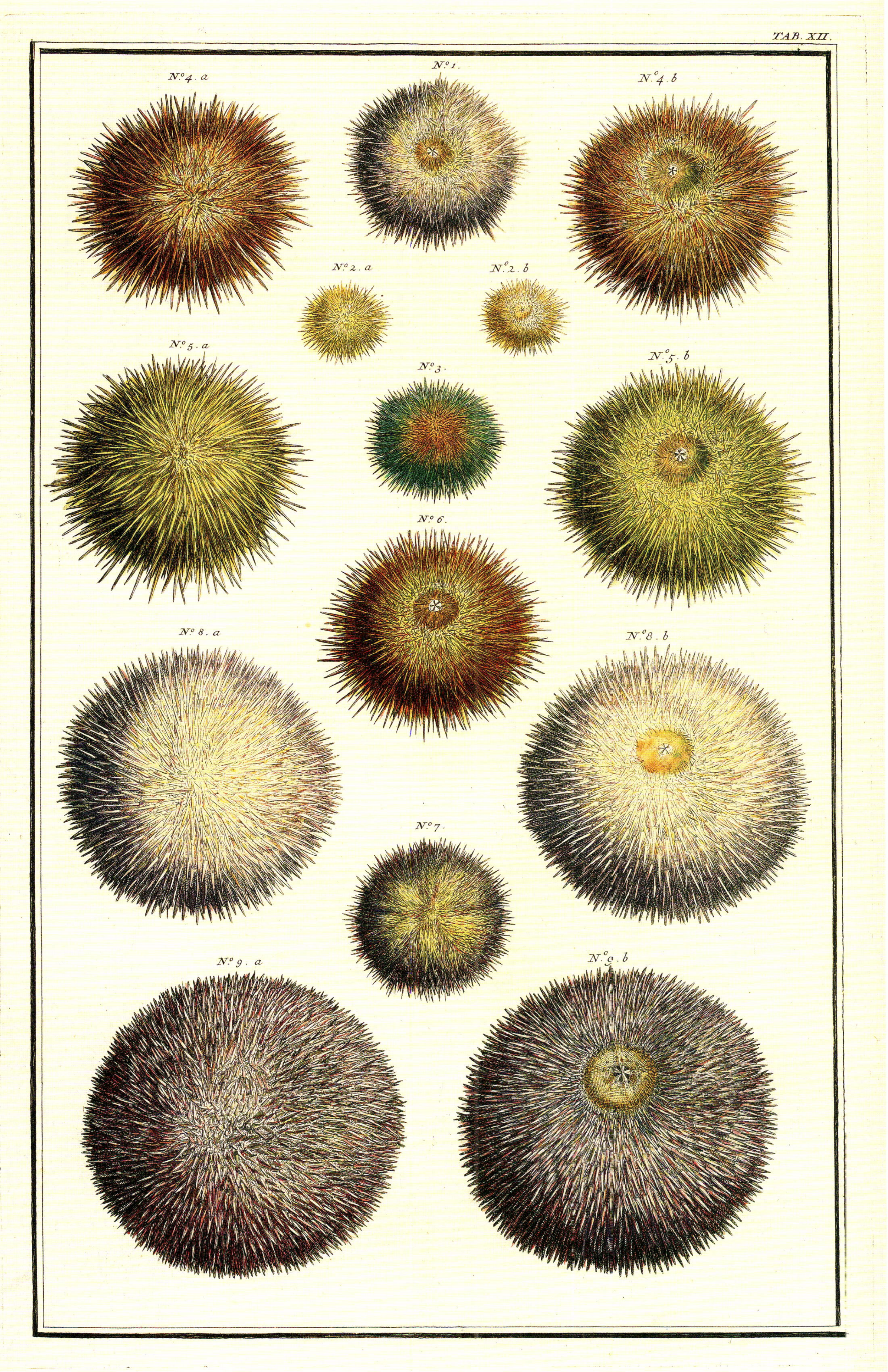

1, 3-4, 6 *Echinus* **2, 7** *Psammechinus miliaris* **5** *Paracentrotus* **8-9** *Echinus esculentus*
1, 3-4, 6 Sea urchins · Seeigel · Oursins **2, 7** Green sea urchins · Strandseeigel · Oursins verts **5** Rock urchin · Steinseeigel · Oursin caillou ou surbaissé
8-9 Edible sea urchins · Essbare Seeigel · Oursins communs comestibles

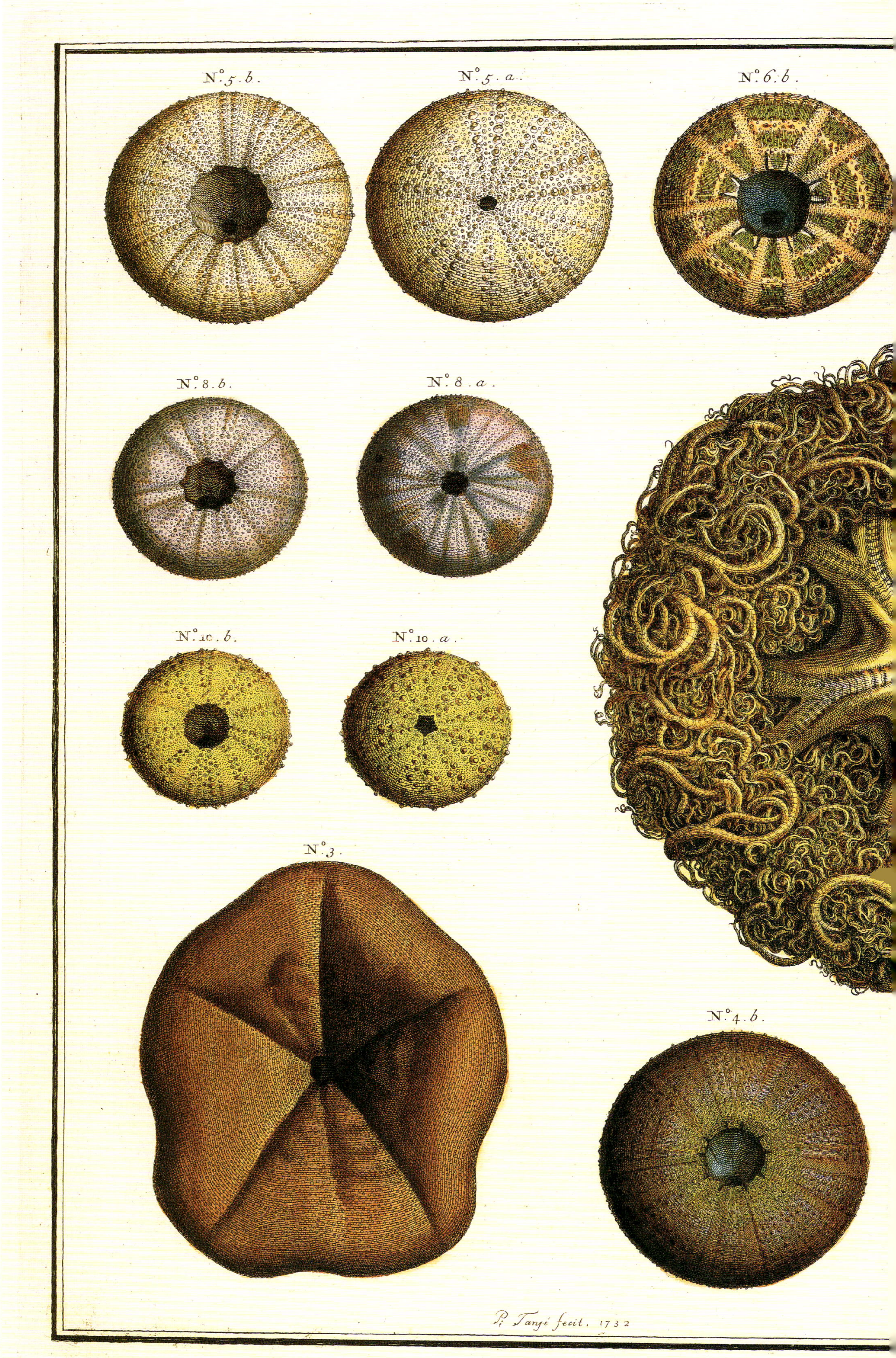

1 *Gorgonocephalus caryi* **2-3** Clypeasteroida **4-9, 11** Echinacea **10** Diadematoida
1 Gorgon's head · Gorgonenhaupt · Gorgonocéphale (Crinoïde) **2-3** Sand dollars · Sanddollars · Dollars des sables **4-9, 11** Sea urchins · Seeigel · Oursins
10 Hatpin urchin · Diademseeigel · Oursin diadème

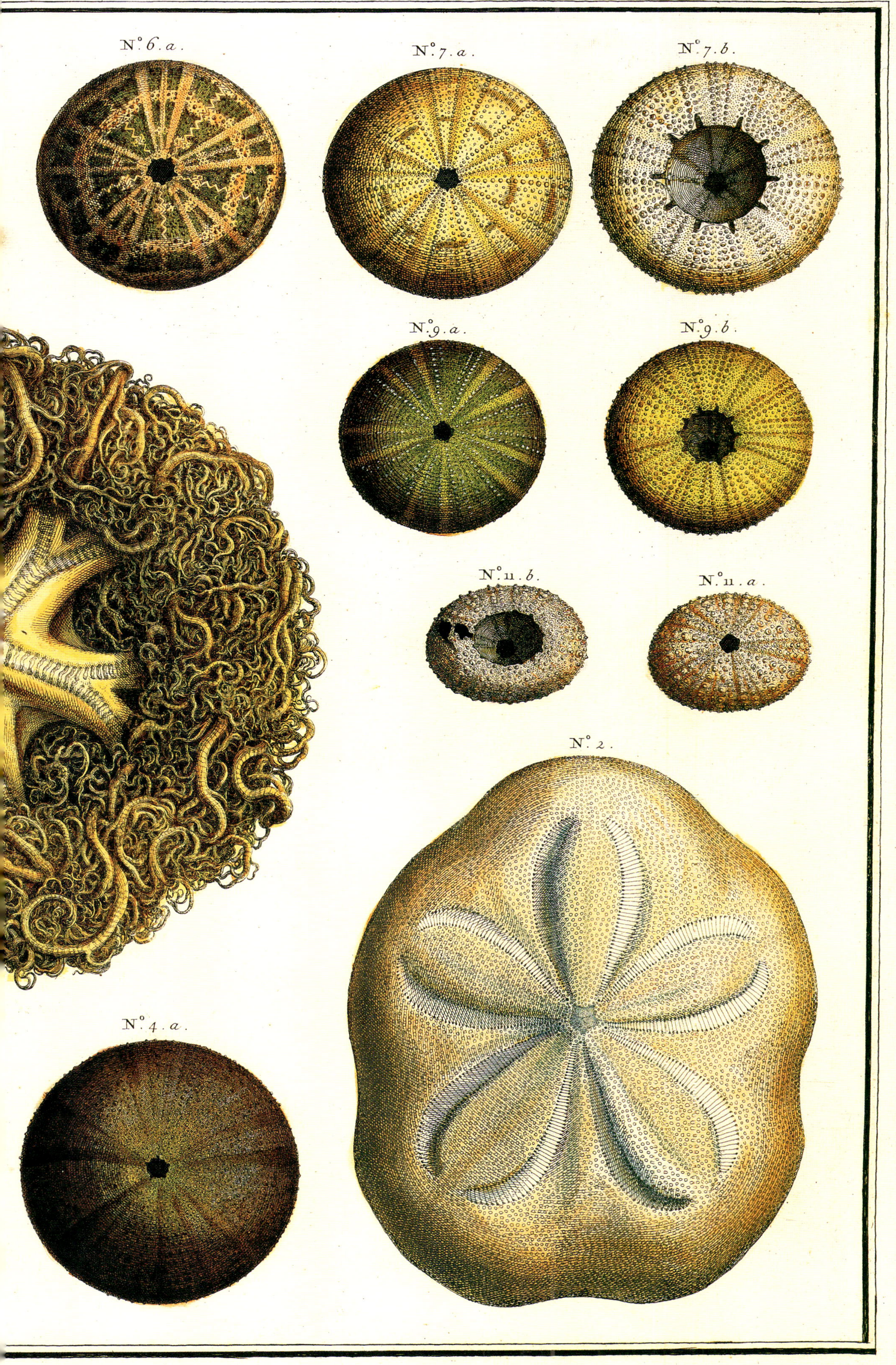
TAB. XI.
N.° 6. a.
N.° 7. a.
N.° 7. b.
N.° 9. a.
N.° 9. b.
N.° 11. b.
N.° 11. a.
N.° 2.
N.° 4. a.

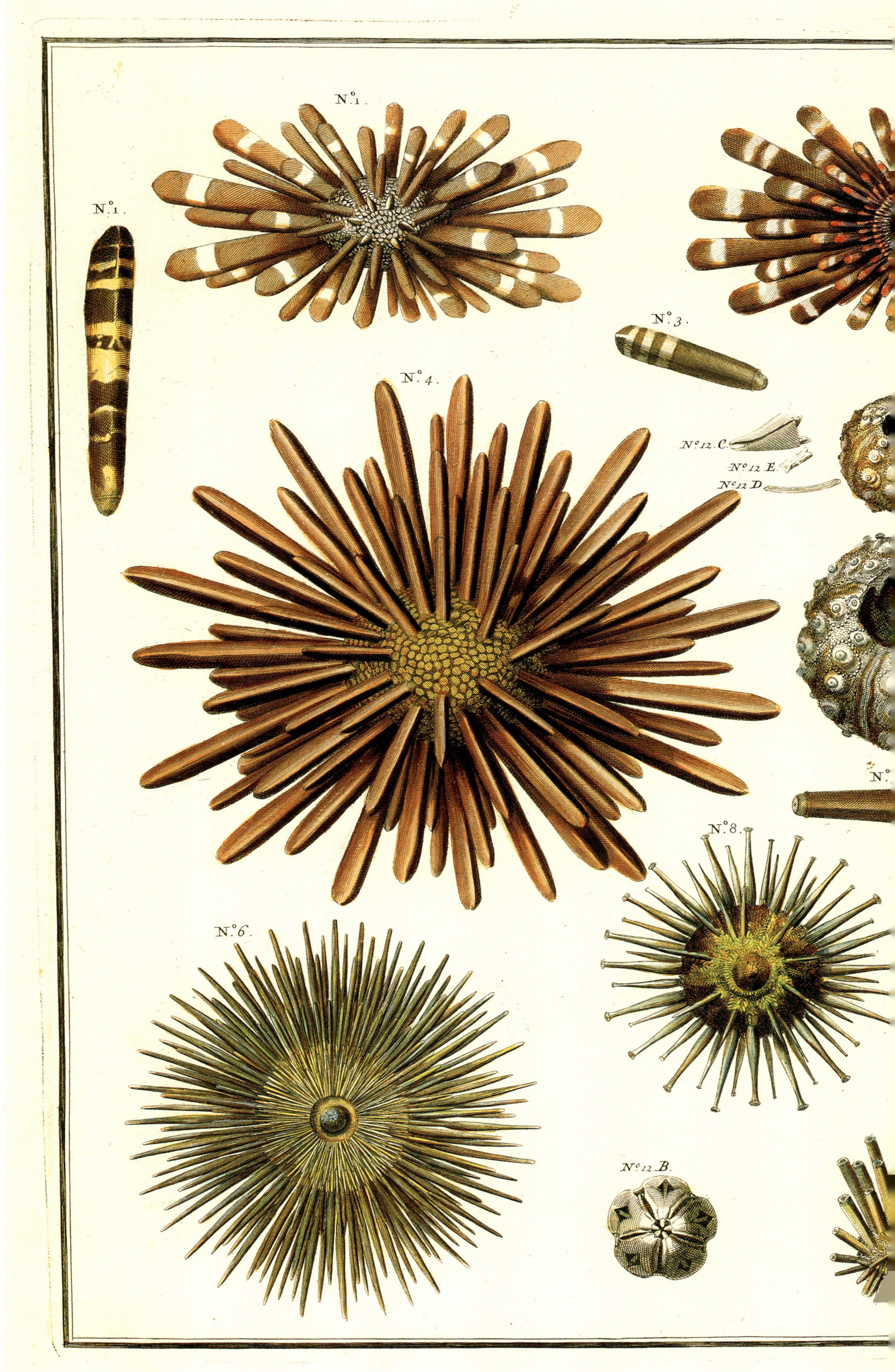

1-2 *Heterocentrotus mamillatus* **3, 12-13** *Heterocentrotus* **4** *Heterocentrotus trigonarius* **5** *Diadema setosum* **6, 8-9** *Diadema* **7** *Echinothrix diadema* **10-11** *Eucidaris*
1-2, 3-4, 12-13 Slate pencil sea urchins · Griffelseeigel · Oursins crayons **5** Long spined sea urchin · Gewöhnlicher Diademseeigel · Oursin diadème **6, 8-9** Hatpin urchins · Diademseeigel · Oursins diadèmes **7** Black sea urchin · Schwarzer Diademseeigel · Oursin diadème noir **10-11** Mine urchins · Lanzenseeigel · Oursins

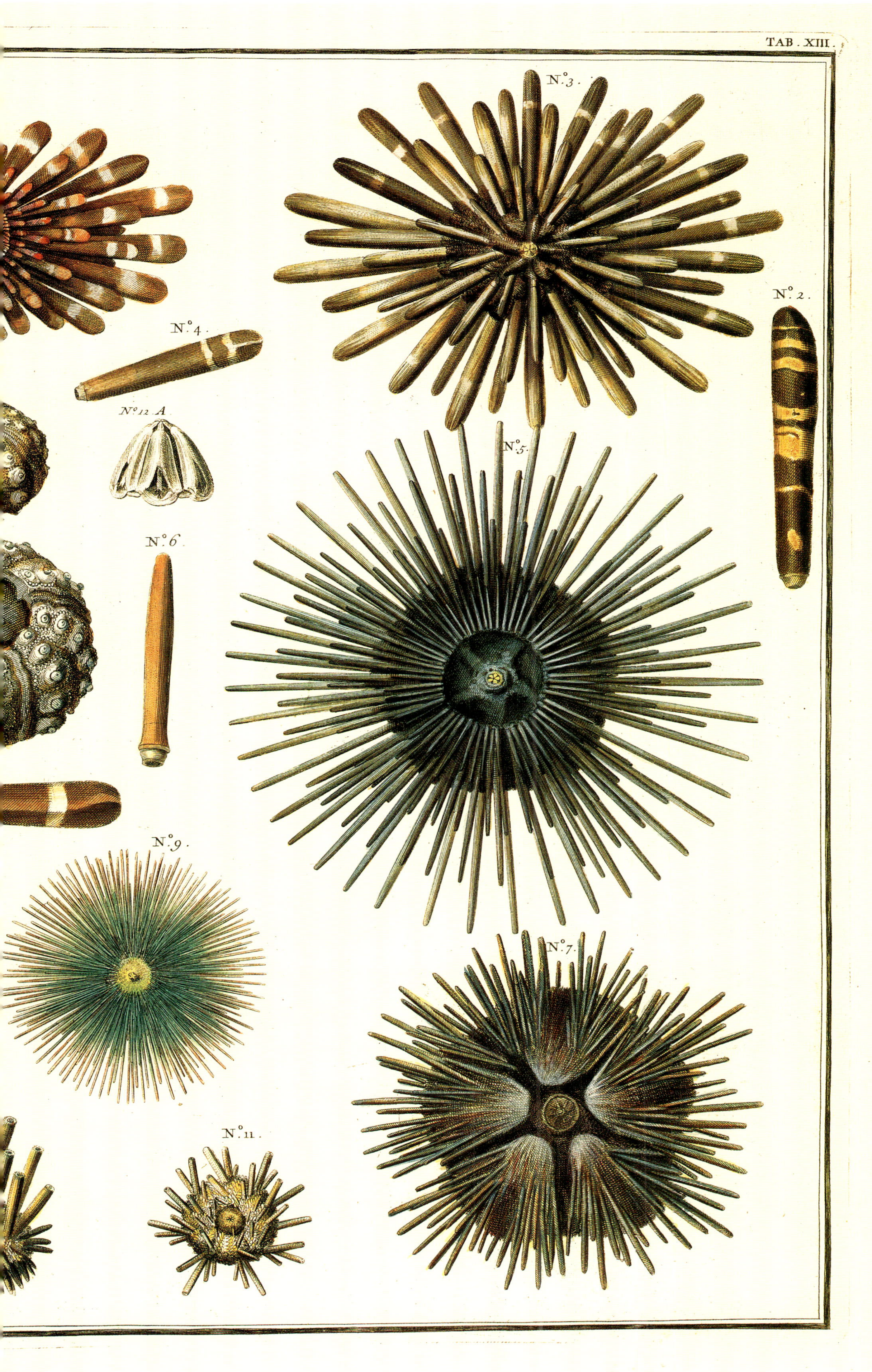
TAB. XIII.
N.° 3.
N.° 2.
N.° 4.
N.° 12 A.
N.° 5.
N.° 6.
N.° 9.
N.° 7.
N.° 11.

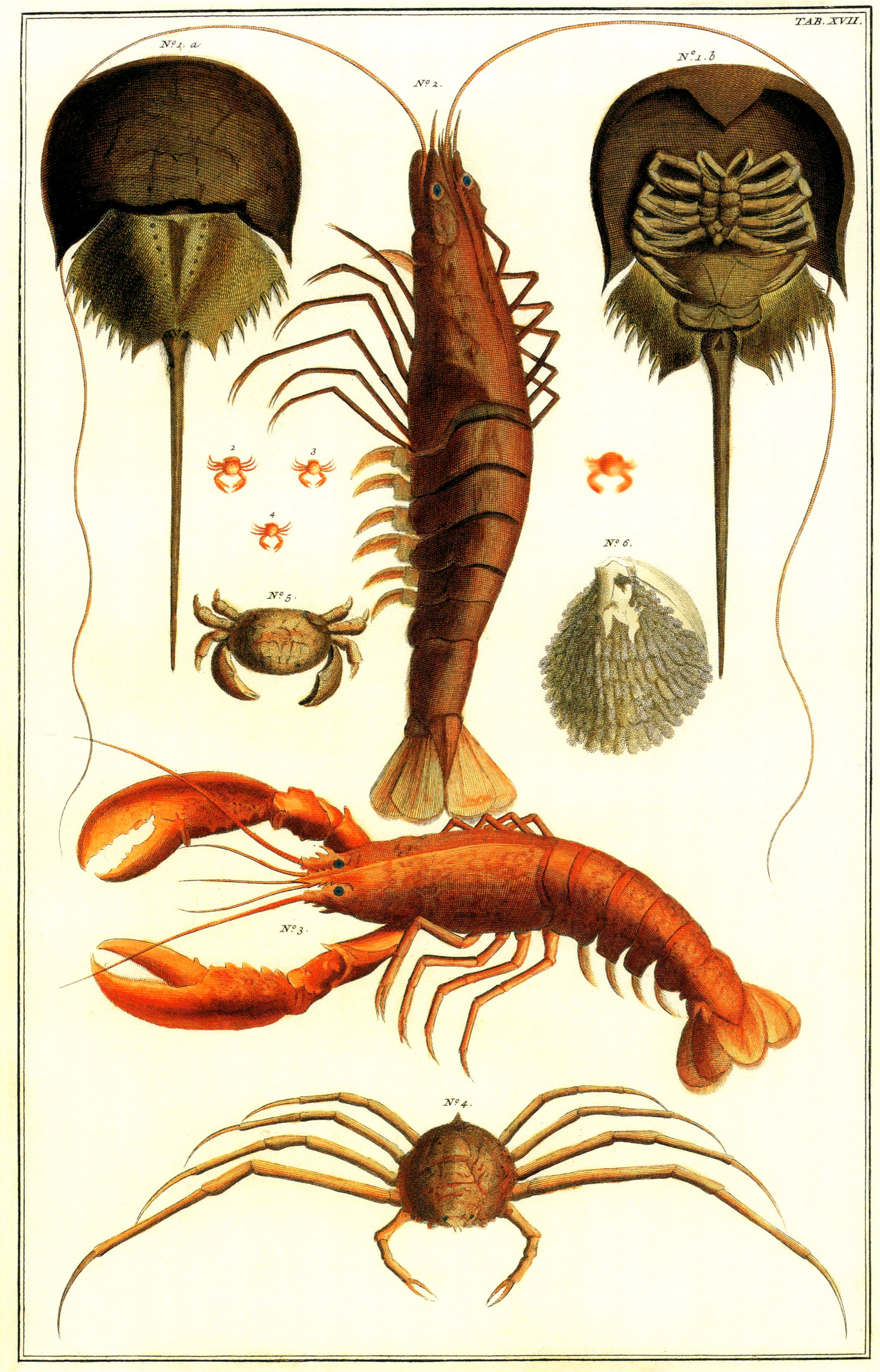

N° 1a, b Xiphosura **N° 2** Penaeidae **N° 3** Homarus **N° 4** Majidae **N° 5** Brachyura **N° 6** Ovum **1-4** Porcellanidae

1a, b Horseshoe crab · Schwertschwanz · Limule (Xiphosure) **2** Penaeid shrimp · Geißelgarnele · Crevette pénéide **3** Lobster · Hummer · Homard **4** Spider crab · Dreieckskrabbe/Seespinne · Araignée de mer **5** Crab · Kurzschwanzkrebs/Echte Krabbe · Crabe **6** Eggs of a crab · Eier eines Krebses · Œufs de crabe **1-4** Porcelain crabs · Porzellankrebse · Crabes porcelaines

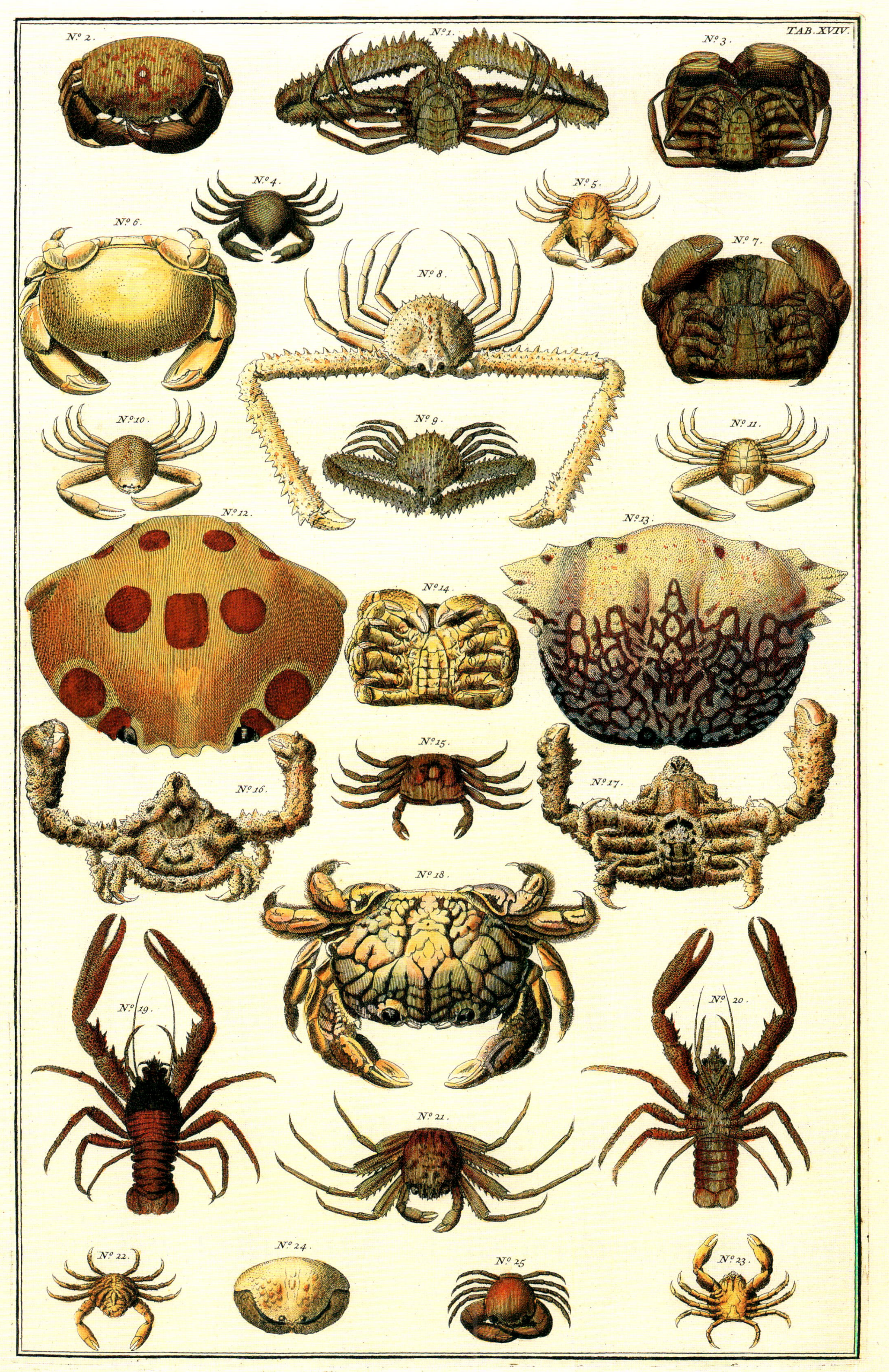

1, 8-9, 16-17 Parthenopidae **2-3, 6-7, 10-11, 14-15, 24-25** Brachyura **4-5** Leucosiidae **12, 18** Xanthidae **13** Calappidae **19-20** Galathe dae **21** Grapsidae **22-23** Majidae
1, 8-9, 16-17 Elbow crabs · Langarmkrabben/Ellbogenkrabben · Crabes parthenopidae **2-3, 6-7, 10-11, 14-15, 24-25** Crabs · Krabben · Crabes **4-5** Purse crabs/Nut crabs/Pepple crabs · Kugelkrabben · Crabes leucosiidae **12, 18** Xanthid crabs/Mud crabs · Rundkrabben · Xanthidés **13** Box crab · Schamkrabbe · Crabe honteux **19-20** Squat lobsters · Furchenkrebse · Galathée **21** Rock crab · Springkrabbe · Grapsidé **22-23** Spider crabs · Dreieckskrabben/Seespinnen · Araignées de mer

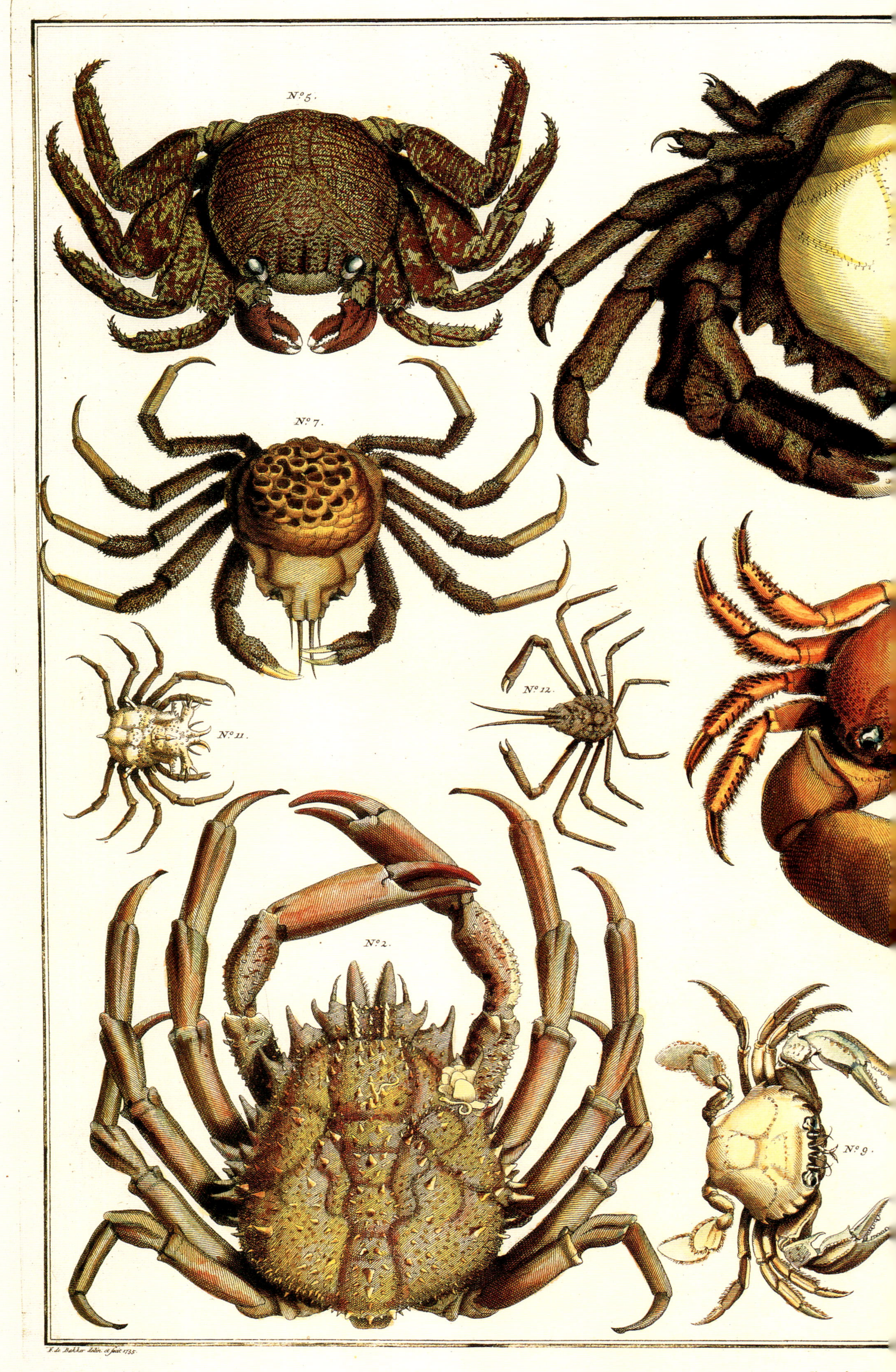

1 Dromiidae **2-3, 7, 11-12** Majidae **4** Gecarcinidae **5-6** Grapsidae **8** *Uca* **9** Portunidae **10** Lithodidae **13** Brachyura

1 Dromid crab · Wollkrabbe · Dromie velue/Dromidé **2-3, 7, 11-12** Spider crabs · Dreieckskrabben/Seespinnen · Araignées de mer **4** Land crab · Landkrabbe · Gécarcinidé **5-6** Rock crabs · Springkrabben · Grapsidés **8** Fiddler crab · Winkerkrabbe · Crabe à signaux **9** Swimming crab · Schwimmkrabbe · Portunidé **10** Lithodid crab · Steinkrabbe · Lithodidé **13** Crab · Krabbe · Crab

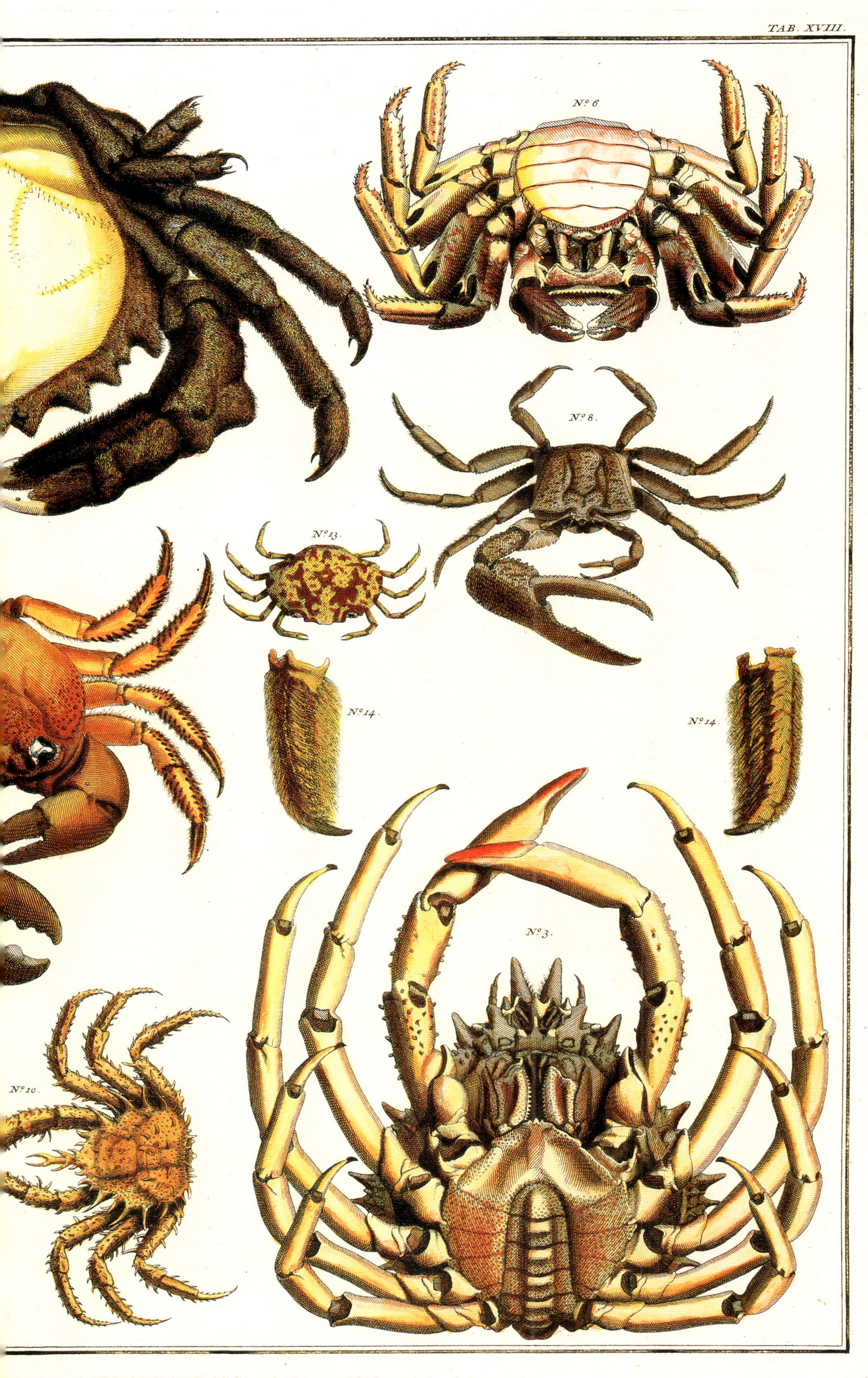
N.° 6
N.° 8
N.° 13
N.° 14
N.° 14
N.° 3
N.° 10

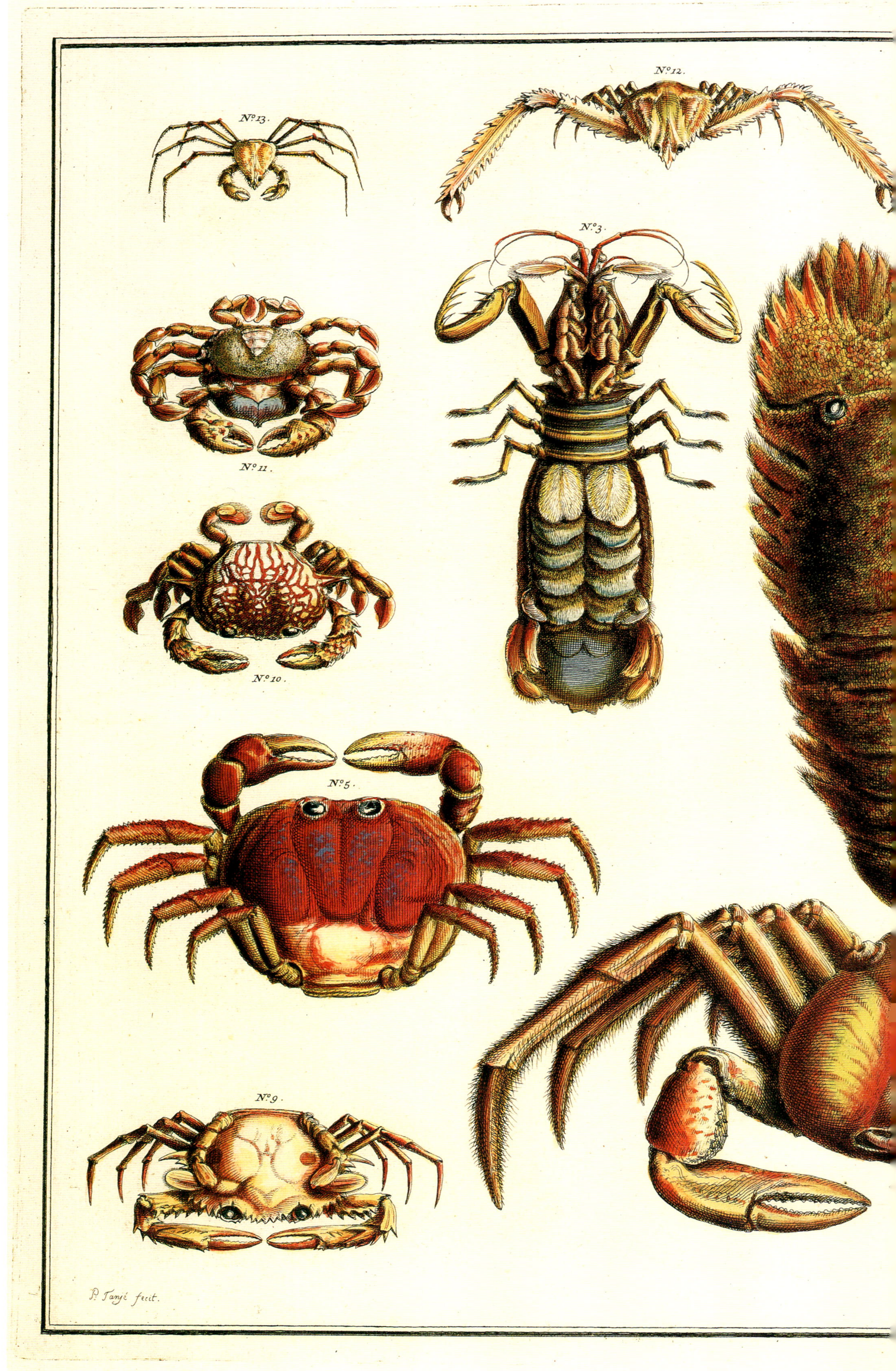

1 Scyllaridae 2-3, 6 Stomatopoda 4-5 Gecarcinidae 7-8, 10-11 Calappidae 9 Portunidae 12 Parthenopidae 13 Majidae
1 Scyllarid · Bärenkrebs · Scyllaridé 2-3, 6 Stomatopods · Fangschreckenkrebse/Maulfüßer · Stomatopodes 4-5 Land crabs · Landkrabben · Gécarcinidés
7-8, 10-11 Box crabs · Schamkrabben · Crabes honteux 9 Swimming crab · Schwimmkrabbe · Portunidé 12 Elbow crab · Langarmkrabbe/Ellbogenkrabbe · Crabe parthenopidae
13 Spider crab · Dreieckskrabbe/Seespinne · Araignée de mer

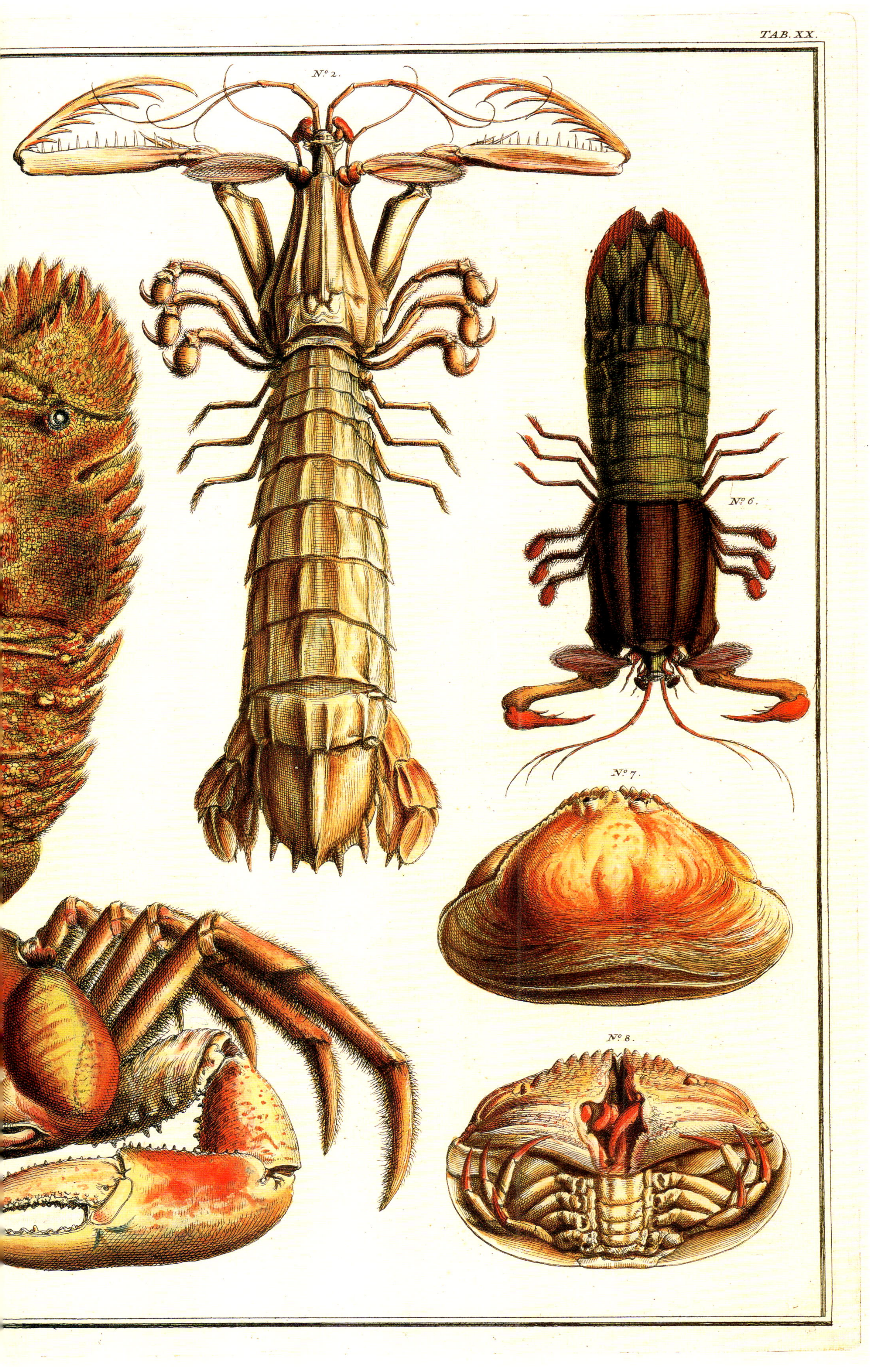
TAB. XX.
N.° 2.
N.° 6.
N.° 7.
N.° 8.

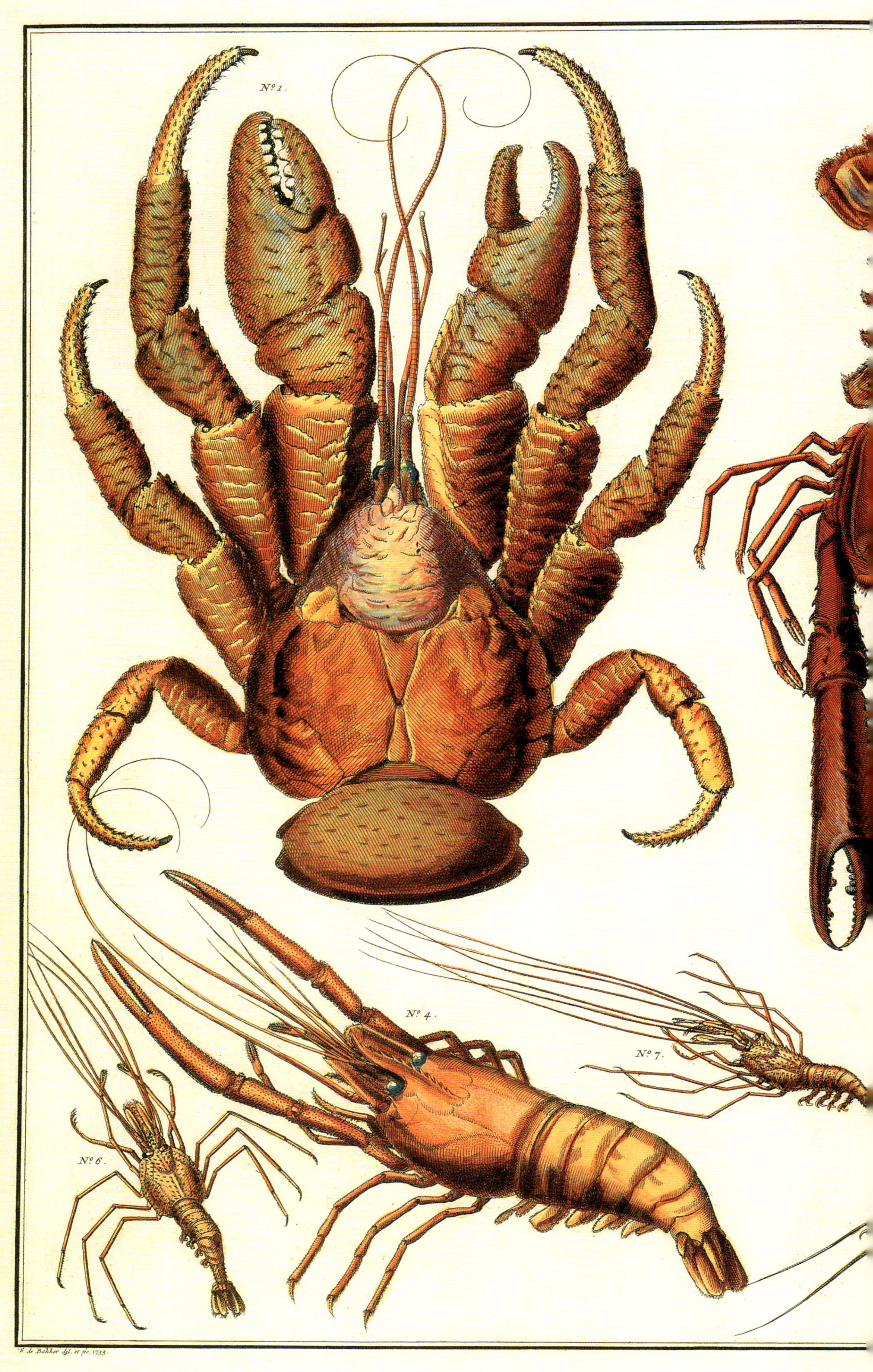

1-2 *Birgus latro* 3 *Nephrops norvegicus* 4, 9-10 Palaemonidae 5 Palinuridae 8 *Crangon crangon* 11 Amphipoda
1-2 Coconut/Robber crab · Palmendieb · Crabe des cocotiers 3 Norway lobster · Norwegischer Hummer/Kaisergranat · Langoustine 4, 9-10 Palaemonid shrimps · Felsengarnelen · Crevettes palémonides 5 Spiny lobster · Languste · Palinuridé 8 Common shrimp · Nordsee-/Sandgarnele · Crevette grise 11 Amphipod · Flohkrebs · Amphipode

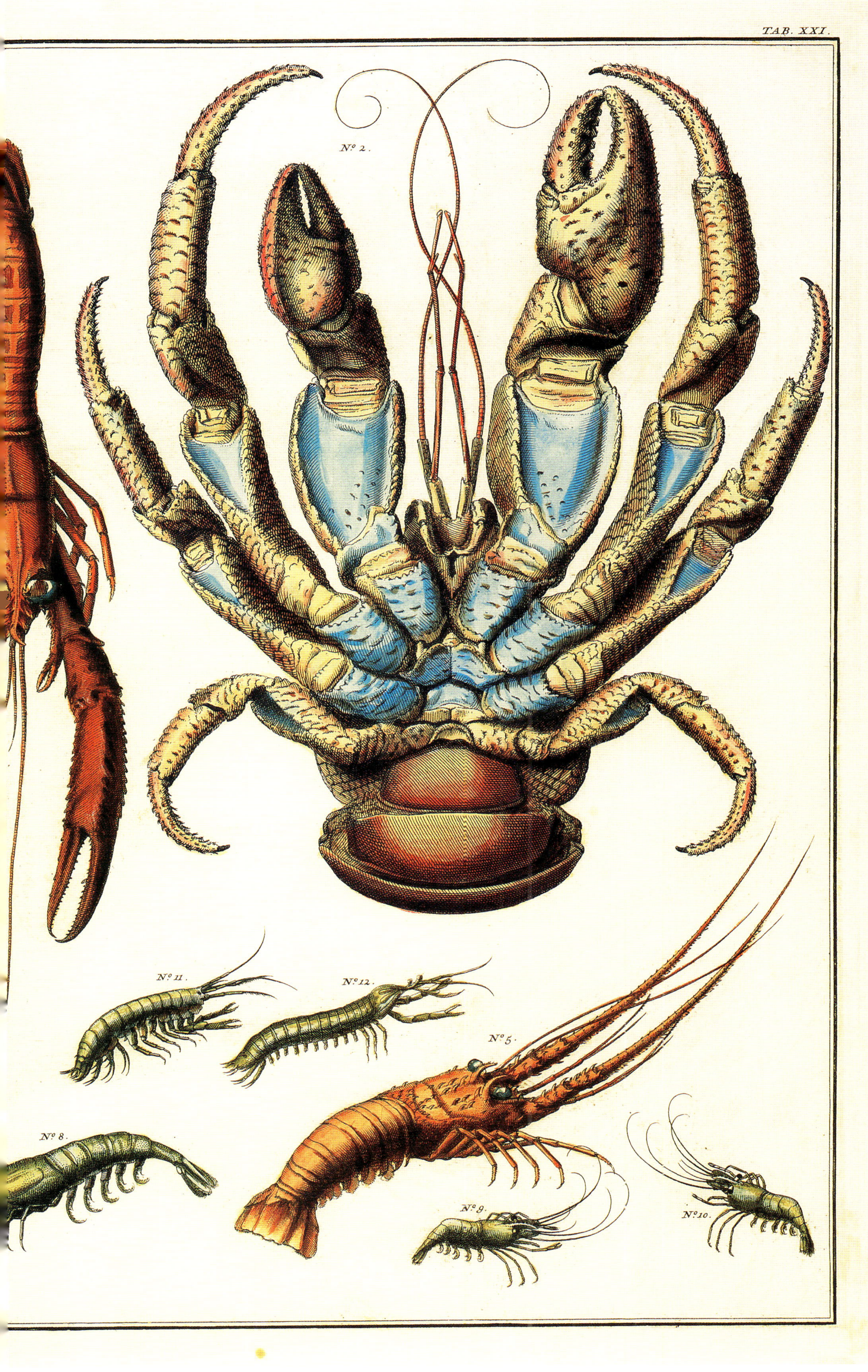
TAB. XXI.
N° 2.
N° 11.
N° 12.
N° 5.
N° 8.
N° 9.
N° 10.

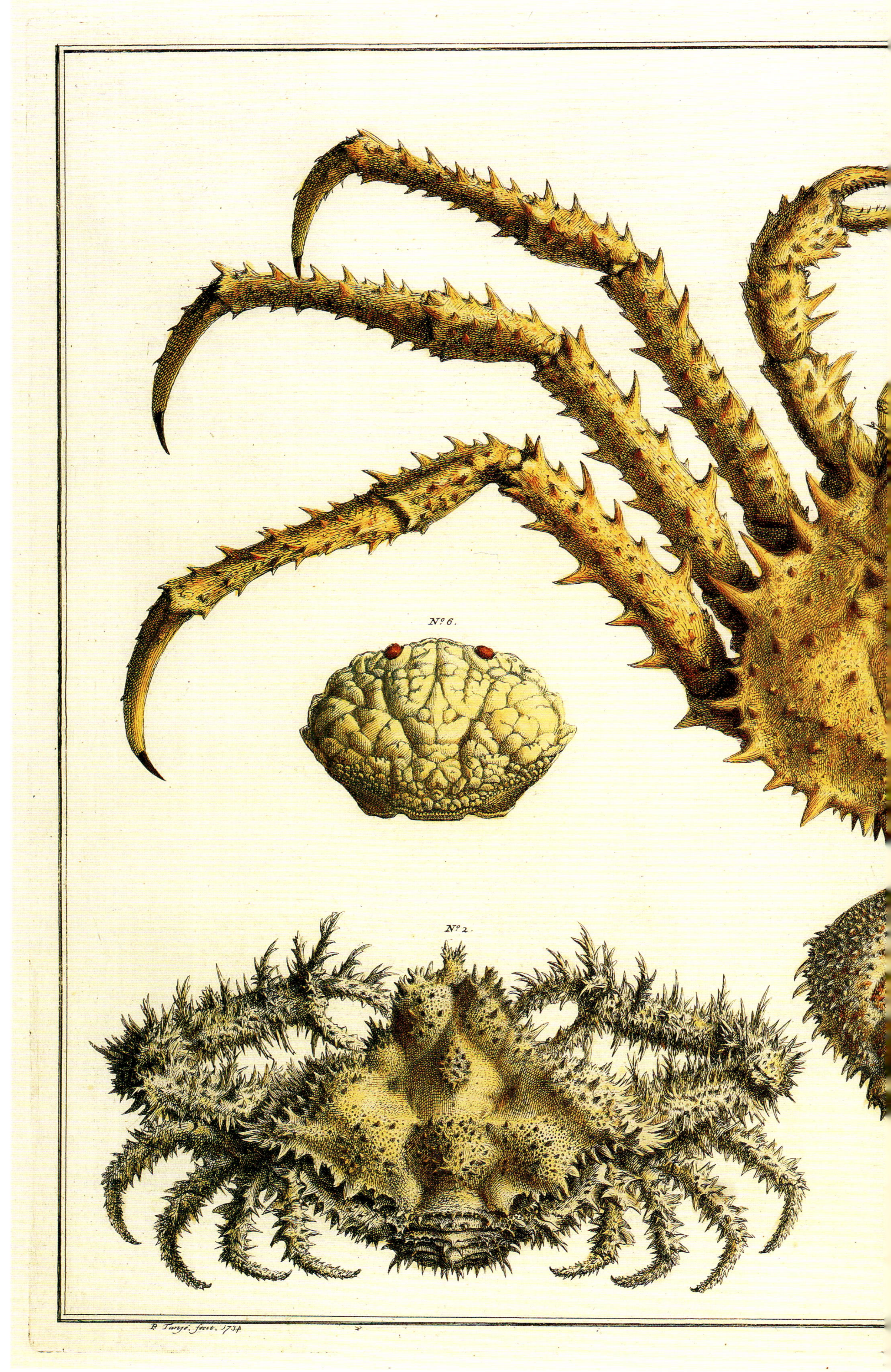

1 Lithodidae 2-3 Parthenopidae 4-6 Brachyura
1 Lithodid crab · Steinkrabbe · Lithodidé 2-3 Elbow crabs · Langarmkrabben/Ellbogenkrabben · Crabes parthenopidae 4-6 Carapaces of crabs · Rückenschilder von echten Krabben · Carapaces de crabes

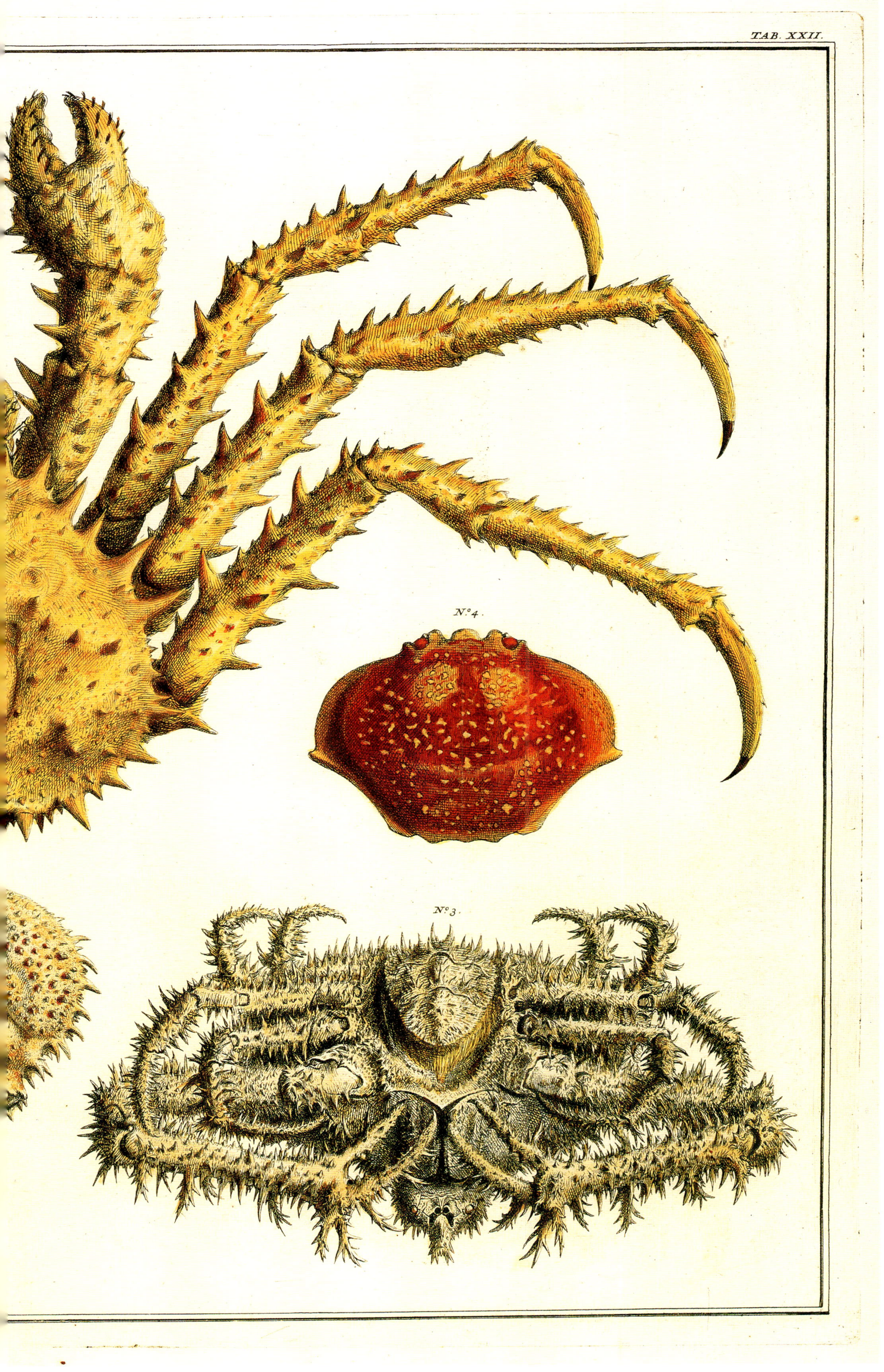
TAB. XXII.
N.° 4.
N.° 3.

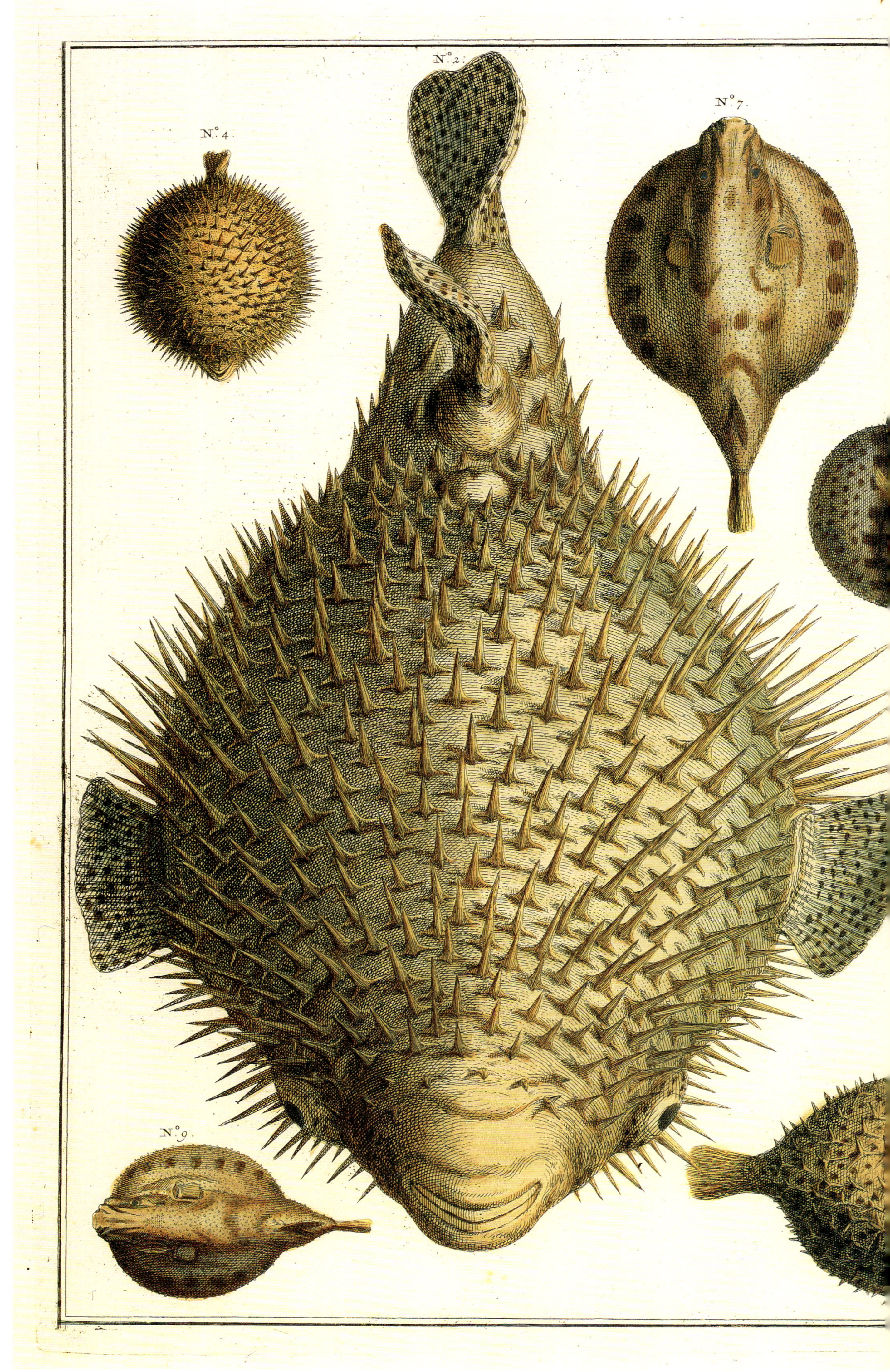

1-2 *Diodon hystrix* 3 *Chilomycterus reticulatus* 4 Diodontidae 5 *Lagocephalus lagocephalus* 6 *Colomesus psittacus* 7-8 Tetraodontidae
Partly poisonous puffer fish from tropical waters, which inflate themselves when threatened · Teilweise giftige Kugelfische aus tropischen Gewässern, die sich bei Bedrohung aufblasen · Poissons-globes des eaux tropicales, partiellement venimeux, qui se gonflent lorsqu'ils sont menacés

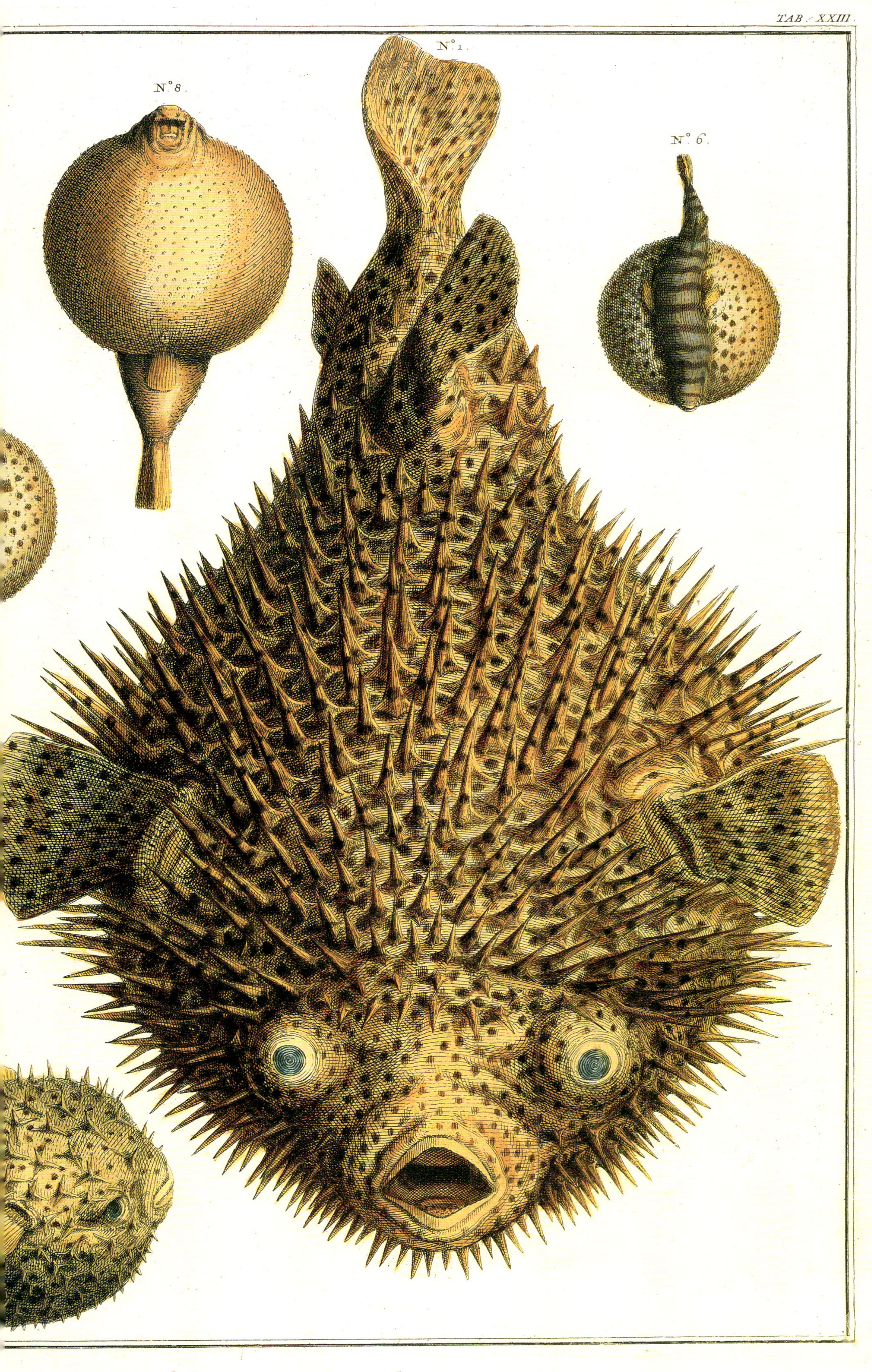
TAB. XXIII.
N°. 1.
N°. 8.
N°. 6.

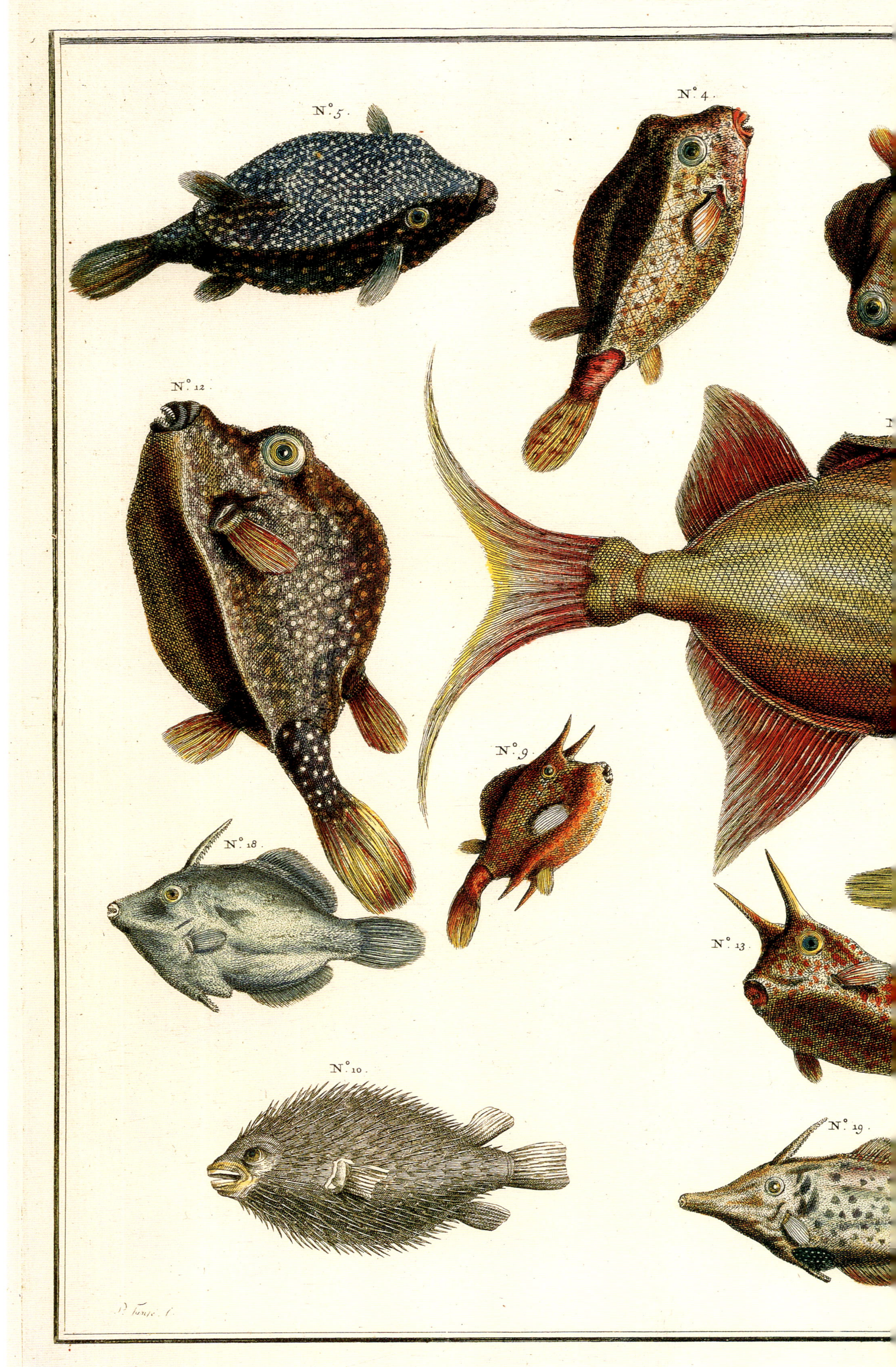

1-2 Tetraodontidae 3-9, 11-13 Ostraciidae 10 *Diodon hystrix* 14, 16 *Balistes* 15, 17 *Rhinecanthus* 18 *Acreichthys* 19 *Oxymonacanthus*
Chiefly tropical coral fish from the Atlantic and Indo-Pacific · Hauptsächlich tropische Korallenfische aus Atlantik und Indopazifik · Principalement des poissons tropicaux vivant dans les récifs de l'Atlantique et de l'aire indopacifique

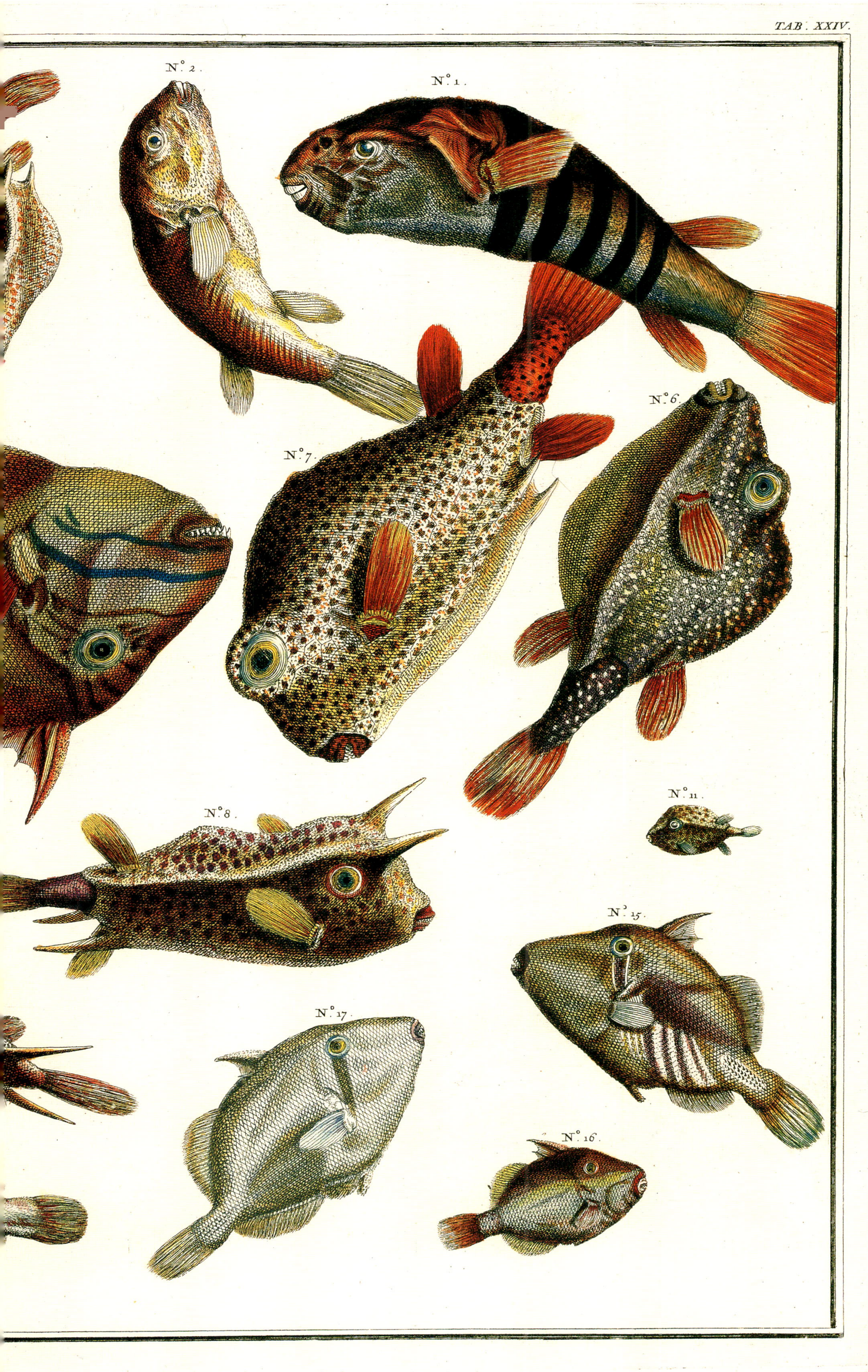
N°. 2.
N°. 1.
N°. 6.
N°. 7.
N°. 11.
N°. 8.
N°. 15.
N°. 17.
N°. 16.

1-4 *Acanthurus* 5 *Pomacanthus* 6-7 *Zanclus* 8 *Heniochus* 9-12, 16, 18 *Chaetodon* 13-14 Perciformes 15 *Platax* 17 *Chelmon*
Tropical coral fish from the Caribbean and Indo-Pacific · Tropische Korallenfische aus Karibik und Indopazifik · Poissons tropicaux vivant dans les récifs aux Caraïbes et dans l'aire indopacifique

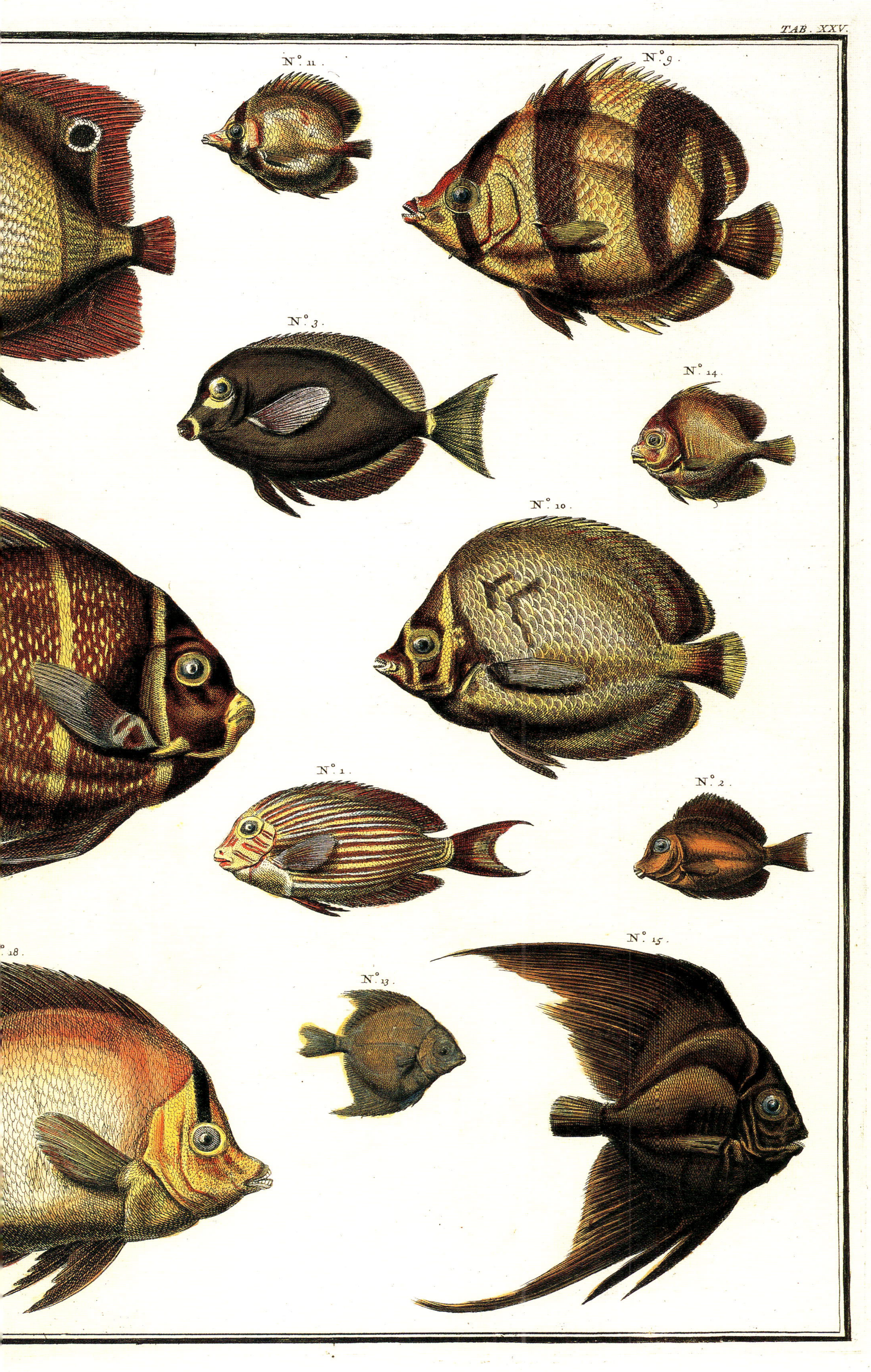
TAB. XXV.
N°. 11.
N°. 9.
N°. 3.
N°. 14.
N°. 10.
N°. 1.
N°. 2.
N°. 15.
N°. 13.
N°. 18.

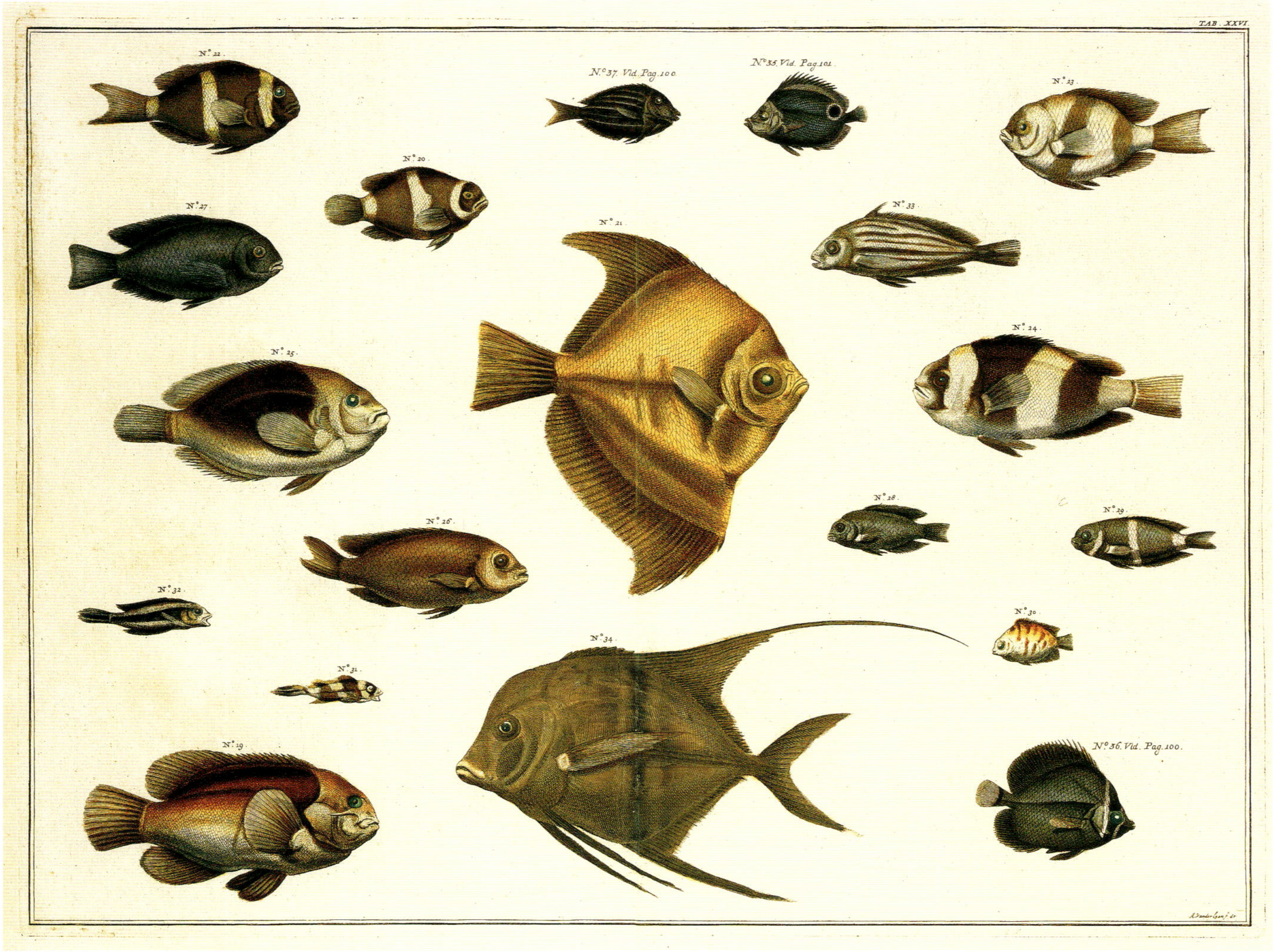

19 *Premnas biaculeatus* 20, 22, 24-25, 29 *Amphiprion* 21 *Monodactylus sebae* 23 *Dascyllus aruanus* 26-28 Pomacentridae 30-32 Perciformes 33 *Equetus acuminatus* 34 *Alectis ciliaris* 35-36 *Chaetodon*
Tropical coral fish from the Atlantic and Indo-Pacific · Tropische Korallenfische aus Atlantik und Indopazifik · Poissons tropicaux vivant dans les récifs dans l'Atlantique dans l'aire indopacifique

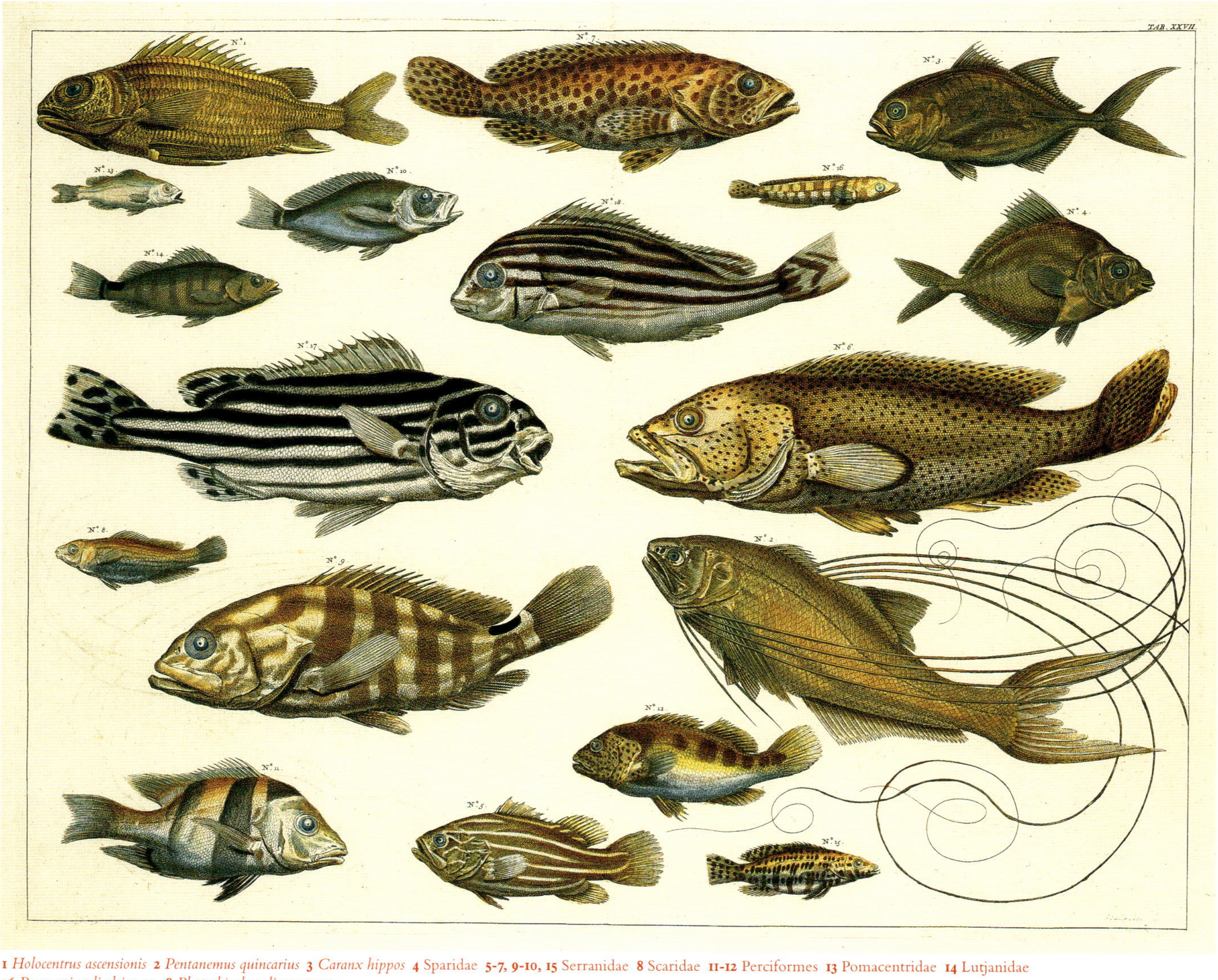

1 *Holocentrus ascensionis* 2 *Pentanemus quincarius* 3 *Caranx hippos* 4 Sparidae 5-7, 9-10, 15 Serranidae 8 Scaridae 11-12 Perciformes 13 Pomacentridae 14 Lutjanidae
16 *Parapercis cylindrica* 17-18 *Plectorhinchus diagrammus*
Tropical fish from the Atlantic and Indo-West Pacific · Tropische Fische aus Atlantik und Indo-Westpazifik · Poissons tropicaux de l'Atlantique et de l'océan Indien et du Pacifique occidental

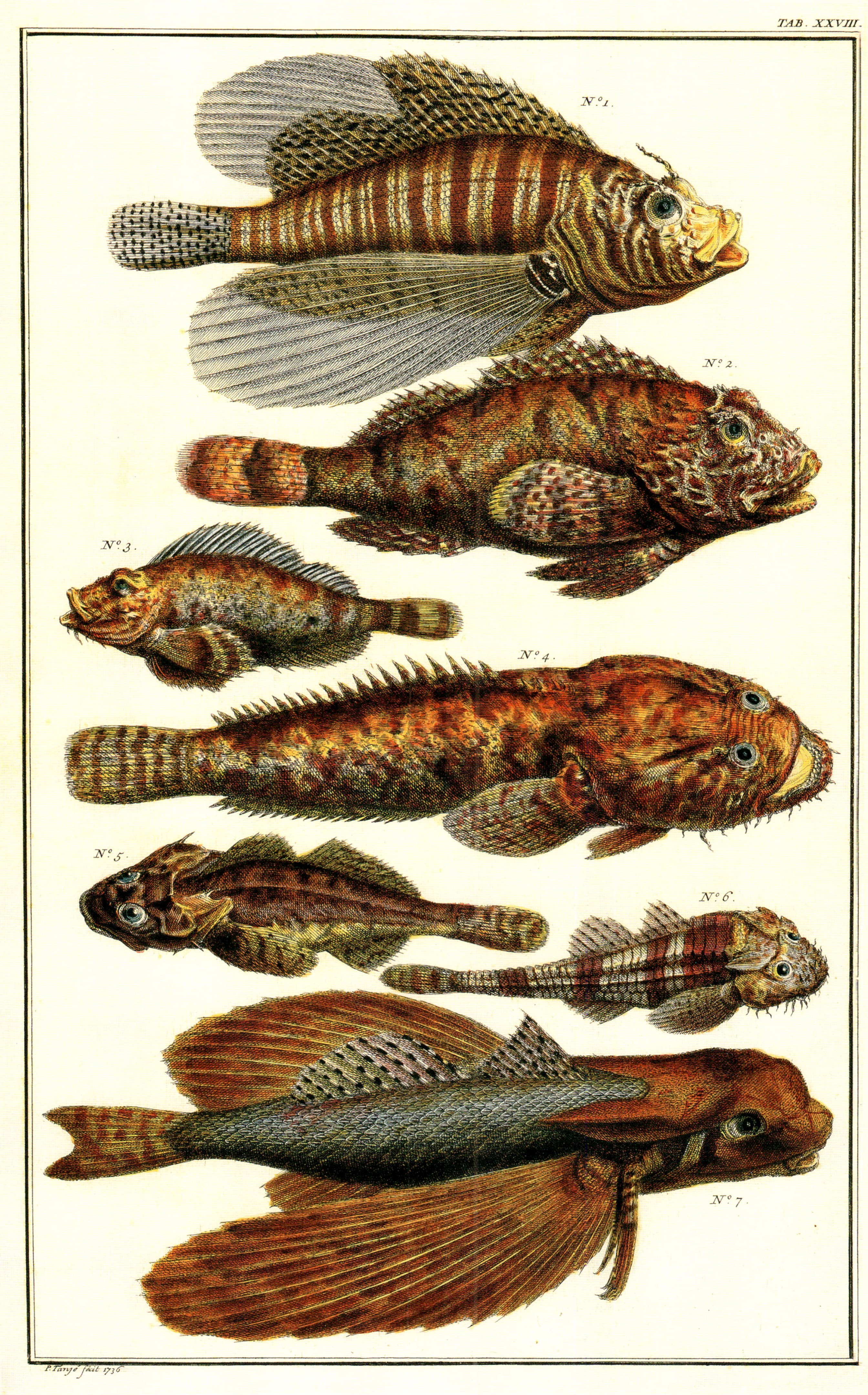

1 *Pterois volitans* 2 *Scorpaena porcus* 3 Scorpaenidae 4 *Allenbatrachus grunniens* 5 *Myoxocephalus scorpius* 6 *Agonus cataphractus* 7 *Dactylopterus volitans*
1 Red lionfish · Rotfeuerfisch · Laffe volant (Seychelles) 2 Brown scorpionfish · Brauner Drachenkopf · Rascasse brune 3 Scorpionfish · Drachenkopf · Rascasse 4 Frogfish · Froschfisch · Baudroie
5 Shorthorn sculpin · Gewöhnlicher Seeskorpion · Chaboisseau à épines courtes (Canada) 6 Hooknose · Steinpicker · Souris de mer 7 Flying gurnard · Flughahn · Poule de mer

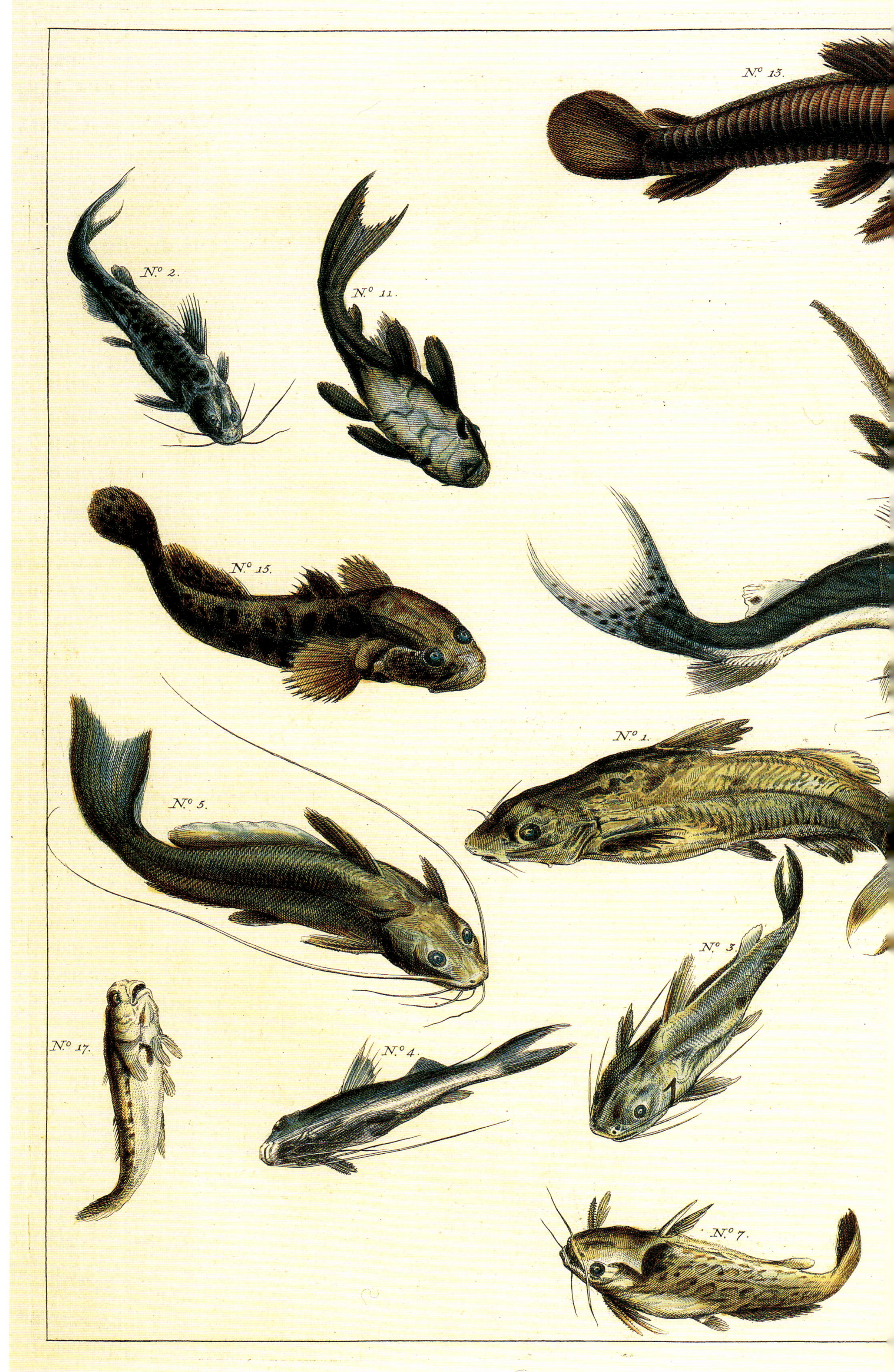

1-5, 8, 12, 17 Siluriformes **6** *Pseudoplatystoma* **7** *Trachelyopterus* **9-10** Aspredinidae **11, 14** Loricariidae **13** *Callichthys* **15-16** Gobiidae **18** Chaetodontidae **19** *Acipenser sturio*
Silurids found in fresh and brackish waters in the Amazon Basin and the north coast of South America · Welsartige Süß- und Brackwasserfische aus dem Amazonasbecken und von der Nordküste Südamerikas · Siluridés trouvés dans les eaux douces et saumâtres du bassin de l'Amazone et sur la côte nord de l'Amérique du Sud

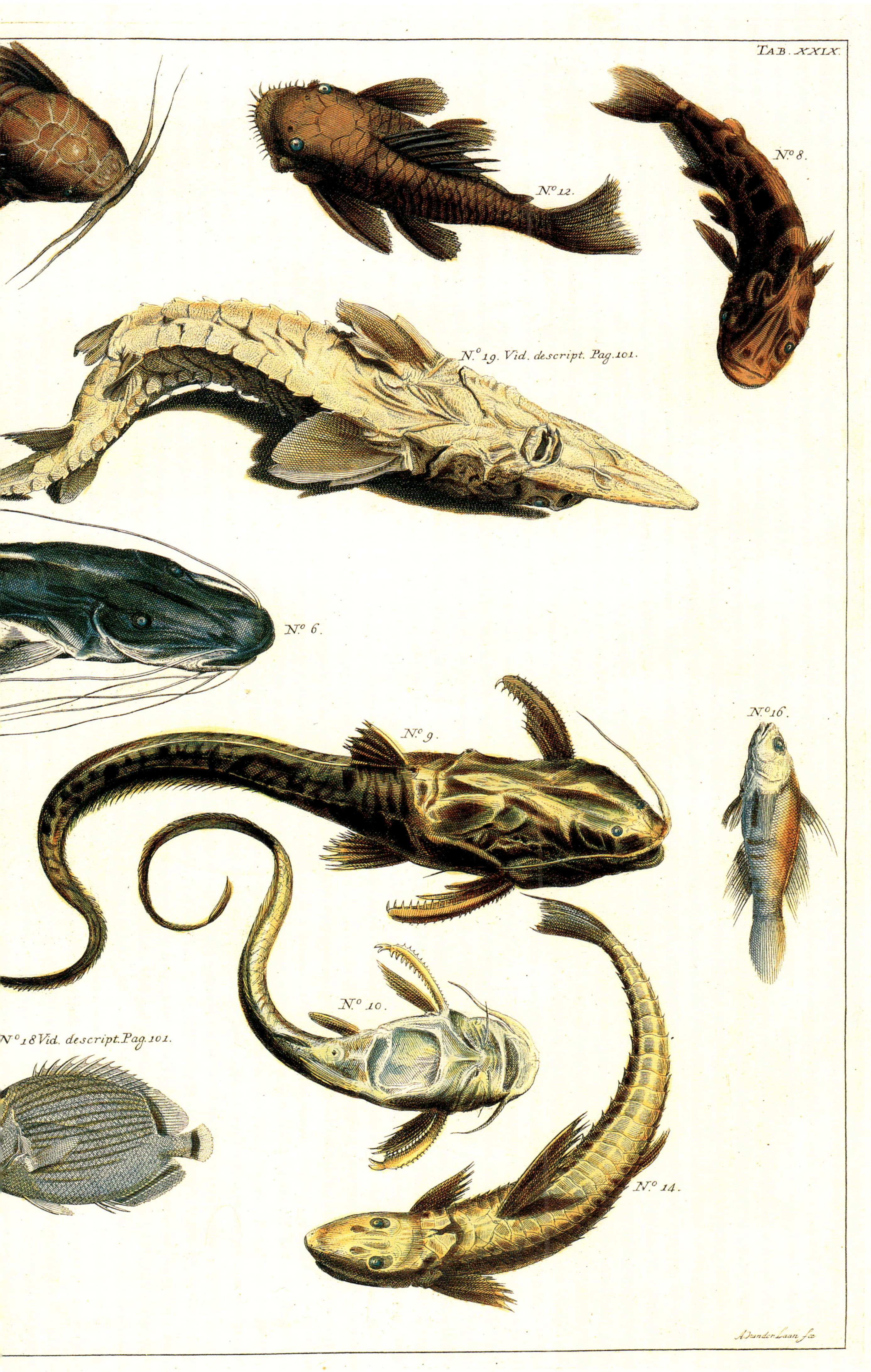
TAB. XXIX.
N.o 12.
N.o 8.
N.o 19. Vid. descript. Pag. 101.
N.o 6.
N.o 16.
N.o 9.
N.o 10.
N.o 18 Vid. descript. Pag. 101.
N.o 14.
A. van der Laan fec.

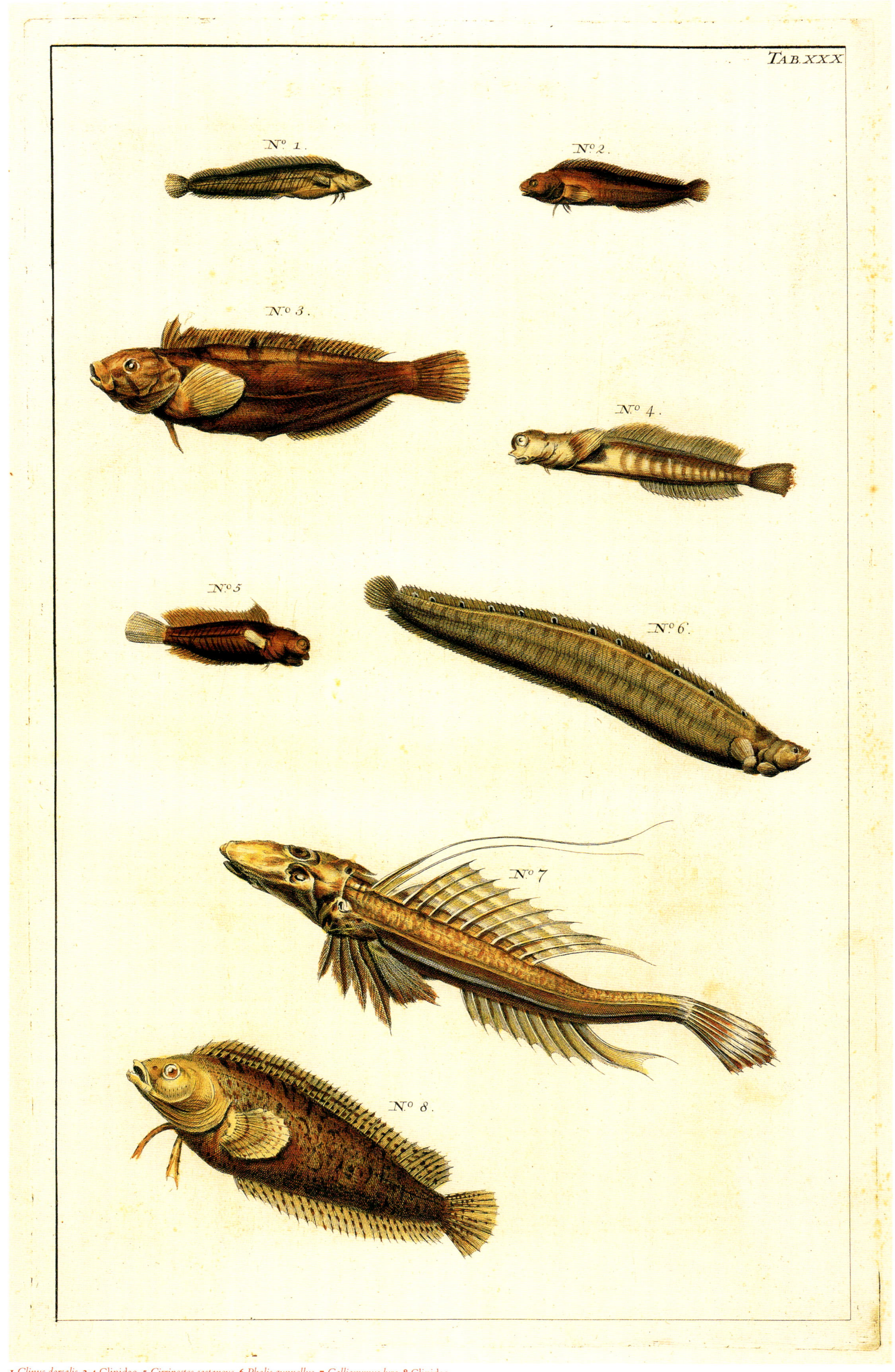

1 *Clinus dorsalis* 2-4 Clinidae 5 *Cirripectes castaneus* 6 *Pholis gunnellus* 7 *Callionymus lyra* 8 Clinidae
Rare fish from temperate waters of both hemispheres · Seltene Fische aus gemäßigten Gewässern beider Hemisphären · Poissons rares vivant dans les eaux tempérées des deux hémisphères

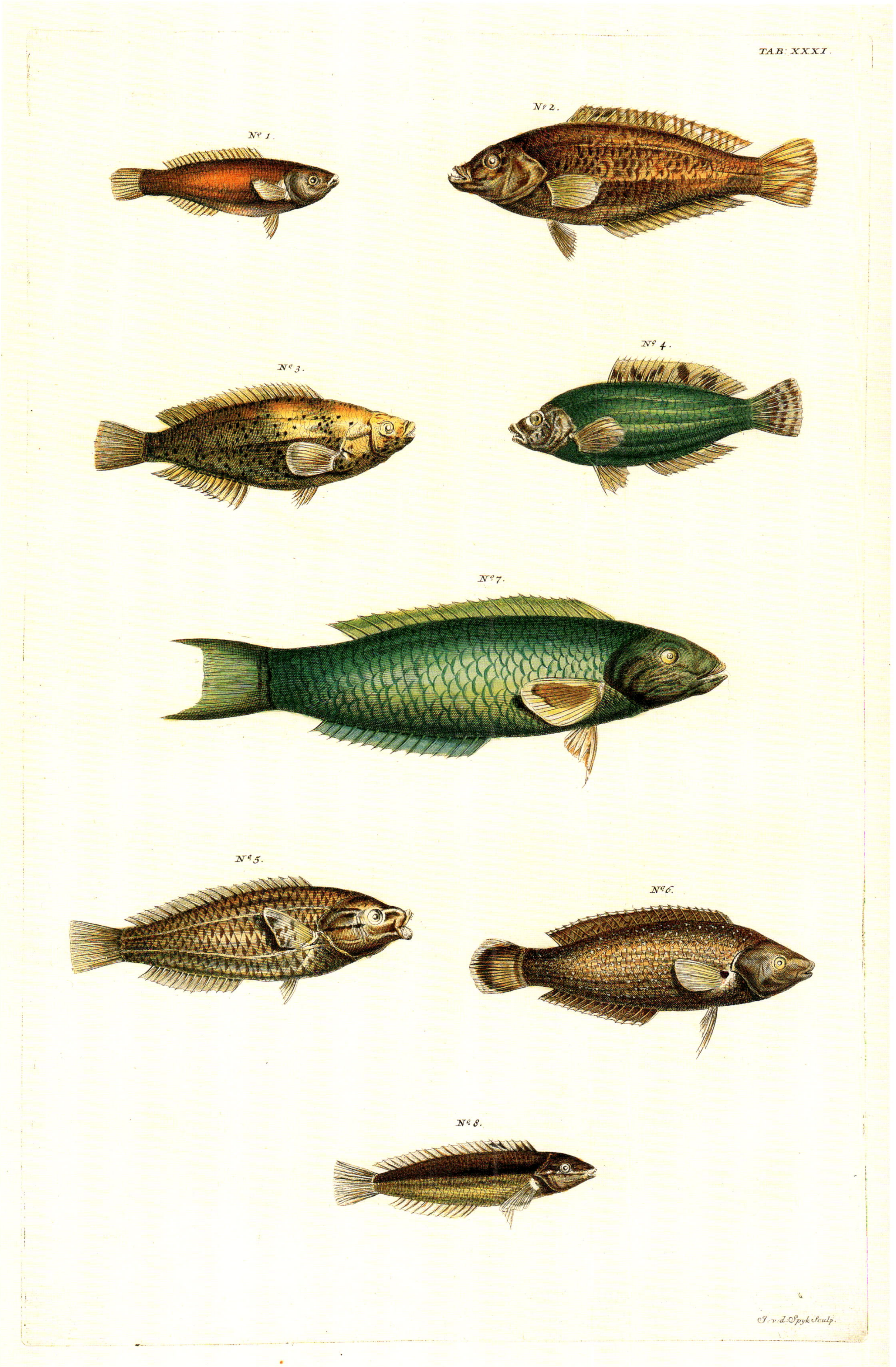

1-4, 8 Labridae 5 *Stethojulis trinlineata* 6 *Halichoeres leucurus* 7 *Thalassoma lunare*
Fish of the Labridae family, from Indo-Pacific coral reefs · Fische aus der Familie der Labridae, aus indopazifischen Korallenriffen · Poissons de la famille des Labridés, des récifs coralliens de l'aire indopacifique

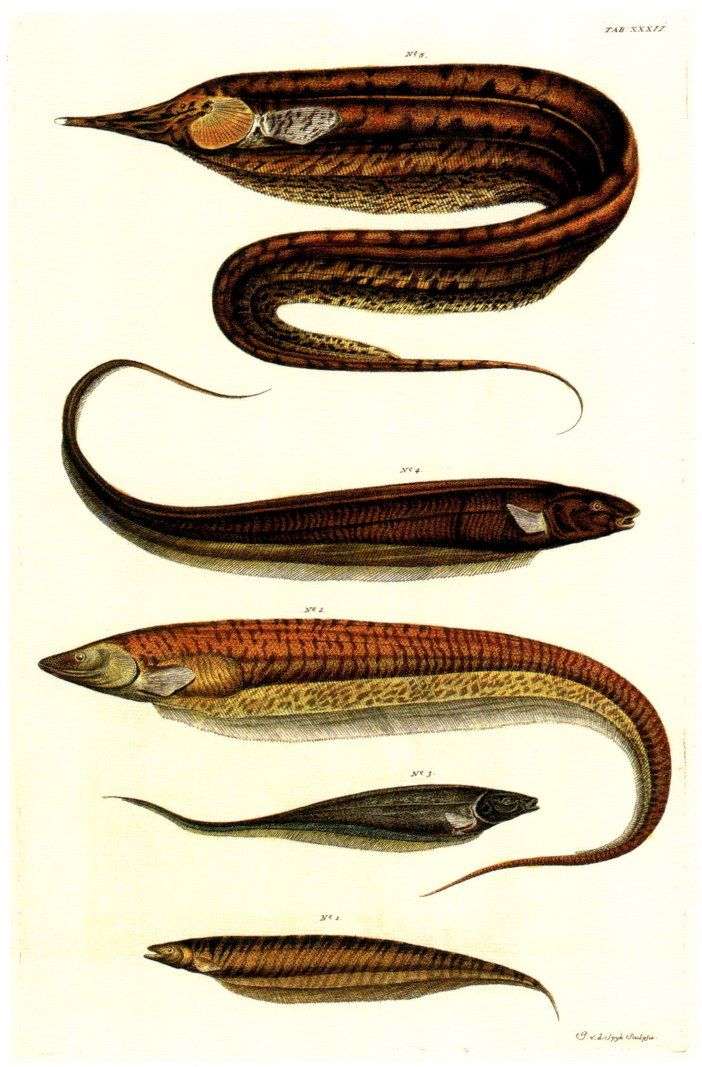

1 *Gymnotus carapo* 2 *Brachyhypopomus* 3 *Sternopygus astrabes* 4 *Sternopygus macrurus* 5 *Rhamphichthyes rostratus*
Weakly electric freshwater fish from the Amazon Basin or Surinam · Messerfische aus dem Amazonasbecken oder Surinam, die schwache elektrische Ströme aussenden · Poissons faiblement électriques des eaux douces du bassin de l'Amazone ou du Surinam

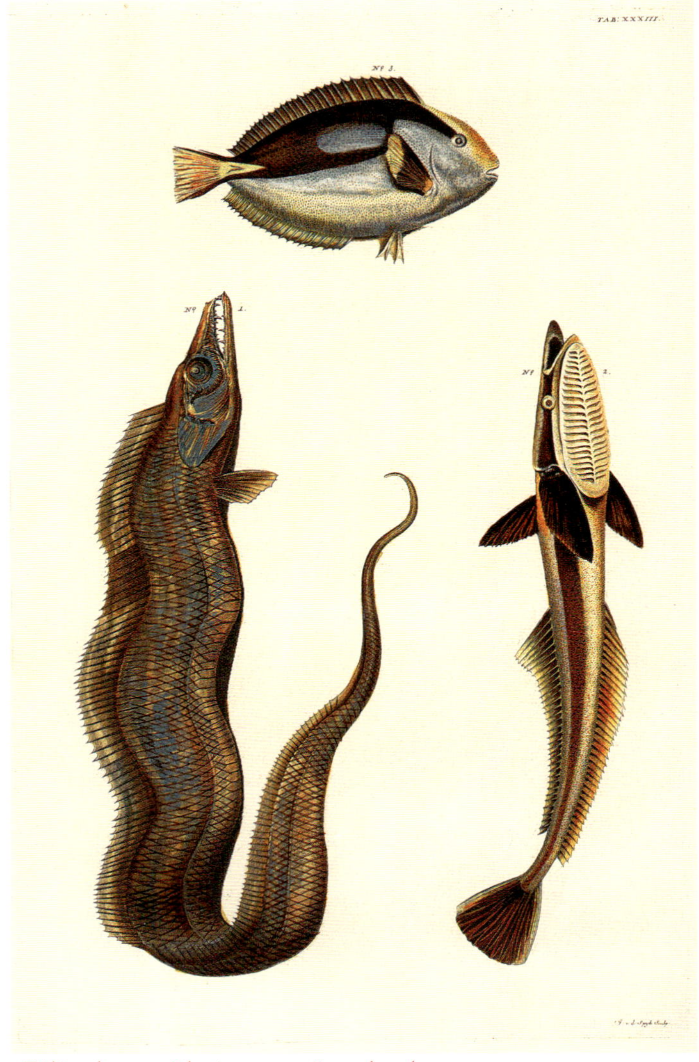

1 *Trichiurus lepturus* 2 *Echeneis naucrates* 3 *Paracanthurus hepatus*
Fish from tropical waters · Fische aus tropischen Gewässern · Poissons d'eaux tropicales

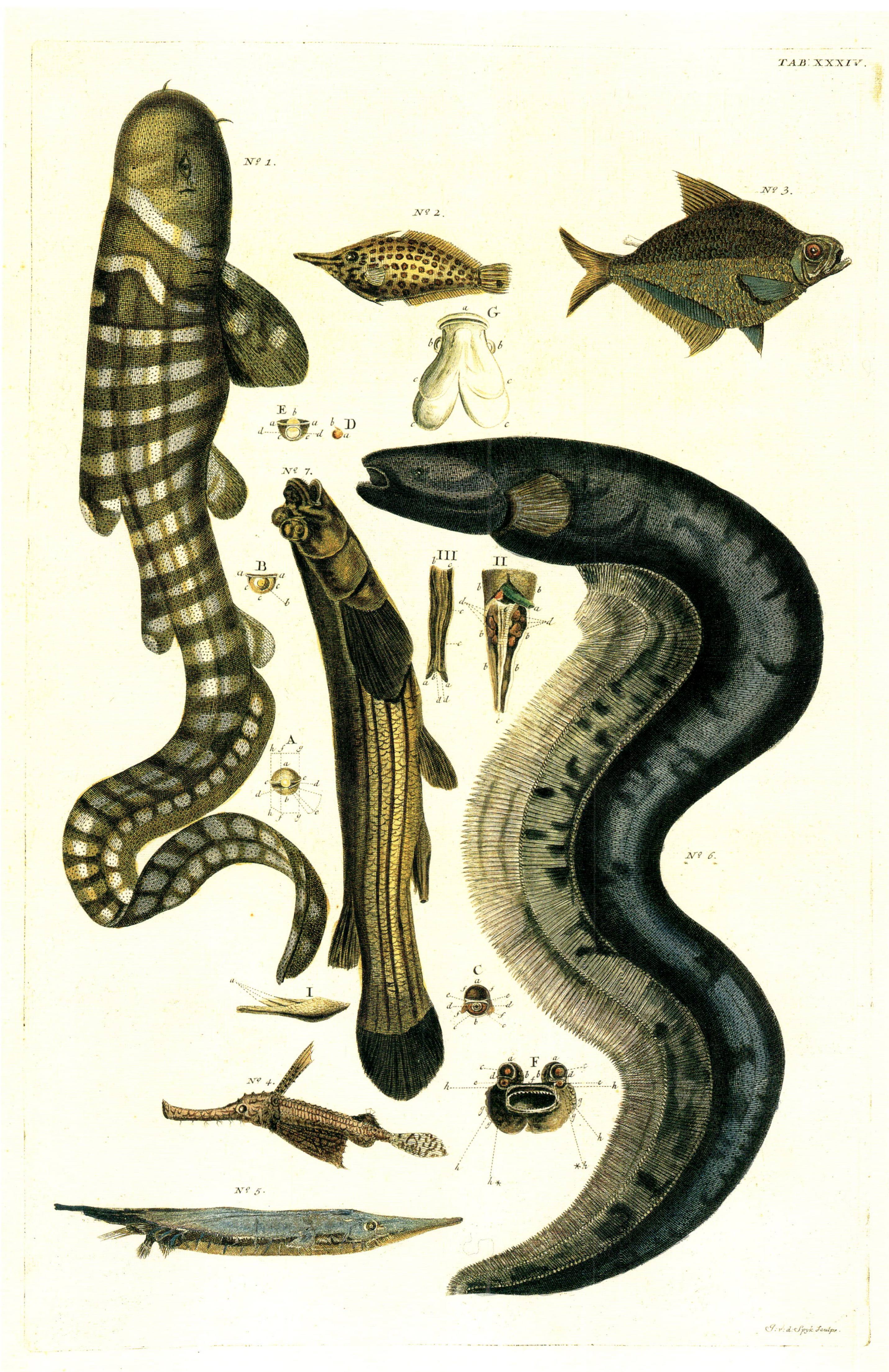

1 Stegostoma fasciatum 2 Stephanolepis hispidus 3 Astyanax bimaculatus 4 Solenostomus cyanopterus 5 Centriscus scutatus 6 Electrophorus electricus 7 Anableps anableps
1 Zebra shark · Pazifischer Zebrahai · Requin zèbre **2** Planehead filefish · Flachkopf-Feilenfisch · Baliste (Mauritanie) **3** Twospot astyanax · Rautensalmler · Yaya (Guyane française)
4 Ghost pipefish · Blauflossiger Röhrenmund **5** Grooved razorfish · Rassiermesserfisch · Poisson-rasoir **6** Electric eel · Zitteraal · Anguille tremblante (Guyane française)
7 Largescale foureye · Vieraugenfisch · Quatre-yeux à grandes écailles

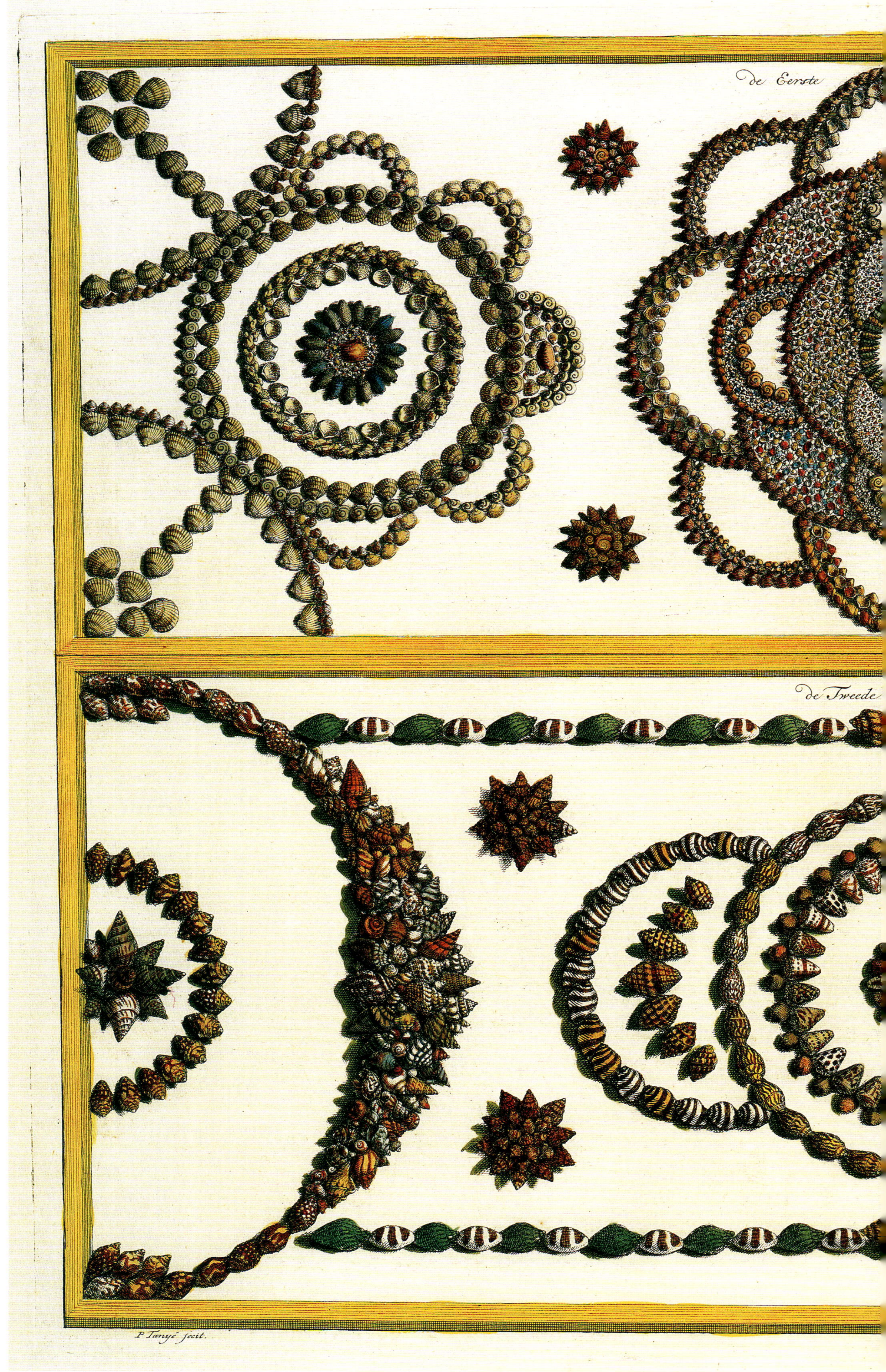

SEBA 1758: »Capsa prima & secunda, in quibus minutissnna Conchyliorum genera, areolarum in modum, concinne digesta exhibentur.«
Various mollusc shells arranged as ornaments · Verschiedene zu Ornamenten angeordnete Gehäuse von Weichtieren · Arrangements ornementaux de diverses coquilles de mollusques

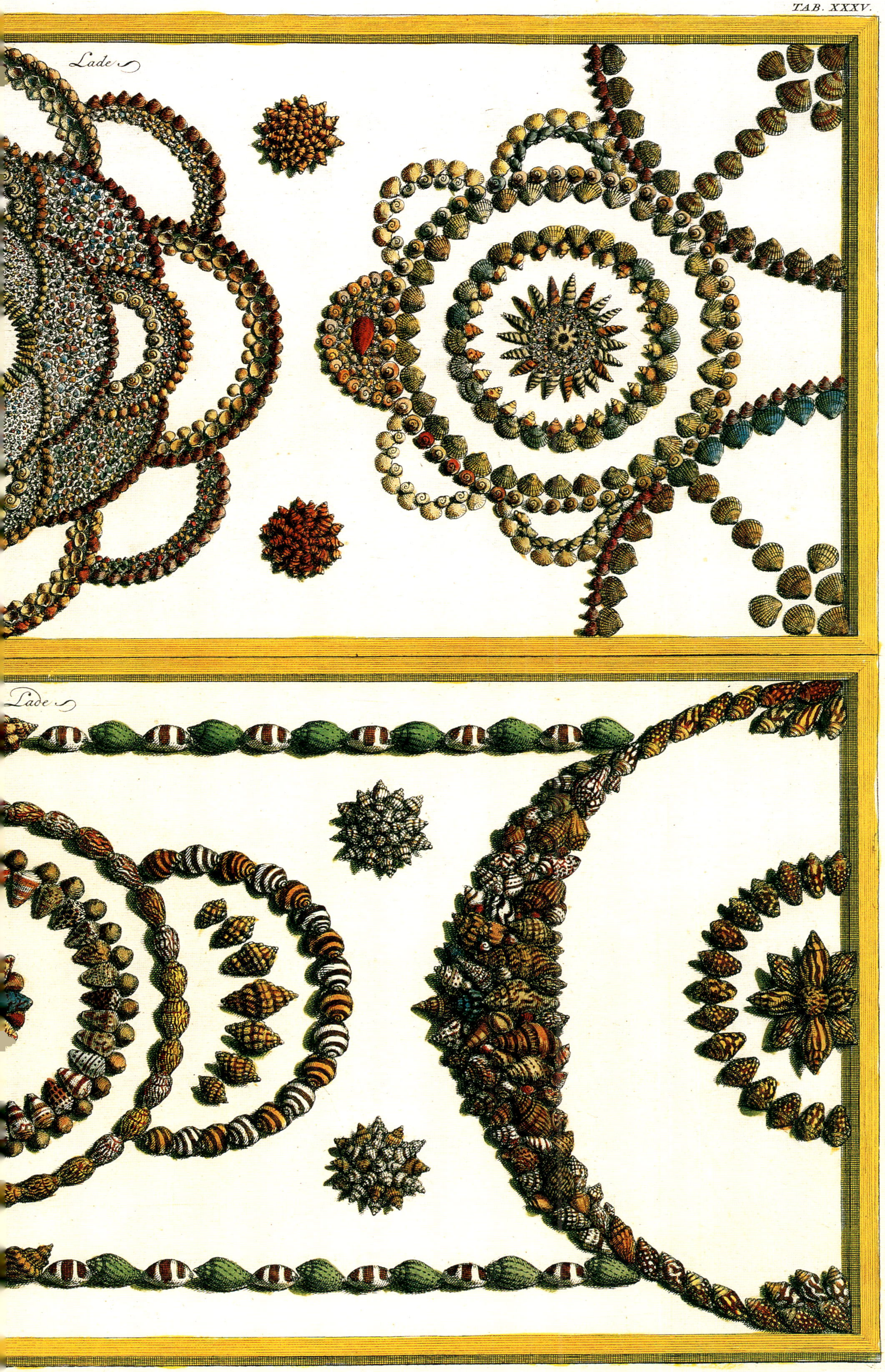

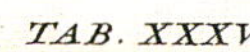

Lade

Lade

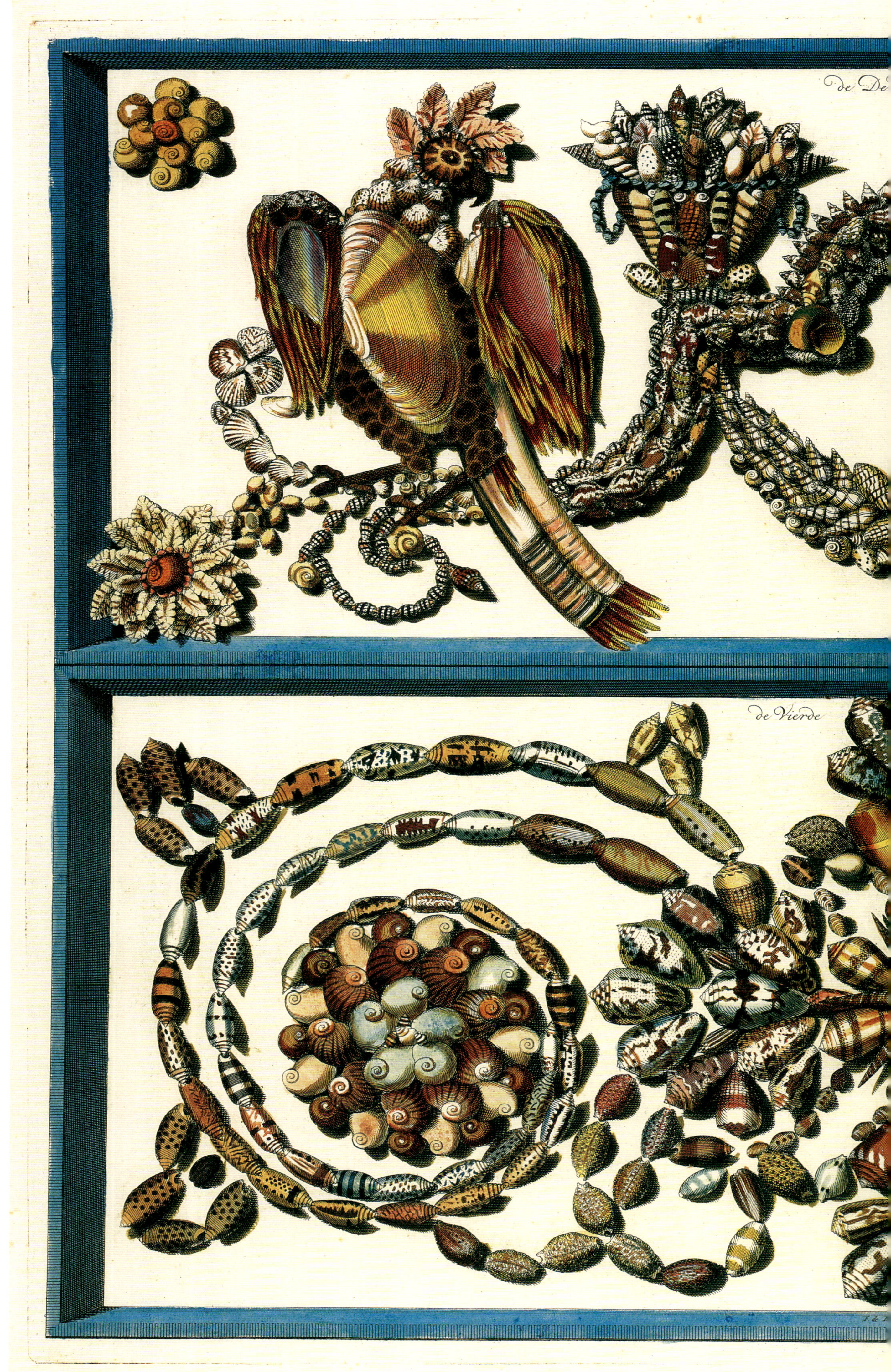

SEBA 1758: »Capsa tertia & quarta, quae majuseula Conchyliorum specimina, familiter, at diverso a superioribus ordine inter se composita monstrant.«
Various mollusc shells arranged as ornaments or garlands with pictorial motifs · Verschiedene zu Ornamenten und Girlanden mit bildhaften Motiven angeordnete Gehäuse von Schnecken und Muscheln · Arrangements ornementaux et en guirlandes de diverses coquilles de mollusques

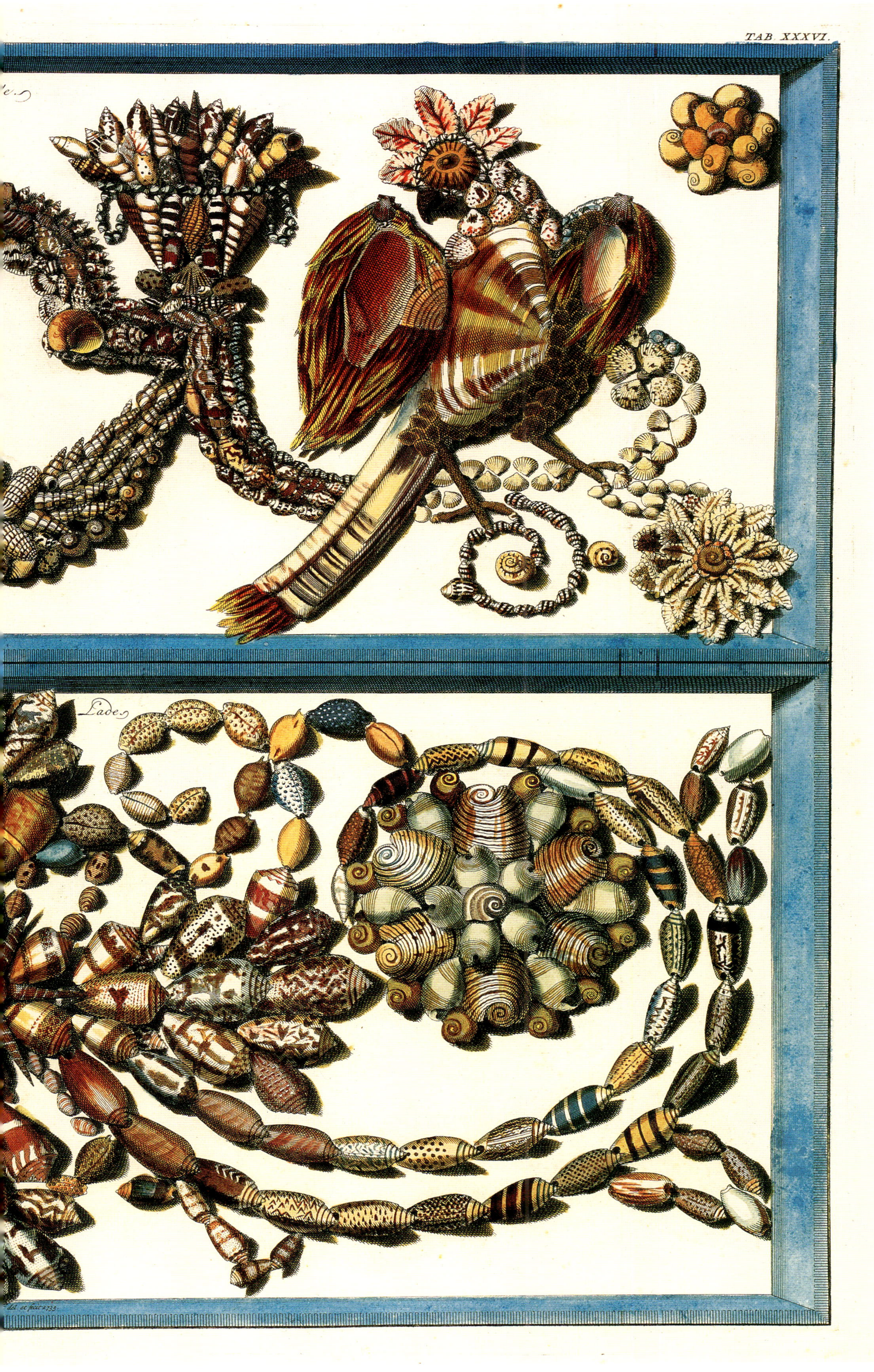
TAB XXXVI.
Lade

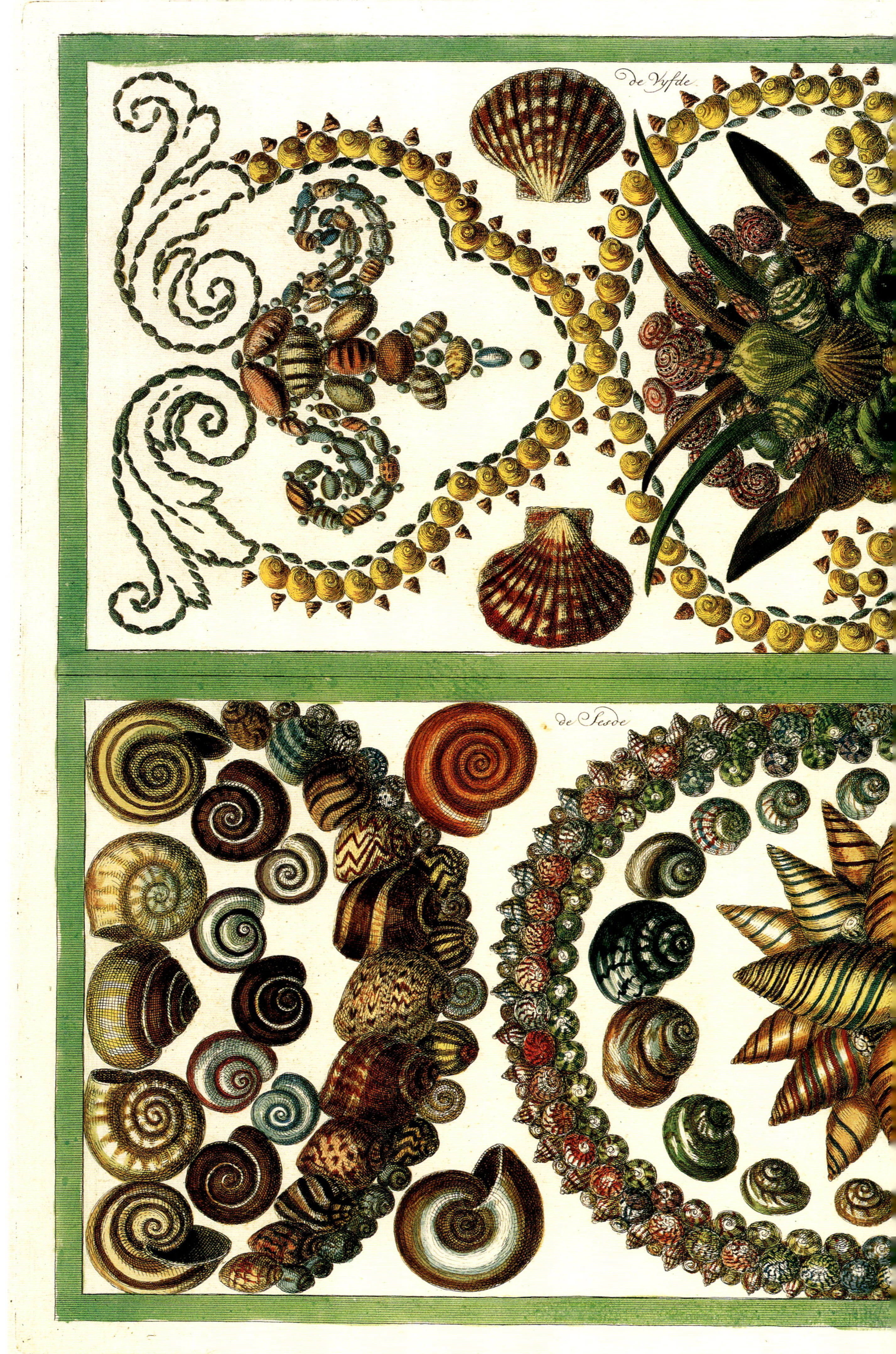

SEBA 1758: »Capsa quinta & sexta, Conchyliis, uti priores, sed alia rursus rationae dispositis, conspicae.«
Ornaments made with mollusc shells, depicting a stylised face · Ornamente aus Gehäusen von Weichtieren mit Darstellung eines stilisierten Gesichts · Arrangement ornemental de coquilles de mollusques représentant un visage stylisé

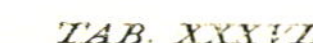
TAB. XXXVII.

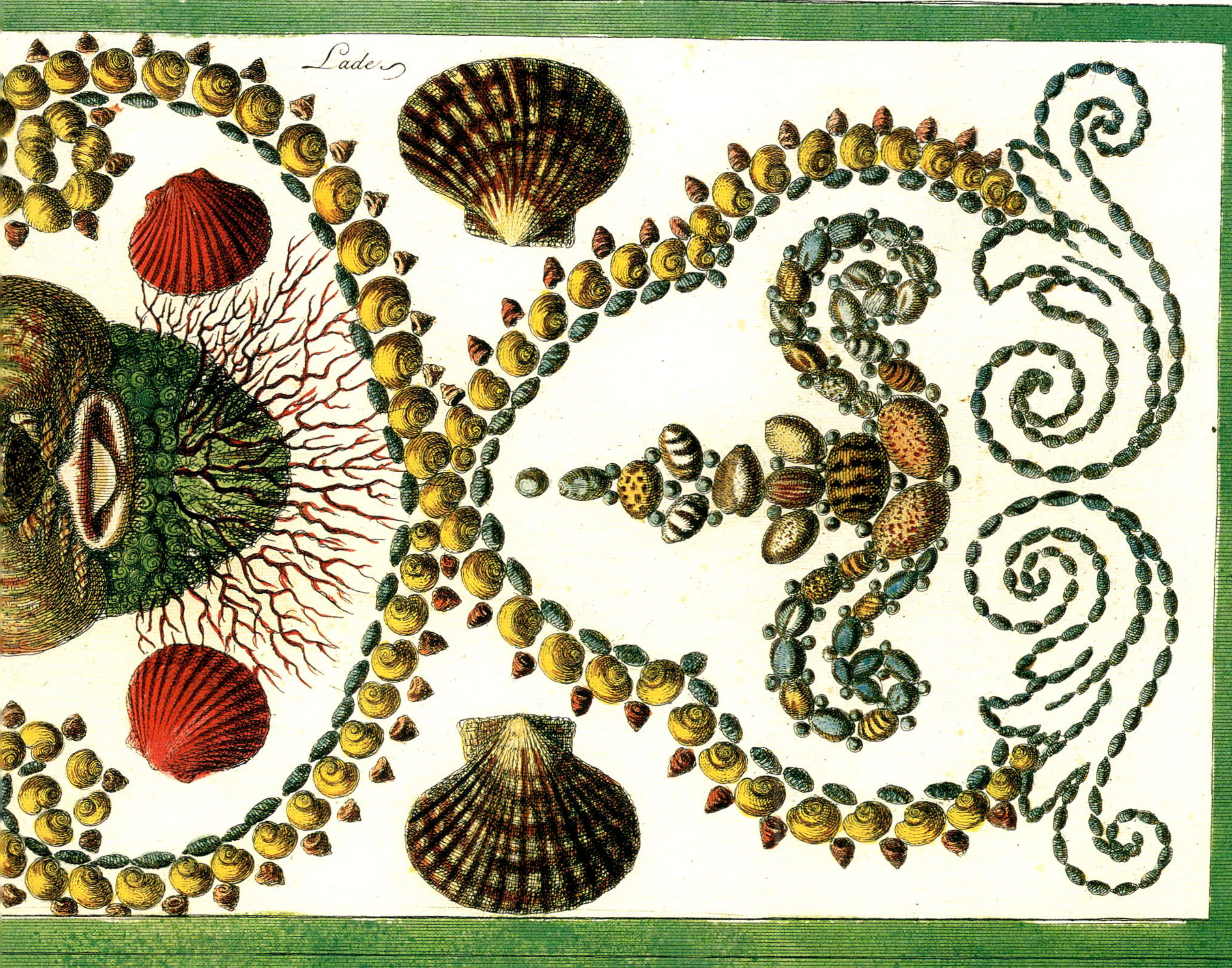
Lade

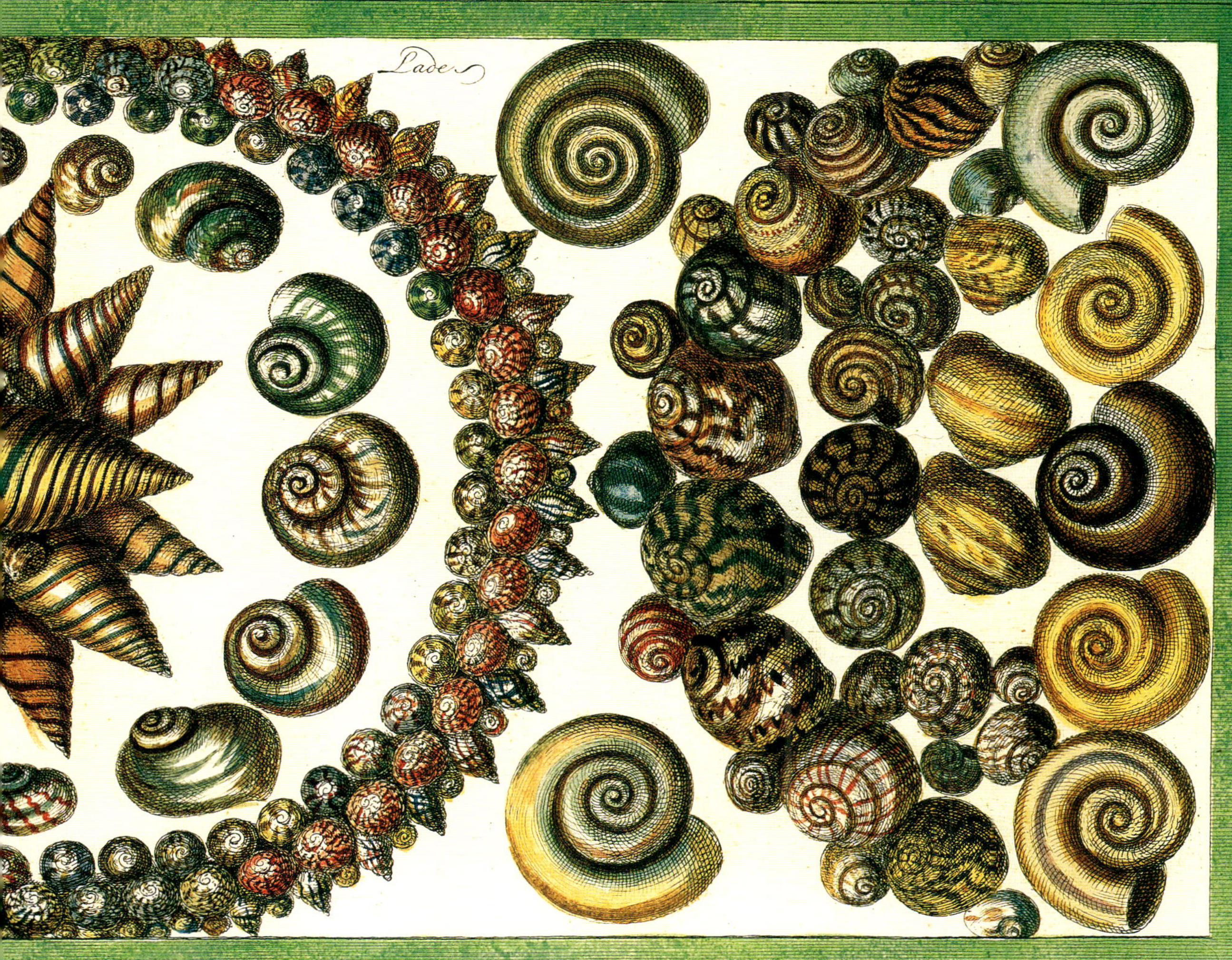
Lade

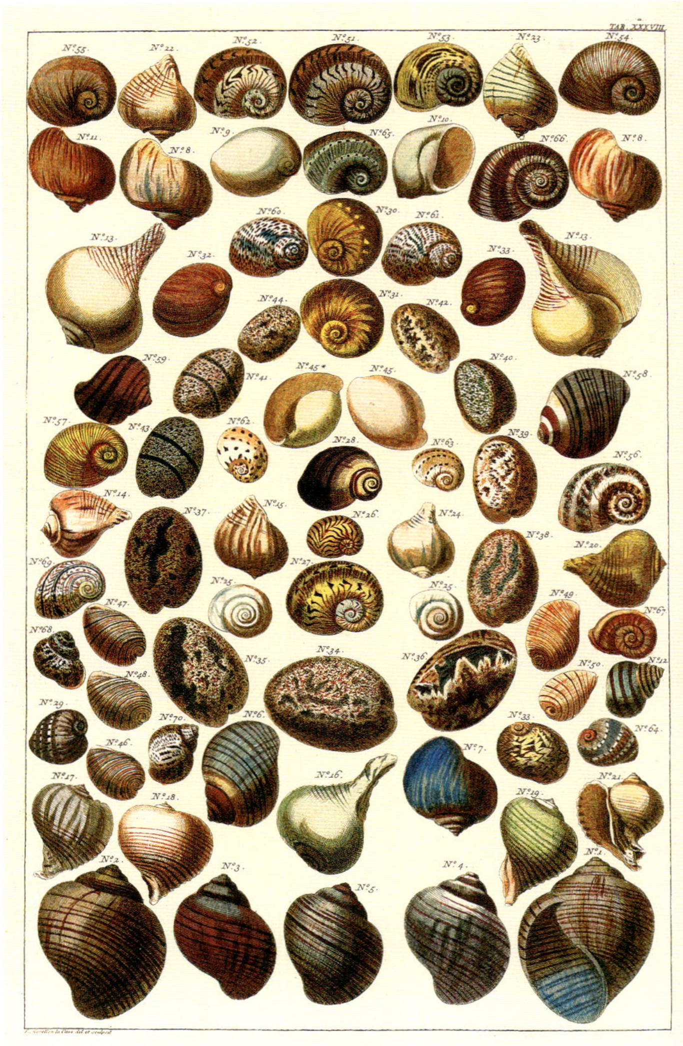

13-16, 18-20, 22-23 *Rapa rapa* **26-27, 51-53, 60-65** *Natica canrena* **31** *Neverita helicoides* **33** *Natica fulminea* **34-44** *Bulla ampulla* **45-45*** *Atys naucum*
Rapa shells, moon shells, spiny conches and cephalaspidean opisthobranchs from the Indo-Pacific, as well as African and American coastal regions · Kopfschildschnecken, Nabelschnecken und Stachelschnecken aus dem Indopazifik sowie afrikanischen und amerikanischen Küstengebieten · Coquilles de rapa, de natices, de murex et d'opisthobranches céphalaspidés de l'aire indopacifique ainsi que des zones côtières d'Afrique et d'Amérique

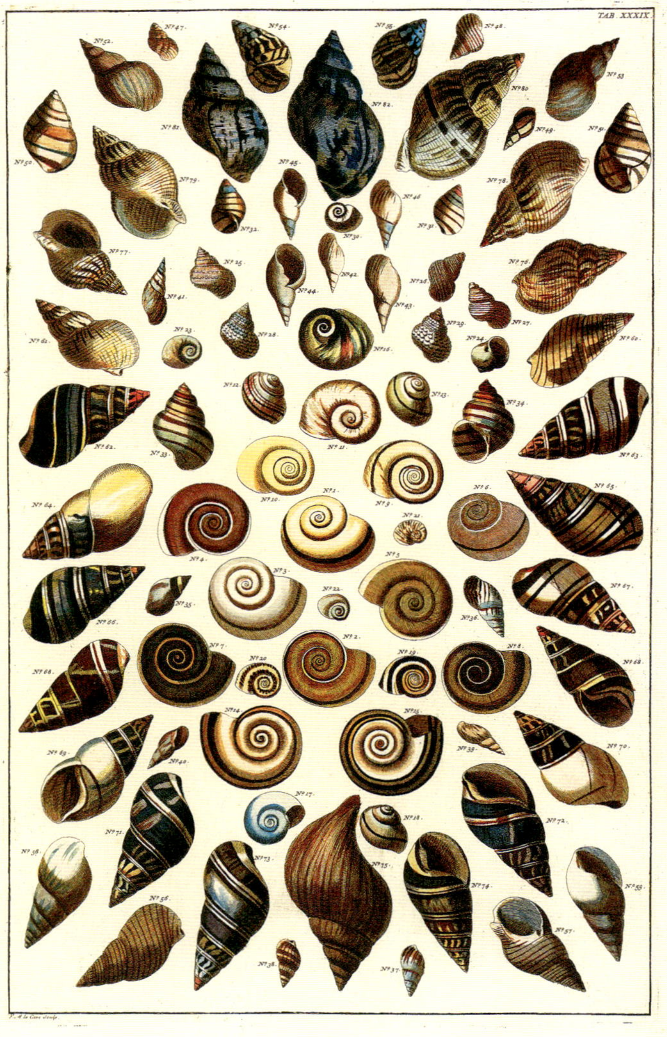

1-3, 9 *Naninia citrina* **16** *Neverita helicoides* **33-34** *Viviparus viviparus* **56-57, 60** *Nassarius glans* **62-74** *Liguus fasciatus* **75** *Neptunea antiqua* **76-82** *Buccinum undatum*
Land, freshwater and sea shells from Europe, North America and Indo-Pacific · Land-, Süßwasser- und Meeresschnecken aus Europa, Nordamerika und dem Indopazifik · Mollusques marins, d'eau douce et terrestres d'Europe, d'Amérique du Nord et de l'aire indopacifique

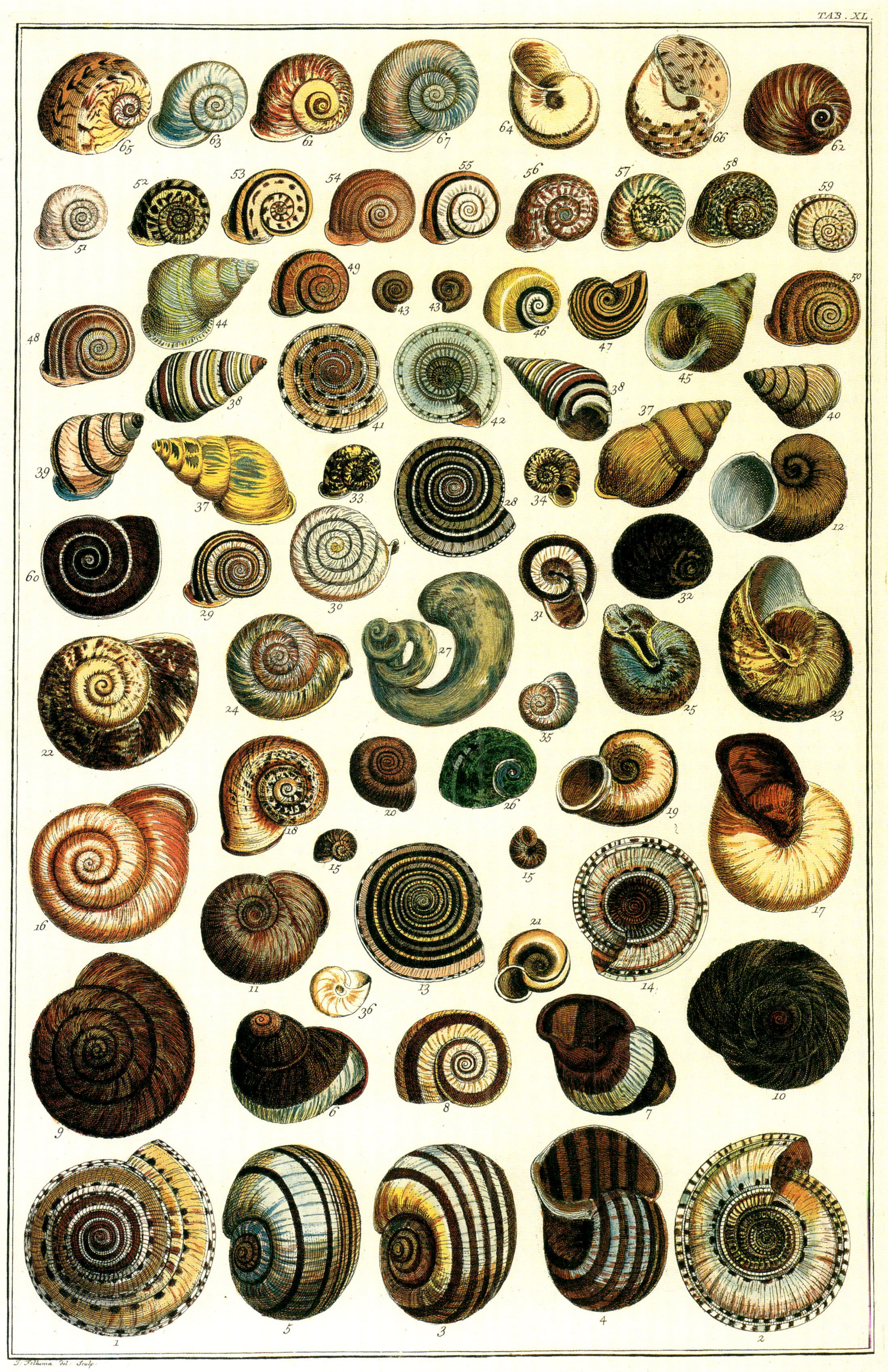

9-10 *Planorbarius* 16-17 *Chloritis* 24-25 Polygyridae 28 *Architectonica perspectiva* 38 *Liguus virgineus* 41-42 *Architectonica picta*
Land, freshwater and sea shells from Europe, Atlantic and Indo-Pacific · Land-, Süßwasser- und Meeresschnecken aus Europa, dem Atlantik und dem Indopazifik · Mollusques marins, d'eau douce et terrestres d'Europe, de l'Atlantique et de l'aire indopacifique

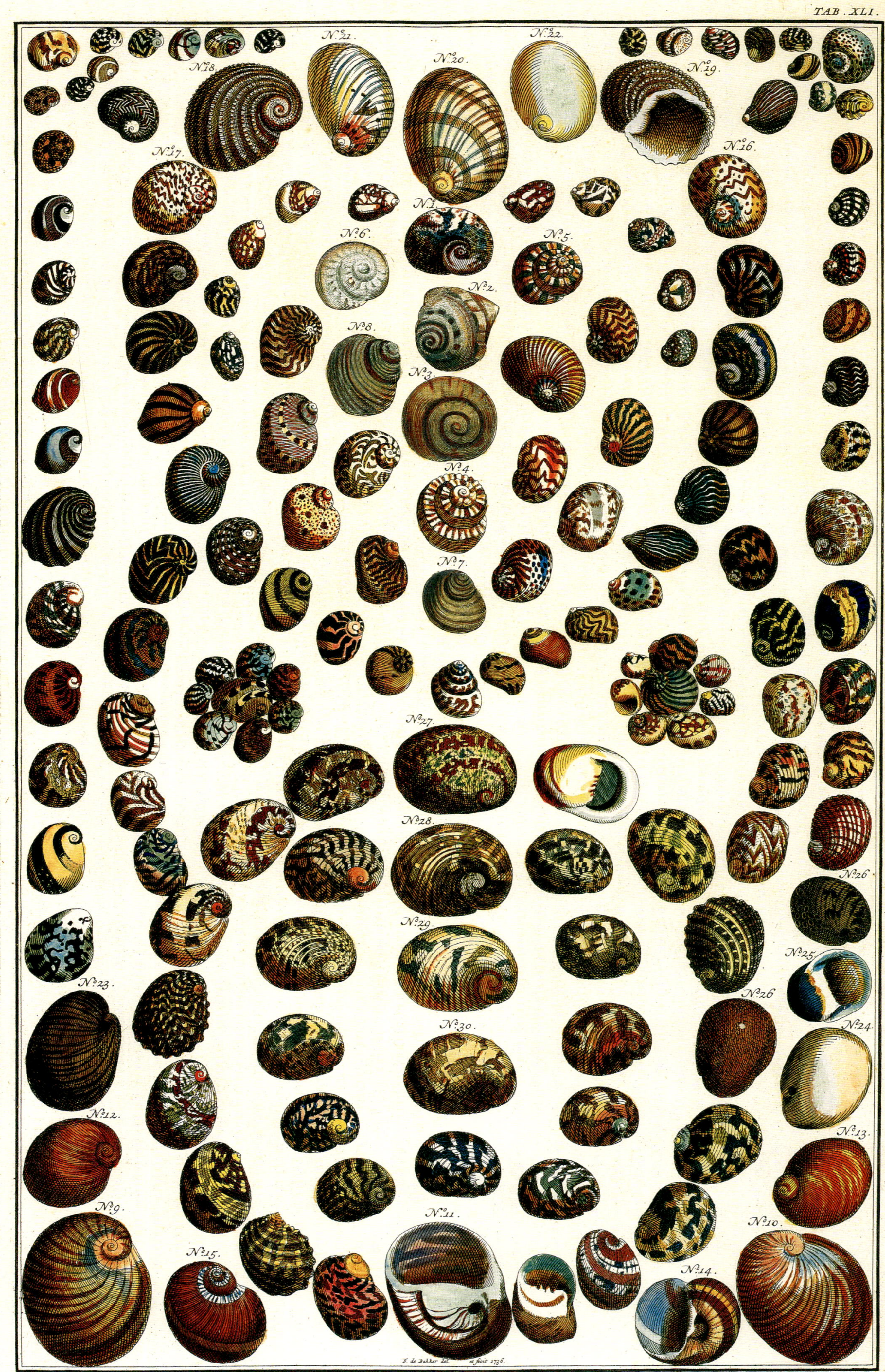

1,5 *Neritina virginea* **4-6** *Gibbula magus* **9-11** *Neverita albumen* **14-15** *Natica vitellus* **18-19** *Neritopsis radula* **20-21** *Polinices melanostomus* **23** *Nerita* **25-26** *Neritina pulligera*
Nerites, top shells and moon shells from the Indo-Pacific, Atlantic and Mediterranean Sea · Schwimmschnecken, Spitzkreiselschnecken und Nabelschnecken aus dem Indopazifik, Atlantik und Mittelmeer · Nérites, troques (gibbules) et natices de l'aire indopacifique, de l'Atlantique et de la mer Méditerranée

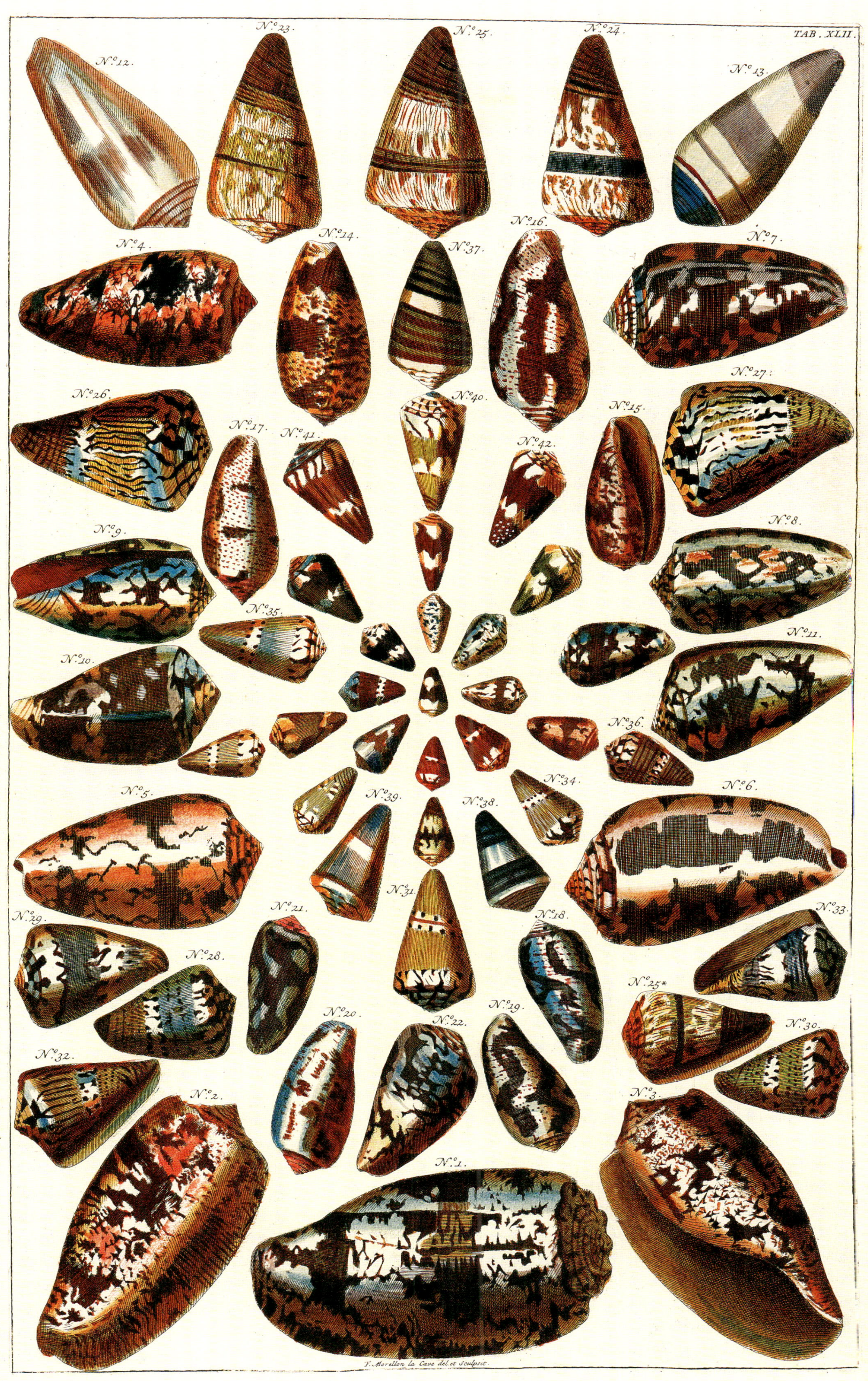

1-42 *Conus* **1-2, 4, 14-15** *Conus geographus* **5-6, 8-9, 16** *Conus striatus* **13** *Conus terebra* **22,** between **10** & **5** *Conus mustelinus* **23-25*** *Conus miles* **26-28, 30, 32-34** *Conus capitaneus* **39** *Conus lividus*
Poisonous cone shells, chiefly from the Indo-Pacific · Giftige Kegelschnecken, überwiegend aus dem Indopazifik · Cônes venimeux, originaires principalement de l'aire indopacifique

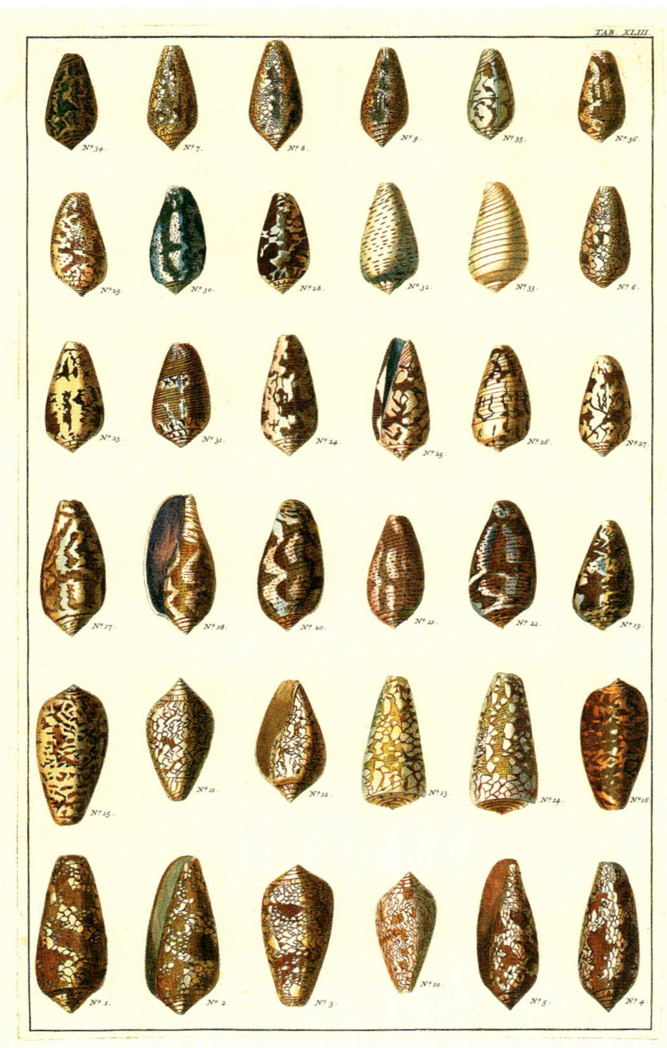

1-36 *Conus* **1-2, 4-5, 10** *Conus textile* **3, 6** *Conus pennaceus* **7-9** *Conus canonicus* **11-12** *Conus retifer* **13-14** *Conus nobilis*
Poisonous cone shells, chiefly from the Indo-Pacific · Giftige Kegelschnecken, überwiegend aus dem Indopazifik · Cônes venimeux, originaires principalement de l'aire indopacifique

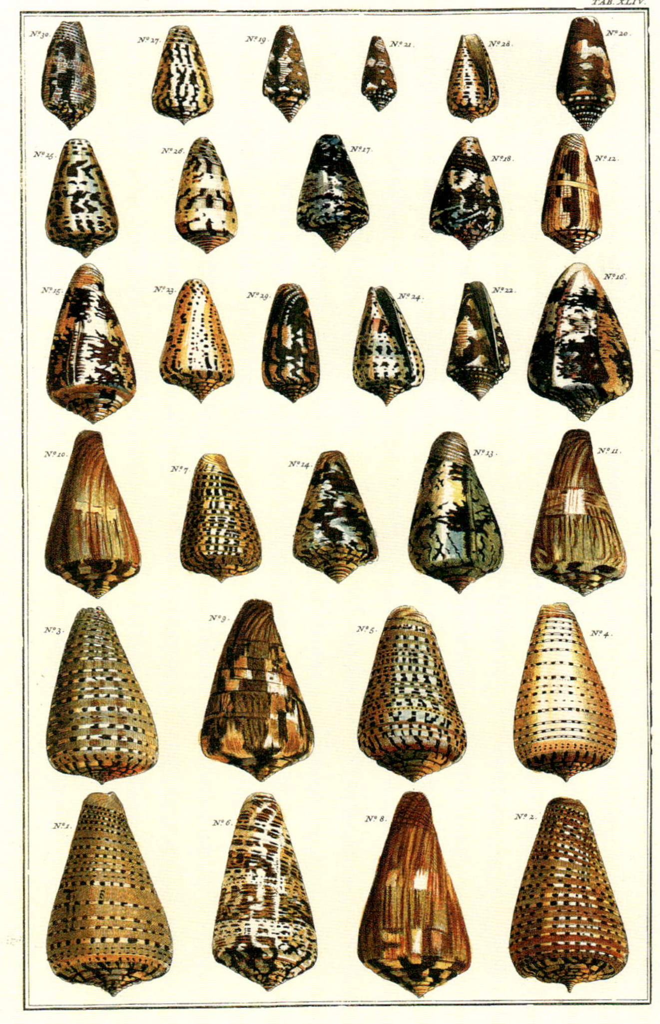

1-30 *Conus* **1-4, 23** *Conus betulinus* **5** *Conus suratensis* **6** *Conus imperialis* **8-11** *Conus vexillum* **15** *Conus ammiralis* **19-21** *Conus aurantius* **24** *Conus spurius*
Poisonous cone shells from the Indo-Pacific and the Caribbean · Giftige Kegelschnecken aus dem Indopazifik und der Karibik · Cônes venimeux, originaires principalement de l'aire indopacifique et des Caraïbes

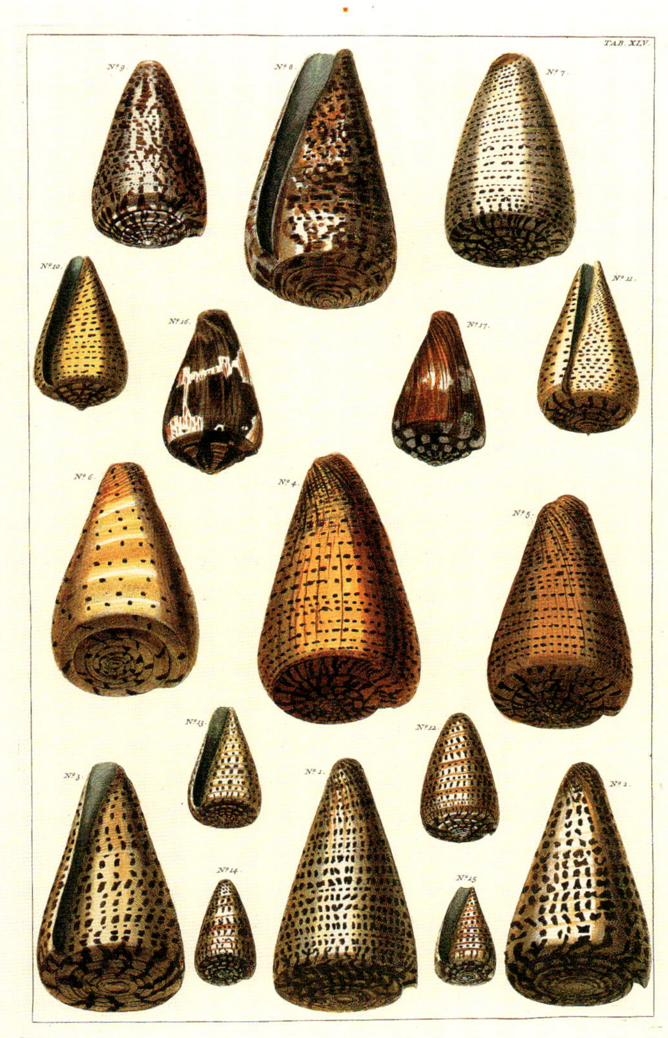

1-17 *Conus* **1-3, 12-15** *Conus litteratus* **6, 10-11** *Conus betulinus* **8** *Conus pulcher*
16-17 *Conus vexillum*
Poisonous cone shells from tropical waters · Giftige Kegelschnecken aus tropischen Meeren · Cônes venimeux des mers tropicales

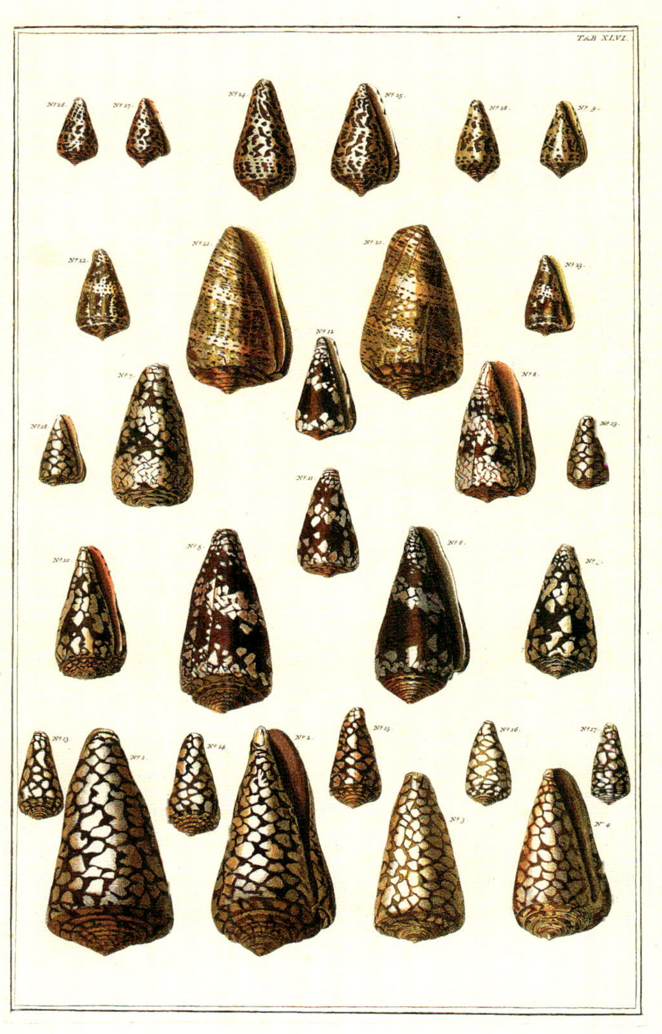

1-29 *Conus* **1-4, 13-19** *Conus marmoreus* **7-8** *Conus vidua* **20-21** *Conus pulcher*
Poisonous cone shells, chiefly from the Indo-Pacific · Giftige Kegelschnecken, überwiegend aus dem Indopazifik · Cônes venimeux, originaires principalement de l'aire indopacifique

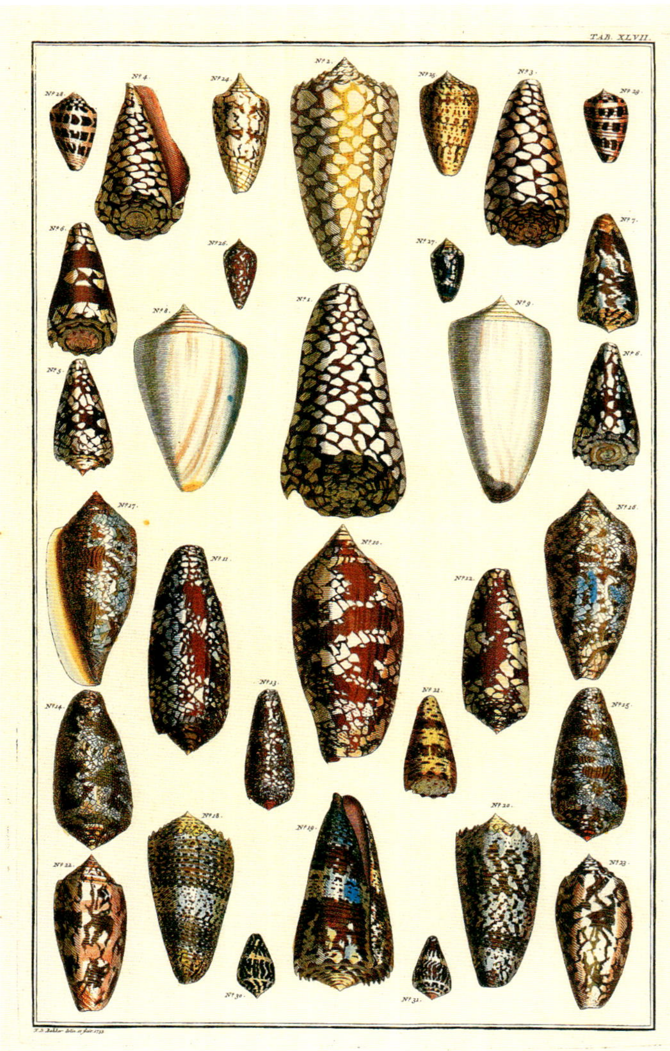

1-31 *Conus* **1-4** *Conus marmoreus* **5-6** *Conus bandanus* **8** *Conus quercinus* **10-12** *Conus aulicus* **13** *Conus aulicus?* **14-17** *Conus textile* **18-21** *Conus imperialis* **22-23** *Conus striatus* **28-29** *Conus ebraeus* **30-31** *Conus chaldeus*

Poisonous cone shells from the Indo-Pacific · Giftige Kegelschnecken aus dem Indopazifik · Cônes venimeux, originaires de l'aire indopacifique

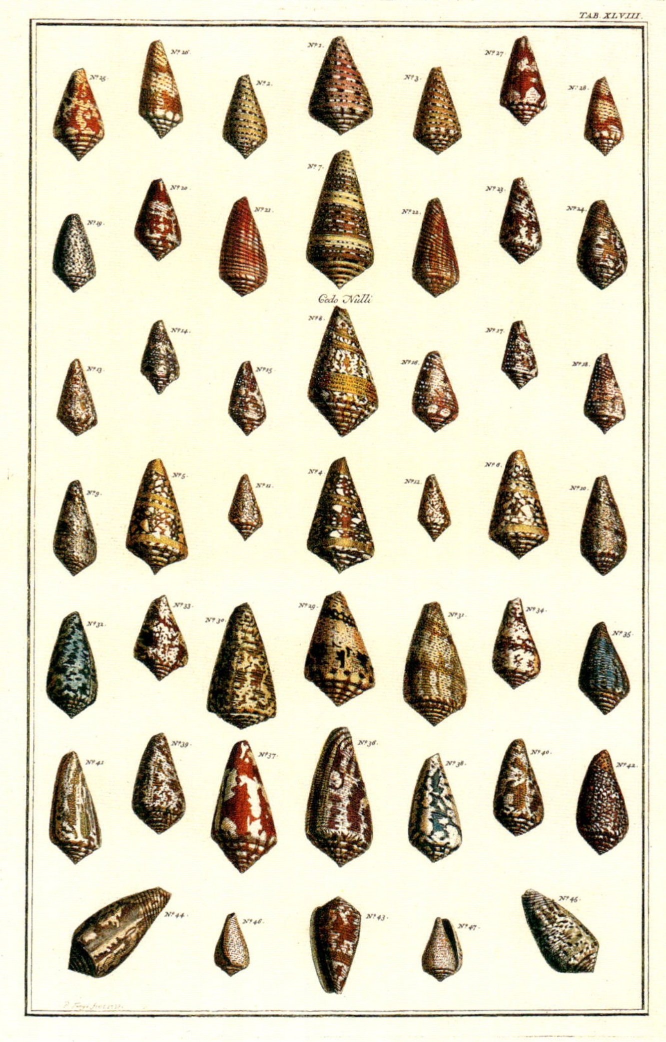

1-47 *Conus* **1-3** *Conus genuanus* **4-7** *Conus ammiralis* **8** *Conus cedonulli* **21** *Conus tenuistriatus* **25, 29** *Conus regius* **27, 37** *Conus aurantius* **42** *Conus dalli*

Cone shells from the Atlantic, Indian Ocean and Pacific · Kegelschnecken aus Atlantik, Indischem Ozean und Pazifik · Cônes originaires de l'Atlantique, de l'océan Indien et du Pacifique

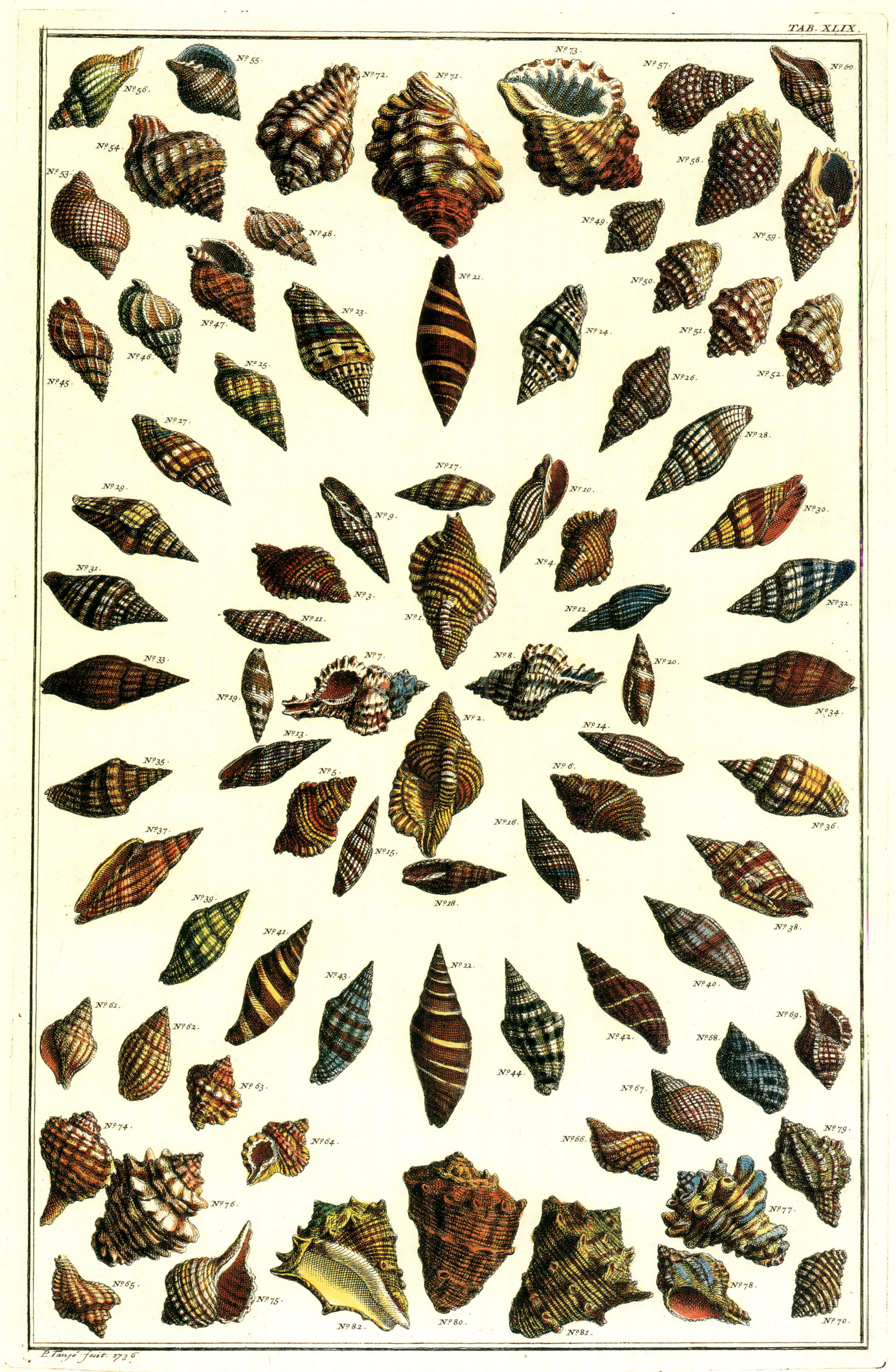

1-6 *Cymatium rubeculum* **11-44** *Vexillum* **11-18** *Vexillum sanguisugum* **19-20** *Vexillum taylorianum* **21-22, 33-34, 41** *Vexillum vulpecula* **23-24** *Vexillum plicarium* **30, 39, 44** *Vexillum rugosum* **45-48** *Phos senticosus* **53, 55** *Cancellaria reticulata* **57-59** *Nassarius papillosus* **63-64, 71-73** *Cabestana cutacea* **76-77** *Vasum turbinellus* **80-82** *Vasum*

Tritons, miter shells, nassas, and vase shells from the Indo-Pacific, Atlantic and Mediterranean Sea · Tritonshörner, Giftwalzenschnecken, Netzreusenschnecken und Vasenschnecken aus dem Indopazifik, Atlantik und Mittelmeer · Tritons, cônes, mitres, nasses et vases de l'aire indopacifique, de l'Atlantique et de la mer Méditerranée

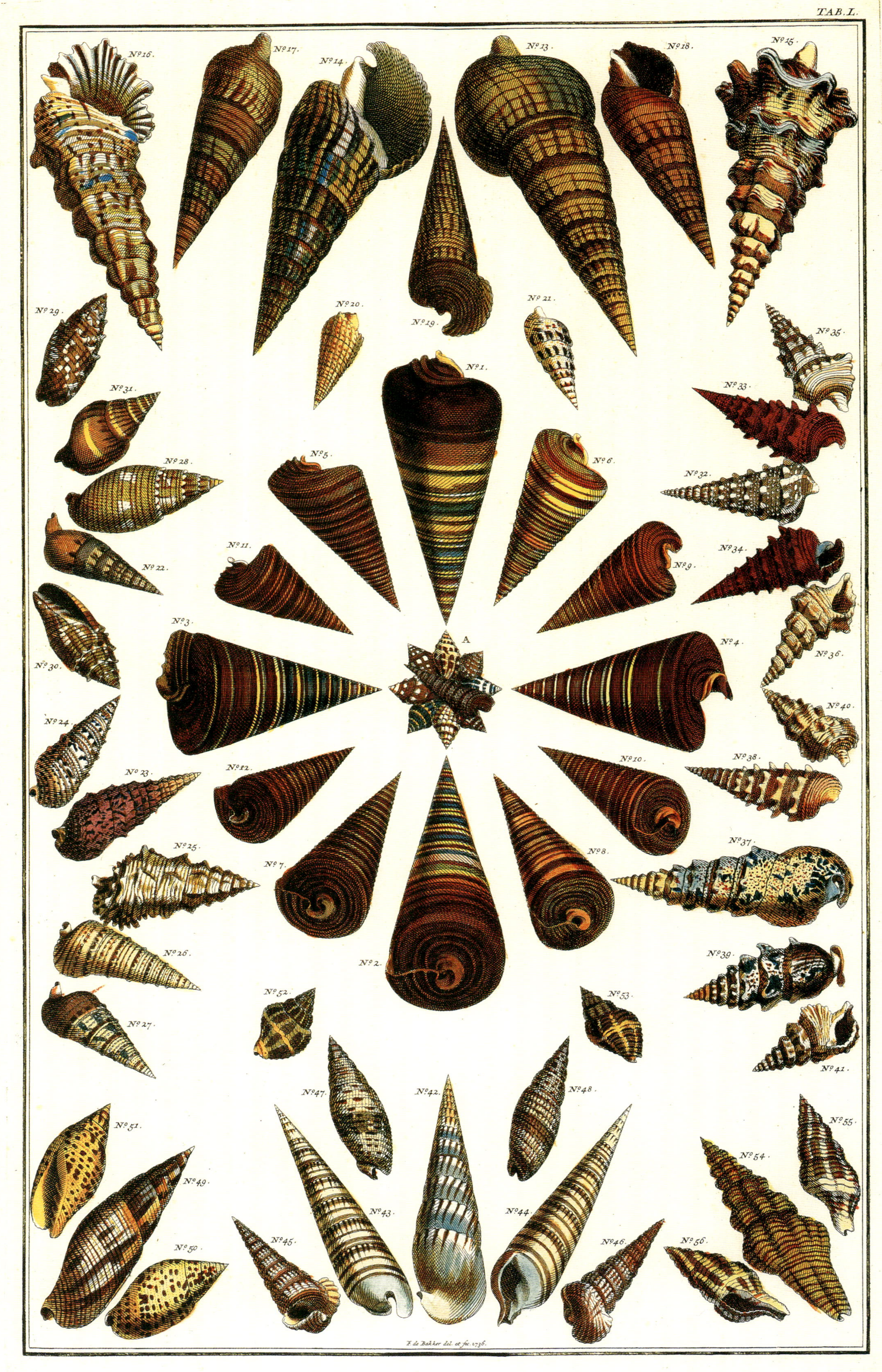

1-12 *Telescopium telescopium* **13-14, 17-19** *Terebralia palustris* **15-16** *Cerithium nodulosum* **22** *Rhinoclavis vertagus* **23-24** *Rhinoclavis sinensis* **26-27** *Neocancilla* **28** *Mitra imperialis* **29-30** *Mitra puncticulata* **31** Buccinidae **32-38, 40** *Cerithium* **37** *Cerithium aluco* **42** *Rhinoclavis* **43-44** *Rhinoclavis fasciatus* **47** *Neocancilla papilio* **48** *Neocancilla granatina* **49** *Mitra incompta* **50-51** *Mitra cardinalis* **52-53** Cantharidae **54** *Latirus infundibulum* **55-56** Latirus nagasakiensis

 Sea shells of different families from the Indo-Pacific · Meeresschnecken verschiedener Familien aus dem Indopazifik · Mollusques marins de différentes familles de l'aire indopacifique

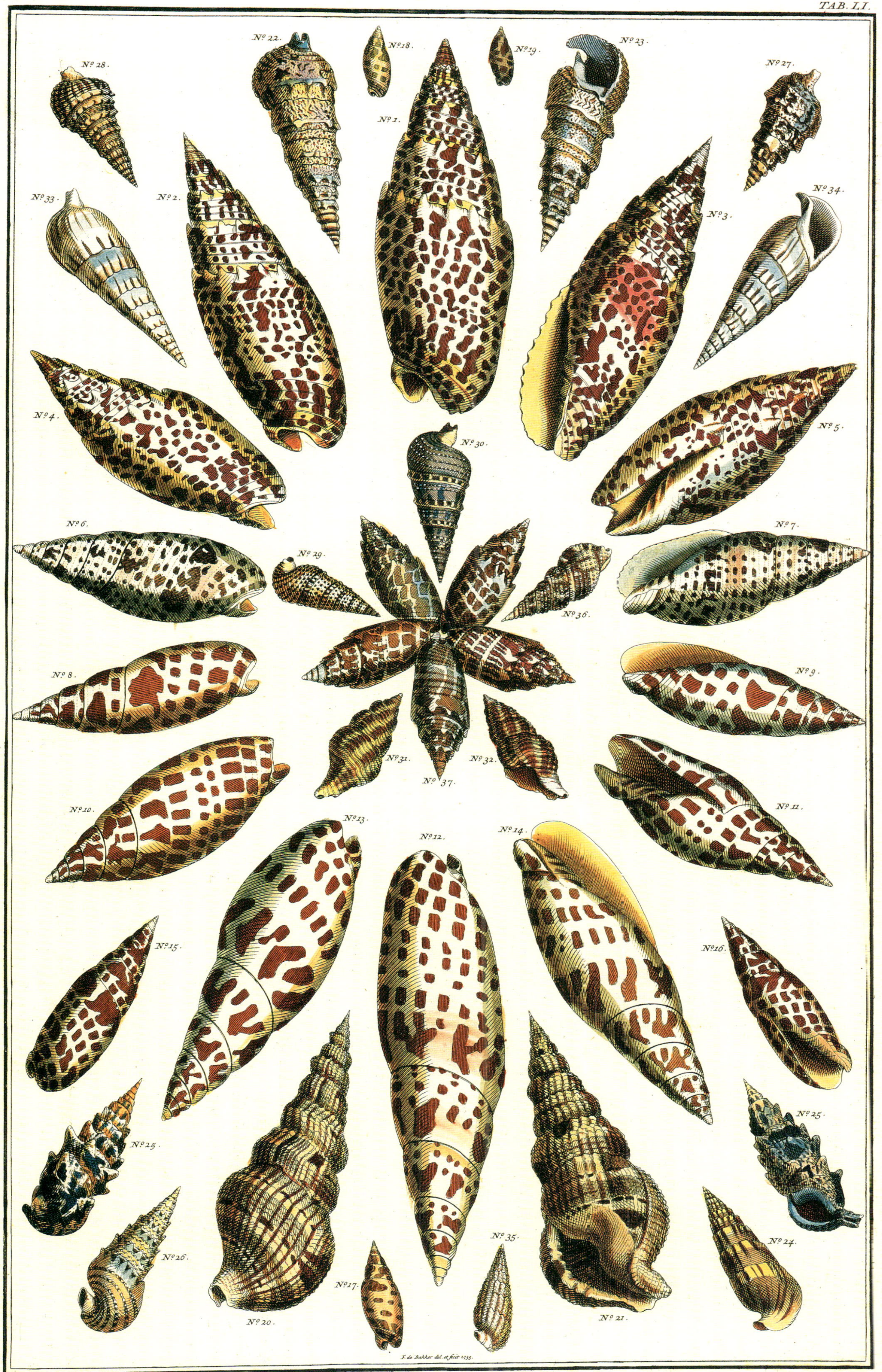

1-5 *Mitra papalis* **6-7** *Mitra cardinalis* **8-16** *Mitra mitra* **17-19** *Mitra* **20-21** *Colubraria muricata* **22-23, 29-30** Cerithiidae **24, 26-27, 35, 38** *Rhinoclavis* **25** *Pseudovertagus aluco* **31-32** *Latirus nagasakiensis* **33-34** *Rhinoclavis fasciatus* **36** *Colubraria* **37** *Mitra stictica*

Miter shells, ceriths and a few other species from the Indo-Pacific · Indopazifische Meeresschnecken, hauptsächlich Bischofsmützenschnecken, Mitras, Nadelschnecken und einige andere Arten aus dem Indopazifik · Mitres, cérinthes (cornets) et autres espèces de l'aire indopacifique

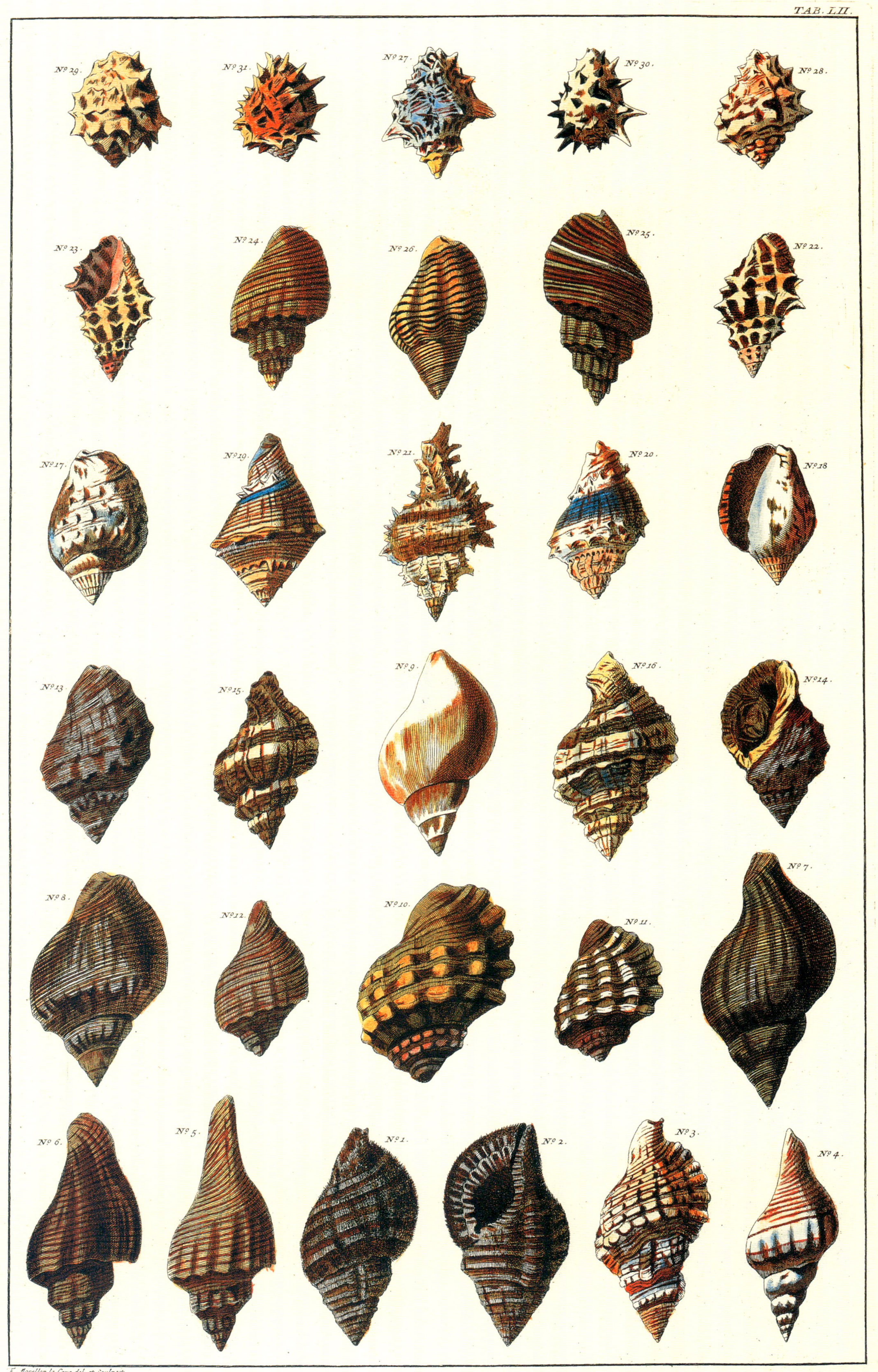

1-3 Ranellidae **5-6** *Hemifusus* **7** Buccinoidea **9** *Neptunea* **10-11** *Cymatium doliarium* **13-14, 27** *Thais* **15-16** Muricidae **17-18** *Strombus pipus* **19-20** Melongenidae **21** *Chicoreus* **22-23** *Thais* **24-25, 28-29** Muricoidea **26** *Cantharus undosus* **30-31** *Drupa*

Sea snails, including murex shells and tritons, chiefly from the Indo-Pacific · Meeresschnecken, hauptsächlich aus dem Indopazifik, darunter Stachelschnecken und Tritonschnecken · Mollusques marins, incluant des murex et des tritons, principalement de l'aire indopacifique

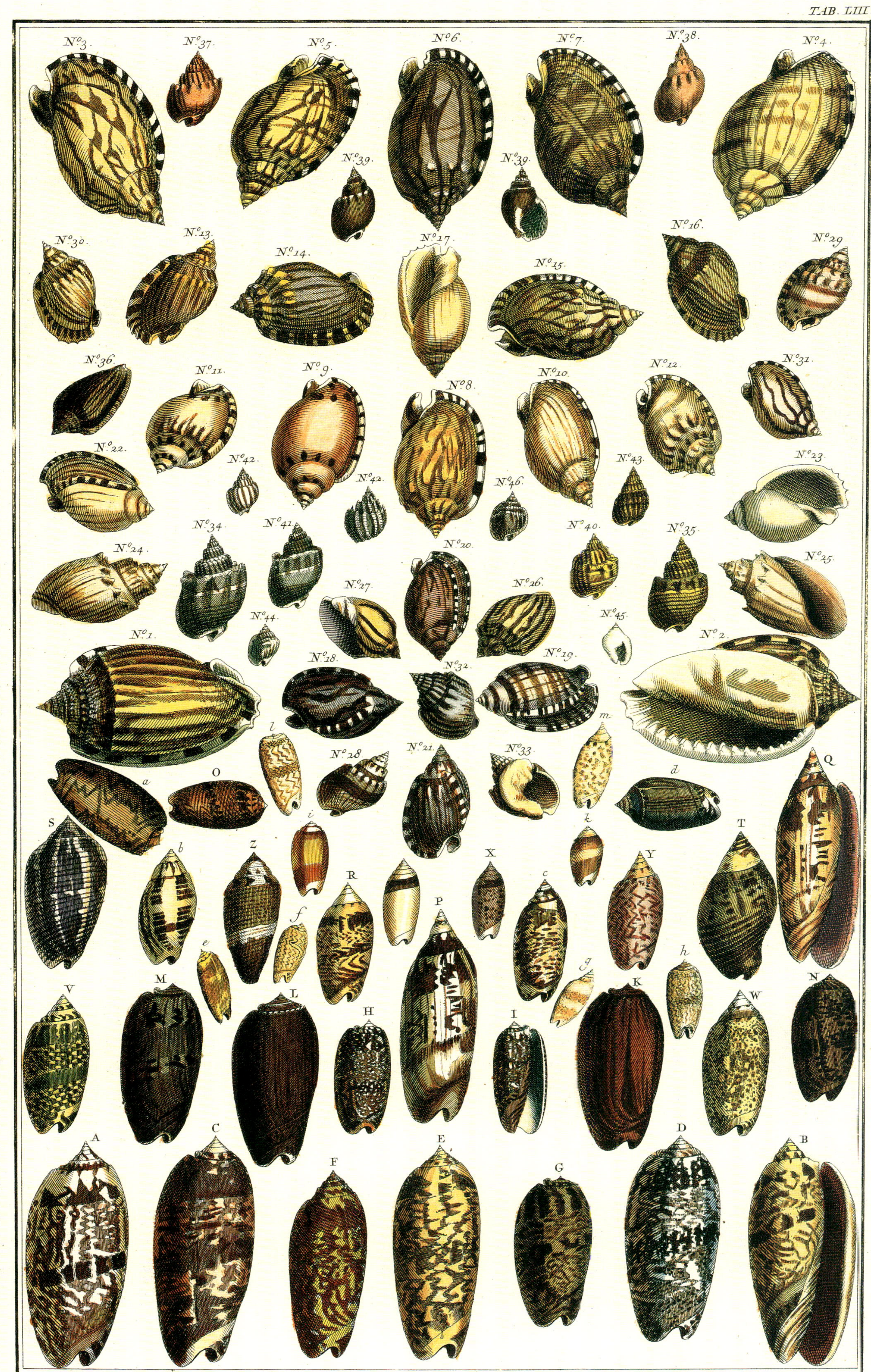

1-16, 18-23, 26-27, 29-31 *Phalium* **24-25** Thiaridae **28, 32-35, 37-46** Nassariidae **A-F** *Oliva miniacea* **G-R, V-Y, a, c-m** Olividae **s, z** *Conus*
Tropical sea shells, including bonnet shells, mud shells, mudcreepers, olive shells, and cone shells · Tropische Meeresschnecken, darunter Helmschnecken, Reusenschnecken, eine Turmdeckelschnecke (Thiaridae), Olivenschnecken (Olividae) und Kegelschnecken (Conidae) · Mollusques marins tropicaux, dont des casques, des nasses, un Thiaridae, des olives et des cônes

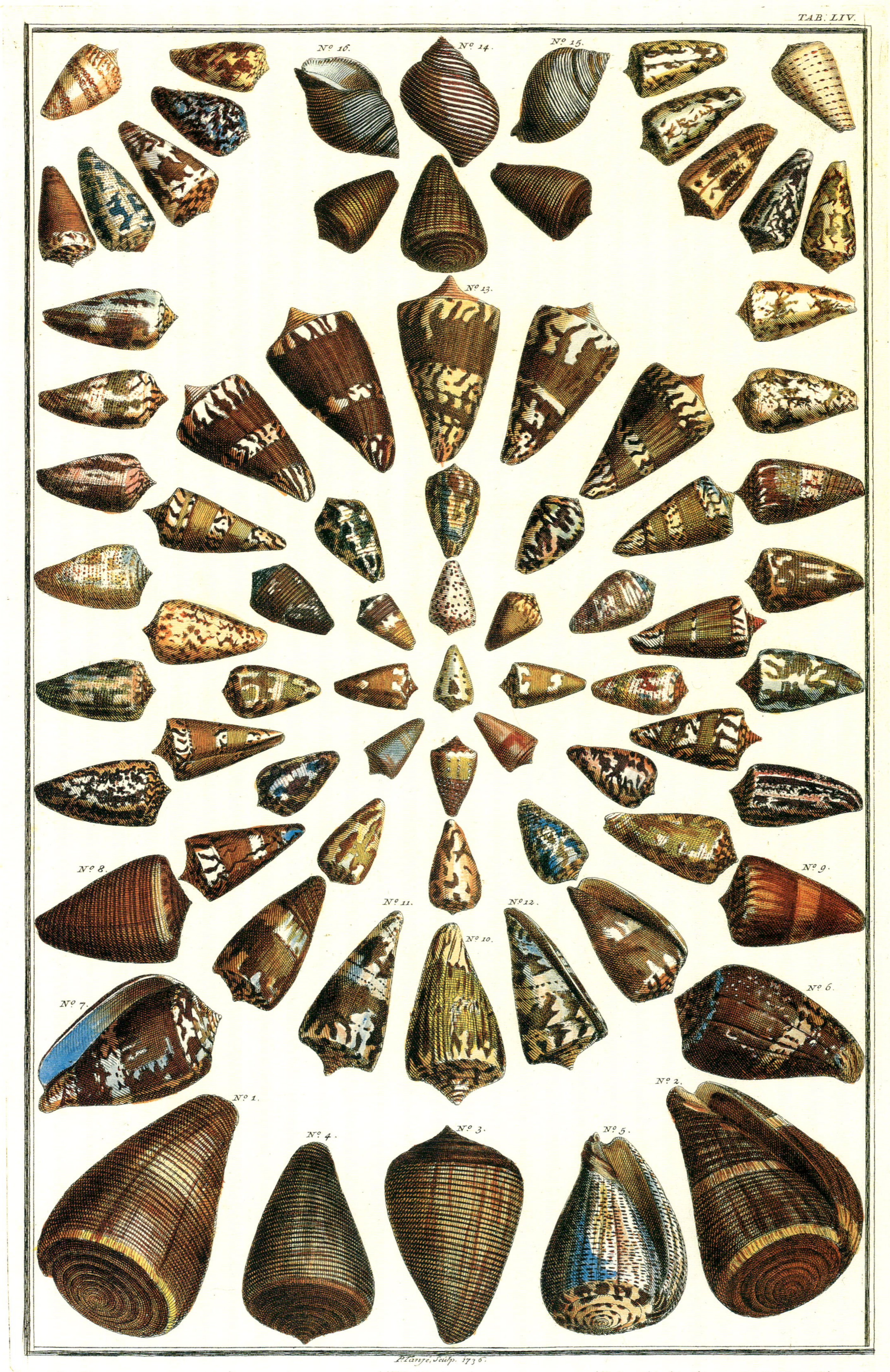

All except 14-16 *Conus* 1-4, below 14-16 *Conus figulinus* 5 *Conus glaucus* 9 *Conus vexillum* 11-13 (next to 7, 8, three shells at both sides of 13) *Conus generalis* 14-16 *Latirogena smaragdula*
Poisonous cone shells and stone shells from tropical seas · Giftige Kegelschnecken und Spindelschnecken aus den tropischen Meeren · Cônes venimeux et fasciolariidés des mers des Tropiques

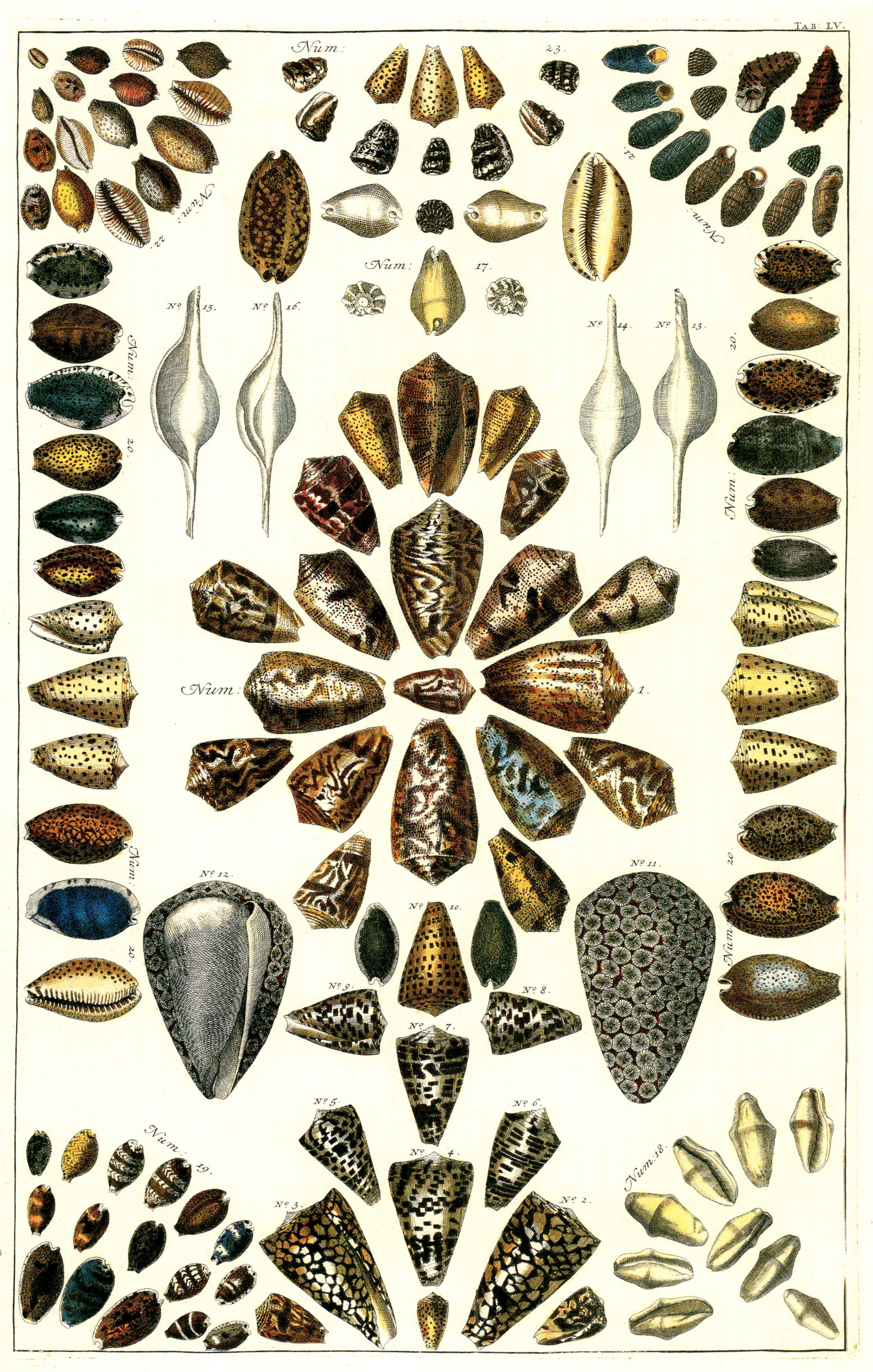

1-12 *Conus* 1 *Conus stercusmuscarum* 2-3 *Conus marmoreus* 4-9 *Conus eburneus* 10, 20 *Conus litteratus* 11-12 *Conus* 13-16 *Volva volva*
17 *Calpurnus verrucosus* 18 *Cyphoma gibbosum* 19 *Cypraea felina* 20 *Conus leopardus* 21 Pupilloidea 22 *Trivia pedicula*
Cone shells and cowries from the Indo-Pacific and West Atlantic · Kegelschnecken und Porzellanschnecken aus dem Indopazifik und dem Westatlantik · Cônes et porcelaines (cyrées et ovules) de l'aire indopacifique et de l'Atlantique occidental

TAB. LVIII.

Neritidae, Naticidae

Nerite shells and moon shells · Schwimmschnecken und Nabelschnecken · Nérites et natices

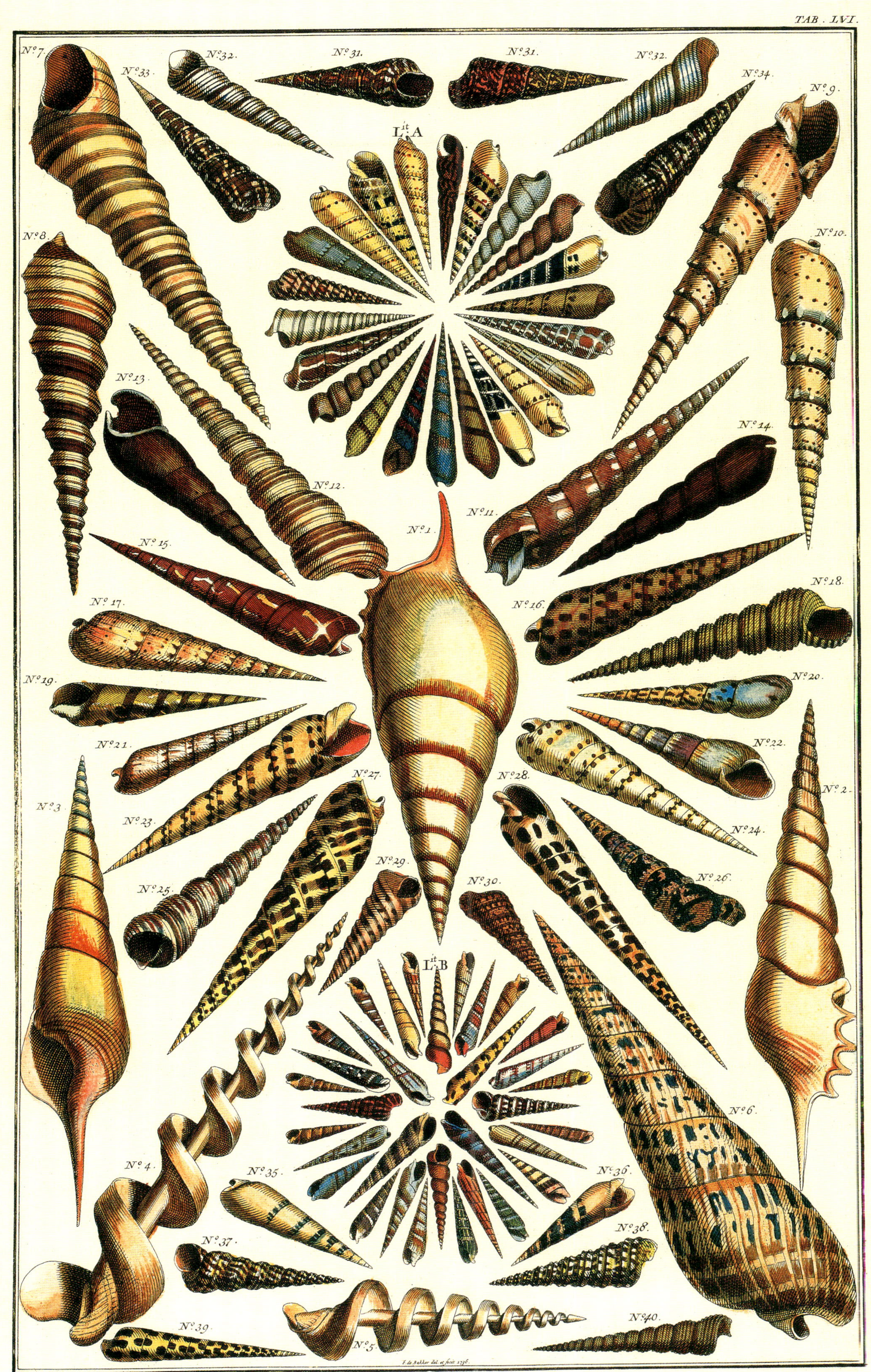

1 *Tibia insulaechorab* 2 *Tibia fusus* 3 *Tibia* 4-5, 8, 17, 19, 22, 41-42, A-B Terebridae 6, 12 *Terebra maculata* 7 *Turritella duplicata* 9-10 *Terebra crenulata*
11 *Terebra guttata* 12, 25 *Turritella terebra* 13-14 *Faunus ater* 15 *Terebra dimidiata* 16, 23-24 *Terebra areolata* 18, 25-26, 29-34, 37-38, 40 *Turritella* 20-21 *Melanoides* 26, 31, 33-34 *Turritella variegata*
Turret shells, auger shells and tibias from the Indo-Pacific and the Caribbean · Indopazifische und karibische Turmschnecken, Schraubenschnecken, Turmdeckelschnecken und Flügelschnecken · Turritelles, térèbres et tibias de l'aire indopacifique et des Caraïbes

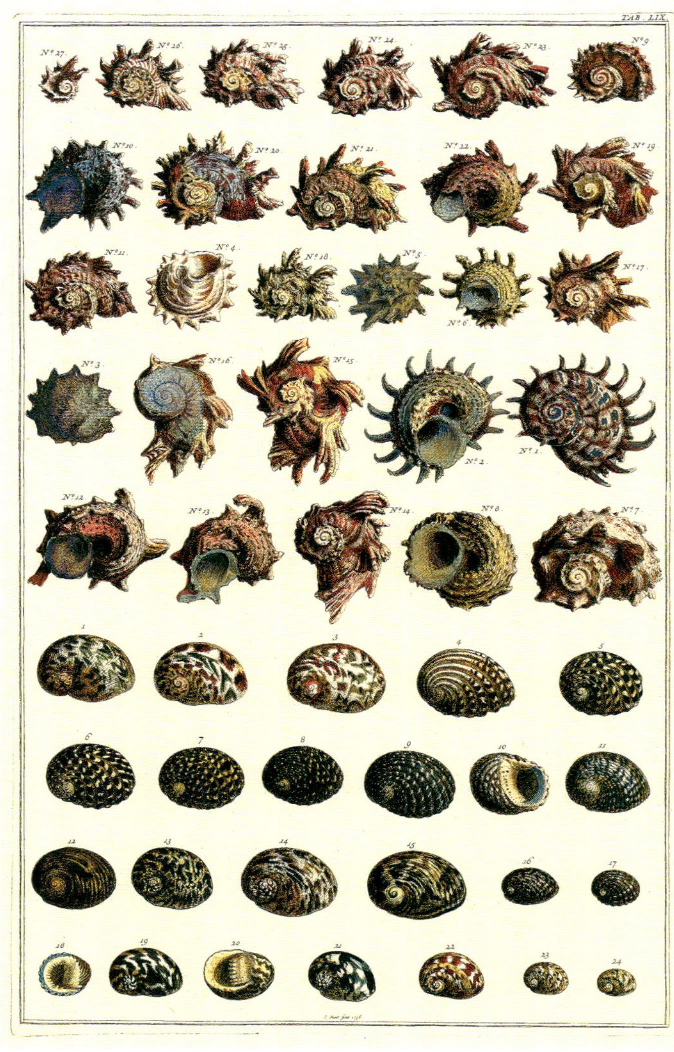

1-3 (bottom) *Nerita polita* **4-18** (bottom) *Nerita exuvia* **19-24** (bottom) *Nerita*
1-2 (top) *Stellaria solaris* **3-4** (top) *Astrea* **5-6** (top) *Astrea calcar*
7-27 (top) *Angaria delphinus, Neorapana muricata*
Nerite shells, star shells and angaria shells from the Indo-Pacific and West Atlantic · Schwimmschnecken, Kreiselschnecken und Stachelschnecken aus dem Indopazifik und dem Westatlantik · Nérites, astreas et anarias de l'aire indopacifique et de l'Atlantique occidental

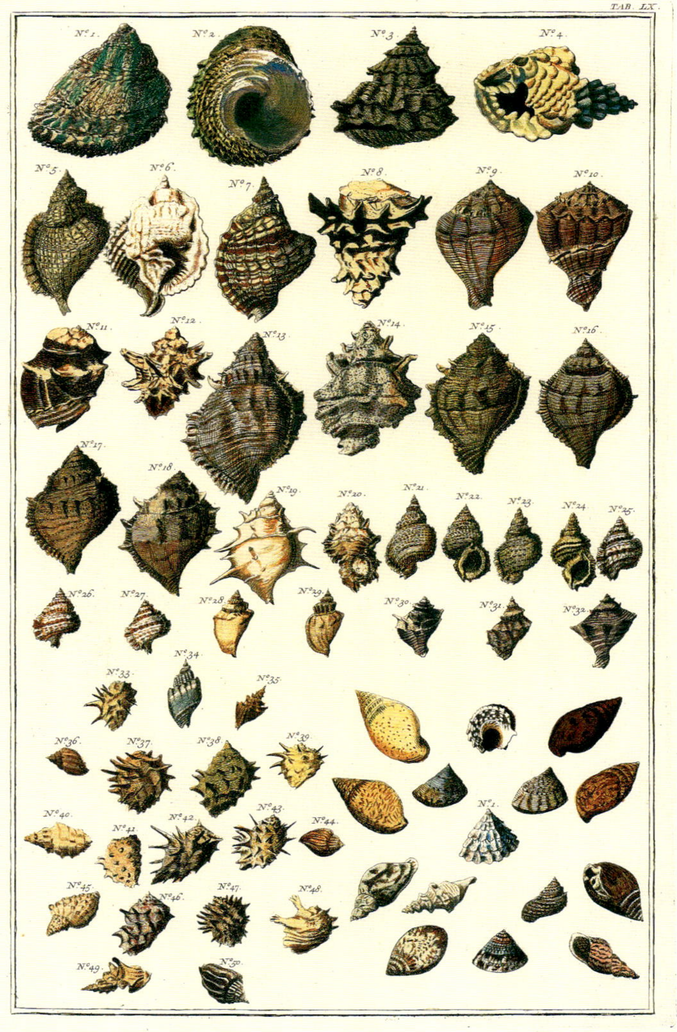

1-2 *Astrea caelata* **3** *Tectarius pagodus* **4-7** *Distorsio anus* **8** *Vasum turbinellus* **9-10** *Bursa*
12 *Thais armigera* **13, 15-18** *Bursa rana* **19** *Bursa echinata* **21-27** *Gyrineum gyrinum*
28-29 *Strombus* **30-32** *Thais* **33, 37-39, 41-43, 46-47** *Drupa* **48** *Drupa grossularia*
Star shells, periwinkles, tritons, vase shells, murex shells and conchs from the Indo-Pacific and West Atlantic · Kreiselschnecken, Strandschnecken, Tritonshörner, Vasenschnecken, Stachelschnecken und Flügelschnecken aus dem Indopazifik und Westatlantik · Astreas, bigorneaux, tritons, vases, murex et strombes de l'aire indopacifique et de l'Atlantique occidental

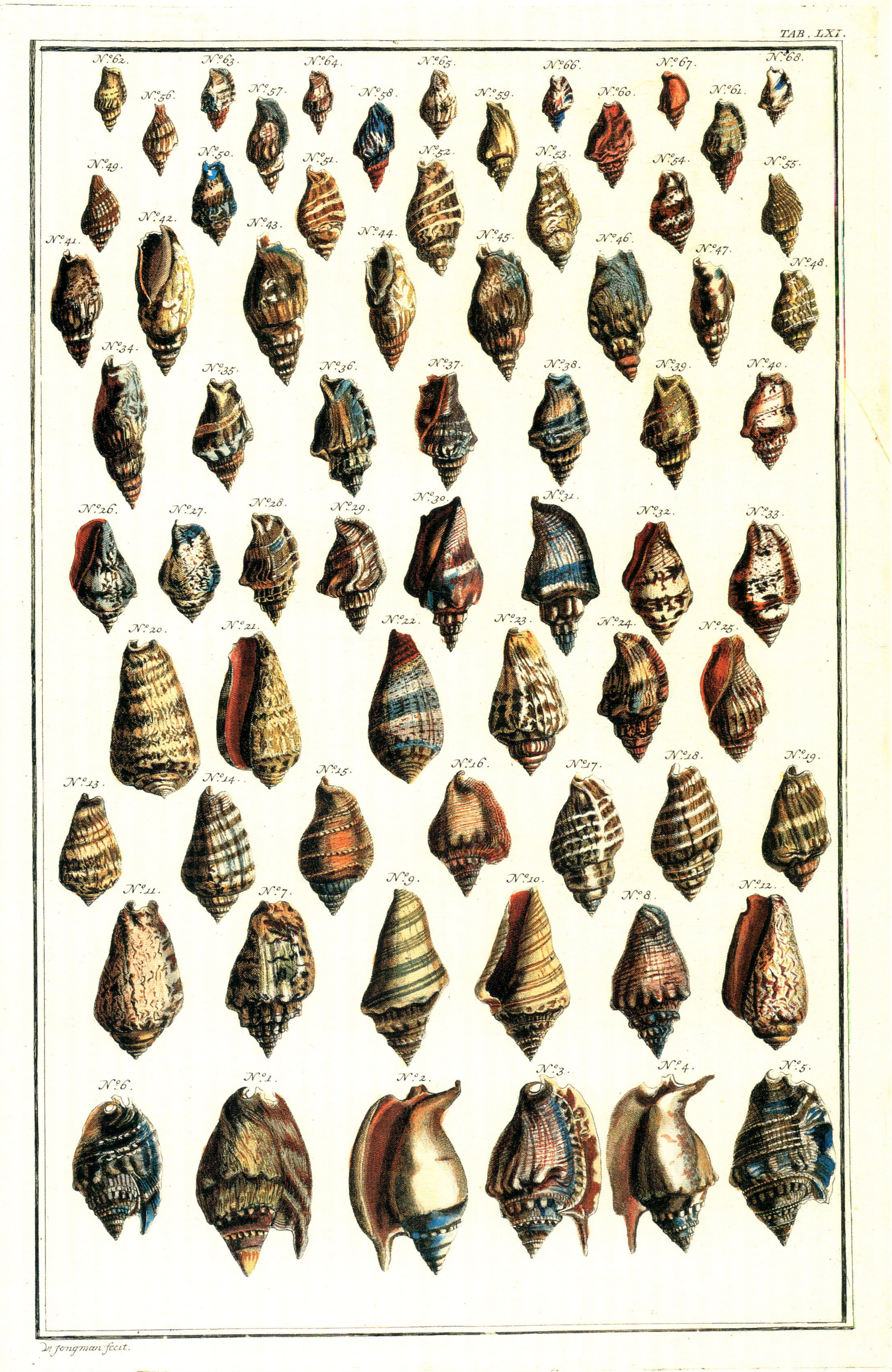

1-6 *Strombus aurisdianae* **7** *Strombus lentiginosus* **8** *Strombus labiatus* **9-10** *Lambis lambis* **11-12, 20-21** *Strombus luhuanus* **13-14, 17-19, 51-53** *Strombus gibberulus* **15-16** *Strombus marginatus* **24, 26-33, 35-39, 50, 57-64, 66-68** *Strombus* **25, 41-47, 55** *Strombus dentatus*
Conchs and spider conch shells from the Indo-Pacific · Flügelschnecken und Spinnenschnecke aus dem Indopazifik · Strombes et coquillage araignée de l'aire indopacifique

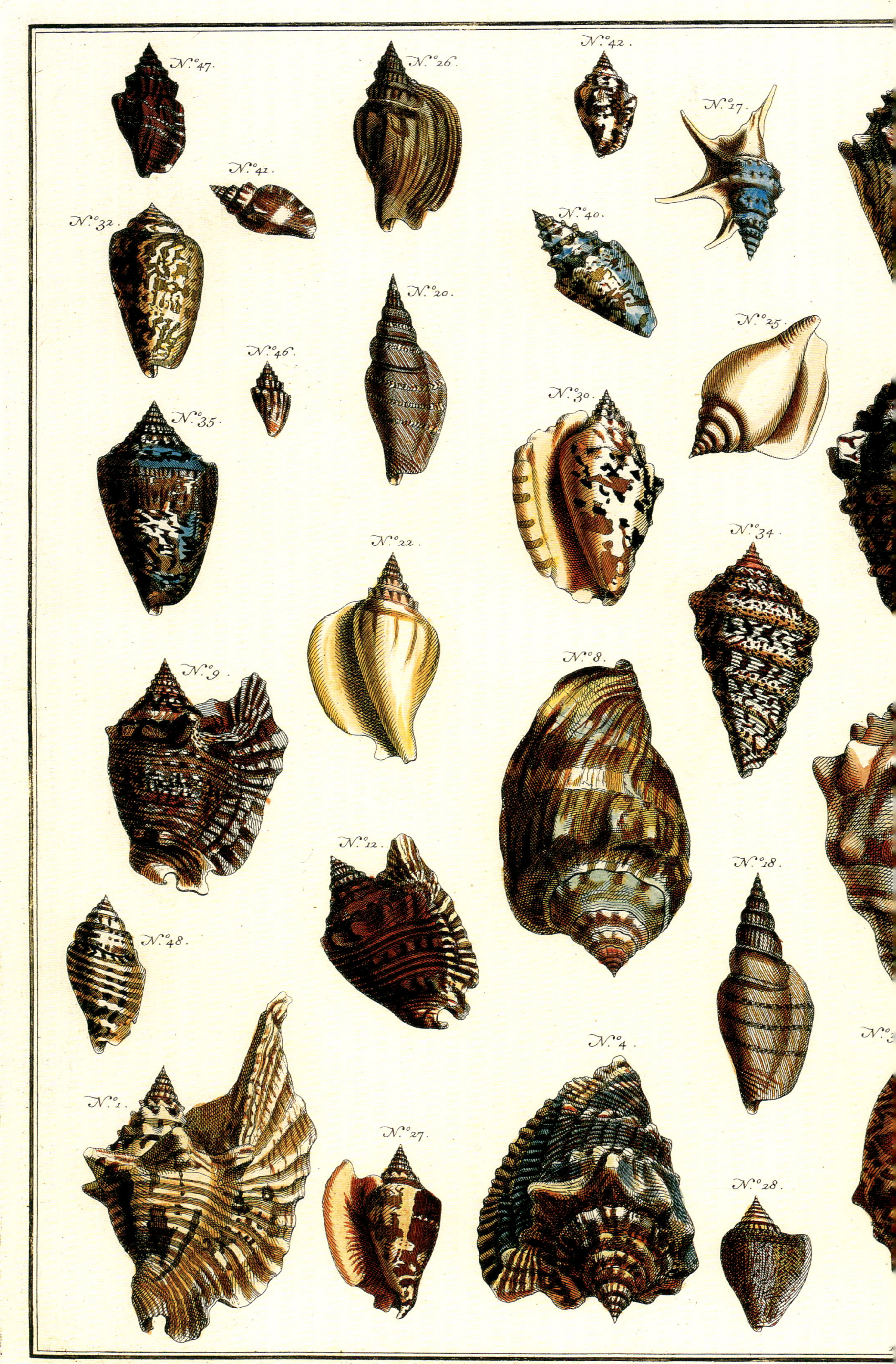

1-16, 18-32, 35-41, 44-50 *Strombus* **1-2, 4-5, 9-10, 12, 14-15, 27, 35-37** *Strombus gallus* **3** *Strombus sinuatus* **6-8** *Strombus fasciatus* **11, 30** *Strombus lentiginosus* **17** *Aporrhais pespelicani* **18-20** *Strombus vittatus* **21-22, 26** *Strombus epidromis* **33** *Lambis* **34** *Lambis chiragra* **41, 45-47** *Strombus urceus* **48, 49** *Strombus gibberulus*

Conchs, spider conch shells and the common pelican's foot · Flügelschnecken, Spinnenschnecken und der Pelikanfuß · Strombes, coquillages araignées et pied de pélican

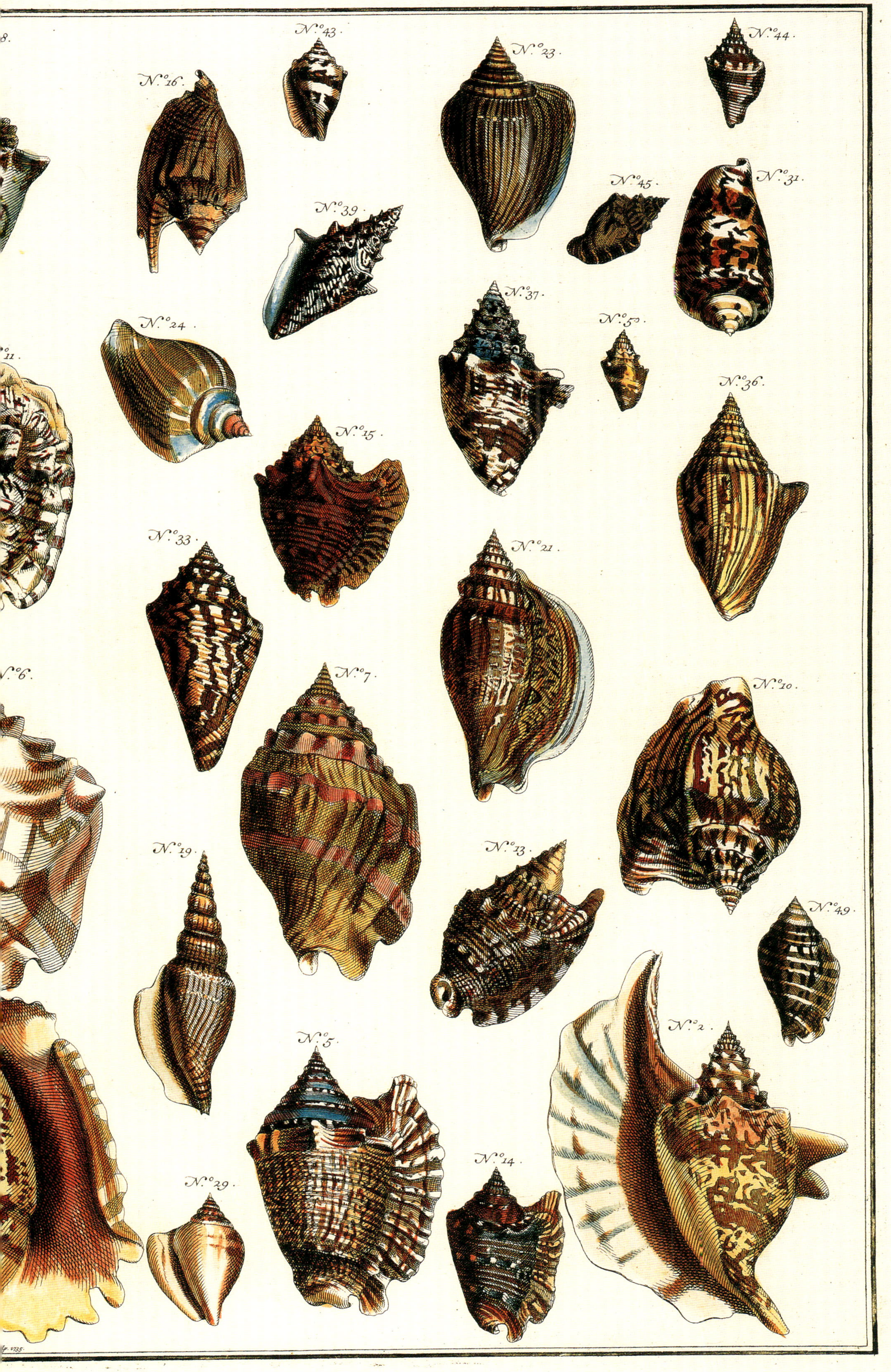
TAB. LXII.
N.° 43
N.° 23
N.° 44
N.° 16
N.° 45
N.° 31
N.° 39
N.° 37
N.° 24
N.° 36
N.° 15
N.° 33
N.° 21
N.° 7
N.° 10
N.° 19
N.° 13
N.° 49
N.° 2
N.° 5
N.° 14
N.° 29

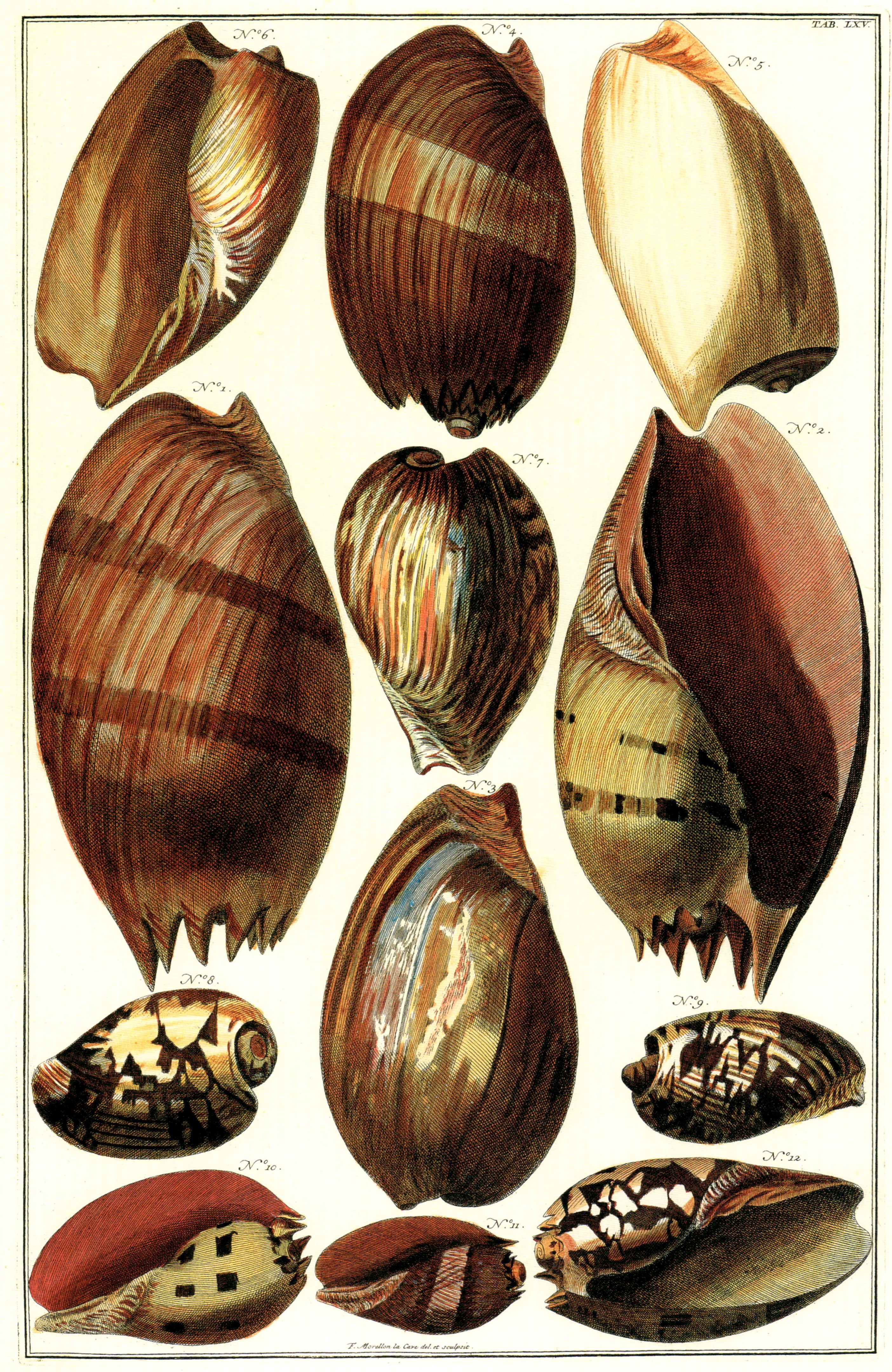

1-2 *Melo georginae* **3** *Melo melo* **4** *Melo broderipii* **5-6** *Cymbium cucumis* **7** *Cymbium pepo* **8-9, 11** *Melo* **10** *Melo aethiopica* **12** *Melo miltonis*
Volutes from the Indo-West Pacific near Australia and Indonesia, and from the Atlantic near West Africa · Walzenschnecken aus dem Indo-Westpazifik bei Australien und Indonesien, und aus dem Atlantik bei Westafrika · Volutes de l'aire indopacifique, près de l'Australie et de l'Indonésie, ainsi que de l'Atlantique près de l'Afrique occidentale

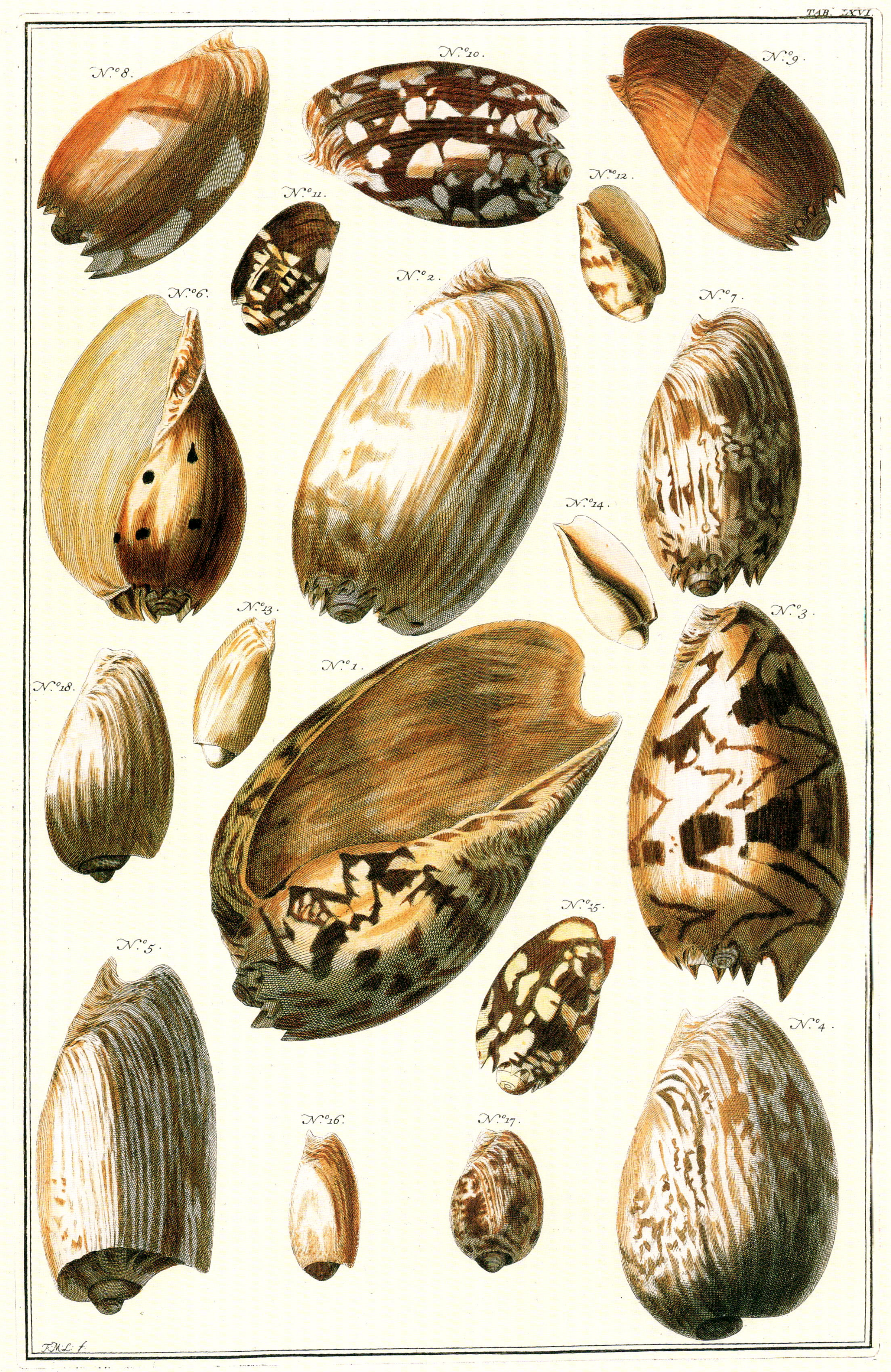

1 Melo amphora **2, 7, 10-12, 15** *Melo miltonis* **4** *Cymbium pepo* **5** *Cymbium cucumis* **6** *Melo aethiopica* **8** *Melo umbilicatus* **9** *Melo broderipii* **13-14, 16** *Cymbium* **18** *Cymbium olla*
Volutes from the tropical seas near West Africa, Indonesia and Australia · Walzenschnecken aus den tropischen Meeren bei Westafrika, Indonesien und Australien · Volutes des mers tropicales près de l'Afrique occidentale, de l'Indonésie et de l'Australie

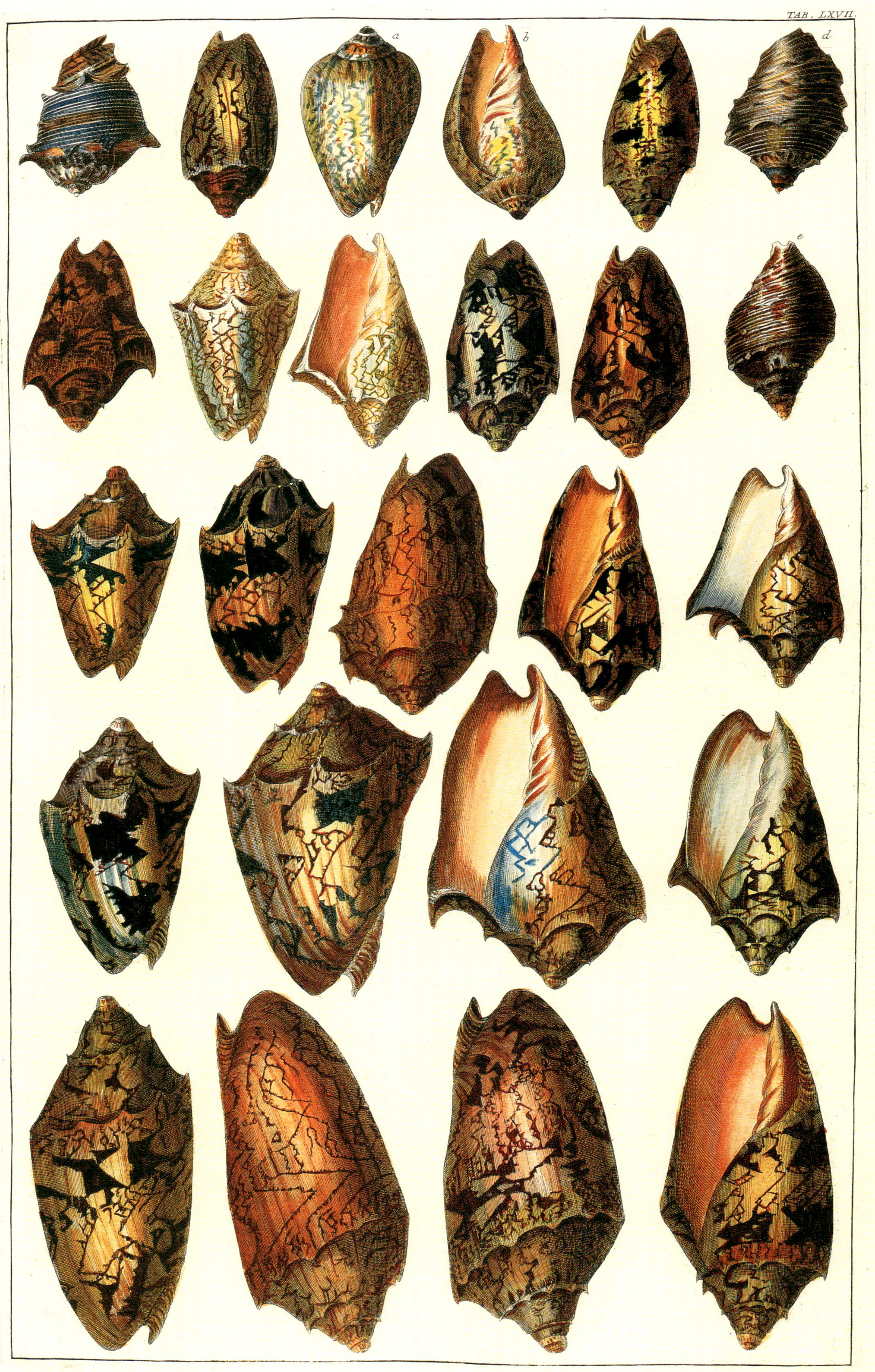

Cymbiola vespertilio
Volutes from tropical seas · Walzenschnecken aus den tropischen Meeren · Volutes des mers tropicales

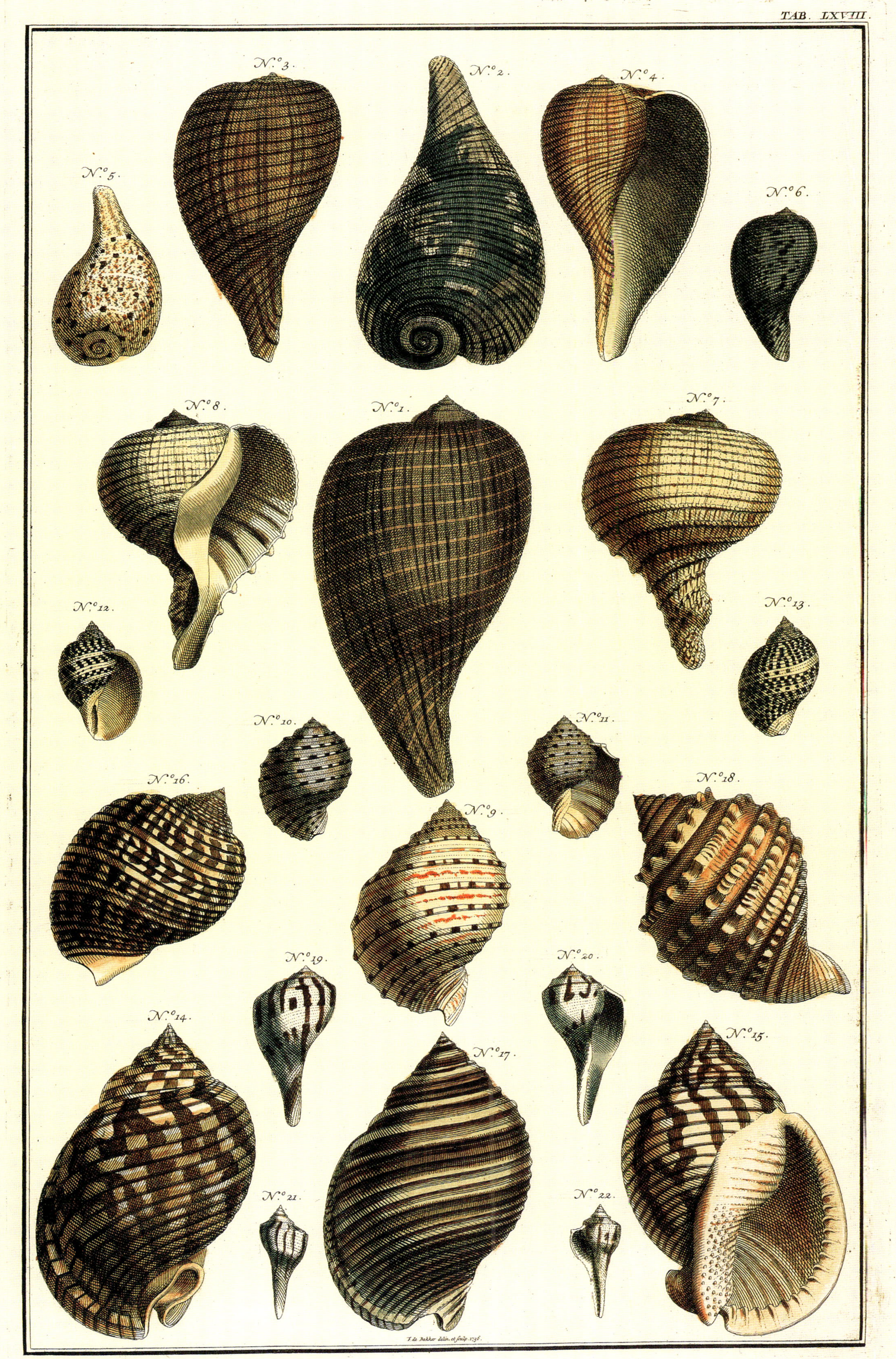

1, 3-4 *Ficus communis* **2** *Ficus* **5** *Ficus variegata* **6** *Ficus subintermedia* **7-8** *Rapa rapa* **9-11** *Tonna dolium* **14-15** *Phalium undulatum* **16** *Tonna perdix* **17** *Galeodea rugosa* **18** *Galeodea echinophora*

Tun shells, helmet shells, fig shells and other sea shells from North-East America, the Mediterranean, and the Indo-West Pacific · Tonnenschnecken, Helmschnecken, Feigenschnecken und andere Meeresschnecken aus Nordost-Amerika, dem Mittelmeer und dem Indo-Westpazifik · Tonnes, casques, figues et a autres mollusques marins du nord-est de l'Amérique, de la mer Méditerranée et de l'océan Indien et Pacifique occidental

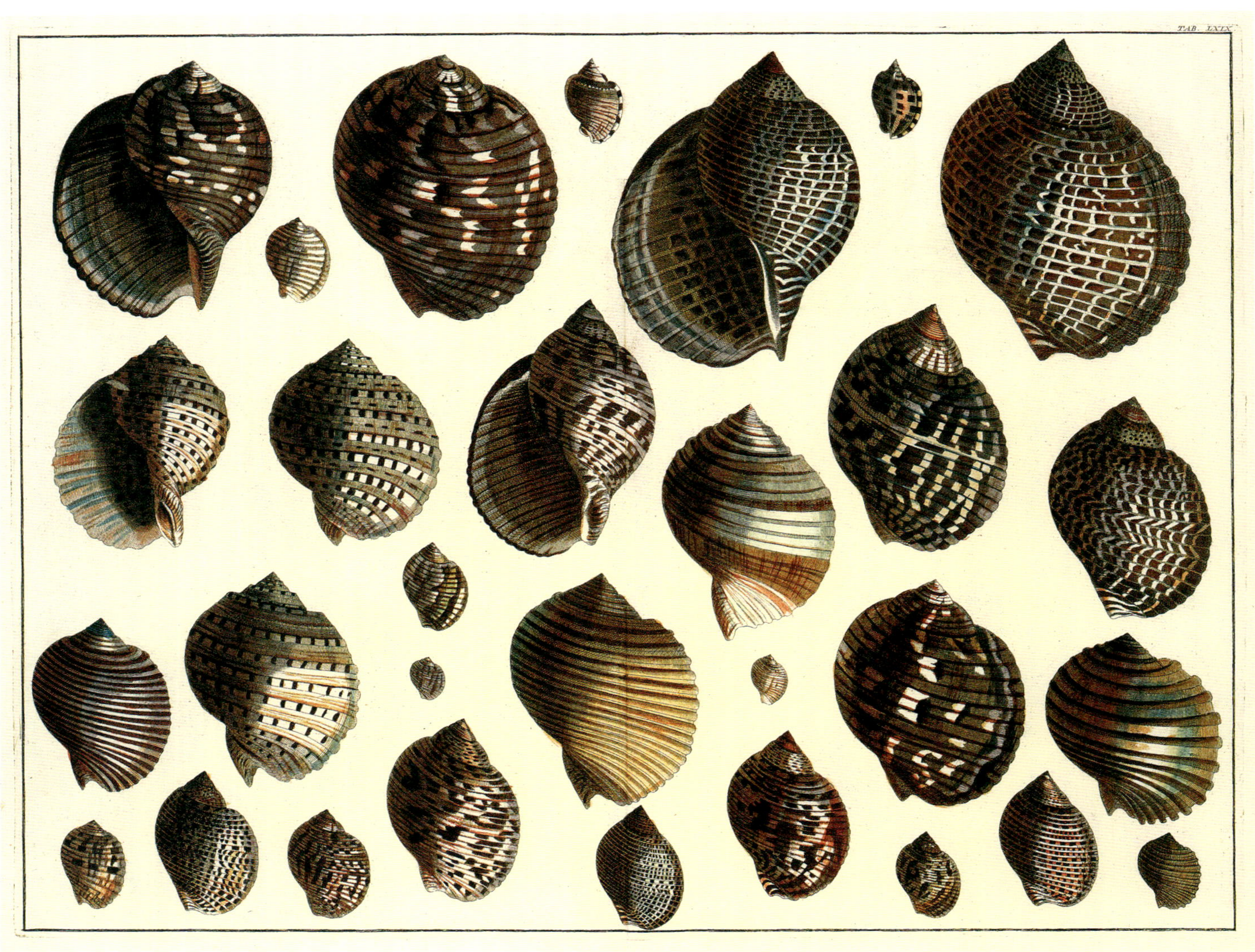

1, 3, 20 *Tonna cepa* 2 *Tonna* 4 *Phalium* 5, 7, 13, 23, 29 *Tonna perdix* 6 *Phalium areola* 8-9, 18 *Tonna dolium* 10, 12 *Tonna maculosa* 11 *Tonna sulcosa* 14-17, 19, 21-22, 24-28 Tonnidae
Tun shells and helmet shells from the Indo-Pacific and West Atlantic · Tonnenschnecken und Helmschnecken aus dem Indopazifik und dem Westatlantik · Tonnes et casques de l'aire indopacifique et de l'Atlantique occidental

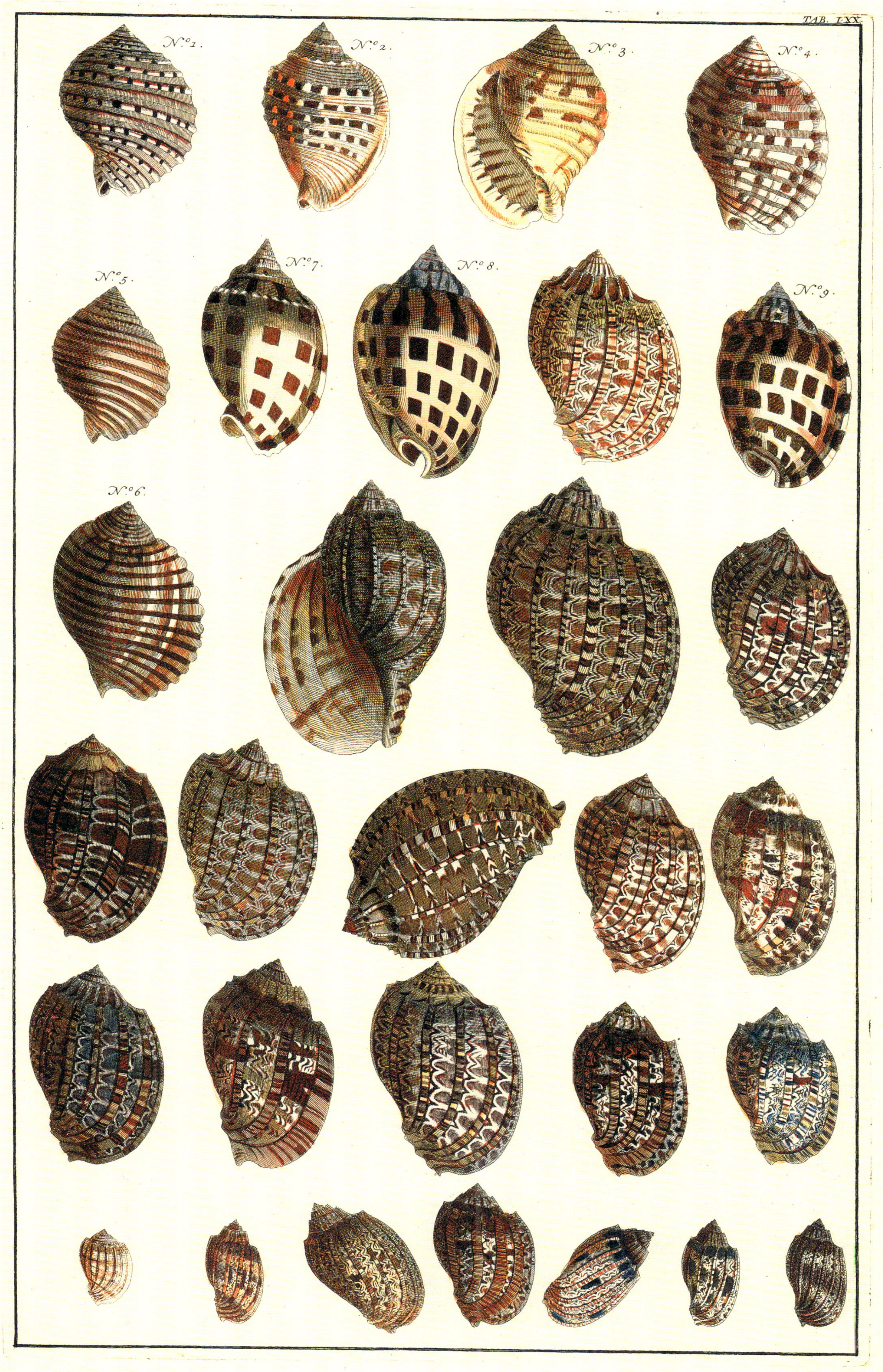

1 *Tonna marginata* 2 *Galeodea echinophora* 3-4 *Malea pomum* 5-6 *Malea ringens* 7-9 *Phalium areola* 10, 13-14, 17-22, 24 *Harpa davidis-complex* 11-12, 16 *Harpa articularis* 15, 23, 27 *Harpa ventricosa* 25-30 *Harpa amouretta*

Tun shells, helmet shells and harp shells from the Indo-Pacific, the Caribbean and the Mediterranean Sea · Tonnenschnecken, Helmschnecken und Harfenschnecken aus dem Indopazifik, der Karibik und dem Mittelmeer · Tonnes, casques et harpes de l'aire indopacifique, des Caraïbes et de la mer Méditerranée

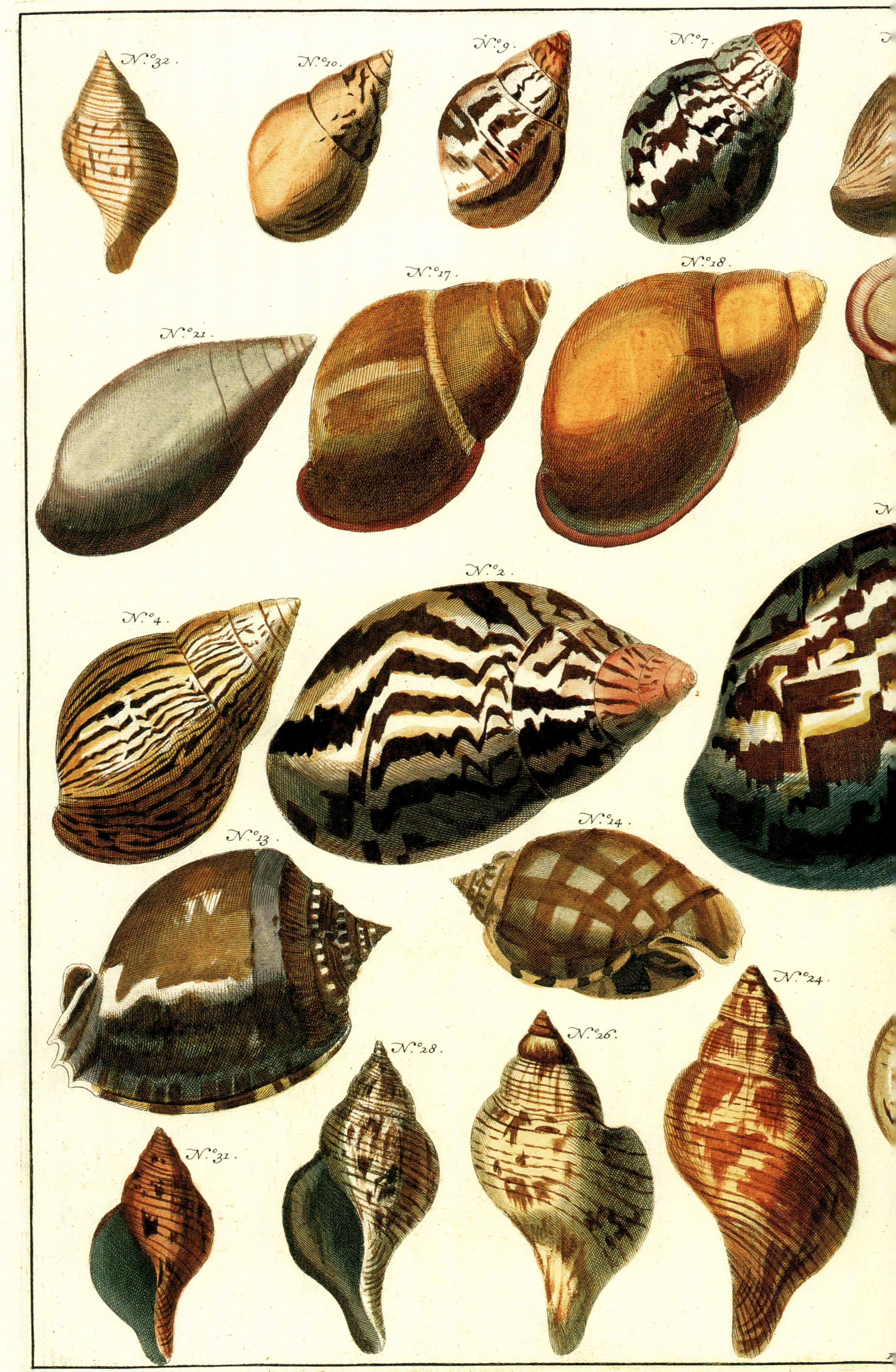

1-3, 7, 9 *Achatina achatina* 4-5 *Achatina* 6 Pulmonata 8 *Archachatina marginata* 10 Bulimulidae 11 *Phalium* 13-16 *Phalium glaucum* 17-20 *Megalobulimus oblongus* 21-22 *Ellobium aurismidae*
Spindle shells and helmet shells from the Indo-Pacific and the Caribbean, and land snails from Africa and South America · Meeresschnecken der Familien Fasciolariidae und Cassidae aus dem Indopazifik und der Karibik, sowie Landschnecken aus Afrika und Südamerika · Fuseaux et casques de l'aire indopacifique et de la mer des Caraïbes, ainsi que des mollusques terrestres (achatines et bulimes) d'Afrique et d'Amérique du Sud

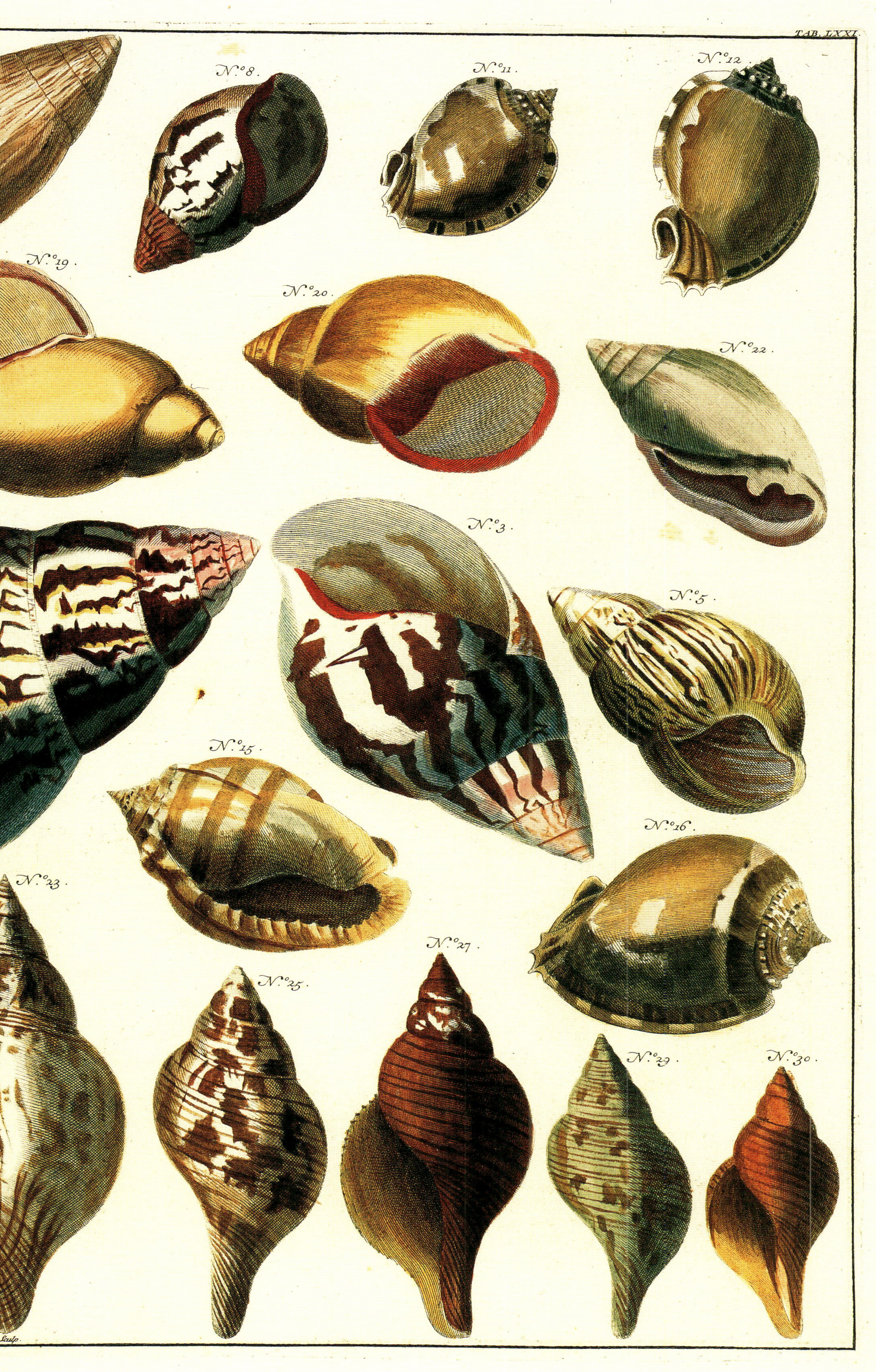
TAB. LXXI.
N.° 8.
N.° 11.
N.° 12.
N.° 19.
N.° 20.
N.° 22.
N.° 3.
N.° 5.
N.° 15.
N.° 16.
N.° 23.
N.° 27.
N.° 25.
N.° 29.
N.° 30.
Sculp.

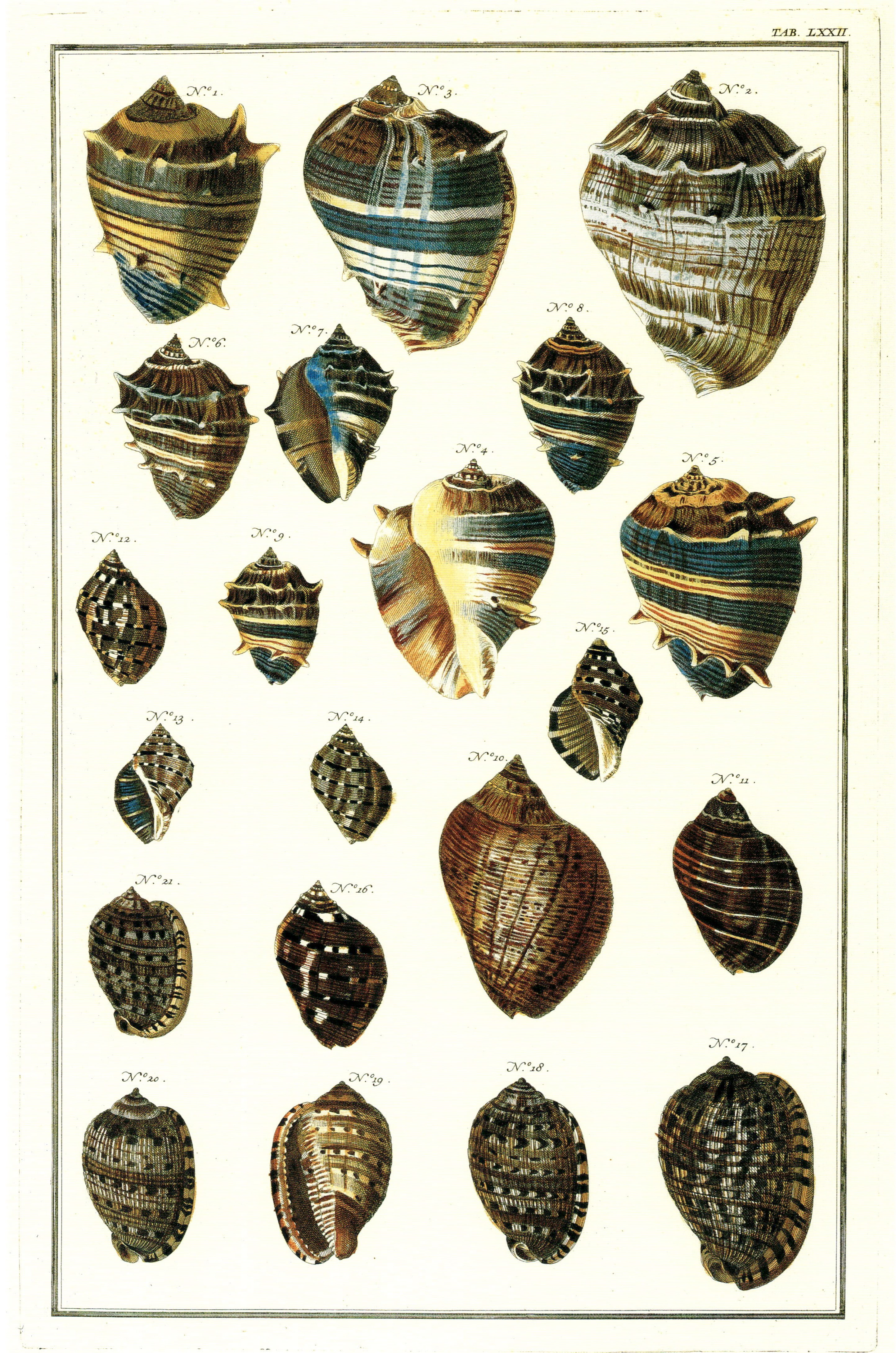

1-9 *Melongena melongena* 10-11 *Purpura persica* 12-15 *Thais haemastoma* 16 *Purpura panama* 17-21 *Cypraecassis testiculus*
Helmet shells and sea shells of the Melongenidae and Thaididae families, from the Indo-Pacific, the Atlantic, the Caribbean and the Mediterranean Sea · Helmschnecken und Meeresschnecken der Familien Melongenidae und Thaididae aus dem Indopazifik, dem Atlantik, der Karibik und dem Mittelmeer · Casques et mollusques marins de la famille des Melongenidae et des Thaididae de l'aire indopacifique, de l'Atlantique, des Caraïbes et de la mer Méditerranée

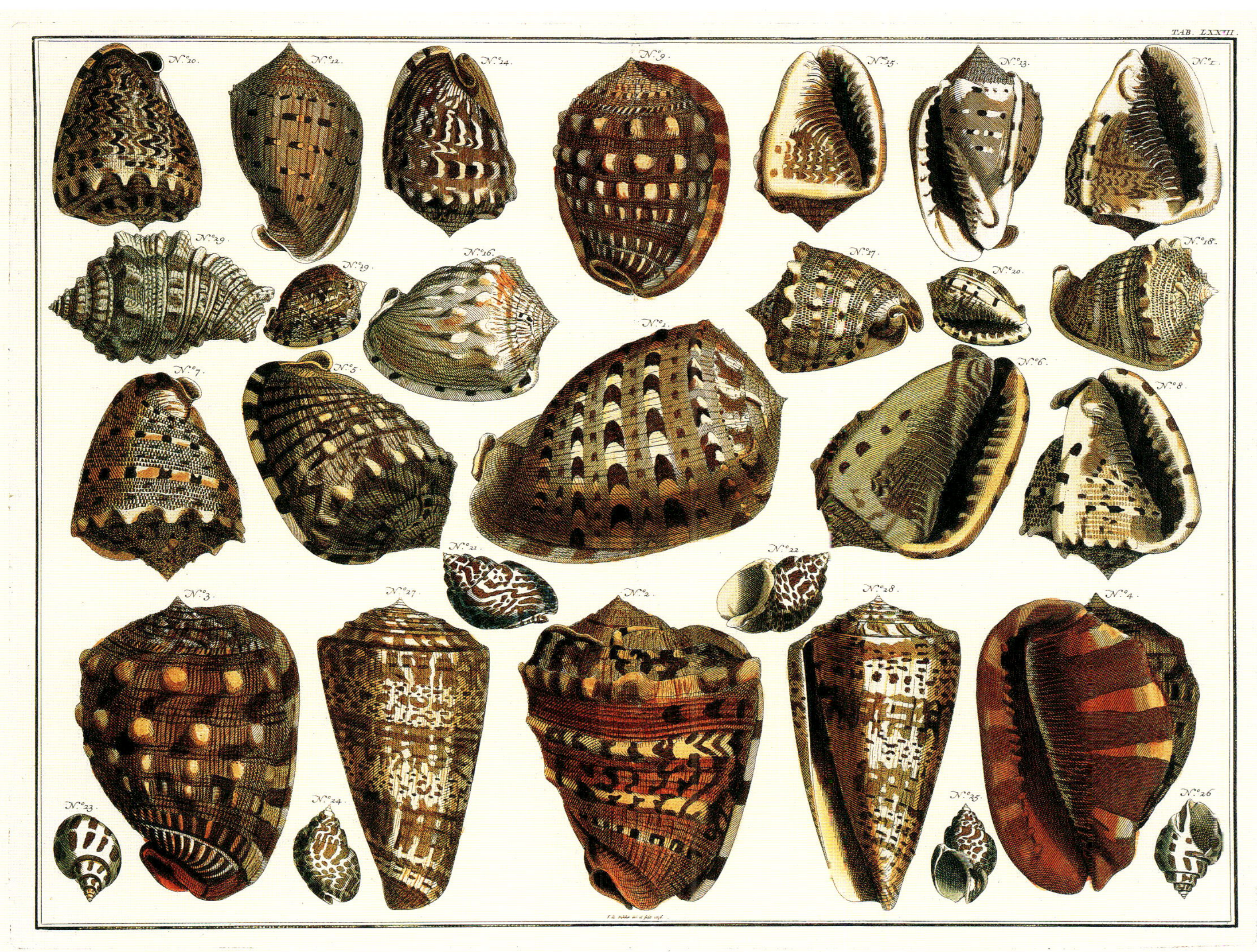

1, 12, 15 *Cassis tessellata* **2** *Cassis tuberosa* **3-4, 9** *Cypraecassis rufa* **5-6, 10-11, 13-14, 16-18** Cassidae **7-8** *Cassis cornuta* **19-20** *Cassis flammea* **21-22, 24-25** *Babylonia spirata* **23, 26** *Babylonia areolata* **27-28** *Conus pulcher*

Helmet shells, cone shell and whelks from the Indo-Pacific, West Africa and the Caribbean · Helmschnecken, Kegelschnecke und Wellhornschnecken aus dem Indopazifik, Westafrika und der Karibik · Casques, cône et buccins de l'aire indopacifique, de l'Afrique occidentale et des Caraïbes

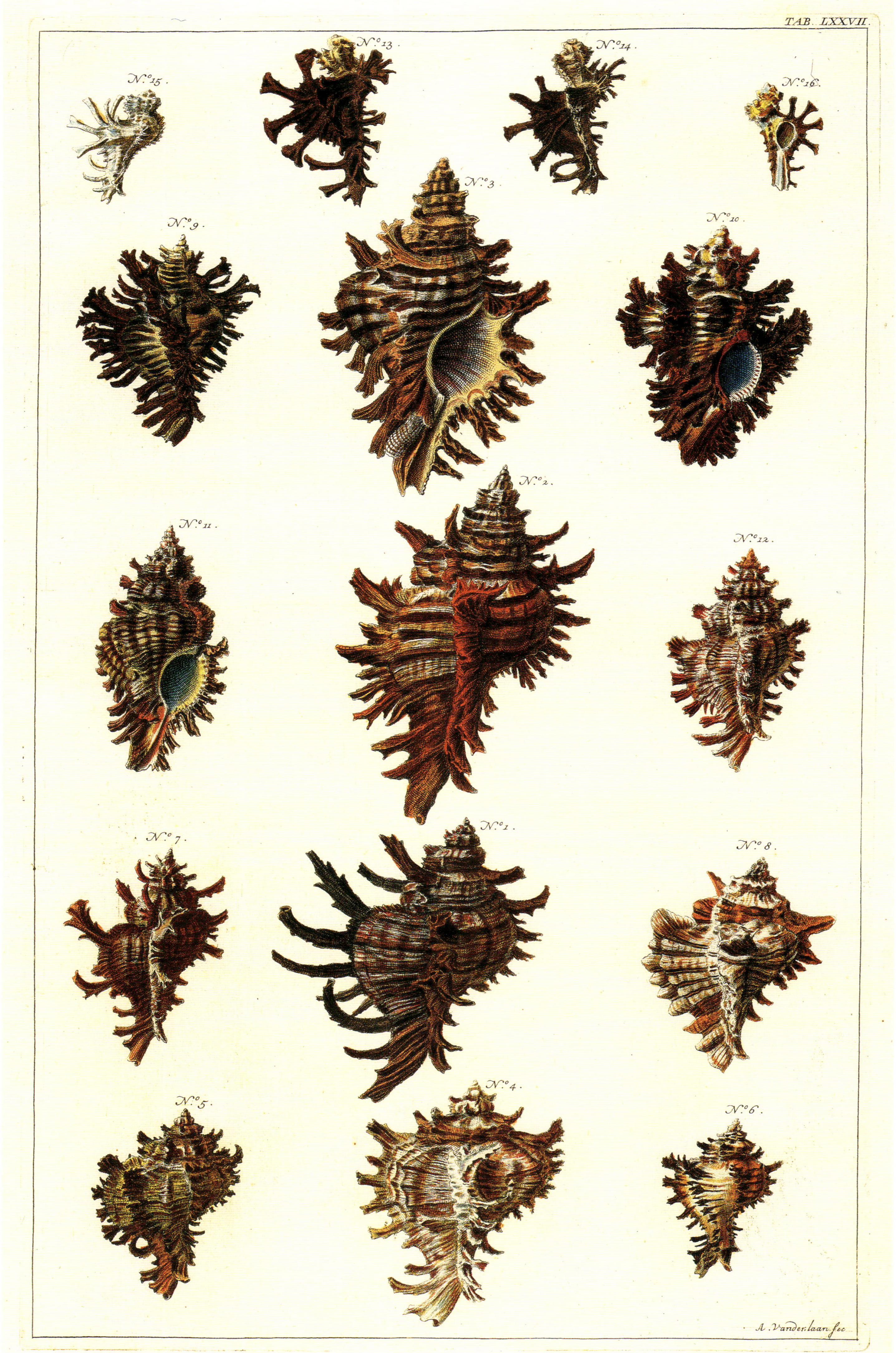

1, 5-6 *Chicoreus cichoreum* 2-3 *Chicoreus brevifrons?* 4 *Chicoreus ramosus* 7, 11-12 *Chicoreus* 8 *Hexaplex* 9-10 *Chicoreus brunneus* 13-16 *Homolacantha scorpio*
Murex shells, chiefly from the Indo-Pacific · Stachelschnecken der Familie Muricidae, hauptsächlich aus dem Indopazifik · Murex (ou rochers), principalement de l'aire indopacifique

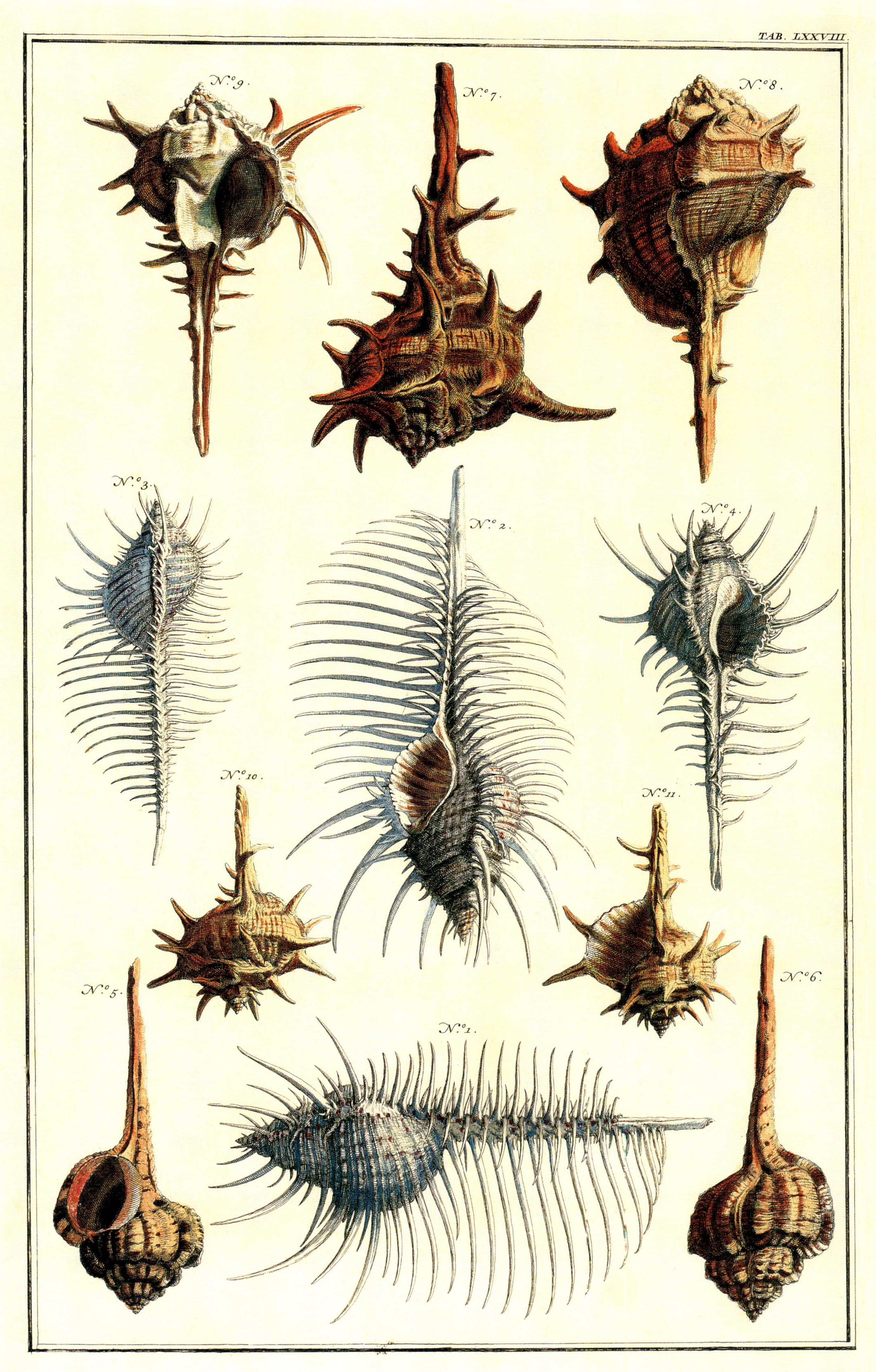

1-3 *Murex pecten* **4** *Murex troscheli* **5-6** *Haustellum haustellum* **7-9** *Bolinus cornutus* **10-11** *Bolinus brandaris*
Murex shells from the Indo-Pacific, West Africa and the Mediterranean Sea · Stachelschnecken der Familie Muricidae aus dem Indopazifik, Westafrika und dem Mittelmeer · Murex peignes et autres murex de l'aire indopacifique, de l'Afrique occidentale et de la mer Méditerranée

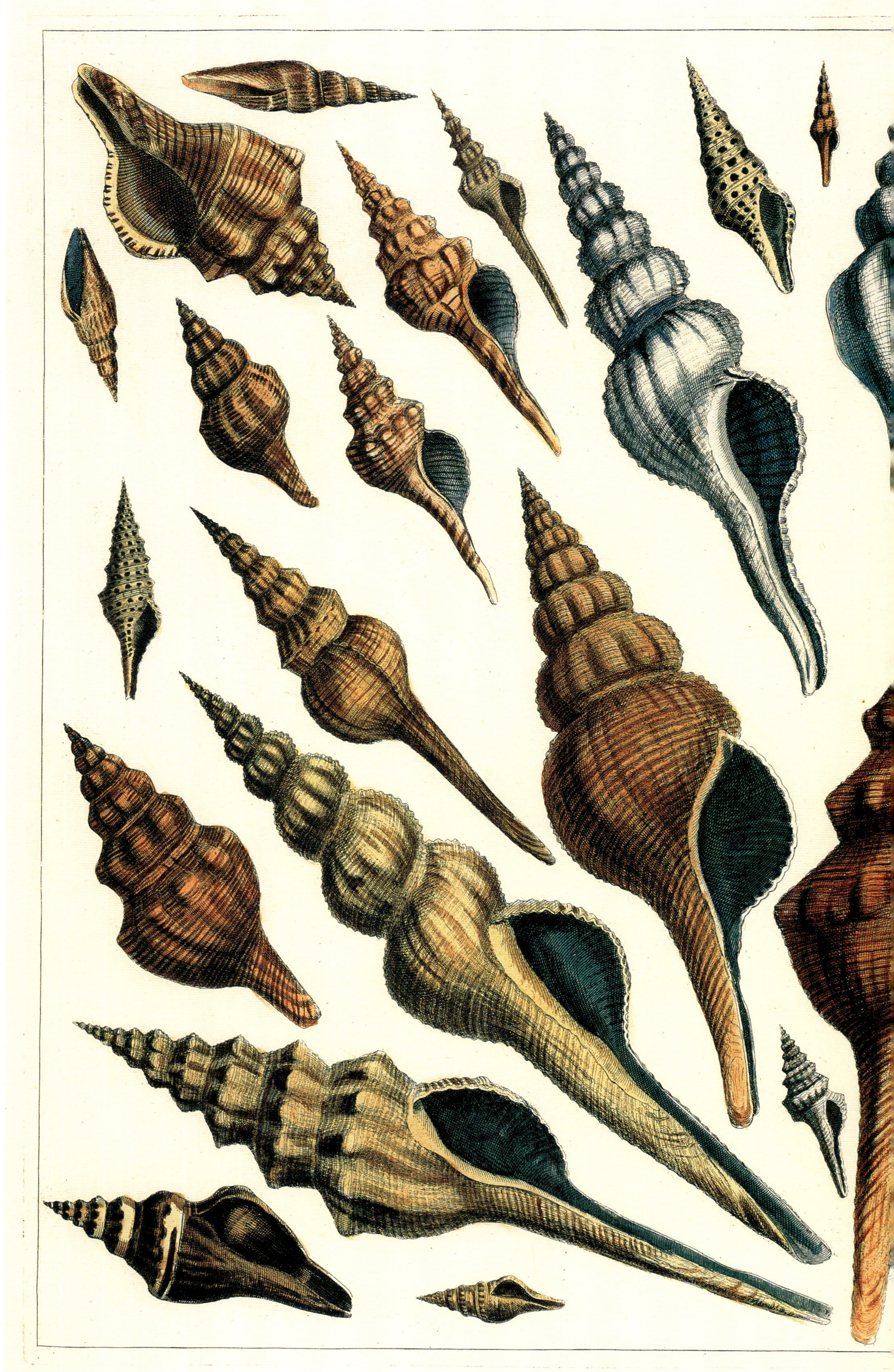

Fasciolariidae, Melongenidae, Turridae
Spindles, crown shells and turrid shells from tropical seas · Spindelschnecken, Kronenschnecken und Turmschnecken aus tropischen Meeren · Fasciolaires ou fuseaux, mélongenidés et turridés des eaux tropicales

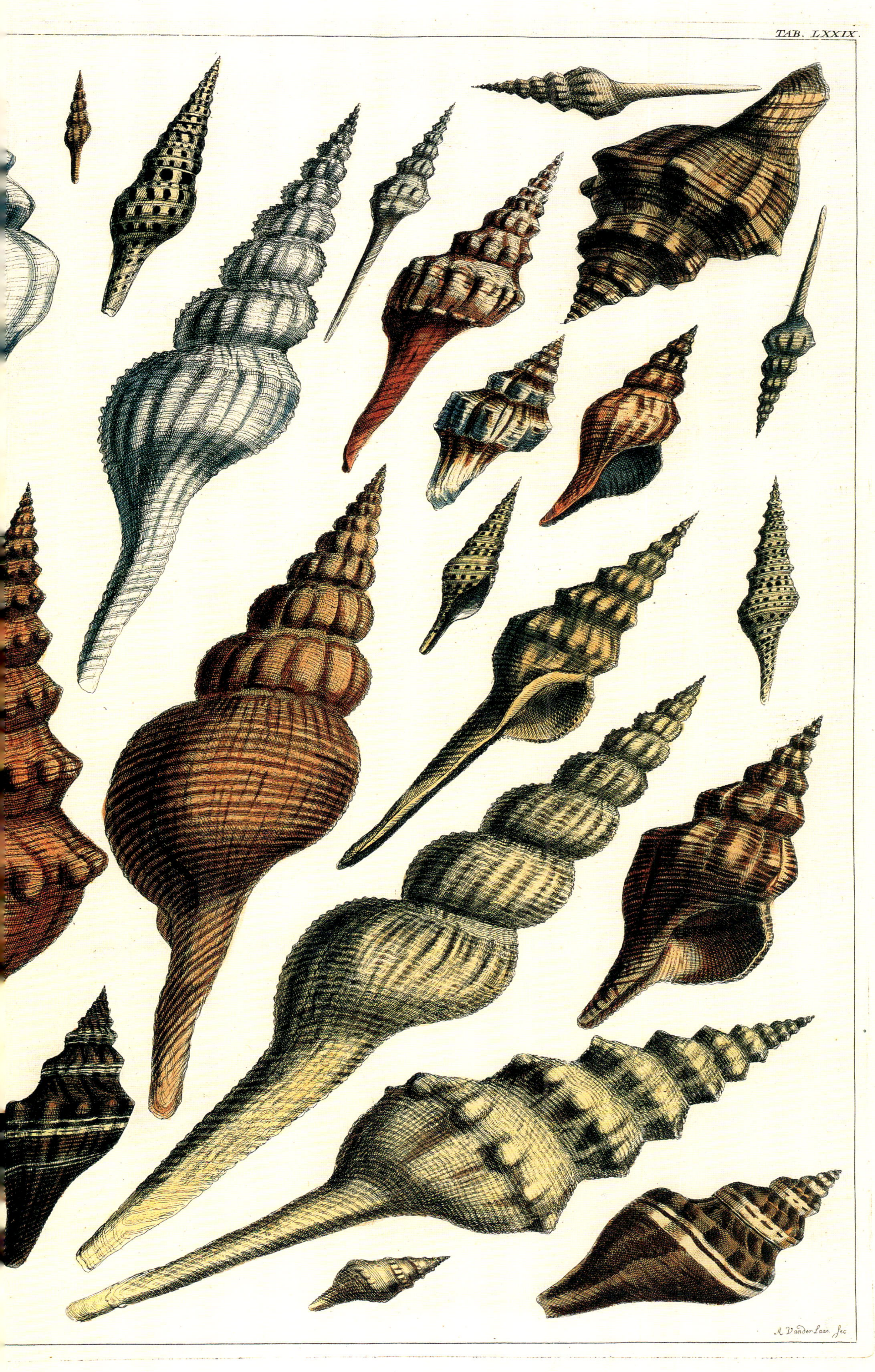
TAB. LXXIX.
A. Vander Laan fec

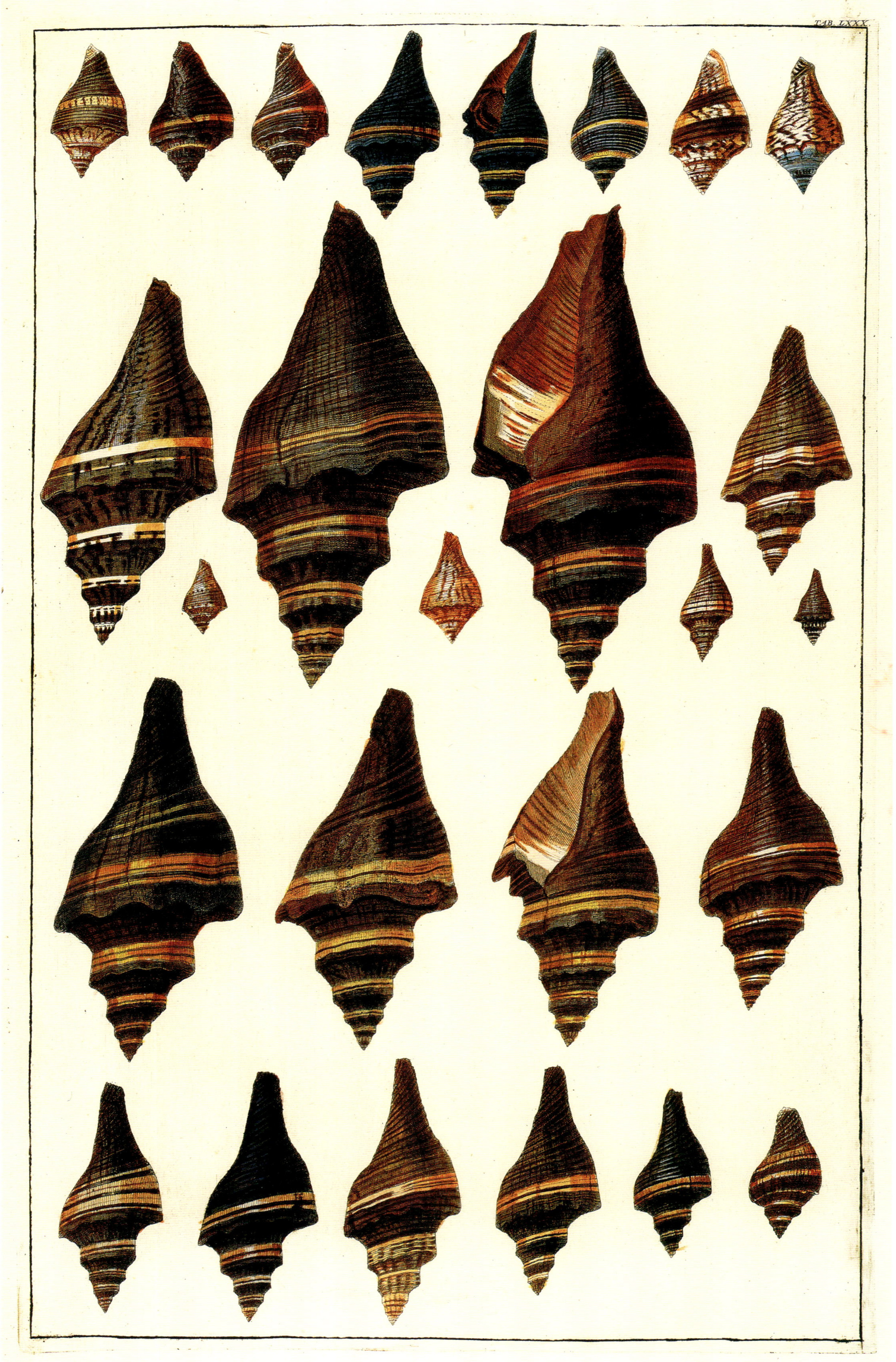

1 -2, 6, 26 *Melongena* 3-5, 9, 11, 13-25 *Pugilina morio* 7-8, 10, 12 Melongenidae
Melongenids from tropical waters · Kronenschnecken aus tropischen Gewässern · Mélongénidés des eaux tropicales

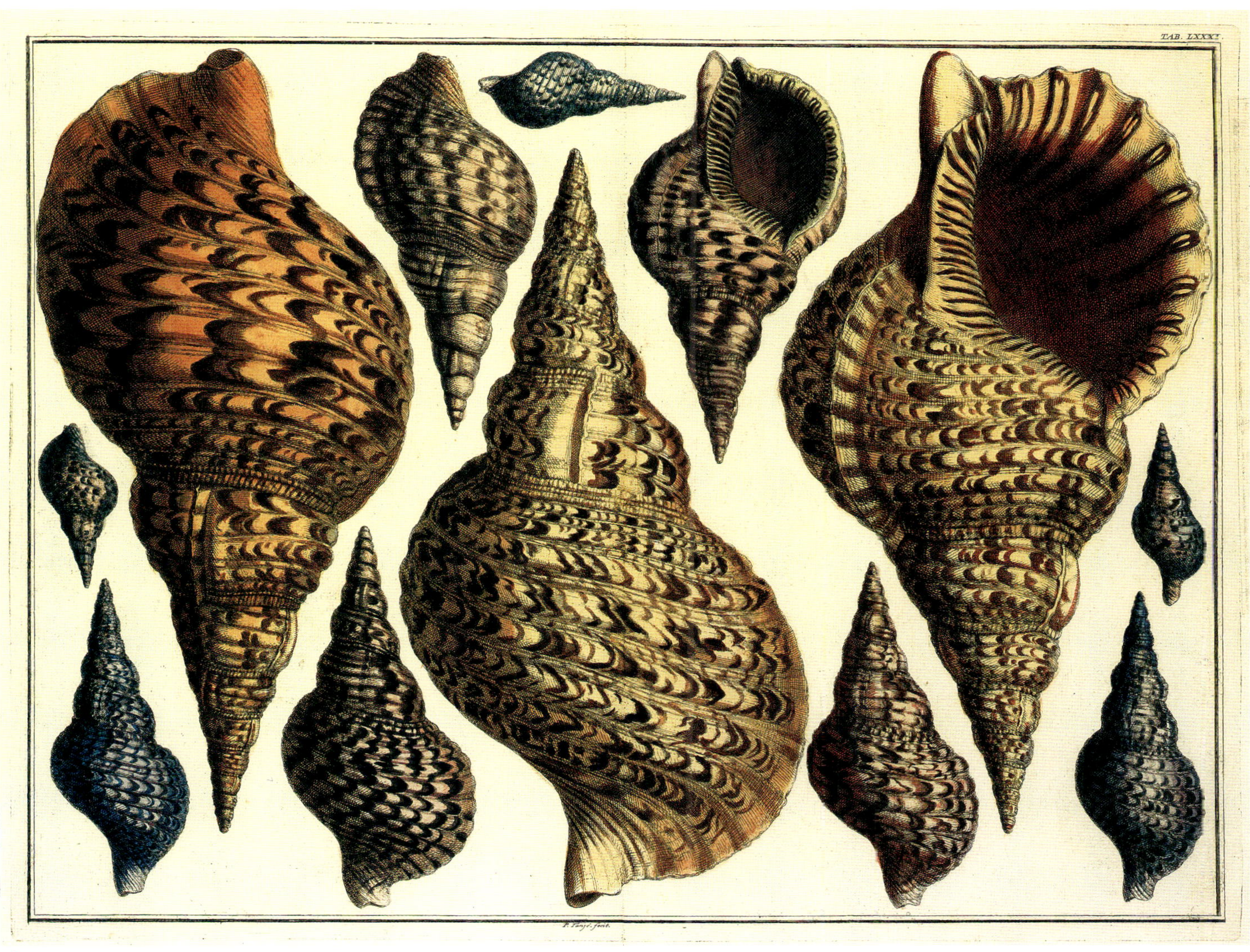

Charonia tritonis
Triton trumpets · Tritonshörner · Grands tritons

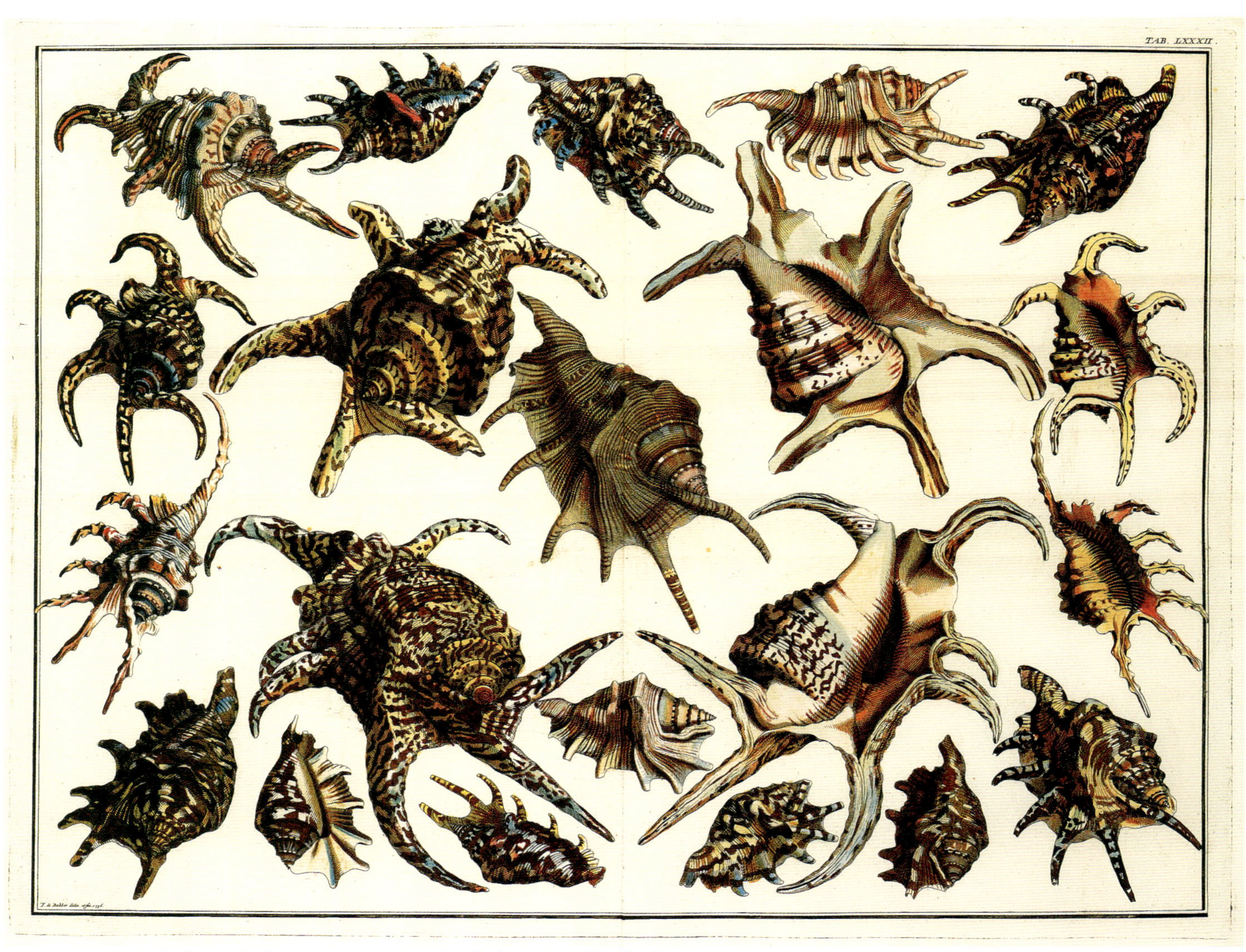

1, 5, 8-13, 17-18, 21 *Lambis lambis* **2, 19** *Lambis scorpius* **3-4, 6-7, 14-15, 20** *Lambis chiragra* **16** *Lambis millepeda*
Spider conchs or lambis shells (Strombidae family), from the Indo-Pacific · Spinnenschnecken der Familie Strombidae aus dem Indopazifik · Coquillages araignées ou lambis (famille des Strombidae) de l'aire indopacifique

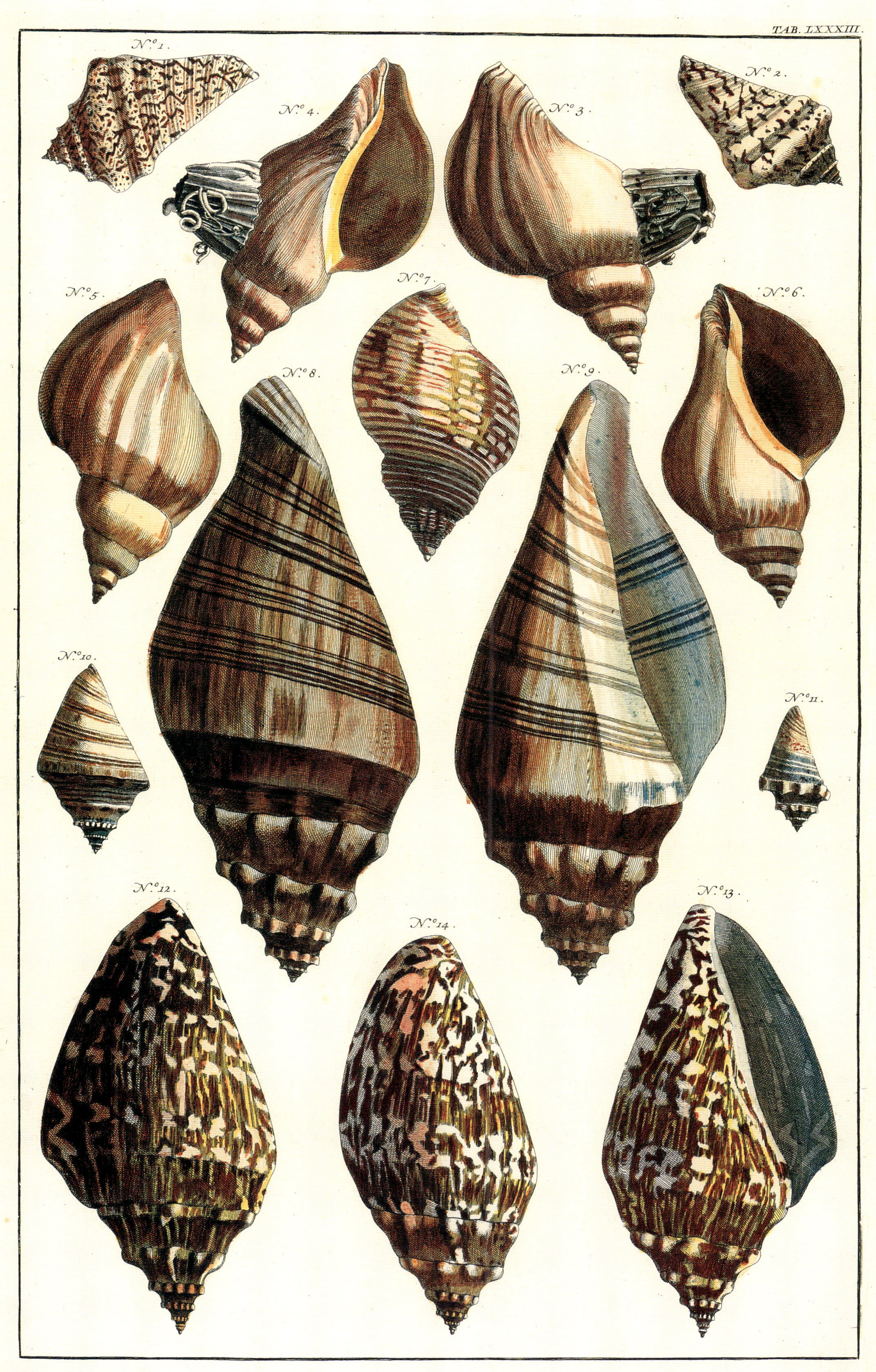

1-2, 12-14 *Lambis lambis* **3-6** *Neptunea antiqua* **7** *Buccinum undatum* **8-9** *Lambis truncata sebae* **10-11** Strombidae
Juvenile spider conchs (Strombidae family) from the Indo-Pacific, and two species of whelk from the northern Atlantic · Jungtiere von Spinnenschnecken der Familie Strombidae aus dem Indopazifik und zwei Wellhornschnecken-Arten aus dem Nordatlantik · Jeunes coquillages araignées ou lambris (famille des Strombidae) de l'aire indopacifique et deux espèces de buccin de l'Atlantique Nord

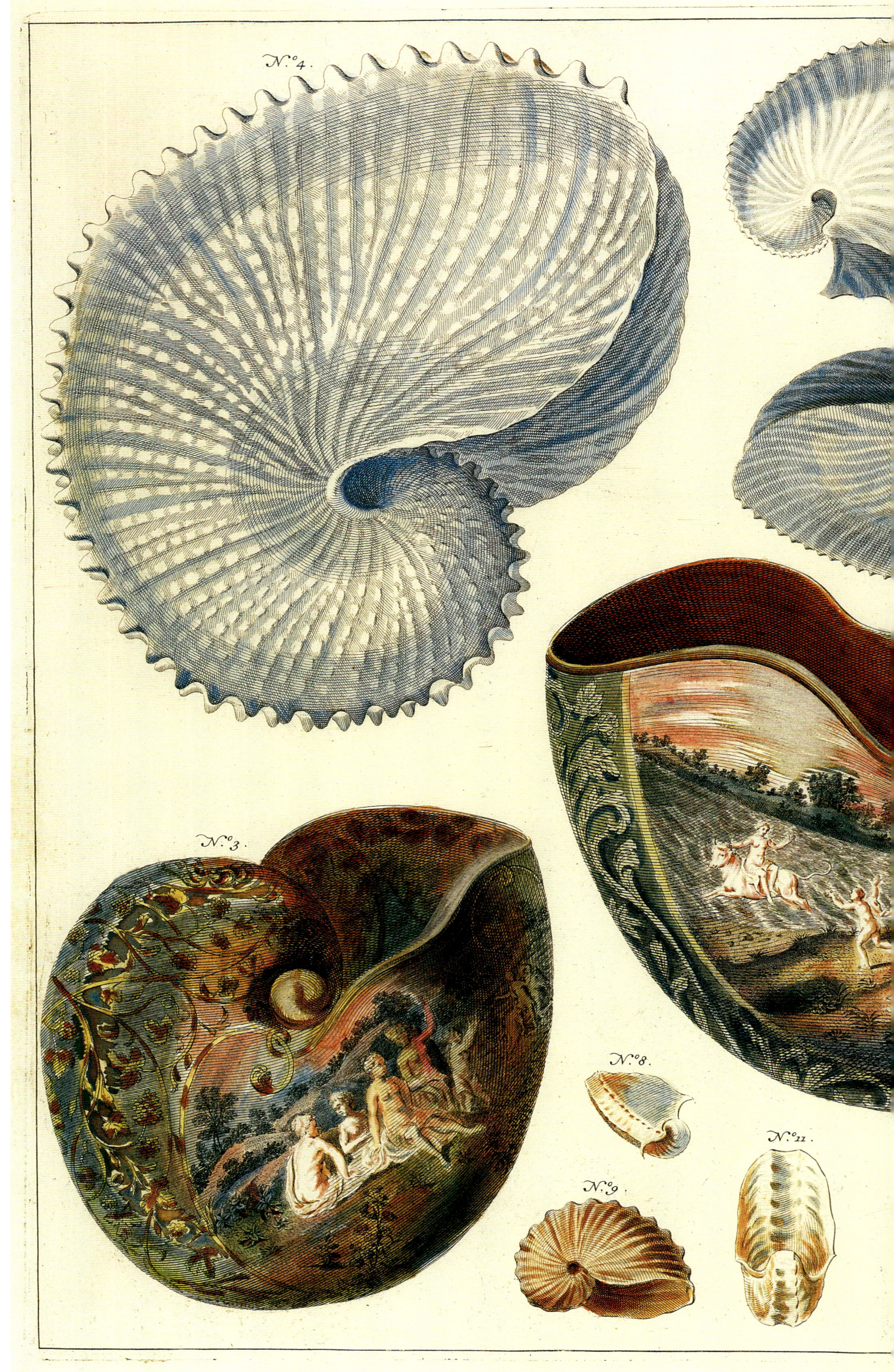

1-3 Nautiloidea **4-12** *Argonauta* **4** *Argonauta nodosa* **5-6** *Argonauta argo* **7** *Argonauta sp.* **9-12** *Argonauta hians*
1-3 Chambered nautilus / Pearly nautilus (etched) · Perlboote (graviert) · Nautiles (décorés et gravés) **4-12** Paper nautilus · Papierboote · Argonautes

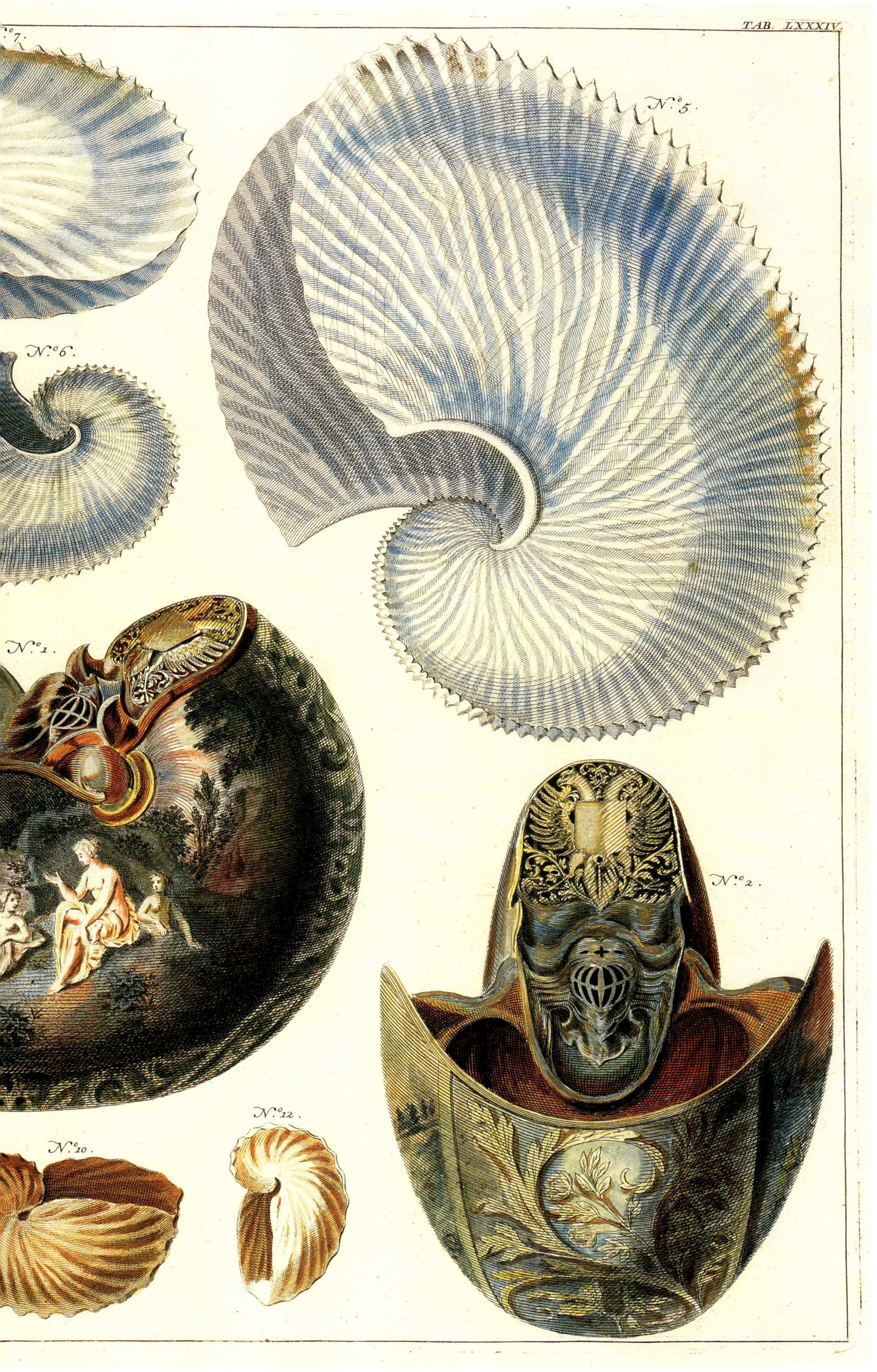
TAB. LXXXIV.
N.°7.
N.°5.
N.°6.
N.°1.
N.°2.
N.°12.
N.°10.

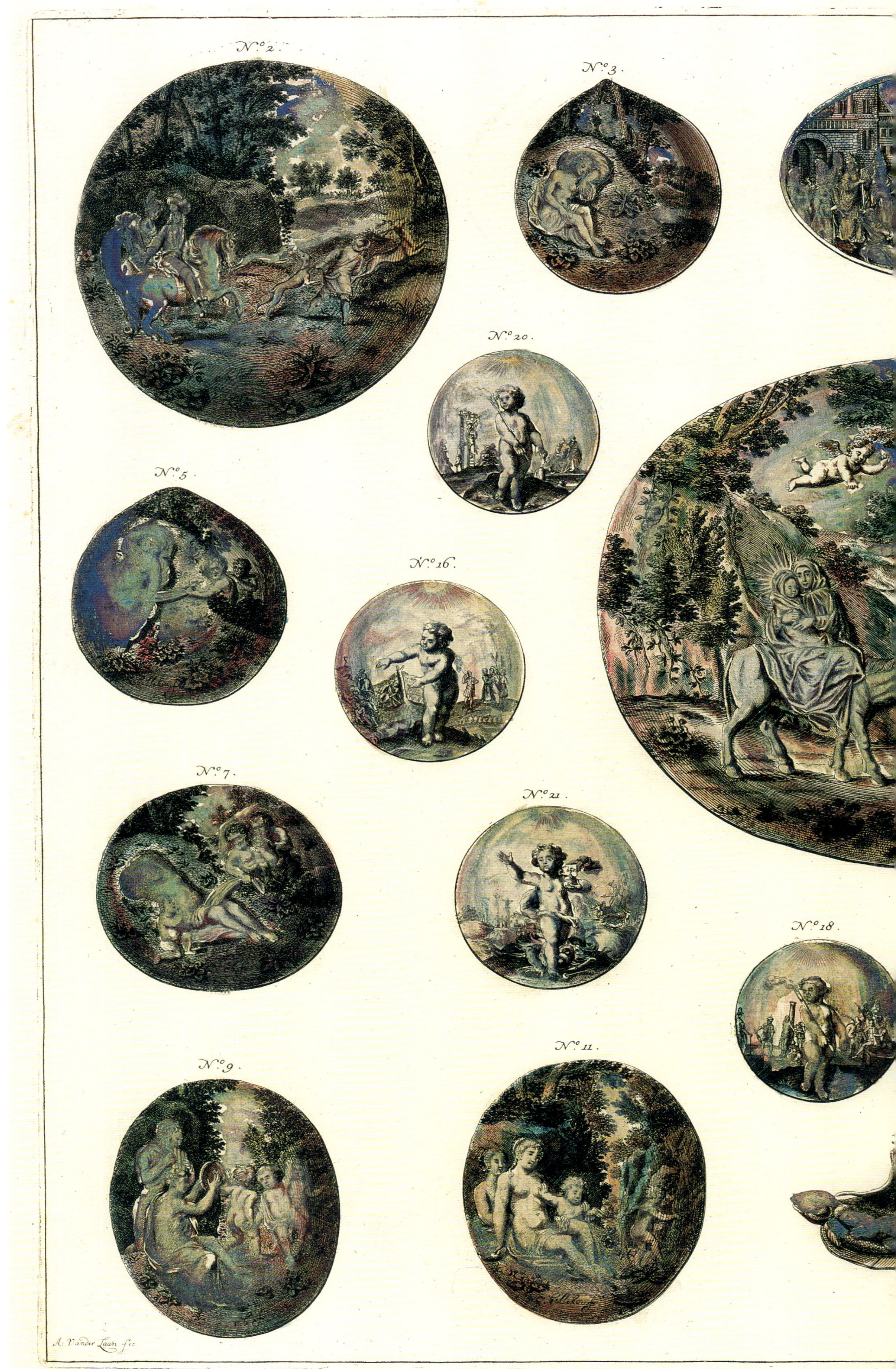

Nautilus
Drawings etched into the mother-of-pearl plates of Nautilus · Ritzzeichnungen auf Perlmuttplättchen von Nautilus · Dessins gravés dans de la nacre de nautile

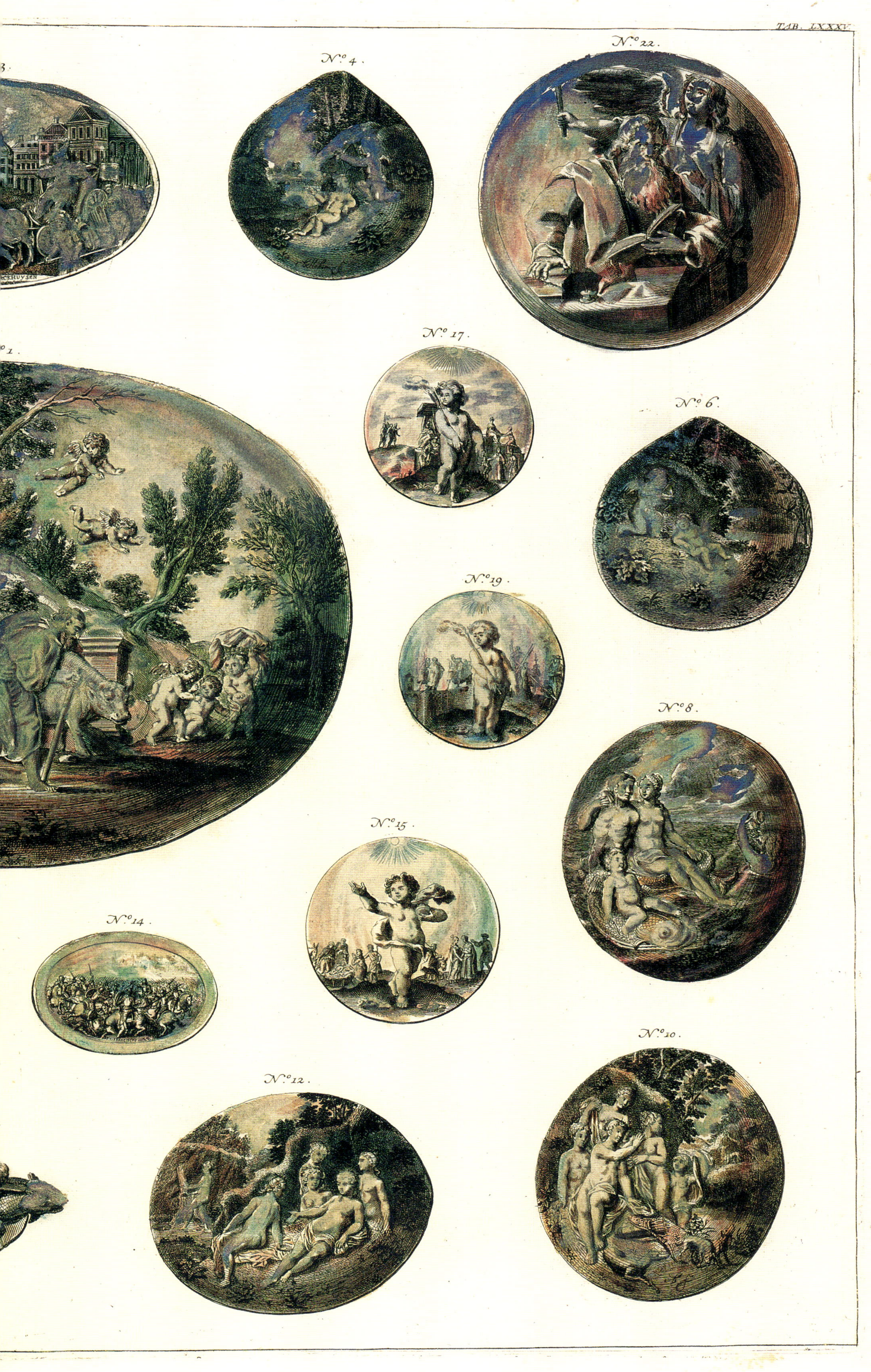
TAB. LXXXV.
N.° 22.
N.° 4.
N.° 17.
N.° 6.
N.° 19.
N.° 8.
N.° 15.
N.° 14.
N.° 10.
N.° 12.

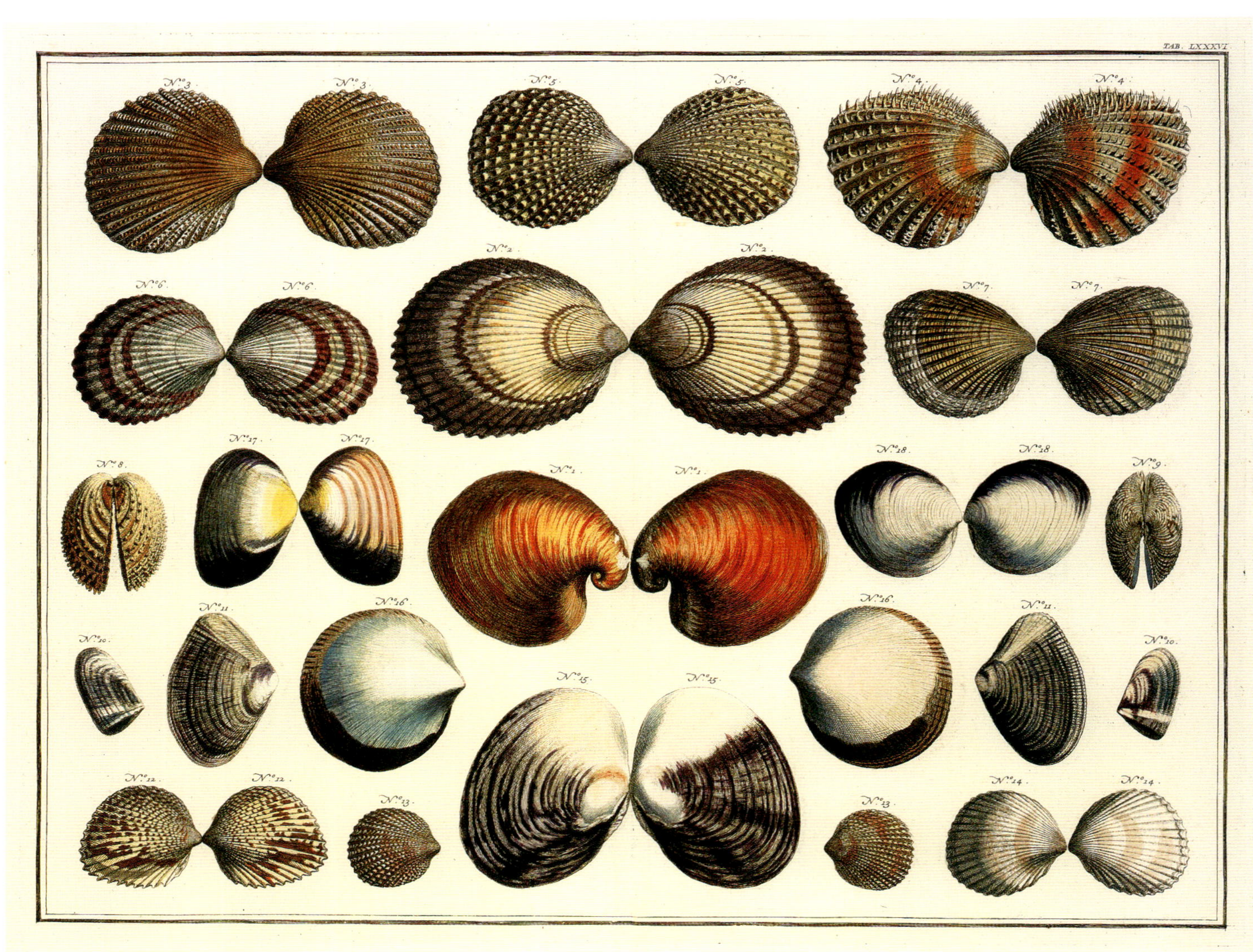

1 *Glossus humanus* 2, 6 *Trachycardium* 3, 13 *Acanthocardia echinata* 4-5, 8 *Acanthocardia aculeata* 7, 14 *Acanthocardia tuberculata* 10-11 *Donax rugosus* 12 *Fragum unedo* 18 *Arctica islandica*
Ox heart, cockles, donax shells and ocean quahog from the Atlantic, Mediterranean Sea and the Indo-Pacific · Ochsenherz, Herzmuscheln, Donaxmuscheln und Islandmuscheln aus dem Atlantik, Mittelmeer und Indopazifik · Cœur de bœuf, coques ou cardiidés, donax et cyprines nordiques de l'Atlantique, de la mer Méditerranée et de l'aire indopacifique

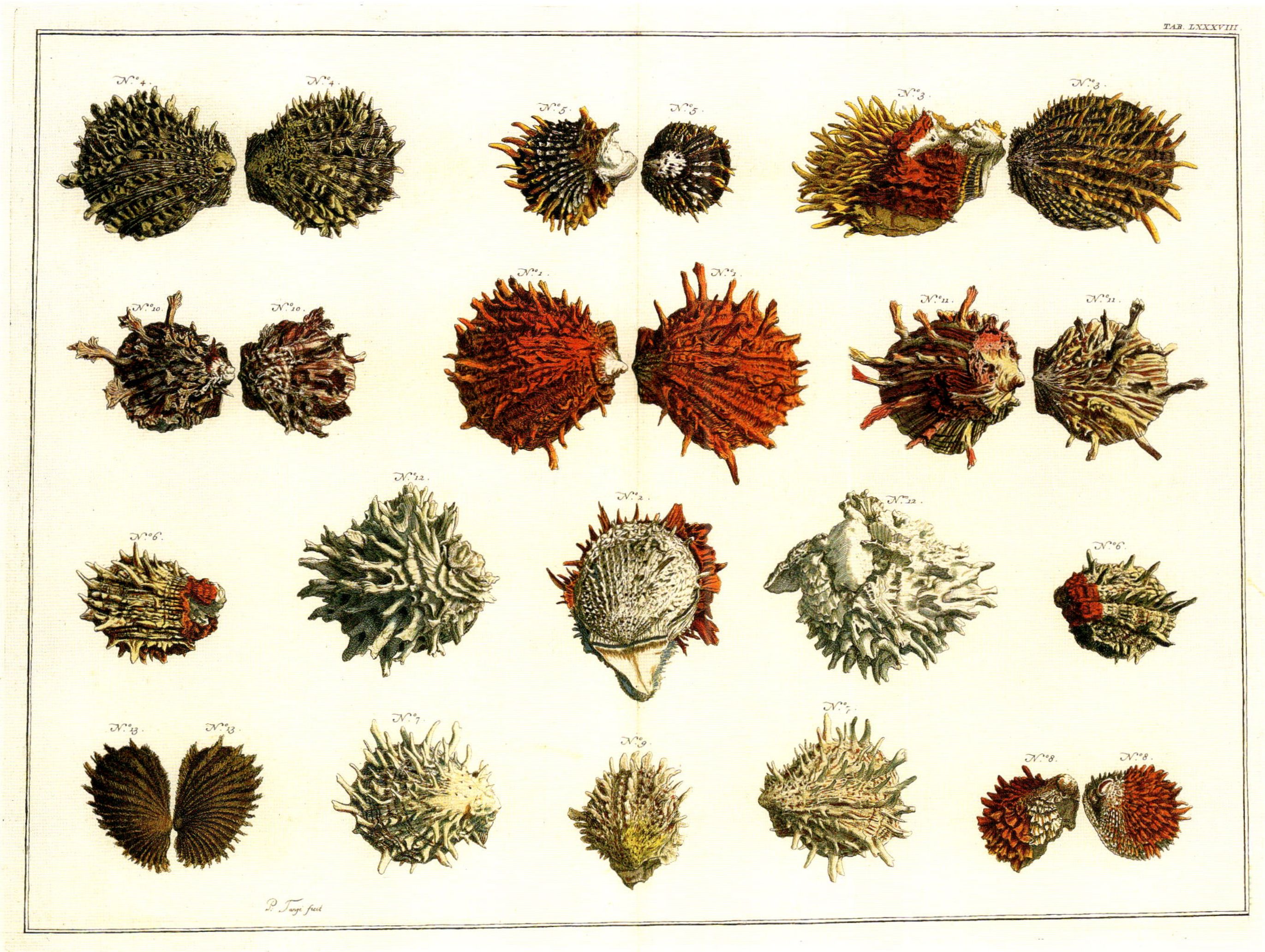

1-7, 9-11 *Spondylus gaederopus* 8 *Chama macerophylla* 12 *Chama lazarus* 13 *Barbatia*
Thorny oysters, Lazarus jewel boxes and an ark shell from the West Atlantic, Mediterranean Sea and the Indo-Pacific · Stachelaustern, Lazarus-Schmuckkästchen und Archenmuschel aus dem Westatlantik, Mittelmeer und Indopazifik · Spondyles pieds d'âne, chames lazarus et arche barbue de l'Atlantique occidental, de la mer Méditerranée et de l'aire indopacifique

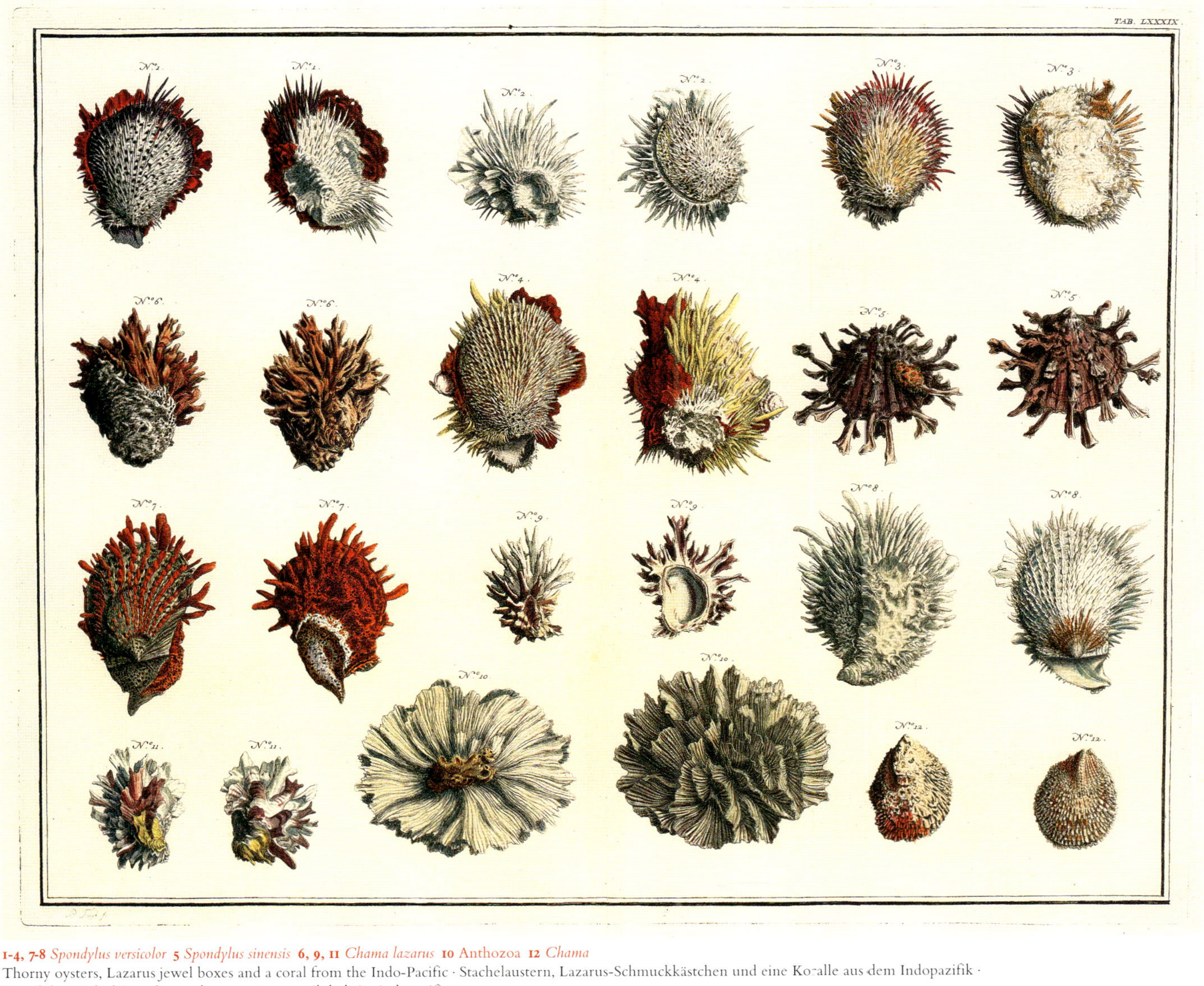

1-4, 7-8 *Spondylus versicolor* 5 *Spondylus sinensis* 6, 9, 11 *Chama lazarus* 10 Anthozoa 12 *Chama*
Thorny oysters, Lazarus jewel boxes and a coral from the Indo-Pacific · Stachelaustern, Lazarus-Schmuckkästchen und eine Koralle aus dem Indopazifik · Spondyles pieds d'âne, chames lazarus et un corail de l'aire indopacifique

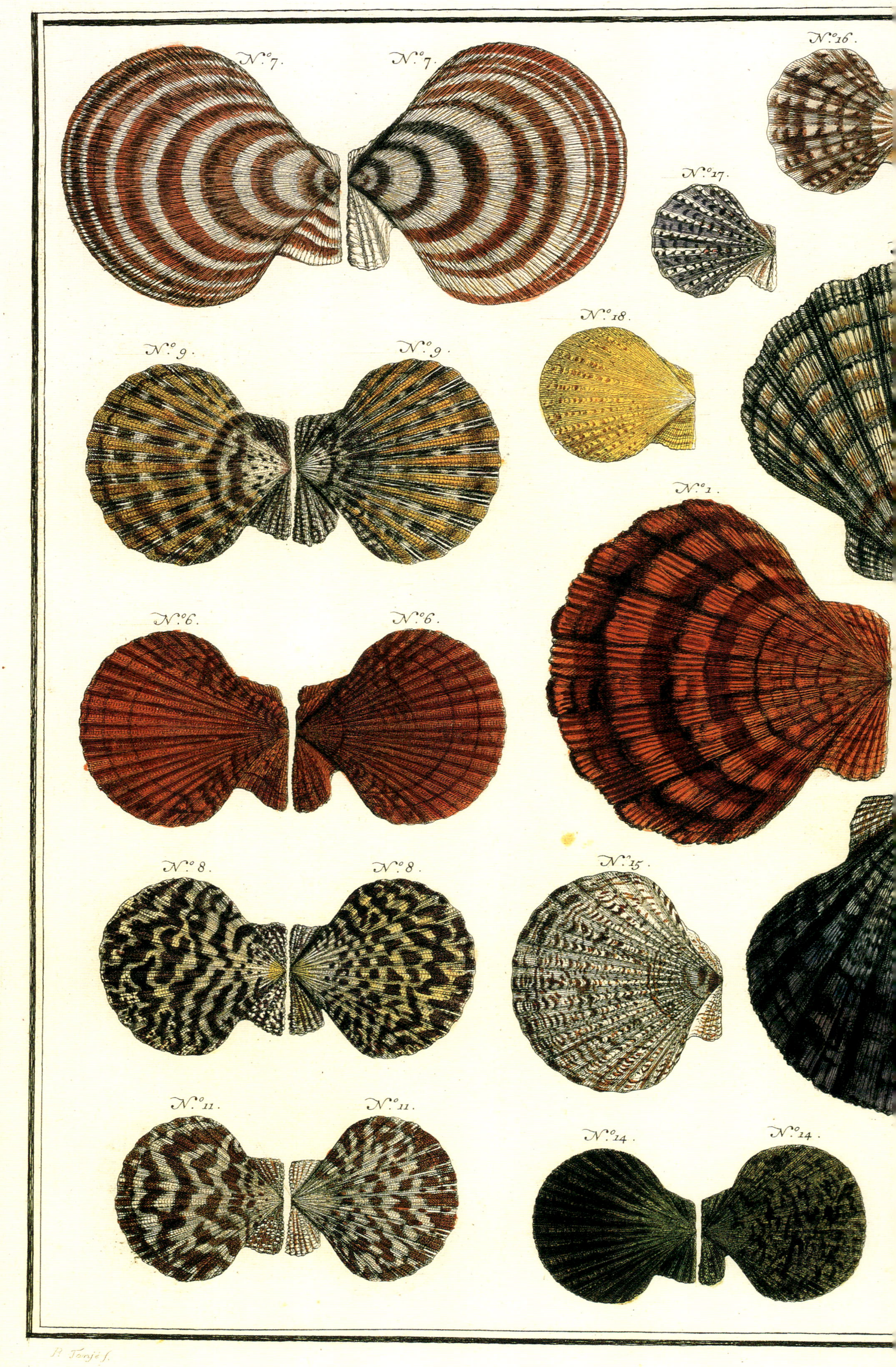

1-5 *Lyropecten nodosa* **7** *Chlamys* **8-12** *Cryptopecten pallium* **13, 18** Pectinidae
Scallops from the West Atlantic and the Indo-Pacific · Kammmuscheln aus dem Westatlantik und Indopazifik · Peignes de l'Atlantique occidental et de l'aire indopacifique

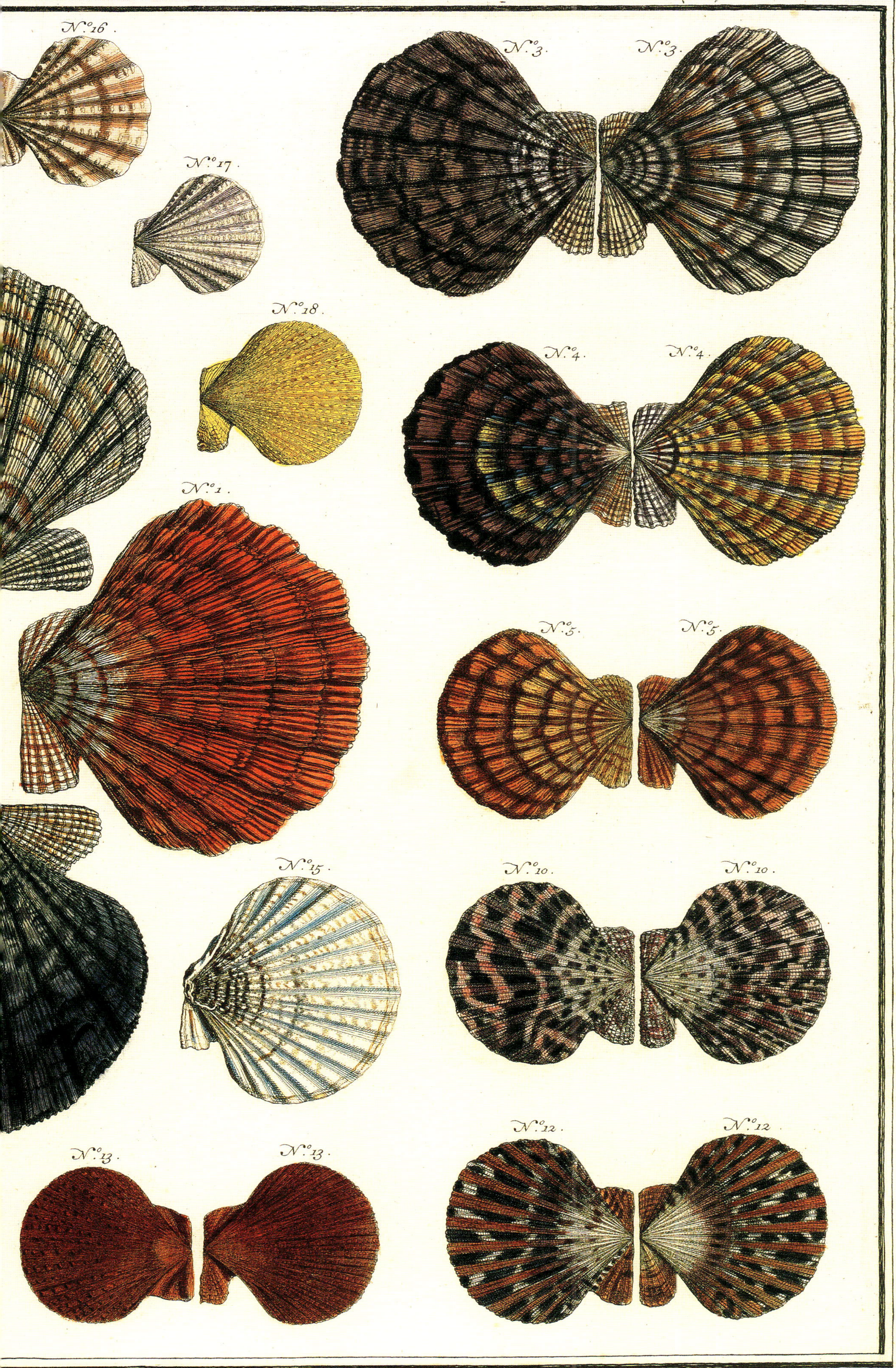
N.° 16.
N.° 17.
N.° 18.
N.° 1.
N.° 15.
N.° 13.
N.° 13.
N.° 3.
N.° 3.
N.° 4.
N.° 4.
N.° 5.
N.° 5.
N.° 10.
N.° 10.
N.° 12.
N.° 12.

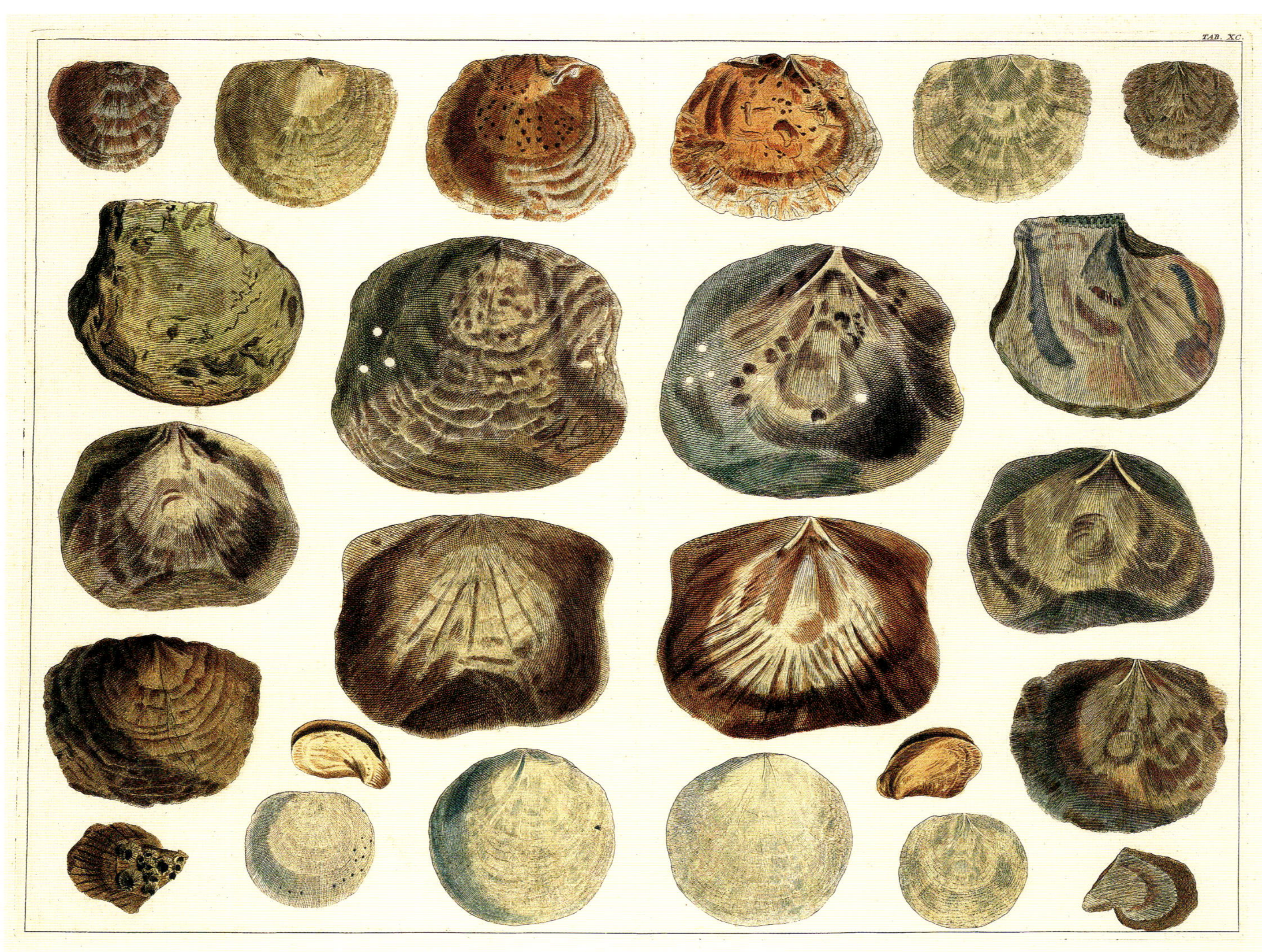

Perna, Placuna sella, Placuna placenta, Anomia ephippium
Mussels, oysters and European jingle shells from the Indo-Pacific, Atlantic and Mediterranean Sea · Muscheln, Austern und Europäische Sattelaustern aus dem Indopazifik, Atlantik und Mittelmeer · Coquillages, huîtres et anomie pelure d'oignon, de l'aire indopacifique, de l'Atlantique et de la mer Méditerranée

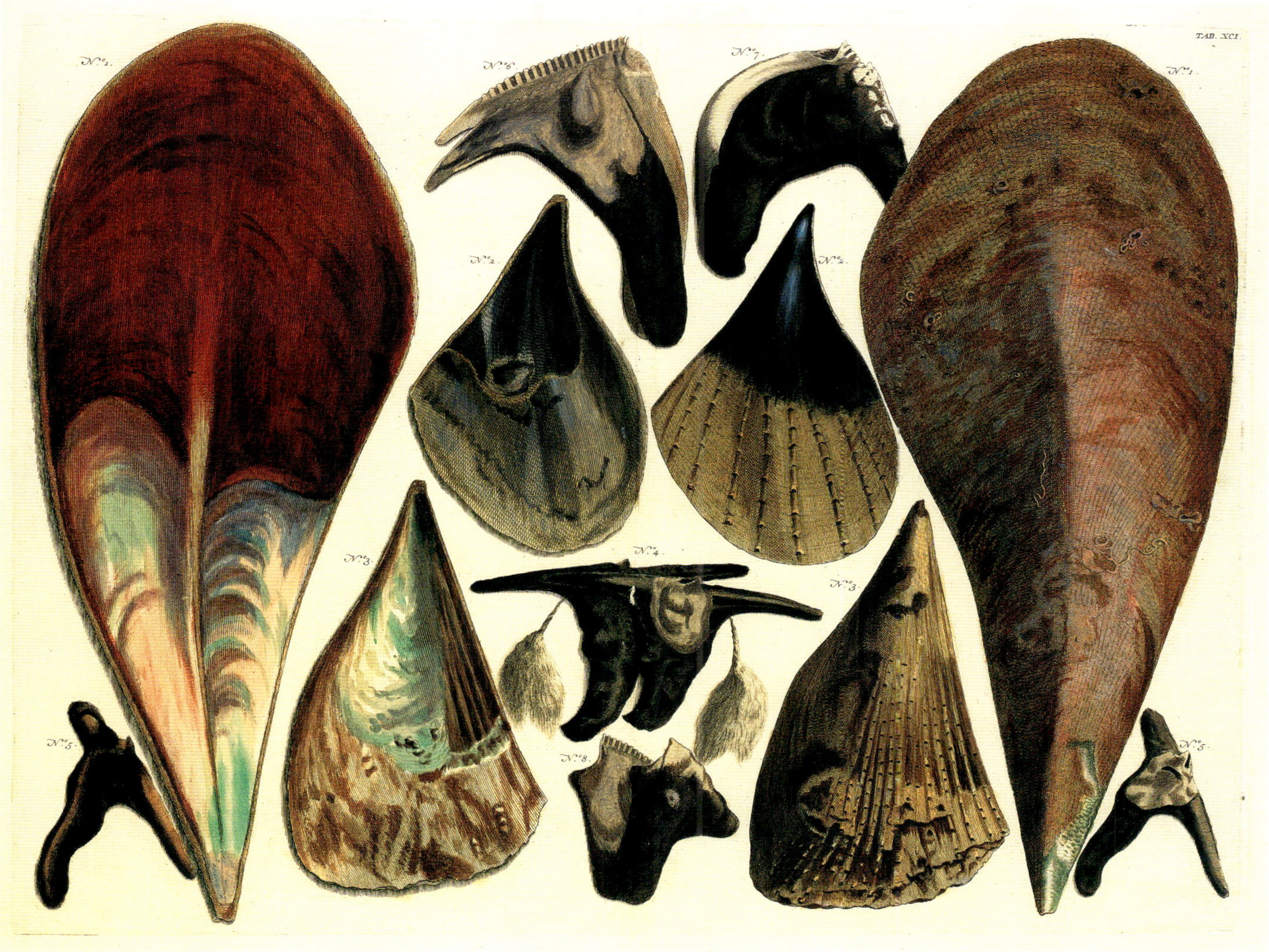

1 *Pinna nobilis* 2 *Atrina vexillum* 3 *Atrina rigida* 4-5 *Malleus malleus* 6-8 *Isognomon isognomon*
Noble Pen shells and other pen shells, hammer oysters and tree oysters from the Mediterranean Sea, Indo-Pacific and West Atlantic · Steckmuscheln, Hammermuscheln und Flügelmuscheln aus dem Mittelmeer, Indopazifik und Westatlantik · Jambonneau hérissé, malleus et autres huîtres nacrées de la mer Méditerranée, l'aire indopacifique et de l'Atlantique occidental

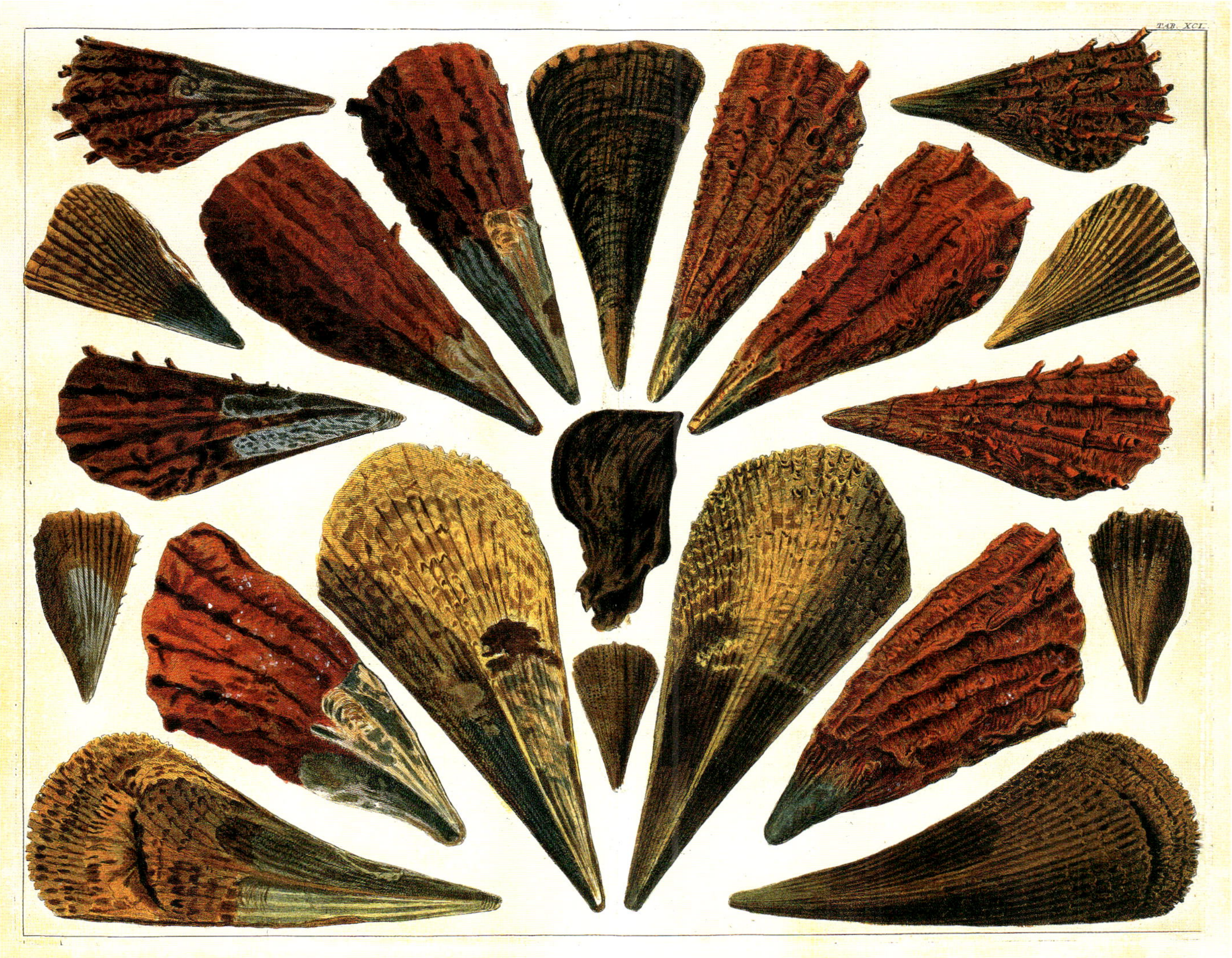

Pinna muricata, Pinna rudis
Prickly pen shells and rude pen shells from the Indian Ocean, Atlantic and Mediterranean Sea · Steckmuscheln aus dem Indischen Ozean, Atlantik und Mittelmeer · Pinnes de l'océan Indien, de l'Atlantique et de la mer Méditerranée

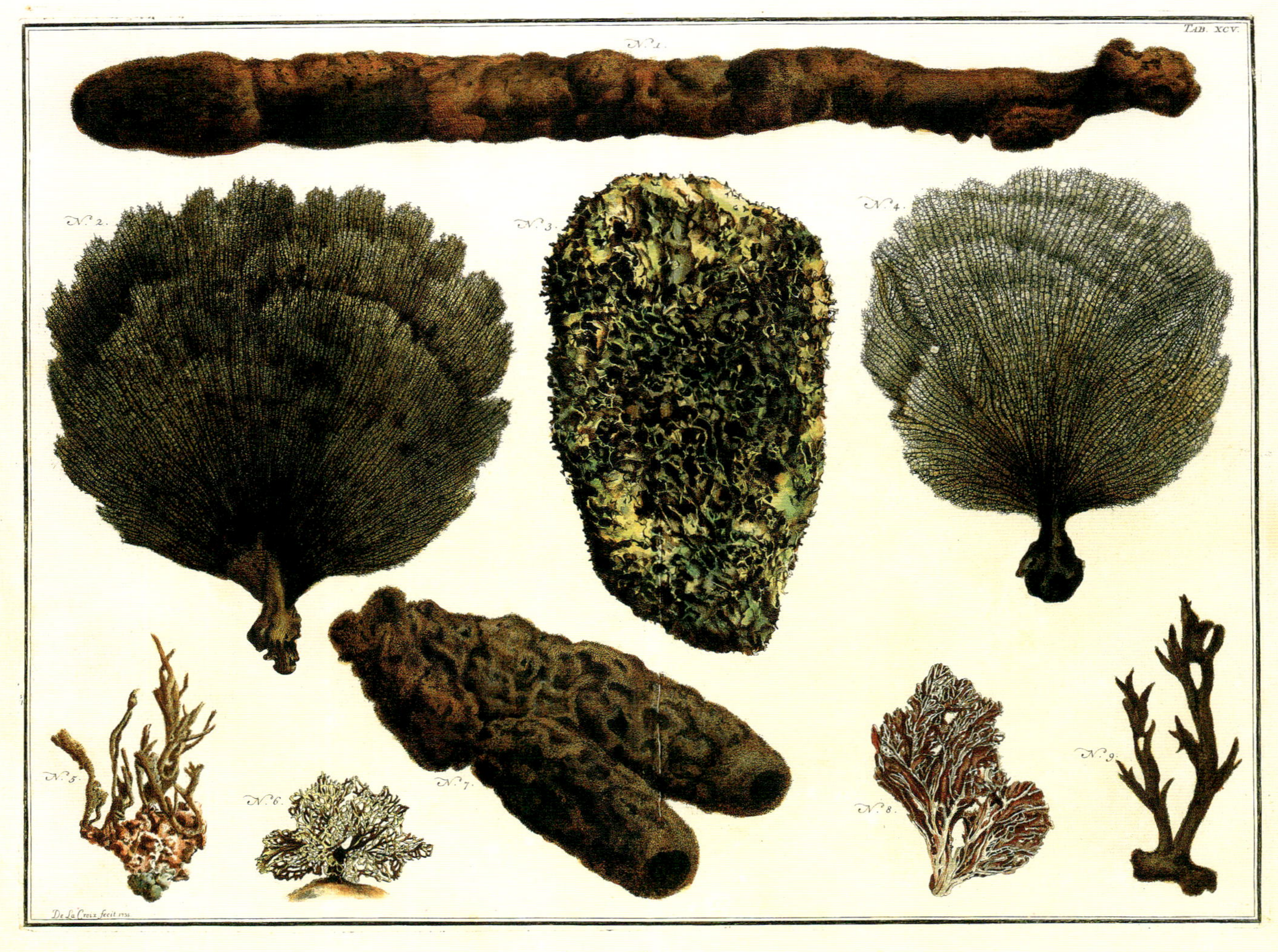

1, 7 *Aplysina fistularis* **2, 4** *Rhipidogorgia flabellum* **3** *Isodictya* **8** *Phakellia ventilabrum* **9** *Axinella cannabina*
1, 7 Yellow tube sponges · Neptunschwämme · Eponges **2, 4** Venus sea fans · Venusfächer · Corbeilles de Vénus ou gorgone **3** Finger sponge · Fingerschwamm · Eponge
8 Chalice sponge · Venusfächer · Corbeille de Vénus ou gorgone **9** Staghorn sponge · Höckriger Geweihschwamm · Eponge

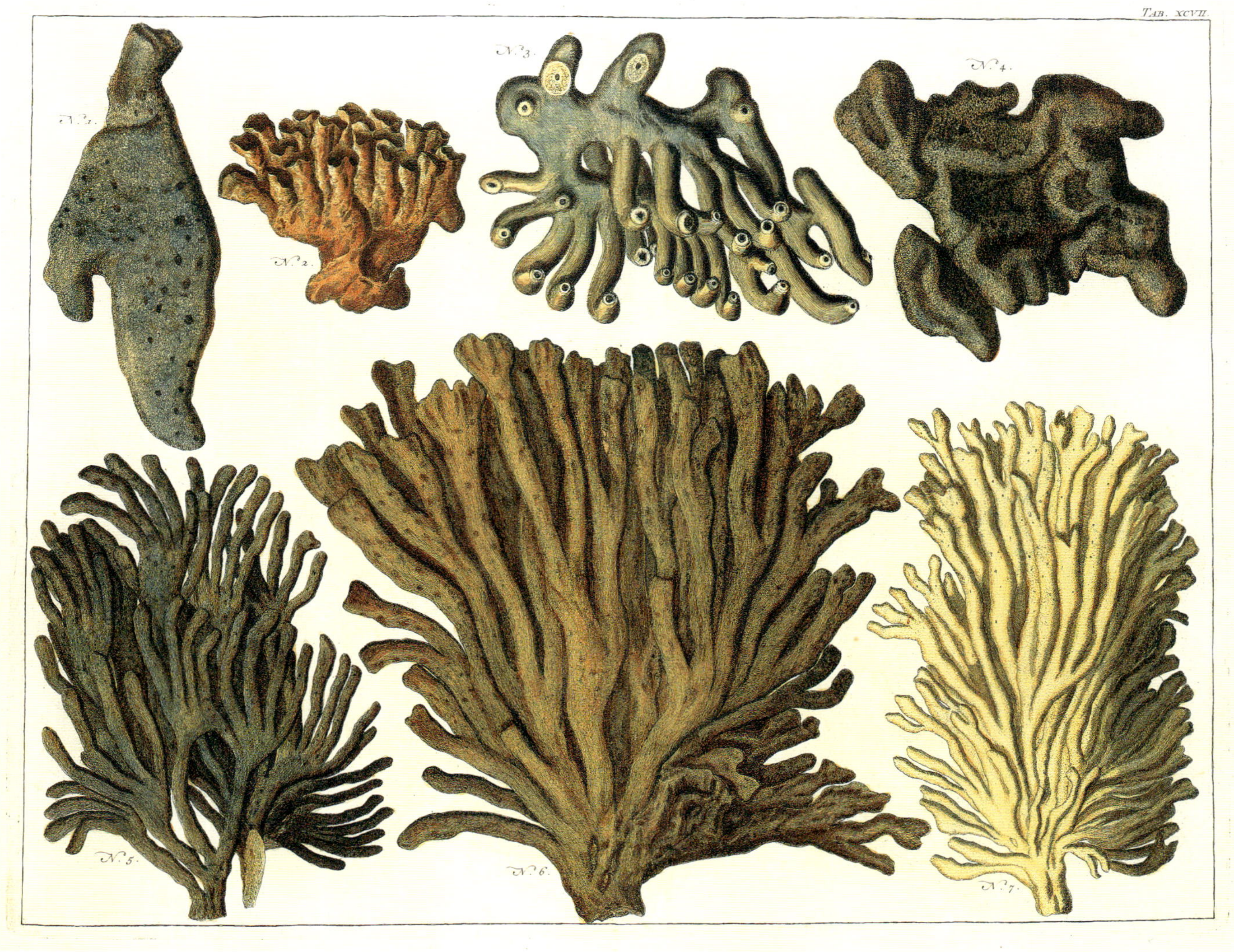

1 *Calyx* **2** *Zoanthus* **3** *Siphonochalina* **4** *Oscarella lobularis* **5-7** *Haliclona oculata*
1 Fan sponge · Schwamm · Eponge **2** Colonial anemone · Krustenanemone · Anémone encroûtante **4** Flesh sponge · Fleischschwamm · Eponge bleue
5-7 Eyed finger sponges/Mermaid's gloves · Geweihschwamm · Chalines/Eponges pourpres

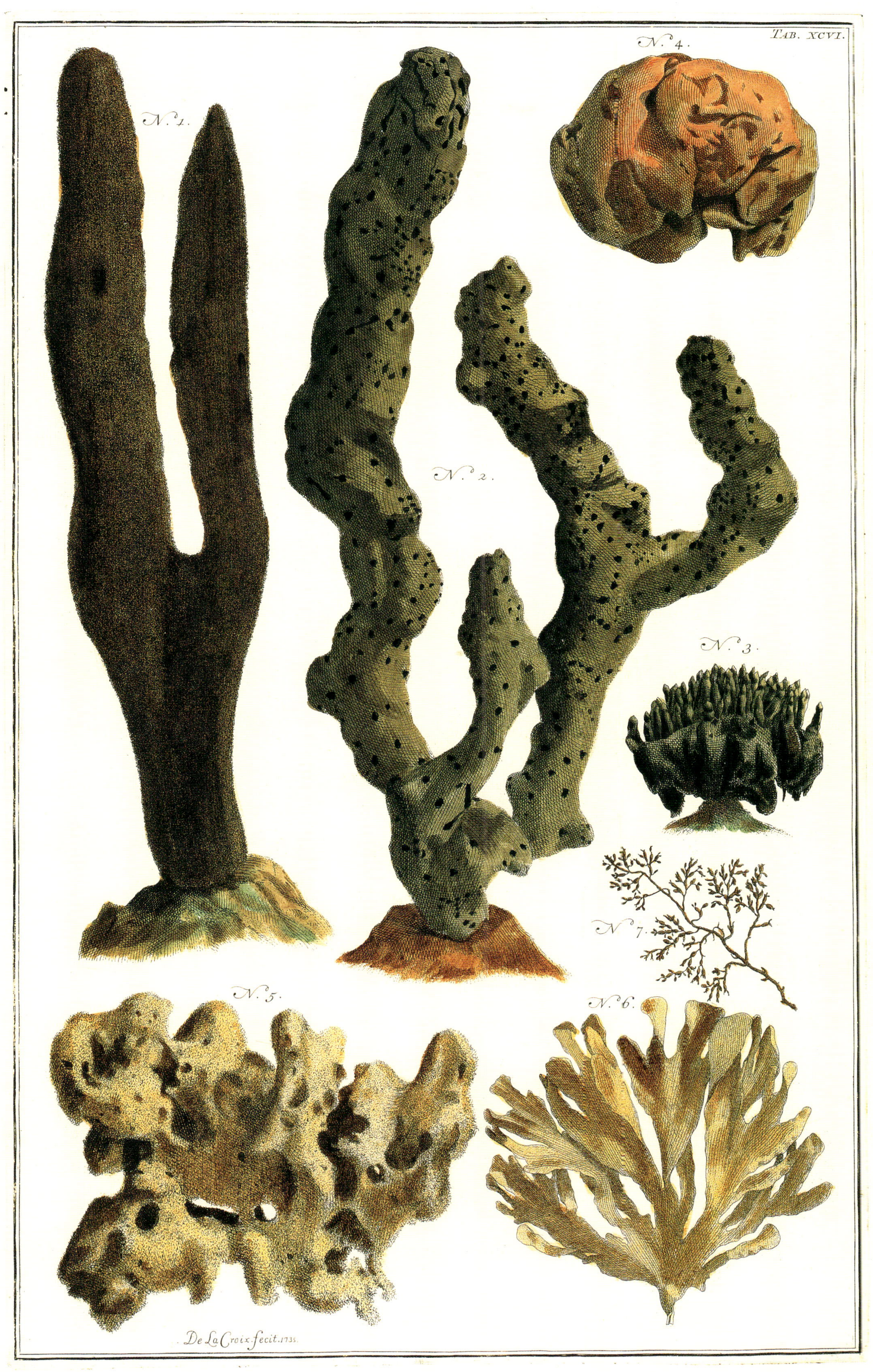

1 *Isodictya quatsinoensis* 2 *Axinella* 3 *Oceanapia* 4 Halichondria panicea 6 Flustra foliacea
1 Finger sponge · Fingerschwamm · Eponge 2 Staghorn sponge · Geweihschwamm · Eponge 3 Sponge oceanopia · Schwamm · Eponge
4 Breadcrumb sponge · Brotkrumenschwamm · Eponge mie de pain 6 Hornwrack · Blättermoostier · Bryozoaires foliacés

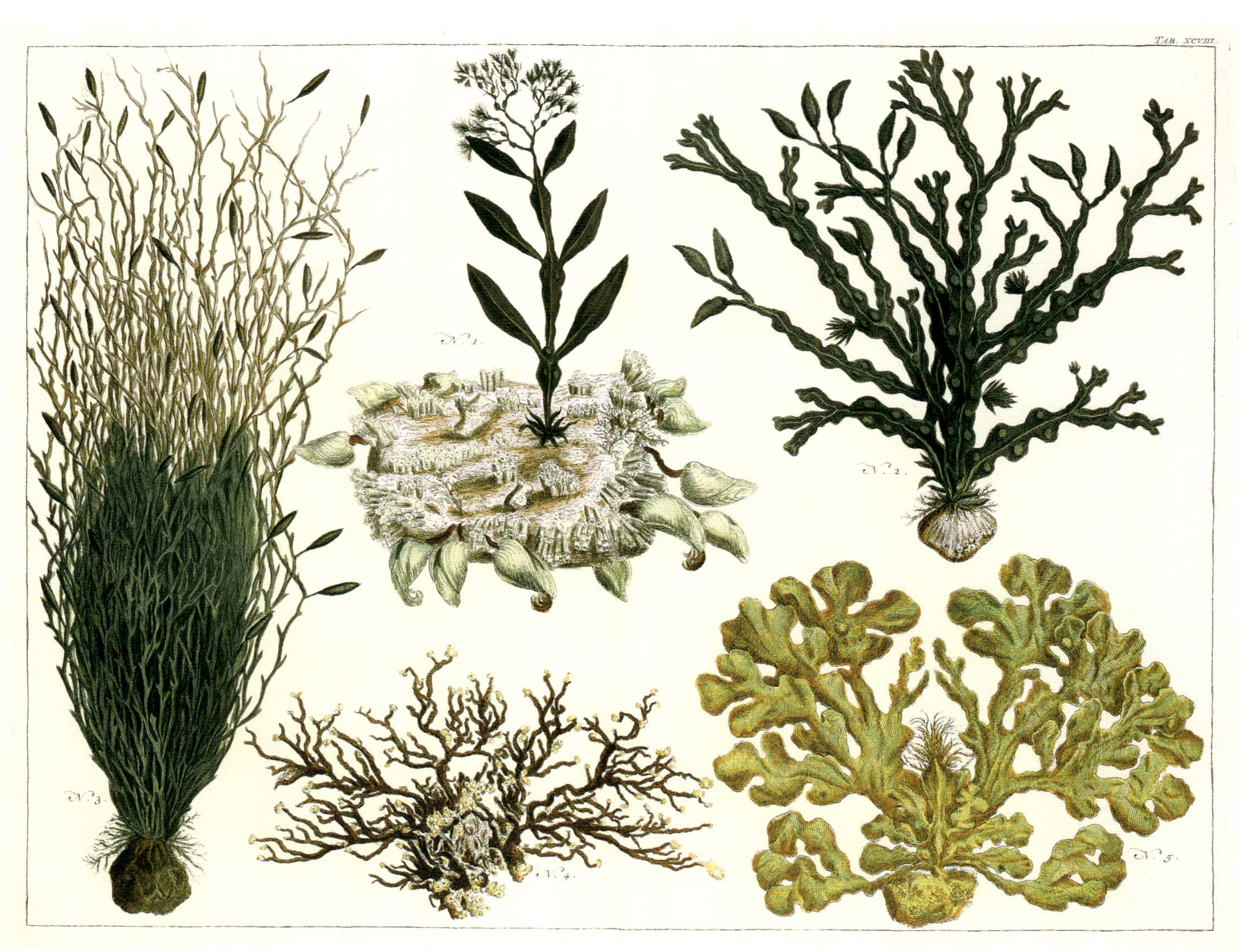

1-3 Plantae **4** *Alcyonidium gelatinosum* **5** *Porella compressa*
1-3 Sea plants · Meeresalgen · Plantes de la mer **4** Gelatinous bryozoan · Gallertmoostier · Bryozoaire gélatineux **5** Moss animal · Korallenmoostier · Bryozoaire

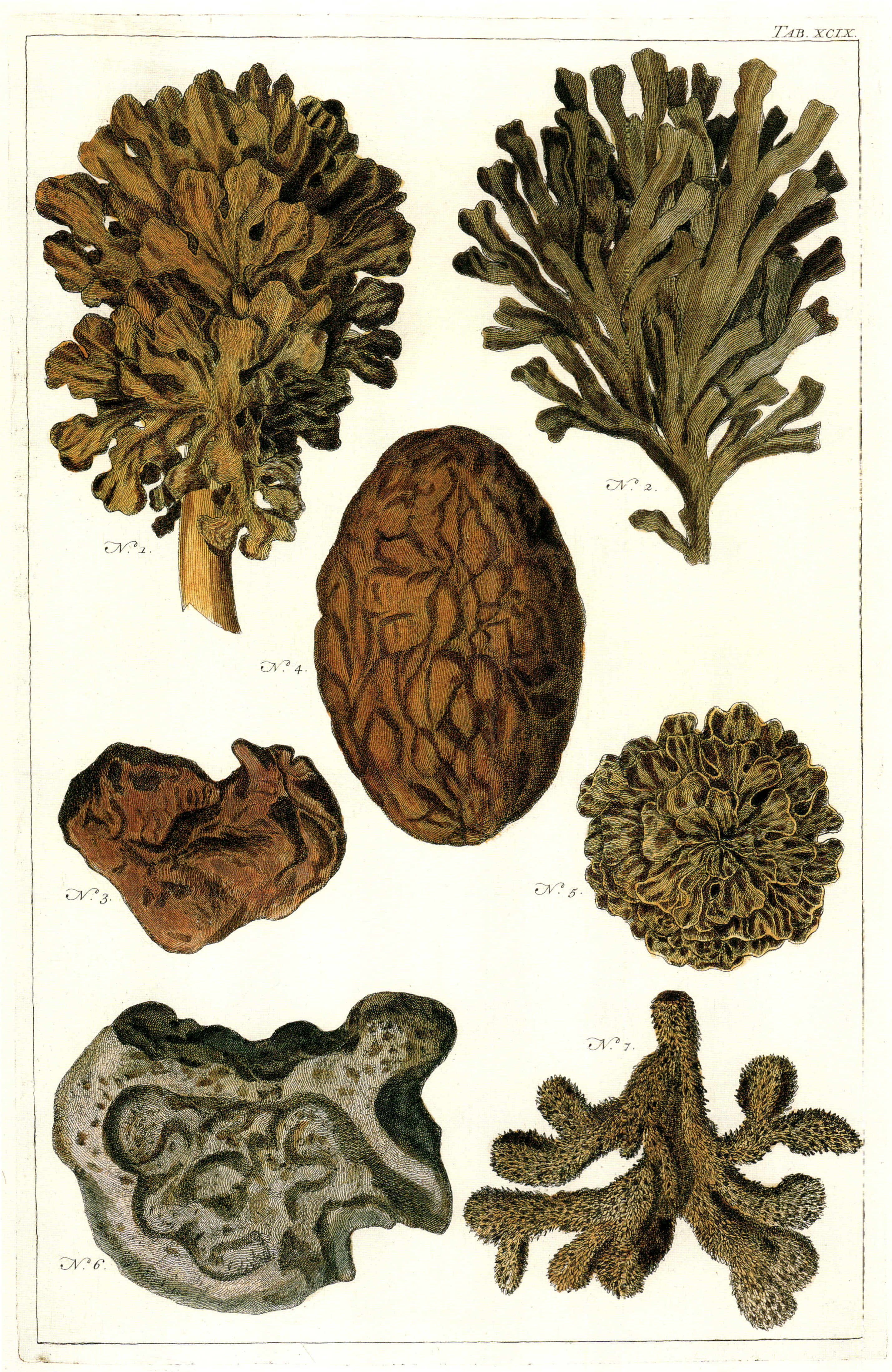

1 *Porella compressa* 2 *Securiflustra securifrons* 3 *Halichondria panicea* 4 *Rosella fibulata* 5 *Turbinaria mesenterina* 7 Porifera
1 Moss animal · Korallenmoostier · Bryozoaire 2 Narrow-leaved hornwrack · Schmalblättriges Moostierchen · Bryozoaire 3 Breadcrumb sponge · Brotkrumenschwamm · Eponge mie de pain
4 Pipe sponge/Chimney sponge · Schwamm · Eponge 5 Lettuce coral · Salatkoralle · Tubinaire jaune 7 Sponge · Schwamm · Eponge

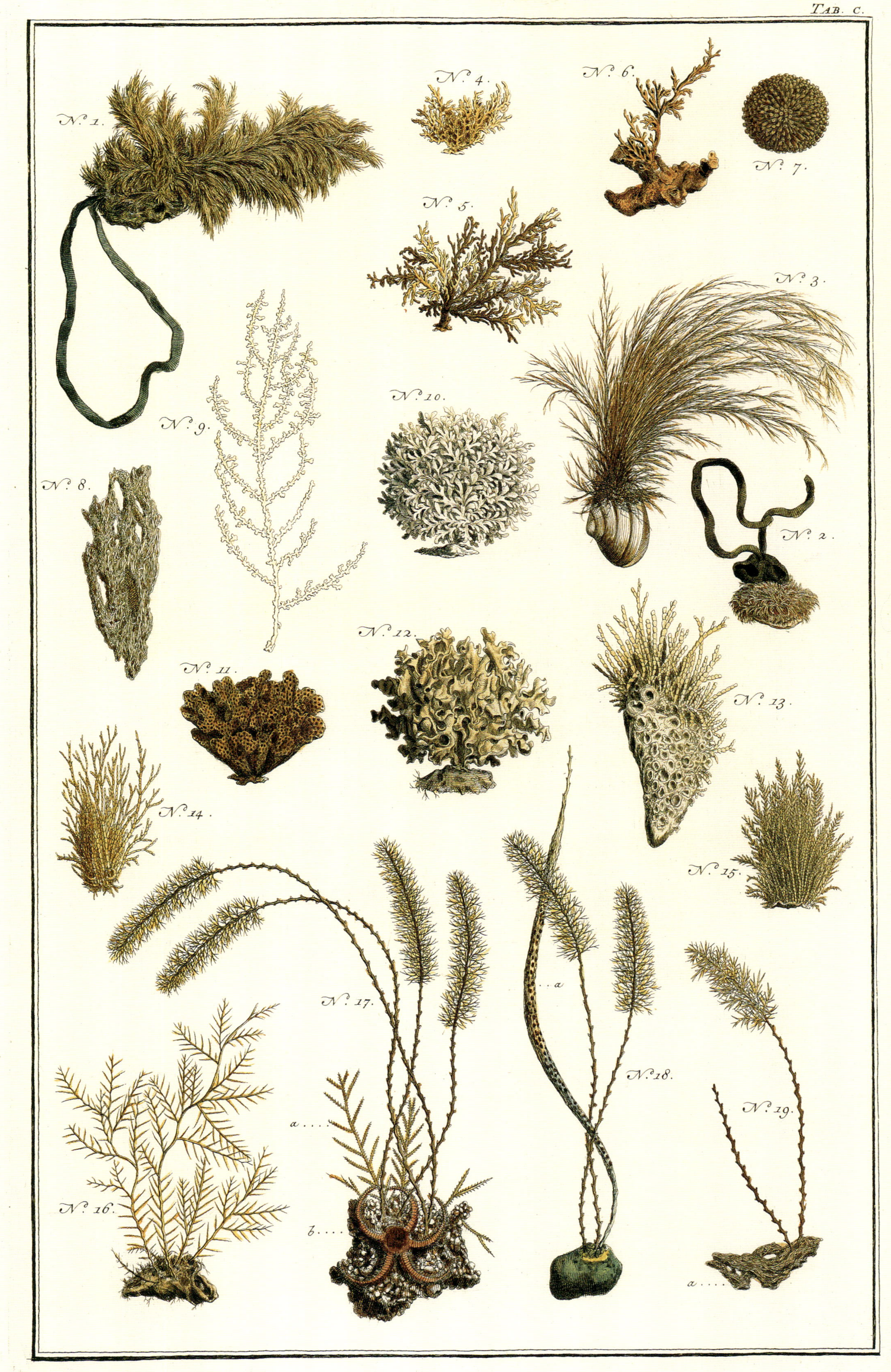

1, 11, 16-19 Cnidaria **2, 9-10, 12** Bryozoa **8** *Filograna* **13-15** *Corallina officinalis* **17a, 18-19** *Thuiaria thuja* **17b** *Ophioderma*
1, 11, 16-19 Cnidarians · Nesseltiere (Korallen) · Cnidaires **2, 9-10, 12** Moss animals · Moostiere · Bryozoaires **8** Sea worm · Röhrenwurm · Salmacine
13-15 Coral weeds · Korallenmoos · Algues **17b** Serpent star · Schlangenstern · Ophiure **17a, 18-19** Bottle brushes · Flaschenputzer Hydroiden · Hydraires

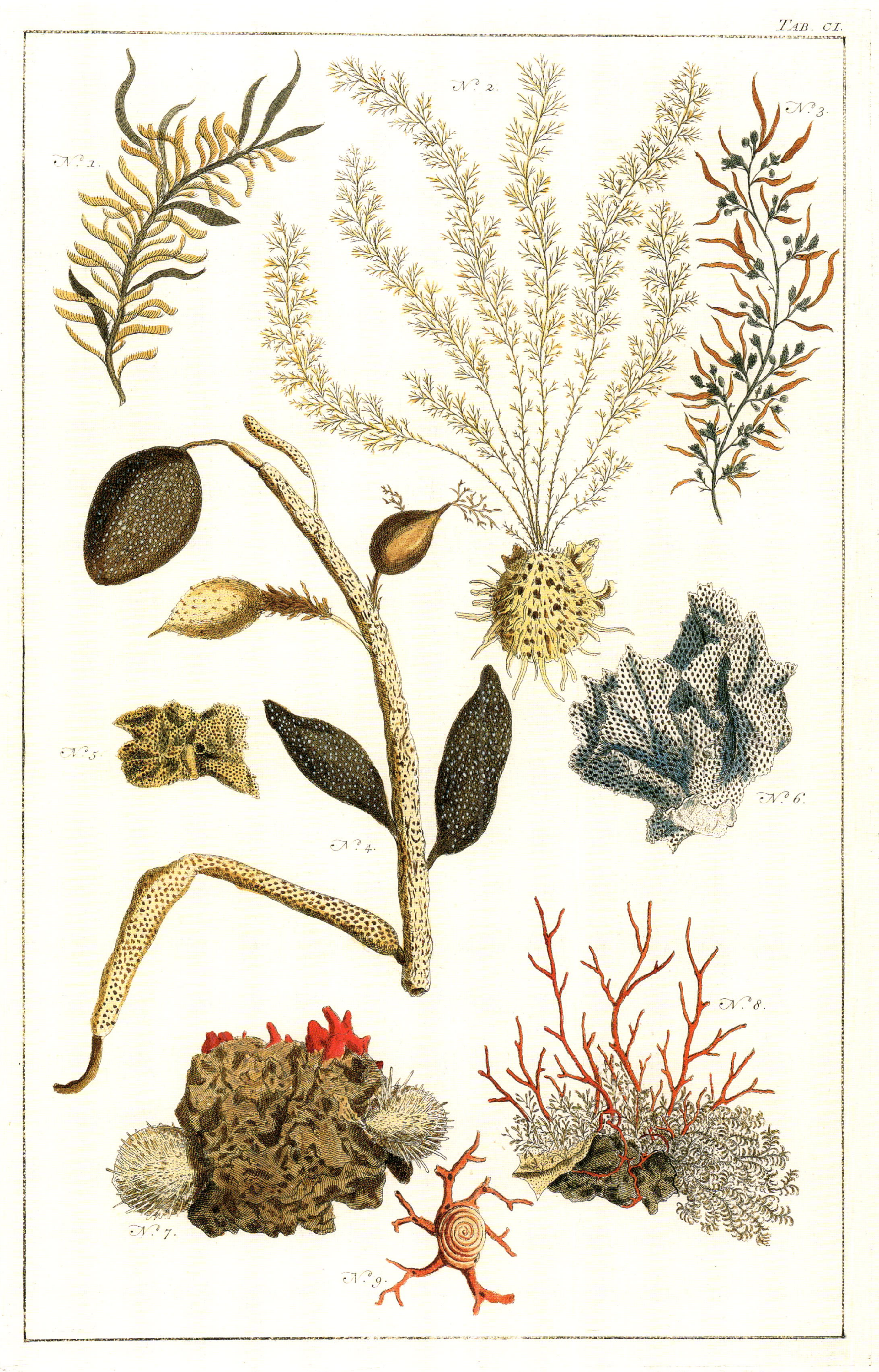

1 Cnidaria 2 *Sertularia cupressina* 3 Plantae 5-6 *Sertella septentrionalis* 8 *Corallium rubrum, Sertularella rugosum* 9 *Smittina cervicornis*
1 Cnidarian · Nesseltier (Koralle) · Cnidaire 2 White weed · Zypressenmoos · Hydroïde 3 Sea plant · Meeresalge · Plante marine 5-6 Sea laces (Moss animals) · Neptunsschleier · Dentelles de Neptune (Bryozoaires) 8 Precious coral with hydroids · Edelkoralle mit Hydroiden · Corail rouge et hydroïde 9 Staghorn bryozoan · Hirschgeweihmoostierchen · Bryozoaire

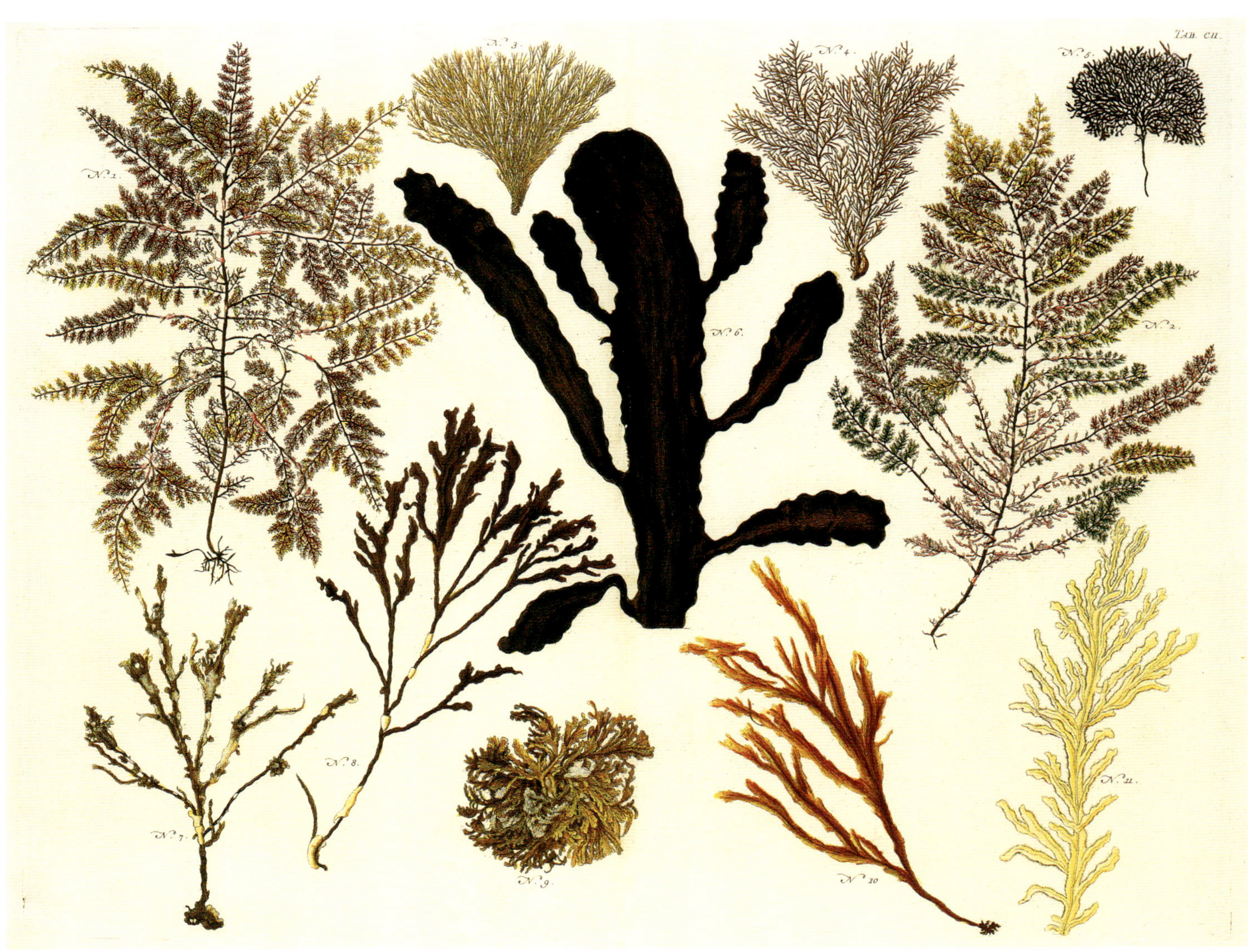

3 Amphisbetia operculata *4 Sertularella spec.* *5 Bugula neritina*
3 Cnidarian · Nesseltier (Koralle) · Cnidaire **4** Hydroid · Hydroid · Hydroïde **5** Moss animal · Moostier · Bryozoaire

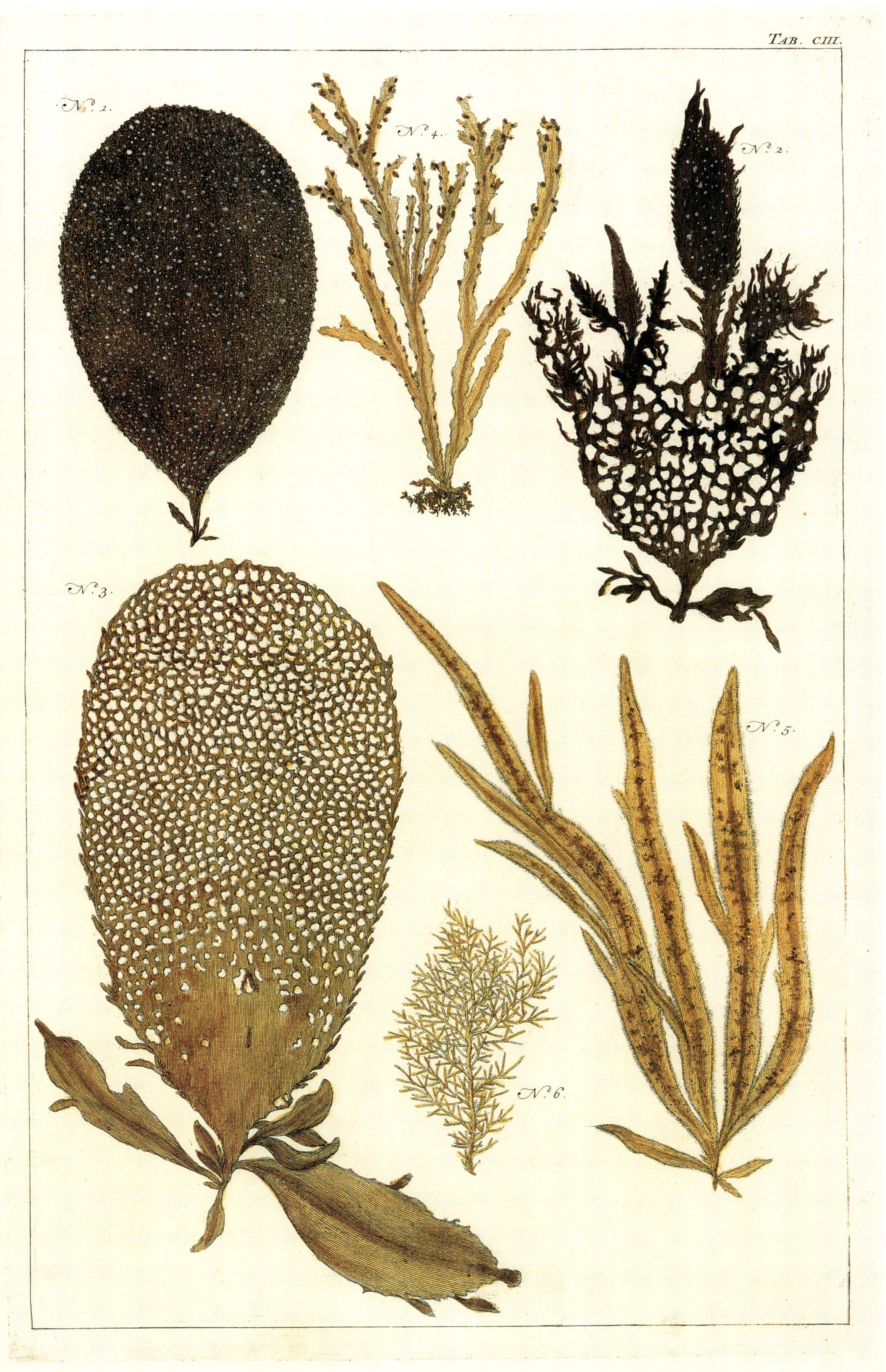

6 *Sertularella gayi*
Sedentary sea organisms, mostly algae · Festsitzende Organismen aus dem Meer, die meisten davon Algen · Organismes marins sédentaires, pour la plupart des algues
6 Hydroid · Hydroid · Hydroïde

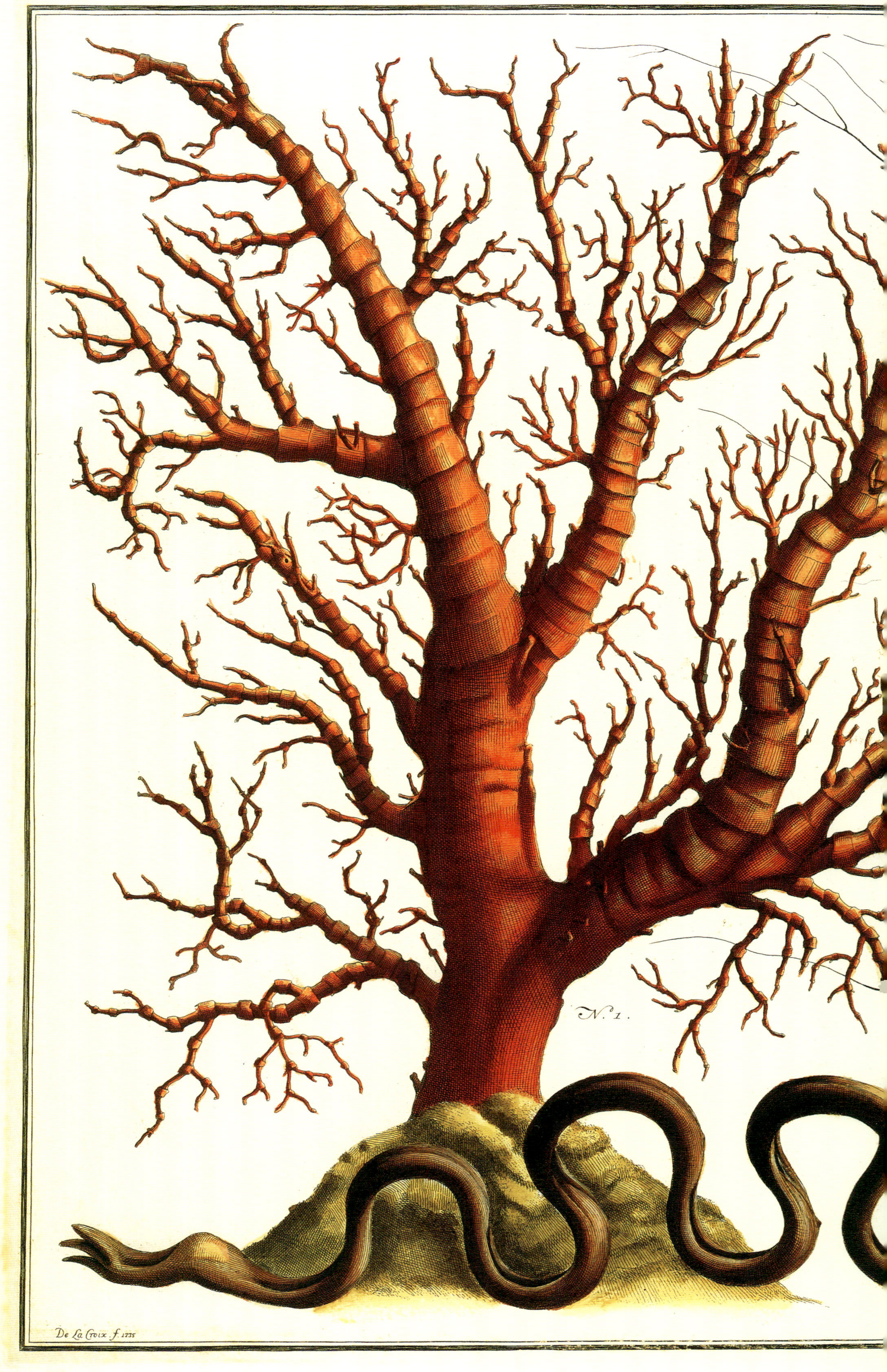

1 *Dendronephythya* 2 *Antipathes*
1 Carnation coral · Rote Lederkoralle · Corail mou 2 Black coral · Schwarze Gorgonie · Corail noir

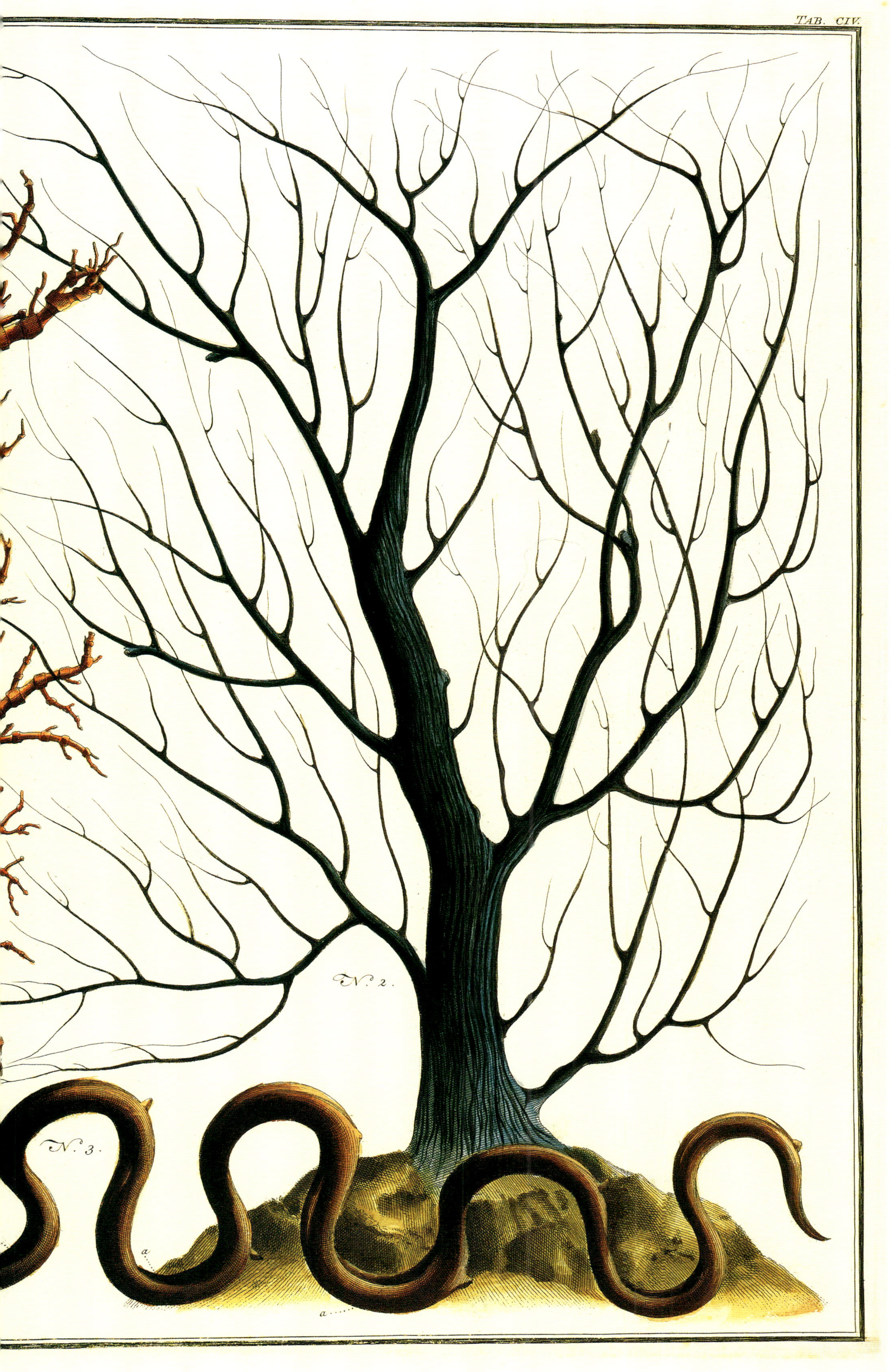
TAB. CIV.
N.° 2.
N.° 3.
a
a

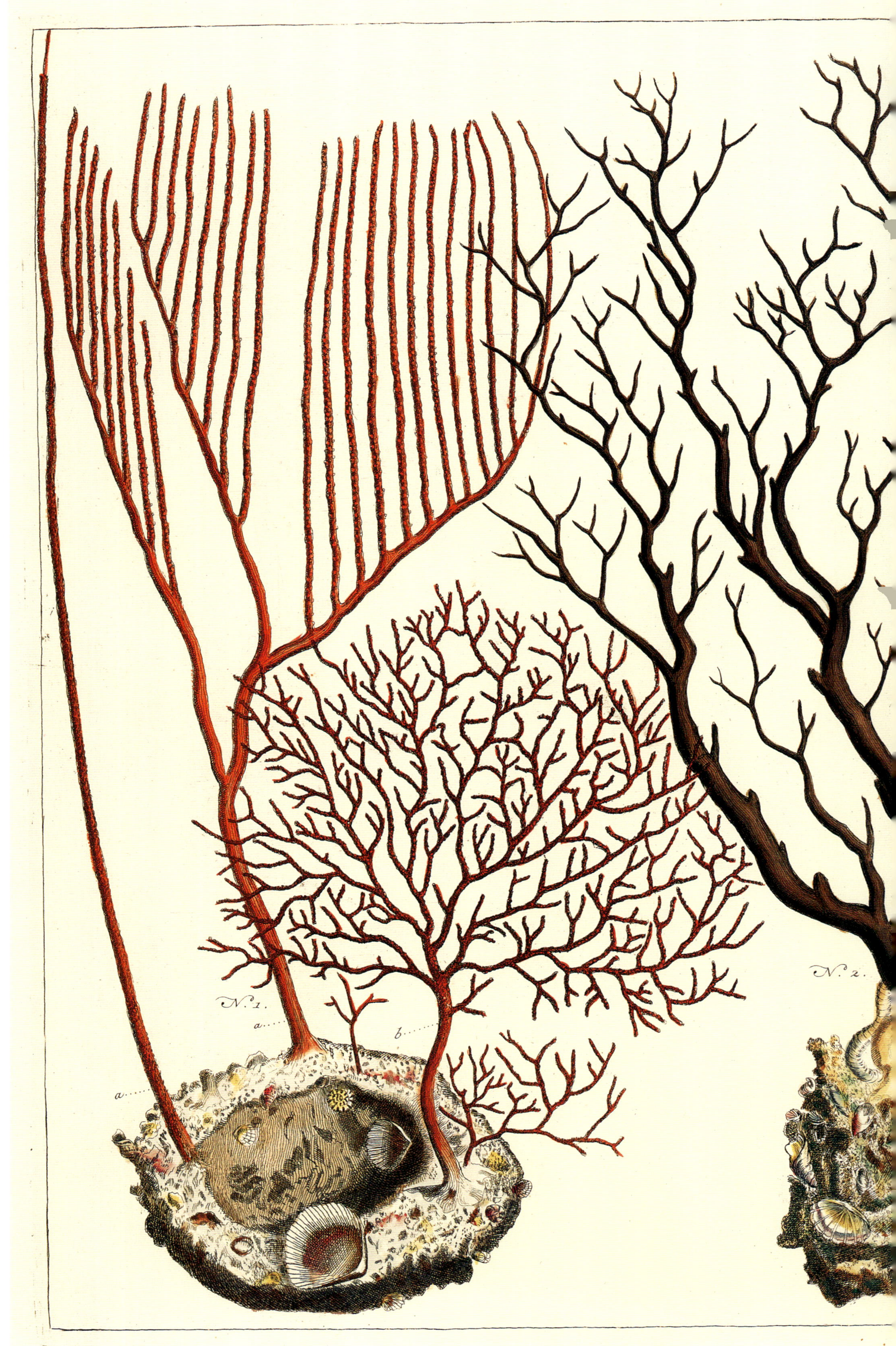

1-4 Cnidaria 1a *Juncella & Ellisella* 1b *Eunicella*
1-4 Cnidarians · Nesseltiere (Korallen) · Cnidaires 1a Sea whip · Seepeitsche · Fouet de mer 1b Violescent sea whip · Rote Gorgonie · Gorgone rouge

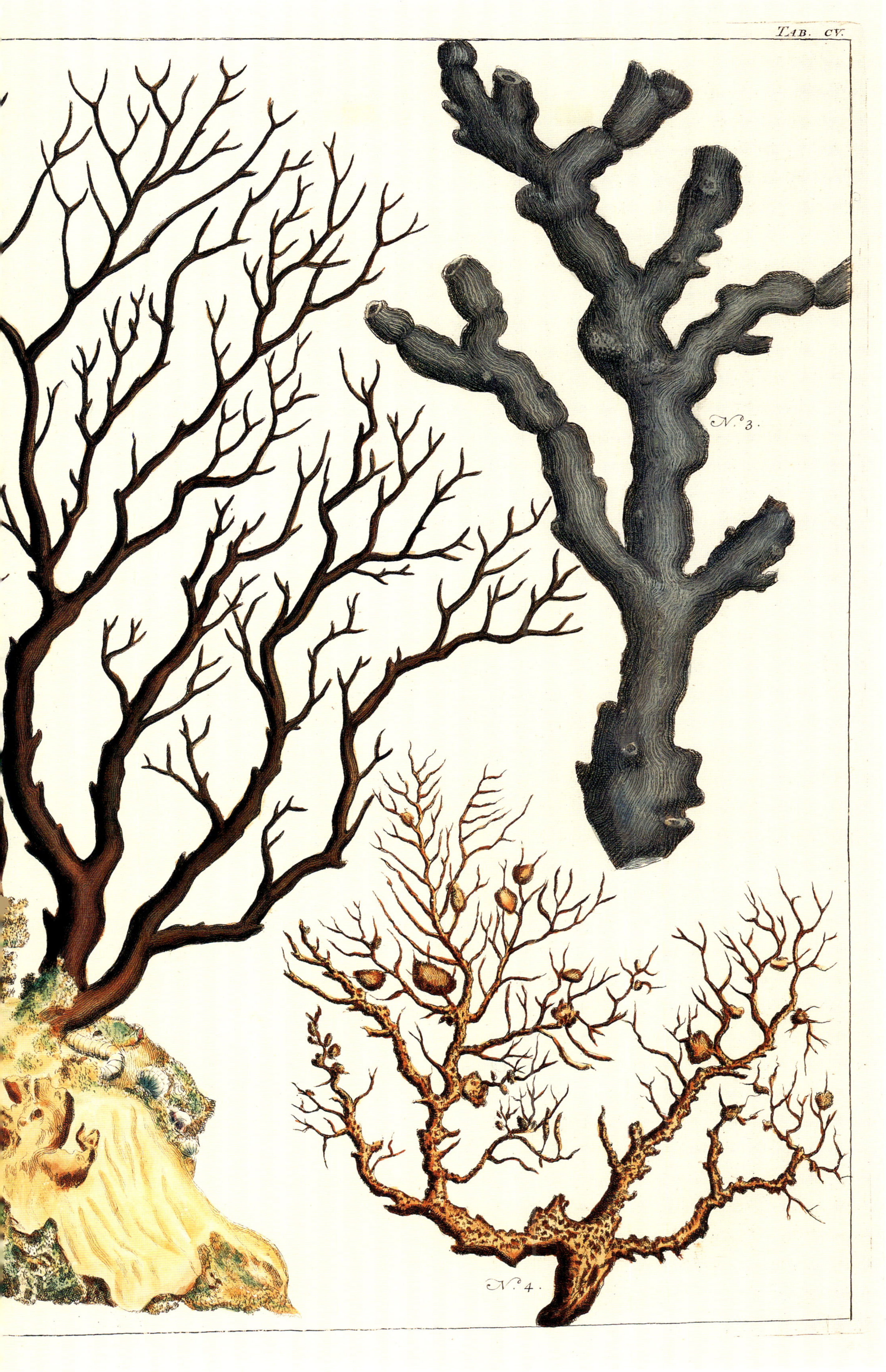
TAB. CV.
N.° 3.
N.° 4.

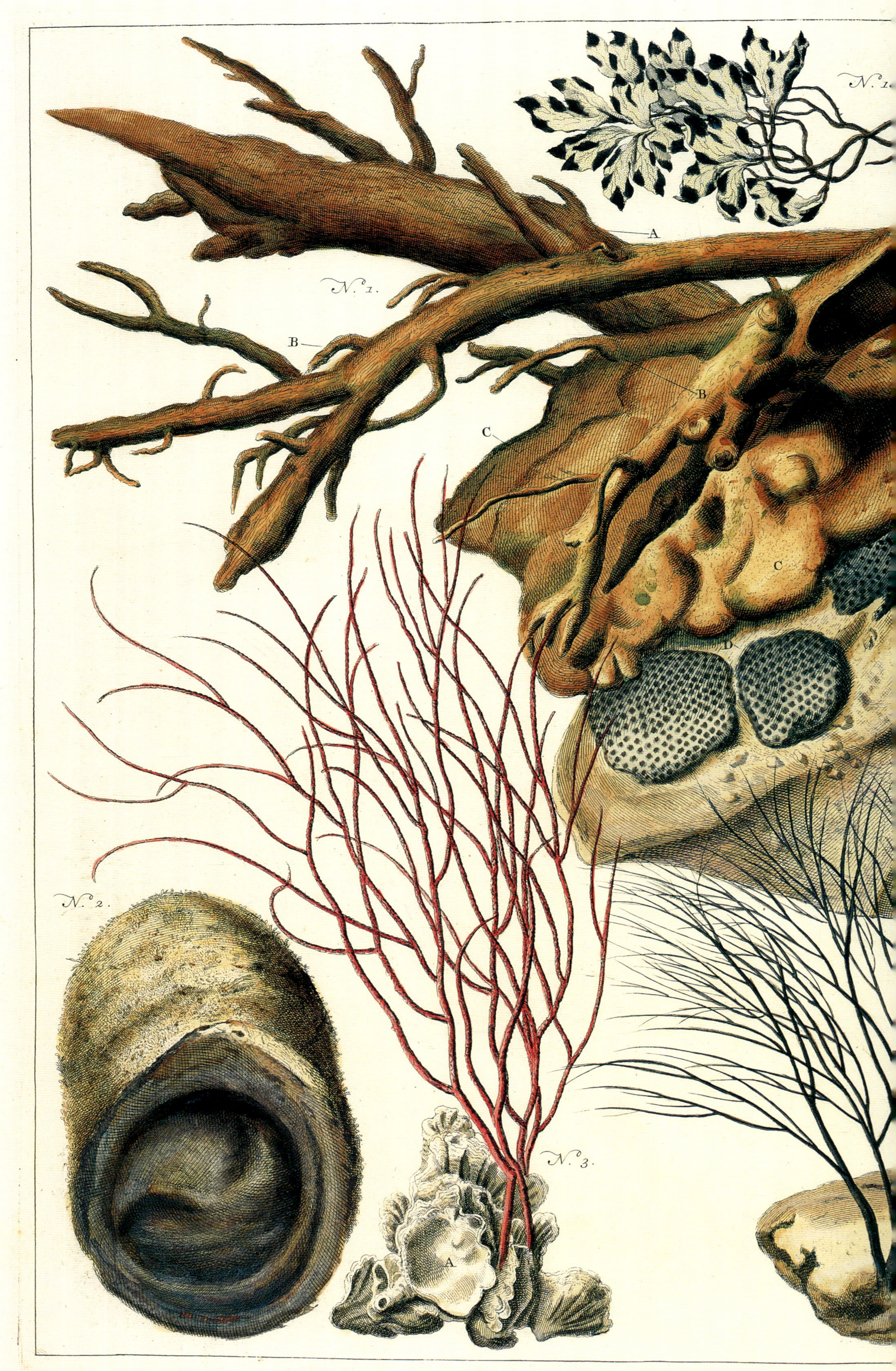

3-6, 8 Cnidaria *3 Lophogorgia ceratophyta* *4 Ellisella* *6 Paramuricea clavata* *8 Antipathes ulex* *9 Caulerpa*
3-6, 8 Cnidarians · Nesseltiere (Korallen) · Cnidaires **3** Orange gorgonian · Orangerote Gorgonie · Gorgone orange **4** Sea whip · Seepeitsche · Fouet de mer **6** Violescent sea whip · Rote Gorgonie · Gorgone rouge **8** Feathery black coral · Schwarze Koralle · Corail noir **9** Caulerpa · Caulerpa · Caulerpa

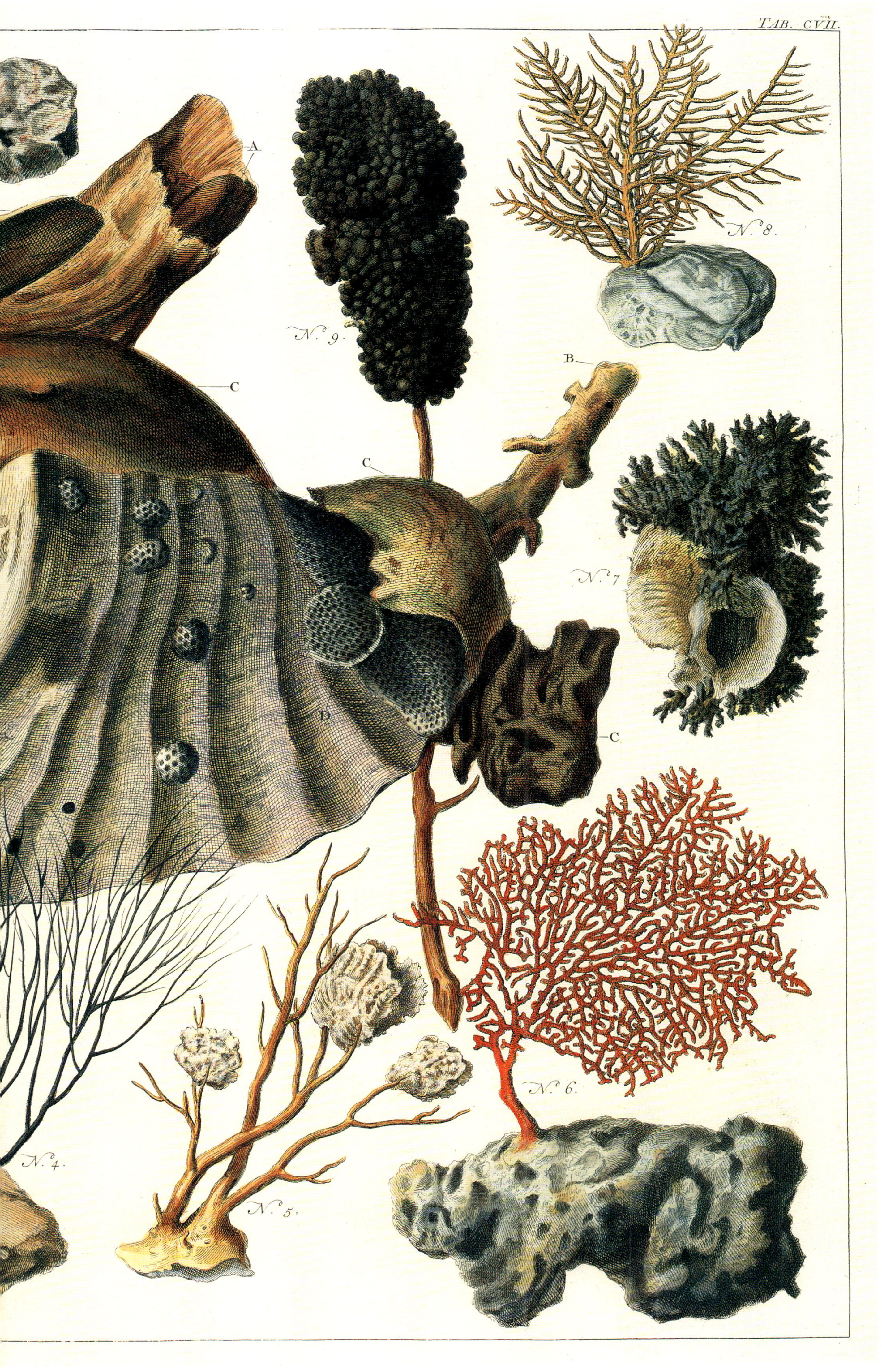
TAB. CVII.
A
N.° 9.
N.° 8.
B
C
C
N.° 7
D
C
N.° 6.
N.° 4.
N.° 5.

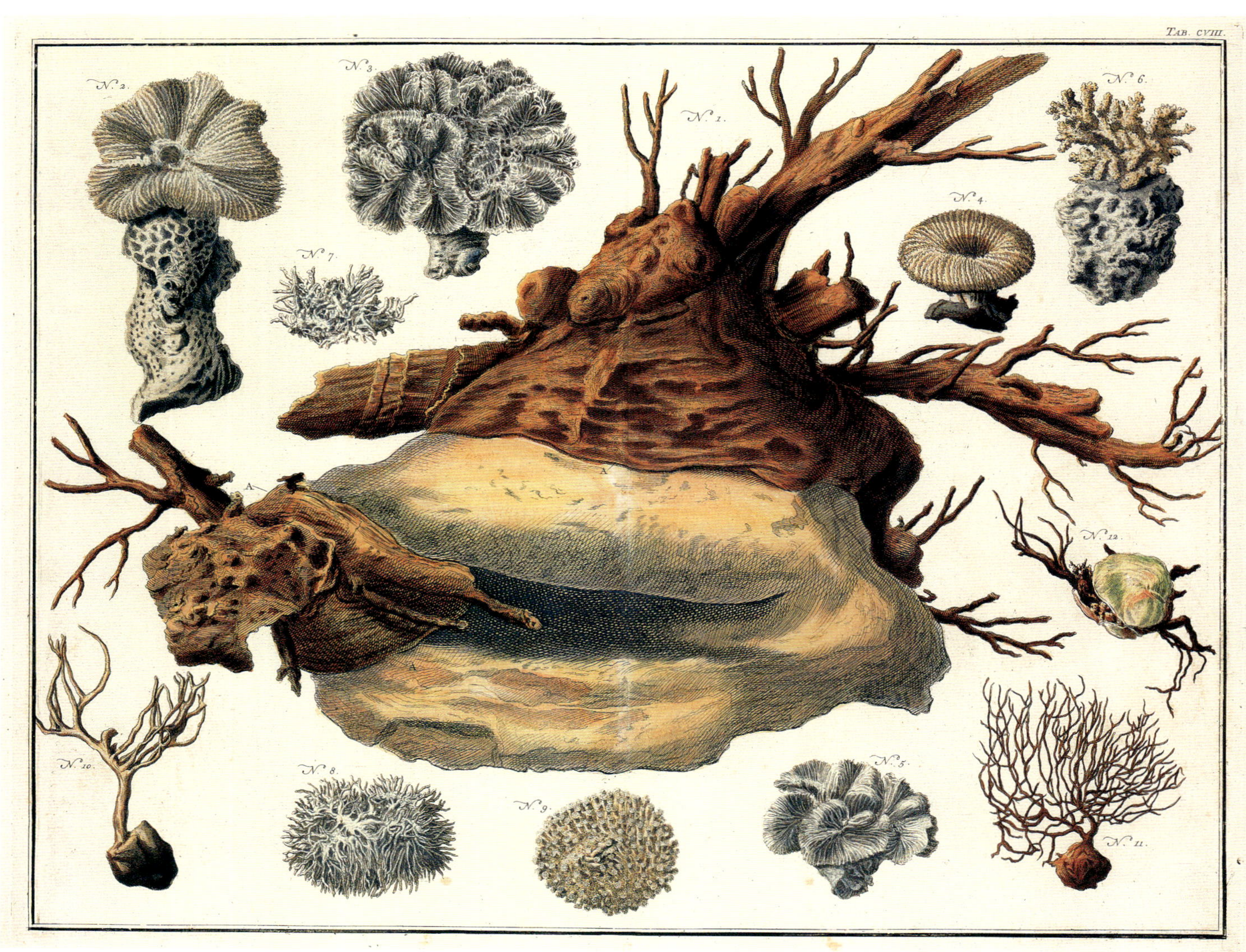

2-11 Cnidaria **2, 4** Sarcophyton **3, 5** *Trachyphyllia* **6** *Pocillopora damicornis* **8** *Seriatopora aculecita* **9** *Astroides* **10** Cnidaria **11** *Gorgonia*
2-11 Cnidarians · Nesseltiere (Korallen) · Cnidaires **2, 4** Toadstools · Pilzlederkorallen · Corail cuir **3, 5** Open brain corals · Wulstkorallen · Trachyphyllidés/coraux cerveaux
6 Raspberry coral · Himbeerkoralle · Corail *Pocillopora damicornis* **8** Needle coral · Nadelkoralle · Corail seriatopora **9** Cup coral · Kelchkoralle · Corail stelliforme
10 Cnidarian · Nesseltier (Koralle) · Cnidaire **11** Gorgonian · Gorgonie · Gorgone

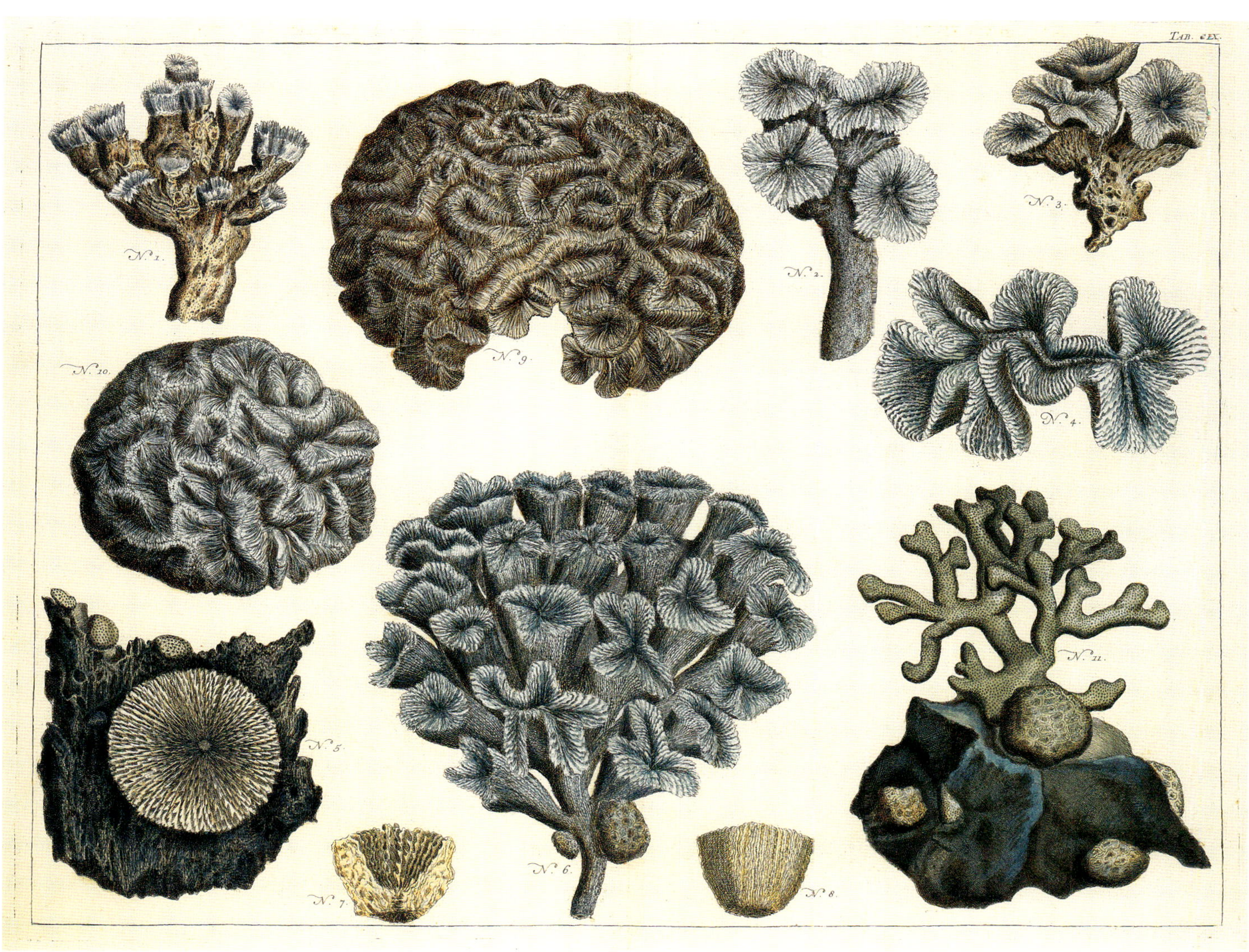

1-11 Cnidaria **1** *Eusmilia fastigiata* **2-3** *Mussa angulosa* **4** *Lobophyllia* **5** *Fungia* **6** *Lobophyllia hemprichii* **9-10** *Colpophyllia* **11** *Porites porites*
1-11 Cnidarians · Nesseltiere (Korallen) · Cnidaires **1** Smooth flower coral · Glatte Blumenkoralle · Corail fleur **2-3** Large flower corals · Atlantische dickstielige Doldenkorallen · Corail fleur **4** Open brain coral · Wulstkoralle · Corail cerveau **5** Plate coral · Pilzkoralle · Corail champignon **6** Brain coral · Doldenkoralle · Corail cerveau **9-10** Brain corals · Hirnkorallen · Coraux cerveaux **11** Finger coral · Fingerkoralle · Corail doigt

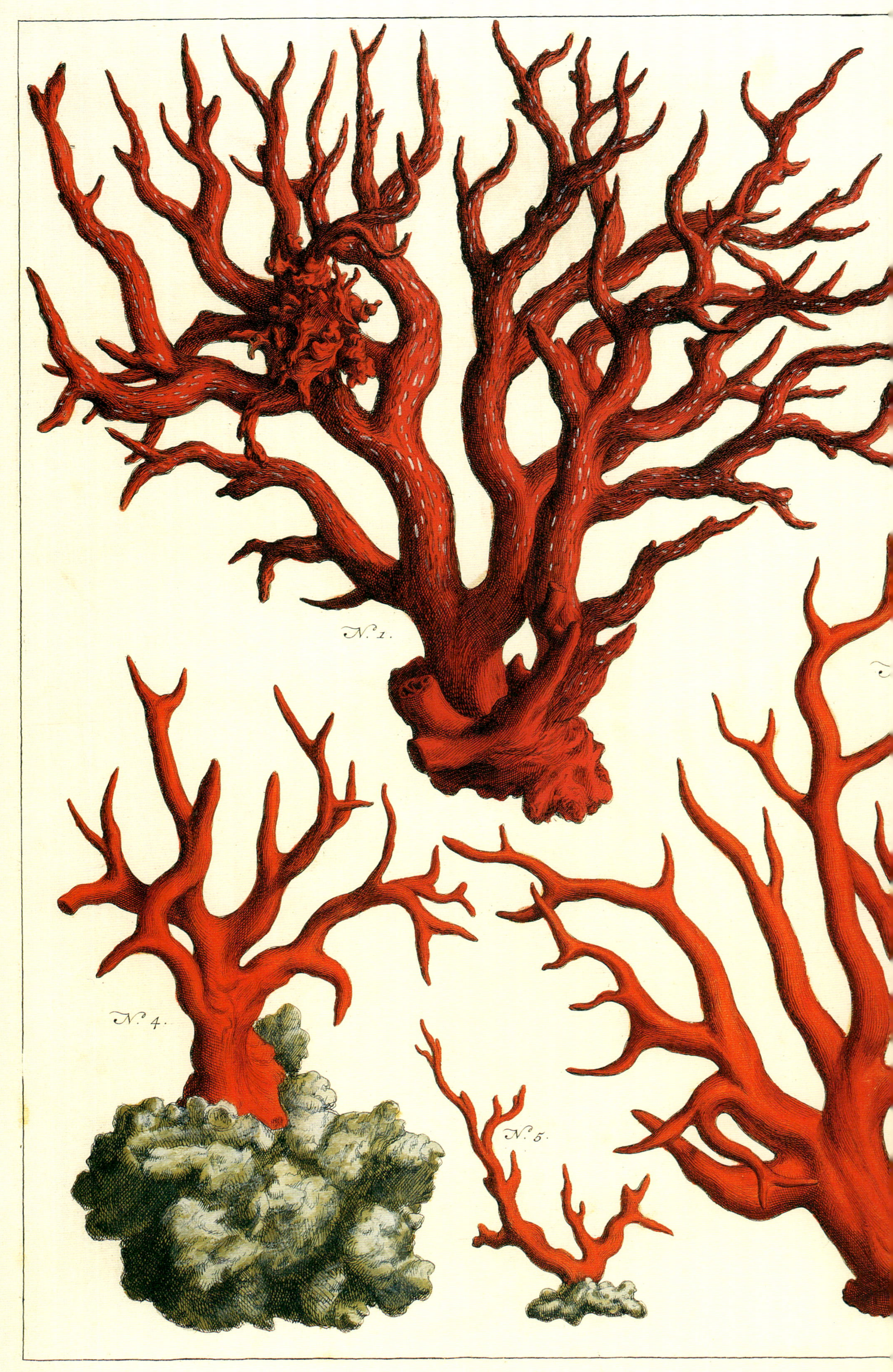

1-7 *Corallium rubrum*
1-7 Precious corals · Edelkorallen · Coraux rouges

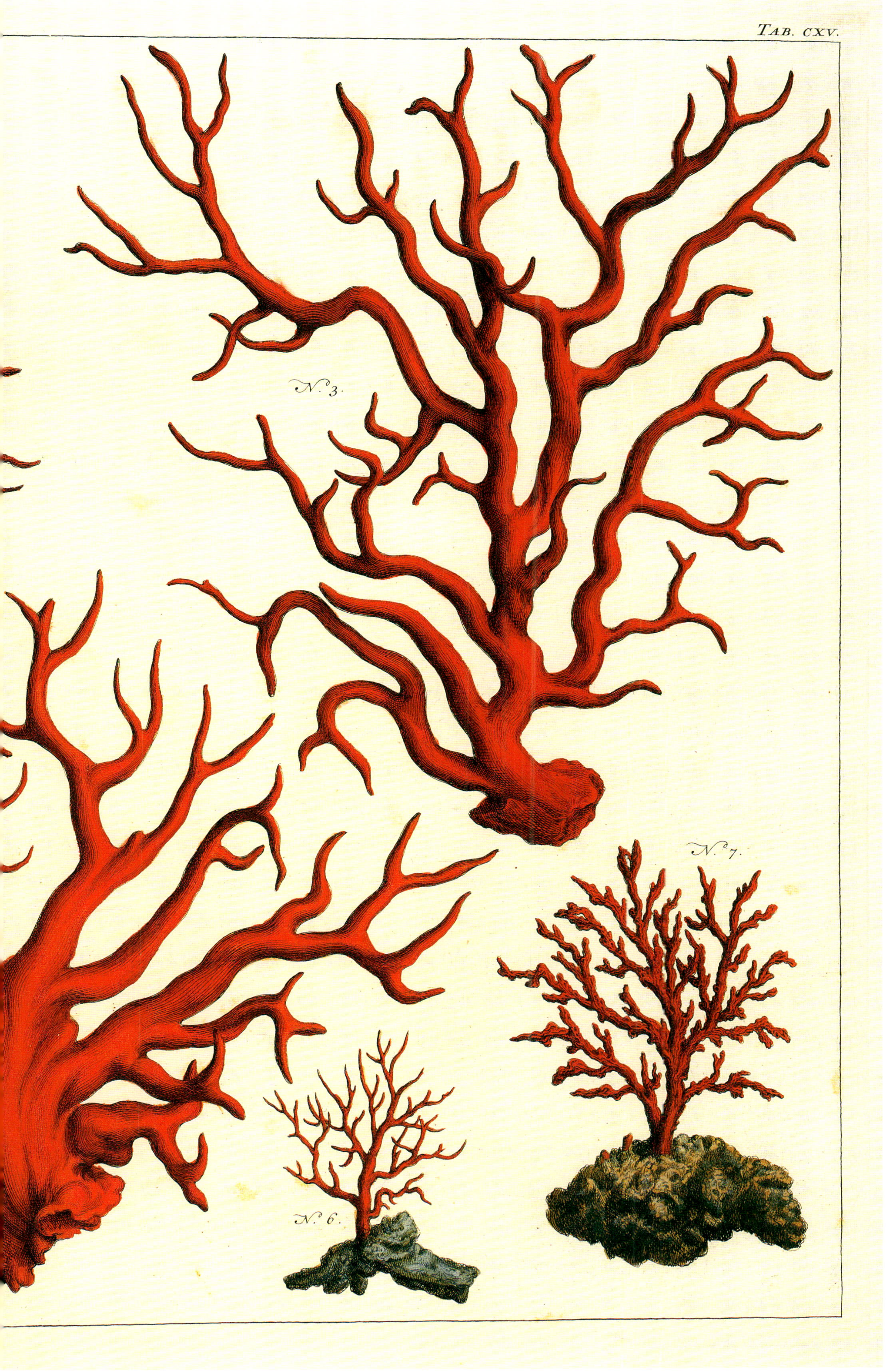
TAB. CXV.
N.° 3.
N.° 7.
N.° 6.

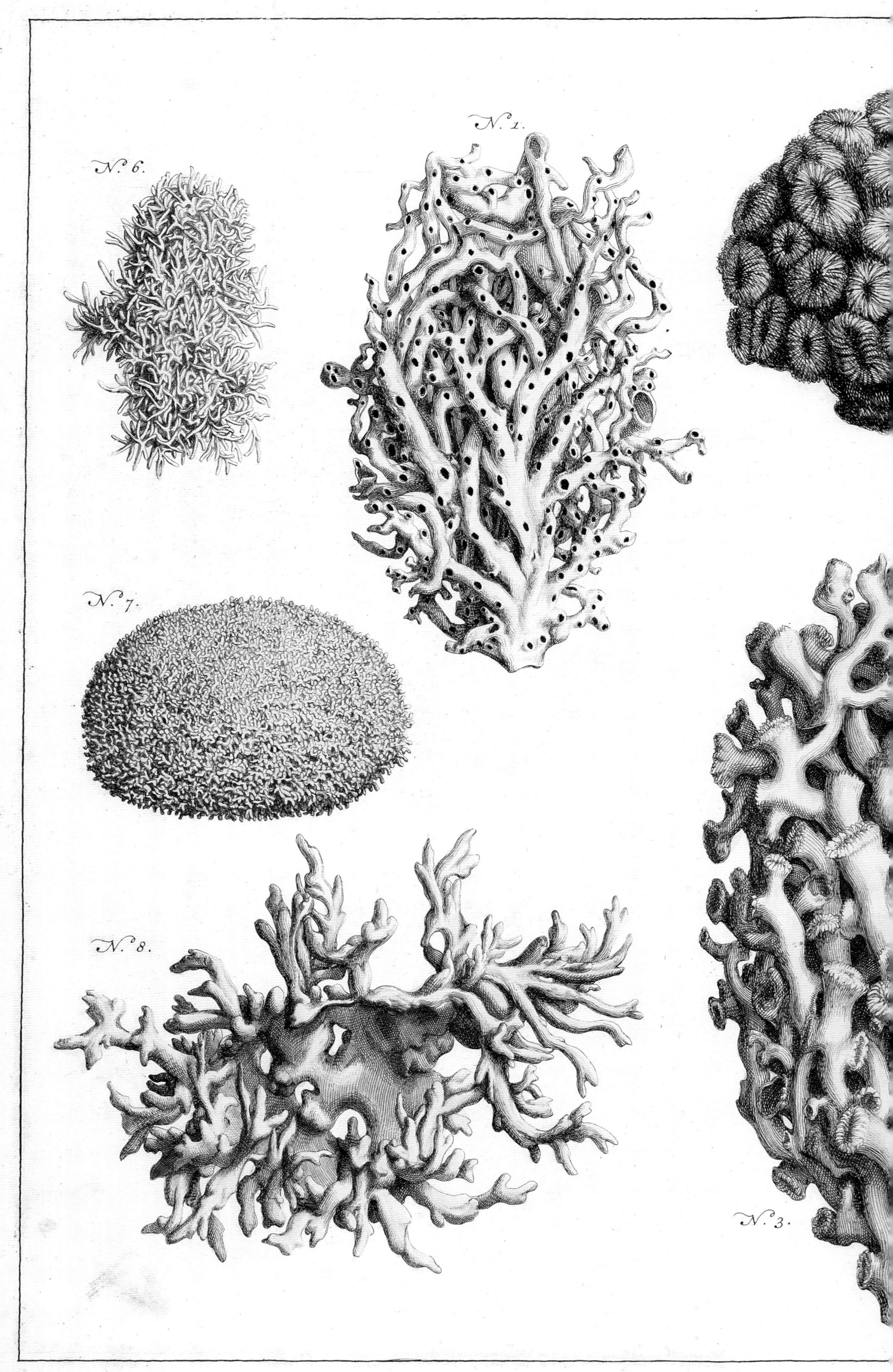

1-8 Cnidaria **1, 2** *Madrepora oculata* **3** *Lophelia prolifera* **4** *Favia* **5** *Acropora* **6** *Seriatopora aculecita*
1-8 Cnidarians · Nesseltiere (Korallen) · Cnidaires **1-2** Ocular corals · Augenkorallen · Coraux blancs **4** Star coral · Sternkoralle · Corail étoile **5** Staghorn coral · Geweihkoralle · Corail bois
6 Needle coral · Nadelkoralle · Corail seriatopora

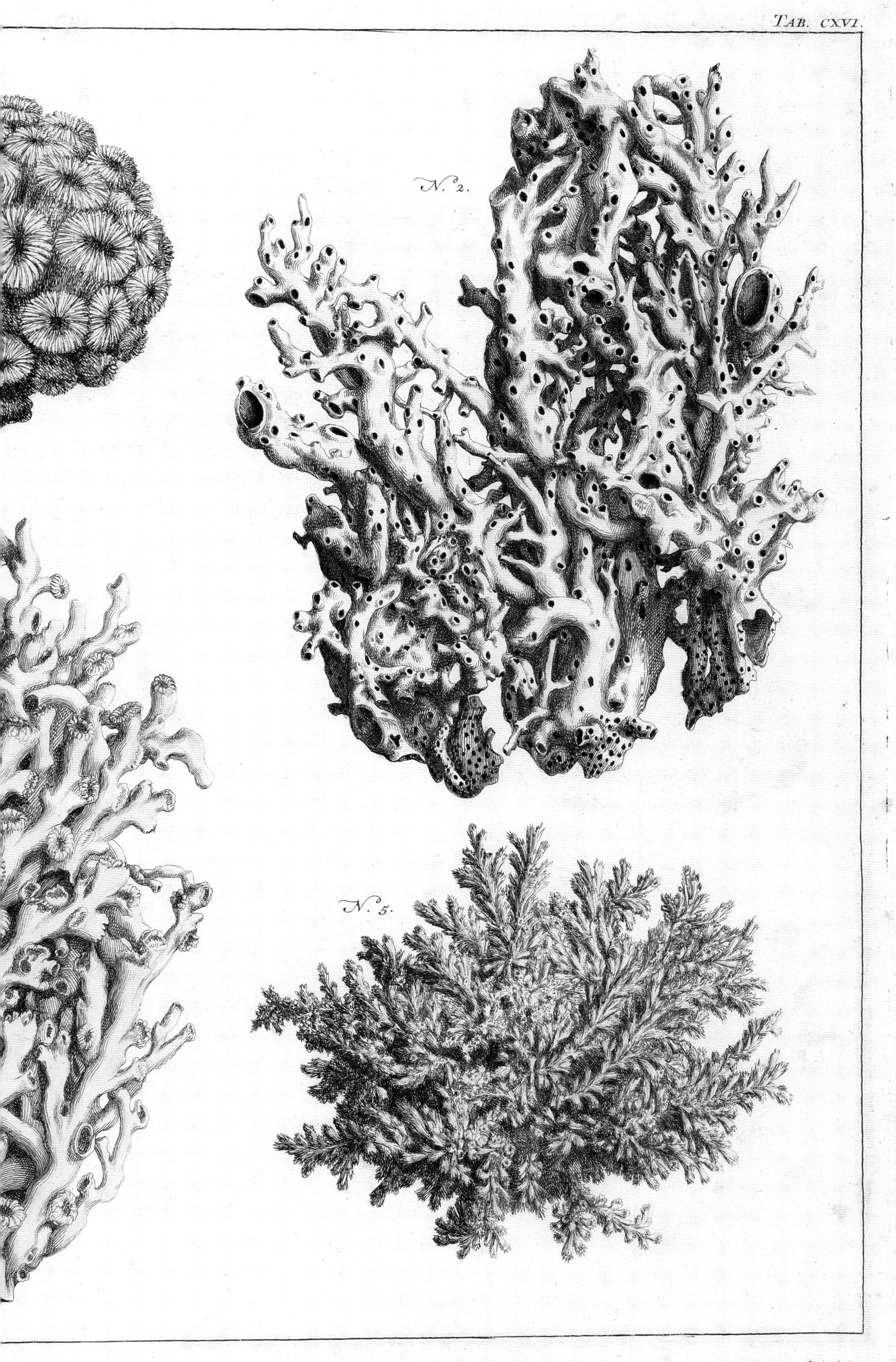
N.° 2.
N.° 5.

LOCUPLETISSIMI RERUM NATURALIUM THESAURI

ACCURATA DESCRIPTIO

ET

ICONIBUS ARTIFICIOSISSIMIS

EXPRESSIO

PER

UNIVERSAM PHYSICES HISTORIAM.

OPUS,

CUI, IN HOC RERUM GENERE, NULLUM PAR EXSTITIT.
EX TOTO TERRARUM ORBE COLLEGIT,
DIGESSIT, DESCRIPSIT, ET DEPINGENDUM CURAVIT

ALBERTUS SEBA,

ETZELA OOSTFRISIUS,

ACADEMIÆ CÆSAREÆ LEOPOLDINO CAROLINÆ NATURÆ CURIOSORUM
COLLEGA XENOCRATES DICTUS; SOCIETATIS REGIÆ ANGLICANÆ,
ET INSTITUTI BONONIENSIS, SODALIS.

TOMUS IV.

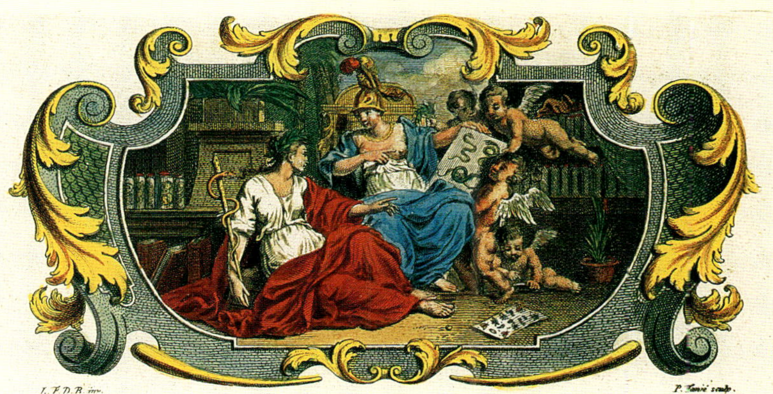

AMSTELAEDAMI,
APUD H. C. ARKSTEUM ET H. MERKUM,
ET PETRUM SCHOUTEN.
MDCCLXV.

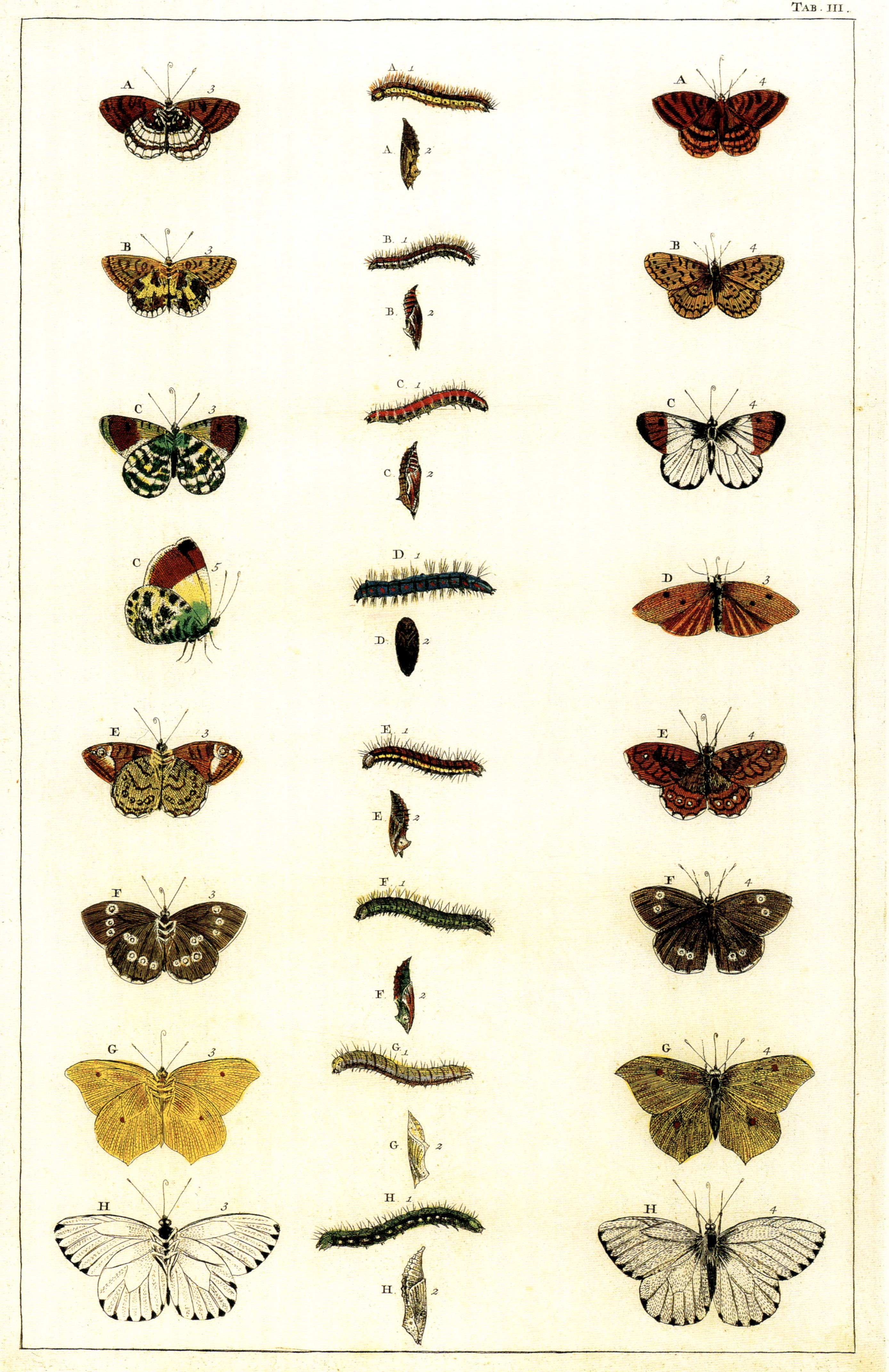

A *Euphydryas maturna* **B** Nymphalidae **C3-5** *Anthocharis cardamines* **D** *Lithosia quadra* **E3-4** Satyridae **F3-4** *Erebia ligea* **G3-4** *Gonepteryx rhamni* **H** *Aporia crataegi*

A Scarce fritillary · Eschenscheckenfalter · Damier du frêne **B** Brush-footed butterfly · Fleckenfalter · Nymphalidé **C3-5** Orange tip · Aurorafalter · Aurore printanière **D** Large footman · Mittelwald-Flechtenbär · Lithosie quadrille **E3-4** Brown · Augenfalter · Satyridé **F3-4** Arran brown · Milchfleck · Grand nègre hongrois **G3-4** Common brimstone · Zitronenfalter · Citron **H** Black-veined white · Baumweißling · Gazé

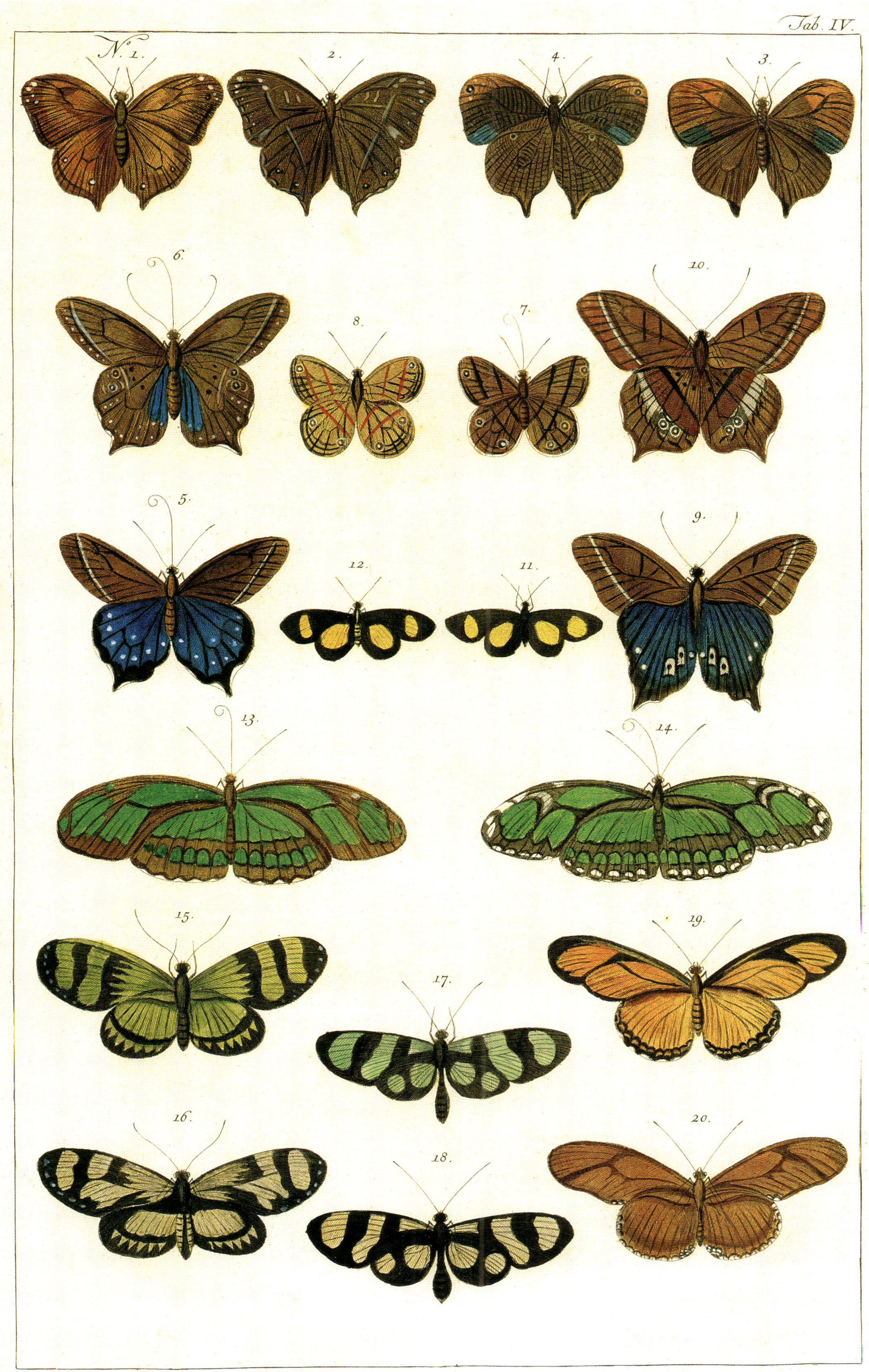

1-4, 7-8 Satyridae 3-4 *Bia actorion* 9-10 *Antirrhea philoctetes* 13-14 *Philaethria dido* 11-12, 15-20 Heliconiidae
Butterflies from tropical America · Tagfalter aus dem tropischen Amerika · Papillons diurnes d'Amérique tropicale

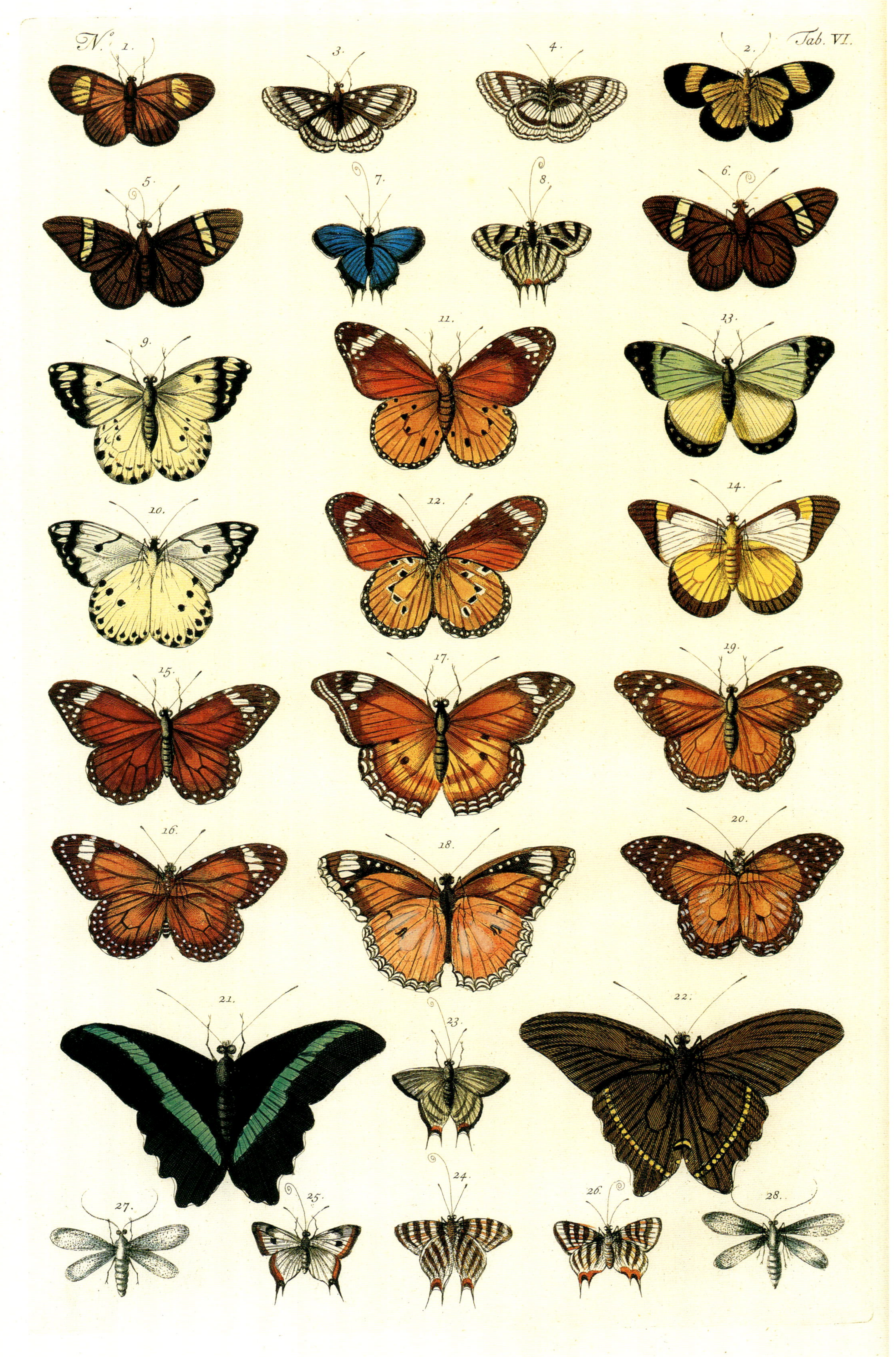

1-2 *Actinote* **7-8, 23-26** Theclinae **9-10** *Belenois calypso* **11-12** *Danaus chrysippus* **13-14** Pieridae **15-16** *Danaus plexippus* **17-18** *Hypolimnas misippus* **19-20** Danaidae **21-22** *Papilio nireus* **27-28** Trichoptera
Tropical butterflies distributed worldwide and caddis flies · Tropische Tagfalter mit weltweiter Verbreitung und Köcherfliegen · Papillons diurnes tropicaux répandus dans le monde entier et trichoptères

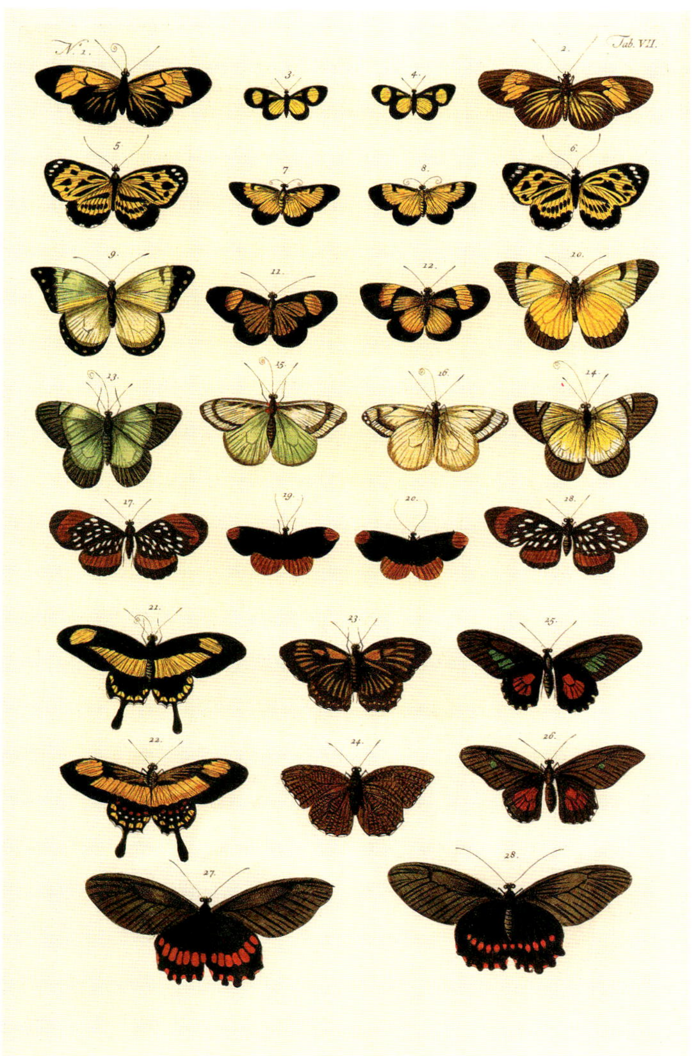

1-2 Papilionoidea **5-6** *Stalachtis calliope* **9-10, 13-16** Pieridae **17-18** *Stalachtis euterpe* **21-22** *Papilio torquatus* **23-24** *Elymnias hypermnestra* **25-26** *Parides aeneas* **27-28** *Parides anchises*
Butterflies from South America and South-East Asia · Tagfalter aus Südamerika und Südostasien · Papillons diurnes d'Amérique du Sud et d'Asie du Sud-Est

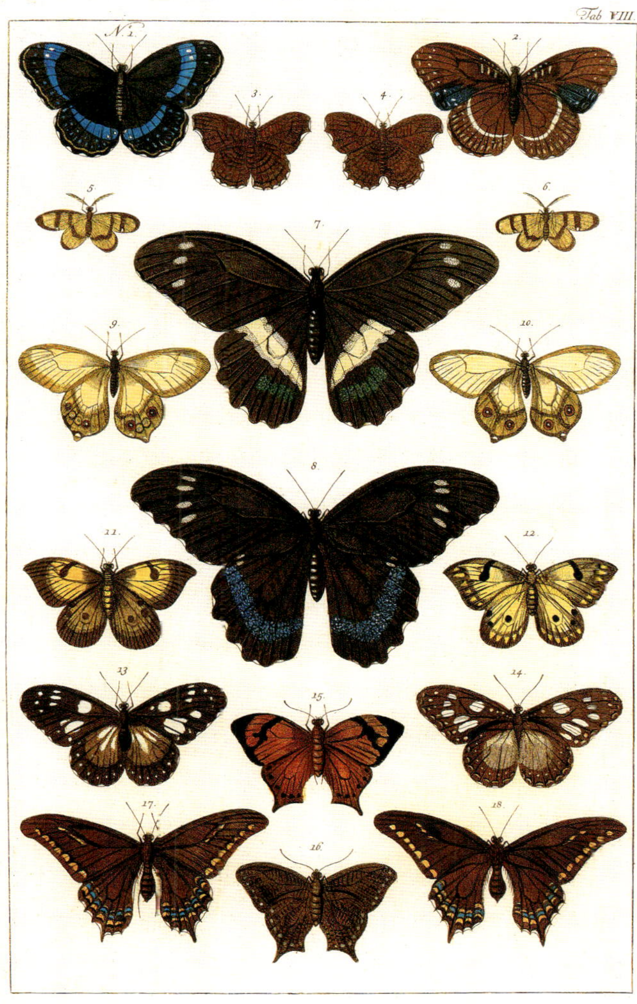

1-2 *Hypolimnas alimena* **7-8** *Papilio gambrisius* **9-10** *Haetera piera* **15-16** Nymphalidae **17-18** *Papilio*
Butterflies distributed variously from South America, the region encompassing the Malay Archipelago and New Guinea to Australia, and worldwide · Tagfalter aus Südamerika vom Malaiischen Archipel und Neuguinea bis nach Australien und mit weltweiter Verbreitung · Papillons diurnes originaires d'Amérique du Sud, de la zone de l'Archipel indomalais et de Nouvelle-Guinée – Australie, et répandus dans le monde entier

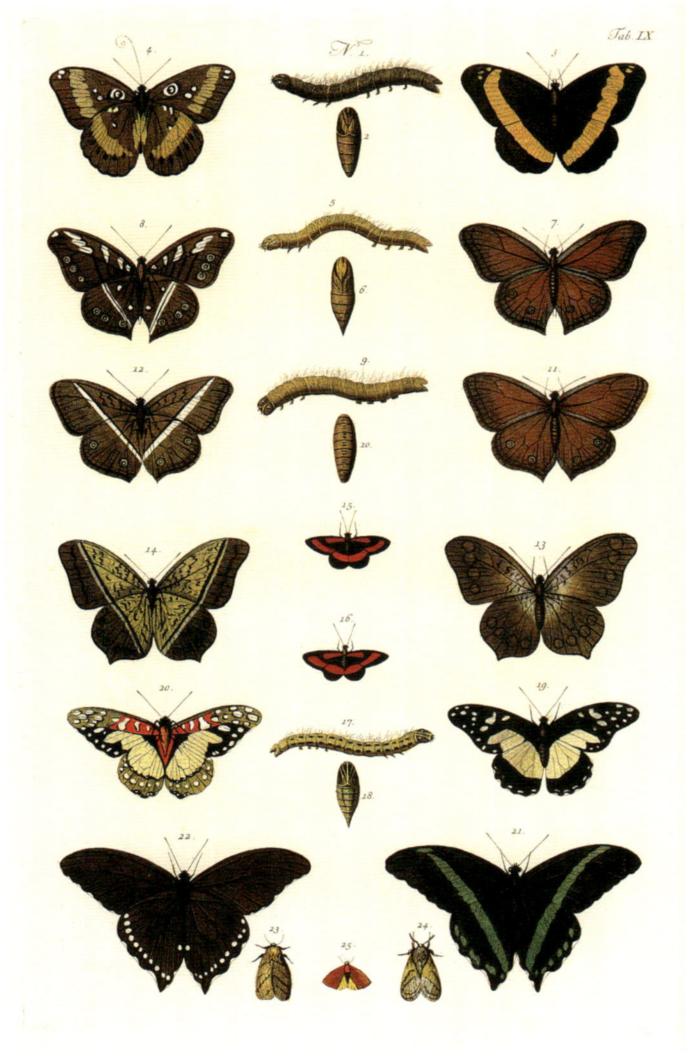

3-4 *Lexias aeropa* **21-22** *Papilio nireus*
Butterflies from the Malay Archipelago and New Guinea · Tagfalter aus dem Malaiischen Archipel und Neuguinea · Papillons diurnes de l'Archipel indomalais et de Nouvelle-Guinée

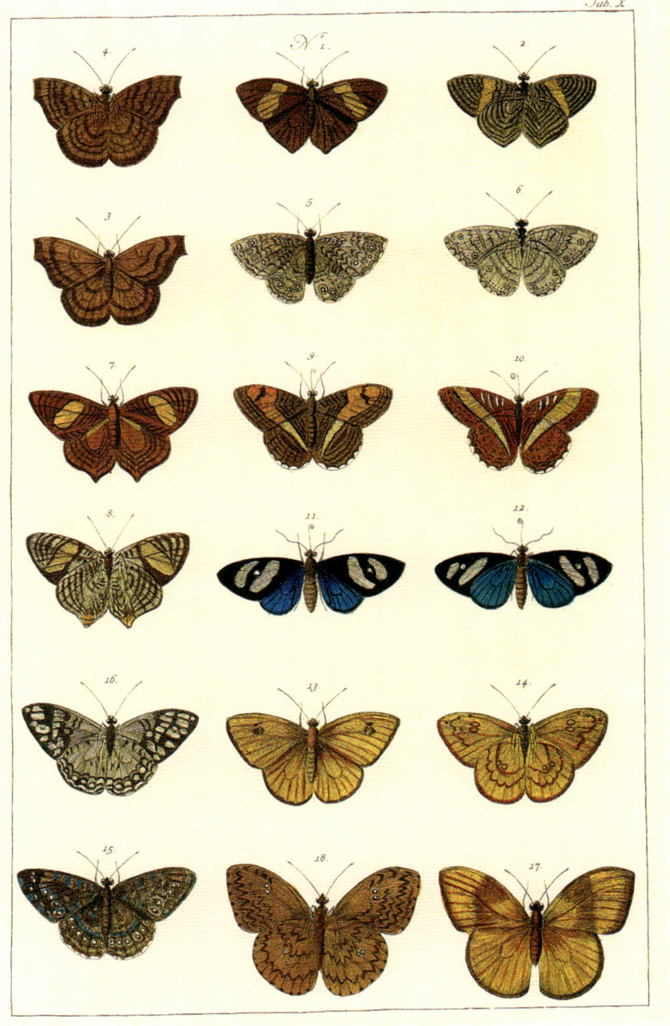

7-8 *Colobura dirce* **11-12** *Heliconius* **13-14, 17-18** *Phoebis sennae*
Butterflies from tropical America · Tagfalter aus dem tropischen Amerika · Papillons diurnes d'Amérique tropicale

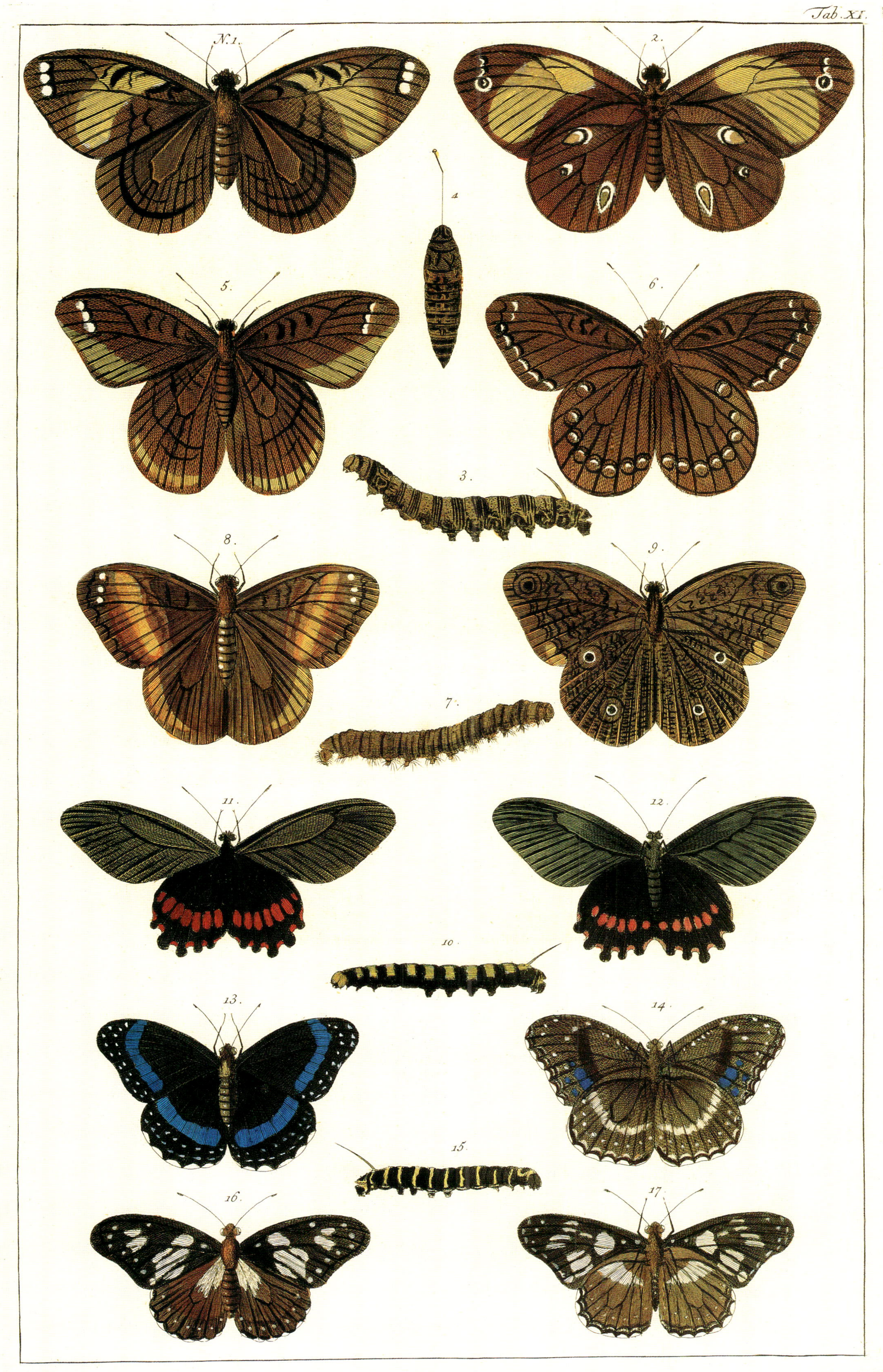

1-2 *Brassolis sophorae* 3-9 Nymphalidae 11-12 *Parides anchises* 13-14 *Hypolimnas alimena* 16-17 Papilionoidea
Butterflies from South America and the region encompassing the Malay Archipelago and New Guinea to Australia · Tagfalter aus Südamerika und vom Malaiischen Archipel und Neuguinea bis nach Australien · Papillons diurnes d'Amérique du Sud et de la zone de l'Archipel indomalais et de Nouvelle-Guinée – Australie

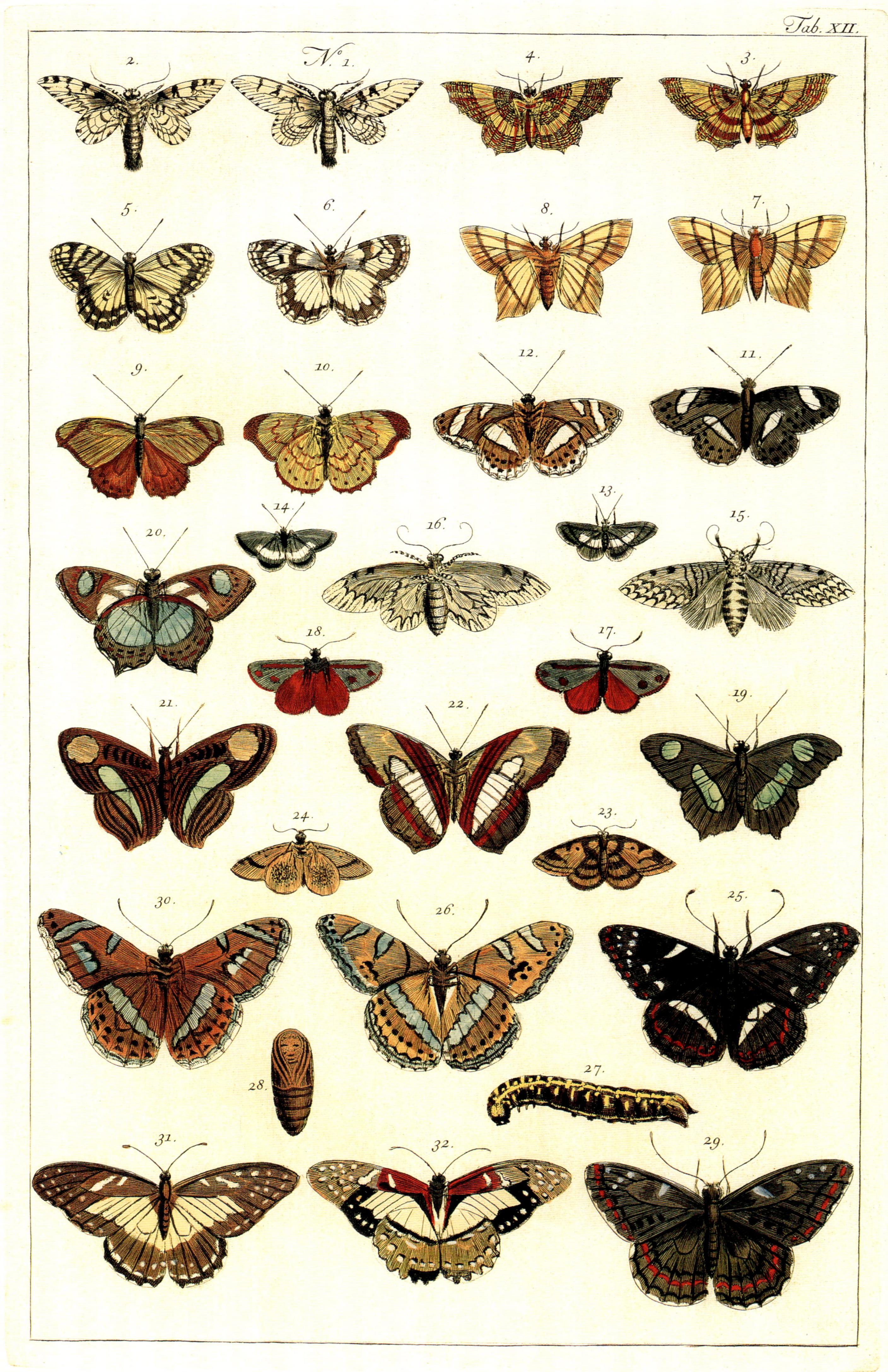

15-16 Sphingidae 17-18 Zygaenidae 19-20 *Pyrrhogyra neaerea* 25-30 *Limenitis populi* 31-32 Nymphalidae
Butterflies and hawkmoths from Europe and tropical Central and South America · Tagfalter und Schwärmer aus Europa und dem tropischen Mittel- und Südamerika · Papillons diurnes et sphinx d'Europe et des zones tropicales d'Amérique Centrale et du Sud

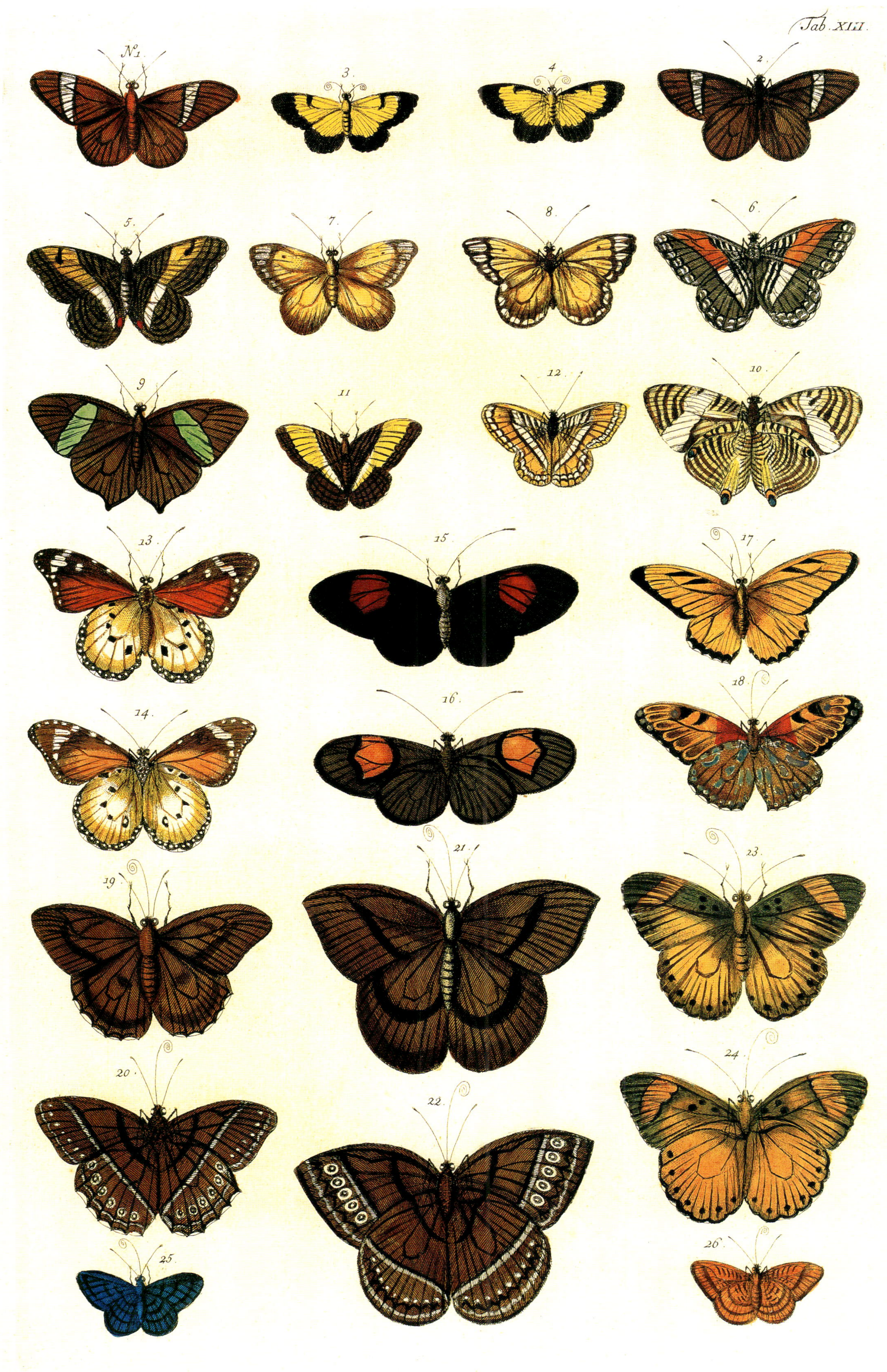

1-2 Brassolinae **5-6** *Adelpha* **9-10** *Colobura dirce* **11-12** *Adelpha cytherea* **13-14** *Danaus chrysippus* **15-16** *Heliconius melpomene* **19-20** Satyridae **21-21** *Euptychia* **25-26** *Emesis lucinda*
Butterflies from the tropics of America and the Caribbean · Tagfalter aus den Tropen Amerikas und der Karibik · Papillons diurnes des zones tropicales d'Amérique et des Caraïbes

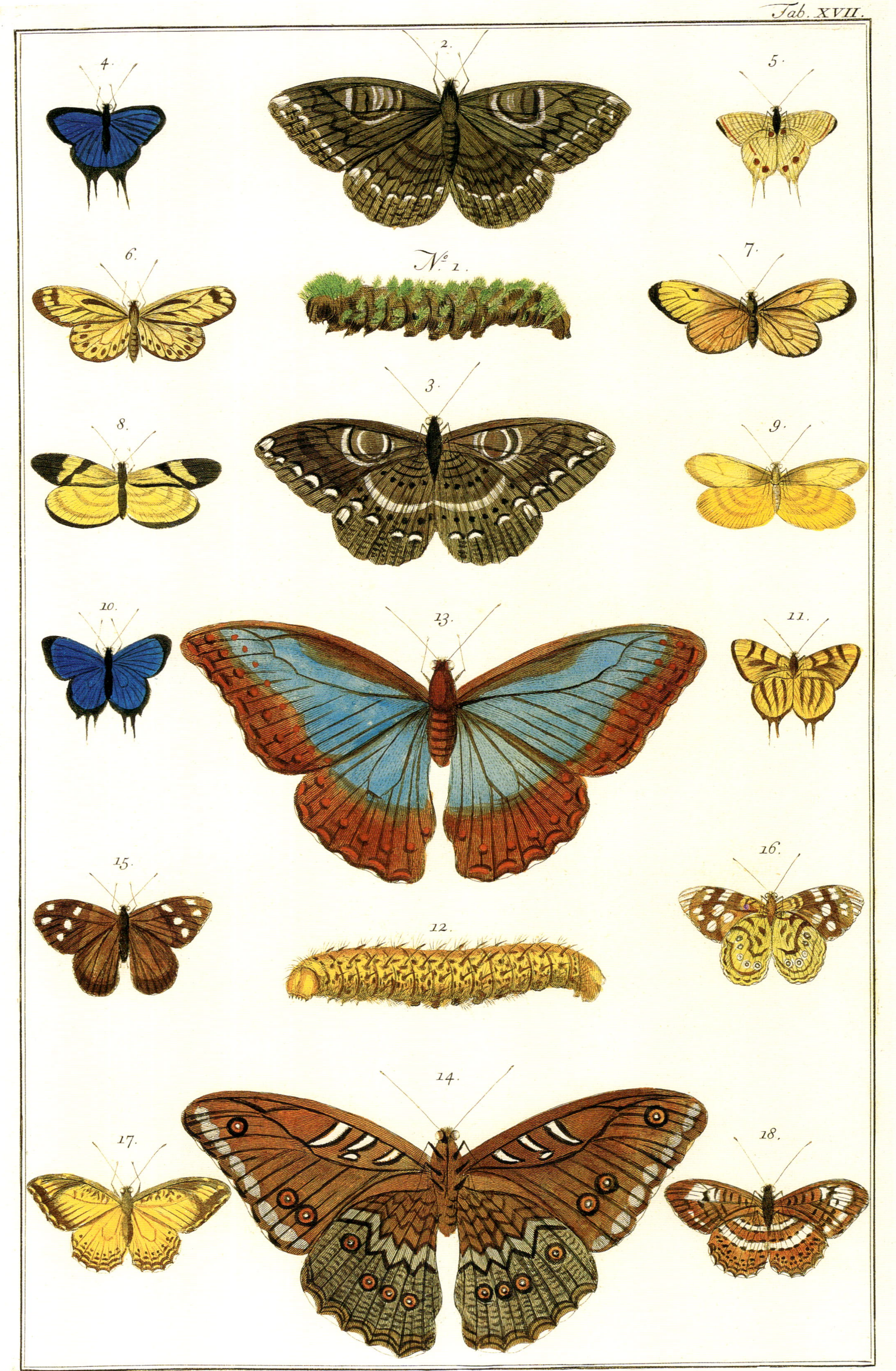

1-3 Papilionoidea? 4-5 Theclinae 8-9 *Enantia melite* 10-11 *Arawacus* 13-14 *Morpho telemachus* 15-16 *Eunica orphise*
Butterflies from tropical Central and South America · Tagfalter aus dem tropischen Mittel- und Südamerika · Papillons diurnes des zones tropicales d'Amérique Centrale et du Sud

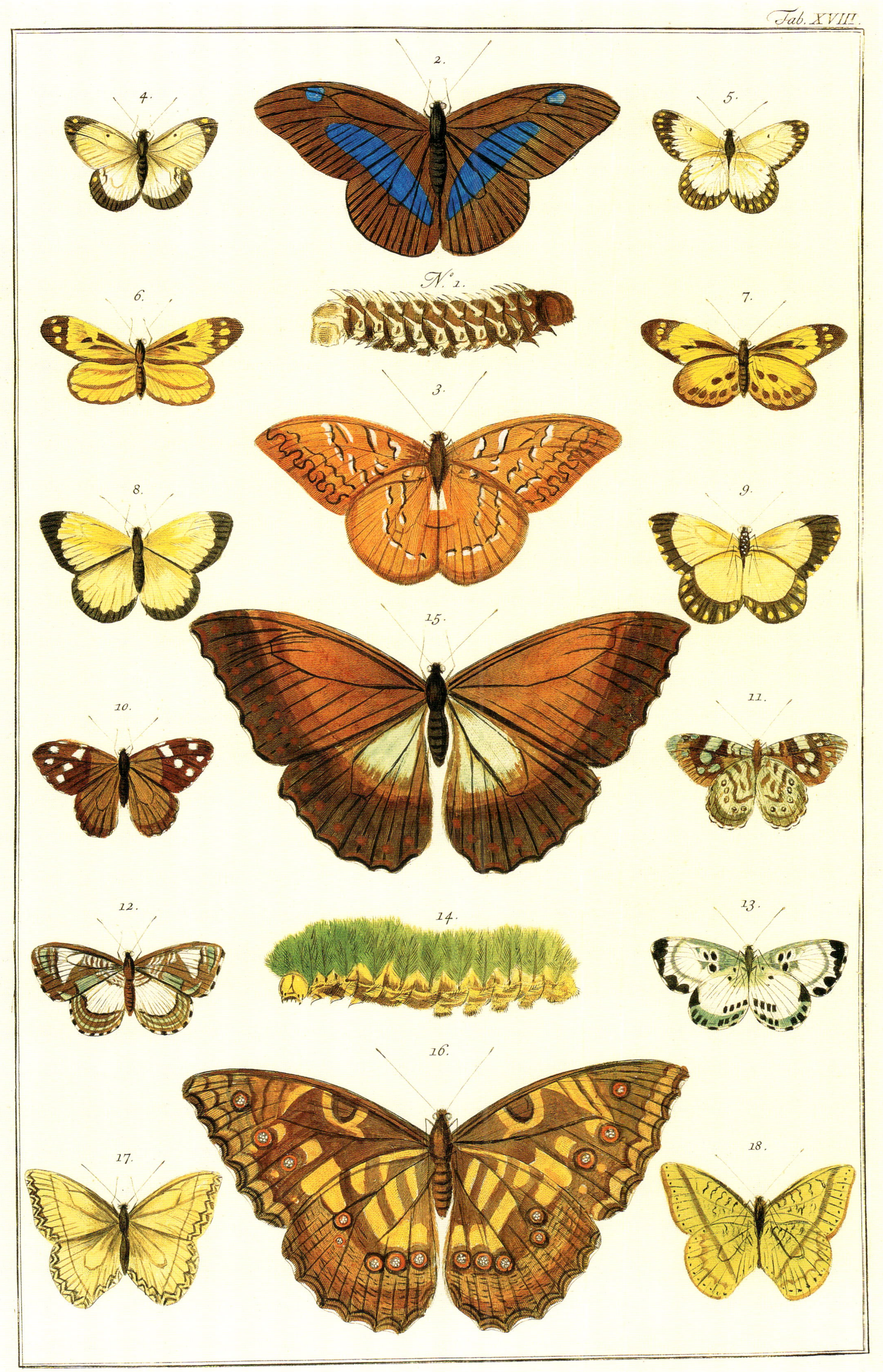

2-3 *Archaeoprepona demophon* **4-5** *Colias* **6-7** *Heliconius hecale* **8-9** *Colias palaeno* **10-11** *Eunica orphise* **15-16** *Morpho telemachus*
Butterflies distributed worldwide · Tagfalter mit weltweiter Verbreitung · Papillons diurnes répandus dans le monde entier

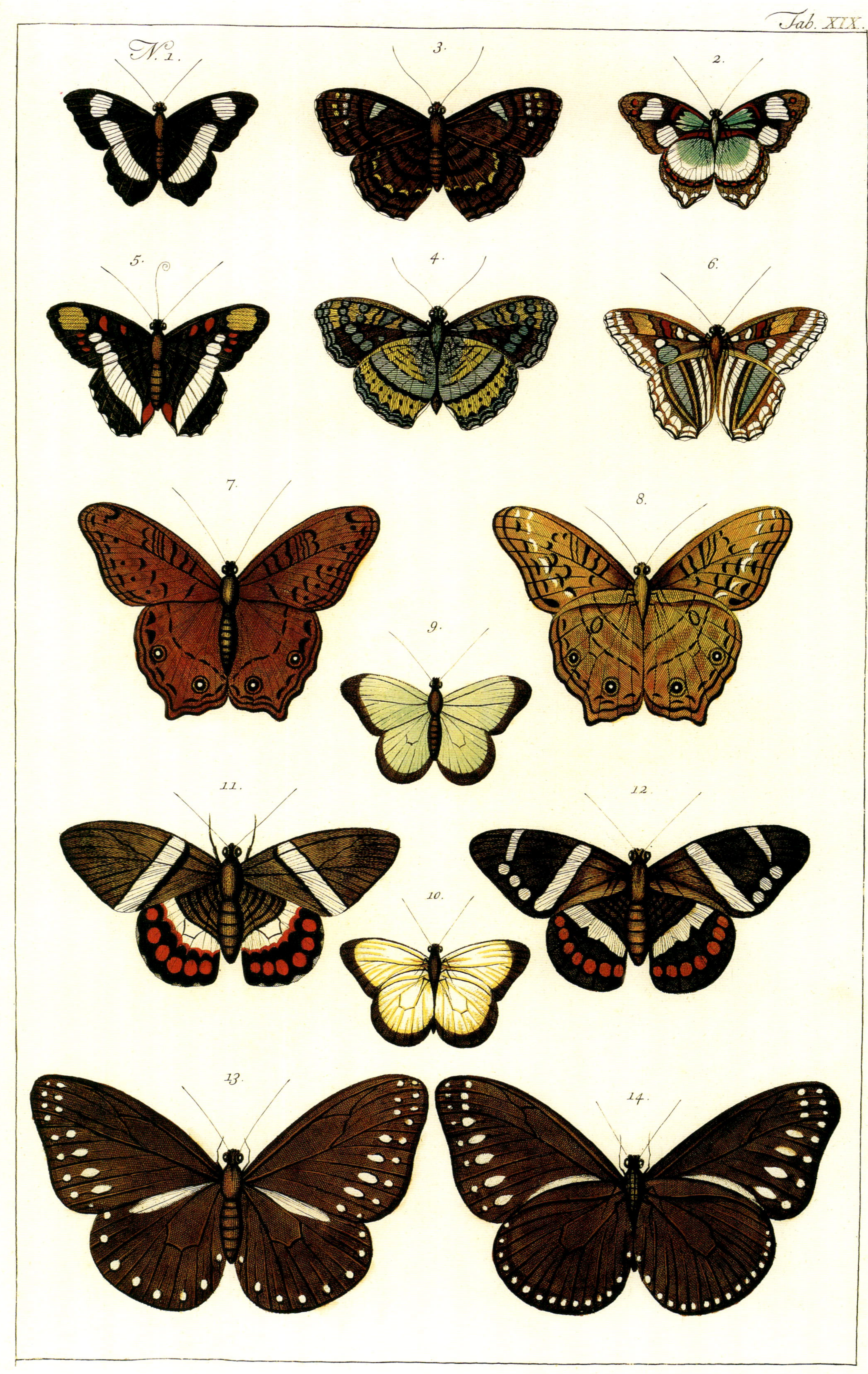

1-2 *Pyrrhogyra neaerea* 7-8 *Vindula arsinoe* 9-10 *Colias* 11-12 *Aeropetes tulbaghia* 13-14 *Euploea midamus*
Butterflies distributed worldwide · Tagfalter mit weltweiter Verbreitung · Papillons diurnes répandus dans le monde entier

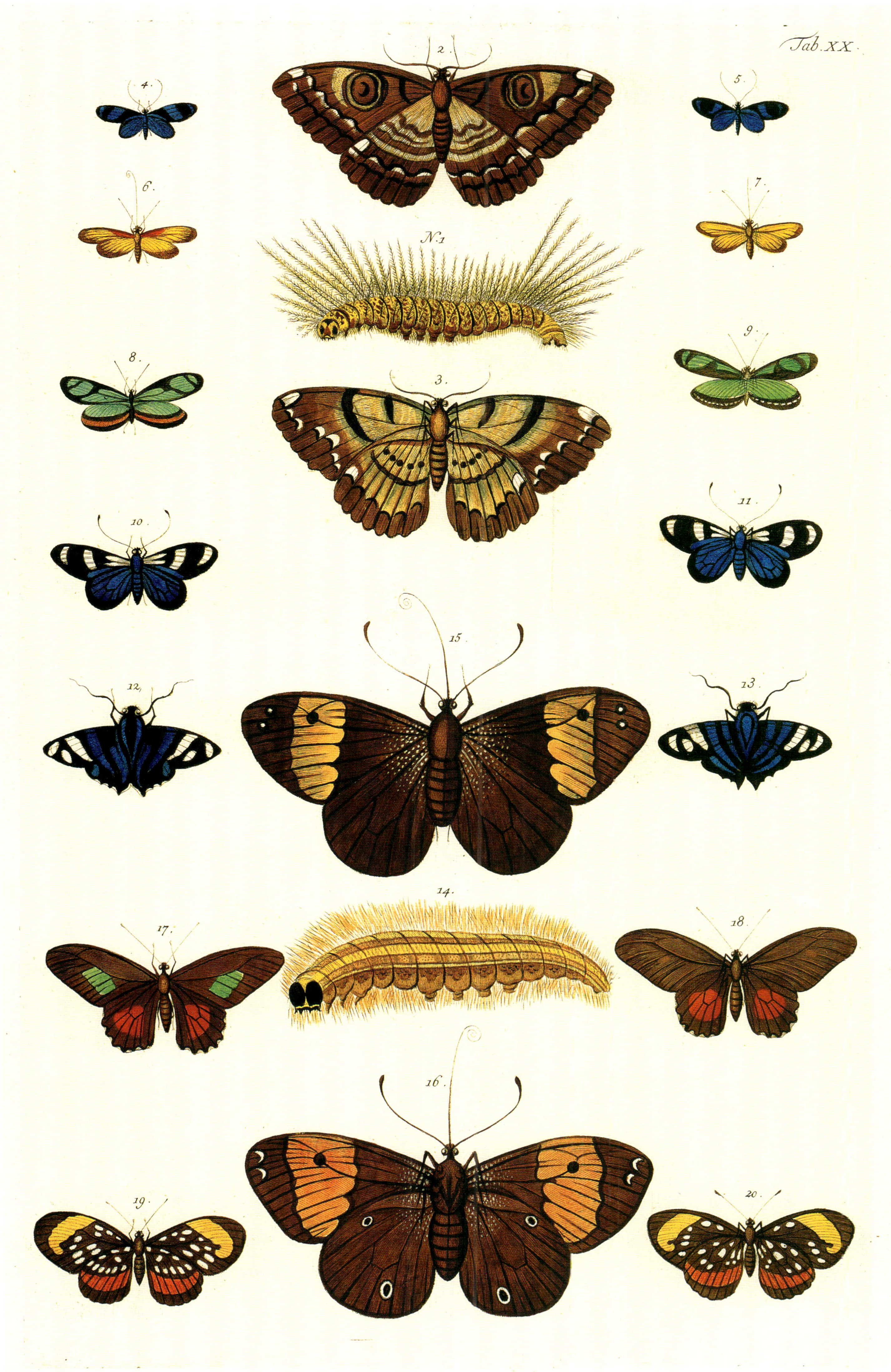

8-9 Riodininae 12-13 *Jemadia gnetus* 15-16 *Brassolis sophorae* 17-18 *Parides aeneas* 19-20 *Stalachtis euterpe*
Butterflies from tropical South America · Tagfalter aus dem tropischen Südamerika · Papillons diurnes des zones tropicales d'Amérique du Sud

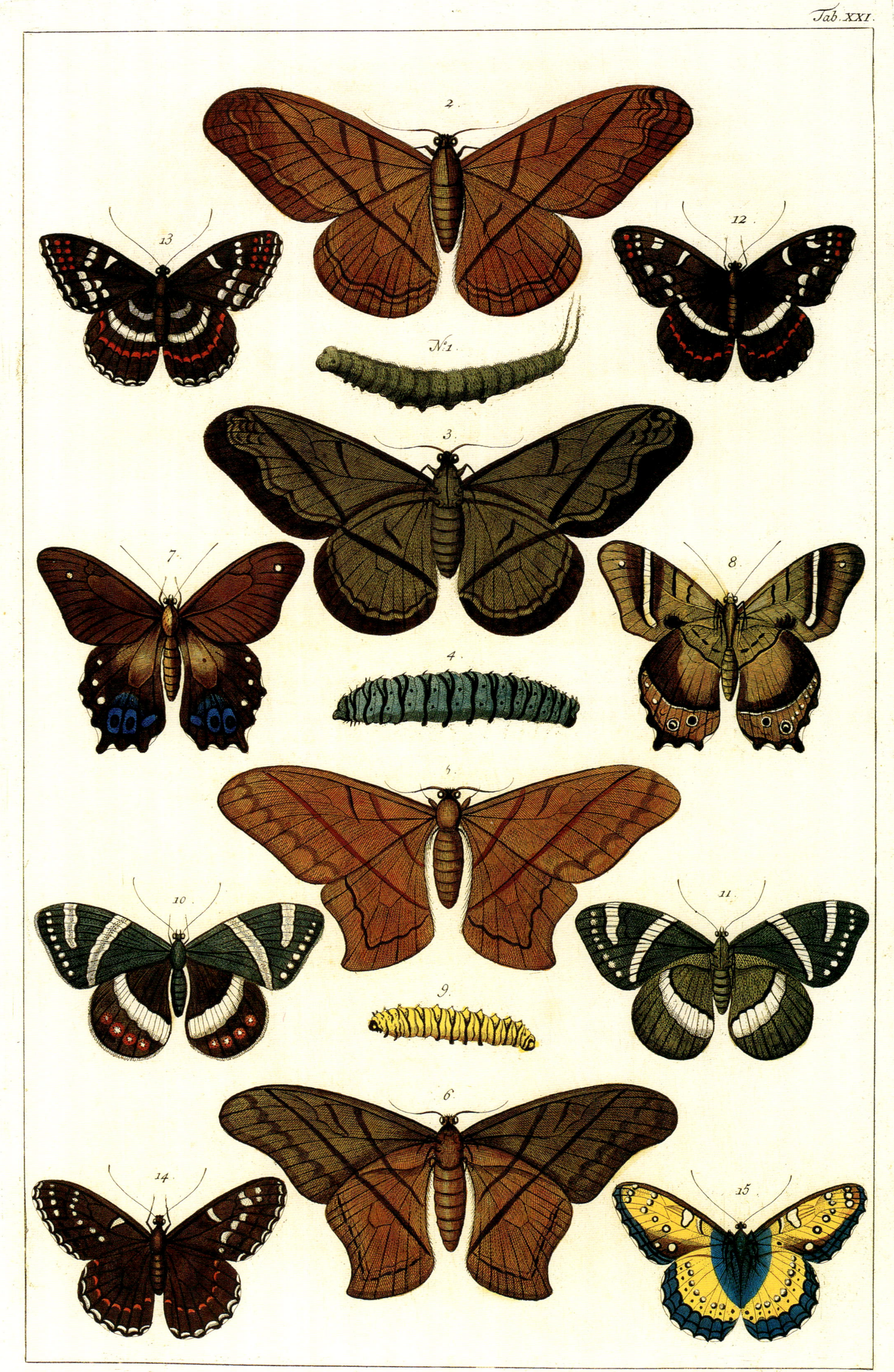

1-3, 5-6 *Arsenura sp.* 7-8 *Antirrhea philoctetes* 12-15 *Limenitis populi*
Butterflies and moths from South America and Eurasia · Tag- und Nachtfalter aus Südamerika und Eurasien · Papillons diurnes et nocturnes d'Amérique du Sud et d'Eurasie

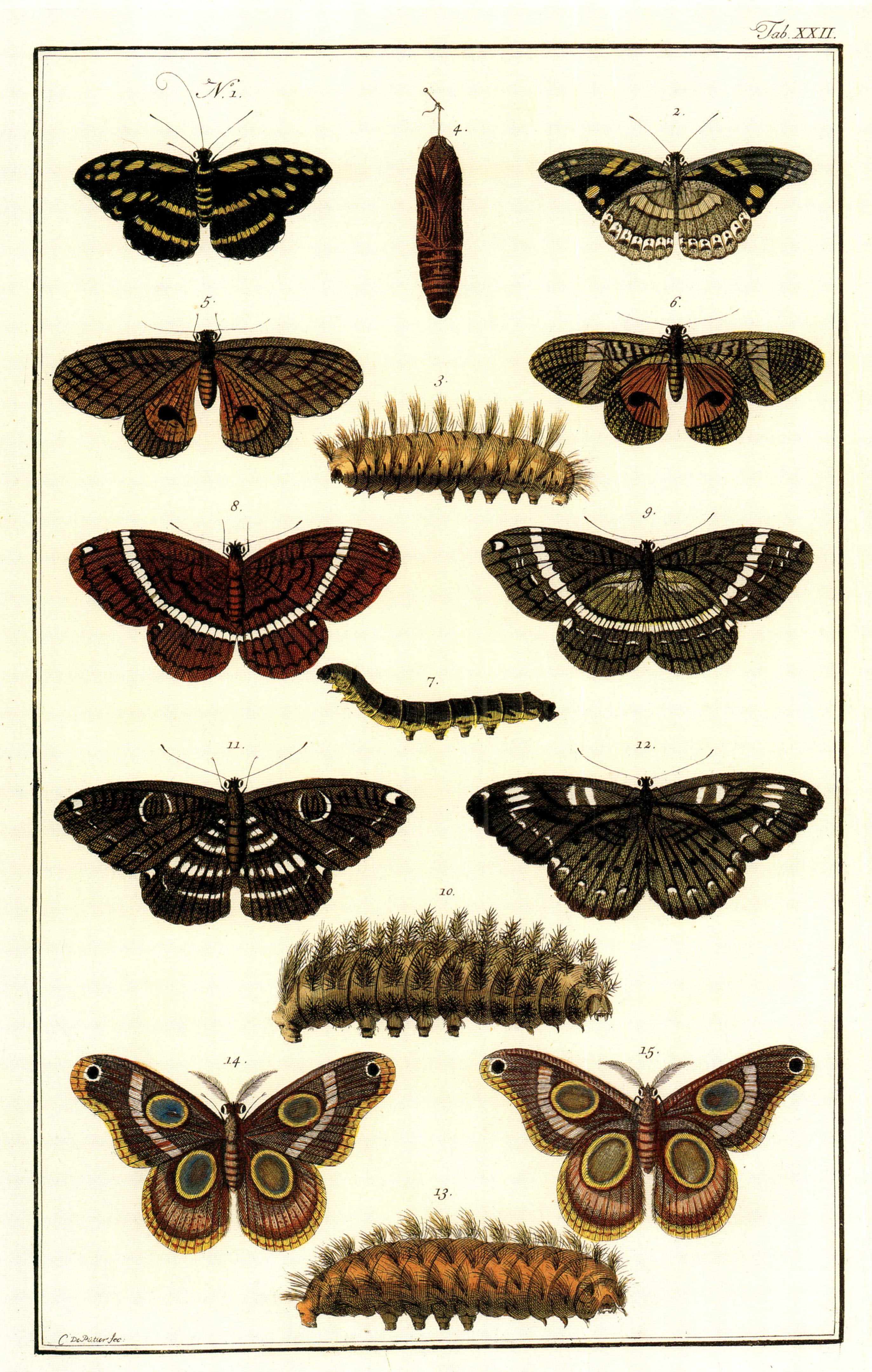

1-2 *Lexias* **14-15** *Rothschildia prionia*
Butterflies from Indonesia and New Guinea and silkmoths from Central and South America · Tagfalter aus Indonesien und Neuguinea sowie Augenspinner aus Mittel- und Südamerika · Papillons diurnes d'Indonésie et de Nouvelle-Guinée ainsi que saturniidés d'Amérique Centrale et du Sud

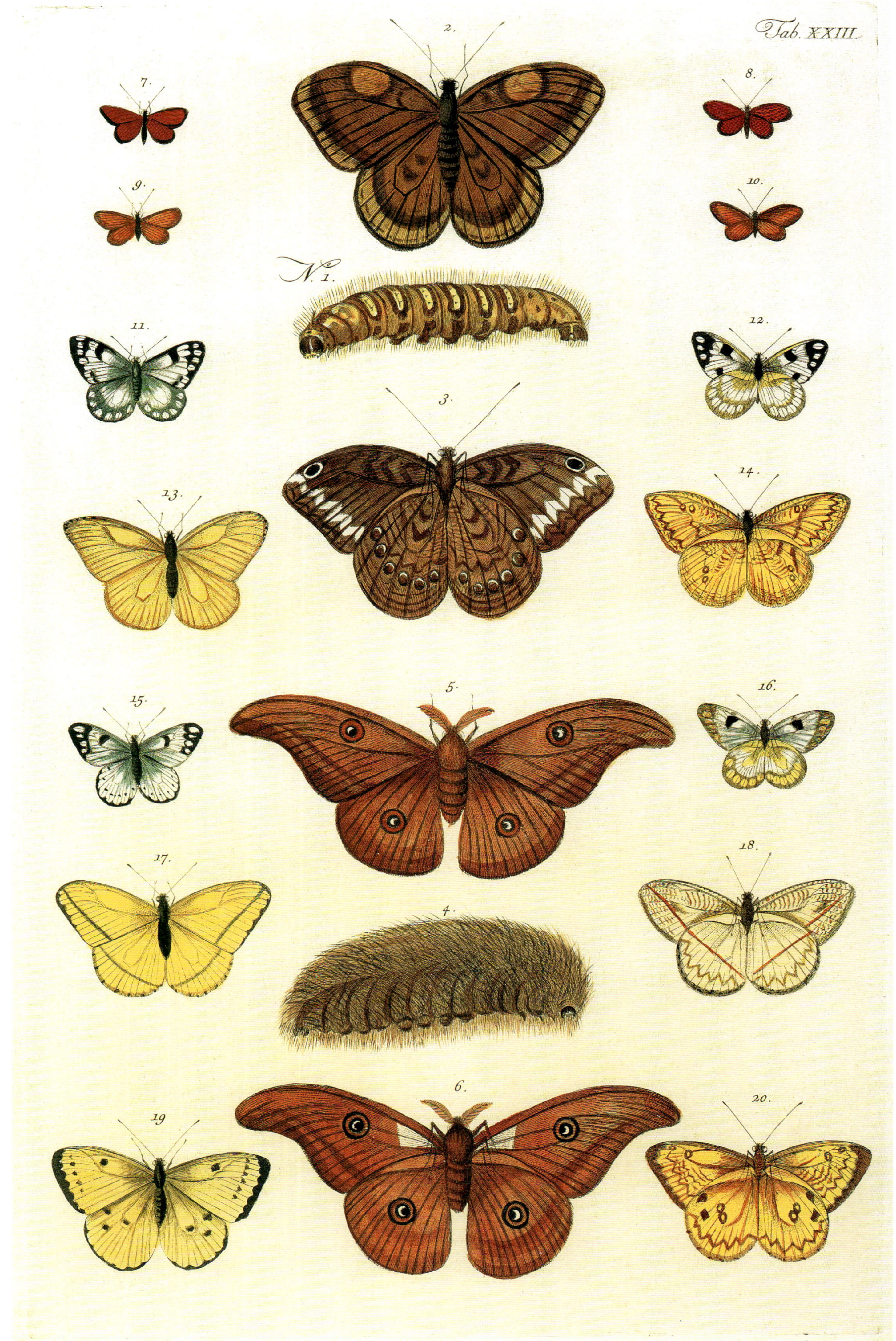

5-6 *Antheraea helferi* 11-12, 15-16 *Pontia daplidice* 13-14, 19-20 *Phoebis sennae* 17-18 *Phoebis trite*
Butterflies from Europe, America and North Africa and silkmoths from South-East Asia · Tagfalter aus Europa, Amerika und Nordafrika sowie Augenspinner aus Südostasien · Papillons diurnes d'Europe, d'Amérique et d'Afrique du Nord ainsi que saturniidés d'Asie du Sud-Est

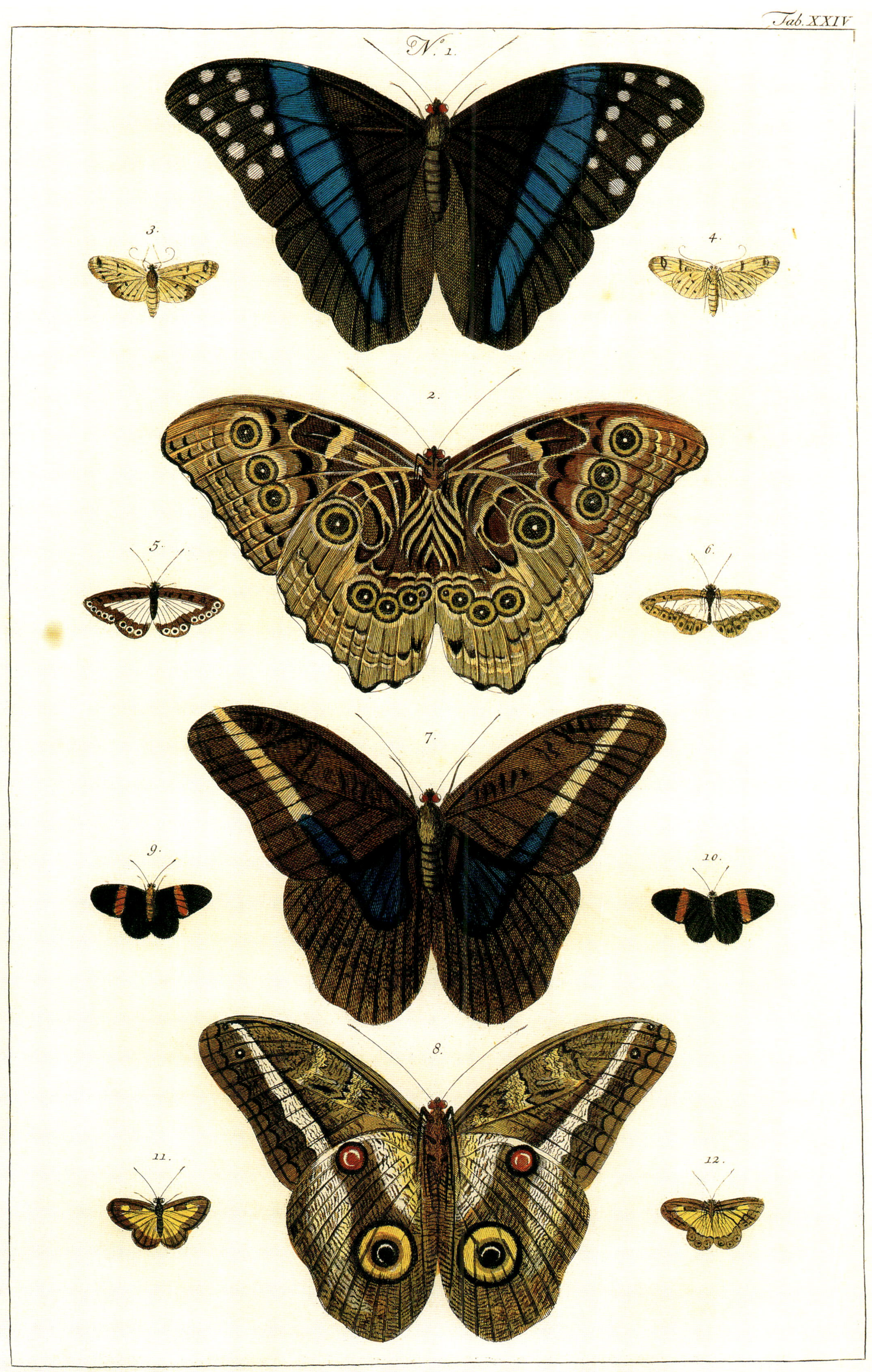

1-2 *Morpho* 5-6 Riodininae 7-8 *Caligo idomeneus* 9-12 Arctiinae
Butterflies and tiger moths from South America · Tagfalter und Bärenspinner aus Südamerika · Papillons diurnes et arctiidés d'Amérique du Sud

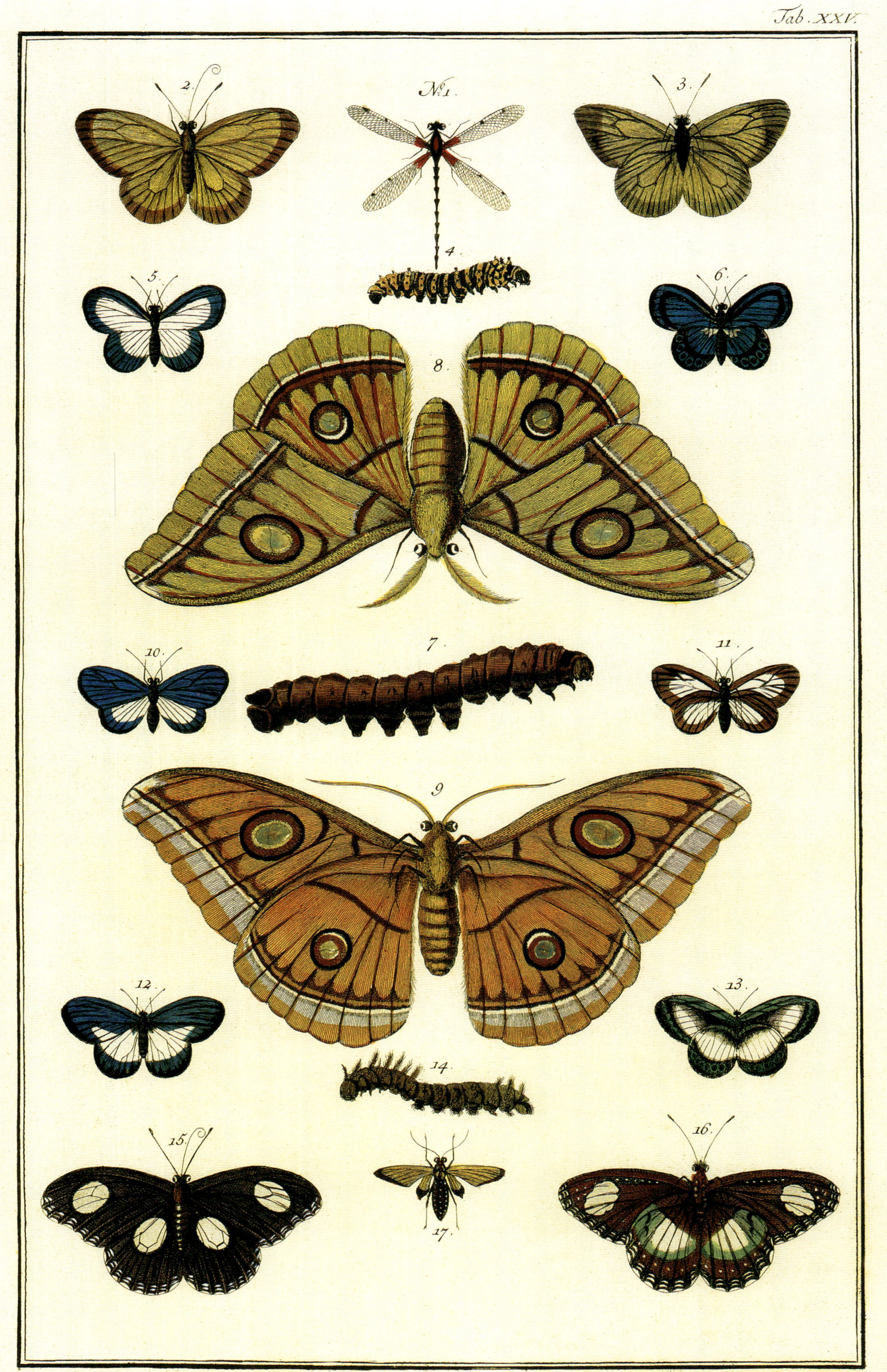

1 Odonata 5-6 *Danis* 8-9 *Antheraea helferi* 10-11 Polyommatinae 12-13 *Danis danis* 15-16 *Hypolimnas bolina* 17 *Trichura coarctata*
One dragonfly, butterflies and silkmoths from South-East Asia to Australia · Eine Libelle, Tagfalter und Augenspinner von Südostasien bis Australien · Une libellule, des papillons diurnes ainsi que des saturniidés de la zone Asie du Sud-Est – Australie

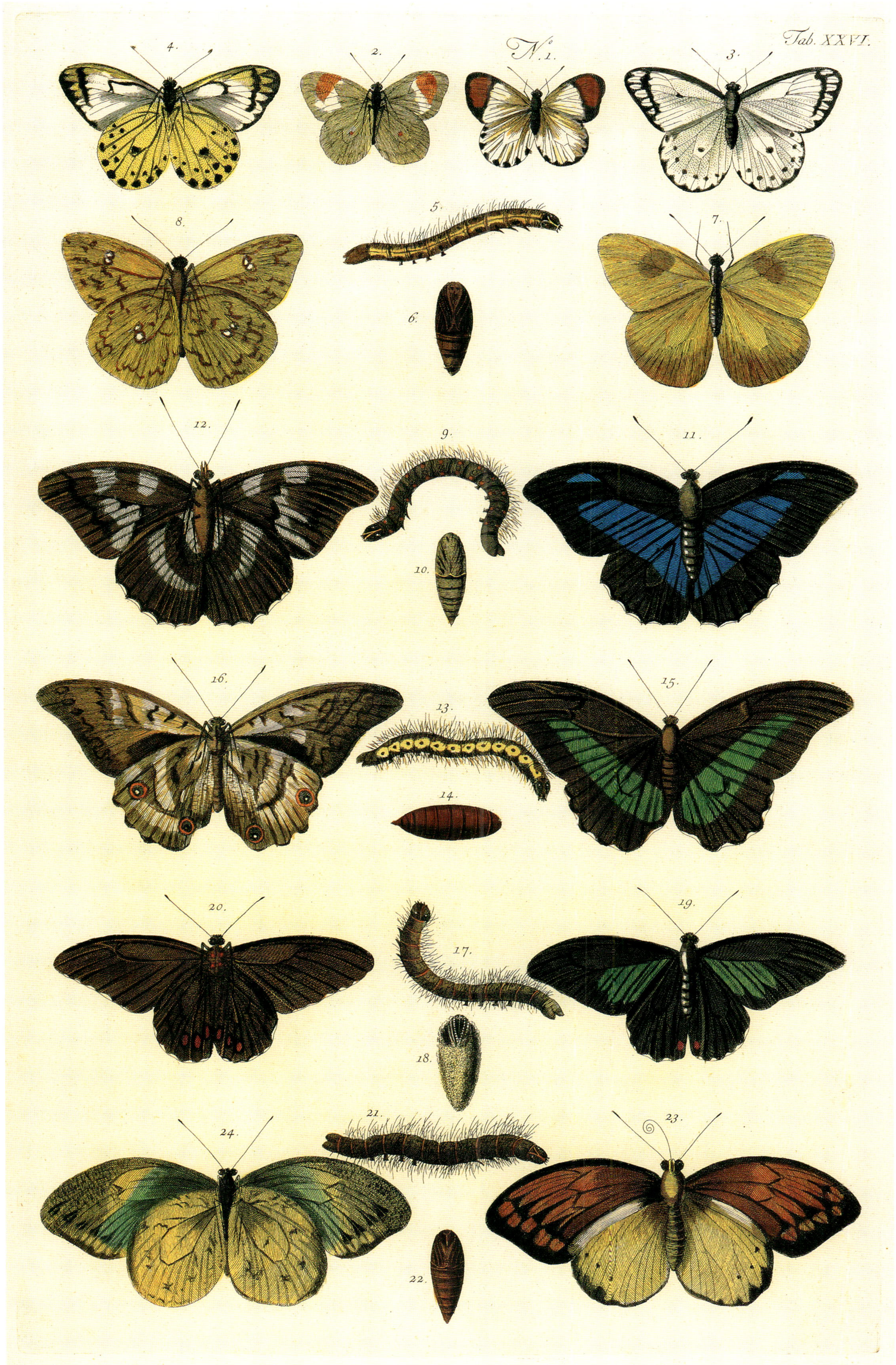

1-2 *Colotis sp.* **3-4** *Belenois calypso* **7-8** Coliadinae **11-16** *Archaeoprepona demophon* **19-20** *Parides sesostris* **21-22** *Hebomoia leucippe*
Butterflies from Africa, Central and South America and the Moluccas · Tagfalter aus Afrika, Mittel- und Südamerika und den Molukken · Papillons diurnes d'Afrique, d'Amérique Centrale et du Sud et des Moluques

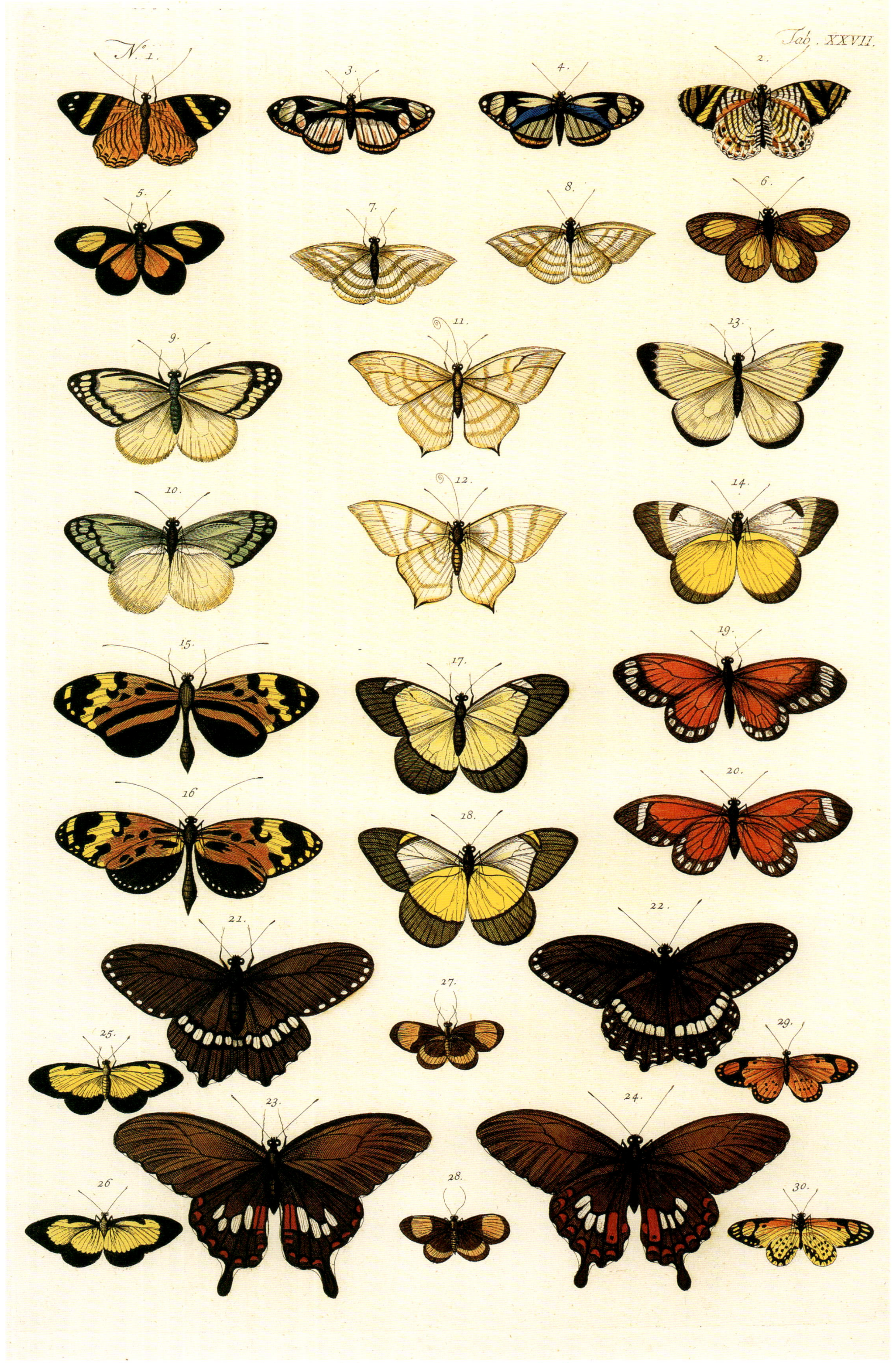

1-2 *Tigridia acesta* **5-6** *Setabis epitus* **9-10** Pierinae **11-12** Coliadinae **13-14** *Melete lycimnia* **15-16** *Melinaea mneme* **21-24** *Papilio polytes*
Butterflies and moths from South America and South-East Asia · Tag- und Nachtfalter aus Südamerika und Südostasien · Papillons diurnes et nocturnes d'Amérique du Sud et d'Asie du Sud-Est

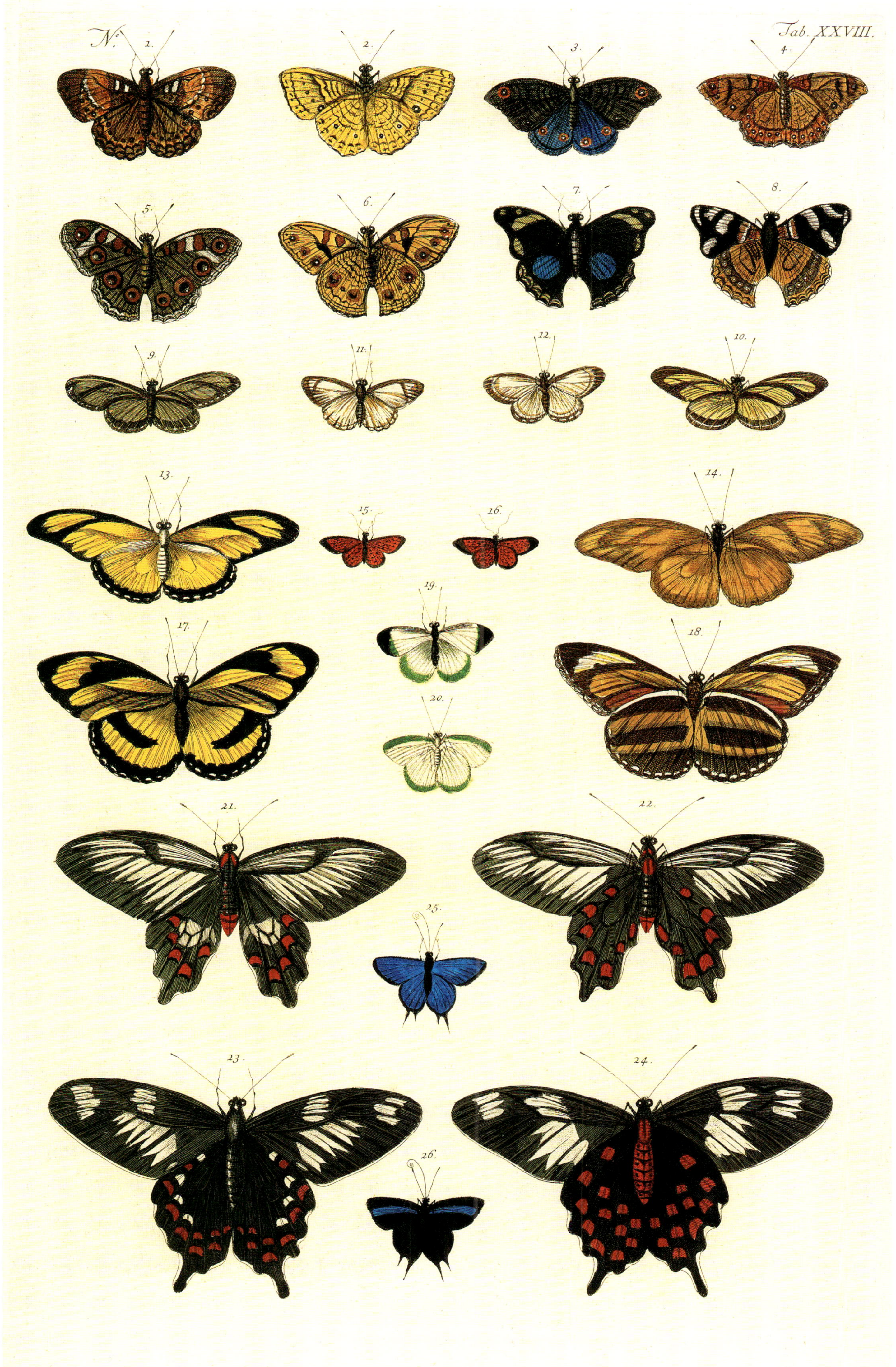

13-14 *Dryas iulia* 17-18 *Dryadula phaetusa* 21-22 *Atrophaneura polydorus* 23-24 *Atrophaneura hector* 25-26 Theclinae
Tropical butterflies distributed worldwide · Tropische Tagfalter mit weltweiter Verbreitung · Papillons diurnes tropicaux répandus dans le monde entier

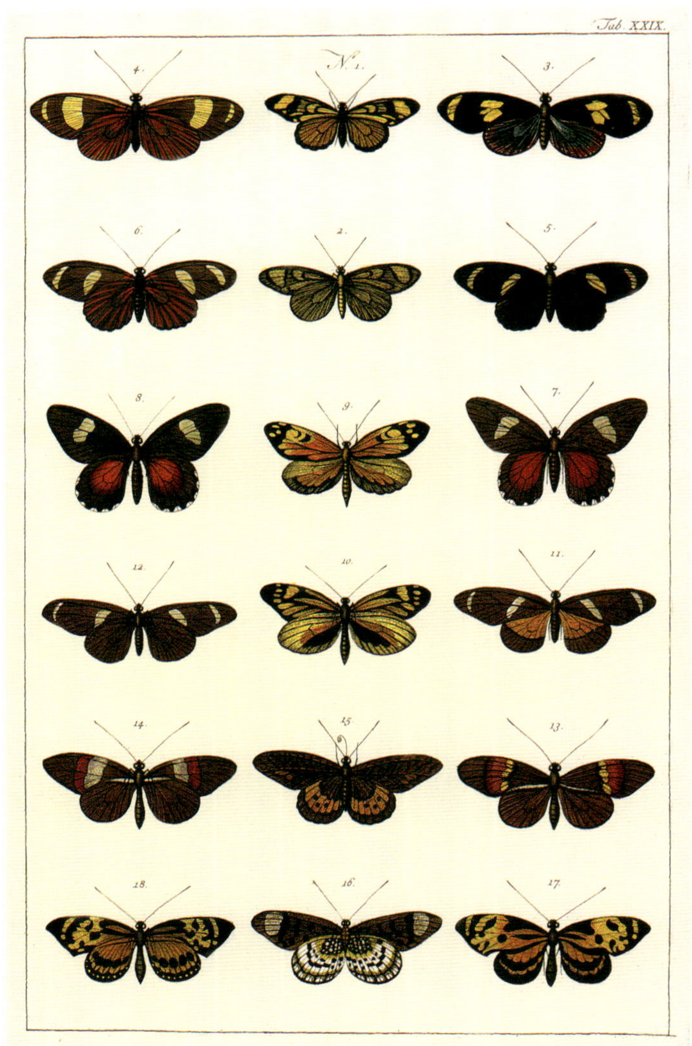

1-2 *Actinote parapheles* **3-4** *Heliconius doris* **5-6** *Heliconius wallacei* **7-8** Papilioninae **9-10** *Dismorphia amphiona* **13-14** *Heliconius heurippa* **15-16** *Acraea egina* **17-18** *Tithorea harmonia*
Butterflies from Africa and tropical Central and South America · Tagfalter aus Afrika und dem tropischen Mittel- und Südamerika · Papillons diurnes d'Afrique et des zones tropicales d'Amérique Centrale et du Sud

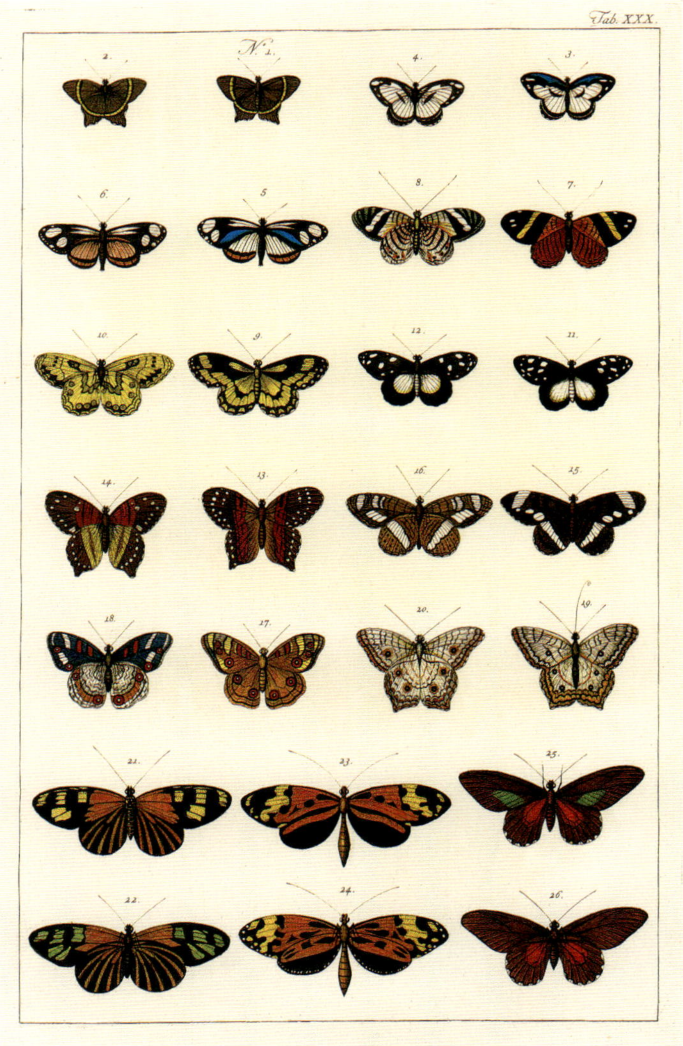

1-2 *Riodina lysippus* **5-6** Ithomiinae **7-8** *Tigridia acesta* **11-12** *Hyalothyrus neleus* **15-18** Nymphalinae **19-20** *Anartia jatrophae* **23-24** *Mechanitis polymnia*
Butterflies from tropical America and the region encompassing Africa to Arabia · Tagfalter aus dem tropischen Amerika und von Afrika bis nach Arabien · Papillons diurnes d'Amérique tropicale et de la zone d'Afrique – Arabie

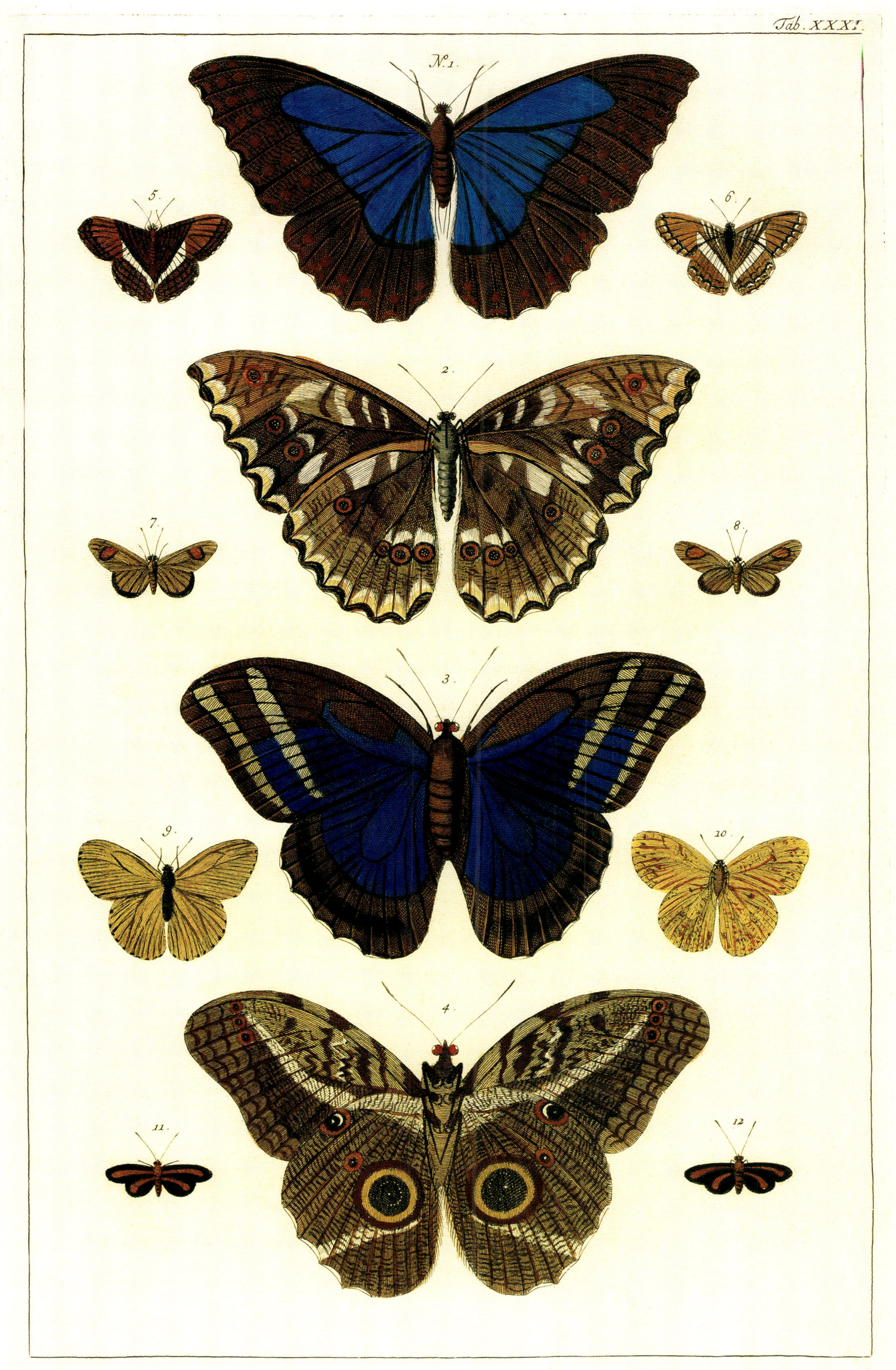

1-2 *Morpho menelaus* 3-4 *Caligo teucer* 5-6 *Adelpha cytherea* 11-12 *Josia sp.*
Butterflies from tropical Central and South America · Tagfalter aus dem tropischen Mittel- und Südamerika · Papillons diurnes des zones tropicales d'Amérique Centrale et du Sud

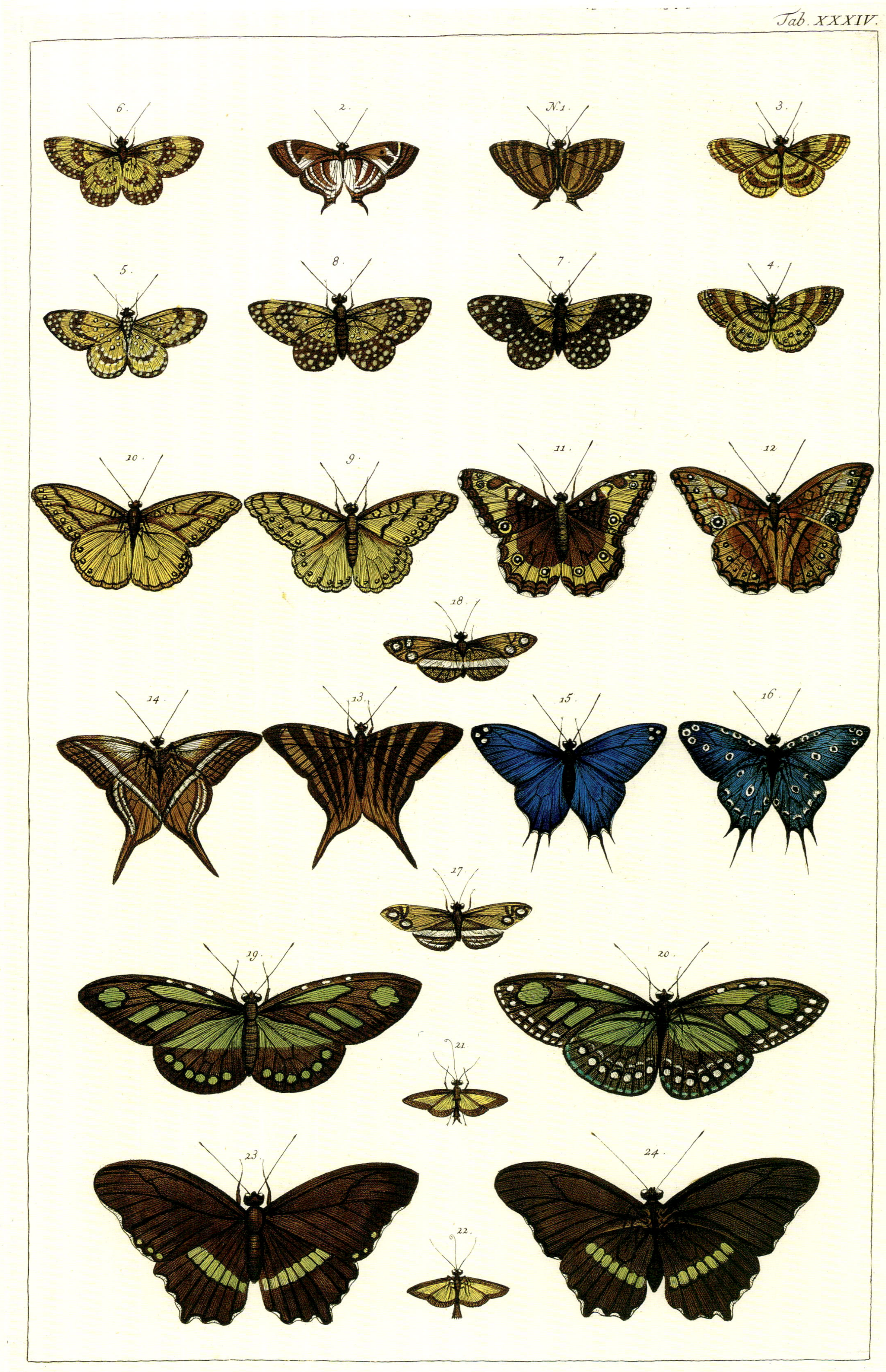

5-8 *Stalachtis phlegia* **13-14** *Marpesia chiron* **15-16** *Pseudolycaena marsyas* **23-24** *Papilio polytes*
Butterflies from America and South-East Asia · Tagfalter aus Amerika und Südostasien · Papillons diurnes d'Amérique et d'Asie du Sud-Est

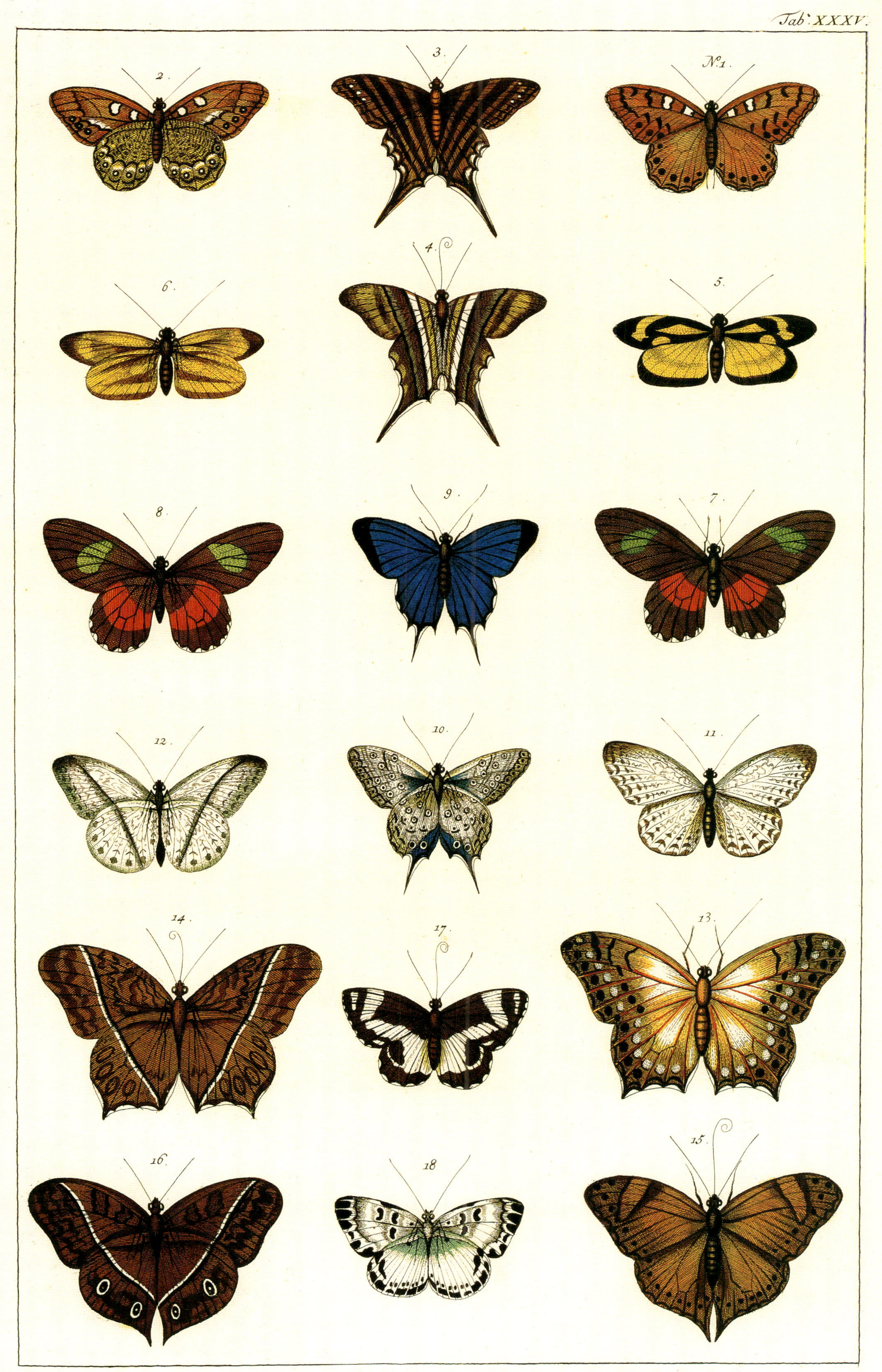

3-4 *Marpesia chiron* **5-6** Arctiinae **7-8** *Parides sp.* **13-14** *Charaxes varanes* **15-16** *Doleschallia bisaltide* **17-18** *Salamis anacardi*
Butterflies from Africa and tropical America, the region encompassing South-East Asia to Australia, as well as one South American moth · Tagfalter aus Afrika und dem tropischen Amerika, von Südostasien bis nach Australien sowie ein südamerikanischer Nachtfalter · Papillons diurnes d'Afrique et d'Amérique tropicale, de la zone d'Asie du Sud-Est – Australie, ainsi qu'un papillon nocturne d'Amérique du Sud

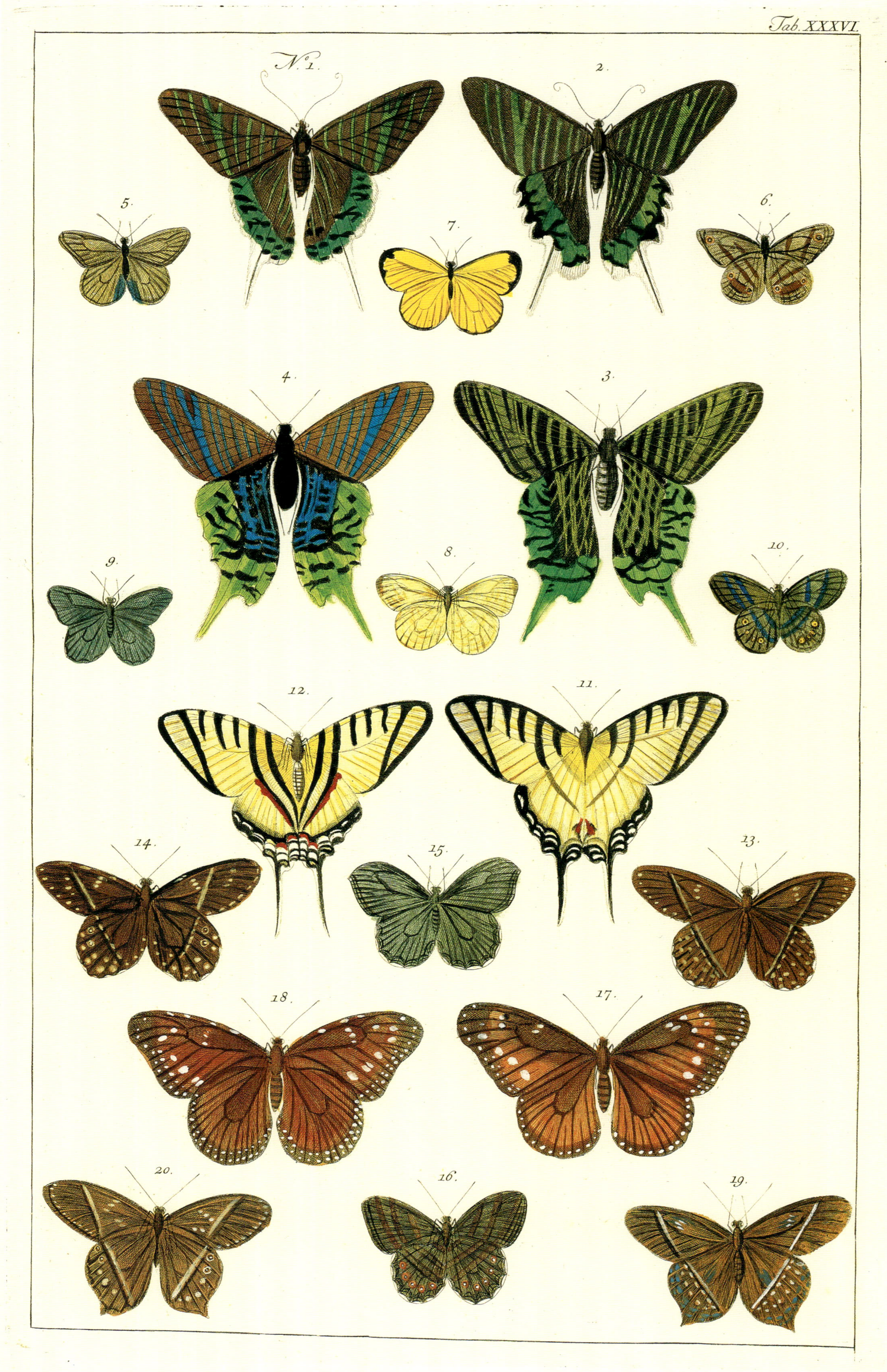

1-4 *Eurytides* **7-8** *Eurema sp.* **11-12** *Eurytides protesilaus* **13-14** *Pierella lena* **17-18** *Danaus eresimus*
Butterflies distributed variously in tropical and subtropical America and worldwide · Tagfalter aus dem tropischen und subtropischen Amerika und mit weltweiter Verbreitung · Papillons originaires d'Amérique tropicale et subtropicale, et répandus dans le monde entier

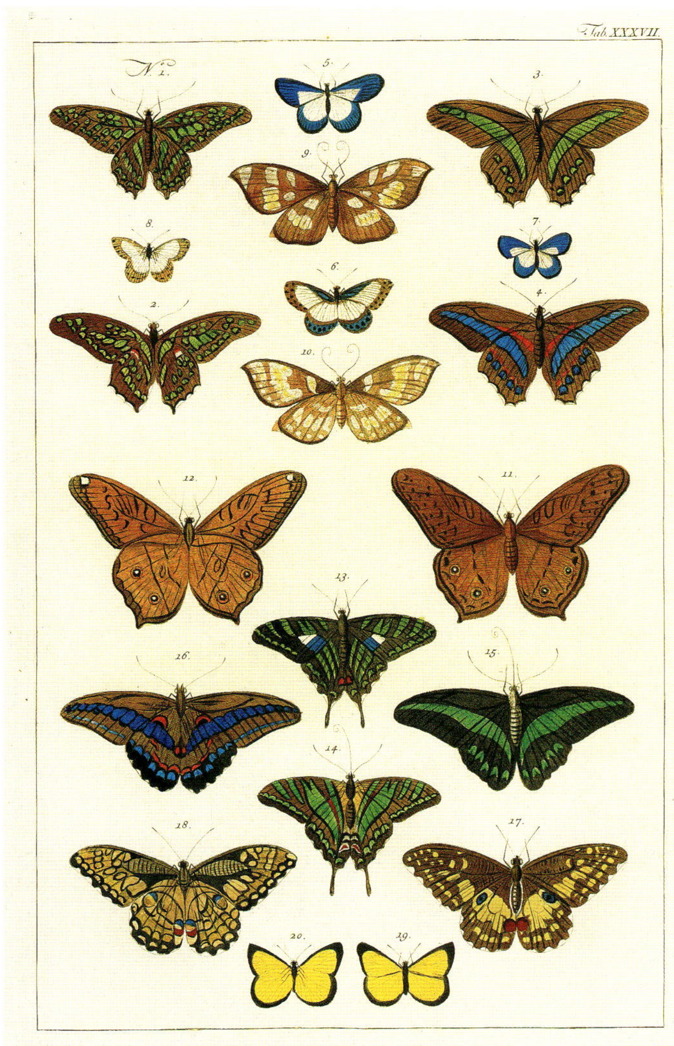

1-2 *Graphium agamemnon* **3-4, 15-16** *Graphium sarpedon* **5-8** *Danis* **9-10** *Draconia peripheta* **11-12** *Vindula arsinoe* **17-18** *Papilio demoleus* **19-20** *Eurema sp.*
Butterflies distributed variously from South-East Asia to Australia, and worldwide · Tagfalter von Südostasien bis nach Australien und mit weltweiter Verbreitung · Papillons diurnes originaires de la zone d'Asie du Sud-Est – Australie, et répandus dans le monde entier

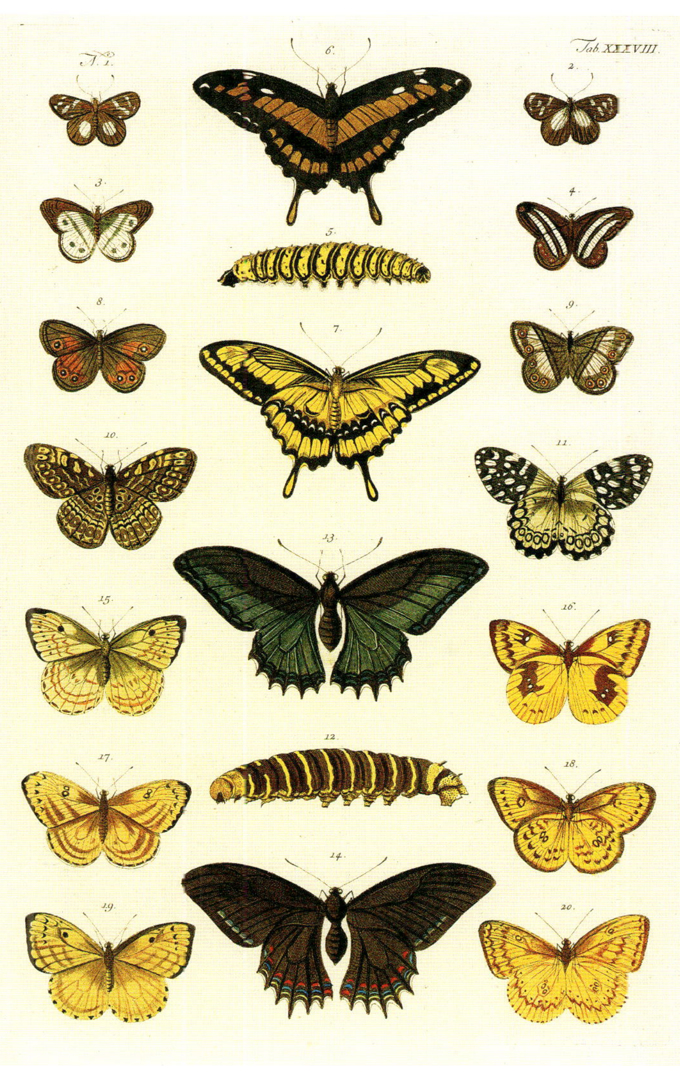

3-4 *Cissia hesione* **6-7** *Papilio thoas* **10-11** *Hamadryas feronia* **13-14** *Papilio androgeus* **15-20** *Phoebis sennae*
Butterflies from tropical and subtropical America · Tagfalter aus dem tropischen und subtropischen Amerika · Papillons diurnes d'Amérique tropicale et subtropicale

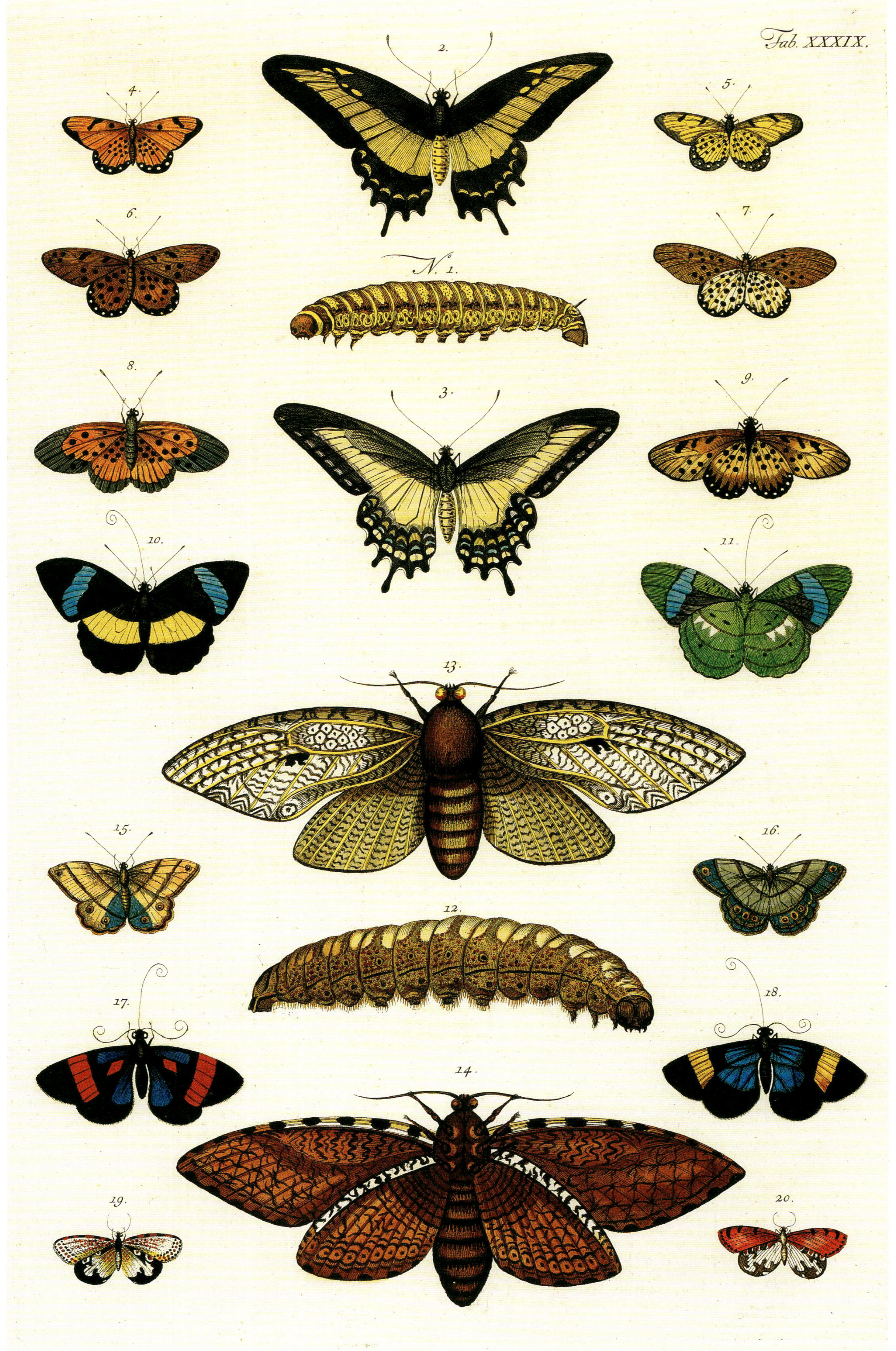

2-3 *Papilio sp.* 4-7 Nymphalidae 8-9 *Acraea horta* 13-14 *Xyleutes strix* 19-20 *Utetheisa ornatrix*
Butterflies from South America and Africa and moths from Malay Archipelago, New Guinea and America · Tagfalter aus Südamerika und Afrika sowie Nachtfalter aus dem Malaiischen Archipel, Neuguinea und Amerika · Papillons diurnes d'Amérique du Sud et d'Afrique, et papillons nocturnes de l'Archipel indomalais, de Nouvelle-Guinée ainsi que d'Amérique

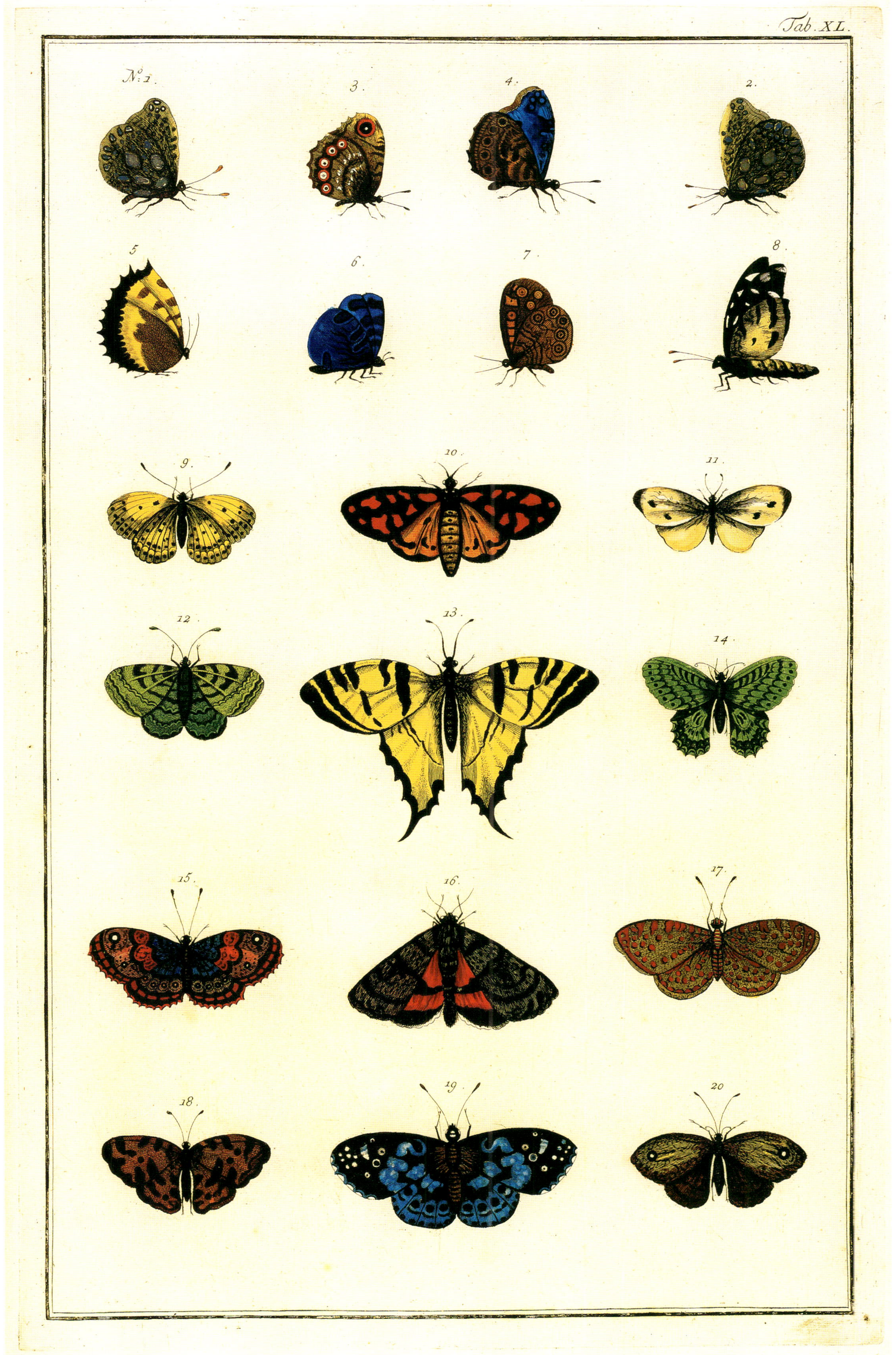

1–12 Lepidoptera 13 *Iphiclides podalirius* 16 *Catocala* 19 *Hamadryas feronia*
Butterflies and moths from Eurasia and America · Schmetterlinge aus Eurasien und Amerika · Papillons et teignes d'Eurasie et d'Amérique

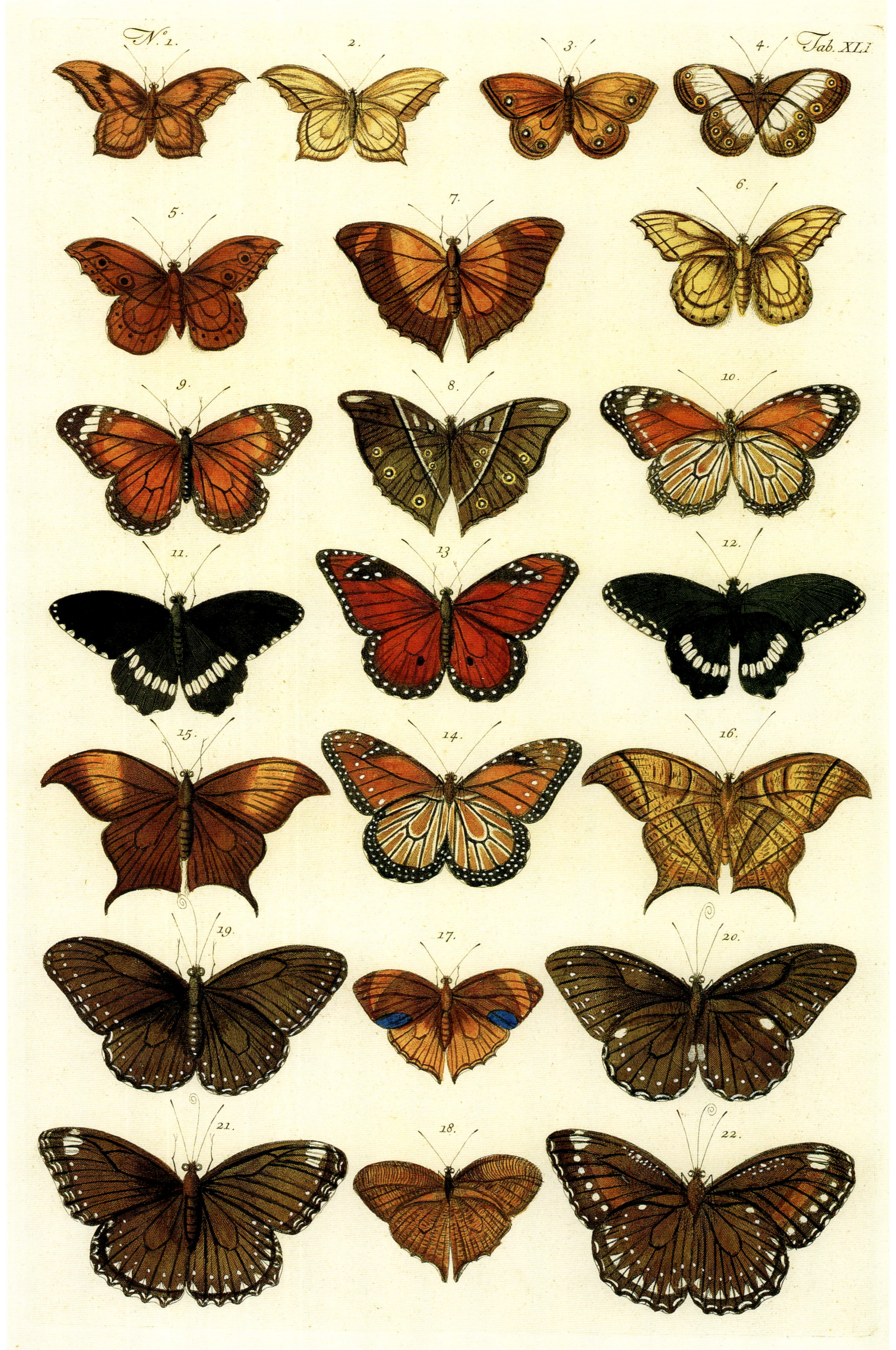

9-10 *Danaus genutia* **11-12** *Papilio polytes* **13-14** *Danaus plexippus* **15-16** *Caerois chorineus* **17-18** *Bia actorion* **19-20** *Hypolimnas bolina*
Tropical butterflies distributed worldwide · Tropische Tagfalter mit weltweiter Verbreitung · Papillons diurnes tropicaux répandus dans le monde entier

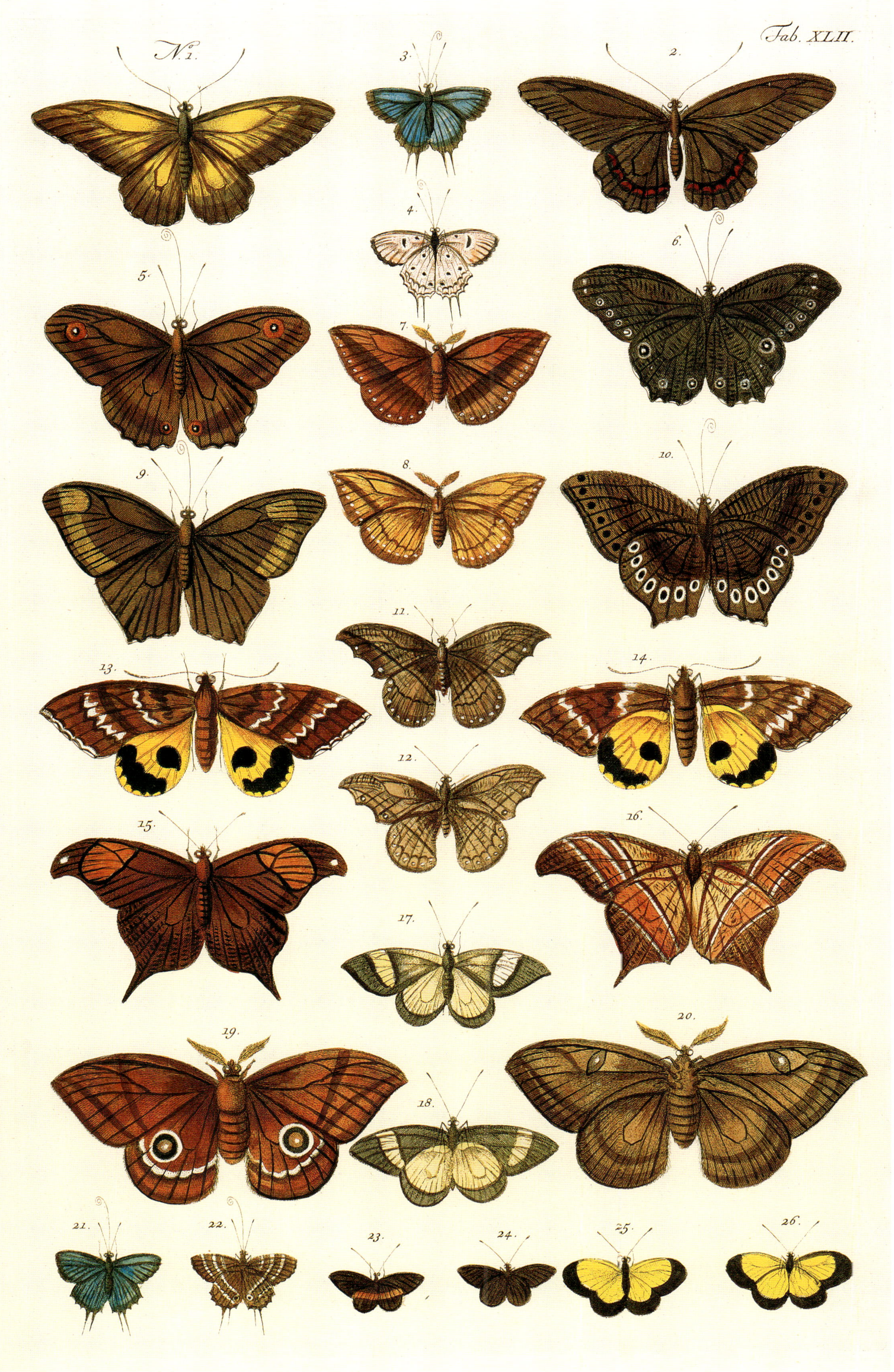

5-6 *Melanitis leda* **15-16** *Caerois chorineus* **23-24** *Stichelia sagaris*
Butterflies and moths from Central and South America and the region encompassing tropical Africa to Australia · Tag- und Nachtfalter aus Mittel- und Südamerika und vom tropischen Afrika bis nach Australien · Papillons diurnes et nocturnes d'Amérique Centrale et du Sud et de la zone d'Afrique tropicale – Australie

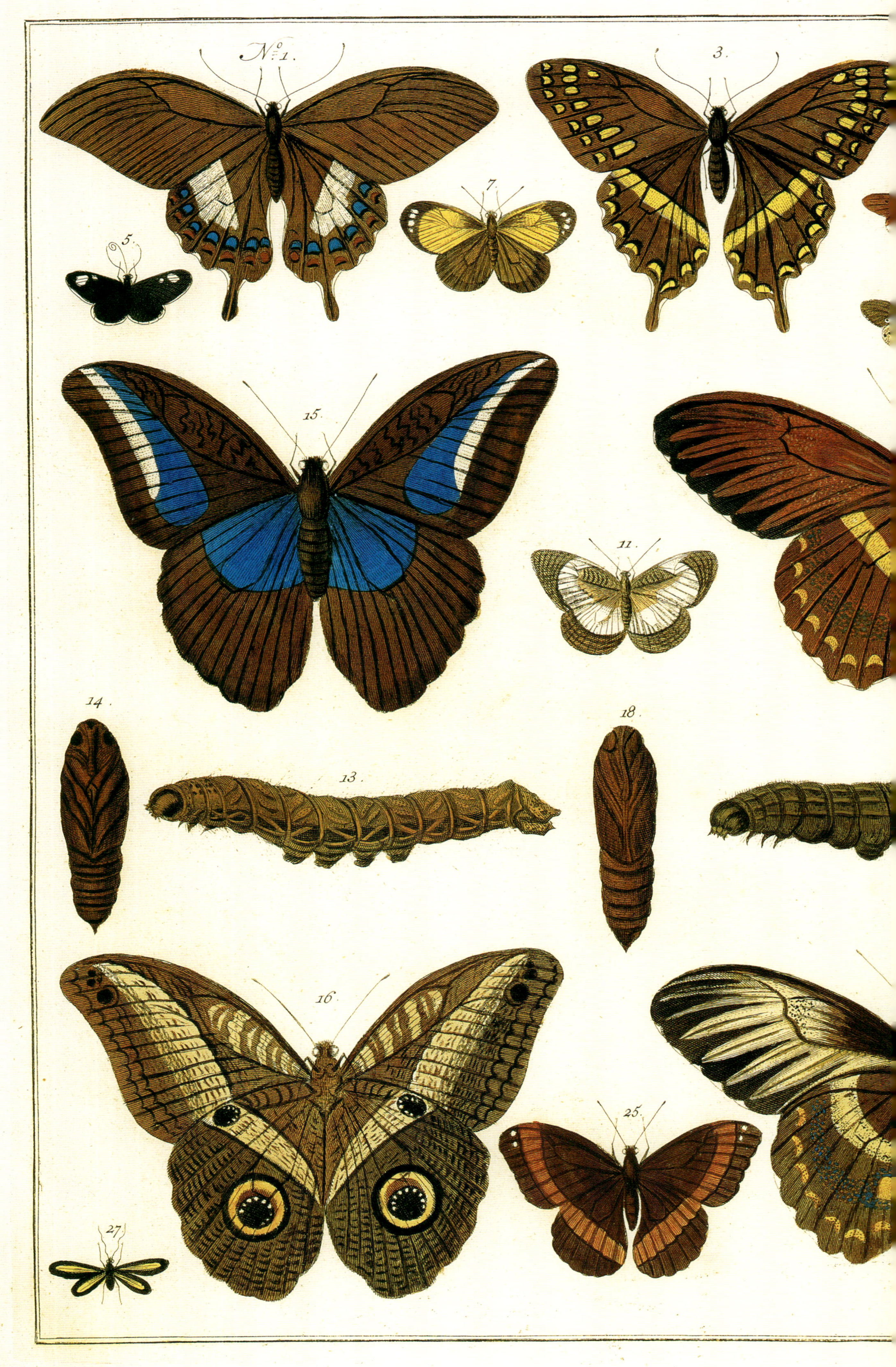

1-4 *Papilio sp.* 15-16 *Caligo idomeneus* 23-24 *Morpho peleides* 27-28 *Josia sp.*
Tropical butterflies and moths from America · Tropische Tag- und Nachtfalter aus Amerika · Papillons diurnes et nocturnes tropicaux d'Amérique

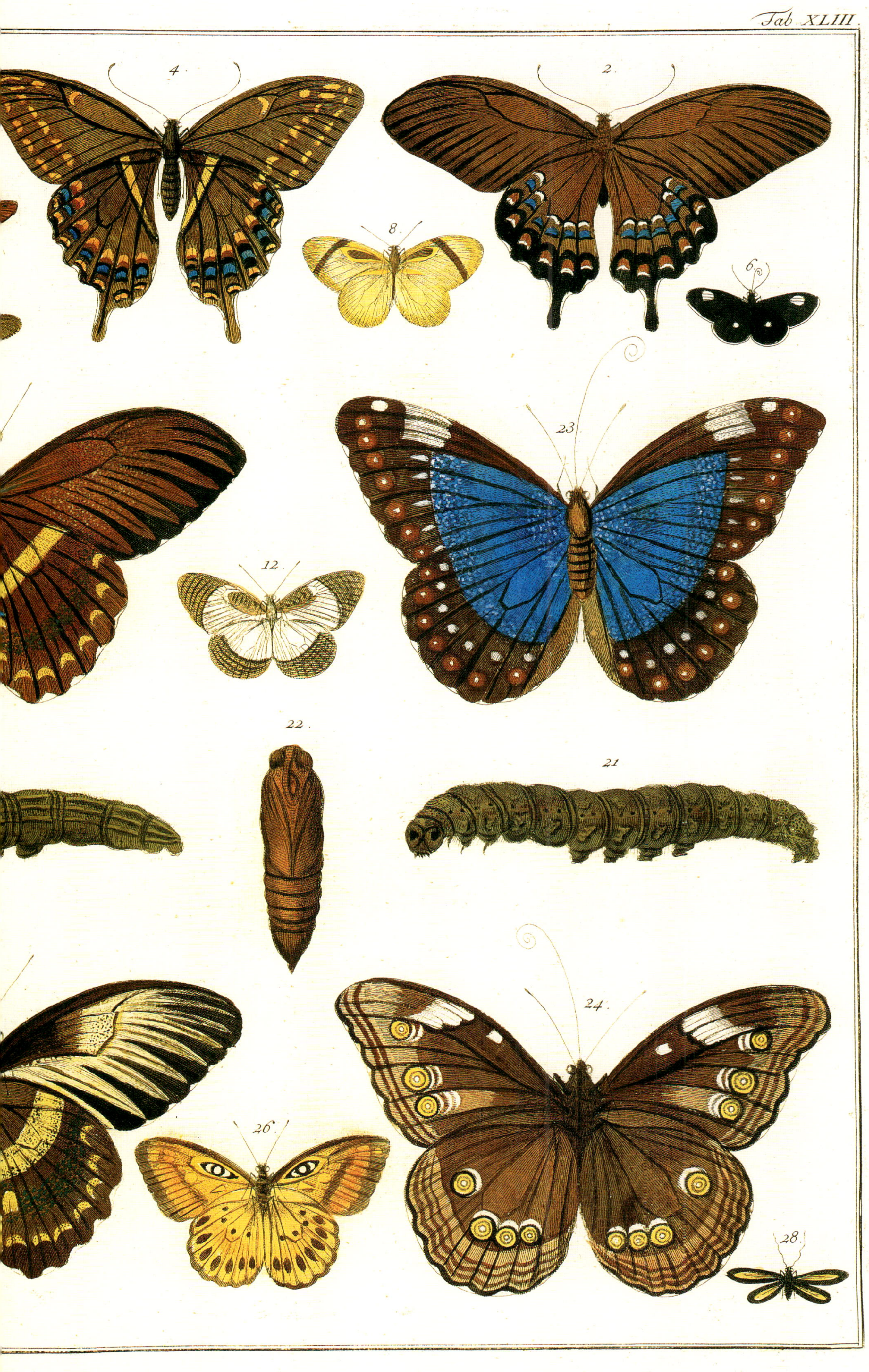
Tab. XLIII.
4.
2.
8.
6.
23.
12.
22.
21
24.
26.
28.

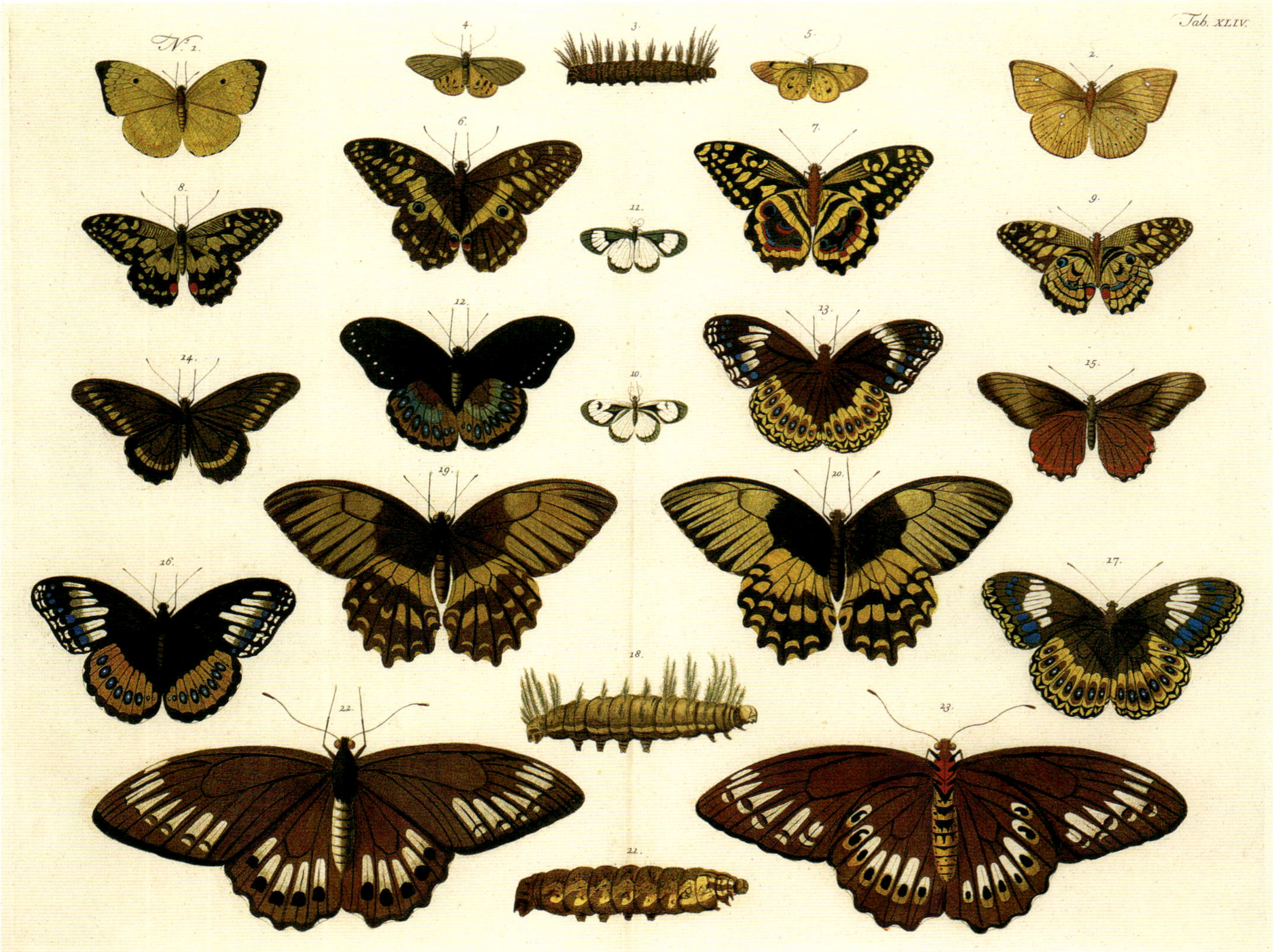

Tab. XLIV.

6-9 *Papilio demolens* **12-13, 16-17** *Hypolimnas pandarus* **14-15** *Battus polydamas* **19-20** *Troides helena* **22-23** *Troides hypolitus*

Butterflies from tropical America and the region encompassing South-East Asia to Australia · Tagfalter aus dem tropischen Amerika und von Südostasien bis nach Australien · Papillons diurnes d'Amérique tropicale et de la zone Asie du Sud-Est – Australie

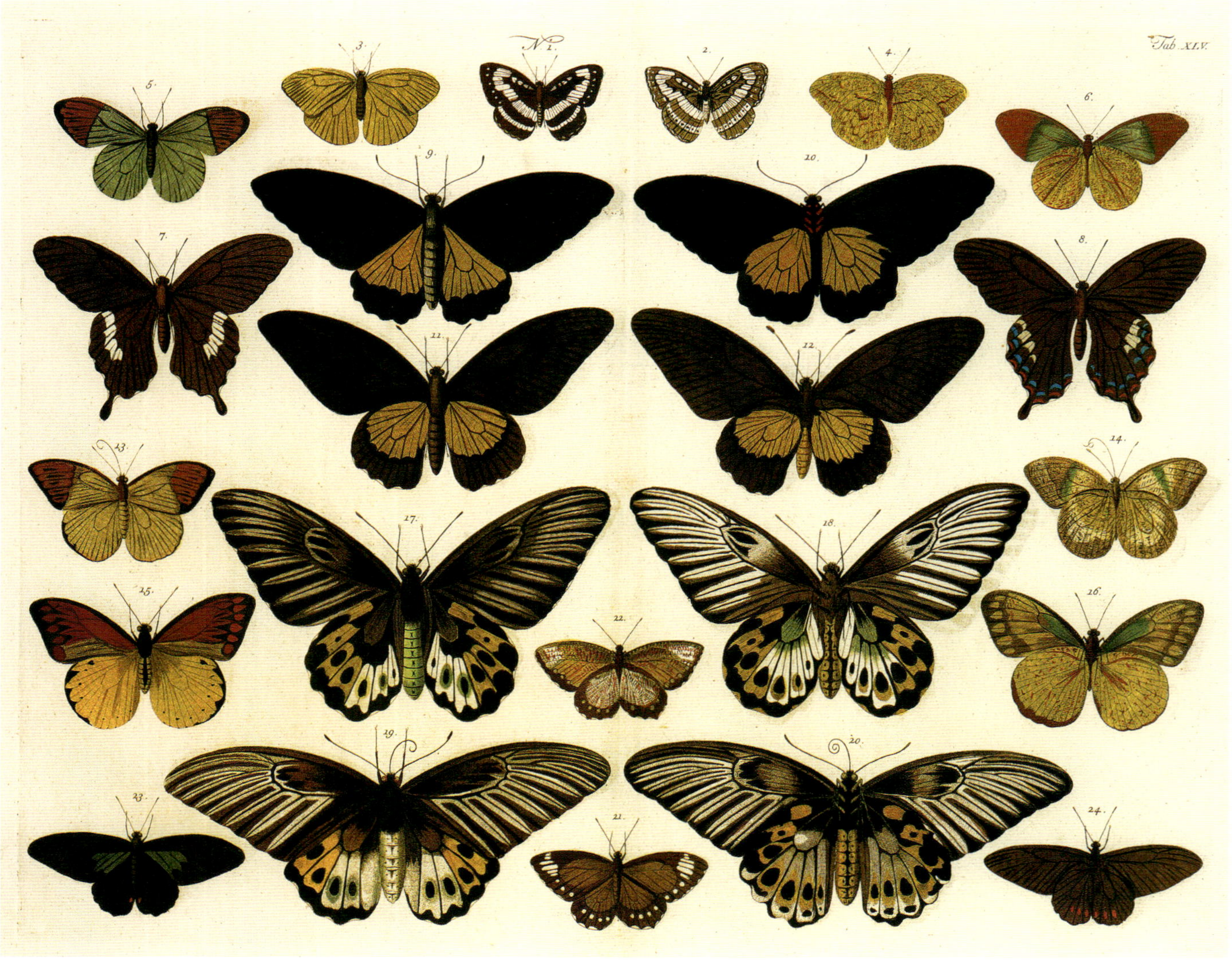

Tab. XLV.

1-2 *Athyma perius* **5-6, 13-14** *Hebomoia glaucippe* **7-8** *Papilio fuscus* **9-12** *Troides helena* **15-16** *Hebomoia leucippe* **17-20** *Troides hypolitus* **23-24** *Parides sesostris*

Butterflies from South-East Asia, North Australia and Central and South America · Tagfalter aus Südostasien, Nordaustralien und Mittel- und Südamerika · Papillons diurnes d'Asie du Sud-Est, d'Australie du Nord et d'Amérique Centrale et du Sud

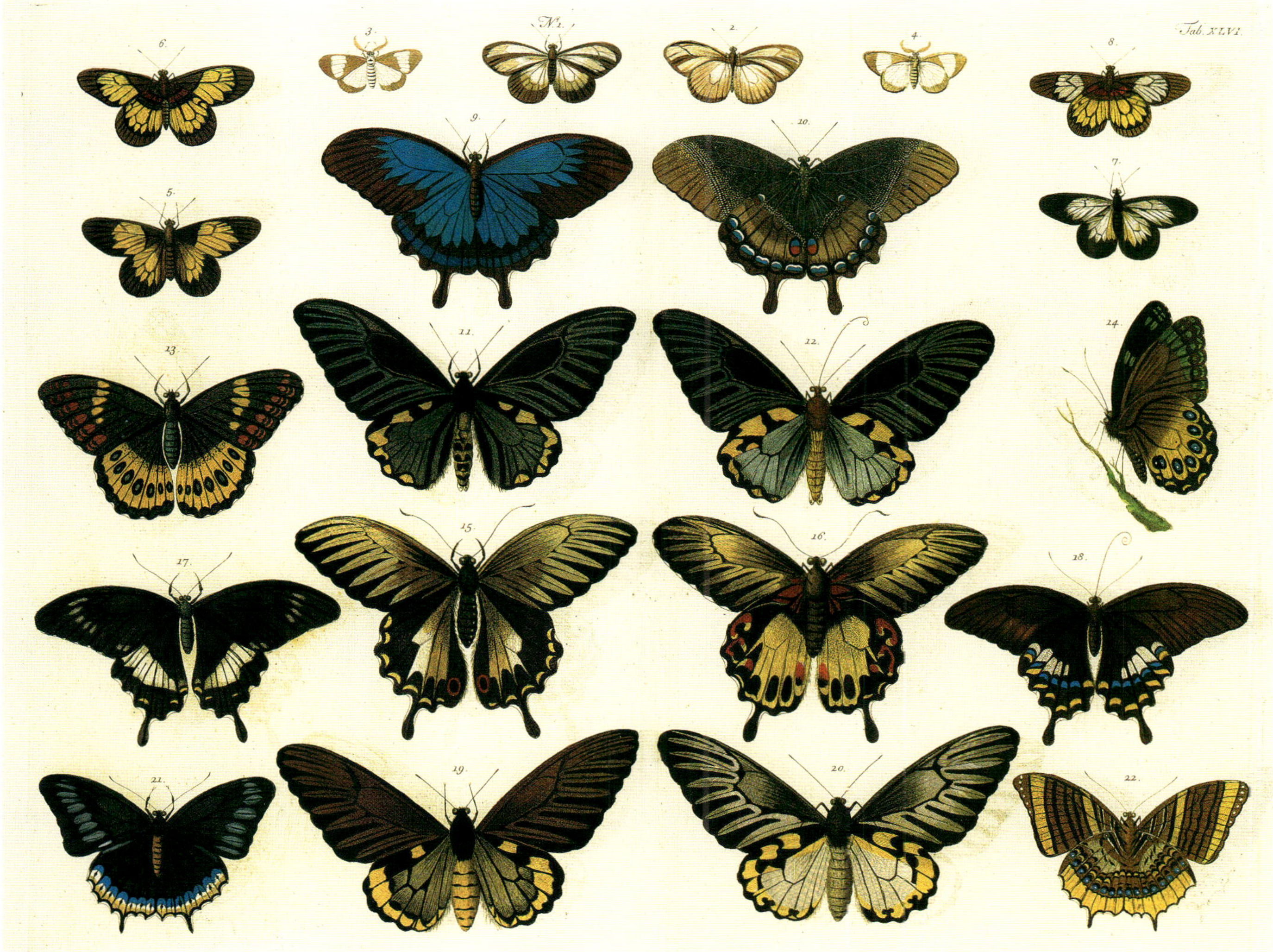

Tab. XLVI.

7-8 *Delias pasithoe* 9-10 *Papilio ulysses* 11-12, 19-20 *Troides hypolitus* 13-14 *Hypolimnas pandarus* 15-16 *Papilio polytes* 17-18 *Papilio helenus* 21-22 *Charaxes jasius*
Butterflies from South-East Asia and North Africa · Tagfalter aus Südostasien und Nordafrika · Papillons diurnes d'Asie du Sud-Est et d'Afrique du Nord

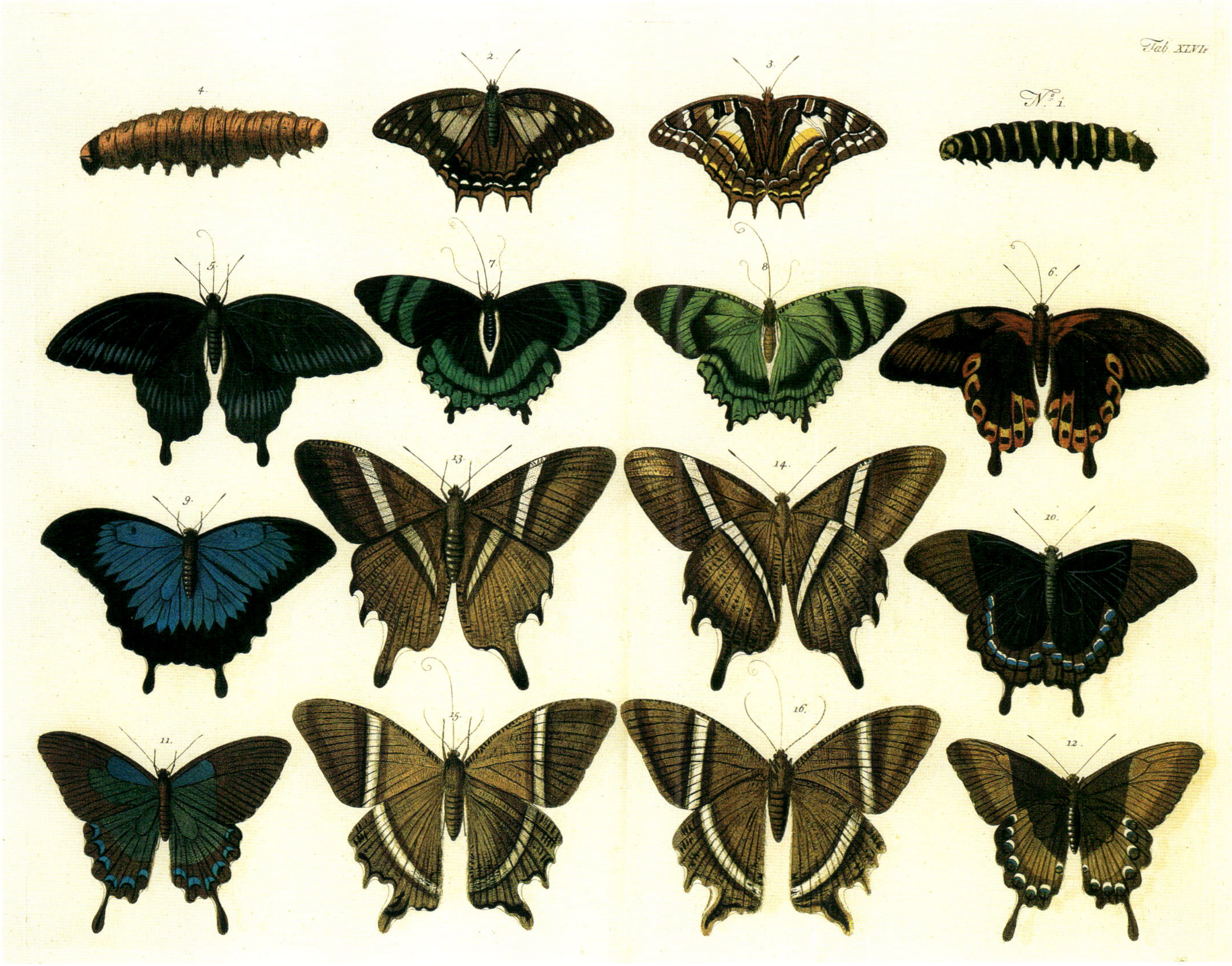

Tab. XLVII.

2-3 *Polyura pyrrhus* 5-6 *Papilio deiphobus* 7-8 *Papilio sp.* 9-12 *Papilio ulysses* 13-14 *Papilio oenomaus* 15-16 *Papilio hipponous*
Butterflies from the Malay Archipelago, New Guinea and Australia · Tagfalter aus dem Malaiischen Archipel, Neuguinea und Australien · Papillons diurnes de l'Archipel indomalais, de Nouvelle-Guinée et d'Australie

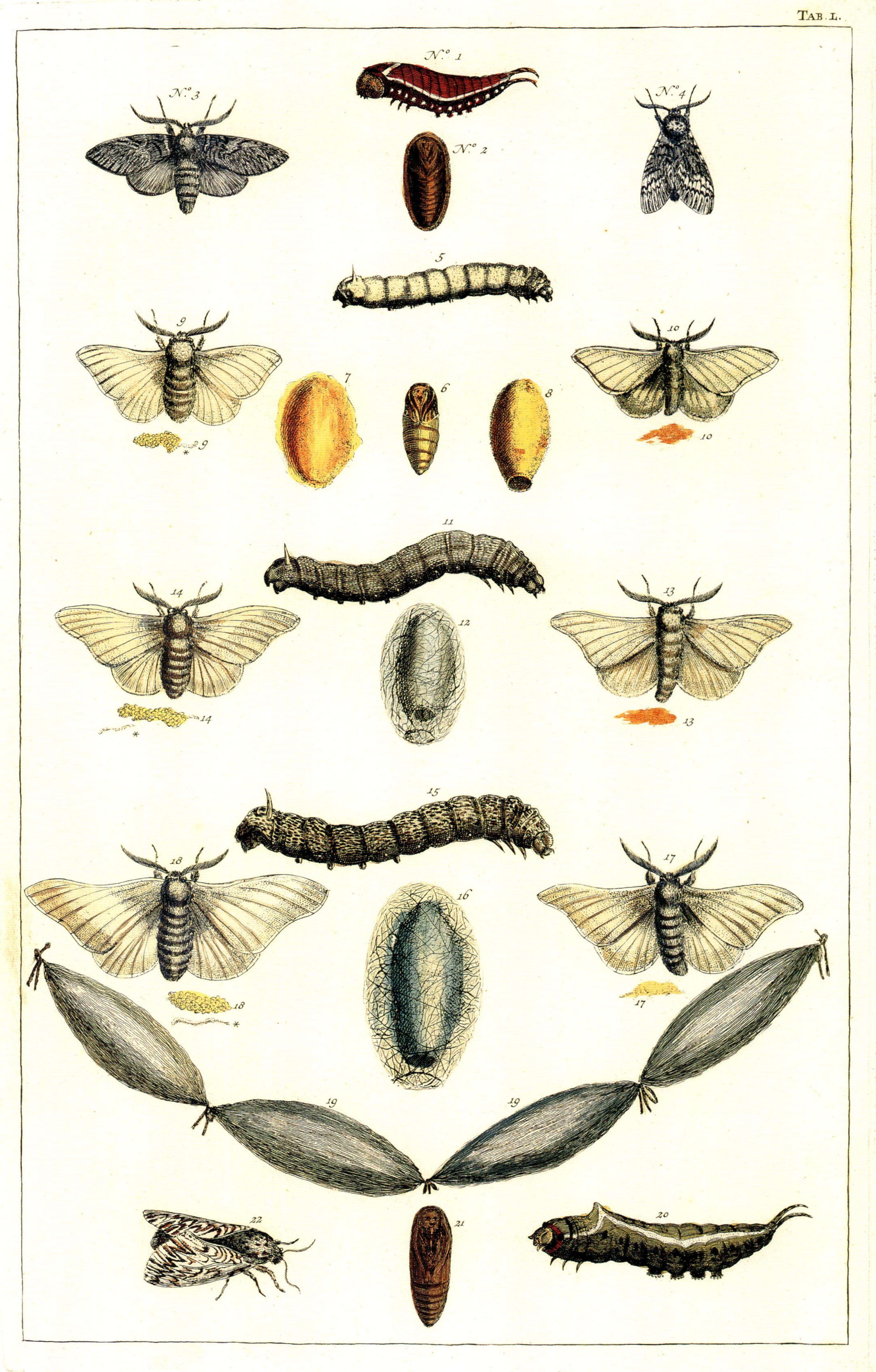

1-4, 20-22 *Cerura vinula* **5-18** *Bombyx mori*
1-4, 20-22 Puss moths · Große Gabelschwänze · Queues fourchues **5-18** Silkworm-moths · Maulbeer-Seidenspinner · Bombyx du mûrier

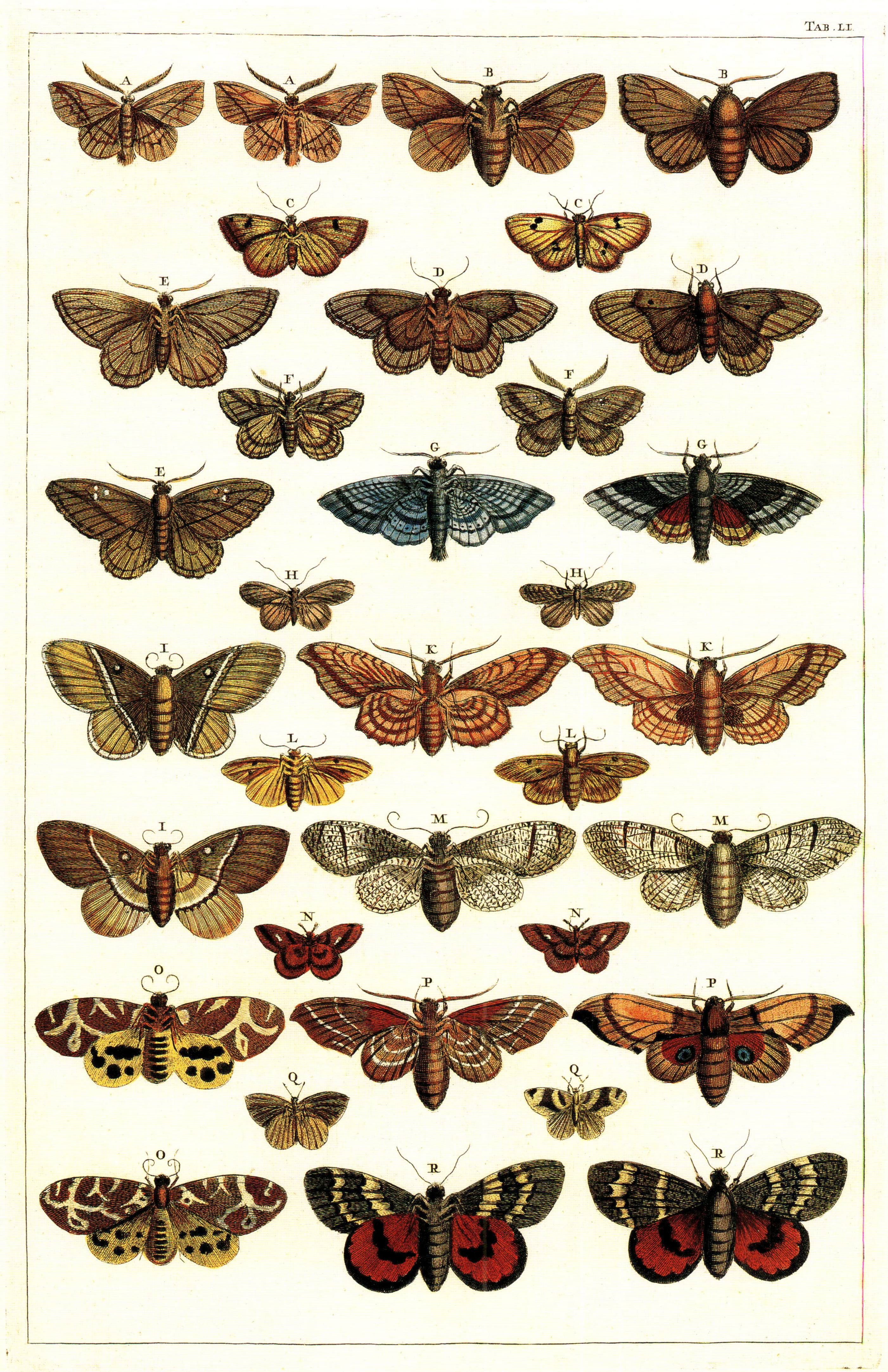

B *Macrothylacia rubi* **C** *Diacrisia sannio* **D** *Lasiocampa quercus* **E-F, I** *Euthrix potatoria* **K** *Marumba quercus* **L** *Lithosia quadra* **M** *Cossus cossus* **N** *Orgyia antiqua* **O** *Arctia caja* **P** *Smerinthus ocellatus*
B Fox moth · Brombeerspinner · Anneau du diable **C** Clouded buff · Rotrandbär · Bordure ensanglantée **D** Oak eggar · Großer Eichenspinner · Minime à bandes jaunes **E-F, I** Drinkers · Grasglucken · Buveuses **K** Oak hawkmoth · Eichenschwärmer · Sphinx du chêne **L** Four-spotted footman · *Lithosia quadra* · Lithosie quadrillé **M** Goat moth · Weidenbohrer · Cossus gâte-bois **N** Vapourer moth · Kleiner Bürstenspinner · Etoilée **O** Garden tiger/Woolly bear · Brauner Bär · Ecaille martre **P** Eyed hawkmoth · Abendpfauenauge · Sphinx demi-paon

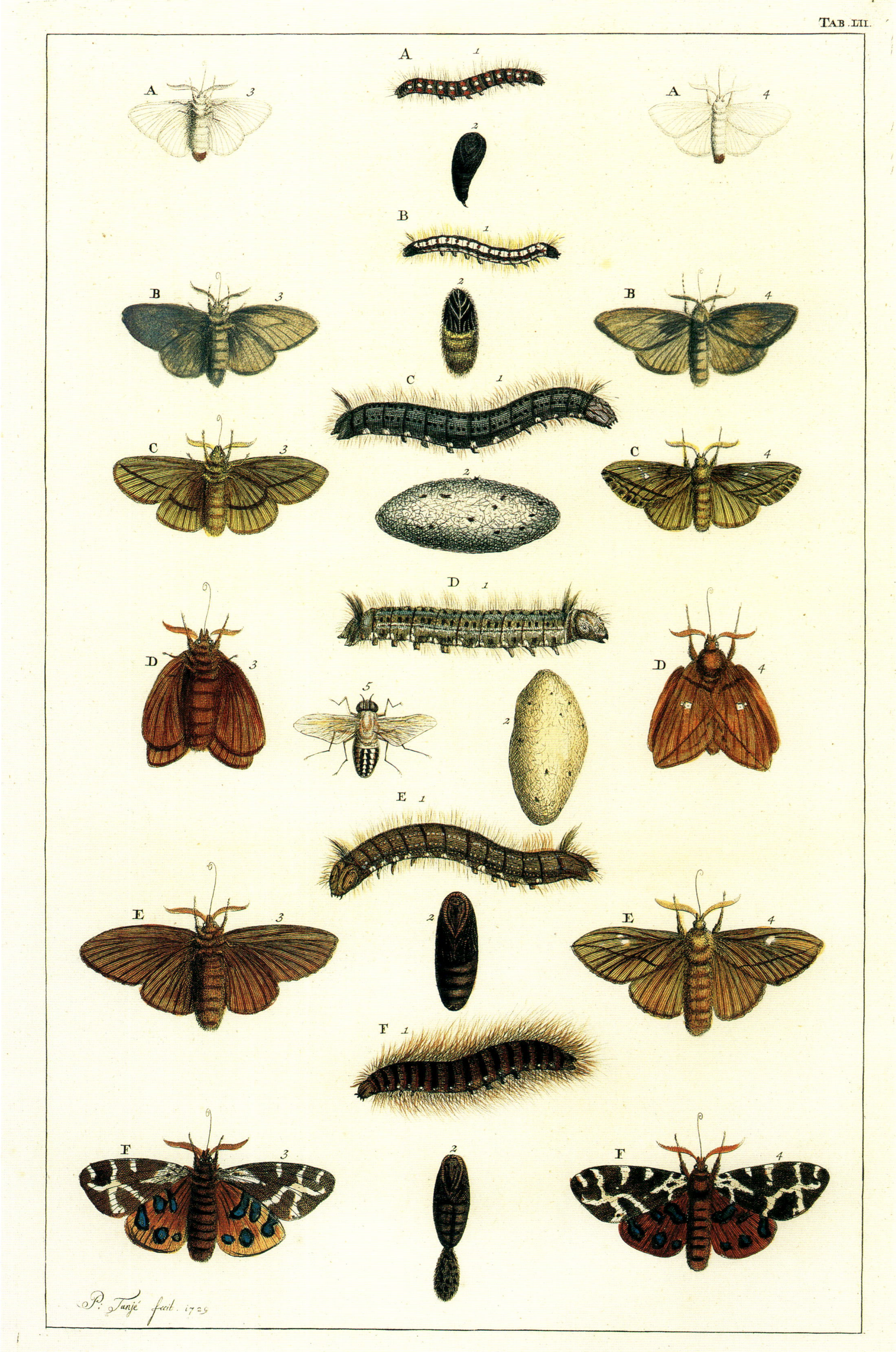

A *Euproctis similis* **B** *Leucoma salicis* **C** *Euthrix potatoria* **D1-4** *Lasiocampa quercus* **D5** Diptera **F** *Arctia caja*
A Yellow-tail · Schwan · Cul-doré **B** White satin moth · Pappelspinner · Papillon satiné **C** Drinker · Grasglucke · Buveuse **D1-4** Oak eggar · Großer Eichenspinner · Minime à bandes jaunes **D5** Fly · Fliege · Mouche **F** Garden tiger/Woolly bear · Brauner Bär · Ecaille martre

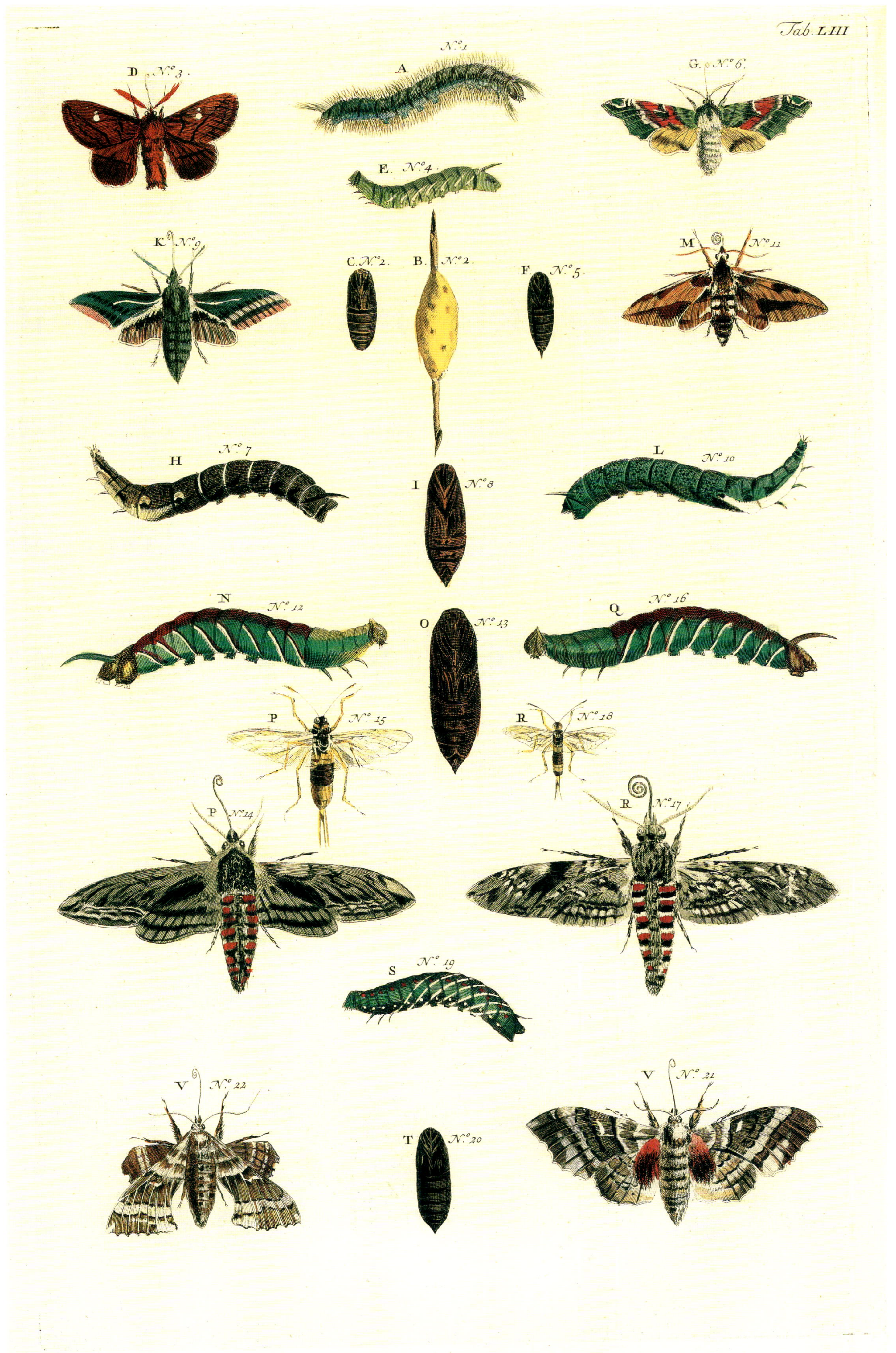

A1-D3 *Euthrix potatoria* **E4-G6** *Mimas tiliae* **H7-K9** *Deilephila elpenor* **L10-M11** *Hyles euphorbiae* **N12-P14** *Sphinx ligustri* **P15** *Urocerus gigas* **Q16, R17** *Agrius convolvuli* **R 18** *Urocerus flavicornis*
A1-D3 Drinker · Grasglucke · Buveuse **E4-G6** Lime hawkmoth · Lindenschwärmer · Sphinx du tilleul **H7-K9** Elephant hawkmoth · Mittlerer Weinschwärmer · Moyen sphinx de la vigne **L10, M11** Spurge hawkmoth · Wolfsmilchschwärmer · Sphinx de l'euphorbe **N12-P14** Privet hawkmoth · Ligusterschwärmer · Sphinx du troène **P15** Giant wood wasp · Riesenholzwespe · Sirex géant **Q16-R17** Morning glory sphinx moth · Windenschwärmer · Sphinx du liseron **R18** Wood wasp · Holzwespe · Sirex

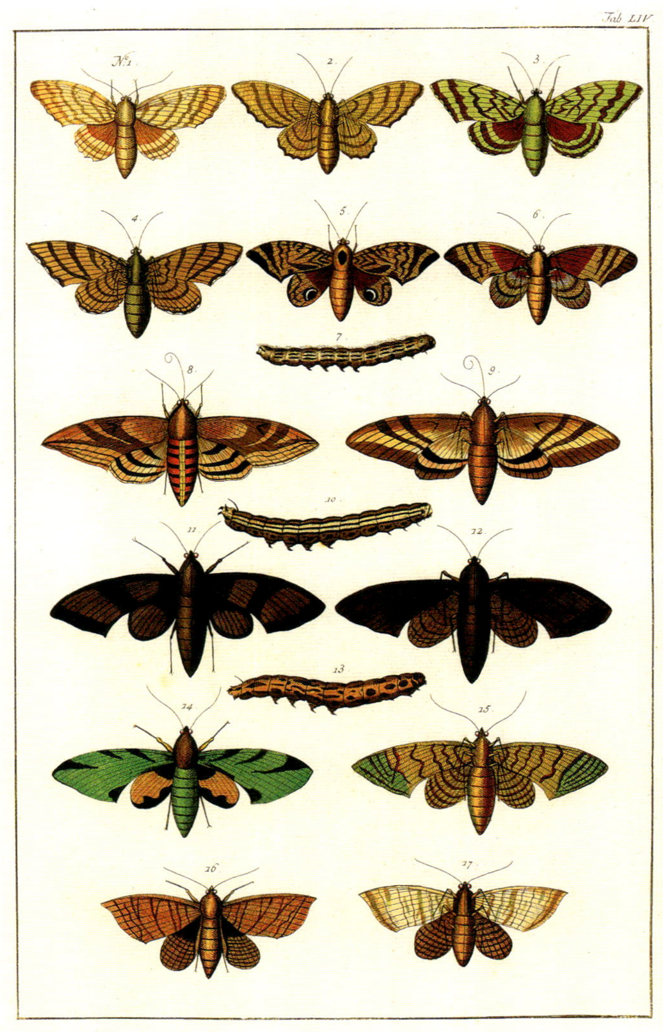

1-2 *Poecilocampa populi* **3-4** Lasiocampinae **5-6** *Smerinthus ocellatus* **7** *Phalera bucephala* **8-9** *Sphinx ligustri* **10-12, 16-17** Sphinginae **13-15** *Hyles nicaea*

1-2 December eggar · Kleine Pappelglucke · Bombyx du peuplier **3-4** Lappet moth · Glucke · Lasiocampiné **5-6** Eyed hawkmoth · Abendpfauenauge · Sphinx demi-paon **7** Buff-tip caterpillar · Ochsenkopf-Raupe · Bucéphale/Lunule (chenille) **8-9** Privet hawkmoth · Ligusterschwärmer · Sphinx du troène **10-12, 16-17** Hawkmoths · Schwärmer · Sphinx **13-15** Mediterranean hawkmoth · Großer Wolfsmilchschwärmer · Sphinx nicéa

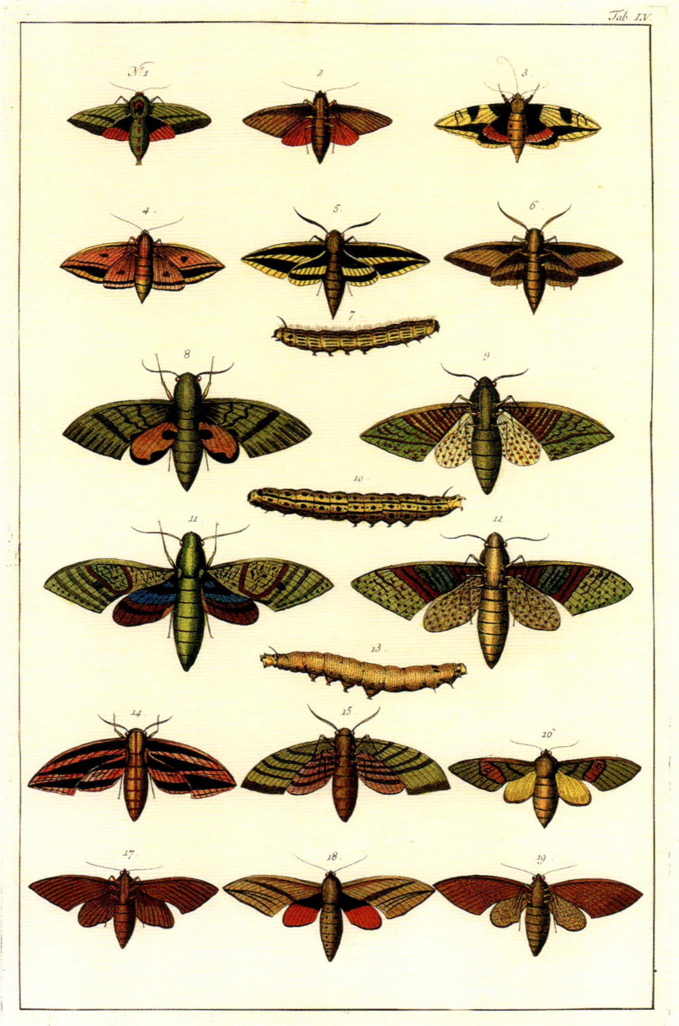

1-19 Sphingidae **1-2** *Deilephila elpenor* **3-4** *Hyles euphorbiae* **7** *Phalera bucephala* **8-10** Sphingidae **11-12** *Eumorpha labruscae*

1-19 Hawkmoths · Schwärmer · Sphinx **1-2** Elephant hawkmoths · Mittlere Weinschwärmer · Moyen Sphinx de la vigne **3-4** Spurge hawkmoths · Wolfsmilchschwärmer · Sphinx de l'euphorbe **7** Buff-tip moth · Mondvogel · Phalère bucéphale/Lunule **11-12** Gaudy sphinx moths · Schwärmer · Sphingidés

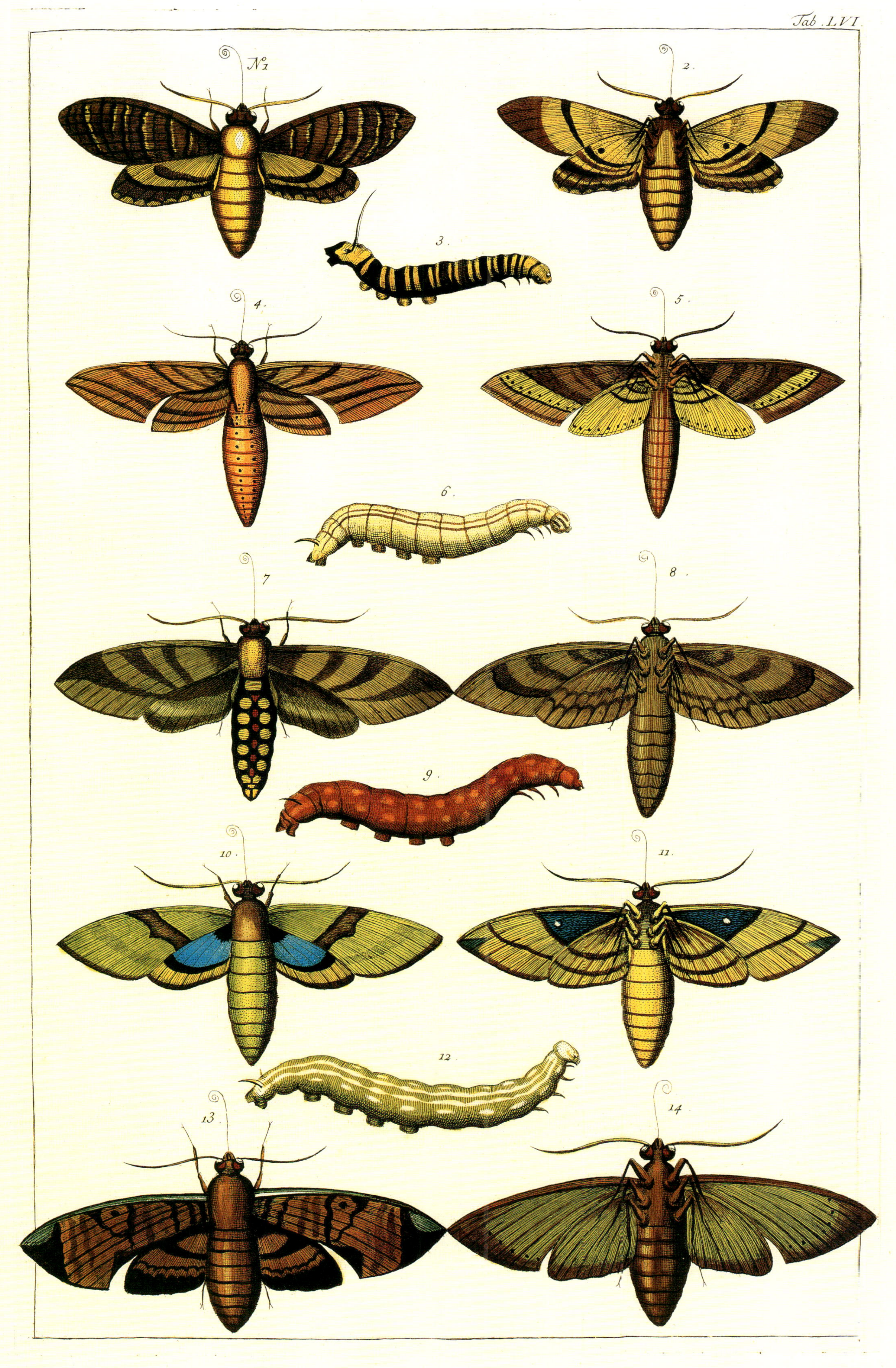

1-14 Sphingidae 1-2 *Acherontia atropos* 7-8 *Manduca occulta* 10-11 *Eumorpha labruscae* 13-14 *Pachylia ficus*
1-14 Hawkmoths · Schwärmer · Sphinx **1-2** Death's head hawkmoth · Totenkopfschwärmer · Sphinx tête-de-mort **7-8** Occult sphinx · Schwärmer · Sphinx **10-11** Gaudy sphinx moth · Schwärmer · Sphingidé **13-14** Fig sphinx · Schwärmer · Sphingidé

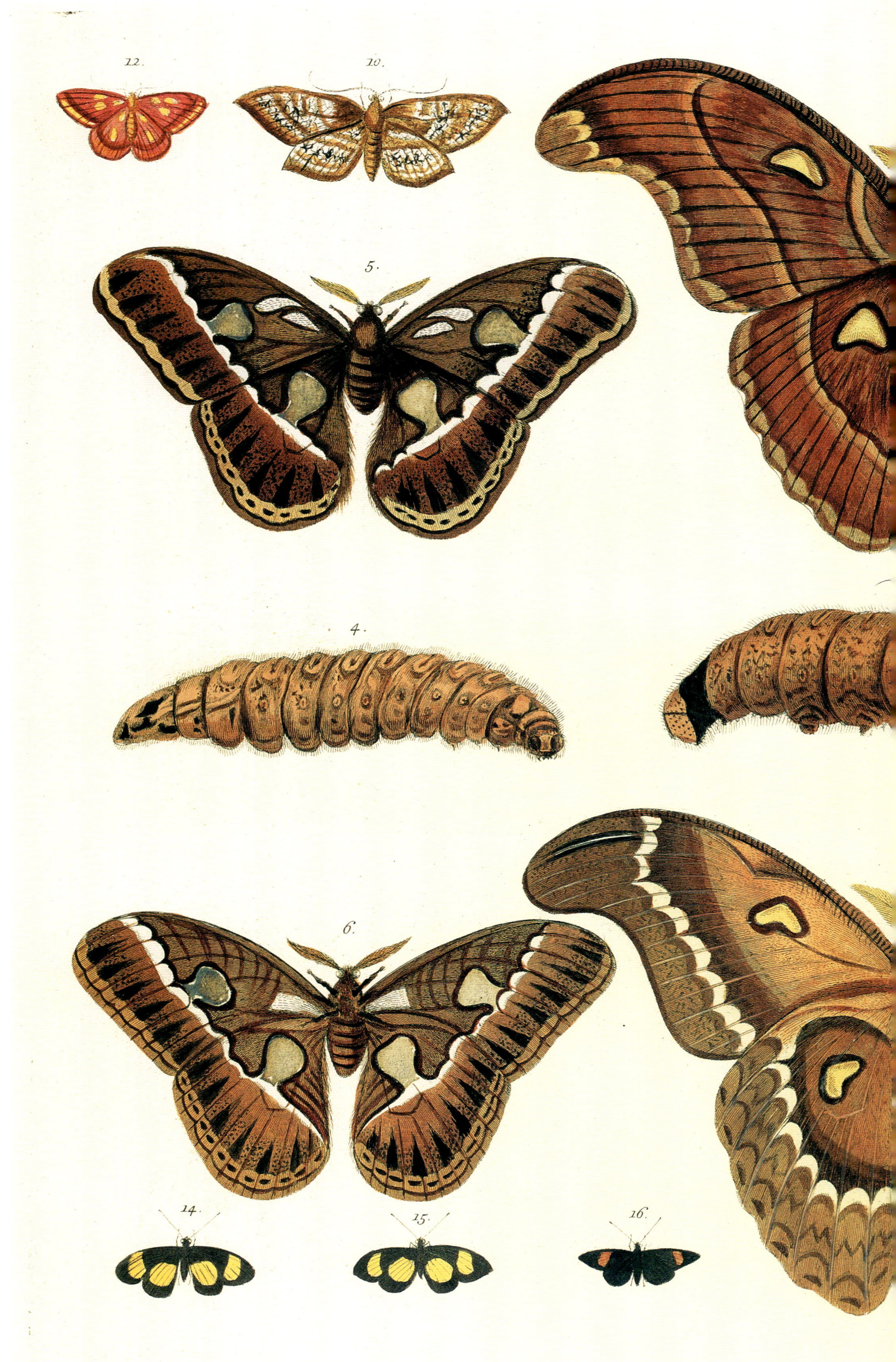

1-3 *Attacus atlas* 4-6 *Rothschildia hesperus* 8-9 *Xyleutes strix* 10-11 *Draconia peripheta* 18-19 *Entheus priassus*
Very large tropical moths from South-East Asia and tropical America · Sehr große tropische Nachtfalter aus Südostasien und dem tropischen Amerika · Très grands papillons nocturnes d'Asie du Sud-Est et d'Amérique tropicale

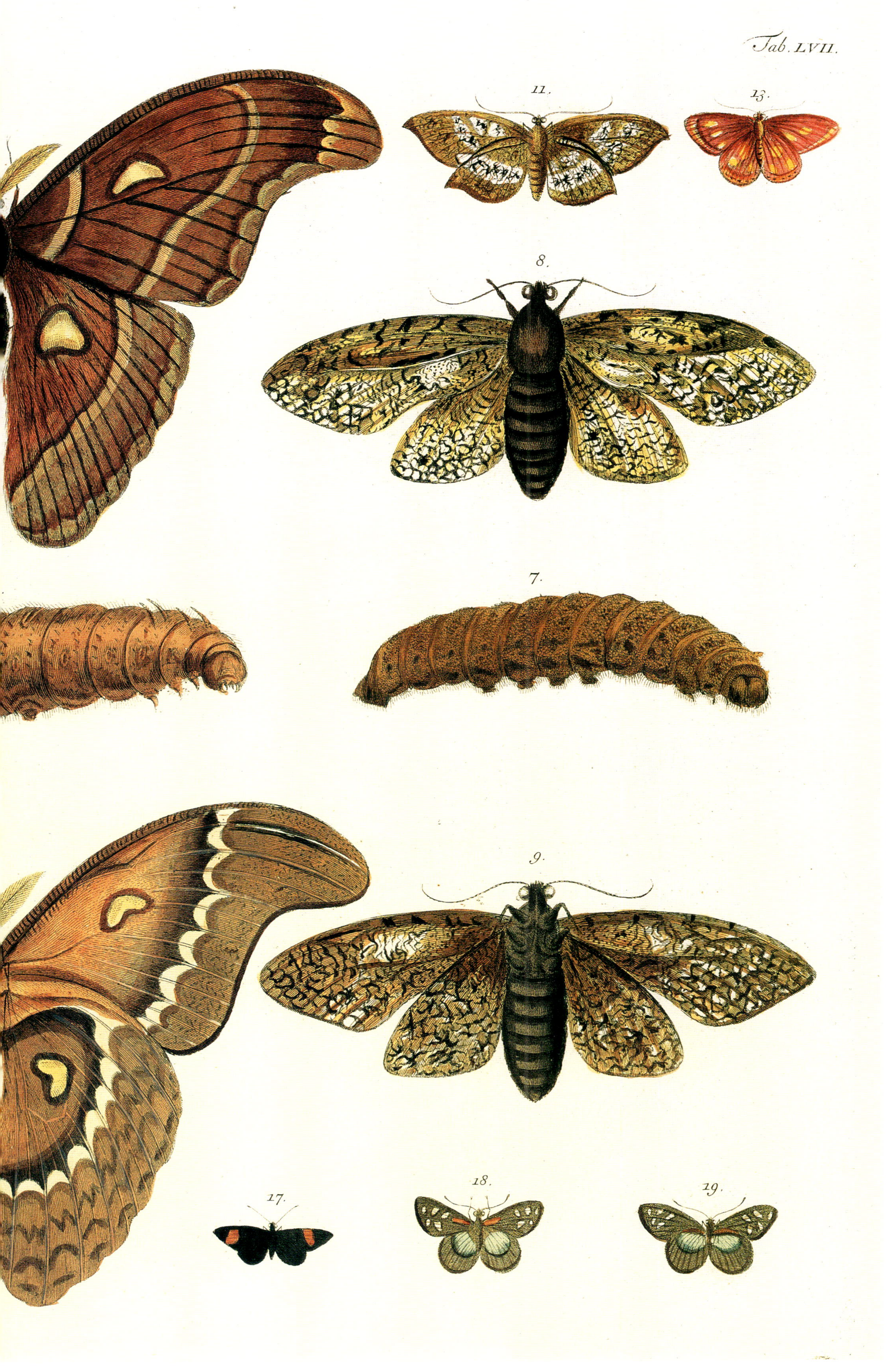
Tab. LVII.
11.
13.
8.
7.
9.
17.
18.
19.

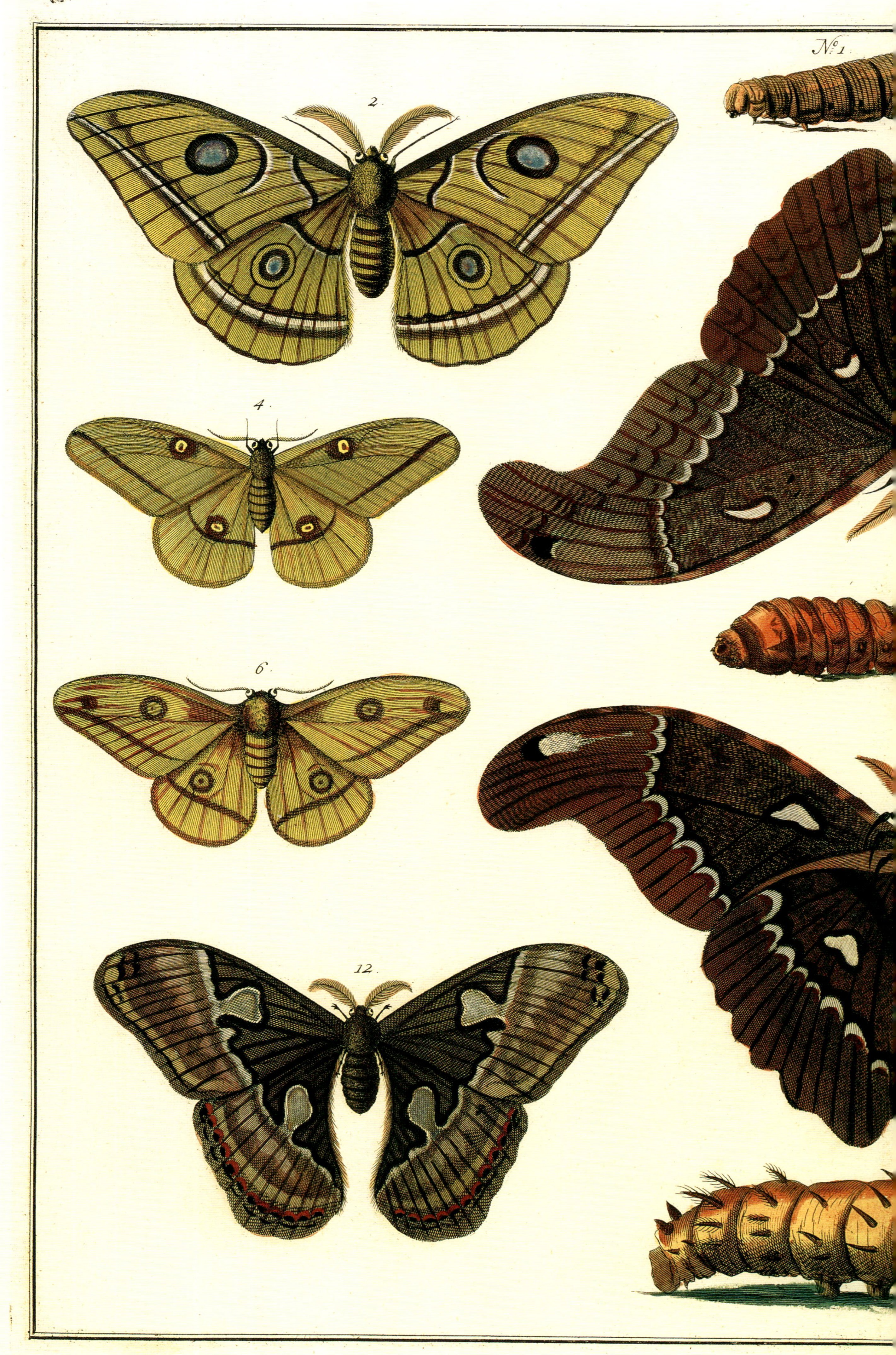

1-7 Saturniidae 8-10 *Attacus atlas* 11-13 *Rothschildia hesperus*
Very large tropical moths · Sehr große tropische Nachtfalter · Très grands papillons nocturnes tropicaux

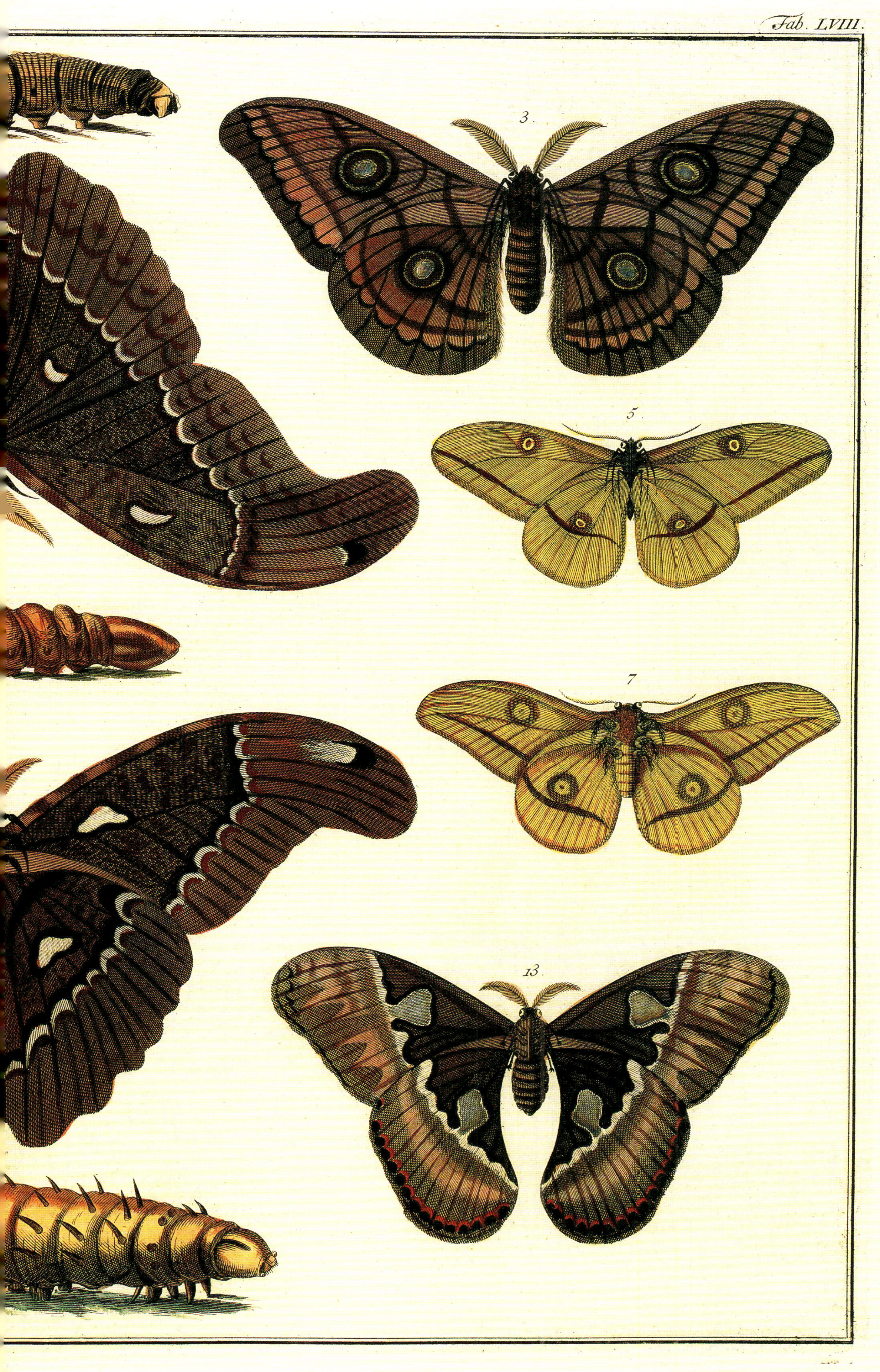
Tab. LVIII.
3.
5.
7.
13.

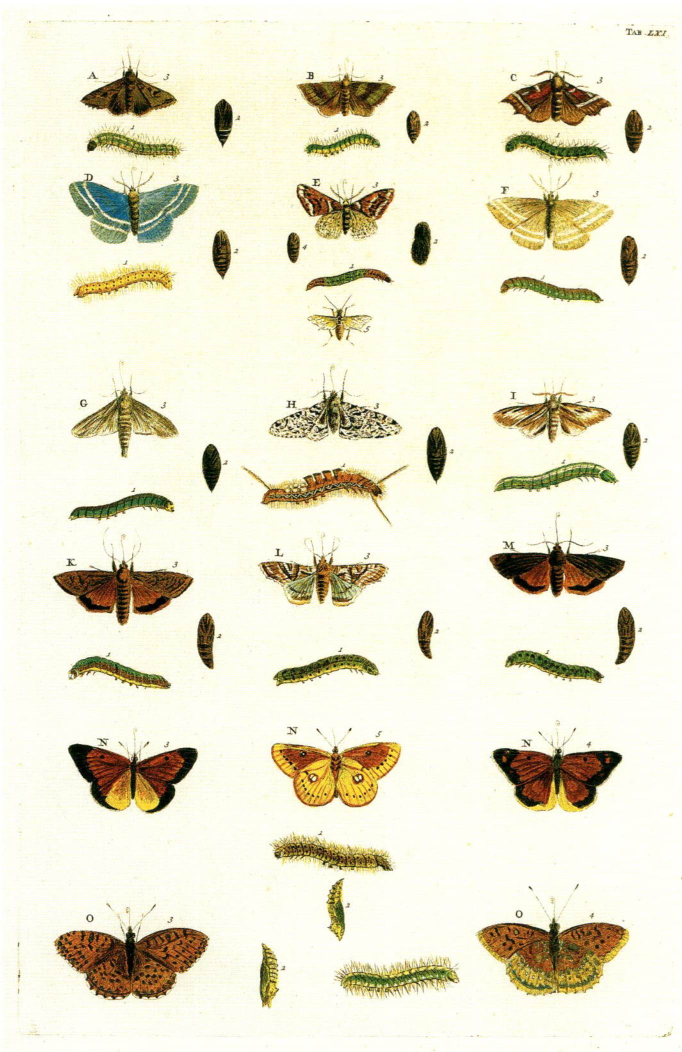

A2, B2, C2, D2 *Conistra rubiginea* **A3, B3, K3, L3, M3** Noctuidae **C3** *Scoliopteryx libatrix* **D3, E3, F3, H3** Geometridae **E5** Tenthredinidae **H1** *Calliteara pudibunda* **N3-5** *Colias croceus* **O3-4** Argynninae
Butterflies and moths from Central Europe with caterpillars and pupae · Tag- und Nachtfalter aus Mitteleuropa mit Puppen und Raupen · Papillons diurnes et nocturnes d'Europe centrale ainsi que chrysalides et chenilles

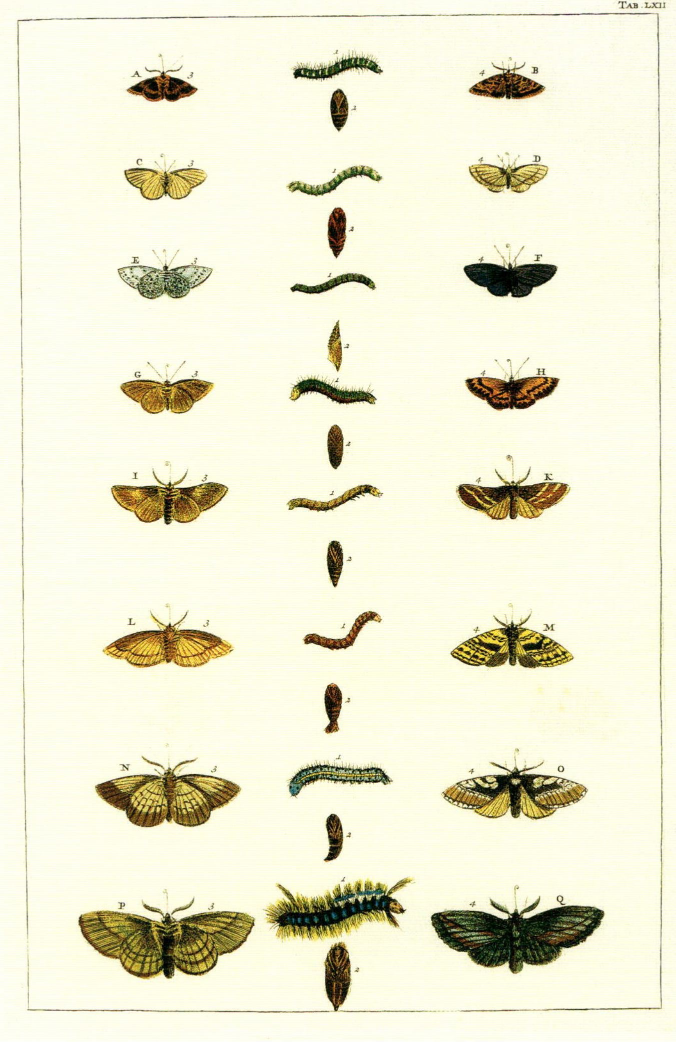

E-F Polyommatinae **P-Q1-4** *Dicallomera fascelina*
E-F Blues butterflies · Bläulinge · Azurés **P-Q1-4** Dark tussocks · Graue Kleespinner · Pattes étendues agathes

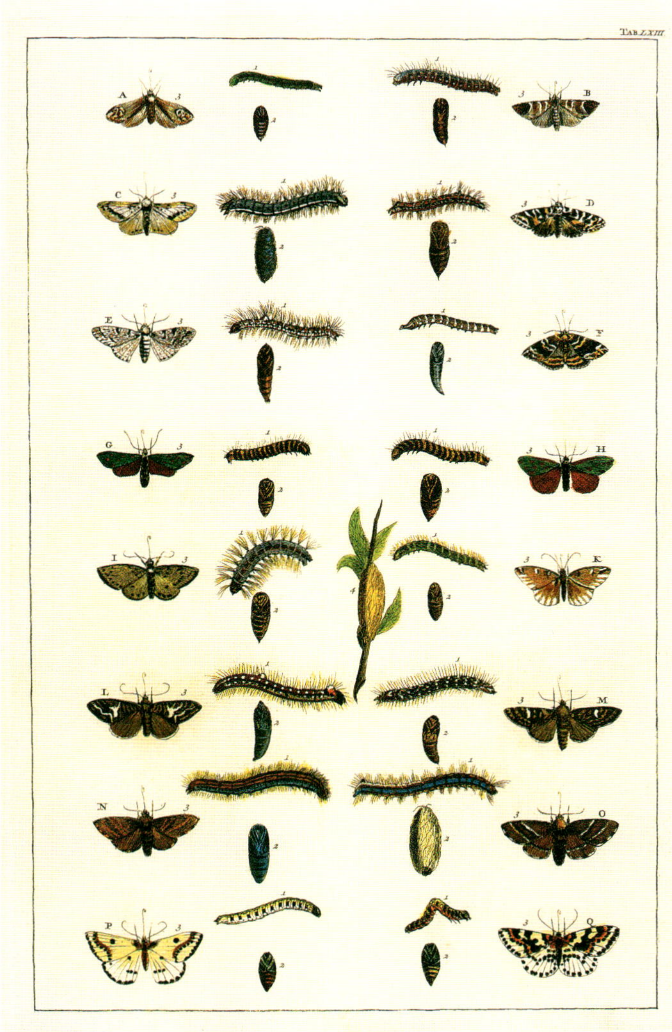

G1, H1-3 *Tyria jacobaeae* **G2-3** *Zygaena sp.* **N1-3** *Malacosoma neustria* **O1-3** *Eriogaster lanestris* **P3, Q1-3** *Abraxas grossulariatus*

G1, H1-3 Cinnabar · Blutbär · Goutte-de-sang **G2-3** Burnet · Widderchen/Blutströpfchen · Zygène **N1-3** Lackey · Ringelspinner · Livrée des arbres **O1-3** Small eggar · Wollafter/Glucke · Bombyx laineux **P3, Q1-3** Currant moth · Stachelbeerspanner · Zérène du groseillier

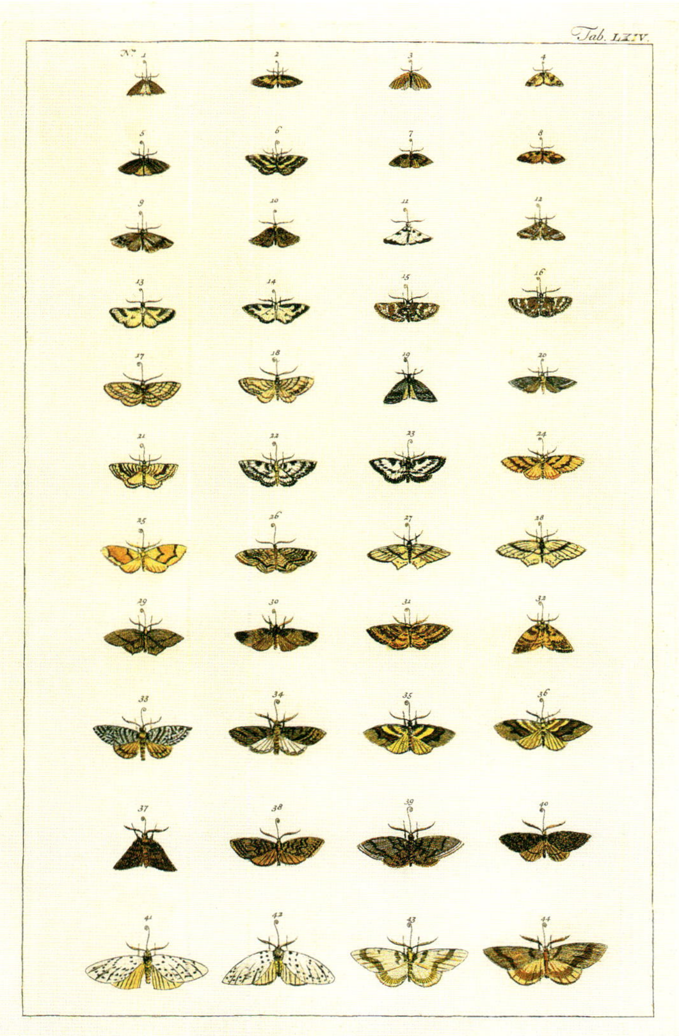

1-5, 7-12 Pyralidae oder Tortricidae **6** *Epirrhoe tristata* **22-23** *Eurrhypara hortulata* **41-42** *Spilosoma lubricipedum*

Moths from Central Europe and North Africa, including pyralids (Pyralidae), tortricids (Tortricidae), geometers (Geometridae) and noctuids (Noctuidae) · Nachtfalter aus Mitteleuropa und Nordafrika, darunter Zünsler (Pyralidae), Wickler (Tortricidae), Spanner (Geometridae) und Eulenfalter (Noctuidae) · Papillons de nuit d'Europe Centrale et d'Afrique du Nord incluant des pyrales (pyralidés), des tordeuses (tortricidés), des géomètres (géométridés) et des noctuelles (noctuides)

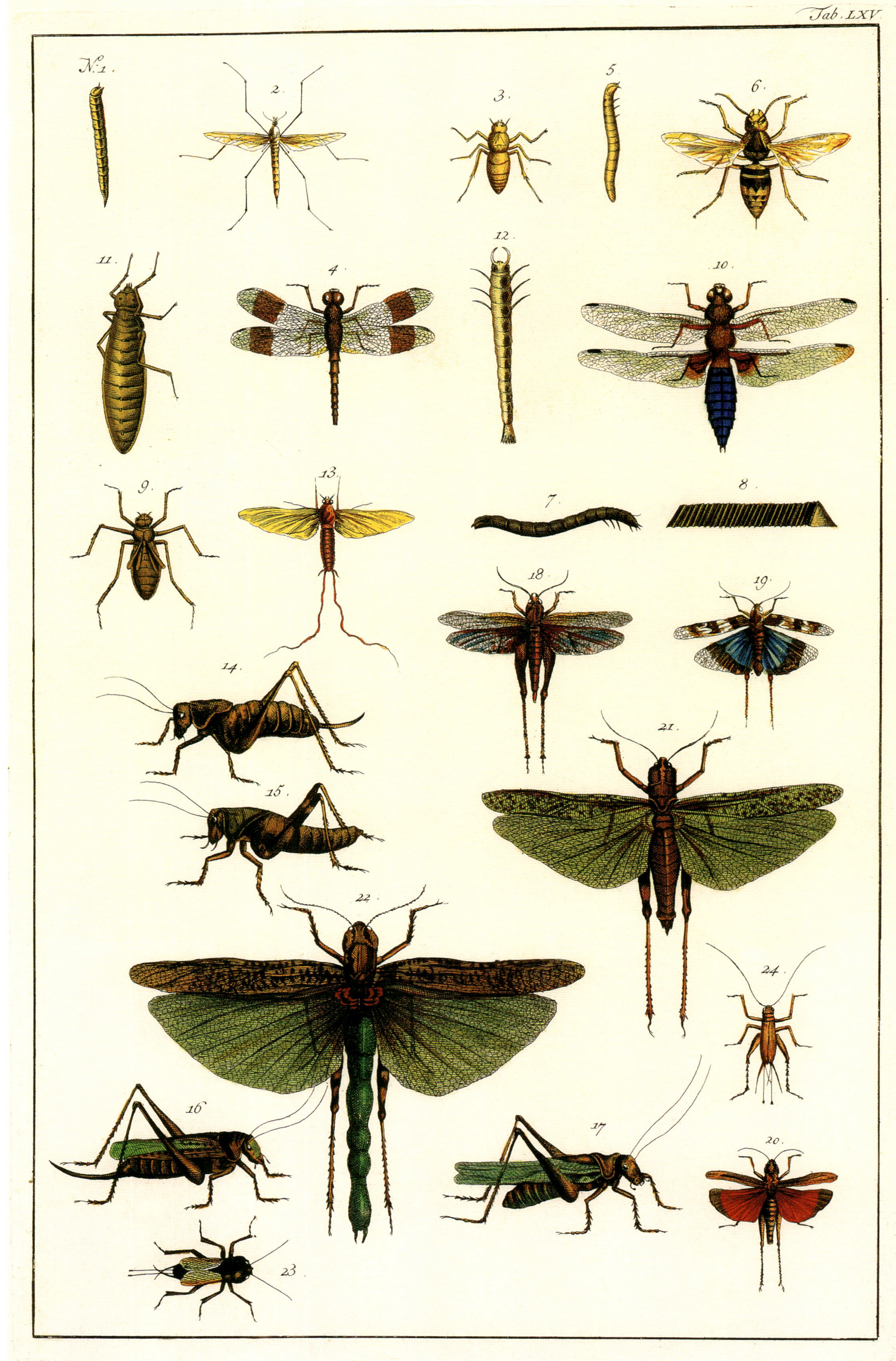

1-2 Tipulidae 3-4, 9-11 Odonata 5, 7-8 Trichoptera 6 Apocrita 12 Dytiscidae 13 Ephemeroptera 14-24 Orthoptera
Various insects and insect larvae, chiefly grasshoppers · Verschiedene Insekten und Insektenlarven, vorwiegend Heuschrecken · Divers insectes et larves d'insectes, principalement des sauterelles

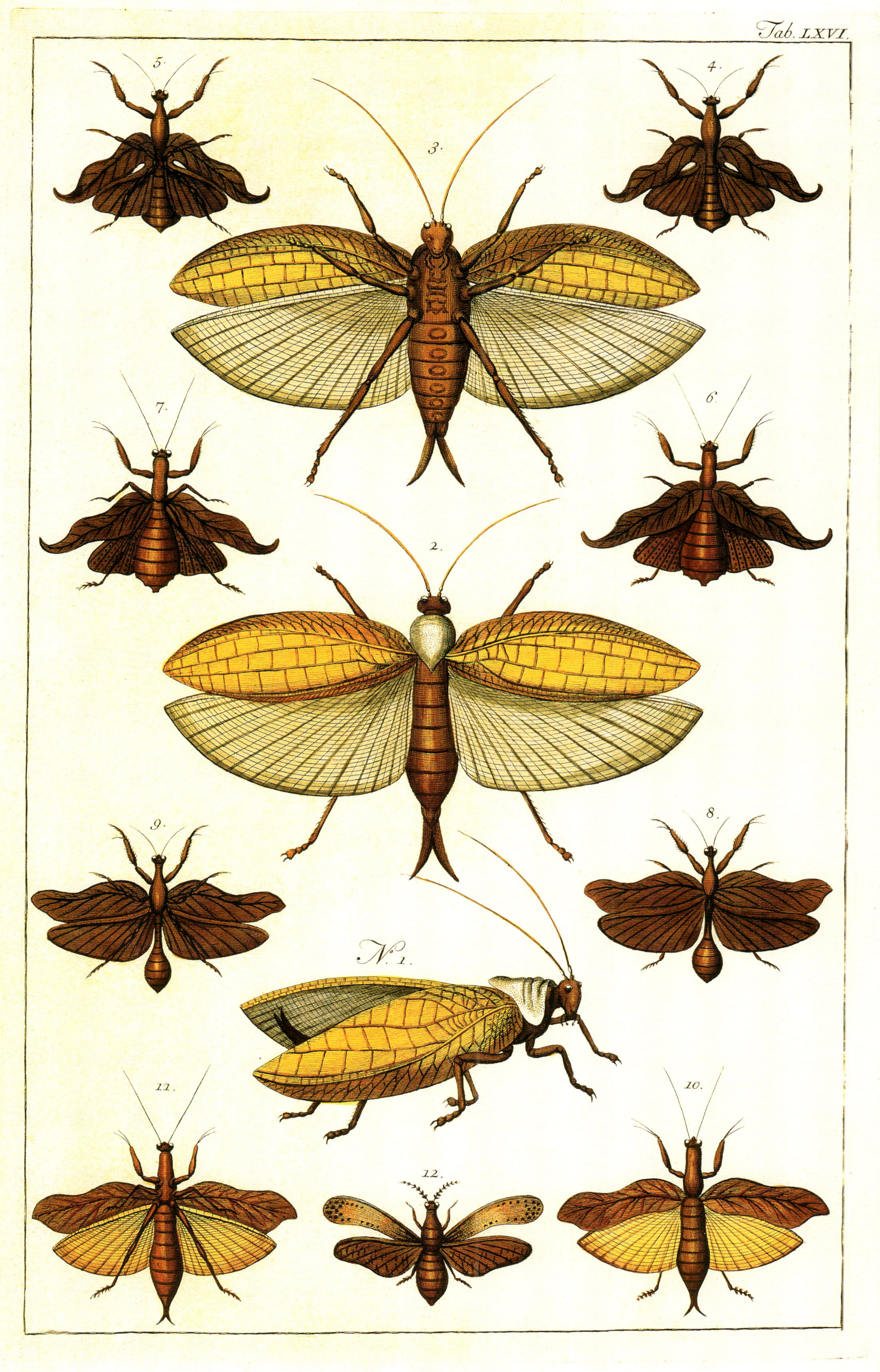

1-3 Ensifera 4-11 Mantodea 12 Hemiptera
1-3 Katydids · Langfühlerschrecken · Ensifères 4-11 Praying mantids · Gottesanbeterinnen · Mantes 12 Cicada · Zikade · Hémiptère

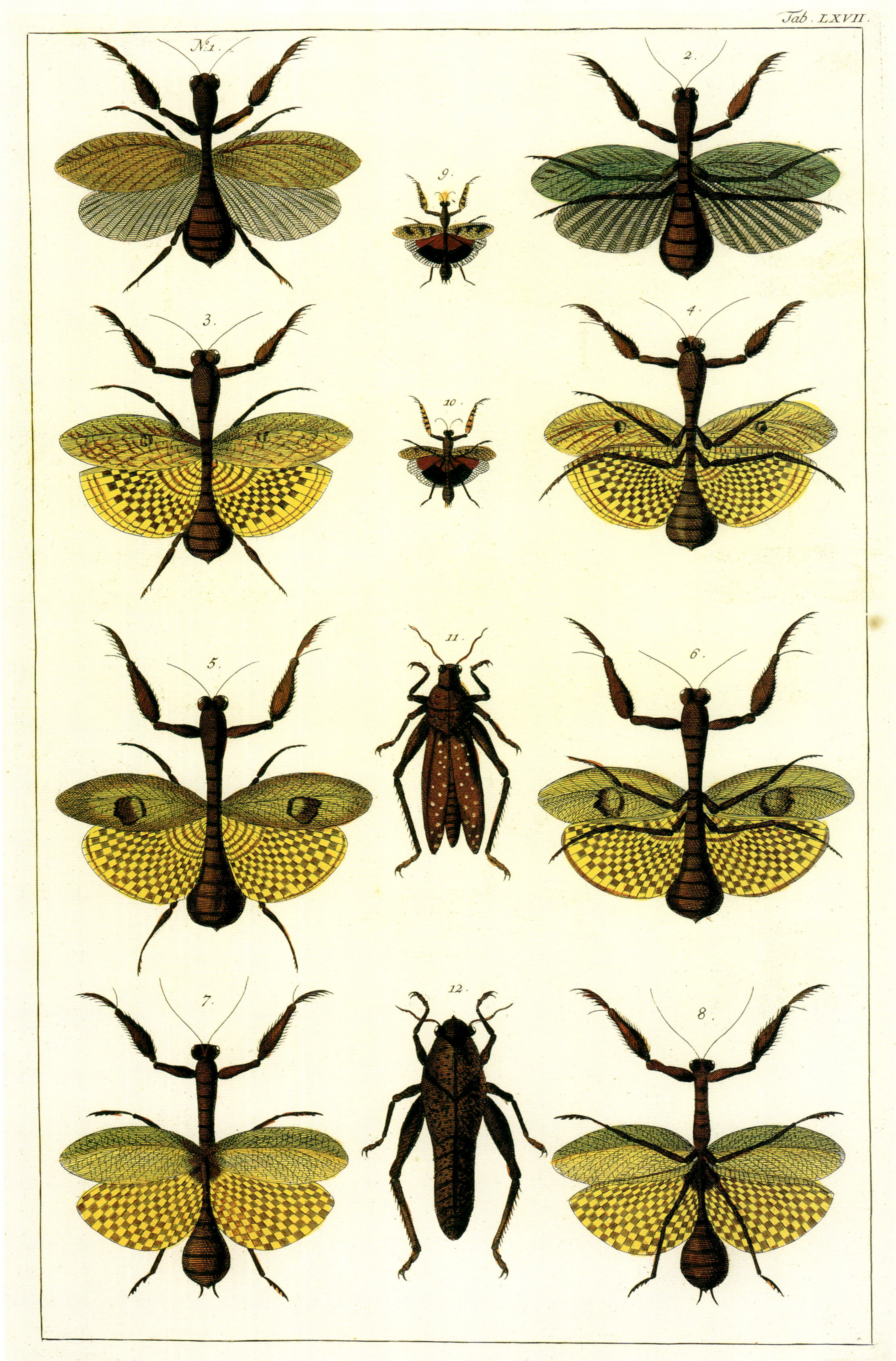

1-10 Mantodea 9-10 *Mantis religiosa* 11-12 Orthoptera
1-10 Praying mantids · Gottesanbeterinnen · Mantes 9-10 European praying mantids · Gottesanbeterinnen · Mantes religieuses 11-12 Grasshoppers · Heuschrecken · Criquets

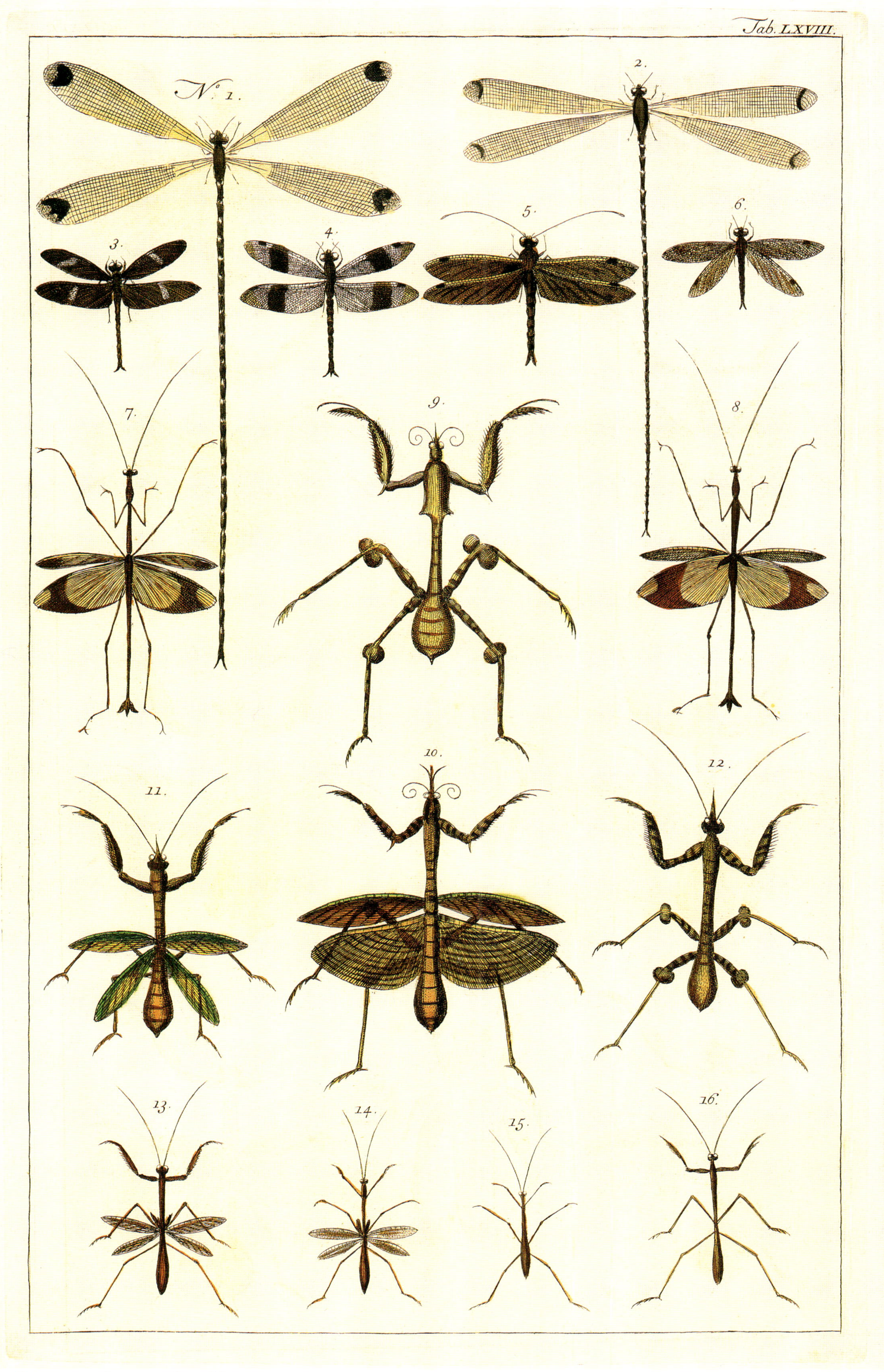

1-6 Odonata **7-16** Mantodea **9-12** *Gongylus gongylodes*
1-6 Dragonflies · Libellen · Libellules **7-12** Praying mantids · Gottesanbeterinnen · Mantes **9-12** Gargoyle mantids/Walking violins · Wandelnde Geigen · Violons ambulants

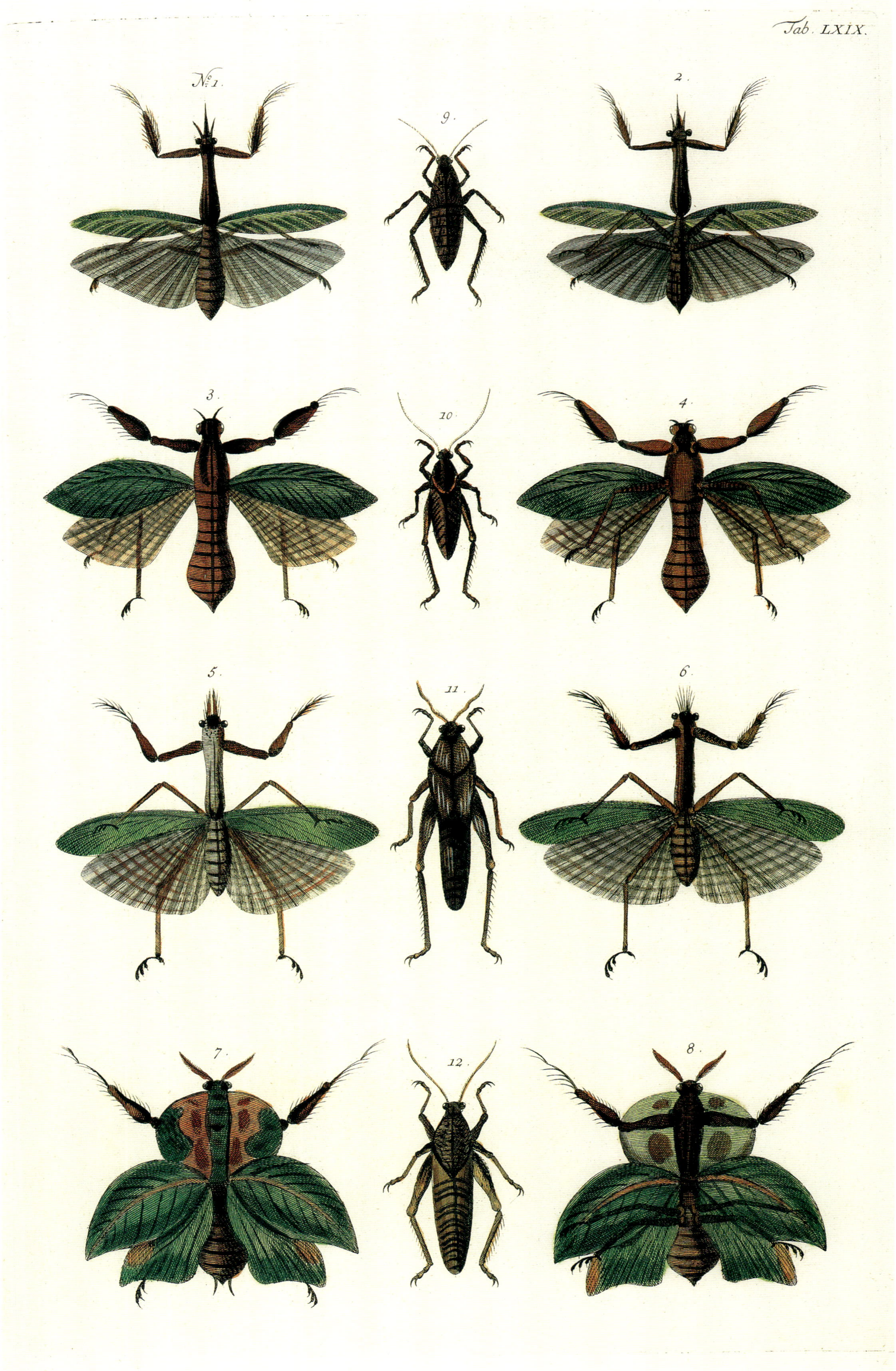

Tab. LXIX.

Nº 1. 2. 3. 4. 5. 6. 7. 8. 9. 10. 11. 12.

1-8 Mantodea **9-12** Orthoptera
1-8 Praying mantids · Gottesanbeterinnen · Mantes **9-12** Grasshoppers · Heuschrecken · Orthoptères

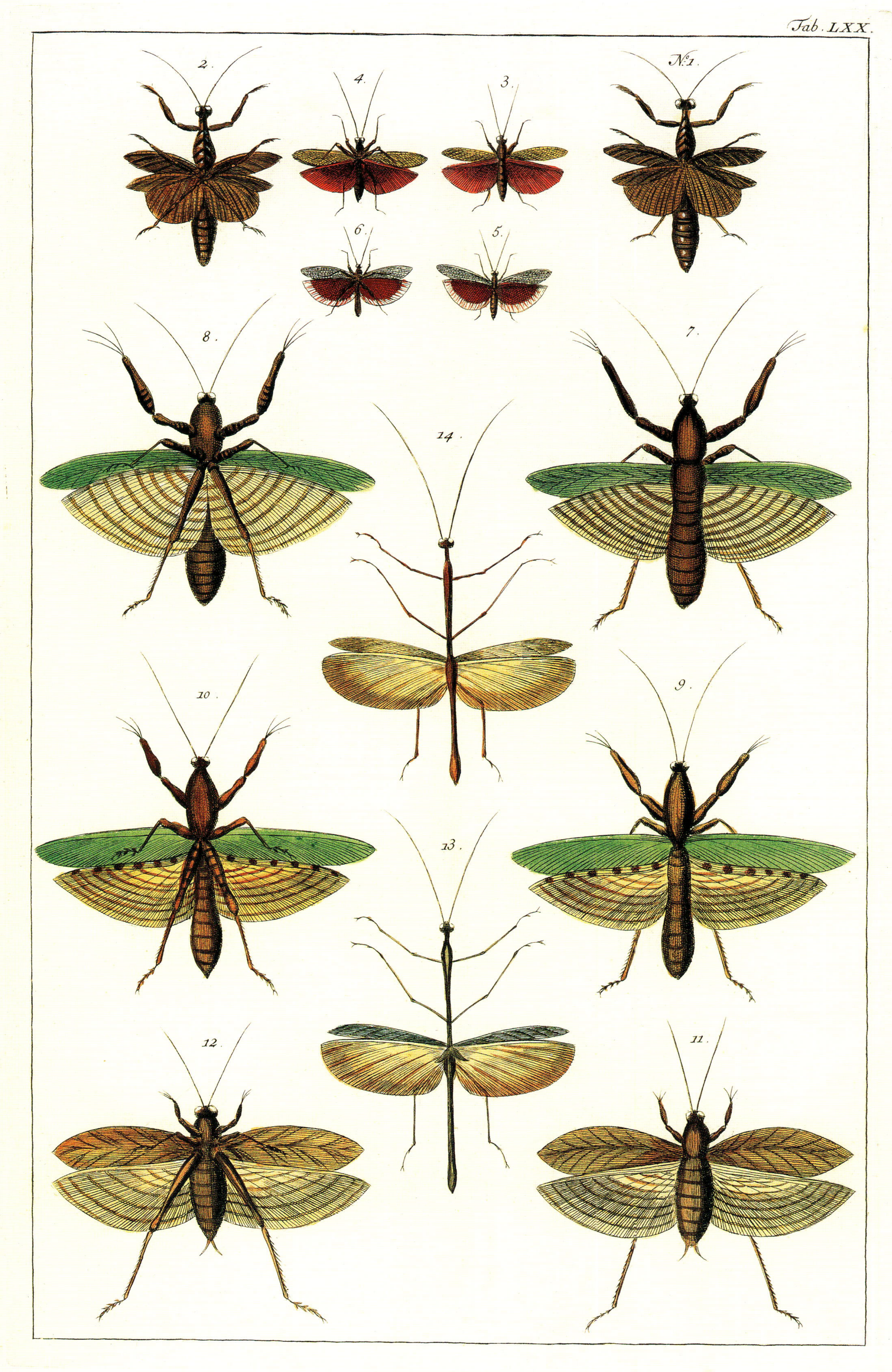

1-2, 7-10, 14-15 Mantodea **3-6, 11-12** Orthoptera **13-14** Phasmatodea
1-2, 7-10, 14-15 Praying mantids · Gottesanbeterinnen · Mantes **3-6, 11-12** Katydids and grasshoppers · Heuschrecken · Sauterelles et criquets **13-14** Stick insects · Stabheuschrecke · Phasmes

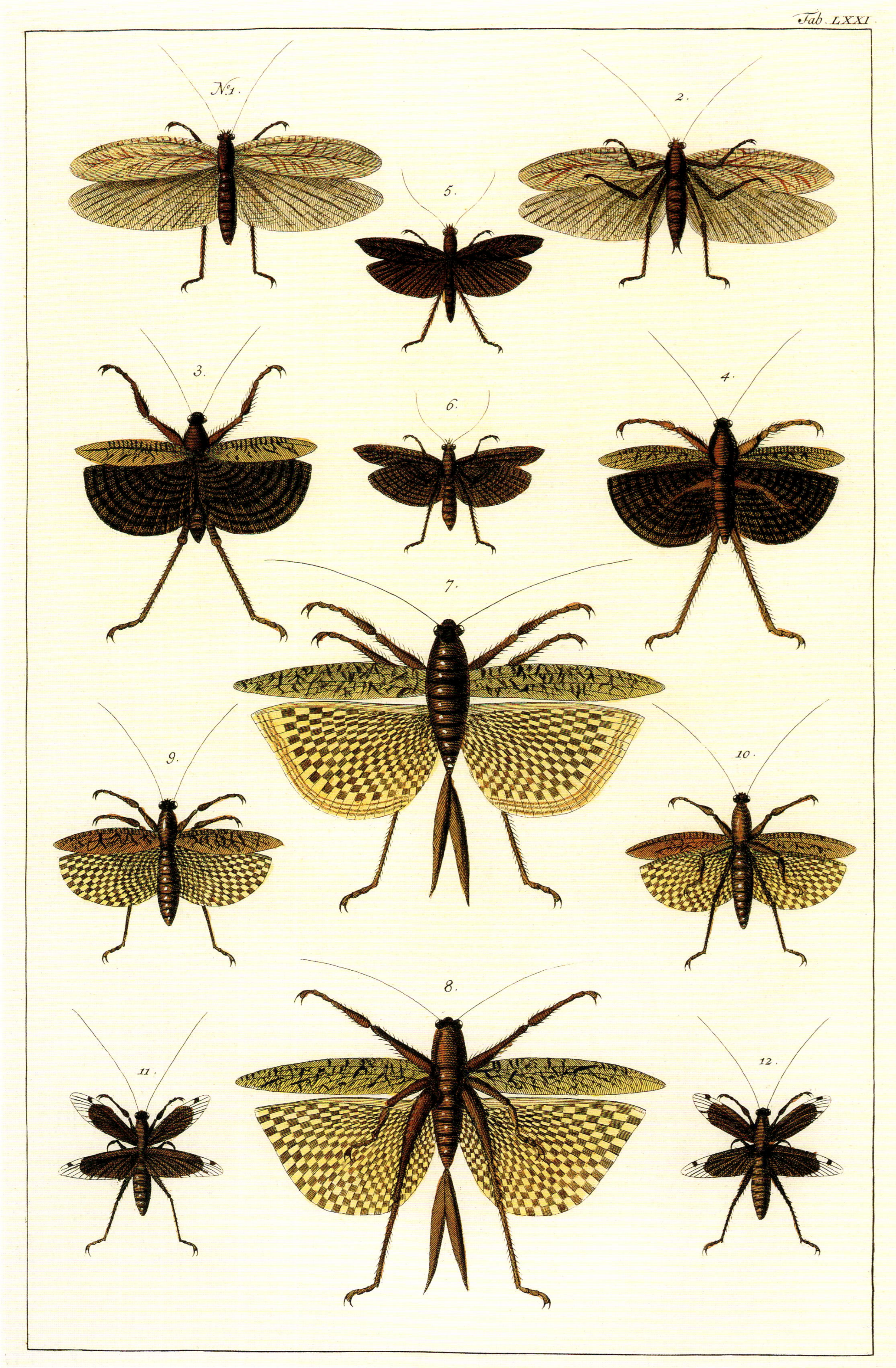

Ensifera
Katydids · Langfühlerschrecken · Sauterelles

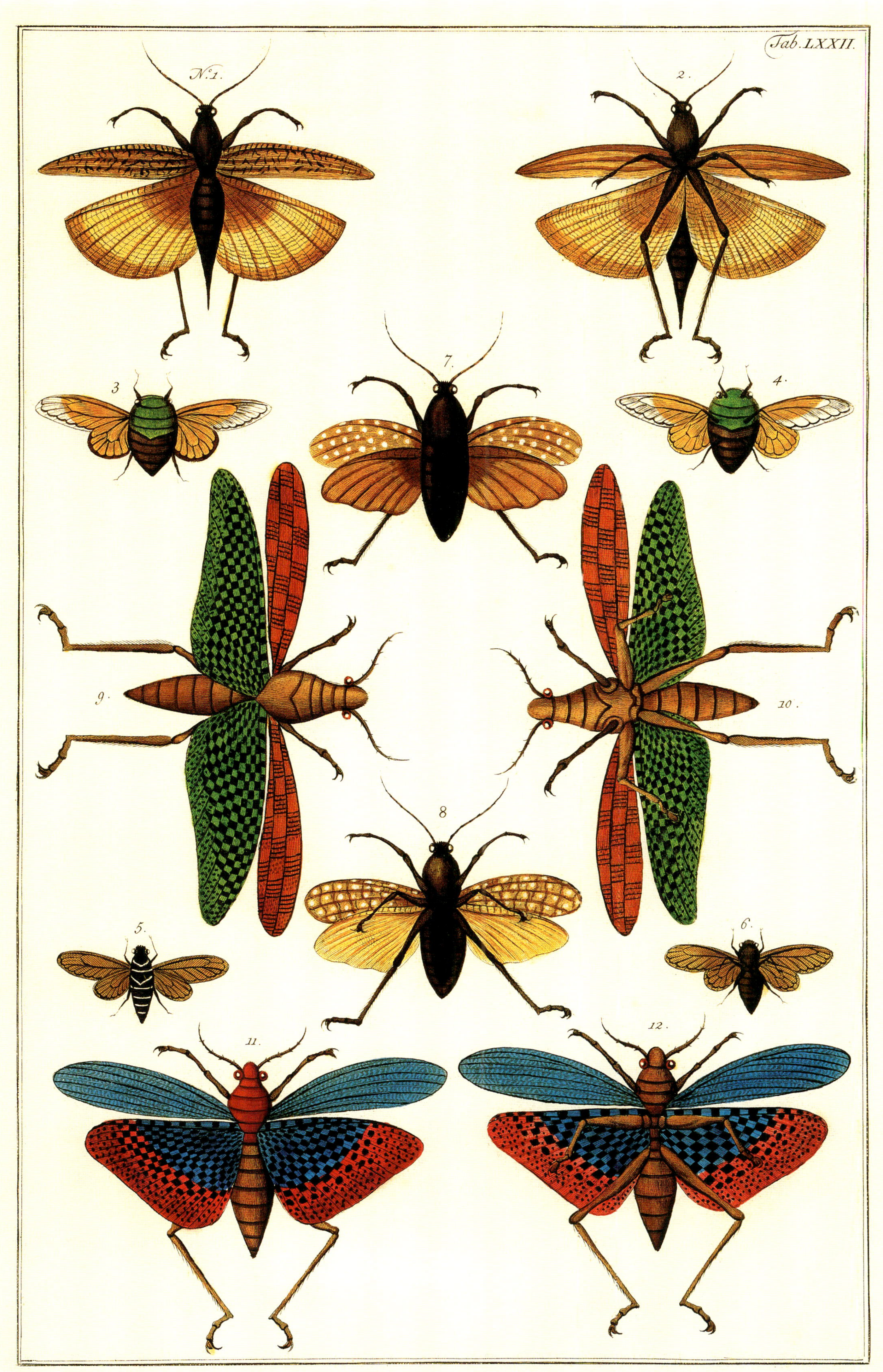

1-2, 9-12 Orthoptera **3-8** Hemiptera **11-12** *Tropidacris cristata*
1-2, 9-12 Grasshoppers · Feldheuschrecken · Orthoptères **3-8** Hemipterans · Wanzen · Hémiptères **11-12** Grasshoppers · Feldheuschrecken · Criquets géants à ailes rouges

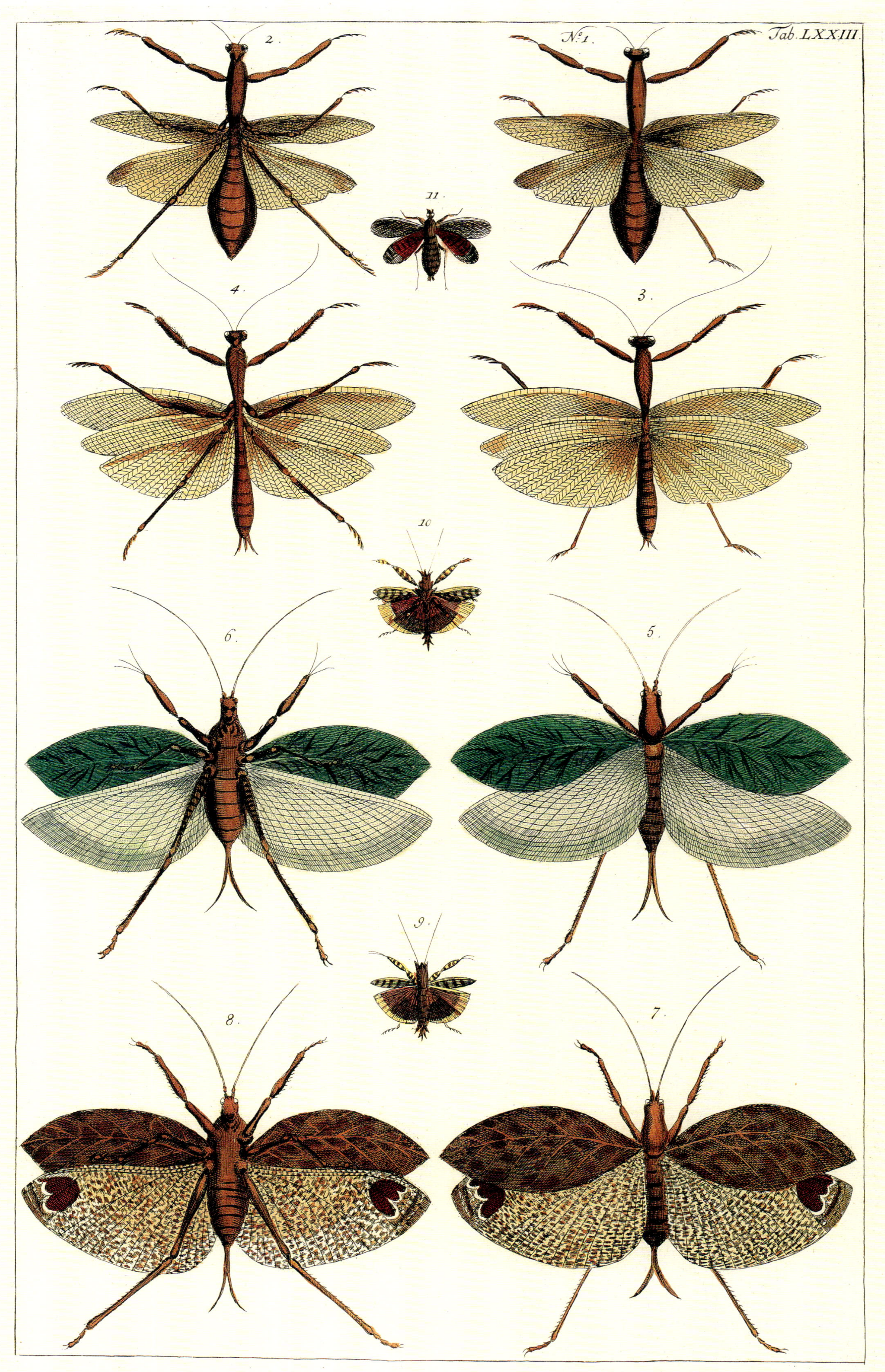

1-4, 9-10 Mantodea **5-8** Ensifera **11** Heteroptera
1-4, 9-10 Praying mantids · Gottesanbeterinnen · Mantes **5-8** Katydids · Langfühlerschrecken · Sauterelles **11** Bug · Wanze · Punaise

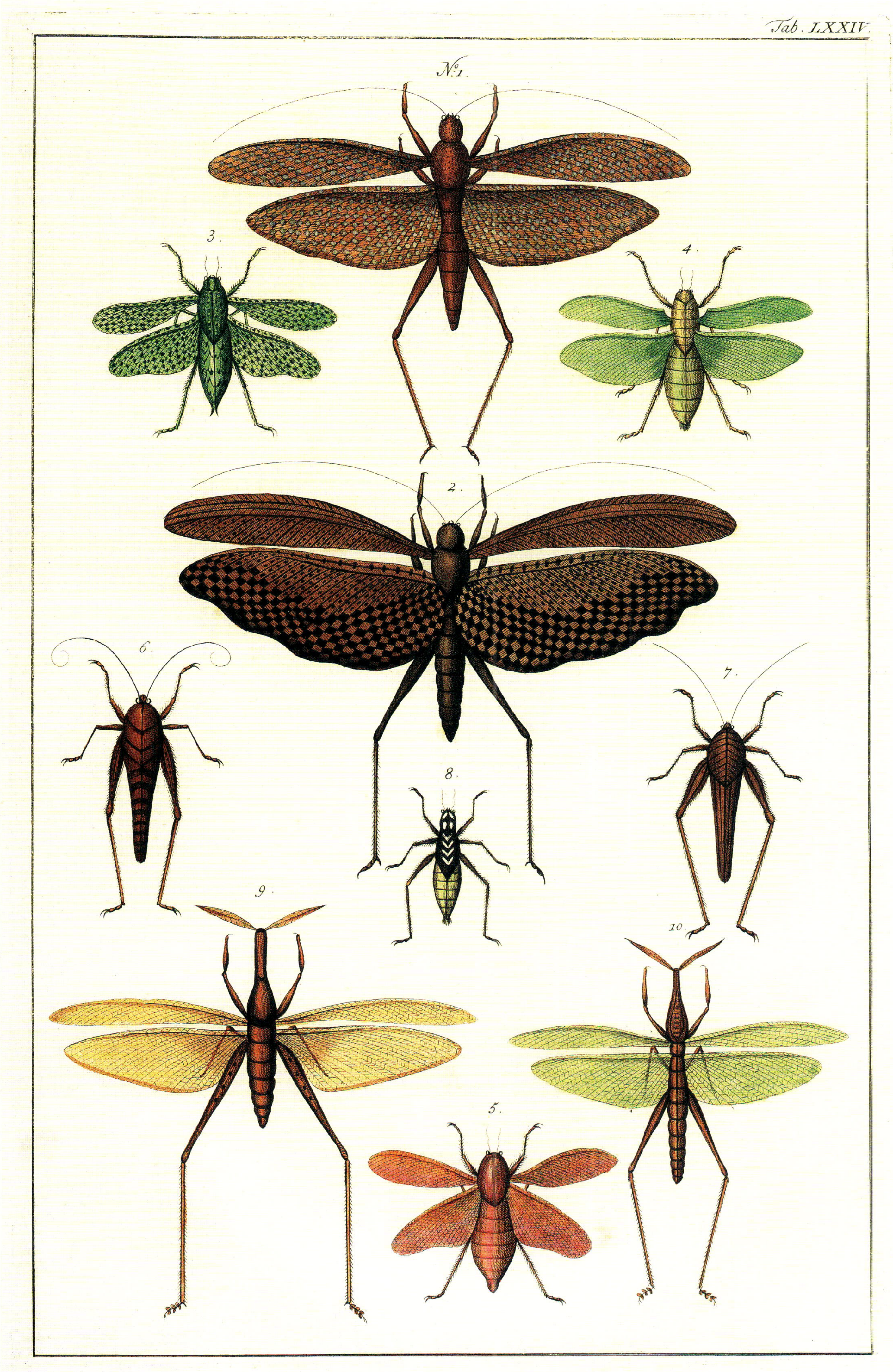

Orthoptera
Grasshoppers, crickets and katydids · Lang- und Kurzfühlerschrecken · Criquets et sauterelles

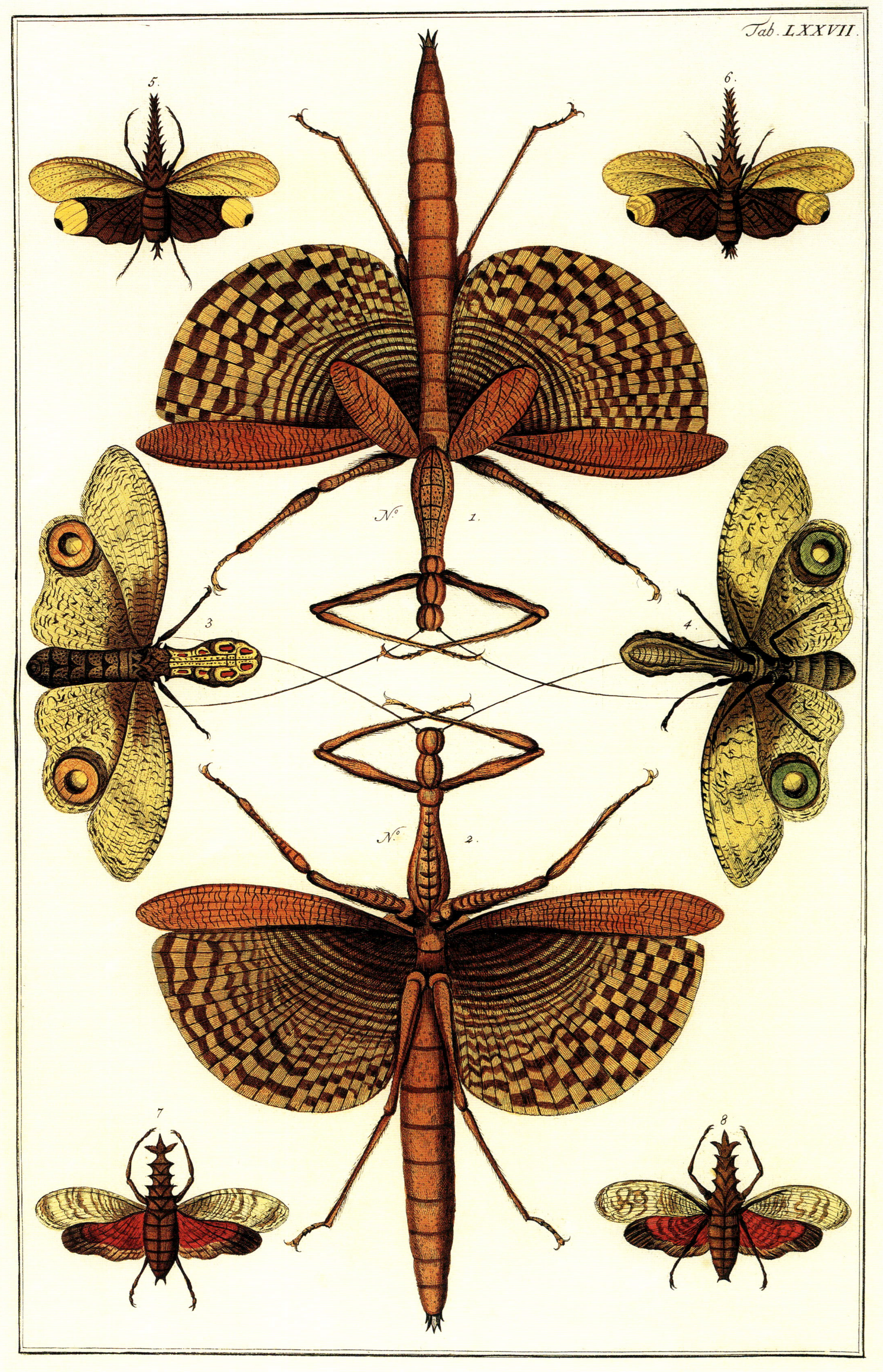

1-2 *Phasma gigas* 3-4 *Fulgora laternaria* 5-8 Auchenorrhyncha
1-2 Walking stick · Stabheuschrecke · Grand phasme ailé 3-4 Greater lanternfly · Großer Laternenträger · Fulgore porte-lanterne 5-8 Cicadas · Zikaden · Homoptères

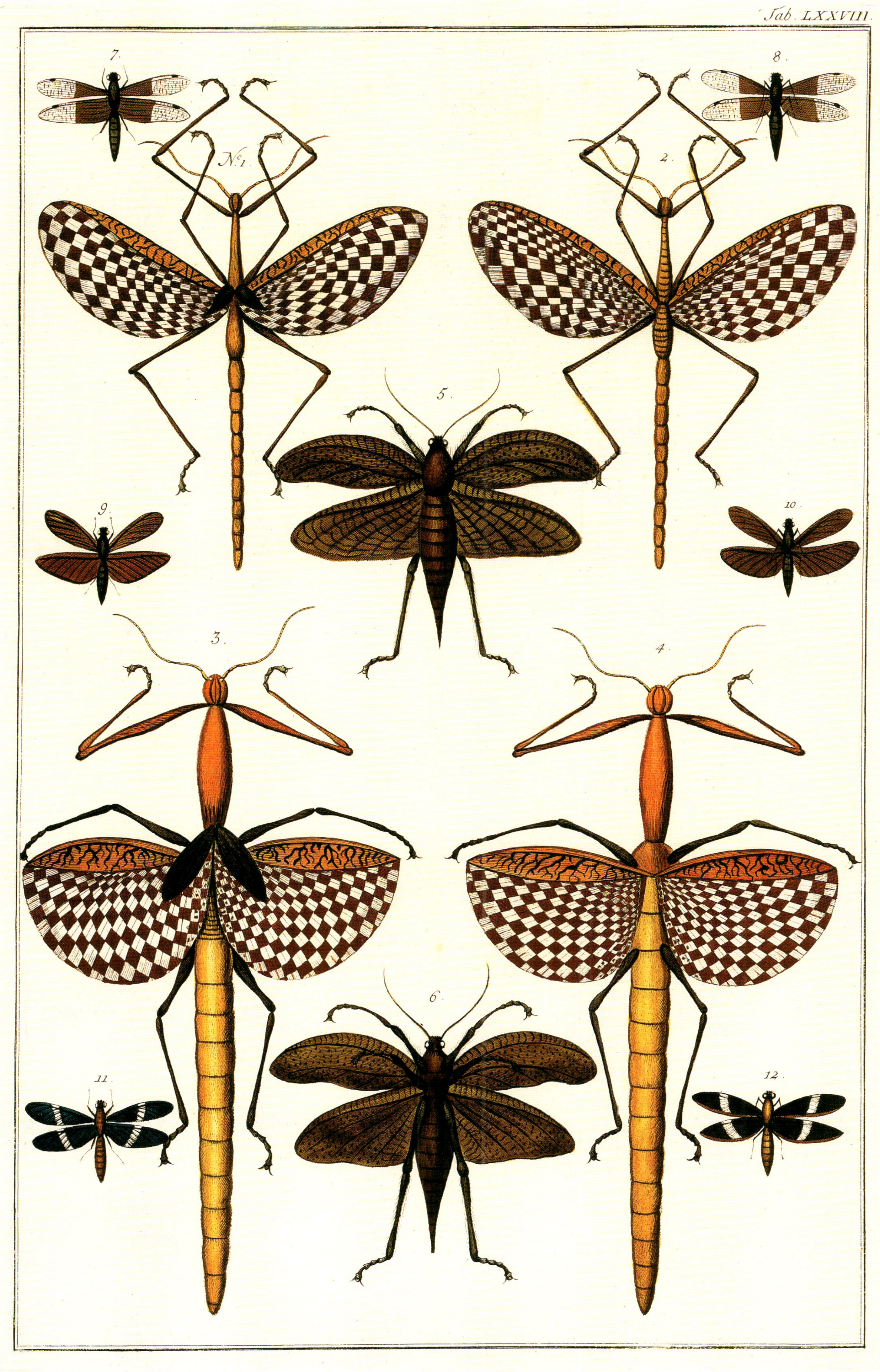

1-4 Phasmatodea 5-6 Ensifera 7-12 Odonata
1-4 Walking stick · Stabheuschrecken · Phasmes 5-6 Katydids · Langfühlerschrecken · Sauterelles 7-12 Dragonflies · Libellen · Libellules

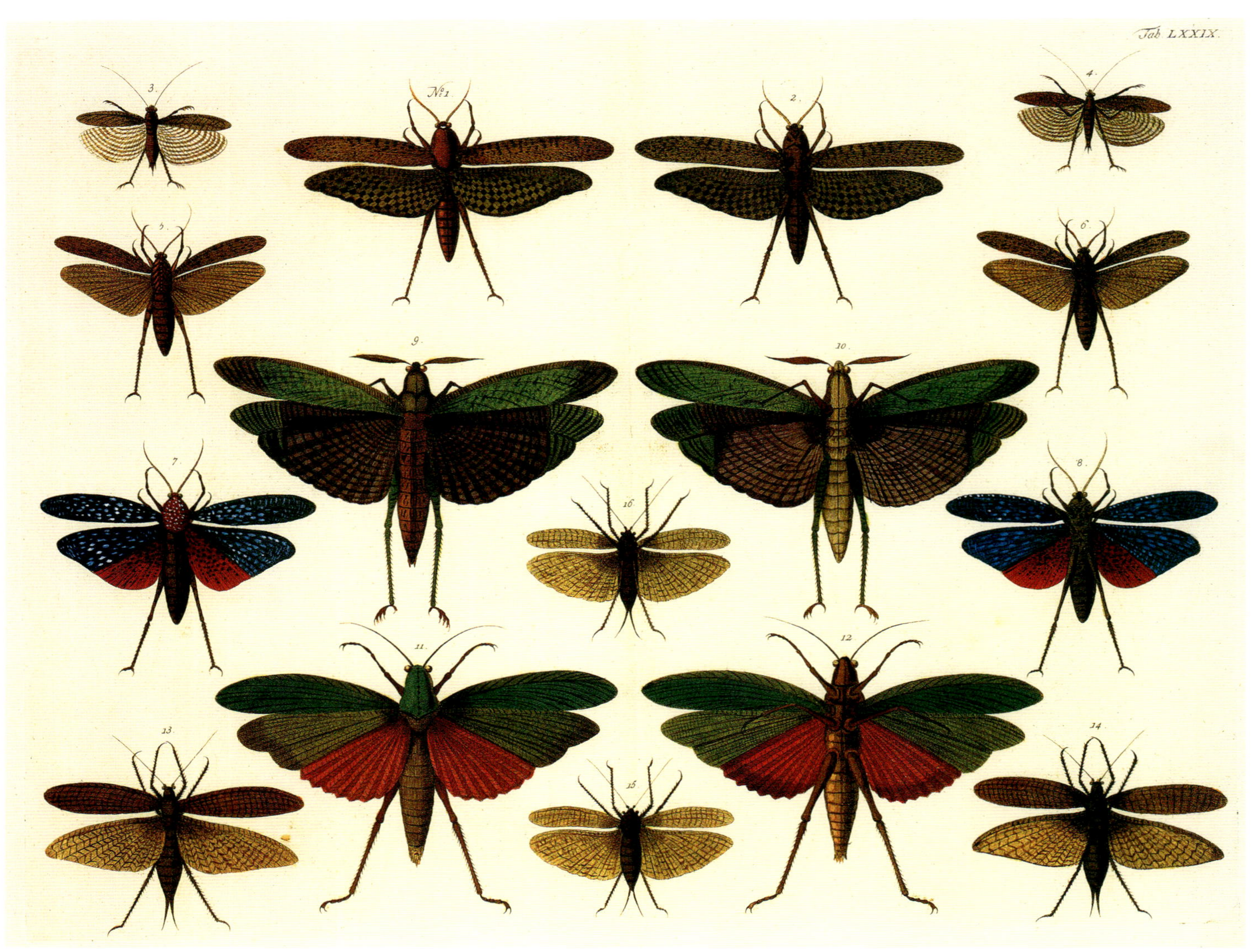

Orthoptera **7-8** *Phymateus morbillosus*
Grasshoppers and katydids · Feld- und Laubheuschrecken · Criquets et sauterelles **7-8** Bush locusts · Wanderheuschrecken · Sauterelles

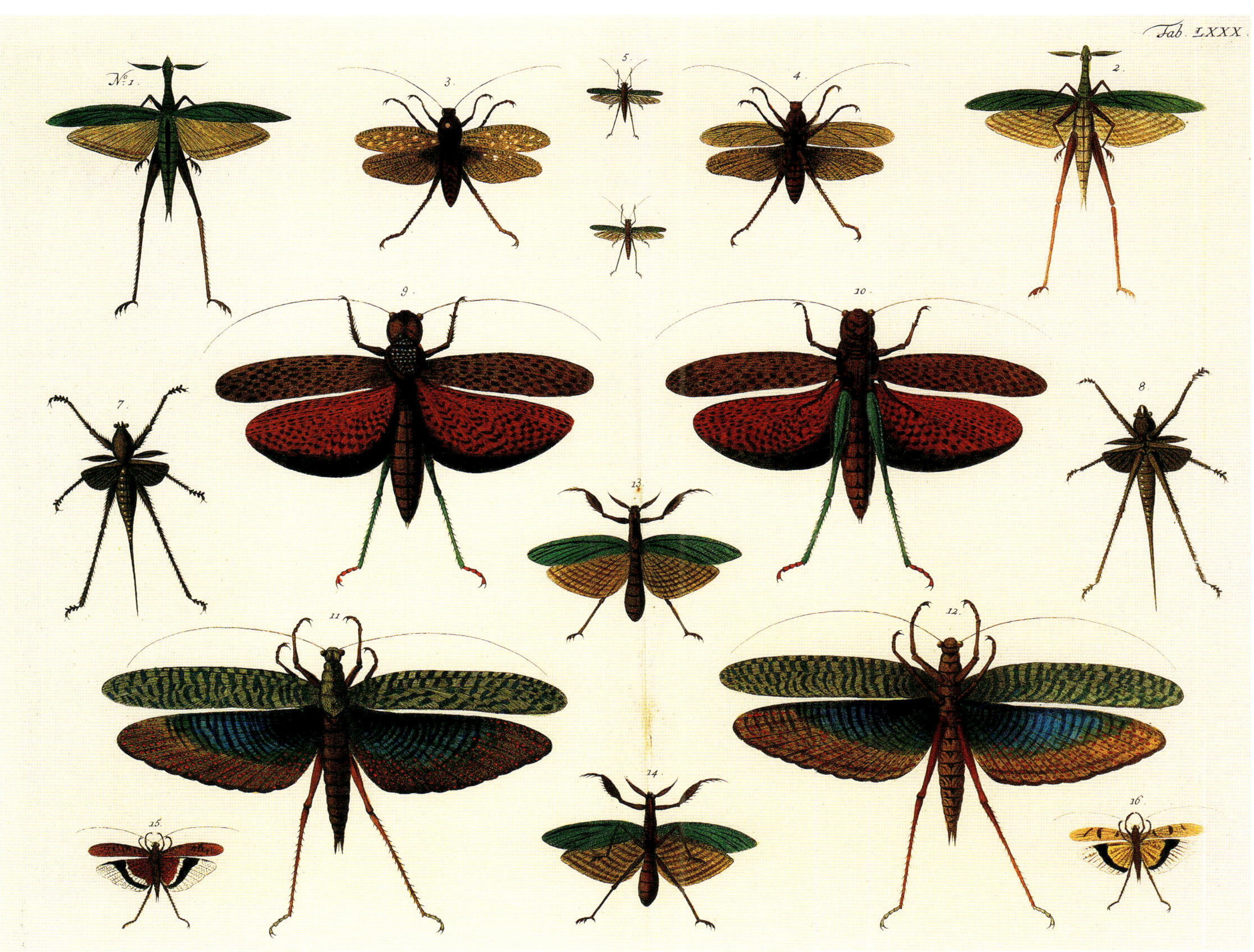

1-12, 15-16 Orthoptera **1-2** *Acrida turrita* **13-14** Mantodea
1-12, 15-16 Grasshoppers and katydids · Feld- und Laubheuschrecken · Criquets et sauterelles **1-2** Mediterranean grasshoppers · Heuschrecken · Criquets **13-14** Praying mantids · Gottesanbeterinnen · Mantes

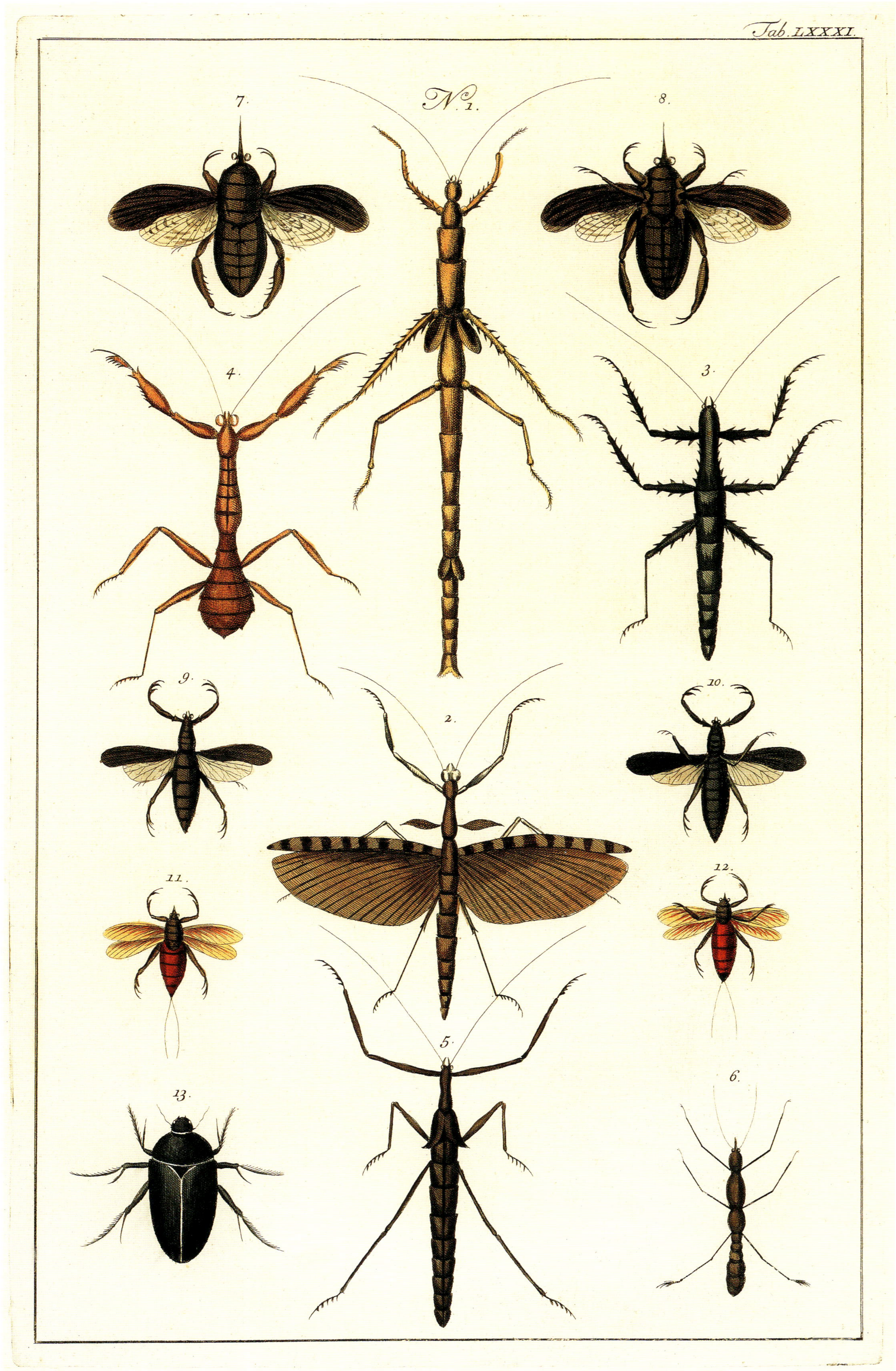

1, 3, 5-6 Phasmatodea **2, 4** Mantodea **7-12** Nepidae **13** Dytiscidae

1, 3, 5-6 Walking sticks · Stabheuschrecken · Phasmes **2, 4** Praying mantids · Gottesanbeterinnen · Mantes **7-12** Water bugs · Wasserwanzen · Punaises aquatiques (Nèpes) **13** Water beetle · Wasserkäfer · Coléoptère aquatique (Dytique)

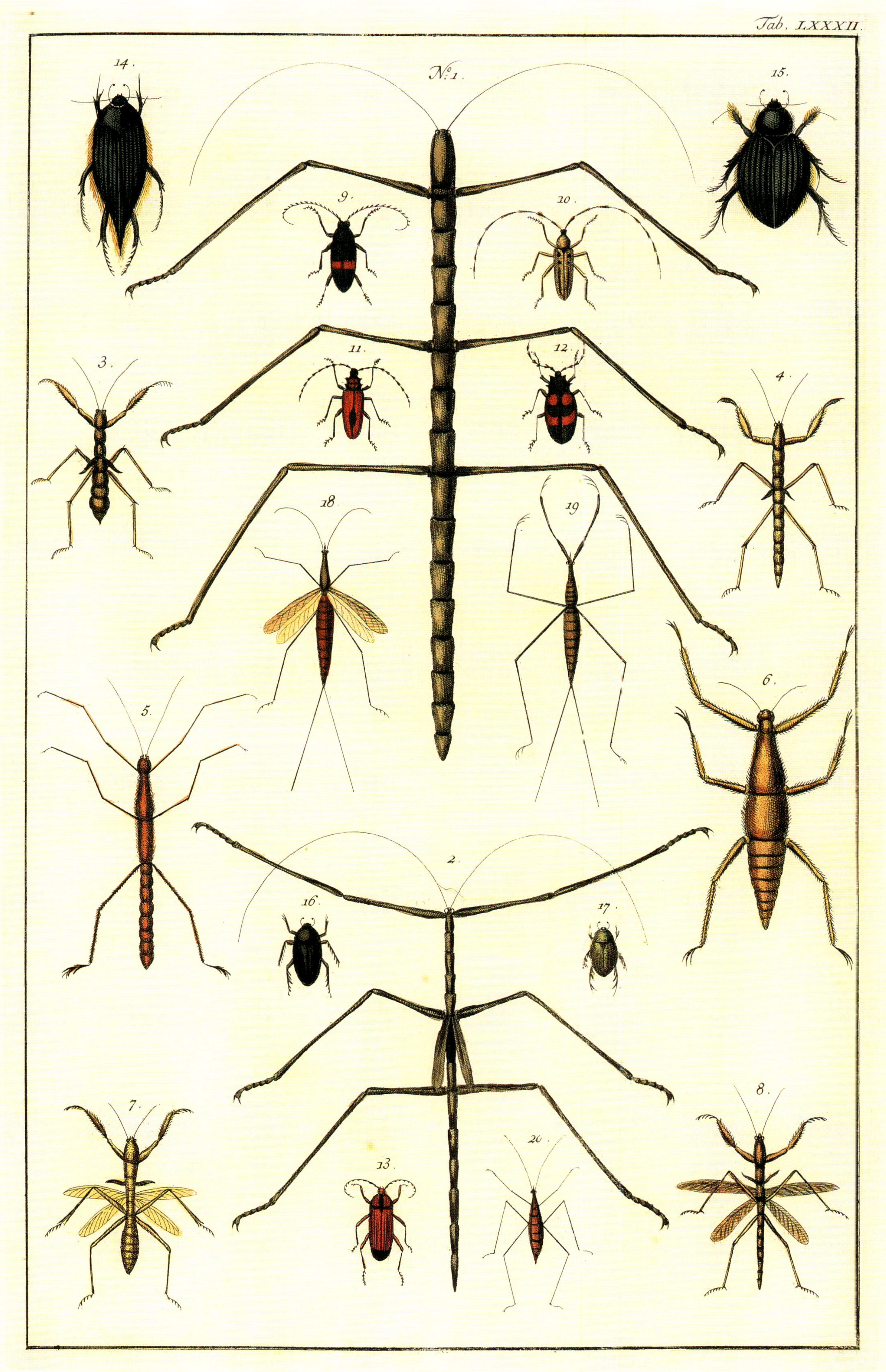

1, 2, 5-6 Phasmatodea **3-4, 7-8** Mantodea **9-17** Coleoptera **18-20** Heteroptera
1, 2, 5-6 Walking sticks · Stabheuschrecken · Phasmes **3-4, 7-8** Praying mantids · Gottesanbeterinnen · Mantes **9-17** Beetles · Käfer · Coléoptères **18-20** Bugs · Wanzen · Punaises

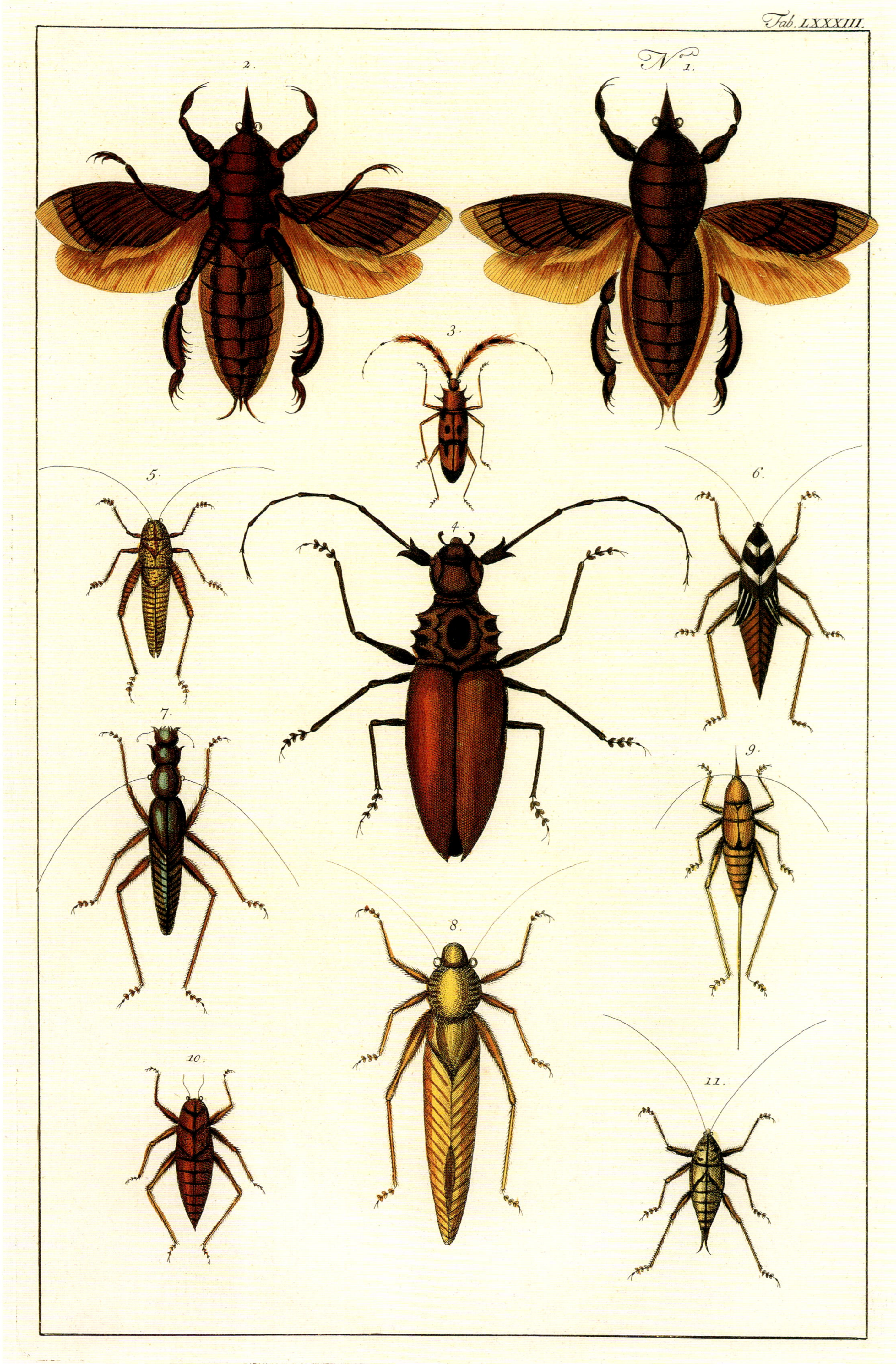

1-2 Nepidae 3-4 Cerambycidae 5-11 Orthoptera

1-2 Water bug · Wasserwanze · Punaise aquatique (Nèpe) 3-4 Longhorn beetle · Bockkäfer · Longicorne 5-11 Grasshoppers and katydids · Heuschrecken · Criquets et sauterelles

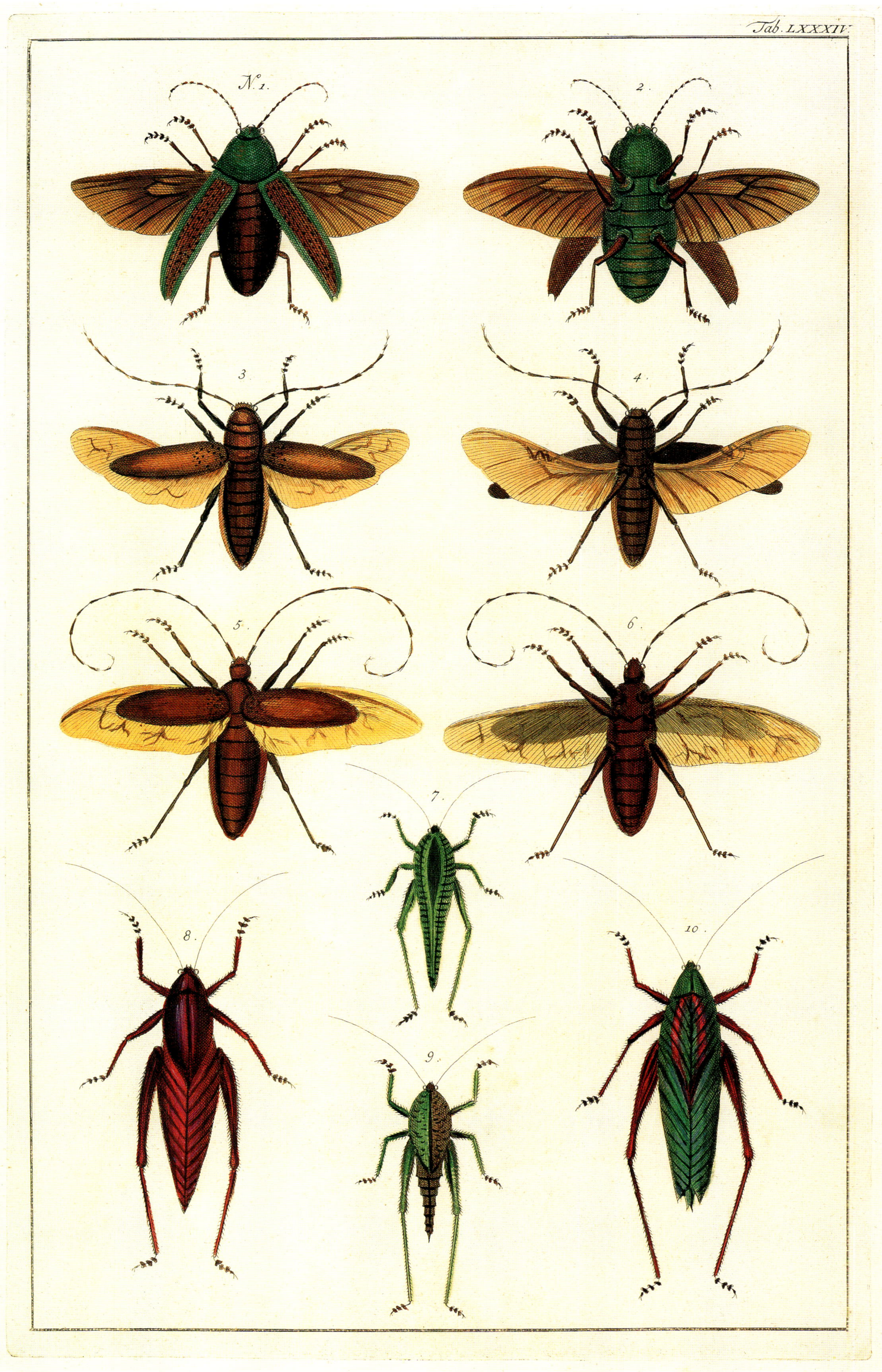

1-6 Coleoptera 7-10 Orthoptera
1-6 Beetles · Käfer · Coléoptères 7-10 Grasshoppers and katydids · Heuschrecken · Orthoptères

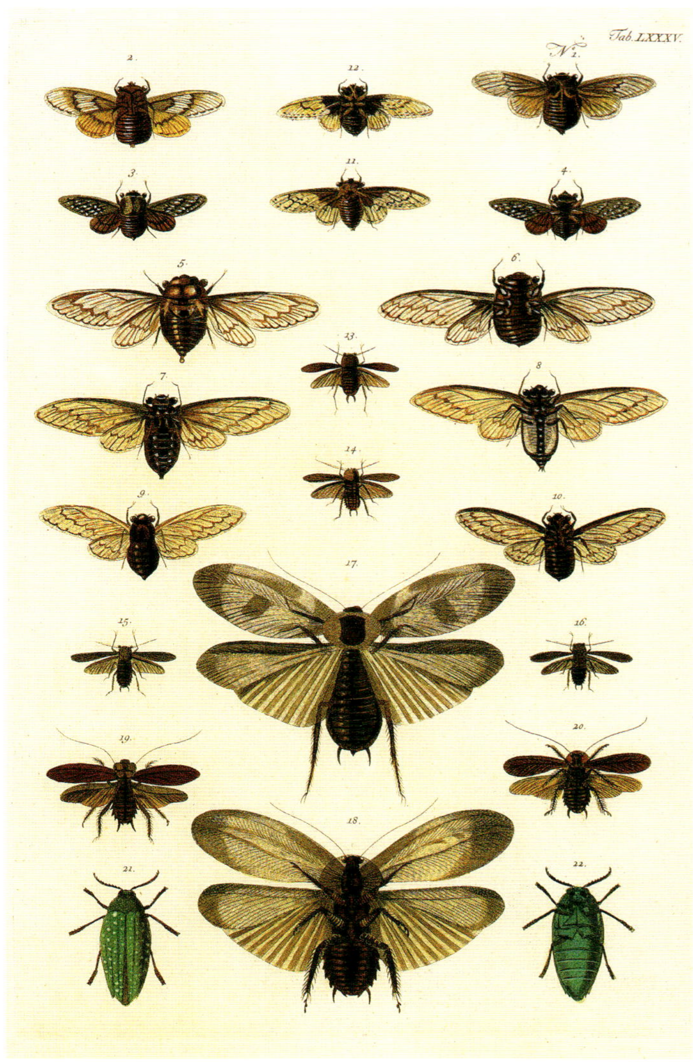

1-12 Auchenorrhyncha **5-6** *Cicada orni* **13-20** Blattodea **17-18** *Blaberus giganteus* **21-22** Buprestidae
1-12 Cicadas · Zikaden · Cigales **5-6** Manniferous cicadas · Mannazikaden/Eschenzikaden · Cigales de l'orne **13-20** Cockroaches · Schaben · Blattes **17-18** Brazilian cockroaches · Brasilianische Schaben · Blattes brésiliennes **21-22** Jewel beetles · Prachtkäfer · Buprestes

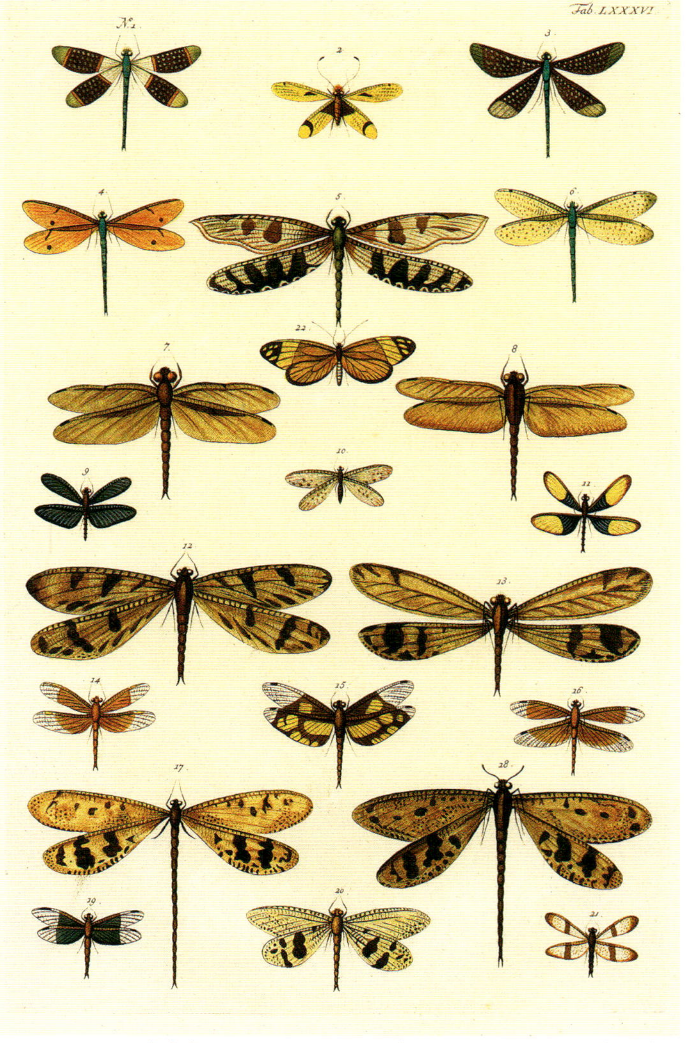

1, 3 Zygoptera **2** Ascalaphidae **4, 6, 9, 11, 14-16, 19, 21** Odonata **5, 12-13, 17-18** Myrmeleontidae **7-8** Anisoptera **10** Planipennia **22** Lepidoptera
1, 3 Damselflies · Wasserjungfern · Demoiselles **2** Lacewing · Netzflügler · Ascalaphe **4, 6, 9, 11, 14-16, 19, 21** Dragonflies · Libellen · Libellules **5, 12-13, 17-18** Ant lions · Ameisenlöwen · Fourmislions **7-8** Dragonflies · Großlibellen · Libellules **10** Neuropterans · Netzflügler · Planipenne **22** Butterfly · Schmetterling · Papillon

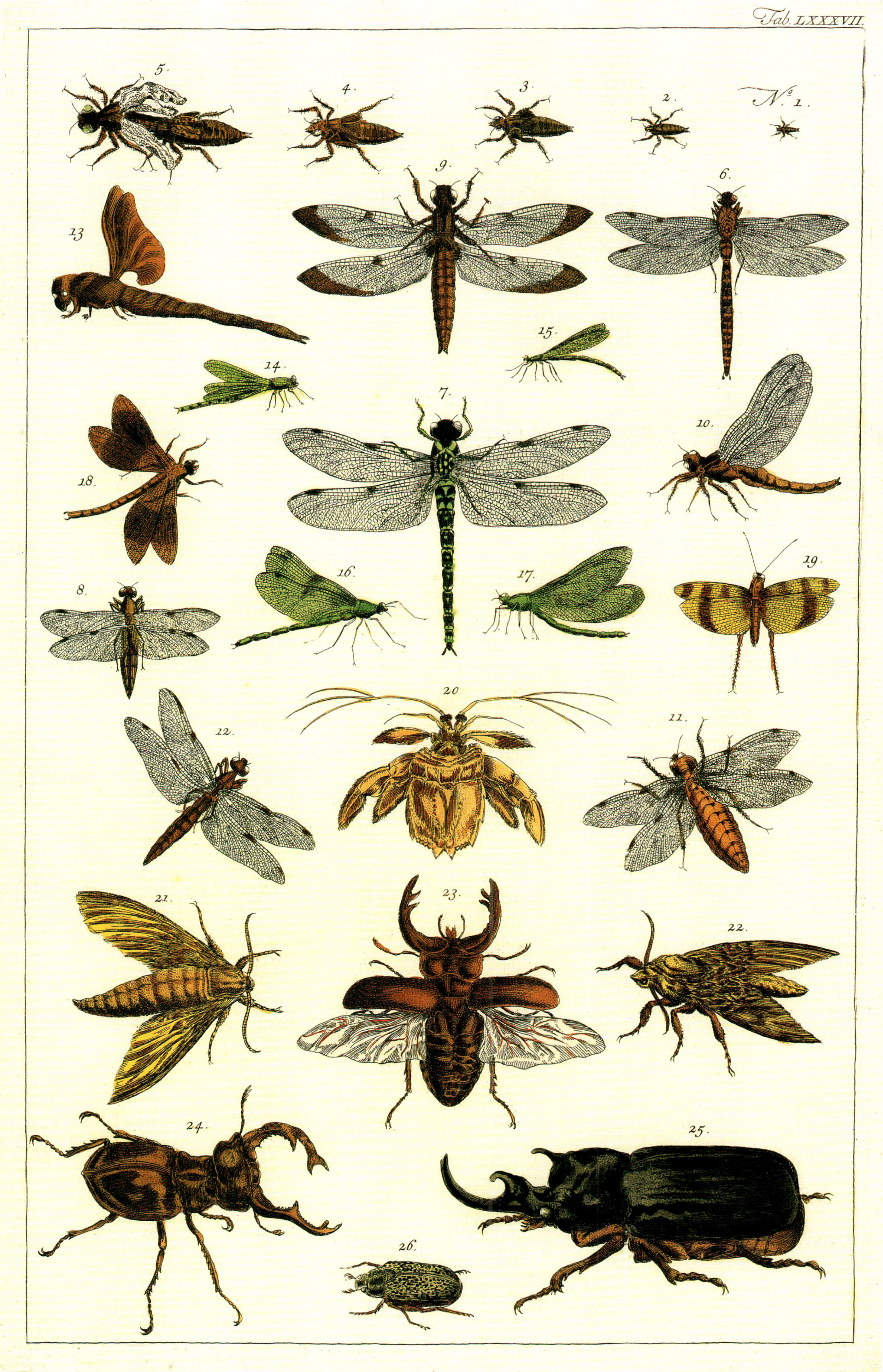

1-18 Odonata 19 Caelifera 20 Crustacea 21, 22 Lepidoptera 23-24 Lucanidae 25 Dynastinae 26 Melolonthinae
1-18 Dragonflies · Libellen · Libellules **19** Grasshopper · Feldheuschrecke · Criquet **20** Crustacean · Krebs · Crustacé **21, 22** Hawkmoths · Schwärmer · Sphinx **23-24** Stag beetles · Hirschkäfer · Lucanes cerfs-volants **25** Hercules beetle · Herculeskäfer · Dynaste hercule **26** May beetle · Maikäfer · Hanneton

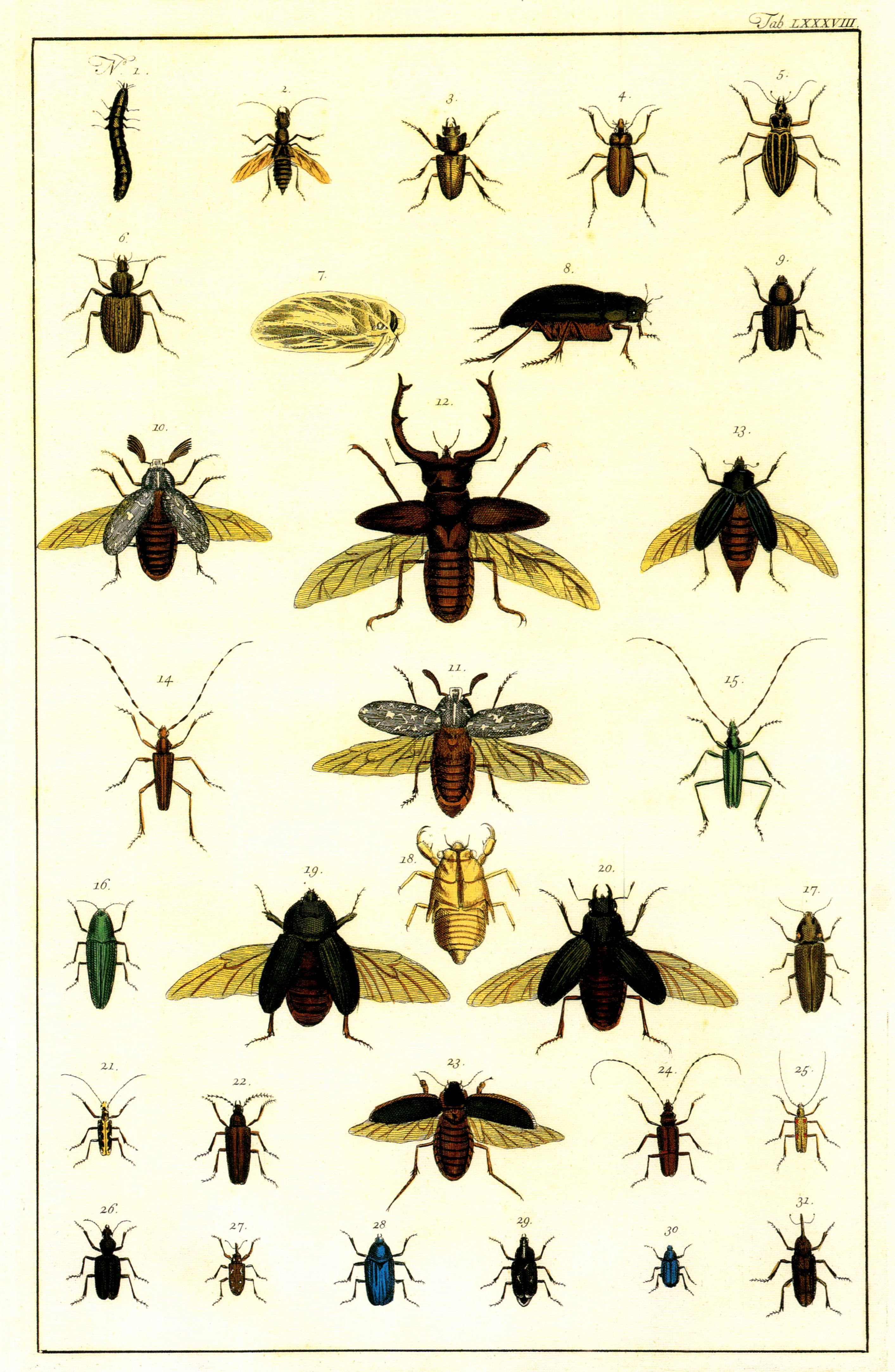

1, 3-4, 8, 21, 25-26, 29-30 Coleoptera **2** Staphylinidae **5-6** Carabidae **9-11, 13, 18-20, 23, 28** Scarabaeidae **12** Lucanidae **14-15, 22** Cerambycidae **16-17** Elateridae **27, 31** Curculionidae

1, 3-4, 8, 21, 25-26, 29-30 Beetles · Käfer · Coléoptères **2** Rove beetle · Kurzflügelkäfer · Staphylin **5-6** Carabids/Ground beetles · Laufkäfer · Carabidés **9-11, 13, 18-20, 23, 28** Cockchafers · Blatthornkäfer · Scarabées **12** Stag beetle · Hirschkäfer · Lucane cerf-volant **14-15, 22** Longhorn beetles · Bockkäfer · Longicornes **16-17** Click beetles · Schnellkäfer · Taupins **27, 31** Weevils · Rüsselkäfer · Charançons

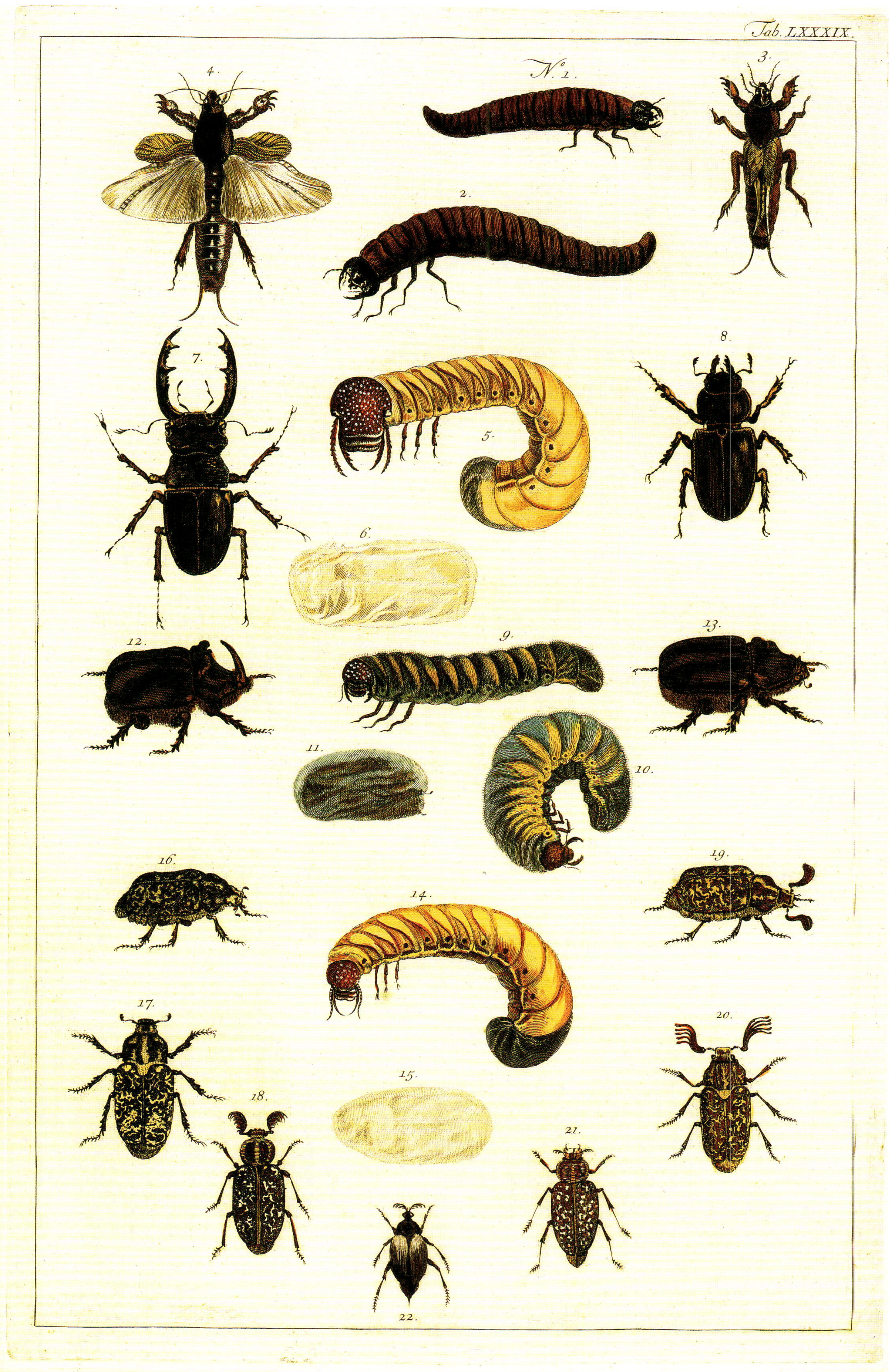

1-2 Hydrophilidae **3-4** *Gryllotalpa gryllotalpa* **5-8** Lucanidae **9-21** Scarabaeidae **22** Rhipiphoridae
1-2 Water-beetles · Wasserkäfer · Hydrophiles **3-4** Mole criquets · Maulwurfsgrillen · Courtilières **5-8** Stag beetles · Hirschkäfer · Lucanes cerfs-volants **9-21** Cockchafers · Blatthornkäfer · Scarabées **22** Wedge-shaped beetle · Fächerkäfer · Rhipiphoridé

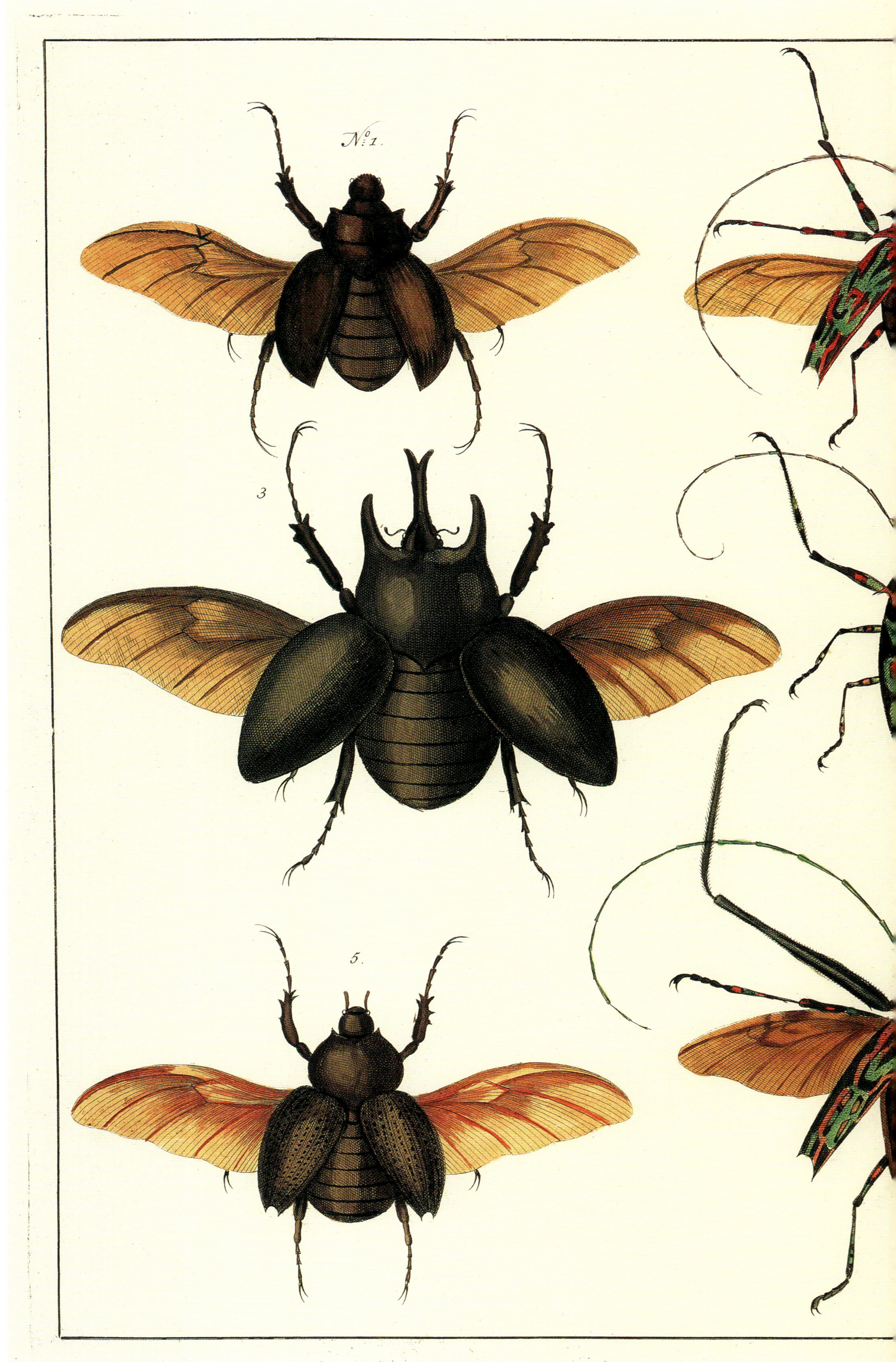

1-6 Scarabaeidae **7-9** Cerambycidae
1-6 Cockchafers · Blatthornkäfer · Scarabées **7-9** Longhorn beetles · Bockkäfer · Longicornes

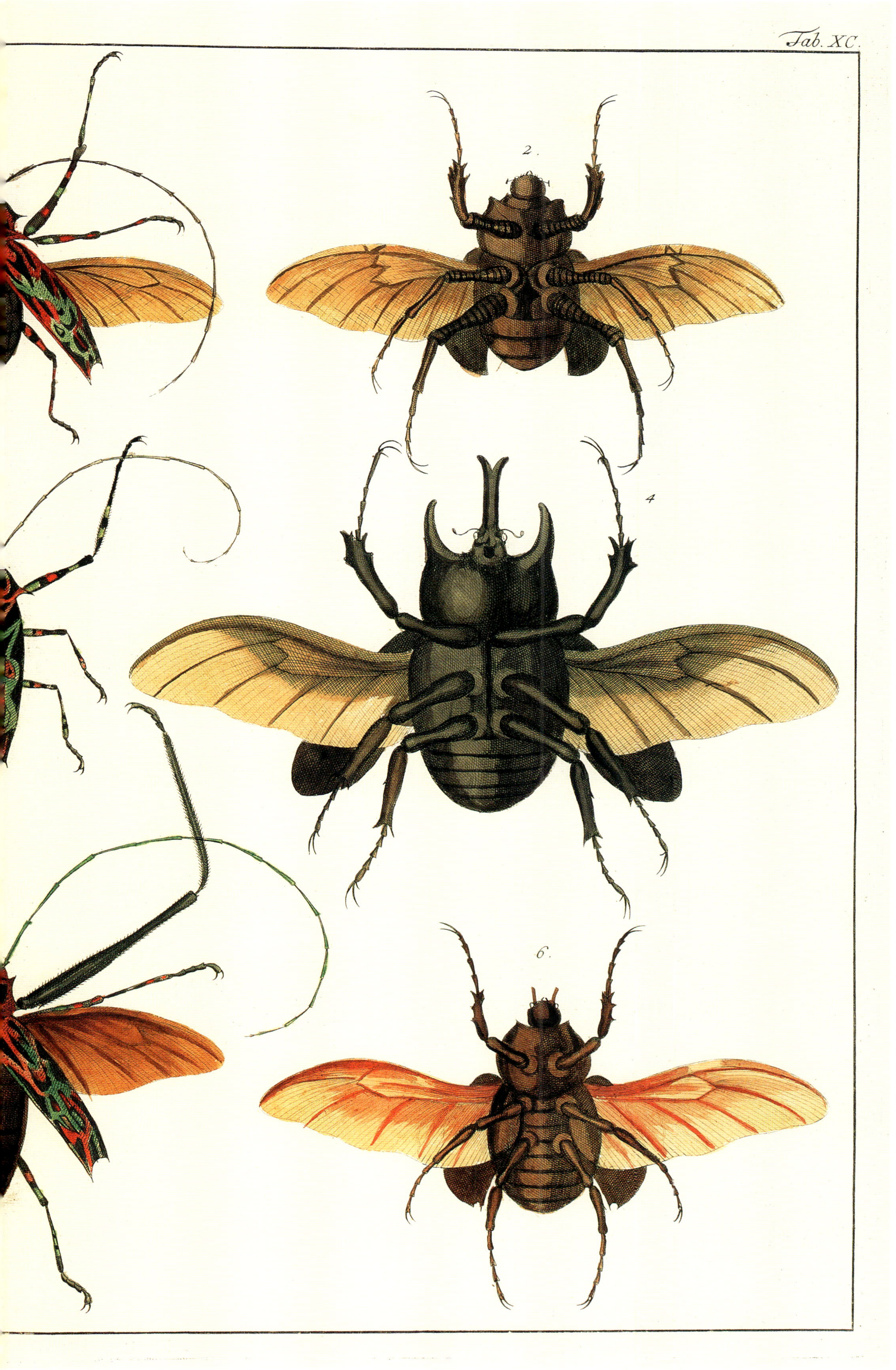
Tab. XC.
2.
4
6.

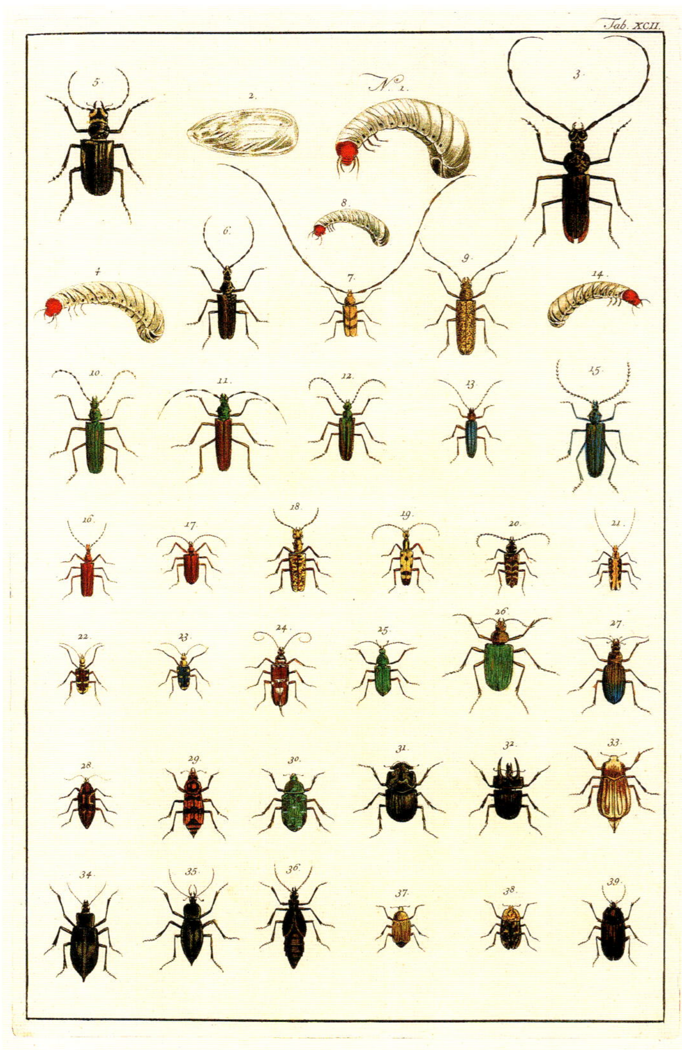

1-2, 4, 8, 14, 31 Scarabaeidae **3, 6-7, 9-13, 15-24** Cerambycidae **25-27** Carabidae **28-30, 33-35, 37-39** Silphidae **32** Geotrupidae **36** Meloidae
1-2, 4, 8, 14, 31 Cockchafers · Blatthornkäfer · Scarabées **3, 6-7, 9-13, 15-24** Longhorn beetles · Bockkäfer · Longicornes **25-27** Carabids/Ground beetles · Laufkäfer · Carabidés **28-30, 33-35, 37-39** Carrion beetles · Aaskäfer · Silphidés **32** Dor beetle · Mistkäfer · Géotrupidé **36** Blister beetle · Ölkäfer · Méloé

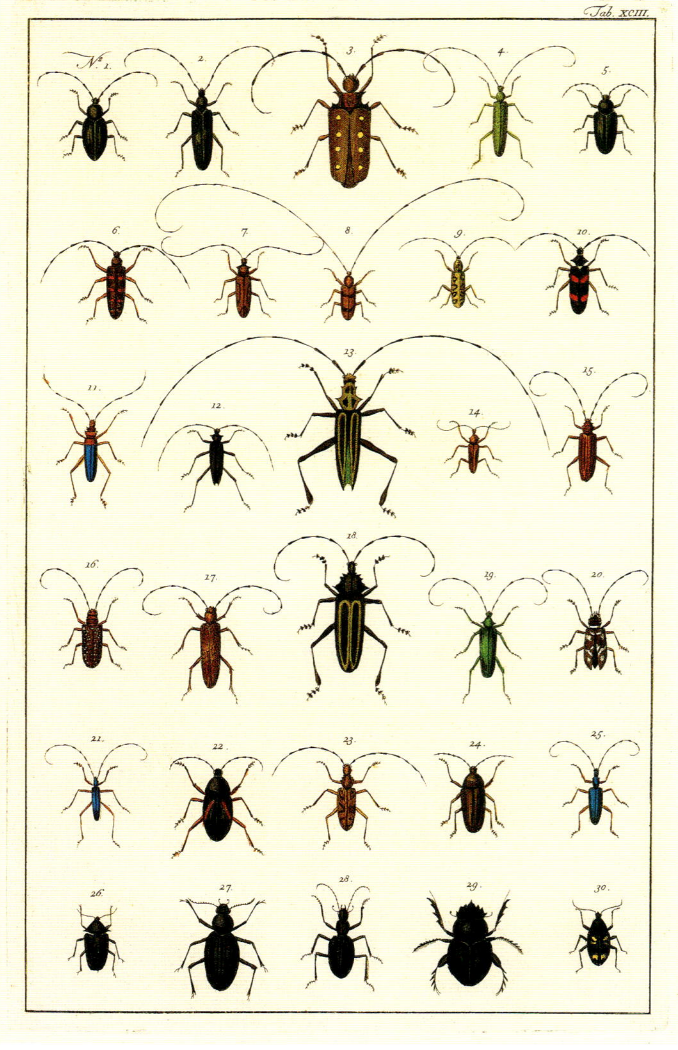

1-25 Cerambycidae **26** Carabidae **27-28** Tenebrionidae **29** Scarabaeidae **30** Silphidae
1-25 Longhorn beetles · Bockkäfer · Longicornes **26** Carabid/Ground beetle · Laufkäfer · Carabidé **27-28** Black beetles · Schwarzkäfer · Ténébrionidés **29** Cockchafer · Blatthornkäfer · Scarabée **30** Carrion beetle · Aaskäfer · Silphidé

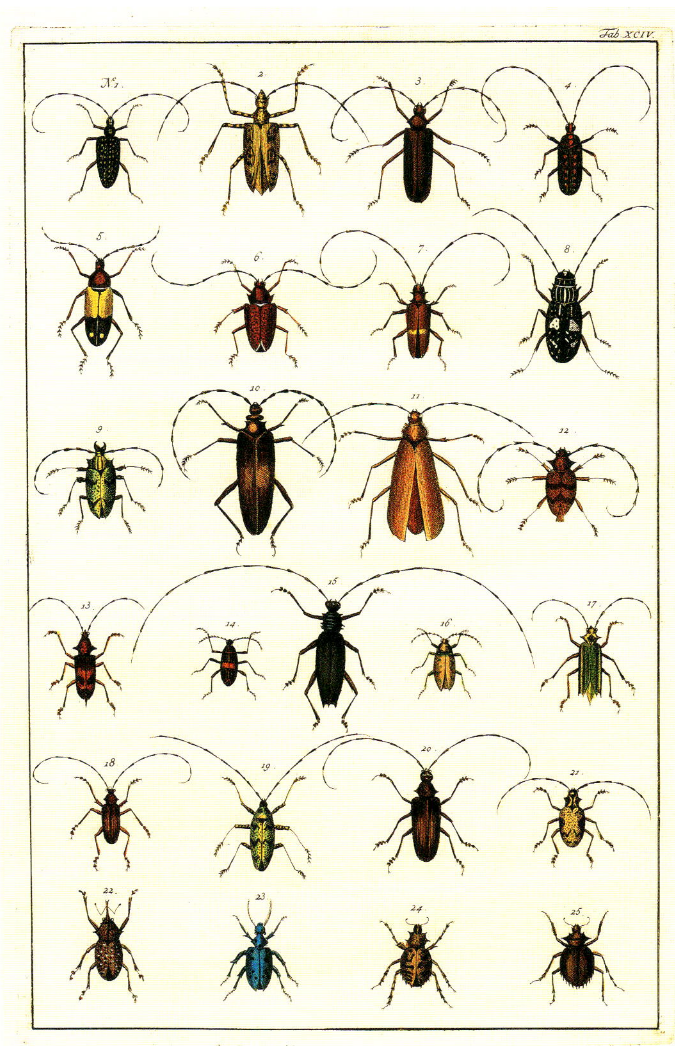

1-13, 15, 17-21 Cerambycidae **14-16** Coleoptera **22** Curculionidae **23** Donacinae
1-13, 15, 17-21 Longhorn beetles · Bockkäfer · Longicornes **14-16** Beetles · Käfer · Coléoptères
22 Weevil · Rüsselkäfer · Charançon **23** Leaf beetle · Schilfkäfer · Chrysomèle (Donacie)

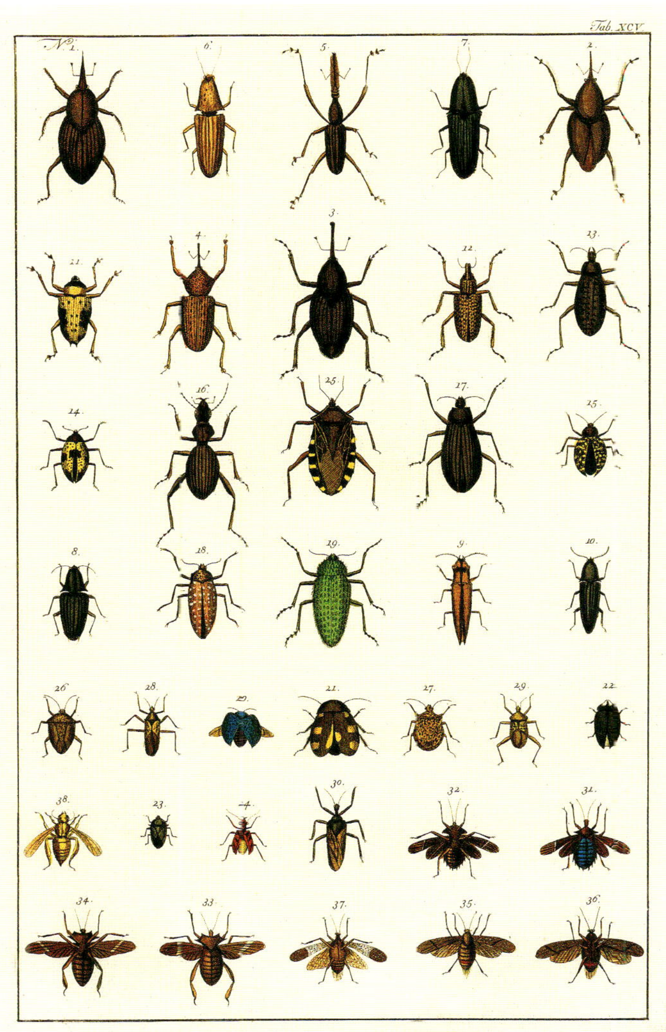

1-5, 12 Curculionidae **6-10** Elateridae **11, 22** Coleoptera **13, 16-17** Carabidae
14-15, 20-21 Chrysomelidae **18-19** Buprestidae **24** Cicindaelinae **38** Aculeata
1-5, 12 Weevils · Rüsselkäfer · Charançons **6-10** Click beetles · Schnellkäfer · Taupins
11, 22 Beetles · Käfer · Coléoptères **13, 16-17** Carabids/Ground beetles · Laufkäfer · Carabidés
14-15, 20-21 Leaf beetles · Blattkäfer · Chrysomèles **18-19** Jewel beetles · Prachtkäfer · Buprestes
24 Tiger beetle · Sandlaufkäfer · Cicindèle **38** Aculeate hymenopterans · Stechimme · Aculéates (Guêpes)

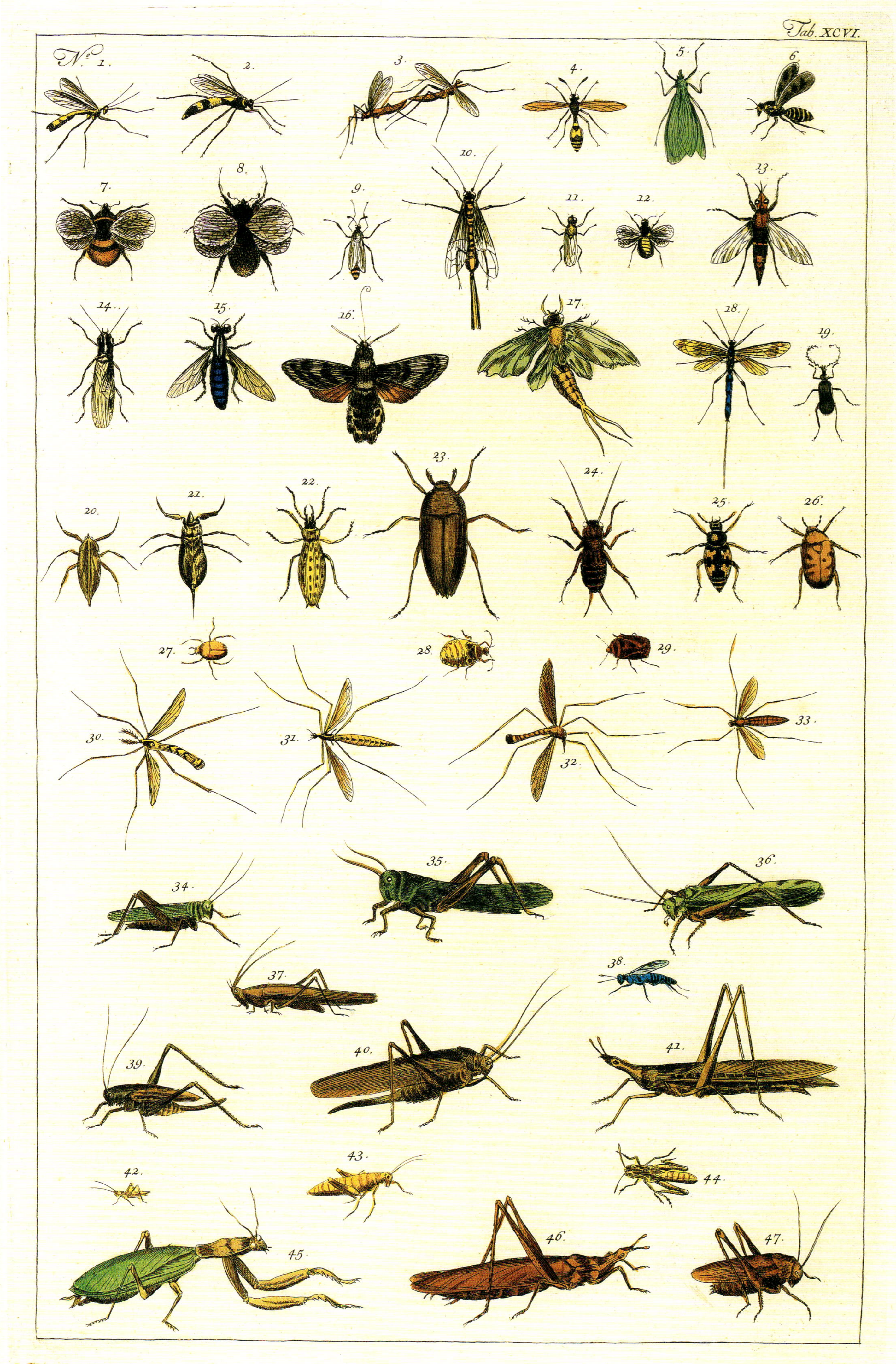

1-2, 4, 6-10, 12, 18, 38 Hymenoptera **3, 11, 13, 15, 30-33** Diptera **14** Plecoptera **17** Ephemeroptera **19, 22-23, 25-27** Coleoptera **28, 29** Heteroptera **34-37, 39-44, 46, 47** Orthoptera **45** Mantodea
1-2, 4, 6-10, 12, 18, 38 Hymenopterans · Hautflügler · Hyménoptères **3, 11, 13, 15, 30-33** Flies · Fliegen · Diptères **14** Stonefly · Steinfliege · Plécoptère **17** Mayfly · Eintagsfliege · Éphémère **19, 22-23, 25-27** Beetles · Käfer · Coléoptères **28, 29** Bugs · Wanzen · Punaises **34-37, 39-44, 46, 47** Grasshoppers and katydids · Heuschrecken · Criquets et sauterelles **45** Praying mantid · Gottesanbeterin · Mante

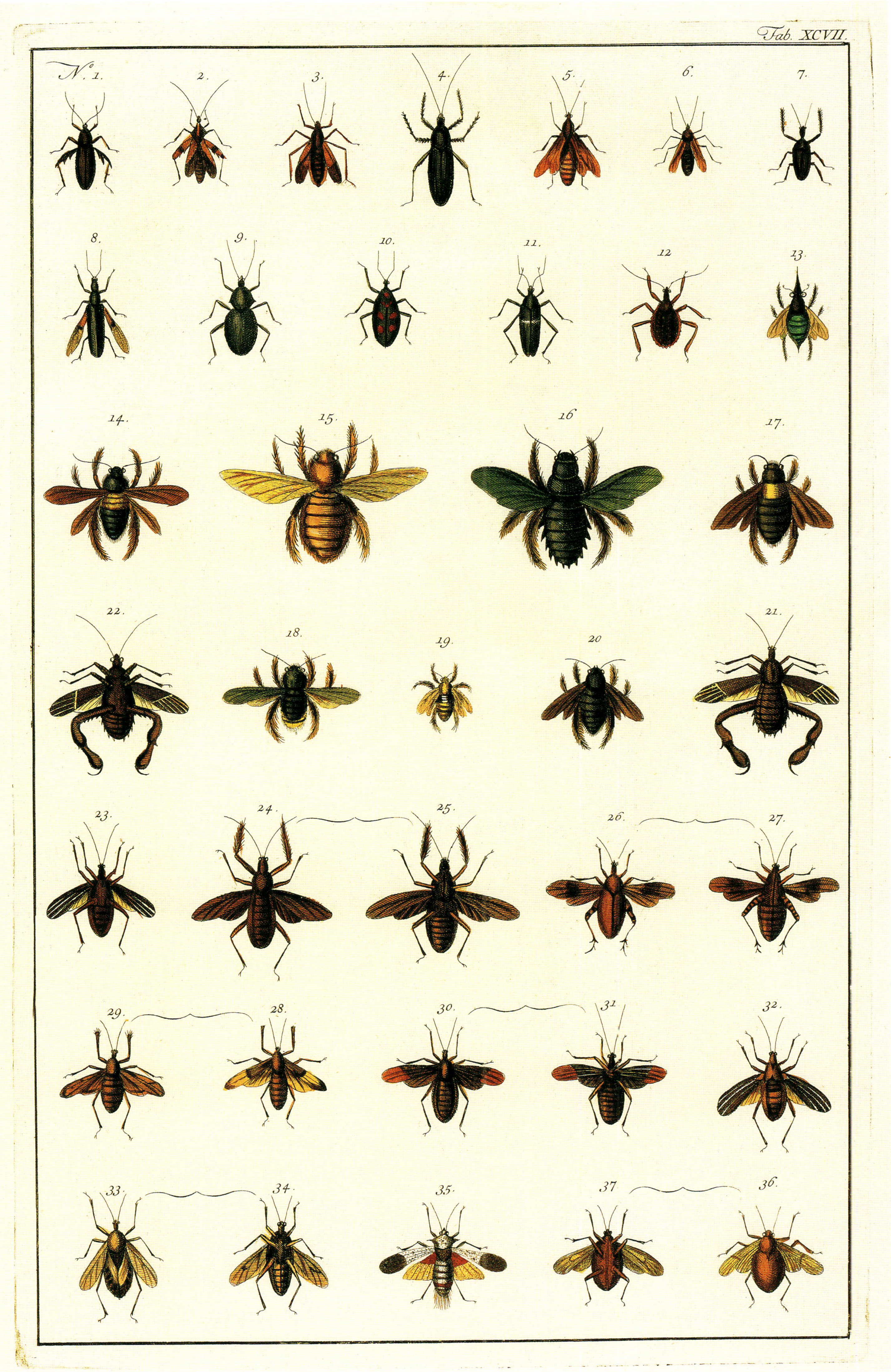

1- 2, 12-13, 21-35 Heteroptera 4, 7-11, 36, 37 Coleoptera 5-6 Hymenoptera 14-20 Apoidea
1-2, 12-13, 21-35 Bugs · Wanzen · Punaises 4, 7-11, 36, 37 Beetles · Käfer · Coléoptères 5-6 Hymenopterans · Hautflügler · Hyménoptères 14-20 Bees · Bienen · Apoïdés

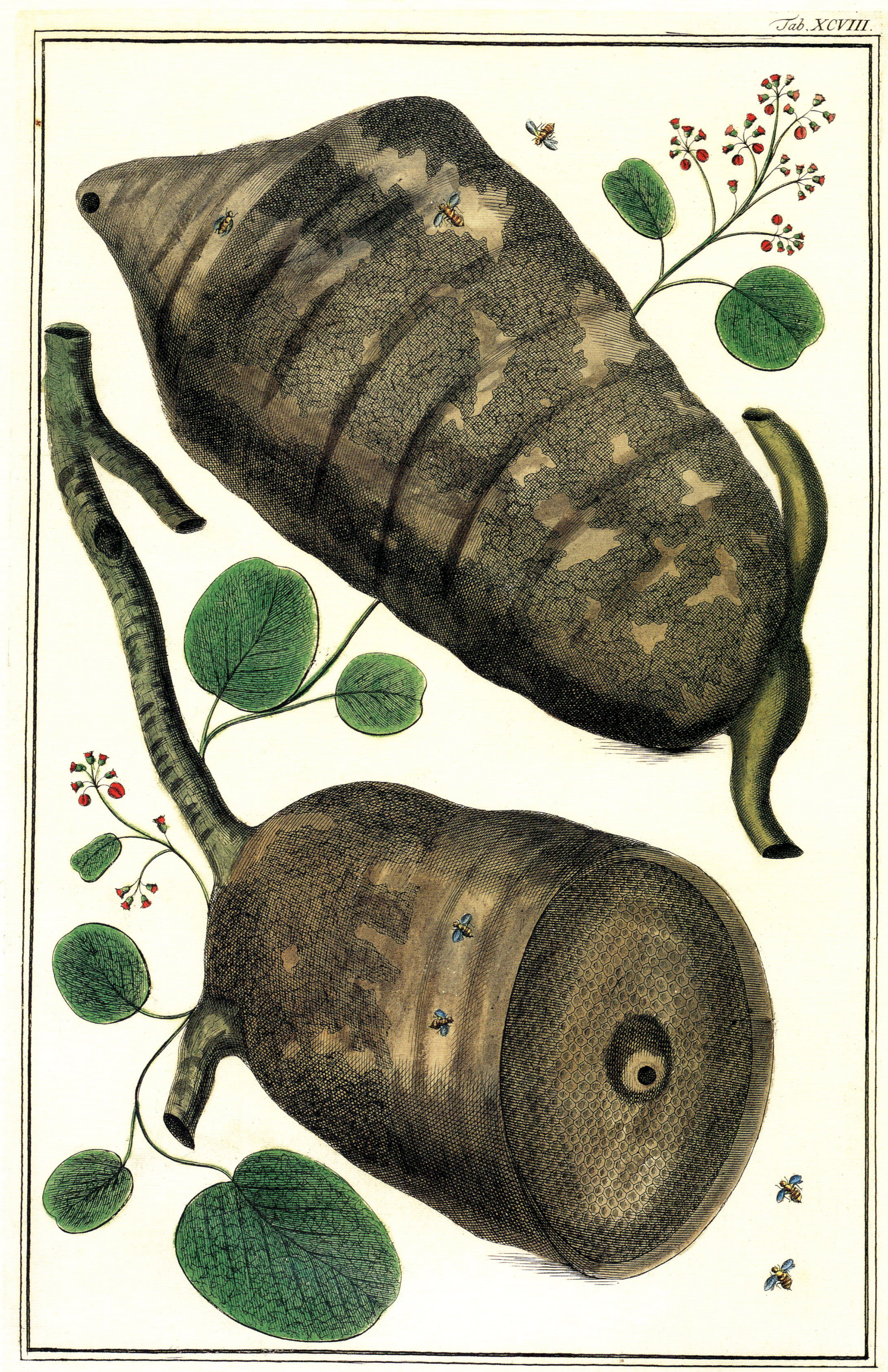

Apoidea
Bee hives · Bienennester · Ruches d'abeilles

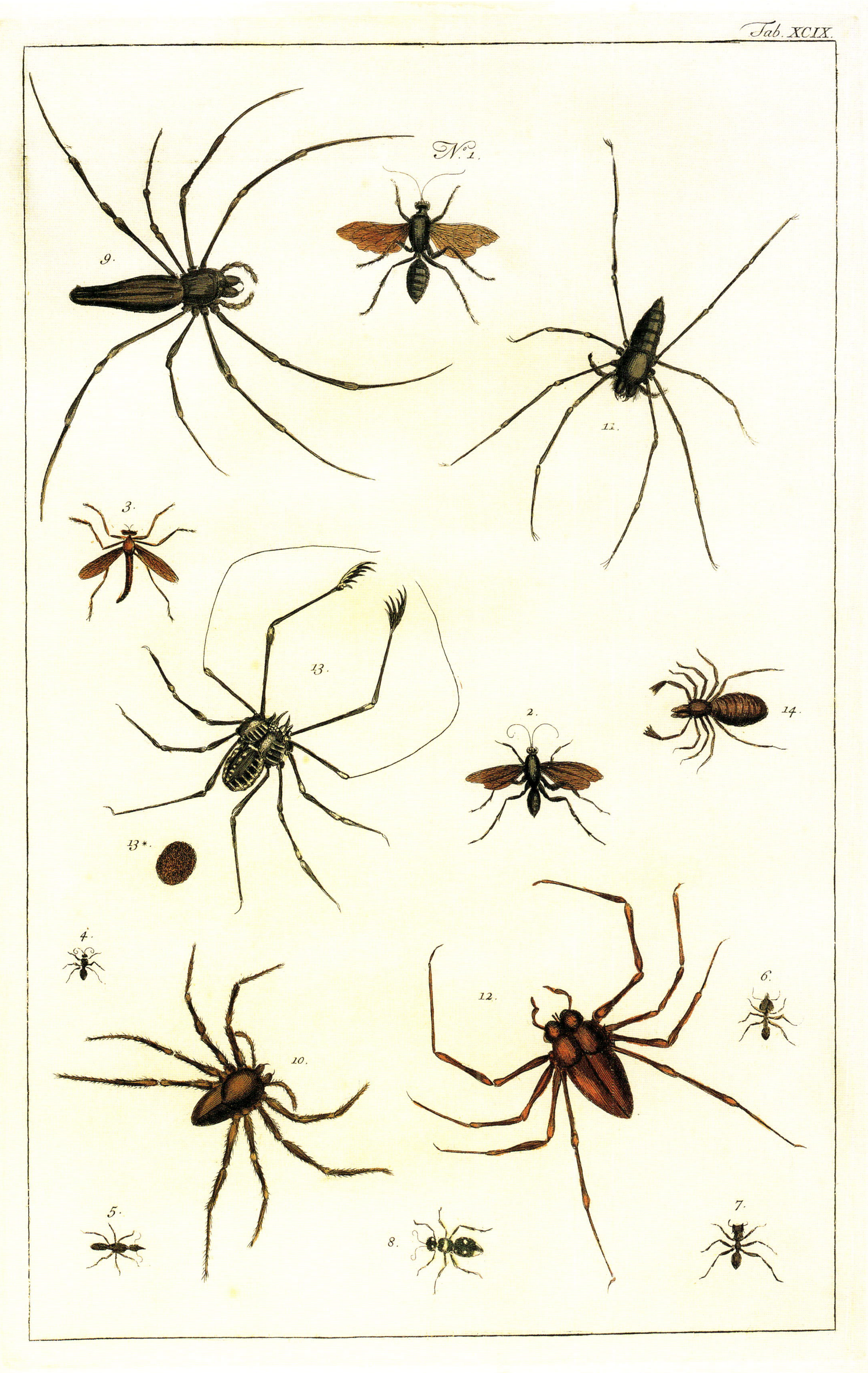

1-2 Pompilidae **3** Diptera **4** Hymenoptera **5-7** Formicidae **8** Mutillidae **9-14** Chelicerata **9-11** Araneae **13** Amblypygi **14** Solifugae
1-2 Spider wasps · Wegwespen · Pompilidés **3** Fly · Fliege · Mouche **4** Hymenopterans · Hautflügler · Hyménoptère **5-7** Ants · Ameisen · Fourmis **8** Velvet-ant · Bienenameise · Mutillidé
9-14 Chelicerates · Spinnentiere · Chélicérates **9-11** Web spiders · Webspinnen · Araignées **13** Tailless whipscorpion · Geißelspinne · Amblipyge **14** Wind scorpion · Walzenspinne · Solifuge

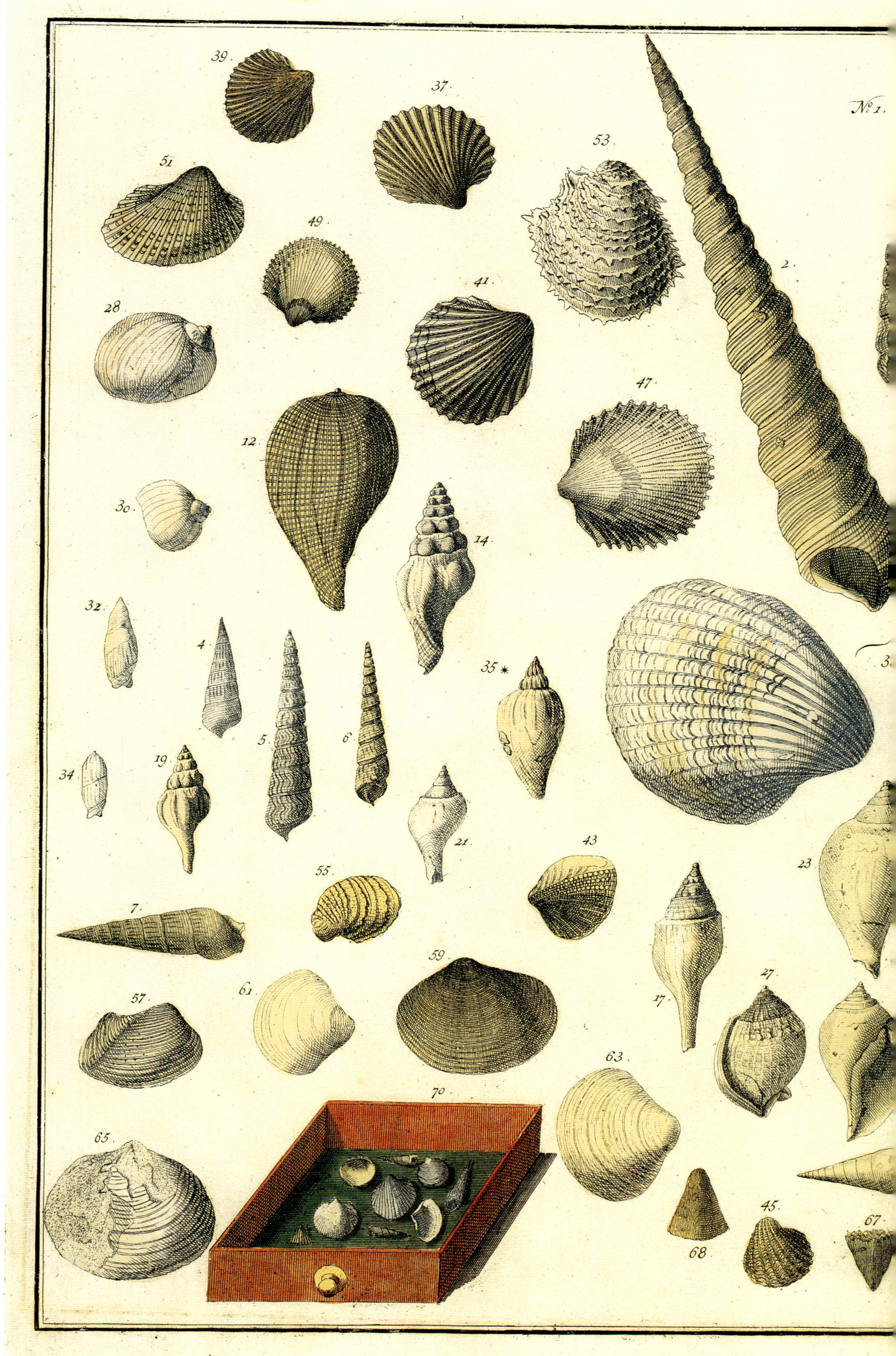

Conchylia marina ex montibus Avenionensibus effossa
Marine shells from the mountains of Avignon · Meeresmuscheln aus den Bergen um Avignon · Coquillages de mer, tirés des montagnes d'Avignon

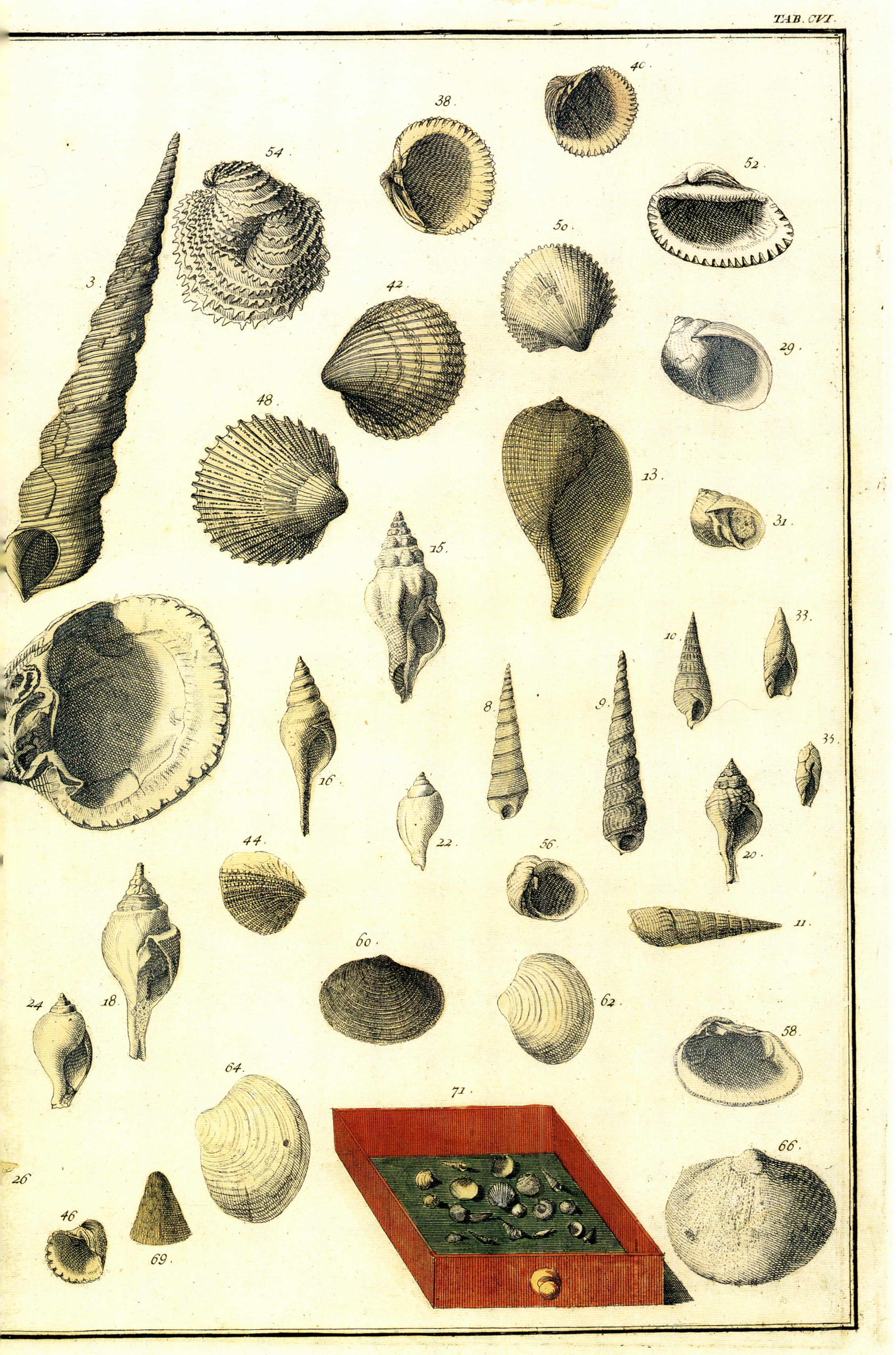
3.
54.
38.
40.
52.
50.
42.
29.
48.
13.
31.
15.
10.
33.
8.
9.
16.
35.
22.
20.
44.
56.
11.
60.
62.
24
18.
58.
64.
71.
66.
26
46
69.

SCIENTIFIC RESEARCH

Georg-August University of Göttingen

Prof. Dr. Rainer Willmann, Göttingen
Prof. Dr. Jes Rust, Bonn
Dr. Volker Wissemann, Jena

Klaus-Dieter Bierwirth
Sven Bradler
Sven-Erik Engmann
Nina Hehn
Dr. Thomas Hörnschemeyer
Rebecca Klug

Hartmut Kutzke (Bonn)
Dr. Wolfgang Mielke
Gisela Vogel
Dr. Sonja Wedmann
Dr. Francisco Welter-Schultes
Sophia Willmann

Important advice and active support was given by
Dr. Yves Finet, Geneva; Bernd Flehmig, Wiesbaden; Christina Förster, Göttingen; Ingo Hausch, Wiesbaden; Lutz Jakob, Ronnenberg; Dr. Bernard Landry, Geneva; Olivier Milhomme, Paris; Dr. Harald Pieper, Kiel; Dr. Helmut Rohlfing, Göttingen; Prof. Dr. Fred-Guenter Schroeder, Göttingen; Dr. Peter Schuchert, Geneva; Dr. Michael Schwerdtfeger, Göttingen; Dr. Michael Stachowitsch, Vienna; Harro Strehlow, Berlin; Hélène Trudel, Geneva; Prof. Dr. Gerhard Wagenitz, Göttingen; Dr. Vollrath Wiese, Cismar.

THE AUTHORS

Dr. Irmgard Müsch
born in 1967, studied art history, history and classical archaeology in Mainz and Berlin. Her 1999 Ph.D. thesis examines Johann Jakob Scheuchzer's *Kupfer-Bibel*, a richly illustrated scientific commentary on the Bible from the early 18th century. She has published on art of the 18th and 20th century, scientific illustrations and *Kunstkammer* pieces.

Prof. Dr. Rainer Willmann
born in 1950, occupies the chair for morphology, taxonomy and evolutionary biology at the Institute of Zoology and Anthropology of the University of Göttingen. In some 120 publications he has addressed the phylogeny of insects, snail evolution, and historical and theoretical issues in biology. He is co-founder of the Research Centre for Biodiversity and Ecology at the University of Göttingen.

Prof. Dr. Jes Rust
born 1963, completed his studies in geology, palaeontology and zoology at Göttingen and Kiel. His thesis dealt with the evolution of fossil snails living in the fresh and brackish waters of prehistoric Greece. His assistantship at the Institute of Zoology in Göttingen between 1993 and 1999 was followed by his appointment in 2001 as professor of invertebrate palaeontology and insect phylogeny at the University of Bonn.

ACKNOWLEDGEMENTS

The publishers would like to thank everyone who made the publication of this work possible.

The *Koninklijke Bibliotheek* in The Hague for kindly lending its copy of the *Locupletissimi rerum naturalium thesauri* for the publication. We would like to thank the staff of the library for all their help, especially *Theo Vermeulen*, who right from the beginning of the project gave his full support, and above all the General Director, *Dr. Wim van Drimmelen*, who made this collaboration possible.

We would also like to thank *Dr. Irmgard Müsch*, Berlin, both for her essay and for placing her specialist knowledge at the disposal of the entire project.

Our particular thanks go to *Prof. Dr. Rainer Willmann*, whose enthusiasm for the publication came from his interest in the history of science, and who suggested working with a team of scientists in order to study the depicted organisms and to annotate the plates. The legends and the extensive and insightful information on the animals and plants were made possible by the effort and commitment of the study group at the Zoological Institute of the Georg-August University in Göttingen under Prof. Willmann's direction. The publication could never have been realised without the work put in by the team. Our thanks are also extended to the co-author *Prof. Dr. Jes Rust*, and *Dr Volker Wissemann*, who undertook the classification of the plants.

We also to wish to express our heartfelt thanks to the other institutes and scientists who gave their active support to this publication, in particular *Dr. Bernard Landry* and *Dr. Yves Finet* of the *Muséum d'histoire naturelle de la Ville de Genève* in Geneva, and *Dr. Michael Stachowitsch* of the Zoological Institute at the University of Vienna.

PHOTOGRAPHIC CREDITS

The copy used for printing belongs to the Koninklijke Bibliotheek, The Hague.
Shelf number: 394 B 26 -29

Niedersächsische Staats- und Universitätsbibliothek, Göttingen: p. 11, 12, 14 (Fig. 6), 18, 21, 22 (Fig. 12), 24
Österreichische Nationalbibliothek, Vienna: p. 22 (Fig. 13)
Stadtbibliothek, Ulm: p. 17 (Fig. 7)
Technische Universität Carolo-Wilhelmina zu Braunschweig, Universitätsbibliothek: p. 17 (Fig. 8)
Ulmer Museum, Ulm: p. 8
Zoölogisch Museum, Universiteit van Amsterdam: p. 14 (Fig. 5)

This edition published by
Barnes & Noble, Inc., by arrangement
with TASCHEN GmbH
2006 Barnes & Noble Books

M 10 9 8 7 6 5 4 3 2 1
ISBN-13: 978-0-7607-8204-0
ISBN-10: 0-7607-8204-0

PROJECT MANAGEMENT
Petra Lamers-Schütze, Cologne

EDITORIAL COORDINATION
Ute Kieseyer, Cologne

TRANSLATION
Anne Hentschel, Göttingen
Malcolm Green, Heidelberg

DESIGN
Claudia Frey, Cologne

PRODUCTION
Ute Wachendorf, Cologne

Printed in China

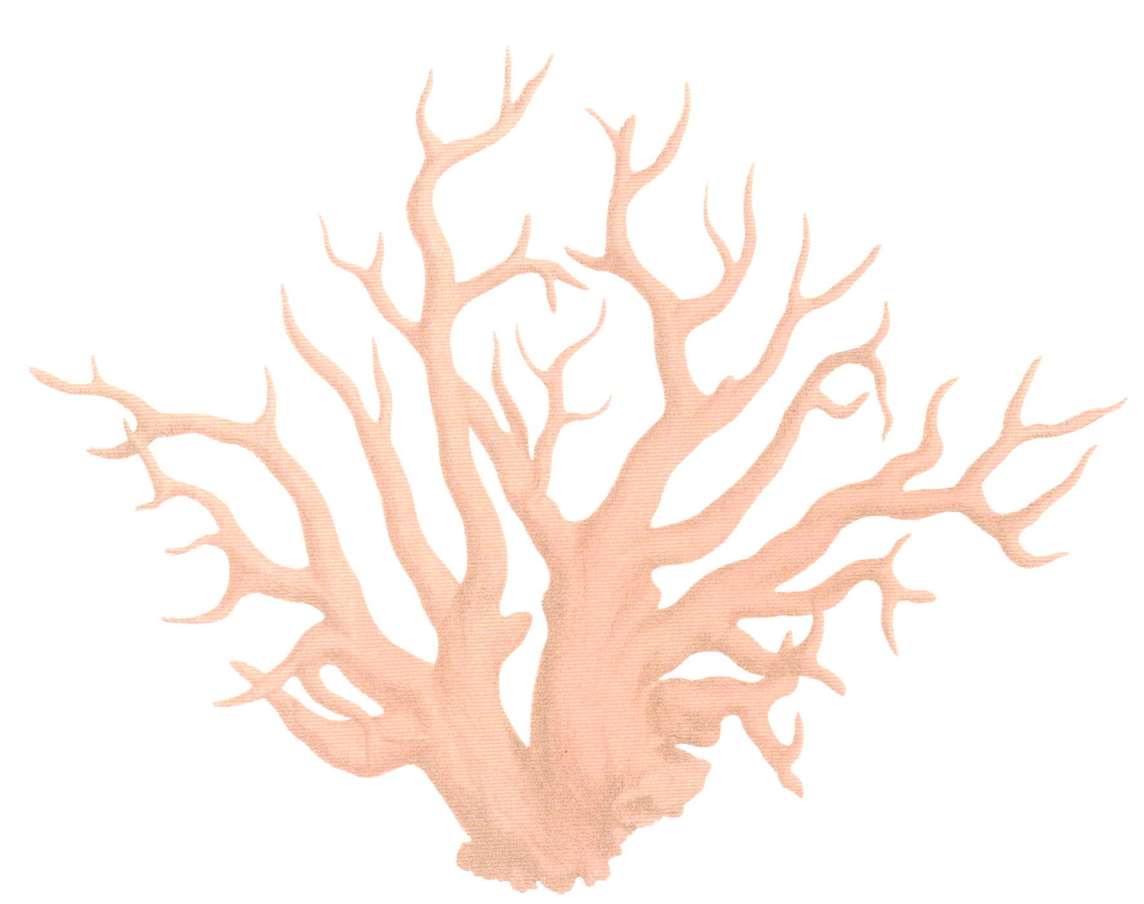